ALASKA NATIVES AND AMERICAN LAWS

D1728545

by
DAVID S. CASE

with chapter 8 by
Anne D. Shinkwin

UNIVERSITY OF ALASKA PRESS
Fairbanks

Originally published as
*The Special Relationship of Alaska Natives to the Federal Government:
An Historical and Legal Analysis*, by the Alaska Native Foundation, 1978.

Revised edition © 1984 University of Alaska Press
All rights reserved.
First printing 3,000 copies, 1984
Second printing 1,000 copies, 1987
Third printing 500 copies, 1997

International Standard Book Number: 0-912006-09-9
Library of Congress Catalog Number: 79-603397

Printed in the United States of America by
Thomson-Shore, Inc. on recycled paper.

This publication was printed on acid-free paper that meets the minimum
requirements of American National Standard for Information Sciences—
Permanence of Paper for Printed Library Materials, ANSI Z39.48-1984.

ACKNOWLEDGEMENTS

Many at the University of Alaska, Fairbanks, have contributed to the completion of this work, and it is a pleasure to acknowledge their contributions. First, I am indebted to Dennis Demmert, Director of Alaska Native Programs, and Gerald McBeath, Chairman of the Political Science Department, for suggesting that I undertake this task and for affording me the time and financial support necessary to complete it. I am also indebted to Professor Anne Shinkwin of the Department of Anthropology for working the research and writing of chapter 8 into an already busy year of field work. Others have reviewed and commented on various portions of the manuscript and proven valuable sources of support. These include especially Professors Michael Gaffney, Russ Currier, Pat Kwachka, Lee Nichols, Eliza Jones, and my dear wife, Dorothy.

I am doubly indebted to Russ Currier who, even after he left the University, agreed to edit the entire work. His patient attention to detail and sensitivity of expression are responsible for many improvements in style which would have been beyond my talents. Finally, but perhaps she should be first, I am indebted to Machelle Wells who speaks to computers and singlehandedly transformed the electronic impulses of my word processor and numerous manuscript changes into camera ready copy. She has the dedication of a marine and the disposition of an angel, characteristics which seem essential in her line of work. I am also grateful to Gerald Mohatt, Dean of the College of Human and Rural Development who made some of Machelle's time available to work on this project.

Many others from the Alaska Native community, state and federal government and the private bar have thoughtfully reviewed various portions of the manuscript for accuracy and completeness. I am particularly grateful for their contributions to chapter 4 ("Allotments and Townsites"), chapter 7 ("Subsistence"), chapter 8 ("Traditional Native Societies"), chapter 9 ("Modern Native Organizations") and chapter 10 ("Native Self-Government"). They are, however, so numerous that to try to acknowledge each individually would be sure to slight some. Each deserves some special praise for taking substantial time from busy lives to review work over which they have no direct control. I hope it is apparent to those who were able to comment that I have taken most of their suggestions into account.

Notwithstanding the assistance of others, I am solely responsible for this work. As is any author's perogative, I have been free to accept or reject the advice of others and to cast the work in my own terms.

David Stanway Case
Fairbanks, Alaska
June 15, 1984

FOREWORD

It is always risky to write a book on such a seemingly complex and volatile topic as the legal rights of Native Americans. It is perhaps doubly risky for a lawyer who is not Native to do so, because his or her motives are inherently suspect. Suffice it to say that, up to a point, one cannot help what other people think. For my part, the best explanation is a personal fascination with the now nearly five hundred-year history of the relationships between two fundamentally different groups of cultures—the aboriginal and the immigrant Americans. Perhaps the most intriguing feature of this history and the relationships born out of it is that *both* groups still persist. It is a phenomenon which perhaps says more about the values of aboriginal cultures than about the technological success of the immigrants.

Writing a book such as this also poses two paradoxical hazards. The first is that it will not say enough, that it will omit some fundamental legal principle or fail to properly criticize a worn-out dinosaur. The second is that it will say too much, that it will prejudice some future argument favoring a particular Native right by accepting as true premises which prove later to be incorrect. These risks, however, are not inherent in the work, but in the uses made of it. There is a tendency, because the law of Native American rights is perceived as complex, to accept any seemingly comprehensive analysis as true and to substitute "authority" for original thought.

This book is, of course, not intended to be a substitute for further thought or analysis of the subject. Rather it is, as the title suggests, a *description* of the interaction of Alaska Natives and American laws. It is not intended primarily to be a criticism of those laws; although, there are ample grounds on which they might be criticized. I leave that for perhaps another time, another place and even other people. Nor is it intended to be a limitation on future legal analysis or political development which may affect the legal status of the Alaska Natives. It is intended, however, to be a beginning point for such independent criticism, analysis or development. Although each chapter focuses on a different aspect of the federal-Native relationship, many statutes and decisions are basic to an understanding of more than one aspect. Those references are made repeatedly, wherever relevant, in order that each chapter be relatively independent. The whole is intended to be a collection, between two covers, of references to and some discussion of the major source material which bears on the legal and political history of the Alaska Natives under the rule of federal and state laws.

This is not to say that the Alaska Natives do not have their own histories, cultures, laws, customs and political life which have survived even under the often adverse conditions imposed by American rule. It is merely to point out that the laws of the American state have, for better or worse, had a bearing on those aspects of Native life which are essential to the persistence of Native communities as distinct cultures. It is my thesis that it is important for both the Native and immigrant cultures to understand the effect of American laws on their continuing relationships. It is important for us all to realize that the rights of Alaska Natives as distinct cultures have had historical protection even under the sometimes hostile laws of the immigrant society. Cultural pluralism in Alaska is not just the product of the happy isolation of Native communities from a burgeoning urban population; it is also the product of a long historical relationship recognized in the laws of the United States. We are, in Alaska in the dwindling days of the twentieth century, in danger of jettisoning that relationship. Before deciding to do so we should understand what it would mean. Hopefully, this book will contribute to that understanding.

TABLE OF CONTENTS
AND
ANALYSIS OF CHAPTERS

PART I
INTRODUCTION

CHAPTER ONE
THE FEDERAL RELATIONSHIP TO ALASKA NATIVES

PART II
ALASKA NATIVE
LANDS AND RESOURCES

CHAPTER TWO
ABORIGINAL TITLE

CHAPTER THREE
RESERVATIONS

CHAPTER FOUR
NATIVE ALLOTMENTS AND TOWNSITES

PART III
FEDERAL
HUMAN SERVICE
OBLIGATIONS

CHAPTER FIVE
HISTORY OF NATIVE SERVICES
AND PROGRAMS IN ALASKA

CHAPTER SIX
NATIVE ENTITLEMENT TO HUMAN SERVICES

PART IV
THE FEDERAL
OBLIGATION TO
PROTECT SUBSISTENCE

CHAPTER SEVEN
SUBSISTENCE IN ALASKA

PART V
NATIVE
SELF–GOVERNMENT

CHAPTER EIGHT
TRADITIONAL ALASKA NATIVE SOCIETIES

CHAPTER NINE
MODERN ALASKA NATIVE
GOVERNMENTS AND ORGANIZATIONS

CHAPTER TEN
"SOVEREIGNTY:" THE ALASKA NATIVE CLAIM
TO SELF–GOVERNMENT

PART I

INTRODUCTION

CHAPTER ONE

THE FEDERAL RELATIONSHIP
TO ALASKA NATIVES

I. The Federal-Native Relationship Generally

A. A Unique Relationship

Chief Justice John Marshall was the first American jurist of stature to define the nature of the federal relationship to the American aboriginal tribes. He concluded in an early opinion that, although the relationship is unlike any other, it resembles that of a ward to his guardian.[1] He was careful not to say that the relationship *is* one of guardianship—only that it *resembles* such a relationship. Because the relationship is unique, the chief justice explained it in terms of the more readily understood figure of speech, which he further expanded by describing the attitude of the Natives and the United States toward each other:

> They look to our government for protection; rely upon its kindness and its power; appeal to it for relief of their wants; and address the president as their great father. They and their country are considered by foreign nations, as well as by ourselves, as being so completely under the sovereignty and dominion of the United States, that any attempt to acquire their lands, or to form a political connection with them, would be considered by all as an invasion of our territory and an act of hostility.[2]

However, the truly unique feature of the relationship is that it also recognizes the internal sovereignty of Native communities. They are, in Chief Justice Marshall's opinion:

> distinct, independent political communities....and the settled doctrine of the law of nations is, that a weaker power does not surrender its independence—its right to self-government— by associating with a stronger, and taking its protection. A weak state, in order to provide for its safety, may place itself under the protection of one more powerful, without stripping itself of the right of government, and ceasing to be a state.[3]

The relationship, therefore, is that of a stronger to a weaker *government.* Although it has admitted failings, this relationship, which acknowledges an inherent right of Natives to self-government even within the borders of the United States, is unique among aboriginal people living within the borders of nation-states.[4]

3

B. Federal "Plenary" Power

Congress, under principles of law laid down by the U.S. Supreme Court, is said to have "plenary" power over Native American communities and their members.[5] This means that Congress has full or "complete" power in the field of Indian affairs. Among other things, this power has been used to prevent Natives from disposing of aboriginal lands without federal consent[6] and to place the political relationship of Native communities to others under the sole authority of federal law.[7] During the early twentieth century, however, the plenary power doctrine became merely an excuse for the exercise of seemingly unfettered or "absolute" power when the Supreme Court held that Congress could unilaterally abrogate an Indian treaty.[8] Several commentators have soundly criticized the exercise of such absolute power in a democratic society,[9] and more recent Supreme Court decisions imply that plenary power is limited by the requirements of the United States Constitution[10] and must also "be tied rationally to the fulfillment of Congress' unique obligation toward the Indians."[11]

That obligation has been variously described as one of "fairness," "trust," or "guardianship" and is the product of the unequal relationship between the federal and Native governments. As the U.S. Supreme Court has described it:

> The recognized relation between the parties [the United States and the Choctaw Nation in this case]...is that between a superior and an inferior, whereby the latter is placed under the care and control of the former, and which, while it authorizes the adoption on the part of the United States of such policy as their own public interest may dictate, recognizes, on the other hand, such an interpretation of their acts and promises as justice and reason demand in all cases where power is exerted by the strong over those to whom they owe care and protection. The parties are not on an equal footing, and that inequality is to be made good by the superior justice which looks only to the substance of the right, without regard to technical rules framed under a system of municipal jurisprudence, formulating the rights and obligations of private persons, equally subject to the same laws.[12]

Thus, the ascendancy of federal power over Native American communities creates an unequal *political* relationship upon which the Native Amercians are compelled to rely. Their reliance requires generally that the federal government adhere to an "overriding duty...to deal fairly with the Indians wherever located,"[13] and "imposes a distinctive obligation of trust incumbent upon the government in its dealings with these dependent and sometimes exploited people."[14] Similar reasoning supports rules of statutory construction, requiring statutes passed for the benefit of Native Americans to be liberally interpreted[15] and those terminating their federal relationship to be narrowly construed.[16]

C. Defining the Relationship

The federal-Native relationship is difficult to define in general terms, because the obligations inherent in the relationship vary with time and specific subject. These obligations have sometimes been termed "trust responsibilities,"[17] but the term is not wholly satisfactory.

In the first place, a "trust responsibility" refers most accurately to obligations arising from a divided property interest in which one party holds and manages the "legal" interest in property for the "equitable" benefit of another.[18] The United States frequently does have a true trust responsibility over Native American resources, and that responsibility frequently requires that funds obtained from the sale or lease of those resources be used to provide specific services.[19] Under these circumstances, it can perhaps be said that the United States has a "trust responsibility" to provide the agreed upon services.[20] However, the courts have not been especially careful in their use of the term "trust," implying there are various "fiduciary,"[21] "guardianship,"[22] or other "obligations of trust"[23] when there is no property relationship involved. The result is a semantic knot, which is impossible to untie by concentrating on the words used to define the relationship.

Clearly there is, in the terms of one opinion, a "unique legal relationship" between the federal government and Native Americans.[24] That relationship is founded on principles of constitutional, international and common law all of which lead to the conclusion that, on a government-to-government basis, Natives are compelled to depend on federal plenary power. They are dependent on the federal government to protect their aboriginal lands and give fair satisfaction to legitimate Native land claims;[25] they depend on the government to provide important human services when the states refuse or are unable to;[26] and they are dependent on the government to protect subsistence resources[27] and tribal government[28] from state or non-Native encroachment.

However, Native dependency alone is not usually sufficient to impose legally enforceable obligations on the United States. Such obligations must first be acknowledged in treaties,[29] statutes,[30] appropriations,[31] executive action,[32] or clear common law principles.[33] Absent *some* acknowledgment, federal obligations to Native Americans appear to be too abstract to permit judicial enforcement.[34]

During the twentieth century, and especially since the 1950's, Congress has enacted a number of statutes, further acknowledging and defining the federal relationship. Many of these have both general and specific relevance to Alaska Natives. These include: P.L. 280 (1953),[35] Indian Civil Rights Act (1968),[36] Alaska Native Claims Settlement Act (1971),[37] Marine Mammal Protection Act (1972),[38] Endangered Species Act (1973),[39] Indian Financing Act (1974),[40] Indian Self-Determination and

Education Assistance Act (1975),[41] Indian Health Care Improvement Act (1976),[42] Indian Child Welfare Act (1978),[43] and Indian Tribal Governmental Tax Status Act.[44] Increasingly, the courts look to statutes such as these to determine specific federal obligations to Native Americans.[45]

II. History of the Alaska Native Relationship

A. Early Years—1867-1905

The federal government did not initially deal with Alaska Natives as dependent Indian communities. In the first place, Article III of the 1867 Treaty of Purchase implied a distinction between "uncivilized tribes" and the other "inhabitants of the ceded territory." The latter, if they remained in the territory, were to be "admitted to the enjoyment of all the rights, advantages and immunities of citizens of the United States," including "the free enjoyment of their liberty, property, and religion." The former were to be "subject to such laws and regulations as the United States may, from time to time, adopt in regard to aboriginal tribes of that country."[46]

Perhaps the implication was that "civilized" Natives, as citizens, would not be subject to federal Indian law; as a matter of law, however, citizenship alone does not terminate the federal-Native relationship.[47] As a matter of judicial practice, nearly all Alaskan Natives appeared to be categorized as "uncivilized," based either on their previous classification under Russian rule[48] or their treatment under nineteenth century U. S. law.[49] Furthermore, the "civilization" issue only became important in naturalization[50] and school attendance[51] cases; it was never used to deny the applicability of federal Indian law to Alaska Natives. However, none of this became clear until the beginning of the twentieth century, so initially the separate treatment of "uncivilized tribes" in the treaty may have given the impression that an indefinite number of Alaska Natives were not subject to the principles of federal Indian Law.

Beginning with the 1884 Organic Act and running through 1900, Congress enacted several statutes purporting to protect "Indians or other persons" in Alaska "in the possession of any lands actually in their use or occupation."[52] It was generally assumed that these acts equated Native possession with non-Native possession and entitled Alaska Natives only to land which was in their individual and actual use and occupancy.[53] The unspoken implication seems to have been that Alaska Natives, unlike other Native Americans, did not have claims of aboriginal title to vast tracts of tribal property.[54] Furthermore, many of the provisions of the Indian Trade and Intercourse Act[55] were arguably not applied to Alaska Native lands until 1948,[56] resulting in early judicial decisions that Alaska did not constitute "Indian country" for purposes of the Indian trade laws.[57]

Most important, until 1905 no distinction was made between Native and non-Native residents of the territory for purposes of federal educational services provided "without regard to race" under the 1884 Organic Act.[58] Furthermore, the federal Bureau of Education, not the Bureau of Indian Affairs, was charged with the education of Alaska Natives. Because there was no Indian agency in Alaska, and Natives were entitled to the same services as non-Natives, the Solicitor for the Department of the Interior held initially that Alaska Natives did not have the same relationship to the federal government as other Native Americans.[59]

Additionally, in In re Sah Quah (1886), the Alaska Federal District Court questioned the sovereign authority of a group of Tlingit Indians to maintain the practice of slavery.[60] The Tlingits argued that as an aboriginal group, they retained internal governing authority exclusive of the laws of the United States. Because slave holding was permitted under Tlingit custom, and because they retained independent sovereignty, the Tlingits contended that federal laws prohibiting slavery did not apply to them. The court held that the Tlingits, as are all residents of the United States, were subject to the Thirteenth Amendment to the United States Constitution. The Department of the Interior has restricted the decision to this narrow holding;[61] however, language in the opinion implies that Alaska Natives were so dependent on the federal government that they did not even have internal governing authority.[62]

B. Middle Period—1904-1971

1. Change in the Relationship—1904-1936

Between 1904 and 1936, the Alaska Native relationship underwent several significant changes. Initially these took the form of administrative actions, judicial decisions, and a few statutory enactments. Then in 1936, Congress applied the comprehensive Indian Reorganization Act to Alaska, thereby equating the status of Alaska Natives to that of Native Americans generally.[63] However, the change was gradual and cumulative over time, manifested initially in administrative actions and judicial decisions which bit by bit acknowledged the existence of a unique legal relationship between the Alaska Natives and the federal government.

Judge Wickersham's 1904 decision in *U.S. v. Berrigan*[64] is perhaps the first official manifestation of the developing relationship. *Berrigan* held that the United States had both the right and the duty to file suit to prevent non-Natives from acquiring lands occupied by Natives, implying that non-Natives could not acquire such lands without the consent of the federal government. From an administrative standpoint, it is most significant that the United States brought this suit in the first place; it indicates an executive determination that the federal government had an obligation to protect Native aboriginal possession from non-Native encroachment. Indeed, Wickersham upheld the authority of the United States to bring the suit in part on the theory that Article III of the 1867 Treaty entitled the Athabascan Natives in this case "to the equal protection of the law which the United States affords to similar aboriginal tribes within its borders."[65]

The year following *Berrigan,* Congress passed what is known as the Nelson Act.[66] This act made explicit what by that time must have been a *de facto* accomplishment—a dual system of education. In 1884, Dr. Sheldon Jackson was appointed General Agent for Education in Alaska to implement the "nonracial" education provisions of the 1884 Organic Act. Dr. Jackson had previously served as the superintendent of Presbyterian missions in Alaska in which capacity he gave special attention to the education and "advancement" of Alaska Natives. He carried this concern over to his duties as General Alaska Agent, and in that capacity supported or established numerous schools in remote Native villages all over Alaska. In time these schools, and the federal teachers staffing them, became the focal points of reindeer herding, health care and a host of other human service programs under the management of the Department of the Interior's Bureau of Education and later the Bureau of Indian Affairs.

Although Congress did not immediately acknowledge them to be "Native" programs, these schools were usually located in Native villages and were in fact intended to benefit only Natives. Then in 1894, Congress made the first appropriation for the Bureau of Education's Alaska Native reindeer programs; these appropriations were maintained and increased annually for the next several years. Thus, when Congress passed the Nelson Act in 1905, it merely acknowledged what by that time had become an accomplished fact—federal services provided to Alaska Natives because of their status as Natives. Appropriations under the Nelson Act were specifically for the "education and support of the Eskimos, Indians and other Natives of Alaska."[67]

Coincident with his "Native" programs, Dr. Jackson encouraged the establishment of executive order reservations for various purposes ranging from the propagation of reindeer to the establishment of schools. The Bureau of Education continued this practice under successive Alaska agents creating in the process some 150 reserves varying in size from less than one acre to several hundred thousand acres.[68] These were established for a variety of specific purposes, but were generally intended for the benefit of Alaska Natives. However, there was some doubt about the authority of the president of the United States to create executive order Native reserves. Furthermore, because they implied exclusive Native usage, they were used to protect Native communities from non-Native incursion and to preserve Native access to hunting, trapping and fishing resources. As a result, controversies frequently arose because exclusive Native fishing rights meant that non-Natives could not fish in reservation waters.

An important case, *Alaska Pacific Fisheries v. U.S.,*[69] arose on the Metlakatla, Annette Island Reserve, and resolved the fishing question in favor of the Natives. Congress established the Metlakatla reserve by statute in 1891,[70] but in 1916 President Woodrow Wilson withdrew all of the waters within 3,000 feet of the shore as an executive order fishing reserve for the Metlakatlan Natives. The United States sued the Alaska

Pacific Fisheries Corporation to prevent them from building a fish trap within the reserved waters. The U.S. Supreme Court affirmed exclusive Native use of those waters on the basis of the 1891 statute, but it was just as important that the lower court opinions[71] affirmed the president's authority to create executive order reserves for exclusive Alaska Native use.

In 1919 Congress prohibited the creation of executive order Indian reserves without legislative consent,[72] but the *Alaska Pacific Fisheries* decisions confirmed the exclusive status of the previously created Alaska reserves and implied that the relationship between Alaska Natives and the federal government was similar to that of Native Americans in the continental United States. Relying on this decision, the Department of the Interior's Solicitor held in 1923 that the department could negotiate a lease for a cannery benefiting the Tyonek Native reserve because:

> The relations existing between [the Natives] and the Government are very similar and in many respects, identical with those which have long existed between the Government and the aboriginal people residing within the territorial limits of the United States....[73]

Prior to this time, Congress had also passed the Alaska Native Allotment Act,[74] permitting any Indian or Eskimo (Aleuts were included in 1956) to acquire up to 160 acres of nonmineral land as an "inalienable and nontaxable" homestead. The allotment act permitted Alaska Natives to acquire individual lands in a manner similar to that afforded other Native Americans under the General Allotment Act of 1887.[75] In 1926, Congress also permitted Alaska Natives to acquire townsite lots[76] because they had been denied title to such lands under a previously enacted statute which had been administratively applied only to non-Natives.[77] Significantly, under the 1926 townsite act, Natives could alienate their townsite lots only with the permission of the Secretary of the Interior; the property was also statutorily protected from taxation and involuntary disposition. Under both the allotment and townsite acts, therefore, Alaska Natives had to rely on the Secretary of the Interior for the administration of their property; in this respect their relationship to the federal government further resembled that of Native Americans in the continental United States.

At last, in 1931 responsibility for the administration of Alaska Native affairs was transferred from the Bureau of Education to the Bureau of Indian Affairs,[78] thereby conforming the Department of the Interior's administrative structure to the by then defined status of the Alaska Natives. The following year the solicitor issued a comprehensive opinion reviewing the "status" of Alaska Natives. He concluded his discussion of the cases, statutes and policies applicable to Alaska Natives as follows:

> From the foregoing it is clear that no distinction has been or can be made between the Indians and other Natives of Alaska

so far as the laws and relations of the United States are concerned whether the Eskimos and other natives are of Indian
origin or not as they are all wards of the Nation, and their
status is in material respects similar to that of the Indians of
the United States. It follows that the natives of Alaska, as referred to in the treaty of March 30, 1867, between the United
States and Russia are entitled to the benefits of and are subject
to the general laws and regulations governing the Indians of
the United States.... [79]

2. Effect of the IRA—1936-1971

The Indian Reorganization Act (IRA) of 1934[80] has been described
as one of the most significant pieces of Indian legislation ever enacted
by Congress.[81] Among other things, it put a stop to further allotment of
Indian lands, permitted the Secretary of the Interior to acquire new lands
in trust for landless Indians or existing reserves, provided money from
a revolving loan fund for economic development, and permitted Native
communities to organize their governments under federal constitutions
and to establish federally chartered businesses or cooperatives. As originally enacted, the IRA did not fully apply to Alaska, and was geared more
to the needs of existing Indian reservations; it was amended in 1936 to
take into account the unique needs of Alaska Natives.[82]

Most Alaska Natives lived in isolated villages, and there were few
large reserves; therefore, the Alaska amendments permitted the Secretary of the Interior to designate "public lands which are actually occupied
by Indians or Eskimos" either as new reservations or as additions to
existing reservations.[83] Because there were relatively few Alaskan reservations and because Alaska Natives were perceived as being organized as villages rather than as "tribes" or "bands," the amendments
also permitted them to organize under federal constitutions and business
charters if they had "a common bond of occupation, or association, or
residence within a well-defined neighborhood, community, or rural district."[84]

The Alaska amendments were apparently intended to place Alaska
Native land ownership and governmental authority on the same footing
as that of other Native American reservations. In a letter supporting the
amendments, then Secretary of the Interior, Harold Ickes, listed three
reasons for establishing Alaska reservations.[85] First, they would define
Alaskan "tribes" by identifying particular groups with the land they occupied; second, they would define geographic limits of jurisdiction so that
Alaska Native communities could exercise powers of local government,
and third, they would enable the United States to segregate Native lands
and resources, thereby preserving the "economic rights" of the Natives.
This last goal seemed to look ahead to an eventual congressional settlement of Alaska Native aboriginal land claims.[86]

The Department of the Interior immediately embarked on a drive to organize Alaska Native villages under IRA constitutions and business charters. By early 1941, thirty-eight Native groups had organized under the Alaska amendments,[87] but none of these were associated with reservations. Then, in 1943, the Department withdrew nearly 1.5 million acres for two Native reserves. The largest of these was Venetie (1,408,000 acres). The Karluk Reserve (near Kodiak island) included within its boundaries all the waters within 3,000 feet from shore, thereby excluding non-Native fishermen from one of Alaska's richest fishing grounds. Almost simultaneously, the department announced plans to create similar reserves on the lands and waters surrounding the southeast Alaskan villages of Kake, Klawock and Hydaburg.

The department attempted to prevent non-Natives from fishing on the Karluk reserve by threatening criminal prosecution under newly issued "conservation" regulations.[88] A group of Kodiak Island packers brought suit *(Hynes v. Grimes Packing Co.),*[89] challenging both the Department's authority to issue the regulations and the legality of the Karluk IRA reserve. The U.S. Supreme Court upheld the department's authority to create such reserves, but prohibited criminal prosecution of non-Native trespassers and characterized the Karluk reserve as a "temporary" withdrawal. As a practical matter, the decision hamstrung the department's ability to enforce exclusive Native fishing on the IRA reserves and called into question the permanent rights the Natives had to such reserves. A subsequent Alaska Federal District Court case *(U.S. v. Libby, McNiell and Libby)* invalidated the Hydaburg reserve on technical grounds and denounced the department's efforts to protect aboriginal title.[90] By that time (1952) Secretary Ickes and others in the Interior Department who supported the reservation program were no longer in office, and Congress was soon to adopt a policy of terminating special federal-Native relationships.[91]

The Alaska reservation policy foundered on litigation and political adversity, casting doubt on both the status of the IRA reserves and on the legitimacy of Alaska Native aboriginal land claims. It was not until 1968 that the Interior Department determined that the Alaska IRA reserves constituted "trust" property for leasing and other BIA administrative purposes.[92] However, there were only six IRA reserves in all of Alaska, and the department carefully avoided the conclusion that non-IRA reserves had a similar status. Instead, federal "trust" responsibilities over executive order reserves were limited to those imposed by specific federal statutes regulating leases on such reserves.[93]

Thus, prior to the Alaska Native Claims Settlement Act, the federal government acknowledged a relatively limited and fragmented land related trust responsibility toward Alaska Natives. Its responsibilities, where they existed, were relatively clear, but narrowly defined. These included statutory trust obligations over Native allotments and fiduciary responsibilities over restricted Native townsites as well as general trust authority over IRA reserves and more specific responsibilities related to leases on executive order reserves. In spite of these limitations, the federal government has, at least since the turn of the century, provided a wide variety of programs and services to Alaska Natives solely because of their status as Natives. It is clear that these programs and services have never been tied to true land and resource "trust" responsibilities.

3. Human Services Under the Snyder Act—1931-1971

A discussed above, the BIA has provided Alaska Natives with a broad range of human services and programs ever since it assumed responsibility for Alaska Native affairs in 1931. Like most Native programs nationwide, these are funded with appropriations made under the broad authority of the Snyder Act.[94] The programs include everything from health care and education to economic development and welfare payments, amounting to millions of dollars annually for Alaska alone. Although such programs in the continental United States are only available to Native Americans living "on or near" reservations, because there were few reservations in Alaska, the programs have always been provided there without regard to reservation status.[95]

In the past, appropriations made for human service programs have been termed "gratuity appropriations" if they were neither associated with treaty rights nor made in exchange for cession of aboriginal lands.[96] The services and programs, authorized under the Snyder Act on the theory that Native Americans were the "wards" of the government,[97] were considered mere privileges (as opposed to rights) which could be withheld at the discretion of federal administrators.[98] However, in a series of decisions in the late 1960's and early 1970's, the U.S. Supreme Court eliminated this "wooden distinction" between rights and privileges, replacing it with the modern theory of statutory entitlement.[99]

Entitlements to federal statutory benefits are now characterized as "expectancies" which, like property, cannot be denied without fair hearings, rulemaking and other "due process" procedures.[100] These requirements sharply limit administrative discretion to deny Native services and programs to their intended beneficiaries;[101] hereby creating federal obligations to provide a wide variety of benefits in strict conformity to the various statutes authorizing them. As will be discussed later, it is in the context of these new statutory entitlements that the "unique legal relationship" and the "overriding duty...*to deal fairly with the Indians*" takes on added importance.[102]

4. Native Subsistence Under the BIA—1931-1971

Even prior to the BIA's assumption of authority in Alaska, the Department of the Interior took some steps to protect Alaska Native subsistence needs. In 1930, for example, 768,000 acres were withdrawn for the Tetlin "vocational education" reserve, the primary purpose of which was to preserve Native hunting and trapping resources.[103] Earlier, international treaties such as the Migratory Bird Treaty with England (1916) and the North Pacific Fur Seal Convention (1911) provided specific, but very limited, exceptions for Native subsistence hunting.[104]

After authority was transferred to the BIA, a small reserve was established on Amaknak Island "for the protection of the fishing rights of Alaska Natives";[105] the IRA reserves were intended to accomplish a similar purpose. The Reindeer Industry Act of 1937 was enacted as an economic development program and more specifically to provide a "means of subsistence for the Eskimos and other Natives of Alaska."[106] Subsequent conservation legislation also provided specific exceptions for Native subsistence needs.[107] On the whole, however, these efforts were uncoordinated and often inconsistent with each other, creating a patchwork of rights and prohibitions, making it impossible to afford consistent long-term protection to Native subsistence needs.

5. Native Government—1931-1971

As noted initially, one of the cardinal features of the federal Native relationship is the recognition of Native internal sovereignty. (See chapter 10) The rule is that unless the United States specifically deprives Native communities of their internal powers of self-government, Native governments retain inherent jurisdiction over their people and territory. Felix Cohen noted in this regard:

> Perhaps the most basic principle of all Indian law, supported by a host of decisions hereinafter analyzed, is the principle that *those powers which are lawfully vested in an Indian tribe are not, in general, delegated powers granted by express acts of Congress, but rather inherent powers of a limited sovereignty which has never been extinguished.* Each Indian tribe begins its relationship with the Federal Government as a sovereign power, recognized as such in treaty and legislation (emphasis in original).[108]

The *Sah Quah* decision, previously discussed, cast doubt of the applicability of this rule to Alaska Natives; however, the importance of that decision seems slight given subsequent administrative, judicial and legislative actions. The BIA has long recognized traditional Alaska Native governments as eligible for federal Native programs and services,[109] and the solicitor has held that Alaska Native communities have inherent authority over the domestic relations of their members.[110] Additionally, extension of the IRA to Alaska and the organization of Native governments under that act equated the status of those governments to that of Native governments generally.[111]

Furthermore, subsequent court decisions and congressional action verify the equivalent status of Alaska Native governments. It was generally presumed that the territory of Alaska had the same jurisdiction over

Alaska Natives as over its other citizens. But in 1957, the Alaska Federal District Court held it had no jurisdiction to try a Native resident of the Tyonek reserve for statutory rape because the Tyonek tribal government had exclusive jurisdiction over its members and territory.[112] Congress responded the following year by extending so-called P.L. 280 over all "Indian Country" in Alaska.[113]

P. L. 280 refers to Public Law 83-280, first enacted in 1953 to extend the criminal and civil jurisdiction of certain states over Natives and Native lands within their borders.[114] The inclusion of Alaska among those states implies that Alaska Natives have inherent powers of self-government, although those powers may now be limited by (or shared with) the State of Alaska. Thus, by the time Alaska became a state (1959), both the courts and Congress had acknowledged that Alaska Native governments historically possessed the same inherent internal authority as Native governments elsewhere.[115] The scope of their present authority may now be subject to practical limits under P. L. 280, but the fact of their existence is confirmed by the necessity of applying P. L. 280 to them.

It should be noted, however, that one problem has always plagued most Alaska Native governments—the lack of a clearly defined territory subject to their jurisdiction. As we have seen, the IRA was intended to remedy this situation by identifying Alaska Native communities with the lands they occupied. Although seventy-one IRA governments were eventually established, the reservations contemplated under the Alaska amendments never became a reality. Even though the IRA governments could provide various services to their resident populations and exercise proprietary authority, as a practical matter, the absence of clearly defined boundaries frustrated their ability to exercise police, taxing and other governmental authority. As will be discussed later, however, it is possible that lands conveyed to ANCSA village corporations could now be subject to the governmental authority of village IRA or traditional governing councils.

C. ANCSA and Its Impact

1. Background

Based on the previous analysis, the federal relationship to Alaska Natives can logically be broken down into four aspects: 1) protection of Native lands; 2) provision of human services; 3) protection of subsistence rights; and 4) promotion of Native government. Beginning with the 1884 Organic Act, the federal government has, by administrative actions, judicial decisions and statutory enactments, defined its relationship to the Alaska Natives in each of these four areas. The federal reservation program, both before and after the IRA, addressed questions of land, subsistence and government. The allotment and townsite acts, on the other hand, more specifically addressed the land relationship. Other statutes, such as the Reindeer Industry Act, were drafted specifically to meet Native subsistence needs. Still other statutes, first the IRA and later P. L. 280, promoted or at least defined the powers of Alaska Native governments. Finally, since before the turn of the century, the federal government has, through continued appropriations for the "education and support" of Alaska Natives, and later under the Snyder Act, provided comprehensive education, health, welfare, economic development and other human services to Alaska Natives solely because of their status as Natives.

This long history of intertwined executive policies, congressional enactments and judicial interpretations has resulted in a relationship as complex, delicate and important as any other that exists between the United States and Native Americans. It has been suggested that the Alaska Native Claims Settlement Act (ANCSA)[116] has somehow terminated this relationship.[117] However, it is clear from the act's subject matter that it only *directly* affects one aspect of the federal-Native relationship—that which relates to land.[118] On the other hand, certain implications of the claims act and events since its passage convey mixed signals as to the future of the relationship. Federal budget reductions in the early 1980's cast some doubt on the future of federal services to Alaska Natives, but the Alaska National Interest Lands Conservation Act (ANILCA), passed in 1980, may further protect Alaska Native subsistence values. By 1984, however, the question of the scope and future of Alaska Native self-government had become the most visible aspect of the federal-Native relationship in Alaska. The emergence of each of these issues in the 1980's can be traced in one way or another to certain provisions of ANCSA.

2. ANCSA and the Land

In the late 1950's and early 1960's, judicial decisions[119] and state land selections under the Alaska Statehood Act,[120] began to jeopardize Alaska Native aboriginal land claims. In the late 1960's, other decisions upheld the existence or the possibility of such claims,[121] and the Secretary of the Interior prohibited further state selections until the question of Native land rights could be resolved.[122] These factors, coupled with the obstacle aboriginal claims posed to the extraction, transport and sale of newly discovered oil reserves, mandated that Native claims be resolved promptly by congressional action.[123]

The legislation which ultimately emerged is unique in the history of Native American aboriginal settlements. It permits conveyance of some 44 million acres of land to Alaska Native corporations, along with a cash payment of nearly $1 billion, in exchange for the purported extinguishment of aboriginal Native claims in Alaska. The final Senate bill (S .35) would have required that part of the cash settlement be used to provide the human services which up to that time had been provided by the federal government.[124] The same bill would have made clear provisions for the protection of Native subsistence values.[125] However, the act which finally emerged from the joint House and Senate Conference Committee made no comprehensive provision for either services or subsistence. Nor did ANCSA address the question of Native government; in all its complexity, the claims act primarily describes the express procedures whereby the land and resource settlement was to be achieved.

3. ANCSA and Other Aspects of the Federal Relationship

a. Section 2(b)

In spite of this relatively narrow purpose (i.e., to settle land claims), ANCSA's policy statements have been read rather broadly by some to imply alteration, indeed termination, of all aspects of the federal relationship. Section 2(b) is the most frequently cited section in support of this proposition.[126] It provides that:

> The *settlement* should be accomplished rapidly, with certainty, in conformity with the *real* economic and social needs of Natives, without litigation, with *maximum participation* by Natives in decisions affecting their rights and property, without establishing any permanent *racially* defined institutions, rights, privileges, or obligations, without creating a reservation system or lengthy wardship or trusteeship, and without *adding* to the categories of property and institutions enjoying special tax privileges or to the legislation establishing special relationships between the United States Government and the *State of Alaska* (emphasis added).[127]

The legislative history of this section appears sparse and unenlightening, but as "Native" legislation[128] it must be read liberally to benefit Natives[129] and may only work a termination of the Native relationship if that appears to be the clear intent of its language or legislative history.[130] Reading this passage with these principles in mind greatly diminishes its pro-termination implications.

In the first place, the "settlement" is the subject of the whole policy statement, and section 4 of ANCSA[131] defines the settlement solely in terms of the extinguishment of titles and claims based on aboriginal rights, titles, use or occupancy of land and water resources. Significantly, the "settlement" does not include resolution of human service or Native government questions. It does extinguish Native hunting and fishing rights, implying resolution of Native subsistence questions; however, the joint House and Senate Conference Committee report and other sections of the act indicate Congress intended that subsistence be protected in other ways. It is also most significant that in 1980 Congress enacted specific legislation aimed to provide more specific protection for subsistence values[132]

It also seems significant that the settlement was to be accomplished "in conformity with the real economic and social needs of Natives." A fair reading of this phrase is that the settlement, although indirectly addressing Native economic and social needs, was not intended to completely satisfy those needs. Indeed, the implication of section 2(c) of the act is that federal Native programs addressing these "real" needs were to be evaluated and their future addressed at a later date.[133] Instead of being a mandate to terminate Alaska Native social services and economic development programs, a liberal reading of this clause indicates that the federal government will continue to meet those needs so long as it is reasonably necessary to do so. Furthermore, the stipulation that Natives should have "maximum participation" in "decisions affecting their rights" implies that the future of Native lands, resources, government, human services and subsistence will be decided in full consultation with the Alaska Natives, not by administrative fiat.

Third, not "establishing permanent racially defined institutions, rights, privileges, or obligations" does not imply that such "institutions," if any, which now exist will be dismantled or that "temporary" ethnic rights are prohibited. More important, however, it has been held in several U. S. Supreme Court cases, all subsequent to the claims act, that unique Native institutions and rights are based on the historical "political" status of Natives and are not, therefore, "racially" defined.

> Federal regulation of Indian tribes, therefore, is governance of once-sovereign political communities; it is not to be viewed as legislation of a " 'racial' group consisting of 'Indians'...."[134]

Thus 2(b) does not even oppose new Alaska Native institutions, rights, privileges or federal obligations associated with them, much less require the disestablishment of those which already exist.[135]

Fourth, the declaration that there is to be no "lengthy wardship or trusteeship" does not eliminate wardship or trusteeship, although it does ambiguously limit the length of either. Moreover, this language more accurately relates to the future status of ANCSA corporate lands rather than the future of Native government or federal services and programs. Native government is not the product of federal wardship but of inherent tribal sovereignty, which the federal government has never totally extinguished. Native sovereignty is the antithesis of wardship, and is the characteristic which sets the government to government relationship of the United States to Natives apart from other relationships, such as those in which the United States provides care and support to needy people. Furthermore, as discussed previously, federal Native services and programs are no longer mere privileges granted to indigent "wards" but statutory entitlements. Congress has the plenary authority to create or withdraw such entitlements, but once established they cannot be administratively limited without rulemaking[136] and other adequate due process.[137]

Finally, not "adding to the categories of property institutions" with special tax privileges does not eliminate special tax privileges for entities such as Native governments, which *already* have such privileges. They are simply not *new* categories. Furthermore, it does seem significant that the "special relationships" disfavored are not those between the United States and *Natives* but rather between the United States and the *State of Alaska*. Admittedly, these policies as well as others stated in section 2(b) are generalized and subject to differing interpretations, but if that is so, then established rules of construction require that these policies be interpreted to benefit Natives, nor can such policies be said to terminate the federal-Native relationship unless they do so clearly. None of the 2(b) policy statements appear to do so. [138]

b. Section 2(c)

This section[139] bears directly on the federal relationship to Alaska Natives when it specifically requires the Secretary of the Interior to make "recommendations for the future management and operation" of "all Federal programs primarily designed to benefit Native people." It is important to note that the provision is divided into two independent clauses.

Clause 1:

> [N]o provision of this Act shall replace or diminish any right, privilege, or obligation of Natives as citizens of the United States or of Alaska, or relieve, replace, or diminish any obligation of the United States or of the State of Alaska, to protect and promote the rights or welfare of Natives as citizens of the United States or of Alaska...

Clause 2:

> [T]he Secretary is authorized and directed together with other appropriate agencies of the United States Government, to make a study of all Federal programs primarily designed to benefit Native people and to report back to Congress his *recommendations* for the future management and operation of these programs within three years of the date of enactment of this Act... (emphasis added).

The language of the first clause remained substantially the same in several bills introduced to settle the claims. It appears as early as 1969 in both the administration bill (HR 13142) and the Federal Field Committee bill (HR10193).[140] With the exception of the final subordinate clause ("as citizens of the United States or of Alaska"), it also appears in a 1969 draft AFN bill[141] and appears in substantially the same form in all the bills introduced in 1971, including HR 10367, which became the Alaska Native Claims Settlement Act.[142]

Although the final language, referring to rights and welfare as "citizens," might be construed as a limitation on the obligation of the United States to protect Native rights and welfare as *Natives,* that concern is really the point of the second clause. The first clause, on the other hand, appears designed to protect rights Natives have to state and federal welfare or other programs available to *all* citizens. [143]

The second clause has a more complex history; its predecessor first appears in the 1969 AFN draft bill and provided that:

> The payments and grants authorized in Section 5 of this Act constitute compensation for the extinguishment of property rights, and shall not be deemed as a substitute for any governmental program otherwise available to Natives of Alaska in accordance with the laws applicable to Indian affairs. [144]

The same language is included in both the House and Senate bills introduced in 1971 on behalf of AFN. [145] Another version of the same clause first appeared in Senate Bill 35, introduced by Senator Jackson in January 1971. There the clause provided that:

> The payments authorized under this Act constitute compensation for the extinguishment of claims to land and shall not be deemed a substitute for any governmental program otherwise available to Indians of Alaska as *citizens of the United States and the State of Alaska* (emphasis added).

If this language had survived, it could imply that Natives, as citizens of the United States and the State of Alaska, would be entitled only to those services and programs available to *other* citizens. The reverse implication is that programs available to them as Natives are eliminated in exchange for the land and money granted under the claims act. [146] The legislative history does not elaborate any further on the question, but the Senate language was deleted in the joint House and Senate conference committee and replaced with the present language.

It seems clear that AFN, in its original draft bill, was attempting to separate the settlement of land claims from Native entitlement to economic and social programs and services. The AFN language would have clearly precluded the claims settlement from being used to terminate such programs and services, but the language of Senator Jackson's bill could have set off the claims settlement against future entitlement to programs and services. The conference committee struck a compromise. A probable interpretation is that Congress chose to preserve the "status quo" of Alaska Native programs until it had the recommendations of the Secretary of the Interior on the future of those programs.

Even though the law "authorized and directed" the Secretary of the Interior to submit his recommendations "within three years," no Interior Secretary has ever complied. Such administrative deriliction is startling, but it is probably now too late to challenge it legally.[147] Although the then Secretary of the Interior, Rogers Morton, did submit a comprehensive description of Alaska Native programs within the required time frame,[148] the letter transmitting it specifically noted that the report did not include any recommendations.[149]

Such an administrative lapse does not prevent Congress from legislating with respect to such programs, and it has done so repeatedly since ANCSA's passage.[150] In the early 1980's, however, Congress also cut the appropriations for certain Alaska Native programs, notably education and welfare assistance.[151] It was not clear in 1984 whether this was the beginning of a policy to terminate Native services in Alaska or merely part of nationwide cuts in such programs, but it is quite clear that there are significant limits on the Interior Secretary's ability to administratively diminish those programs. Section 2(b) requires there be "maximum participation of Natives in decisions affecting their rights"; almost certainly continued entitlement to Native programs and services is among those rights. To administratively reduce Native entitlement without involving Natives in such a decision also appears contrary to the federal government's judicially recognized "overriding duty...to deal fairly with the Indians wherever located."

The U.S. Supreme Court, in part on such reasoning, has prevented the Secretary of the Interior from denying general assistance payments to certain needy Native Americans, because congressional appropriations were made on the assumption such Natives would receive the assistance.[152] In a similar case in Alaska, the Ninth Circuit Court of Appeals has required the BIA to continue funding welfare assistance payments to needy Natives where it was not crystal clear that Congress had acquiesced in the Interior Department's decision to cut the program.[153] The latter case may be especially significant, because it illustrates a judicial reluctance to accept administrative attempts to reduce Alaska Native programs in the absence of especially clear congressional authority.

III. The Modern Relationship

A. The Abstract Relationship

In a general and somewhat abstract sense, there is an enduring relationship between the federal government and Native Americans. That relationship has historically been described as one of "wardship," "guardianship," "trust" and more recently "fairness." Felix Cohen suggests that in this general sense, "wardship" is descriptive of the unequal *political* relationship of Native "tribes" (as governments) to the federal government.[154] This relationship, because it is unequal, necessarily implies a federal duty of protection[155] and by a "natural extension" is also a source of federal plenary power over Native Americans.[156] The U.S. Supreme

Court summed it up this way in the late nineteenth century:

> From their very weakness and helplessness, so largely due to the course of dealing of the Federal Government with them and the treaties in which it has been promised, there arises the duty of protection, and with it the power.

* * * *

> The power of the General Government over these remnants of a race once powerful, now weak and diminished in numbers, is necessary to their protection.... It must exist in that government, because it never has existed anywhere else, because the theatre of its exercise is within the geographical limits of the United States because it has never been denied, and because it alone can enforce its laws on all tribes. [157]

More modern Supreme Court decisions have established that, while the exercise of this authority for the protection of Native interests is committed to the broad political discretion of the executive branch and Congress, [158] it is also limited by the U. S. Constitution and its use must be "tied rationally to the fulfillment of Congress' unique obligation toward the Indians."[159] That means, for example, that neither Congress nor the executive branch can take recognized Indian property rights without paying for them. [160] So long as Congress and the executive act within these limits, however, their actions in the field of Indian affairs are not generally subject to judicial scrutiny. [161]

One strength of the abstract relationship is that it permits wide congressional and executive latitude in fashioning and providing Native American programs and benefits. Because they are based on a unique *political* relationship, such programs and benefits are not held to be racially discriminatory, even though they exclusively benefit members of a distinct racial group. [162] In this abstract sense, the relationship has been applied to Alaska as a source of federal authority to provide programs and services, [163] protect Native lands, [164] protect Native children, [165] confirm Native sovereign immunity[166] and uphold Native contracting preferences. [167]

On the other hand, that same flexibility permits Congress to narrow the scope of Native sovereignty, [168] abrogate previous Indian treaties, [169] or refuse to provide compensation for the taking of "unrecognized" aboriginal title. [170] It also permits the secretary to refuse to exercise his discretionary authority on behalf of Natives, unless a congressional statute, treaty, appropriation or other requirement obligates him to do so. It is through these vehicles that Congress "recognizes" and defines the abstract federal relationship in such terms that it can be enforced, if need be, as a specific federal obligation. It is in such specific congressional actions as these that are frequently found the more specific and enforceable aspects of the federal relationship.

B. The Specific Aspects

1. General

Because there were no treaties between Alaska Natives and the federal government, statutory manifestations (including appropriations) of their federal-Native relationship are very important. As we have seen, however, the absence of statutes does not eliminate federal authority over Alaskan Native affairs nor necessarily prevent the executive branch from acting on their behalf. On the other hand, statutory (and regulatory) descriptions afford an opportunity for both the federal government and Alaska Natives to define their respective obligations and expectancies, thereby ensuring more likely future realization of both.

As previously discussed, even prior to ANCSA, a number of federal statutes were enacted specifically for Alaska Native benefit; similarly, appropriations under the Snyder Act have long included *all* Alaska Natives within the scope of their intended benefits. However, since 1971, there has been a veritable explosion of statutory provisions specifying Alaska Natives as the beneficiaries of federal, Native American programs. These statutes manifest all four aspects of the federal relationship to Alaska Natives: 1) protecting Native lands and resources, 2) providing human services, 3) protecting subsistence values, and 4) promoting Native government.

2. Protecting Native Lands and Resources

One commentator has noted that ANCSA "fundamentally reduced" federal trust responsibilities over Alaska Native lands

> as the for-profit corporation was substituted for a more protective entity, and as the Congress fashioned an equitable method for distributing the vast amount of land and funds among variously placed and situated Native individuals and organizations. [171]

Section 2(b) of the act also clearly requires that the settlement be accomplished without creating a "lengthy trusteeship." However, as noted earlier, federal trusteeship prior to the act was fragmented and varied in scope depending on the particular statute or previous executive action under which it was exercised. ANCSA cut away these tangled responsibilities, at least as they related to reserves, and replaced them with the as yet undefined responsibilities of the various Native corporations to their stockholders and to each other. [172]

Because ANCSA restricts alienation of village and regional corporation stock,[173] it is possible for dissenting shareholders to prevent disposition of "all or substantially all" of a corporation's assets. Under state law, such dispositions (other than in the "ordinary course of business") require approval of two-thirds of the shareholders and afford dissenters the right to be "bought out."[174] Since the ANCSA stock cannot be sold until 1992, the dissenters' shares cannot be bought which means they could effectively block any extraordinary disposition of corporate assets.[175]

Other provisions of the act required regional corporations to review village corporation articles of incorporation and budgets during the first five years following the act.[176] Still other provisions permitted regional corporations to withhold from a village indefinitely distributions from the Alaska Native Fund indefinitely unless the affected village corporation submitted a satisfactory "plan" for the use of those funds.[177] It has been suggested that regional corporation negligent approval of a wasteful or otherwise inappropriate plan could, under some circumstances, render the regional corporation liable for any resulting loss to village corporation shareholders.[178] Similarly, another provision of the act permitted regional corporations to review and advise village corporations on "land sales, leases or other transactions prior to any final commitment" for a period of ten years after the act.[179] If a regional corporation negligently rendered advice on such transactions to a village corporation's detriment, it seems likely the regional corporation would then be liable to the village corporation or its shareholders for any resulting damages.[180]

Finally, regional corporations have substantial obligations to each other under section 7(i) of the act and to the village corporations and at-large shareholders under section 7(j).[181] Section 7(i) provides for a division among "all twelve regional corporations" of seventy percent of "all revenues received" from any one region's subsurface estate or timber resources. Congress chose this mechanism to assure an equitable distribution among Alaska Natives of the value of the lands to be conveyed under ANCSA,[182] but it proved deceptively simple and fraught with ambiguity. For example, it was not clear whether "all revenues" was the same as "net income," nor, if they were the same, was it clear how the costs of development would be calculated for determining net income. Such issues spawned a spate of lawsuits among the regional corporations[183] which were ultimately resolved in the massive "7(i) agreement," which the twelve in state regional corporations signed in 1982.[184]

Under section 7(j), fifty percent of the revenue each regional corporation receives as 7(i) distributions must be passed on to the village corporations and to the regional corporation's at-large shareholders on a per capita basis.[185] Although section 7(j) appears broadly enough worded to require a similar distribution of "all other net income," the Alaska Federal District Court has held that the 7(j) distributions apply only to revenues attributable to the 7(j) distributions each regional corporation *receives*.[186] That is to say it does not include either revenue derived from other sources (e.g., investments) or revenue attributable to the thirty percent of the 7(j) revenue *retained* by the regional corporation making a 7(j) distribution. [187]

Perhaps none of these obligations amount to a "trust responsibility" for the regional corporations, but they are important statutory obligations with perhaps perpetual significance. Similarly, the Alaska Federal District Court has also held that the federal government does not have a "trust responsibility" in its management of ANCSA selected lands prior to conveyance. [188] But even this does not mean that the government has no land-related obligations under the act or trust responsibilities under other federal Native land laws. For example, the courts soundly rebuffed the government's early attempt to impose numerous easements on the lands to be conveyed because such easements were beyond the intent of ANCSA. [189] The courts have also required the Secretary of the Interior to adhere to specific due process requirements in determining village rights to ANCSA benefits in part because section 2(b) of ANCSA requires the "maximum participation" by Natives in decisions affecting their rights and property."[190] Such decisions imply that the other general ANCSA policy requirements have more force than their facile generality may initially imply. Moreover, the courts have also held that the federal government retains a "trust responsibility" for the administration of restricted townsites and allotments under earlier legislation. [191]

3. Providing Human Services

As discussed earlier, [192] sections 2(b) and 2(c) of the claims act manifest specific congressional concern for the future of Alaska Native human service programs. When the act was passed, it was acknowledged that Alaska Natives were among the most disadvantaged of United States citizens. In this context, Congress specifically required that the settlement be accomplished "in conformity with the real economic and social needs of Natives" and that there be "maximum participation by Natives in decisions affecting their rights." Furthermore, the act required the Secretary of the Interior to make recommendations to Congress "for the future management and operation" of those programs "primarily designed to benefit Native people." In the context of recognized Alaska Native needs, these policies can hardly be dismissed as mere window dressing. Similar general policy statements, when connected with an acute and obvious need, have been held sufficient to impose an obligation on the government to meet that need. [193]

In spite of these policies, beginning in the 1980's, the federal government initiated several deep cuts in funding for Alaska Native programs—notably education and welfare payments. Closure of all BIA schools in Alaska now appears certain by 1985. [194]

However, attempts to terminate a substantial BIA financial assistance program met with judicial obstacles. [195] Given the importance ANCSA attaches to the "real social and economic needs of Natives," it is perhaps not too surprising that the court in this case refused to accept the government's argument that Congress had cut the funding for the federal program even though the state's program which was to replace it did not provide even closely comparable benefits. It is also significant that in circumstances even less compelling than these the Ninth Circuit Federal Court of Appeals (which is the federal appellate court for Alaska) has required the BIA to hold a due process hearing prior to terminating funding of another Native welfare program. [196] A subsequent Alaska case also held that the federal government had a "trust responsibility" under the so called Bartlett Housing Act to build adequate houses with money appropriated for Alaska Native housing. [197]

The claims act policies aside, the BIA has assumed an obligation to provide human services on a broader scope to Alaska Natives than to other Native Americans. As discussed earlier, most Native programs and services are provided under the general authority of the Snyder Act. [198] In the continental United States, these services are provided only to otherwise eligible Natives who reside "on or near" a reservation. Owing to the absence of reservations in Alaska, the BIA has always provided these services to *all* Alaska Natives. [199] It has been suggested by some that the scope of the Alaska service obligation might now be restricted to ANCSA corporation shareholders or some other restricted class of Native beneficiaries. However, the U.S. Supreme Court's decision in *Morton v. Ruiz* makes it plain that in order to accomplish any such restriction, the Interior Department would have to at least promulgate regulations according to the requirements of the federal Administrative Procedure Act. [200] Additionally, any such regulations affecting Alaska Natives would, under ANCSA, require "maximum participation of Natives" in their formulation.

Finally, it should be noted that at least four major enactments since the claims act have specifically recognized the right of Alaska Natives to benefit from general legislation enacted for the benefit of Native Americans. The Indian Financing Act (1974), [201] Indian Self-Determination Act (1975), [202] Indian Health Care Improvement Act (1976), [203] and the Indian Child Welfare Act (1978)[204] recognize variously Alaska Native villages, groups, regional corporations or village corporations as eligible for their benefits. In so doing, each of these enactments manifests the federal government's continuing special relationship to Alaska Natives. In both general and specific terms, each statute imposes obligations on federal administrators charged with the implementation of the programs mandated under each piece of legislation. [205]

4. Protecting Subsistence Rights

Although ANCSA extinguished Alaska Native hunting and fishing rights, it is clear from its legislative history that Congress also intended that the lands conveyed under the act as well as state and federal policies were to be used to promote and maintian Alaska Native subsistence values. [206] Furthermore, subsequent to ANCSA, the courts have held that special Native subsistence exemptions found in numerous federal wildlife treaties and statutes manifest a federal "trust responsibility" to protect Alaska Native subsistence values. [207]

Just as important, however, is the enactment in 1980 of Title VIII of the Alaska National Interest Lands Conservation Act (ANILCA). [208] This statute provides a preference and other protections for subsistence uses of wild, renewable resources by "rural Alaska residents" on federal public lands within Alaska. But it goes beyond that to require the state to establish the same range of protections on state and private lands in order to exercise state fish and game management authority on federal lands. [209] In some sense ANILCA it is a "settlement" of Alaska Native fishing and hunting rights, because it affords the predominately Native population of rural Alaska a unique set of protections and preferences for off-reservation subsistence uses of wildlife. However, ANILCA is unique in the field of United States Indian legislation because it also extends these same protections to non-Native rural residents who participate in the predominately Native subsistence economy.

One question which ANILCA does not clearly resolve, however, is the question of state and tribal authority over fishing and hunting on lands controlled by Alaska Native corporations or tribal governments. [210] It does seem likely that, in the absence of either reservations or federal statutes prohibiting state authority over Native hunting and fishing, that tribal governments would be able to exercise only concurrent jurisdiction over subsistence resources. This issue, however, is part of the more general question of the scope of Native self-government in Alaska in the post-ANCSA era.

5. Promoting Native Government

At least since the days of John Marshall, the relationship between the federal government and Native American "tribes" has been characterized as that of one government to another. Federal recognition of a Native community as eligible for federal programs and services provided to Natives because of their status as Natives is one manifestation of this relationship. Once eligibility is recognized, the federal government will then attempt to define the government with which it will deal in providing the particular program or service. In some circumstances, as with the Tlingit and Haida Central Council in southeast Alaska, it will mandate the establishment of a new government. [211] In other cases, as with the Alaska traditional village councils, it will recognize governments already in place or create a more formalized relationship with such governments under the Indian Reorganization Act. [212]

Although ANCSA established new Native corporations to manage the benefts flowing from the act, it did not thereby disestablish pre-existing traditional, IRA or congressionally created Native governments. [213] Furthermore, the Native profit and nonprofit corporations established throughout the state do not appear to have either defined or implied powers of social or political governance. Those powers are held either by state organized municipalities or by Native governments and sometimes by both in the same community. However, because Alaska Native governments have seldom been identified with specific territory, they have, as a practical matter, been unable to clearly define the scope of their authority. The Alaska amendments to the Indian Reorganization Act were intended to resolve that problem with reservations, but only six IRA reserves were created, and those were revoked under ANCSA.[214]

Nevertheless, in a 1958 case involving the Tyonek reserve, where there was an identity of territory with a Native government, the Alaska Federal District Court held that the Tyonek council had the same internal governing powers as any Native government.[215] Shortly thereafter, Congress applied P.L. 280 to Alaska, authorizing the state to assume a large measure of civil and criminal jurisdiction over "Indian country" in Alaska.[216] It is not clear whether the state and its subdivisions have acquired exclusive or merely concurrent civil or criminal jurisdiction under P.L. 280. Nor is it clear whether the state's jurisdiction extends to general regulatory matters or is confined to judicial adjudication of civil disputes. At least on reservations, the leading federal cases have narrowly interpreted P.L. 280 to prevent local taxation of on-reservation personal property[217] or local zoning of reservation lands.[218] On the other hand, P.L. 280's legislative history indicates that Congress (probably mistakenly) assumed that, at least in Alaska, the state would acquire exclusive *criminal jurisdiction*.[219]

However, the scope of the state's civil jurisdiction seems less extensive. For example, P.L. 280's grant of civil jurisdiction requires that Native "ordinances and customs" be given "full force and effect" in Alaska state courts.[220] The Alaska State Supreme Court has also consistently interpreted P.L. 280 narrowly to deny state civil jurisdiction over tribal or individual trust or restricted property[221] and as not constituting a waiver of tribal sovereign immunity.[222] The latter case involved the sovereign immunity of the Metlakatla reservation IRA government; subsequent state court decisions involving non-reservation Alaska Native governments have found waivers of sovereign immunity in more tenuous circumstances[223] and even suggested that an Alaska IRA was not a federally recognized "tribe."[224] The Alaska Federal District Court, on the other hand, has confirmed the jurisdiction of an Alaska Native tribal court to adjudicate the ownership of tribal artifacts,[225] and affirmed the sovereign immunity of the Tlingit and Haida Central Council, a non-IRA, non-reservation tribal government.[226]

Although it is possible that either legislation or litigation will be necessary to finally resolve some questions, it is possible that ANCSA has opened the way for Alaska Native governments to exercise civil and even criminal authority over village corporation lands. In the Tyonek decision previously discussed, the Alaska Federal District Court, relying on previous U.S. Supreme Court decisions, held that the Tyonek Natives were not subject to general federal criminal jurisdiction because the land they occupied was "set aside for the use of and [was] governed by an operational tribal unit."[227] Significantly, the U.S. Supreme Court decision on which the district court relied does not require that the Native land be "set aside" but only that it be "owned or occupied by an Indian nation or tribe of Indians."[228] Conceivably, ANCSA village lands fall within this definition, permitting a traditional or IRA Native government to exercise governmental (although not proprietary) authority over village corporation lands. It is also significant in this regard that, even subsequent to ANCSA, the Secretary of the Interior has delegated governmental authority to Alaska Native villages to enforce the federal Indian liquor laws within Native townsites.[229]

On the other hand, even lack of territory does not work a dissolution of Native government for other purposes—particularly those related to the provision of certain governmental services. Furthermore, recent legislation specifically recognizes the eligibility of Alaska Native "villages" for economic development,[230] self-determination,[231] health care;[232] and child welfare[233] grants, contracts and jurisdiction. Since 1982, the Secretary of the Interior has also included nearly 200 Alaska Native entities in the annual publication of "Indian tribes which are recognized as receiving services from the Bureau of Indian Affairs."[234] These congressional statutes and continued executive recognition of Alaska Native governments all manifest a continuing federal policy which recognizes Alaska Native tribes or villages as "distinct cultural and governmental entities" having a "unique government to government relationship" with the United States.[235]

IV. General Conclusions

Although the Alaska Native Claims Settlement Act significantly affects the relationship of Alaska Natives to the federal government, it is by no means the only legislation which affects that relationship either historically or recently. Furthermore, ANCSA is in many respects more important for what it does *not* say about certain aspects of the federal-Native relationship than for what it does say. The implication of these significant omissions is that the future of federal economic and social services, Native subsistence, and Native government will be determined under existing and future legislation and upon previously established legal principles specific to these issues.

Even as to lands and resources, ANCSA may impose certain obligations on the Secretary of the Interior to faithfully implement the claims act. After conveyance, it also seems likely that the regional corporations will retain certain obligations for the guidance of village corporations as well as responsibility for the proper distribution of resource profits among regional and village corporations. Given the restrictions on the alienation of ANCSA stock, it is also probable that ANCSA corporations are subject to extraordinary limitations on their ability to dispose of corporate assets. It is also plain that the federal government retains a land related "trust responsibility" for the administration of restricted Native townsite and allotted lands.

Furthermore, ANCSA clearly contemplates that the future of federal Native programs in Alaska will be the subject of future congressional action based on the "maximum participation" by Natives in any decisions affecting their rights to such programs and services. Legislation enacted since ANCSA affecting Native economic development, education, social services, health care, child welfare and a host of other matters has been specifically applied to Alaska Natives. Thus, one implication of both ANCSA and more recent legislation is that the full range of federal Native programs will remain applicable to Alaska Natives and that those Natives will participate fully in major decisions affecting the future of those programs. Although federal budget cuts in the early 1980's cast a cloud on the future of these programs, there has been judicial resistance to enforcing these cuts in the absence of very clear congressional intent. The courts have also held, subsequent to the claims act, that federal agencies have a "trust responsibility" to scrupulously administer these programs for Native benefit.

Even though a comprehensive approach to the question of Native subsistence escaped the authors of the claims act, both the Natives lobbying for the act and the Congress passing it clearly contemplated that the future of Native subsistence would be sensitively handled so as to protect access to those renewable resources historically vital to Native physical and cultural survival. Subsequent court decisions have characterized federal obligations for Native subsistence under certain conservation statutes as a "trust responsibility," and in 1980 Congress enacted comprehensive subsistence protections favoring (predominately Native) "rural Alaska residents" as a part of ANILCA. However, the question of tribal jurisdiction over these resources in Alaska is perhaps not fully resolved.

Finally, ANCSA is silent on the future of Alaska Native self-government, but previous legislative authority exists for the continued formal organization of Native governments under the Indian Reorganization Act and for the exercise of their governmental authority subject to P.L. 280 and other federal legislation. Subsequent to ANCSA, the Self-Determination Act has been made specifically applicable to Alaska, encouraging the strengthening of Native self-government. Under one view, Alaska Native traditional or IRA governments could exercise civil and even criminal authority over village lands which are owned or occupied by Natives under ANCSA. Even absent such territorial jurisdiction, Alaska Native governments still have the potential to provide significant types of governmental services to the residents of their communities.

Thus, when considering the relationship of Alaska Natives to the federal government, one must be conscious not only of the recent present but also of past legislation, policies and legal principles which have conceived the present and which, to a remarkable degree, continue to determine the nature of the unique legal relatioship between those Natives and the government. That relationship is one of many parts, here divided into a convenient four, and the principles applicable to one part may not imply a similar resolution of issues affecting others. Thus, for example, extinguishment of land claims under ANCSA, does not similarly extinguish claims of Native governing authority established on other legal principles or defined by previous legislation. Similarly, resolution of land claims has little logical relationship to the continued entitlement of Natives to statutory economic and social benefits. The following chapters and their sundry sub-parts more fully analyze the history and laws which have created and shaped the several aspects of the federal relationship to Alaska Natives.

ENDNOTES

[1] Cherokee Nation v. Georgia 30 U.S. (5 Pet.) 1, 17 (1831).

[2] Id. at 17-18.

[3] Worcestor v. Georgia, 31 U.S. (6 Pet.) 515, 559-560 (1830).

[4] See generally *Law and Indigenous Populations,* 27 Buffalo L. Rev. 581 (State University of New York: Buffalo, 1978), several articles analyzing and comparing the legal status of North and South American Native people. See also B. A. Keon-Cohen, *Native Justice in Australia, Canada, and the U.S.A.: A Comparative Analysis,* 7 Monash U.L. Rev. 250 (Monash University: Clayton, Victoria, Australia, 1981).
There are, of course, indigenous people who have achieved national independence, notably in Africa, but also in New Guinea and certain islands in the South Pacific. Greenlandic Inuit have also obtained a measure of "home rule," but for certain purposes remain subject to Danish law. See e.g., G. Alfredson, *Greenland and the Law of Political Decolonization,* 25 German Yearbook of International Law 290 (Berlin: Dunckner & Humblot, 1982); P. Jull, *Greenland Lessons of self-government and development,* VII Northern Perspectives 1 (Ottawa: Canadian Arctic Resources Committee, 1979); O. Olesen, *Home Rule for Greenland* (Ottawa: Department of Indian and Northern Affairs).

[5] F. S. Cohen, *Handbook of Federal Indian Law,* (Charlottesville, Va.: Michie Bobbs-Merrill, 1982) at 217-220.

[6] Johnson v. M'Intosh, 21 U.S. (8 Wheat.) 543 (1823). See also chapter 2, "Aboriginal Title."

[7] *Worcester v. Georgia,* note 3, above, at 561.

[8] Lone Wolf v. Hitchcock, 187 U.S. 553, 565 (1903).

[9] See e.g., R. L. Barsh and J. Y. Henderson, *The Road* (Berkley: University of California Press, 1980) at 112-134; R. T. Coulter, "The Denial of Legal Remedies to Indian Nations Under U. S. Law," *Rethinking Indian Law* (National Lawyers Guild, 1982) at 105-106.

[10]United States v. Sioux Nation, 448 U.S. 371 (1980), awarding $117 million in damages and interest for the congressional abrogation of the 1868 Treaty of Fort Laramie without just compensation.

[11]Delaware Tribal Business Committee v. Weeks, 430 U.S. 73, 85 (1977). See generally Cohen (1982), note 5, above, at 217-228. See also *Federal Plenary Power in Indian Affairs After Weeks and Sioux Nation,* 131 U. of Penna. L. Rev. 235 (1982).

[12]Choctaw Nation v. United States, 119 U.S. 1, 28 (1886).

[13]Morton v. Ruiz, 415 U.S. 199 (1973), obligation to provide welfare benefits to nonreservation Indians.

[14]Seminole Nation v. U.S., 286, 296 (1942), obligation to ensure that trust funds paid to tribal leaders were used for tribal benefit.

[15]E.g., Alaska Pacific Fisheries v. U.S., 248 U.S. 78, 89 (1918).

[16]E.g., Menominee Tribe of Indians v. U.S., 391 U.S. 404 (1968).

[17]Cohen (1982), note 5, above, at 220.

[18]Scott, Austin Wakeman, *The Law of Trusts* (Boston: Little Brown and Company, 1967) at 3-4.

[19]Id. at 773. See e.g., Quick Bear v. Leupp, 210 U.S. 50 (1908), in exchange for transfer of Indian land, the federal government agreed to use the purchase price for education of Indian children at Catholic school.

[20]Cohen (1982), note 5, above, at 677-678.

[21]E.g., Rockbridge v. Lincoln 449 F. 2d 567, 570 (1971).

[22]E.g., U.S. v. Kagama, 118 U.S. 375 (1896).

[23]E.g., *Morton v. Ruiz,* note 13 above, at 236.

[24]White v. Califano, 437 F. Supp. 543, 557, n.9 (D.C.S.D. 1977), aff'd. 581 F. 2d 697 (8th Cir. 1978).

[25]Alaska Public Easement Defense Fund v. Andrus, 435 F. Supp. 664, 671 (D.C. Ak. 1977), Alaska Natives held dependent on congressional "protection and good faith" in the resolution of their land claims.

[26]C.f. *Morton v. Ruiz,* note 13, above.

[27]C.f. U.S. v. Winans, 198 U.S. 371 (1905). See also People of Togiak v. U.S., 470 F. Supp. 423, 427-428 (D.C. D.C. 1979).

[28]E.g., Williams v. Lee, 358 U.S. 217 (1959).

[29]E.g., *Choctaw Nation v. U.S.*, note 12, above.

[30]E.g., Metlakatla v. Egan, 369 U.S. 45 (1962), protection of Native fishing under federal regualtions on Alaska statutory reserve. See also *White v. Califano,* note 24, above, obligation to provide health care under Indian Health Care Improvement Act.

[31]E.g., *Morton v. Ruiz,* note 13, above, obligation to provide welfare benefit payments to Indians living "on or near" a reservation, because congressional appropriations for such assistance were based on understanding that such Indians would receive assistance.

[32]E.g., In re McCord, 151 F. Supp. 132 (D.C. AK 1957), federal prosecution of Alaska Native resident of executive order reserve prohibited because it was land "set aside for the use of and...governed by an operational tribal unit."

[33]E.g., Edwardsen v. Morton, 369 F. Supp. 1359 (D.C.D.C. 1973), federal obligation to protect alleged aboriginal claims of Alaska Natives.

[34]See e.g., Tee-Hit-Ton Band of Indians v. U.S., 348 U.S. 272 (1955), unrecognized aboriginal title not compensable under the Fifth Amendment. See also Gila River, Pima-Maricopa Band of Indians v. U.S., 427 F. 2d 1194 (Ct. Cls. 1970), holding, absent some statute, there was no obligation to provide health and other services to Native American plaintiffs.

[35]Act of August 15, 1953, P.L. 83-280, 67 Stat. 589, codified as amended at 18 USCA 1162, 28 USCA 1360 and 25 USCA 1321 and 1322, conferring a measure of state criminal and civil jurisdiction over Indians and "Indian country".

[36]Act of April 11, 1968, P.L. 90-284, 82 Stat. 77, codified as amended at 25 USCA 1301 et seq.

[37]Act of December 18, 1971, P.L. 93-203, 85 Stat. 689, 43 USCA 1601 et seq.

[38]Act of October 21, 1972, P.L. 92-522, 86 Stat. 1027, 16 USCA 1361 et seq.

[39]Act of December 28, 1973, P.L. 93-2056, 87 Stat. 884, 16 USCA 1531 et seq.

[40]Act of April 12, 1974, P.L. 93-262, 88 Stat. 77, 25 USCA 1451 et seq.

[41]Act of January 4, 1975. P.L. 93-638, 88 Stat. 2203, 25 USCA 450 et seq.

[42]Act of September 30, 1976, P.L. 94-437, 90 Stat. 1400, 25 USCA 1601 et seq.

[43]Act of November 8, 1978, P.L. 95-608, 92 Stat. 3069, 25 USCA 1901 et seq.

[44]Act of January 14, 1982, Title II, P.L. 97-473, 96 Stat. 2607, as amended and codified at scattered parts of 26 USCA.

[45]E.g., McClanahan v. Arizona State Tax Commission, 411 U.S. 164, 172 (1973), the limits of state power over Native governments is defined by applicable treaties and statutes. See also *White v. Califano,* note 30, above.

[46]Treaty of March 30, 1867, 15 Stat. 539.

[47]See e.g., U.S. v. Sandoval, 231 U.S. 28, 48 (1913). See also *Status of Alaska Natives,* 53 I.D. 593, 605-606 (1932).

[48]See U.S. v. Berrigan, 2 Ak. Rpts. 442 (D.C. Ak. 1904).

[49]See discussion of the distinction between "civilized" and "uncivilized" in chapter 2, V B3, below " 'Civilized' and 'Uncivilized'."

[50]In re Minook, 2 Ak. Rpts. 200 (1904).

[51]Davis v. Sitka School Board, 3 Ak. Rpts. 481 (1908).

[52]These Acts include:

> The Organic Act of May 17, 1884, sec. 8, 23 Stat. 24.
> The Act of March, 3, 1881, sec. 14, 26 Stat. 1095.
> The Homestead Act of May 14, 1898, sec. 7, 20 Stat. 412.
> The Act of June 6, 1900, sec. 217, 31 Stat. 330.

[53]See e.g., *Alaska Lands-Indian Occupancy,* 13 L.D. 120 (1891). See also Sutter v. Heckman, 1 Ak. Rpts. 188 (D.C. Ak. 1901).

[54]See Miller v. U.S., 159 F. 2d, 1005 (9th Cir. 1947), characterizing Alaska Native land claims as individual not tribal claims.

[55]Act of June 30, 1834, 4 Stat. 729, as amended and repealed in part.

[56]Act of June 25, 1948, c. 645, 62 Stat. 757, as amended, 18 USCA 1151. This was a revision and codification of Title 18 of the U.S. Code (Crimes and Criminal Procedure) into positive law, and broadly defined the meaning of "Indian country" for purposes of federal criminal law. Under this act, Indian country includes all reservations, allotments and "dependent Indian communities." The latter term is broad enough to include most Alaska Native villages and has been judicially interpreted to apply to federal civil jurisdiction and tribal jurisdiction also, DeCoteau v. Dist. County Court, 420 U.S. 425, 427, n.2 (1975). The significance of the amendment is that many provisions of the trade and intercourse act applied only to Indian country. Thus, broadening the definition expanded the scope of the trade and intercourse act in Alaska. See also the historical note following 25 USCA 217. See generally Cohen (1982), note 5, above, at 27-46, discussing the history of the Indian country concept in the trade and intercourse act.

[57]U.S. v. Seveloff, 1 Ak. Fed. Rpts 64 (1872); Waters v. Campbell, 1 Ak. Fed. Rpts. 91 (1876).

[58]Act of May 17, 1884, sec. 13, 23 Stat. 24.

[59]*Alaska-Legal Status of Natives,* 19 L.D. 323 (1894).

[60]In re Sah Quah, 1 Ak. Fed. Rpts. 136 (1886).

[61]"Powers of Indian Tribes," 55 I.D. 14, 24 (1934). See also F. S. Cohen, *Handbook of Federal Indian Law,* (1942; reprint, New York: AMS Press, 1972) at 124, n. 11.

[62]In re Sah Quah, note 60, above, at 140. See also Cohen (1942), note 61, above, at 405, n. 78.

[63]Id. at 406. See also Cohen (1982), note 5, above, at 751-752.

[64]Note 48, above.

[65]Id. at 445. See also U.S. v. Cadzow, 5 Ak. Rpts 125 (D.C. Ak. 1914) and note 6, above, and accompanying text.

[66]Act of January 27, 1905, 33 Stat. 617.

[67]See generally chapter 5, "History of Native Services and Programs in Alaska."

[68]See generally chapter 3, II B, "Metlakatla and the First Executive Order Reserves."

[69]248 U.S. 78 (1918).

[70]Act of March 3, 1891, sec. 15, 26 Stat. 1101, 25 USCA 495.

[71]U.S. v. Alaska Pacific Fisheries, 5 Ak. Rpts. 484 (D.C. Ak. 1916); aff'd. Alaska Pacific Fisheries v. U.S., 250 F. 274 (9th Cir. 1917).

[72]Act of June 30, 1919, sec. 27, 41 Stat. 34, 43 USCA 150.

[73]*Leasing of Lands Within Reservations Created for the Benefit of the Natives of Alaska,* 49 L.D. 592, 593 (1923).

[74]Act of May 17, 1906; 34 Stat. 197, as amended, 43 USC 270-1 (1970), repealed with savings clause by the Alaska Native Claims Settlement Act of December 18, 1971, P.L. 92-203, sec. 18, 85 Stat. 710, 43 USCA 1617.

[75]Act of February 8, 1887, 24 Stat. 388, 25 USCA 331 et seq., also known as the "Dawes Act" after its chief sponsor.

[76]Act of May 25, 1926, 44 Stat. 629, 43 USC 733-736 (1970), repealed with a savings clause by the Federal Land Policy and Management Act (FLPMA) of October 21, 1976, sec. 703, 90 Stat. 2789.

[77]The Act of March, 3, 1891, 26 Stat. 1095, 1099, 43 USC 732 (1970), repealed by FLPMA, note 76, above, permitted occupants of Alaska townsites to acquire title to individual lots by making application to a federal trustee for survey, subdivision and deeds. See generally chapter 4, III, "Native Townsites."

[78]Secretarial Order 494, March 14, 1931.

[79]53 I.D., note 47, above, at 605 (1932).

[80]Act of June 18, 1934, 48 Stat. 984, 25 USCA 461 et seq.

[81]70 Mich. L. Rev. 955 (1972). See generally Cohen (1942), note 61, above, at 84-87 and Cohen (1982), note 5, above, at 144-152.

[82]Act of May 1, 1936, 49 Stat. 1250, 25 USCA 473a.

[83]25 USC 496 (1970), repealed by sec. 704 of FLPMA, note 76 above.

[84]25 USCA 473a. Cohen noted that the Federal Credit Union Act (12 USCA 1759) was the basis for the "common bond" criteria. See Cohen (1942), note 61, above, at 414, n. 209. See also Cohen (1982), note 5, above, at 751-752.

[85]H. Rpt. No. 2244, 74th Cong., 2nd sess. at 4 (1936).

[86]See chapter 3, II D-F, for a detailed discussion of IRA policies.

[87]Cohen (1942), note 61, above, at 414.

[88]See chapter 3, II F3, "Karluk."

[89]337 U.S. 86 (1949).

[90]107 F. Supp. 697, 699 (D.C. Ak. 1952).

[91]House Concurrent Resolution 108, 67 Stat. B132 (1953), specifically adopted "termination" of certain tribes as a policy for the eighty-third Congress.

[92]See "Native Village of Karluk and the reservation of Karluk," Memorandum of the Regional Solicitor, Anchorage (January 22, 1968).

[93]See e.g., *Oil and Gas Leasing on Lands Withdrawn by Executive order for Indian Purposes in Alaska,* 70 I.D. 166 (1962).

[94]Act of November 2, 1924, 42 Stat. 208, 25 USCA 13.

[95]See *Morton v. Ruiz,* note 13, above, at 212.

[96]See Cohen (1942), note 61, above, at 237-238. See also Cohen, note 5, above, at 673-678.

[97]C.f. U.S. v. Sandoval, 231 U.S. at 47 (1913). See also *Leasing of Lands Within Reservations Created for the Benefit of the Natives of Alaska,* 49 L.D. 592 (1923) and 53 I.D., note 47, above, at 605.

[98]C.f. Cohen (1942), note 61, above, at 173 and 327-238. See also Cohen (1982), note 5, above, at 677-678.

[99]See e.g., Goldberg v. Kelly, 397 U.S. 471 (1970), entitlement to welfare. See also Board of Regents v. Roth, 408 U.S. 564, 571 (1972), where the Supreme Court clearly stated its rejection of the right-privilege doctrine.

[100]See generally *Goldberg v. Kelly*, note 99, above, due process hearing prior to denial of welfare benefits, and *Morton v. Ruiz*, note 13, above, rule-making required prior to denial of BIA welfare benefits to certain off-reservation Indians. Compare Pence v. Kleppe, 529 F. 2d 135 (1976), due process required prior to denial of Alaska Native allotment for same reasons as required in *Goldberg v. Kelly.*

[101]Of course, limiting discretion does not altogether deny administrative authority to curtail statutory programs if there is a rational necessity for doing so. That is especially true when appropriations are insufficient to meet the demand for the entitlement. However, to be valid such limits must be imposed fairly and on a rational basis. Dandridge v. Williams, 397 U.S. 471 (1970).

[102]See chapter 6, "Native Entitlement to Human Services."

[103]E.O. No. 5365, June 10 1930.

[104]See chapter 7, II B, "Preemptive Treaties."

[105]E.O. No. 6044, February 23, 1933.

[106]Act of September 1, 1937, 50 Stat. 900, 25 USCA 500 et seq.

[107]See chapter 7, II C, "Preemptive Statutes."

[108]See generally Cohen (1942), note 61, above, at 122. Accord Cohen (1982), note 5, above, at 231. See also U.S. v. Wheeler, 435 U.S. 313, 322-323 (1978).

[109]See generally chapter 5, I A and B, relating to Bureau of Education and Bureau of Indian Affairs.

[110]*Validity of Marriage by Custom Among the Natives or Indians of Alaska*, 54 I.D. 39 (1932).

[111]See 46 Fed. Reg. 1668-1676 (January 7, 1981); 46 Fed. Reg. b 38351-38352 (July 27, 1981), redesignated at 47 Fed. Reg. 13327 (March 30, 1982); 25 CFR Parts 81 and 82, establishing new regulations for organization of IRA governments and specifically including "Alaska Native entities" as "Tribes," 25 CFR 82.1(w). See also 48 Fed. Reg. 56862 at 56865 (December 23, 1983), listing Alaska Native entities. But see R. Price, "Native Rights A Report to the Alaska Statehood Commission" (Juneau: Alaska Department of Law, 1982) at 74-75, implying that Alaska Native villages may not have the powers of tribal governments. See also Board of Equalization for the Borough of Ketchikan v. Alaska Native Brotherhood and Sisterhood, Camp No. 14, 666 P.2d 1015, 1023 (Ak. 1983), Rabinowitz J., dissenting, suggesting that the Ketchikan Indian Corporation IRA is not a "tribe."

[112]In re McCord, 151 F. Supp. 132 (D.C. Ak. 1957). But see U.S. v. Booth, 161 F. Supp. 269 (D.C. Ak. 1958), denying the exclusive jurisdiction of Metlakatla over a drunk driving offense and specifically distinguishing In re McCord. *U.S. v. Booth* appears to have no current vitality; see Atkinson v. Haldane, 569 F.2d 151 (Ak. 1971), upholding Metlakatla's sovereign immunity.

[113]Act of August 15, 1953, P.L. 83-280, 67 Stat. 589, as amended by P.L. 85-615 (1958). "Indian country" is defined at 18 USCA 1151.

[114]See 18 USCA 1162 (criminal jurisdiction) and 28 USCA 1360 (civil jurisdiction).

[115]P.L. 280 was amended in 1970 to return concurrent jurisdiction to Metlakatla over lesser criminal offenses. (Act of November 25, 1970, P.L. 91-523, 84 Stat. 1358). The implication of this action is that, contrary to the holding in *U.S. v. Booth*, (note 112, above), Metlakatla did exercise inherent governing authority prior to the application of P.L. 280 to Alaska.

[116]Act of December 18, 1971, P.L. 92-203, 85 Stat. 689, 43 USCA 1601 et seq., as amended.

[117]C.f. R. D. Arnold, *Alaska Native Land Claims*, (Anchorage: Alaska Native Foundation, 1976) at 279-280. Mr. Arnold does not allege the relationship is terminated; he only reports that others do so.

[118]The status of Alaska Native water rights under the Alaska Native Claims Settlement Act is not included in this discussion. See generally K. Stoebner, *Alaska Native Water Rights as Affected by the Alaska Native Claims Settlement Act*, 4 American Indian Law Journal, No. 3 (Institute for the Development of Indian Law: Washington, D.C., March 1978) at 1.

[119]Most notably Tee-Hit-Ton Band of Indians v. U.S., 348 U.S 272 (1955), denying the compensability of unrecognized aboriginal title.

[120]Act of July 7, 1958, 72 Stat. 339, as amended.

[121]See Tlingit and Haida Indians of Alaska v. U.S., 177 F. Supp. 452 (1959) and Alaska v. Udall, 420 F. 2d 938 (9th Cir. 1969).

[122]PLO 4582, 34 Fed. Reg. 1025 (January 23, 1969).

[123]See e.g., M. C. Berry, *The Alaska Pipeline: The Politics of Oil and Native Land Claims*, (Bloomington: Indiana University Press, 1975).

[124]S. 35, sec. 8. See S. Rep. 92-405, 92nd Cong., 1st sess., at 9-13 and 57-68.

[125]Id., sec. 15, and S. Rep. 92-405 at 33-36 and 81-82.

[126]C.f. *Authority to Determine Eligibility of Native Villages After June 18, 1934*, 81 I.D. 316, 325 (1974).

[127]43 USCA 1601(b).

[128]The Department of the Interior has also characterized ANCSA as "Native" legislation. See *1977 Convention—Alaska Federation of Natives*, (Anchorage: Alaska Federation of Natives, 1978) at 26, remarks of James A. Joseph, Undersecretary of Interior. Compare 81 I.D., note 126 above.

[129]Alaska Public Easement Defense Fund v. Andrus, 435 F. Supp. 664, 671 (D.C. Ak 1977).

[130]Menominee Tribe of Indians v. U.S., 391 U.S. 404 (1968).

[131]16 USCA 1603. See also 1601(a).

[132]See chapter 7, "Subsistence in Alaska."

[133]16 USCA 1601(c). See note 139, below, and accompanying text.

[134]U.S. v. Antelope, 430 U.S. 641, 646 (1976), citing Morton v. Mancari, 417 U.S. 535 (1975), right to preferential employment. See also Fisher v. District Court, 424 U.S. 381 (1976), exclusive jurisdiction of tribal court over adoption proceedings.

[135]Alaska Chapter, Associated General Contractors of America, Inc. v. Pierce, 694 F.2d 1162, 1168-1169, n.10 (9th Cir. 1982), upholding Indian preference contracting because it is based on the "political" status of Alaska Natives.

[136]*Morton v. Ruiz,* note 13, above.

[137]E.g., Fox v. Morton, 515 F. 2d 254 (9th Cir. 1974).

[138]See Price, note 111, above, at 71-72, concurring generally in this analysis.

[139]16 USCA 1601(c).

[140]Hearings on HR 13142 and HR 10193 before the House Subcommittee on Indian Affairs of the Interior and Insular Affairs Committee, 91st Cong., 1st sess., August 4-6 at 4 and September 9, 1969 at 6.

[141]Id. at 55-56.

[142]Hearings on HR 3100 (Aspinal Bill), HR 7039 (AFN Bill), HR 7432 (Administration Bill) House Subcommittee on Indian Affairs of the Interior and Insular Affairs Committee, 92nd Cong., 1st sess., May 3-7, 1971, at 18 and 44. Hearings on S.35 (Jackson Bill) and S.835 (Harris Bill), Senate Committee on Interior and Insular Affairs, 92nd Cong., 1st sess., February 18 at 6 and March 16, 1971, at 178. See also HR 10367 sec. 1(4), passing the House October 20, 1971.

[143]See Hamilton v. Butz, 520 F. 2d 709 (9th Cir. 1975), eligibility for food stamps notwithstanding ANCSA cash benefits, noting also that section 2(g) of the act required that ANCSA not be interpreted as terminating federal grant or loan programs in Alaska.

[144]See Hearings on HR 13142 and HR 10193, note 140, above, at 55-56.

[145]HR 7039, sec. 2(c) and S. 835, sec. 2(c), note, 142 above.

[146]Indeed S. 1830, the 1970 predecessor to S. 35, contained specific language terminating most federal Native programs in Alaska within five years. Although

S. 1830 passed the Senate in the 91st Congress, it did not pass the House and died. Specific termination of services was not a feature of the bills introduced in 1971 in the 92nd Congress. See 116 Cong. Rec. 24208-24237 and 24377-24426 for debates on the termination provisions of S. 1830.

[147]See 13th Regional Corp. v. Department of the Interior, 654 F.2d 758 (D.C. Cir. 1980), denying mandamus relief to compel the Secretary of the Interior to include non-resident Alaska Natives in the 2(c) program study, because the plaintiffs waited too long to bring the suit.

[148]*2(c) Report: Federal Programs and Alaska Natives,* (Anchorage, Ak.: Robert R. Nathan Associates, circa 1975).

[149]Letters from Rogers C.B. Morton to House Speaker Carl Albert and Senate President Nelson Rockefeller, April 22, 1975, on file in the Office of the Secretary, Department of the Interior, Washington, D.C. The 2(c) Report also states specifically: "No effort was requested or made to formulate policy recommendations for resolving the issues identified" in the Report. *2(c) Report,* note 148, above, at vii.

[150]See notes 40-44, above, and accompanying text.

[151]See chapter 5, II B3, "Statehood, Self-Determination and School Transfers" and IV D2b "Attempts to Terminate General Assistance."

[152]*Morton v. Ruiz,* note 13, above.

[153]Wilson v. Watt, 703 F.2d 395 (9th Cir. 1983), granting a preliminary injunction, but not deciding whether Congress had actually cut the appropriation for the program.

[154]Cohen (1942), note 61, above, at 170.

[155]See Cohen (1982), note 5 above, at 207.

[156]Cohen (1942), note 61, above, at 170.

[157]U.S. v. Kagama, 118 U.S. 375, 383-385 (1885) Upholding the authority of the federal government to exercise criminal jurisdiction over Native Americans.

[158]U.S. v. Sandoval 231 U.S. 28 (1913), liquor prohibition on Pueblo Indian lands.
See also U.S. v. Candelaria, 271 U.S. 432 (1925), protection of Pueblo Indian lands and U.S. v. Chavez, 290 U.S. 354 (1933), federal prosecution for larceny of Pueblo Indian property.

[159]Morton v. Mancari, 417 U.S. 535, 555 (1974), Indian employment preference tied rationally to federal obligations. See also Delaware Tribal Business Committee v. Weeks, 430 U.S. 73 (1977). See generally Cohen (1982), note 5, above, at 221.

[160]U.S. v. Sioux Nation, 448 U.S. 371 (1980).

[161]U.S. v. Holliday, 70 U.S. (3 Wall.) 407 (1852), recognition of Natives is a political question left to the executive and Congress.

[162]See e.g., *Morton v. Mancari,* note 159 above.

[163]53 I.D. note 47, above.

[164]E.g., U.S. v. Berrigan, 2 Ak. Rpts. 442 (D.C. Ak 1904).

[165]Application of Angus, 655 P. 2d 208 (Or. Ct. App. 1982); cert. den. *sub nom* Woodruff v. Angus, 52 USLW 3263 (1983).

[166]Cogo v. Central Council of Tlingit and Haida Indians, 465 F. Supp. 1286 (D. Ak. 1979).

[167]Alaska Chapter, Association of General Contractors of America v. Pierce, 694 F.2d 1162 (9th Cir. 1982).

[168]*U.S. v. Kagama,* note 157, above, upholding removal of certain "major" crimes from trial jurisdiction.

[169]*Lone Wolf v. Hitchock,* note 8, above.

[170]Tee-Hit-Ton Band of Indians v. U.S., 348 U.S. 272 (1955).

[171]M.E. Price, *Region-Village Relations Under the Alaska Native Claims Settlement Act,* 5 UCLA-Alaska L. Rev. 58, 61 (1975).

[172]See generally, Cohen (1982), note 5, above, at 756-757.

[173]43 USCA 1606(h)(1).

[174]AS 10.05.435 et seq., relating to dissenters' rights in the dispositon of "all or substantially all" of a corporation's assets other than in the "ordinary course of business."

[175]See also AS 10.05.417, relating to dissenters' rights in the case of mergers and consolidations. Dissenters are prohibited from exercising these rights with respect to mergers or consolidations "effected prior to December 19, 1991" under the Act of January 2, 1976, P. L. 94-204, sec. 30, 89 Stat. 1148, 43 USCA 1627(b). See also AS 10.05.005(c), regarding ANCSA corporation shareholder approval requirements for mergers and consolidations.

[176]43 USCA 1607(b).

[177]43 USCA 1606(l). See also Price, note 171, above, at 63.

[178]See id. at 73-75.

[179]43 USCA 1613(c)(5).

[180]See Price, note 171, above, at 245.

[181]43 USCA 1606(i) and (j).

[182]See generally Aleut Corp. v. Arctic Slope Regional Corp., 484 F. Supp. 862 (D.C. Ak. 1980), 7(i) broadly construed to effect equitable distribution of revenues.

[183]See generally Cohen, note 5, above, at 748-750.

[184]See Aleut Corp. v. Tyonek Native Corp., 725 F. 2d 527 (9th Cir. 1983), district court did not abuse its discretion in denying village corporation motion to intervene to enjoin 7(i) settlement. The settlement was judicially approved in Aleut Corp. v. Arctic Slope Regional Corp., A-75-53 Civ. (D. Ak. 1983).

[185]43 USCA 1606(j). The distribution formulas are specified in sections 7(k) and (m), 43 USCA 1606(k) and (m).

[186]Ukpeagvik Inupiat Corp. v. Arctic Slope Regional Corp., 517 F. Supp. 1255 (D. Ak. 1981).

[187]During the first 5 years after ANCSA, 7(j) required that 55% of the money received from the Native Fund and 7(i) distributions (if any) be distributed as well. See generally Arnold, note 117, above at 212-228.

[188]Cape Fox Corp. v. U. S., 456 F. Supp. 784 (D. Ak. 1978), government does not have a trust responsibility to manage a timber harvest contract for the ANCSA corporation's benefit prior to conveyance; rev'd. on jurisdictional grounds, 648 F. 2d 399 (9th Cir. 1981).

[189]Alaska Public Easement Defense Fund v. Andrus, 435 F. Supp. 664, (D.C. Ak 1977).

[190]Koniag v. Kleppe, 405 F. Supp. 1360 (D.C.D.C. 1975), due process required adversary proceeding to determine village entitlement to ANCSA benefits in part because section 2(b) [43 USCA 1601(b)] required "maximum participation" of Natives in decisions affecting their rights and property, aff'd *sub nom* Koniag v. Andrus, 580 F. 2d 601, (D.C. Cir. 1978); cert. den. 439 U.S. 1052.

[191]Carlo v. Gustafson, 512 F. Supp. 833 (D. C. Ak. 1981), Alaska Native Townsite Act imposes a trust responsibility on the federal government and restricted townsite lots compared to allotments for jurisdictional purposes. See generally chapter 4, III, "Native Townsites."

[192]See notes 126-151, above, and accompanying text.

[193]See White v. Califano, note 24 above, requiring the Secretary of the Interior to provide hospital care to an insane Native given the general policies of the Indian Health Care Improvement Act (25 USCA 1602).

[194]See chapter 5 II B3, "Statehood, Self-Determination and School Transfers."

[195]*Wilson v. Watt,* note 153, above, and chapter 5, IV D 2b, "Attempts to Terminate General Assistance."

[196]Fox v. Morton, 404 F. 2d 254 (9th Cir. 1974), hearing required prior to defunding of a Tribal Work Experience Program.

[197]Eric v. Secretary of U.S. Department of Housing and Urban Development, 464 F. Supp. 44 (D.C. Ak. 1978).

[198]See notes 94-101, above, and accompanying text.

[199]See *Morton v. Ruiz,* note 13, above, at 212.

[200]Act of September 6, 1966, P.L. 89-554, 80 Stat. 381, as amended and codified at 5 USCA 551 et seq.

[201]Act of April 12, 1974, P.L. 93-262, 88 Stat. 77, 25 USCA 1451 et seq.

[202]Act of January 4, 1975, P.L. 93-638, 88 Stat. 2203, 25 USCA 450 et seq.

[203]Act of September 30, 1976, P.L. 94-437, 90 Stat. 1400, 25 USCA 1601 et seq.

[204]Indian Child Welfare Act of November 8, 1978, P.L 95-608, 92 Stat. 3069, 25 USCA 1901 et seq.

[205]See generally chapter 6, "Native Entitlement to Human Services."

[206]See chapter 7, III B, "The Effect of ANCSA," and also Cohen (1982), note 5, above, at 759, n. 166.

[207]See chapter 7, II D, "Trust Responsibility for Subsistence."

[208]Act of December 2, 1980, P.L. 96-487, Title VIII, 94 Stat. 2371, 16 USCA 3111 et seq.

[209]See chapter 7, III D, "ANILCA."

[210]See chapter 7, V, "Possibilities for Tribal Control."

[211]See chapter 9, II D, "Tlingit and Haida Central Council."

[212]See id. II C, "Traditional and IRA Governments."

[213]See e.g., Price, note 171, above, at 70.

[214]See generally chapter 3, regarding the history of Alaska reservations.

[215]In re McCord, 151 F. Supp. 32 (D.C. AK. 1957), Tyonek was an executive order reserve—not an IRA reservation.

[216]P.L. 83-280, Act of August 15, 1953, ch. 505, 67 Stat. 588, now codified as amended in scattered parts of 18 and 28 USCA. See 28 USCA 1360 (mandatory civil jurisdiction) and 18 USCA 1162 (mandatory criminal jurisdiction), applied to Alaska by the Act of August 8, 1958, P.L. 85-615, 72 Stat. 545. Other provisions of P.L. 280 not related to Alaska were repealed and substantially reenacted as part of the 1968 Indian Civil Rights Act of April. 11, 1968, P.L. 90-284, Title IV, 82 Stat. 78, codified at 25 USCA 1321-1326.

[217]Bryan v. Itasca County, 426 U.S. 373 (1976).

[218]Santa Rosa Band of Indians v. Kings County, 532 F. 2d 655 (9th Cir. 1976).

[219]See generally chapter 10.

[220]28 USCA 1360(c).

[221]Ollestead v. Tyonek, 560 P. 2d 31 (Ak. 1977), tribal trust assets; Heffle v. Alaska, 633 P. 2d 264 (Ak. 1981), individual restricted allotment lands.

[222]Atkinson v. Haldane, 569 P. 2d 151 (Ak. 1977).

[223]Native Village of Eyak v. G.C. Contractors, 658 P.2d 256 (Ak. 1983), sovereign immunity of traditional Alaska Native village assumed for the sake of argument, but held to have been waived by a contractual arbitration clause.

[224]Board of Equalization for the Borough of Ketchikan v. Alaska Native Brotherhood and Sisterhood, Camp No. 14, 666 P. 2d 1015, 1023 (Ak. 1983), Rabinowitz J., concurring.

[225]Johnson v. Chilkat Indian Village, 457 F. Supp 384 (D. C. Ak. 1978).

[226]*Cogo v. Central Council of Tlingit and Haida Indians,* note 166, above.

[227]*In re McCord,* note 215, above, at 136.

[228]*U.S. v. Chavez,* note 158, above, at 364.

[229]Village of Chalkyitsik, 48 Fed. Reg. 21378 (Thursday, May 12, 1983) and Village of Northway, 48 Fed. Reg. 30195 (June 30, 1983). See also "Liquor Ordinance, Village of Allakaket, Alaska," Op. Assoc. Sol. Ind. Aff. (October 1, 1980), concluding that all lands selected by an ANCSA village corporation were subject to such delegated tribal jurisdiction.

[230]25 USCA 1451 et seq., Indian Financing Act. See also 25 CFR Parts 101, 103 and 286.

[231]25 USCA 450 et seq., Indian Self-Determination Act. See also 25 CFR Parts 271-274.

[232]25 USCA 1601, Indian Health Care Improvement Act.

[233]Indian Child Welfare Act, note 204, above, as implemented by 25 CFR Part 23. See also *Application of Angus,* note 165, above, at 212, n. 9, holding that application of the Indian Child Welfare Act was constitutional because the Sitka Community Association (an Alaska Native IRA) was a "tribe."

[234]47 Fed. Reg. (No. 227) 53130, 53133 (Wednesday, November 24, 1982); republished without qualification, 48 Fed. Reg. (No. 248) 56862, 56865 (Friday, December 23, 1983). See also 25 CFR 81.1(w), defining "Tribe" to include "Alaska Native entities" listed in the Federal Register for purposes of eligibility to reorganize under the IRA.

[235]25 CFR Part 32 ("Indian Education Policies") at 32.1, referring to "Alaska Native entities" and at 32.2, characterizing "Alaska Native villages" as having a "unique government-to-government relationship" with the federal government and as being "distinct cultural and governmental entities." See also "Indian Policy," statement by the President of the United States (Office of the Press Secretary: The White House, January 24, 1983). See generally P.A. Barcott, *The Alaska Native Claims Settlement Act: Survival of a Special Relationship,* 16 Univ. of San Francisco L. Rev. 157 (Fall 1981).

PART II

ALASKA NATIVE
LANDS AND RESOURCES

CHAPTER TWO

ABORIGINAL TITLE

I. Introduction

From the earliest days of the United States, federal efforts to protect, recognize or extinguish aboriginal or "Indian" title acknowledge the existence of a special relationship between the United States and Native Americans. Access to new lands and new resources were among the primary reasons the immigrant Europeans colonized the American continents. The fact the aboriginal inhabitants occupied those same continents and controlled access to their resources was one of the first and most persistent obstacles to expansion of the immigrant population in the new world. State, federal and private efforts to acquire aboriginal lands and resources needed for expansion are the genesis of federal Indian law and the special legal obligations which the federal government recognizes toward Native Americans.[1]

Both political reality and moral principle led early North American immigrants to seek aboriginal lands and resources by negotiation rather than conquest. The early colonists faced a hostile natural environment and could ill-afford open conflict with the then stronger and more numerous aboriginal inhabitants. Additionally, the Puritans in New England and the Quakers in Pennsylvania chose on principle to purchase rather than take the aboriginal lands they needed.[2]

Similarly, because of military necessity and principles of international law, the British sovereign chose to purchase rather than conquer aboriginal lands. After the American Revolution, the United States government succeeded to the political and territorial claims of Great Britain, and assumed the place of the British Government *vis a vis* the aboriginal inhabitants.[3] Throughout the revolution, the Americans also cultivated alliances with the aboriginal tribes on the East Coast and were to some extent obligated to those tribes for their assistance or at least non-opposition during the war.[4]

With this history in mind, it is not difficult to see why the relationship between the federal government and Native Americans became more one of equals before the law rather than of conquerors and conquered.[5] From the earliest days, the relationships between the immigrants and aboriginal cultures were, out of necessity and principle, based on one of the basic instruments of Anglo-American law—the contract. Nowhere is the use of this instrument more apparent than in the treaties, agreements and statutes where, by mutual consent and the exchange of promises, the aboriginal inhabitants agreed to the extinguishment of portions of their vast claims to the lands and resources of the American Nation.

John Marshall was the first American jurist to define the essential principles of the aboriginal title doctrine. Distinctive federal obligations to Native Americans are derived from those principles; therefore, the historical existence of aboriginal title in Alaska is one measure of the extent to which those obligations are also owed Alaska Natives. Furthermore, the ways in which the federal government has met these obligations in Alaska also afford a perspective on the scope of the more general "special relationship" existing between the federal government and the Natives of Alaska.

A. Generally

According to the principles of federal Indian law, aboriginal title (also called Indian title, Indian right of occupancy, etc.) is first of all group or tribal title.[6] It differs from fee simple title in that aboriginal title is only the right of exclusive occupancy and does not include the ultimate fee, the ability to freely convey the occupied land.[7] Aboriginal occupants may sell their lands, but only the federal government or those authorized by it may purchase such lands. This basic rule is founded on early principles of international law.

B. The Rule of Discovery

The aboriginal title concept grew from the competition among the so-called discovering nations which colonized and eventually came to control the lands and the original inhabitants of the American continents. The sixteenth, seventeenth and eighteenth centuries were periods of intense international competition for the assumed wealth of the new world. Recognizing that competition among themselves would be destructive of their individual interests, the "discovering" nations adopted a rule among themselves to control their inevitable strife.

This "rule of discovery" held that the nation first landing on or discovering a land in the new world acquired title to the land and dominion over the original inhabitants exclusive of any other *discovering nation*. The fact the original inhabitants were not a party to this agreement is the root of the aboriginal title concept. The discovering power had exclusive title to the land *only* among other European powers, but that title was subject to the possessory interests of the aboriginal inhabitants. While each discovering power had title against any other discovering power, that fact alone did not affect the land status of the aboriginal inhabitants. At most, the rule of discovery only gave the discovering power the exclusive authority to extinguish aboriginal possessory rights.[8] Chief Justice John Marshall defined both the negative and positive aspects of aboriginal title in two early U.S. Supreme Court cases, *Johnson v. M'Intosh*[9] and *Worcester v. Georgia.*[10]

C. M'Intosh—The Exclusive Right of Purchase

Johnson v. M'Intosh affirms the exclusive authority of the federal government to convey title to aboriginal lands subject only to the Indian right of occupancy or "aboriginal title." In this case, a non-Native had acquired land from an Indian tribe by conveyance. Subsequently, the defendant acquired title to the land through a patent from the United States. The plaintiff sued claiming that his title from the Indian tribe was earlier and therefore better. The issue was whether the plaintiff's title from the Indian tribe could be recognized in the United States courts. In determining that the title from the tribe could not be recognized, Chief Justice Marshall set forth the basic principles of aboriginal title.

Because there could only be one sovereign over the land, Marshall had to choose between the United States and the Indian tribe in determining which title should take precedence. He reasoned that because the United States had the same title that Great Britain had acquired (i.e., that of a discovering power), the United States had "ultimate dominion" over the land, and therefore sole authority to convey it, "while yet in possession of the natives." Although the title which the United States conveyed would always be subject to the Indian right of occupancy until that right was extinguished, it was, Marshall concluded, the United States and not the Indian tribe which had the power to convey the land:

> All our institutions recognize the absolute title of the crown, subject only to the Indian right of occupancy, and recognize the absolute title of the crown to extinguish that right. This is incompatible with an absolute and complete title in the Indians.

> The British government, which was then our government, and whose rights have passed to the United States, asserted a title to all the lands occupied by the Indians, within the chartered limits of the British colonies. It asserted also a limited sovereignty over them, and the exclusive right of extinguishing the title which occupancy gave to them. These claims have been maintained and established as far west as the river Mississippi, by the sword. The title to a vast portion of the lands we now hold, originates in them. It is not for the courts of this country to question the validity of this title, or to sustain one which is incompatible with it. [11]

Thus even though the aboriginal inhabitants may still occupy their lands, the United States can convey those lands to another. Because there can only be one holder of the ultimate fee, no other government or person may acquire legal title to aboriginal lands unless the United States conveys the title. It also follows that the aboriginal occupants are powerless to convey legal title to their lands to any other entity except the United States. This disability is one of the major distinctions between aboriginal and fee simple title.

D. Worcester—Protection Against States and Others

Subsequent cases emphasize the positive aspects of aboriginal title.[12] *M'Intosh* established the federal government's ultimate fee in aboriginal lands and the resulting limitation of aboriginal title to a right of occupancy. *Worcester v. Georgia* emphasized the exclusivity of the aboriginal right as against state governments (and by implication other third parties).

The issue in *Worcester* was the authority of the State of Georgia to control activity on the lands of the Cherokee Nation within the borders of the state. Georgia had prosecuted and imprisoned a missionary, Worcester, who had worked among the Cherokees without first obtaining a state license. Worcester argued that the Cherokee lands were not within Georgia's jurisdiction because those lands had been guaranteed to the Cherokee Nation in treaties with the United States which, under the Constitution, were superior to the laws of Georgia. Georgia argued that the continued existence of the Cherokee Nation within the State's borders was repugnant to Georgia's sovereignty.[13]

Relying in part on the rule of discovery and aboriginal title as analyzed in *M'Intosh,* Marshall held that the laws of Georgia were void within the borders of the Cherokee Nation.[14] In reaching that conclusion, Marshall found that the United States had succeeded to the position of the English King *vis a vis* title to the Cherokee lands and therefore had the exclusive right to purchase such lands as the Cherokees were willing to sell.[15]

Worcester is an important case from the standpoint of aboriginal title, because it alludes to the protection aboriginal possession affords Native lands against state interference. Unless the United States or the Natives themselves extinguish title to aboriginal lands, state governments (and private persons) deal with such lands without legal authority and under the peril of becoming trespassers. Thus, while the rule of discovery limits the ability of Native Americans to sell their lands to whomever they wish, *Johnson v. M'Intosh*, the same rule limits the legal authority of any besides the United States to interfere with aboriginal possession.

E. Three Elements

Three elements of the federal-Native relationship emerge from the rule of discovery and Marshall's analysis of aboriginal title. The first is a federal obligation to protect the Indian right of occupancy from incursion or trespass. The second is the power of the federal government to extinguish aboriginal title—usually by purchase with some form of tribal consent. Extinguishment is usually a two-step process involving both extinguishment of the right of occupancy for large tracts of land in exchange for money and "recognition" of a *permanent property* right to occupy a smaller tract called a "reserve." "Recognition" of this property right produces the third element—the right to compensation for any further taking of the reserved (recognized) lands.

II. The Obligation to Protect Aboriginal Title

A. Common Law Principle

A correlative to the principle that only the sovereign has power to convey the land is the principle that he also has the obligation to protect aboriginal possession from invasion by another. In *M'Intosh*, Justice Marshall derived this obligation from the very limits imposed on Indian property rights by the rule of discovery, concluding that:

> The Indian inhabitants are to be considered merely as occupants *to be protected, indeed, while in peace, in the possession of their lands,* but to be deemed incapable of transfering the absolute title to others (emphasis added). [16]

Justice Marshall also notes that the federal obligation to protect Native lands grows out of the historical reliance of the aboriginal people on a stronger power for protection:

> The general law of European sovereigns, respecting their claims in America, limited the intercourse of Indians, in a great degree, to the particular potentate whose ultimate right of domain was acknowledged by the others....

> The consequence was that their supplies were derived chiefly from that nation, and their trade confined to it. Goods, indispensable to their comfort, in the shape of presents, were received from the same hand. What was of still more importance *the strong hand of government was interposed to restrain the disorderly and licentious from intrusions into their country, from encroachments on their lands,* and from those acts of violence which were often attended by reciprocal murder.

> The same stipulation, entered into with the United States is undoubtedly to be construed in the same manner. They received the Cherokee Nation into their favor and protection (emphasis added). [17]

Were it not for the federal obligations growing out of aboriginal dependency on federal protection, the positive aspects of aboriginal title would be nullilfied. Absent the protection of federal law, aboriginal lands would fall easy prey to the avarice of land speculation and expanding state jurisdiction. However, these are not only threats to aborigianl possession but also to federal sovereignty. If the federal government truly has "ultimate dominion" over aboriginal lands, then others cannot invade those lands without threatening the government's ultimate authority. There is, therefore, a very practical reason for the federal government to protect aboriginal lands, beyond the moral and legal requirements imposed by aboriginal lands, beyond the moral and legal requirements imposed by Native American political dependency.

To summarize, *M'Intosh* and *Worcester* form the foundation for the common law obligation of the federal government to protect aboriginal lands from trespass. This obligation is based on principles of international law which governed the conduct of the discovering nations toward each other in the colonization of the new world. The rule of discovery, however, does not define the relationship of the discovering powers to the aboriginal inhabitants. That task was left to the individual powers:

> The relation between the Europeans and the natives was determined in each case by the paricular government which asserted and could maintain this pre-emptive privilege (exclusive right to purchase aboriginal title) in the particular place. [18]

As to aboriginal title, *M'Intosh* and *Worcester* define the particular relationship which developed between the government of the United States and those Native American communities within its borders. Without congressional action prohibiting them, these principles extend to the aboriginal inhabitants of newly acquired territories. In this manner the power of the United States over aboriginal lands and its obligation to protect those lands became part of the common law of the nation. These principles prohibit all except the federal government from interfering with the aboriginal right of occupancy and obligate the federal government to protect aboriginal lands from trespass. [19] As we shall also see, the obligation attaches even if the trespass is committed with the authorization of the federal government. [20]

B. The Statutory Requirements

What one commentator has characterized as the "formative years of American Indian Policy" ended in 1834 with the enactment of the last Trade and Intercourse Act. [21] This was the last of a long line of similar acts beginning in 1790 under the administration of George Washington. These acts were prior to and contemporaneous with Marshall's aboriginal title decisions. Sometimes called the Indian Nonintercourse Acts, they protected Indian aboriginal land rights by requiring federal authorization for disposition of aboriginal lands to individuals or states. They thus form a statutory basis for the protection of aboriginal title independent of the common law foundation laid by Marshall.

Of the first of these acts, George Washington said in a 1790 speech to the Senecas:

> Here, then, is the security for the remainder of your lands. No State, no person, can purchase your lands, unless by some public treaty, held under the authority of the United States. *The General Government will never consent to your being defrauded, but it will protect you in all your just rights....* But your

great object seems to be the security of your remaining lands; and I have, therefore, upon this point, meant to be sufficiently strong and clear, that, in future, you cannot be defrauded of your lands; that you possess the right to sell, and the right of refusing to sell your lands; that, therefore, the sale of your lands, in future, will depend entirely upon yourselves. But that, when you may find it for your interest to sell any part of your lands, the United States must be present, by their agent, and *will be your security that you shall not be defrauded in the bargain you may make* (emphasis in original).[22]

In 1975, relying on the act's intent and protective purposes as well as George Washington's contemporaneous interpretation of the act, the Maine District Court held that the act created a trust responsibility in the Secretary of the Interior on behalf of the Passamaquoddy Indians. The secretary was required to pursue Indian claims for unauthorized taking of their lands in violation of the Trade and Intercourse Act.

Some provisions of the Trade and Intercourse Act were not initially applicable to Alaska owing to the act's original definition of "Indian country." These provisions related primarily to criminal activities (importing liquor etc.) in Indian country, which as defined in the 1834 act included only U.S. territory east of the Rocky Mountains. The act's legislative history made it clear that it was to apply to subsequently acquired territory only by specific congressional enactment. Although Congress later extended the Intercourse Act to the then Territories of Oregon, New Mexico and Utah,[23] the act's Indian country provisions were not initially extended to Alaska.

In 1872, the Oregon District Court, then the federal court for Alaska, dismissed federal prosecutions under sections 20 and 21 of the Intercourse Act (prohibiting importation of liquor into Indian country) and held that Alaska was not Indian country under the terms of the act.[24] The next year, Congress amended the Act to specifically apply only sections 20 and 21 to Alaska.[25] In 1876 the Oregon District Court held that although sections 20 and 21 did apply to Alaska, other portions of the act did not because had Congress wished to apply the whole act to Alaska it would have done so.[26] Twentieth century amendments to the Indian country definition have probably eliminated the force of these decisions.[27]

In any event, the reported decisions have never limited the Intercourse Act's restrictions on the alienation of tribal lands to the changing definition of Indian country.[28] The act provides in part:

No purchase, grant, lease, or other conveyance of lands, or of any title or claim thereto, from any Indian nation or tribe of Indians, shall be of any validity in law or equity, unless the same be made by treaty or convention entered into pursuant to the Constitution.[29]

Whether or not Alaska was historically "Indian country" for other purposes, Alaska Native aboriginal title was probably subject to the same statutory protection afforded other Native Americans.

III. Extinguishment of Aboriginal Title

A. Purchase and Conquest

Unless aboriginal possessory rights are extinguished, they remain a "cloud" on the discovering power's title and thus on anyone else's title received through that power. Once again the rule of discovery provides the solution. As John Marshall described it in *M'Intosh:*

> The United States, then, have unequivocally acceded to that great and broad rule by which its civilized inhabitants now hold this country. They hold and assert in themselves, the title by which it was acquired. They maintain, as all others have maintained, that discovery gave an exclusive right to extinguish the Indian title of occupancy, either by purchase or by conquest; and gave also a right to such a degree of sovereignty as the circumstances of the people would allow them to exercise.[30]

It is also well settled that in addition to purchase or conquest aboriginal title may be extinguished by the tribe's voluntary abandonment of its lands or by the death of all the members of the tribe.[31]

As mentioned earlier, the practice, originating with the English monarch out of both necessity and principle, was to purchase aboriginal lands. The United States, succeeding in all respects to the position of the English King, has continued that practice throughout the last two hundred years. Although Congress, under the rule of discovery, could legally extinguish aboriginal title without compensation (the modern equivalent of conquest), political reality and moral principle usually prevent it from doing so.

B. Congress and Its Intent

Clear government action to extinguish aboriginal title is the best evidence that aboriginal title has been extinguished. The methods of extinguishment are various and need not always involve government action (as when lands are voluntarily abandoned); however, when the government acts to extinguish aboriginal title, it must do so clearly to be effective. As the U.S. Supreme Court said of ambiguous congressional action creating a reserve for the Walapai Indians of Arizona:

> We find no indication that Congress by creating that reservation intended to extinguish all of the rights which the Walapais had in their ancestral home. That Congress could have ef-

fected such an extinguishment is not doubted. *But an extinguishment cannot be lightly implied in view of the avowed solicitude of the Federal Government for the welfare of its Indian wards* (emphasis added). [32]

It is also well established that the government cannot inadvertently extinguish aboriginal titles:

> The relevant question is whether the governmental action was intended to be a revocation of Indian occupancy rights, not whether the revocation was effected by permissible means. [33]

IV. Recognition and Other Rights to Compensation

A. Recognized and Unrecognized Aboriginal Title

The federal practice of extinguishing aboriginal title by purchase must be distinguished from the obligation of the government to pay compensation for the taking of property under the Fifth Amendment to the United States Constitution. [34] Aboriginal title, because it is only a right of occupancy, is not considered to be "property" in the meaning of the Fifth Amendment. Thus the Fifth Amendment does not prevent the government from extinguishing aboriginal title without paying compensation for it.

Whether aboriginal title is compensable or not has come to depend on whether Congress has "recognized" a *permanent* right to a particular tract of land. The Supreme Court decision [35] which finally and clearly decided that only "recognized" title is compensable is heavily criticized, but it is nonetheless the law of the land. [36]

B. Jurisdictional Acts

In addition to recognizing permanent possessory rights, Congress has often authorized Indian tribes to sue for compensation for prior takings by either third parties or the federal government. Such jurisdictional acts [37] do not constitute recognition of permanent aboriginal possessory rights. Rather, they manifest the consent of Congress to a suit against the United States for breach of its fiduciary obligation to protect Native possessory rights which have been previously lost. Jurisdictional acts specify the sort of claims to which Congress has consented suit and thereby define the limits of the court's jurisdiction over those claims. Unlike claims based on the Fifth Amendment (i.e. claims for the taking of recognized aboriginal title), claims based on jurisdictional acts require that the claimant prove not only exclusive aboriginal use and occupancy but also that such use and occupancy has been diminished and damages suffered as a result. [38]

V. Aboriginal Title In Alaska

A. Introduction

The principles of aboriginal title just discussed have been applied to Alaska Native lands in several cases. However, some court decisions have so interpreted the 1867 Treaty of Purchase and other federal laws relating to Alaska Native land rights as to confuse the Alaska aboriginal title question. Other decisions, both old and new, have held that the federal government has both the power and duty to protect Alaska Native claims based on aboriginal title. Additionally, the federal Court of Claims, in an important decision, has held that the Tlingit and Haida Indians of southeast Alaska had extensive aboriginal land claims.

The Alaska Native Claims Settlement Act (ANCSA) extinguished nearly all claims which might be based on aboriginal title. Yet federal litigation protecting Alaska Native lands from trespass, coupled with recognition of Tlingit and Haida aboriginal land claims supports the conclusion that prior to ANCSA the Natives of Alaska possessed their lands under valid claims of aboriginal title. If that is true, then it also follows that the Natives of Alaska have historically occupied the same position under American law as other Native Americans with similar claims.

The legal questions surrounding aboriginal title in Alaska begin with the 1867 Treaty of Cession between the United States and Russia. The courts have interpreted Articles III and VI of the treaty alternately both to confirm and to deny Alaska Native aboriginal title. Other congressional acts protecting Native occupancy have also been interpreted alternately to protect either aboriginal or individual (i.e., non-aboriginal) Native title. The resulting confusion is perhaps what is responsible for the appearance of doubt as to the legitimacy of Alaska Native aboriginal land claims. These rather technical doubts aside, the general lesson gleaned from the history and disposition of aboriginal claims in Alaska is that, like other aboriginal Americans, Alaska Natives held claims to vast tracts of land by aboriginal title. [39]

B. Treaty of 1867

Early on the morning of March 30, 1867, Secretary of State, William H. Seward, and Minister for the Russian Czar, Edward de Stoeckl, executed the treaty whereby the United States purchased what was then called Russian America. [40] The ratifications of both governments were exchanged and the treaty proclaimed on June 20, 1867. [41] The treaty is frequently characterized as a "quitclaim" whereby the United States acquired "whatever dominion Russia had possessed immediately prior to cession." [42] Thus, if Alaska Natives held thier lands by aboriginal title under Russian rule, their aboriginal possession continued under United States rule unless extinguished in the treaty or subsequent federal legislation. The treaty had two provisions which became relevant in litigation involving Alaska Native aboriginal title.

1. "Private Property" Provision

Article I of the treaty described the land rights being conveyed; Article VI provided that in consideration for those rights, the United States would pay the Russian government $7,200,000 in gold. For that amount, and in addition to the rights themselves, the Russian government guaranteed that:

> The cession of territory and dominion herein made is hereby declared to be free and unencumbered by any reservations, privileges, franchises, grants or possessions, by any associated companies, whether corporate or incorporate, Russian or any other, or by any parties, except *merely private individual property holders;* and the cession hereby made, conveys all the rights, franchises, and privileges now belonging to Russia in the said territory or dominion, and appurtenances thereto (emphasis added).

This guarantee is somewhat unusual in a treaty. Correspondence between Seward and de Stoeckl confirms that the guarantee was aimed specifically at extinguishing the title of the Russian-American Fur Company to its Alaskan corporate property. The Court of Claims, in *Tlingit and Haida Indians of Alaska v. U.S.* traces the history of this provision in minute detail.[43]

Secretary of State Seward requested the guarantee because of problems which arose in the Oregon Territory (purchased from Britain) when the Oregon treaty was held to confirm the title of the Hudson's Bay Company to its Oregon property. The United States wished to avoid a similar situation in Alaska.[44] Even though this may have been Seward's main objective, he chose to word the treaty very broadly so as to include all corporate possibilities. Given the fact that aboriginal title is by definition "tribal" or group title, the language might be considered broad enough to include the extinguishment of Indian title as well.[45] For the reasons discussed below, however, it is unlikely that this language extinguished aboriginal title.

2. Indian Law Provision

Article III of the treaty directly addresses the status of the Natives then living in Alaska. The treaty divides the inhabitants of Alaska into two broad categories: (1) the "uncivilized" tribes and (2) all other inhabitants:

> The inhabitants of the ceded territory, according to their choice, reserving their natural allegiance, may return to Russia within three years; but if they should prefer to remain in the ceded territory, they, *with the exception of uncivilized native tribes,* shall be admitted to the enjoyment of all the rights,

advantages and immunities of citizens of the United States, and shall be maintained and protected in the free enjoyment of their liberty, property, and religion. *The uncivilized tribes will be subject to such laws and regulations as the United States may, from time to time, adopt in regard to aboriginal tribes of that country* (emphasis added).

The last sentence of Article III has been held to apply the whole body of federal Indian and statutory law to the "uncivilized" tribes of Alaska.[46] This logically should include the obligation to protect aboriginal title previously discussed. Unfortunately, the "merely private individual property holder" language of Article VI casts a cloud over this interpretation. As we shall see, however, twentieth century court decisions clear up this confusion.

3. "Civilized" and "Uncivilized"

The characterization of certain tribes in Alaska as "uncivilized" seemed to imply that there were other tribes who were "civilized." Under this interpretation, members of the "uncivilized tribes" would not be U.S. citizens, whereas other "inhabitants" of the ceded territory would enjoy "all the rights, advantages and immunities" of U.S. citizenship. The importance of the distinction for purposes of the aboriginal title doctrine is that up until the Citizenship Act of 1924[47] "civilization" for Native Americans generally included abandonment of tribal relations.[48] Since aboriginal title is by definition "tribal" title, one possible implication drawn from the Treaty of Cession was that whole groups of Alaska Natives (i.e., "civilized tribes") did not possess aboriginal title.

As interpreted by one court, the distinction was derived from the Russian categorization of Alaska Natives under the last Russian-American Fur Company charter. The charter specifically defined the relationships the company was to have with the inhabitants of the territory and divided those inhabitants into three categories: (1) dependent, (2) semi-dependent and (3) independent. The dependent people were those who adopted the Russian way of life, lived in Russian communities and were perhaps married to Russian men or women. They were considered to be subjects of the Russian czar and entitled to all the rights of a Russian citizen. The semi-dependent people were those who associated with the Russians from time to time, lived near their communities, but were distinguished from the dependent people by their refusal to adopt the Russian Orthodox faith. Finally, the independent people were those over whom Russia exercised no dominion and who were for all practical purposes free of Russian control. The intent of the Treaty of Cession was to admit those entitled to Russian citizenship also to U.S. citizenship. Under this reasoning, those categorized under Russian rule as semi-dependent or independent might appear to be classed as "uncivilized tribes" in the 1867 treaty.[49]

On the other hand, in terms of the legal thought of the time, it is probably inconsistent to speak of a distinction between "civilized" and "uncivilized" *tribes*. Generally, whether an individual Native American was "civilized" or not did not depend on the adoption of non-Native culture, but on the disassociation of the individual from the tribal community.[50] Civilization, abandonment of tribal relations and citizenship were often synonymous under U.S. naturalization statutes common to the period of the Russian-American treaty. Therefore, it seems likely that the distinction between "uncivilized tribes" and other "inhabitants" mentioned in Article III of the treaty was intended to be consistent with the then current requirements of Native American citizenship and not intended to create a whole new category of "civilized tribes" (not even mentioned in the treaty) whose members, although tribal, were to be denied the unique rights characteristic of Native Americans generally.

This conclusion is also consistent with the contemporaneous interpretation of the treaty by those who negotiated and implemented it. For example, in a handwritten memorandum almost certainly placed before the president's cabinet on March 15, 1867, Secretary Seward said simply that under the treaty, "The Indians [were] to be on the footing of Indians domiciled in (the) U.S."[51] In his own explanation of Article III, dated April 19, 1867, Ambassador de Stoeckl distinguished only between "Russians" and "savage tribes" and as to the latter noted that: "[I]t was impossible for me to stipulate anything in their favor. This would be in a way for us to reserve the right of intervention in the ceded territory."[52]

Finally, the census of the territory taken seemingly in 1868 indicated the following population groups:

Russians and Siberians	483
Creoles and halfbreeds	1,421
Native tribes	26,843
Americans (not troops)	150
Foreigners (not Russians)	200
	29,097

During the U.S. Army's early occupation of Alaska, people wishing to remain and become citizens were permitted to register and file declarations, but in practice citizenship was granted to only limited numbers. An early Navy report notes that in 1879 there were 247 "citizens by treaty"; by 1880 the number had dropped to 229.[53] From these numbers and the treaty negotiator's own explanations, it seems likely that few if any Natives were considered to be citizens under the terms of the treaty.

In Alaska, the civilized/uncivilized distinction turned out to have more effect in the area of civil rights and entitlement to education than in the application of general principles of federal Indian law. Prior to the Citizenship Act of 1924, whether an Alaskan Native had been dependent under Russian rule or independent became relevant in determining whether an individual or his descendants were U.S. Citizens by operation of the Treaty of Cession.[54] Later, under the Nelson Act,[55] education in "white" territorial schools was permitted for "children of mixed blood who lead a civilized life." Education of Indians and Eskimos remained under the control of the Secretary of the Interior. In accord with Native American naturalization statutes, the Alaska court also interpreted this act to require Alaska Natives to abandon their tribal relations as the price of being "civilized."[56]

4. A Confusion of Cases

Although the Article III mandate to apply federal Indian law to the "uncivilized" Natives of Alaska was not always followed, at least two cases[57] specifically protecting aboriginal title do rely on the Article III language. They apply the common law principles of *M'Intosh* and cases growing out of *Worcester* to protect Alaska Native lands from non-Native incursions. Two other cases,[58] which do not address the protection issue, imply that Native lands can be conveyed to non-Natives without first being conveyed to the federal government. Under the principles laid down in *M'Intosh*, that is seemingly possible only if the aboriginal title to those lands had first been extinguished and the lands somehow granted back to the Natives. By relying on certain federal statutes which superficially appear to guarantee Alaska Natives some sort of new land rights, these two cases conclude that Alaska Natives could convey lands without prior extinguishment of aboriginal title.

A fifth case, *Miller v. U.S.*,[59] states that Article VI of the 1867 treaty extinguished aboriginal title and that the rights guaranteed Natives under subsequent federal statutes entitled them to individual compensation for federal taking of the lands they occupied. In *Tee-Hit-Ton Band of Indians v. U.S.*,[60] the United States Supreme Court interpreted *Miller* as holding that federal legislation subsequent to the 1867 treaty "recognized" aboriginal title in Alaska and specifically disapproved *Miller* on these grounds. The U.S. Supreme Court held that federal legislation subsequent to the 1867 treaty merely maintained the *status quo* as to Indian title at the time of the treaty.[61] However, the Supreme Court did not decide whether or not the 1867 treaty in fact extinguished aboriginal title. Subsequent decisions of the court of claims[62] and the Washington, D.C. United States District Court[63] have either held or assumed that Alaska Native aboriginal title was not extinguished by the 1867 treaty.

ANCSA has now extinguished most (perhaps all) Alaska Native claims founded on aboriginal title. Nevertheless, the history of the controversy surrounding aboriginal land claims in Alaska is important because it manifests one important aspect of the federal-Native relationship. Reading Article III of the 1867 treaty and all of the cases together, the most satisfactory legal conclusion is that prior to ANCSA the Alaska Natives held their lands in Alaska by right of aboriginal possession. Whenever directly confronted with the question, the federal courts have held that, as with all Native Americans, the United States had both the right and the duty to protect Alaska Native aboriginal title.

Each of the major cases mentioned above bear further analysis. Two of these *(U.S. v. Berrigan* and *U.S. v. Cadzow)* rely in part on common law aboriginal title principles and hold that the United States has both the power and the duty to protect Alaska Native aboriginal lands. The other two cases *(Sutter v. Heckman* and *Worthen Lumber Mills v. Alaska-Juneau Gold Mining Company)* concern disputes between private landowners one of whom had acquired title to disputed lands from a prior Native occupant. Both cases hold that under certain federal statutes the Native occupants had the power to convey their lands to private parties.

C. The Obligation of Protection

1. Sutter v. Heckman (1901)

This case did not involve the question of aboriginal title per se. It was a dispute between two fish packers over the use of a beach for a setnet site. Sutter claimed a right to use the beach because he had acquired title to the adjoining land by conveyance from its Indian occupants in 1888. Heckman claimed he had the right to use the beach and obstruct Sutter from setting his beach nets, because, under the principles of Indian law, the Indians did not have the power to convey the land to Sutter. The court found that the Indian occupants had the power to convey legal title to Sutter.

The court relied on section 8 of the 1884 Organic Act which provides that:

> [T]he Indians or other persons in said district *shall not be disturbed in the possession of any lands actually in their use or occupation or now claimed by them* but the terms under which such persons may acquire title to such lands is reserved for future legislation by Congress (emphasis added). [64]

The court determined that the 1884 act, by guaranteeing Indian possession of lands "actually in their use or occupation," also permitted Indian occupants to convey title to such lands. The decision ignores Justice Marshall's *M'Intosh* decision, which holds that an Indian occupant cannot convey title to a non-Indian. Perhaps for that reason, the Ninth Circuit affirmed *Heckman* without adopting the district court's right to convey theory. [65]

2. United States v. Berrigan (1905)

In this decision, Judge Wickersham specifically disapproved the reasoning in *Heckman* and upheld the federal obligation to protect aboriginal occupancy on two grounds. The Natives in this lawsuit were Athabascans living in what is now Delta Junction. After a gold discovery at the headwaters of the Little Delta River, the defendants in the case attempted to purchase the Indian land at a nominal price to be paid in the future. The defendant gold seekers were in the process of removing the Indians from the land when the United States filed suit to enjoin them.[66]

Wickersham determined on the basis of their previous relationship with the Russian government that these Athabascans were "uncivilized native tribes at the date of the Treaty with Russia." He therefore determined that under Article III of the 1867 treaty these Natives were "entitled to the equal protection of the law which the United States affords to similar aboriginal tribes within its borders."[67] These laws of general applicability include the federal common law obligation to protect aboriginal title.

Judge Wickersham also found that by a series of special enactments Congress had further provided "for the protection of the Indian right of occupancy upon the public domain in Alaska."[68] The defendants apparently argued that under these same acts (such as the 1884 Organic Act) as interpreted in *Heckman,* the Natives acquired the power to convey their title to private parties. Wickersham reasoned that if such were the rule, the statutory protection afforded the Indian right of occupancy would be meaningless.[69] If entitled to convey their lands away, the Natives themselves could nullify the protection Congress sought to give them:

> Such a rule would completely nullify the act of Congress, or at least permit the Indian to do it, and thus leave him prey to the very evil from which Congress intended to shield him. Congress alone has the right to dispose of the lands thus specially reserved for his occupancy, and any attempt to procure him to abandon them is void. He is a dependent ward of the government, and his reserved lands are not subject to disposal or sale or abandonment by him.[70]

3. U.S. v. Cadzow (1914)

In this case, the Alaska District Court again upheld the right and duty of the United States to protect Alaska Native title. In *Cadzow,* non-Native traders at Ft. Yukon claimed to have purchased a cabin from a Native in the Ft. Yukon Native village. The traders were planning to further encroach on the Native village by building a trading post within the village area. The United States sued to enjoin further encroachment on the Native occupied lands.[71]

Relying on *Berrigan* as well as *M'Intosh* and other U.S. Supreme Court decisions upholding the government's obligation to protect its dependent wards, the court held that the *Cadzow* defendants:

> ...by purchasing a cabin of an Indian occupant, did not aquire any title whatever thereto, and could be removed therefrom at the suit of the United States, if such action were deemed advisable.[72]

Like *Berrigan, Cadzow* also supports its conclusion with the congressionl enactments between 1884 and 1900, guaranteeing continued Native possession of lands then in their "actual use or occupation."[73] The important factor in both cases is not that these statutes grant new land rights to Natives or new powers to the federal government to protect those rights. These statutes merely confirm to the Natives of Alaska what was always theirs under federal Indian common law—aboriginal title to the lands they occupied. On the basis of *Cadzow* and *Berrigan,* Alaska Natives at the first of the 20th century seemed to have the same claims to aboriginal title as Native Americans in the rest of the nation. A Ninth Circuit Court of Appeals decision soon clouded this picture.

4. Worthen Lumber Mills v. Alaska-Juneau Gold Mining Company (1916)

This Ninth Circuit decision follows *Cadzow* by only two years. As in the *Heckman* case, a non-Native landowner (Alaska-Juneau Gold Mining) claimed the right to use tidelands because it had acquired the upland by grant from a previous Indian occupant. The dispute did not involve the right or obligation of the United States to protect aboriginal title, but was merely a dispute between two private businesses over their respective rights to use tidelands.

Like *Heckman* this court also relied on section 8 of the 1884 Organic Act. The Ninth Circuit did not think that:

[I]t was the purpose of this act *merely to protect the possession of the Indians* of lands which they then occupied in Alaska, and to *deny them the power to convey* others their right of occupation. It was an act, not only for the benefit of the Indians, but also for the white settlers.

The Act made no distinction between the rights of the white settlers and the rights of the Indians, and it is not to be presumed that Congress intended thereby to deprive either the power to exercise rights which they had *theretofore possessed* (emphasis added).[74]

It is not clear from the opinion exactly what rights to the land the Indians had "theretofore possessed." The implication is that these rights were something different from aboriginal possessory rights, because the opinion held that the Indians were able to convey title to the non-Native gold mine owners under the 1884 act. The impression also is given that the 1884 act somehow put Alaska Natives and non-Natives on the same footing as far as land ownership was concerned. That is, both Natives and non-Natives had the same rights to the land they were using and occupying, and Congress only reserved the power at some future date to determine exactly how they would acquire title to the land.

The court makes no distinction between Native aboriginal use and occupancy and the more recent use and occupancy of the immigrant settlers. In failing to do so, decisions like *Heckman* and *Worthen Mills* imply that Alaska Native possession is the same as non-Native possession and based on the same principles. In other words, they reduce the concept of aboriginal possession of vast tracts of land to the Anglo-American concept of fee title to carefully defined plots. Although it is not so held in either *Heckman* or *Worthen Mills,* the implication is that somehow vast claims of aboriginal title are not possible in Alaska. This interpretation does not withstand careful analysis.

5. Critique and Analysis

Berrigan and *Cadzow* interpret section 8 of the 1884 Organic Act as merely supporting the authority of the federal government to protect aboriginal occupancy.[75] Additionally, both decisions recognize that federal Indian common law requires the same result.[76] Because both these decisions speak in terms of the 1884 Organic Act "protecting" the "Indian right of occupancy," they are also consistent with an interpretation that the 1884 Organic Act merely maintains the status quo of aboriginal title following the 1867 treaty. Only if aboriginal title exists after the treaty would there be any Indian right of occupancy to protect.

Heckman and *Worthen Mills,* on the other hand, interpret the 1884 act to confer some different sort of *non-aboriginal* land rights on Alaska Natives. The exact nature of these rights is not clear, but the assumption appears to be that they are the same as those guaranteed non-Natives. The assumption is incorrect unless the point is to strip Native lands of their aboriginal (communal) ownership; although it is perhaps theoretically possible for the 1884 act to permit individual Natives to possess lands on the same basis as non-Natives.

The 1884 act guarantees that "the Indians or other persons shall not be disturbed in the possession of any lands actually in their use or occupation or now claimed by them." However, because of the rule of discovery and the concept of aboriginal title described in *M'Intosh,* Native communal use, occupation and claims to land are legally different from individual Native or non-Native use, occupation and claims. Therefore, when the 1884 Organic Act protects "Indians or other persons" in their possession of Alaska lands, it is perhaps protecting two different types of possession. As to Native communities, the act protects possession based on aboriginal occupancy; as to both Native and non-Native individuals, the act protects possession based on more recent occupancy, subject, however, to overriding claims of aboriginal title.

Only if aboriginal (communal) title were first extinguished could it be replaced by a new sort of individual right of occupancy. Under the *M'Intosh* rationale, Alaska Native communities could have held their land by aboriginal title unless such title was extinguished and would have been prohibited from conveying title to their lands to private parties.[77] The

1884 act did not clearly extinguish aboriginal title and neither *Heckman* nor *Worthen Mills* held that aboriginal title was otherwise extinguished. So long as Alaska Native communities held their lands by aboriginal title, they could not legally convey title to these lands. The *Worthen Mills* and *Heckman* cases simply do not make legal sense, unless it is on the theory that the Organic Act merely preserved the status quo as to aboriginal title under the 1867 treaty without determining the precise property rights of individual Natives or non-Natives. As discussed below, this is also the position of the United States Supreme Court.

D. Preserving the Status Quo

Between 1947 and 1955, both the Ninth Circuit and the U.S. Supreme Court considered the impact of the 1884 Organic Act on Alaska Native aboriginal title. The Ninth Circuit specifically held that the 1884 act "recognized" individual "Indian title" in Alaska Native lands for Native occupants. The U.S. Supreme Court specifically disapproved that decision and held that the 1884 act merely preserved the status quo as of the 1867 treaty.

1. Miller v. U.S. (1947)

In *Miller v. U.S. (1947)*, individual Tlingit Indians occupying land in Juneau contested condemnation proceedings which the United States brought against their lands. The United States argued that since the Indians at most held their land by "unrecognized" aboriginal title, the United States could extinguish their title without compensation. [78] The government also argued that since aboriginal title could only be tribal title, the appellant *individual* Indians had no standing to oppose the condemnation. [79]

. In meeting these two arguments, the Ninth Circuit Court of Appeals first stated in dictum [80] that the "merely private individual property holder" language in Article VI of the 1867 treaty extinguished tribal and, therefore, aboriginal title. [81] The court then went on to hold that the 1884 act and acts similar to it constituted congressional recognition of appellants' title as that of "individual" Indians:

> As we have already pointed out, however, the only sound basis for relief that the appellants have is not based upon original Indian title. The true foundation of their right is the repeated congressional *recognition* of the occupancy or possession of the land by the (individual) "Indians" who were on the land at the time the act of 1884 was passed (emphasis in original). [82]

By finding that the 1867 treaty extinguished Alaska Native aboriginal title, the *Miller* court supplied the premise missing in *Worthen Mills* and *Heckman.* By then characterizing the 1884 act as "recognition" of *individual* Indian title, the opinion put Alaska Natives in the same position as non-Native landholders. Like non-Natives, Alaska Natives were entitled to convey the lands they occupied and to compensation for government taking.[83] One suspects, however, that the geographic extent of potential Native land claims was thereby limited to the carefully defined plots of the immigrant culture. *Miller* was a strange case in the context of federal Indian law.[84] The U.S. Supreme Court twice disapproved it.

2. Tee-Hit-Ton Band of Indians v. U.S. (1955)

Tee-Hit-Ton Band of Indians v. U.S. (1955) was an appeal to the United States Supreme Court by a band of Tlingit Indians. They claimed a right to compensation under the Fifth Amendment for timber taken by the federal government from their lands within the Tongass National Forest. The Tee-Hit-Ton argued in part that they were entitled to Federal compensation, because, as held in *Miller,* section 8 of the 1884 Organic Act "recognized" their right to permanent occupation of the lands from which the timber was taken.[85]

Without deciding whether the 1867 treaty extinguished aboriginal title, the Supreme Court held, on the basis of legislative history, that the 1884 act did not grant the Tee-Hit-Ton "any permanent rights in the lands of Alaska occupied by them."[86] The Court also held that, as to Alaska Native land rights, the 1884 Act "was intended merely to retain the *status quo* until further congressional or judicial action was taken."[87] On that basis, the Court re-emphasized its earlier disapproval of *Miller's* holding that the 1884 act constituted recognition of a compensable (individual) Native interest in occupied lands.[88]

Thus, unless the 1867 treaty extinguished it, the Tee-Hit-Ton (and by implication other Alaska Natives) held their lands at most by "unrecognized" aboriginal title. The Court concluded, after analyzing several of its previous cases, that federal taking of unrecognized aboriginal title was not compensable under the Fifth Amendment.[89] However, the *Tee-Hit-Ton* Court specifically avoided deciding whether the 1867 treaty extinguished Alaska Native aboriginal title. In so doing, it left open the question of whether Alaska Natives had any claim to the lands they occupied in Alaska.[90] As Justice Douglas recognized in dissent, that ambiguity left Alaska Native aboriginal land claims in a precarious position.[91] The major Alaska aboriginal title decisions[92] could all fall into the vortex surrounding the *Miller* extinguishment dictum.

If the *Miller* dictum was wrong, Alaska Native aboriginal title, although unrecognized, could still be protected under *Berrigan* and *Cadzow* until further congressional action was taken to "recognize" permanent Native rights in the land. If the dictum was right, Alaska Natives would have neither federally protected "unrecognized" rights nor federally compensable "recognized" rights. Such a result would simply be absurd, and one not contemplated in either *Heckman, Worthen Mills* or *Miller.*

Each of those cases determined that the 1884 act conferred some sort of recognized property interest on Alaska Natives. In *Heckman* and *Worthen Mills,* the interest enabled Natives to convey their lands to third parties. In *Miller* that interest entitled Alaska Natives to compensation for federal taking of their lands. Because *Tee-Hit-Ton* disapproved the recognized property interest held to exist in *Miller* it also cast doubt on the interest recognized in *Heckman* and *Worthen Mills.*

Berrigan and *Cadzow,* on the other hand, are consistent with *Tee-Hit-Ton's* conclusion that the 1884 Organic Act merely preserved the *status quo,* provided that the 1867 treaty did not extinguish aboriginal title. In 1959, the federal court of claims held that the treaty did not extinguish Tlingit and Haida aboriginal title. Since then the federal District Court in Washington, D.C., has also decided *Edwardsen v. Morton* in which it was found that the Inupiat Eskimos held their lands by aboriginal title. These two cases along with other recent statutes and cases relevant to Alaska Native aboriginal title are discussed below.

E. Events After Statehood

Immediately prior to Alaska statehood and perhaps owing to the confusion of cases just discussed, there was serious doubt as to the existence of Alaska Native aboriginal title.[93] Shortly after statehood, in the first case where the issue was squarely presented, the court of claims determined that the Tlingit and Haida Indians held virtually all of Southeast Alaska by aboriginal title.

1. Tlingit-Haida Land Claims

Under a special jurisdictional act,[94] the Tlingit and Haida Indians became entitled to sue the United States for loss of their aboriginal lands. In 1959, soon after Alaska Statehood, the court of claims held that the Tlingit and Haida Indians had been deprived of their aboriginal land by the acts of the United States. In the course of doing so, the court adopted the extensive findings of fact made by the Indian Claims Commission. These findings demonstrate that the Article VI "private property" clause of the 1867 treaty was intended to extinguish title to corporate property belonging to the commercial enterprises then operative in Alaska. It was not intended to extinguish aboriginal title. Furthermore, Seward's correspondence subsequent to the treaty indicates that the Natives of Alaska were to be treated in all respects as the Natives of the contiguous states.[95] Based on these findings of fact, the court of claims concluded that:

> The use and occupancy title of the Tlingit and Haida Indians...was not extinguished by the Treaty of 1867 between the United States and Russia...nor were any rights held by these Indians arising out of their occupancy and use extin-

guished by the Treaty. The negotiations leading up to the Treaty and the language of the Treaty itself shows that it was not intended to have any effect on the rights of the Indians in Alaska and it was left to the United States to decide how it was going to deal with the Native Indian population of the newly acquired territory.[96]

Court of claims decisions are not necessarily precedent for other federal courts. However, these findings of fact are so persuasive and the conclusion so obvious it is probable that, prior to ANCSA and given proper jurisdictional acts, every Alaska Native community could have successfully pursued claims based on aboriginal title. Article III of the treaty, by guaranteeing that the law generally applicable to American Indians would also apply to Alaska Natives, virtually assures that the principles laid down by Justice Marshall would have applied to Alaska Natives as well. Thus, *Tlingit-Haida* significantly reverses the adverse impact of *Miller* and further confirms the validity of *Berrigan* and *Cadzow*.[97]

2. The Statehood Act and Kake v. Egan

Sections 4 and 6(b) of the Alaska Statehood Act are both relevant to the question of aboriginal title. Section 4 provides in pertinent part:

As a compact with the United States said State and its people do agree and declare that they forever disclaim all right and title...to any lands or other property (including fishing rights), the right or title to which may be held by any Indians, Eskimos, or Aleuts (hereinafter called natives) or is held by the United States in trust for said natives; that all such lands or other property (including fishing rights), the right or title to which may be held by said natives or is held by the United States in trust for said natives, shall be and remain under the absolute jurisdiction and control of the United States until disposed of under its authority, except to such extent as the Congress has prescribed or may hereafter prescribe, and except when held by individual natives in fee without restrictions on alienation....

In *Kake v. Egan*,[98] the plaintiff villages of Kake and Angoon claimed that this provision guaranteed them aboriginal fishing rights free of state regulation and control. In deciding against the villages, the United States Supreme Court held that the legislative history behind the Statehood Act showed that this section was intended neither to grant new rights nor deny old rights but rather to preserve the status quo. In this respect, the decision is reminiscent of the similar *Tee-Hit-Ton* conclusion about the 1884 Organic Act; however, because it comes after the *Tlingit-Haida* decision, *Kake* reinforces (at least historically) the argument for the existence of aboriginal title. That is because the Tlingit Indians of Kake were among those confirmed as having aboriginal title in *Tlingit-Haida*. Therefore, the "status quo" guaranteed by the Statehood Act is the status quo of aboriginal title. Of the legislative intent behind section 4, the Supreme Court found that:

> [Congress's] concern was to preserve the status quo with respect to *aboriginal* and possessory claims so that statehood would neither extinguish them nor recognize them as compensable (emphasis added). [99]

Events growing out of another section of the statehood act compelled Alaska Natives to test the continuing validity of their own claims to aboriginal title.

Section 6(b) of the statehood act permitted the State of Alaska to select up to 102,550,000 acres of "vacant, unappropriated and unreserved" public lands in Alaska. On the basis of their continuous use and occupancy, Natives all over Alaska protested the state's selections to the United States Department of the Interior. Partly in response to these protests and in order to protect Native land rights, the Secretary of the Interior, Stewart Udall, informally suspended the issuance of patents and tentative approvals of state land selections in 1966. [100] The state sued the Secretary of the Interior *(State of Alaska v. Udall)* to compel him to issue the patents and tentative approvals. The Athabascan Native village of Nenana intervened as a party defendant asserting its claim to the state-selected lands "on the basis of aboriginal use, occupancy and continued possession."[101]

The Alaska District Court granted a state motion for summary judgment, because it found that past and present Native use did not prevent the land from being "vacant, unappropriated and unreserved" as was required for state selection under section 6(b). [102] In 1969, the Ninth Circuit found that in order to uphold the district court's summary judgment it would have to hold that:

> [U]nder no circumstances could Indian trapping, hunting, and camping...constitute a condition which would deprive the selected lands of being "vacant, unappropriated, and unreserved."[103]

Specifically citing section 8 of the 1884 Organic Act and *Berrigan*, the Ninth Circuit reversed the district court and remanded the case for trial. The citation to both *Berrigan* and the 1884 act is significant, because, coming just two years before ANCSA, it put the Ninth Circuit on record as supporting the *Berrigan* conclusion that the 1884 act "provided for the protection of the Indian right of occupancy upon the public domain in Alaska."[104] The practical effect of the *Udall* decision was to ensure long and protracted court battles before the state could select its land. However, by the time of this decision, the first legislation proposing a settlement of the Alaska Native land claims had been introduced in Congress. In view of that fact, the court, in remanding the case to the Alaska District Court, suggested that future proceedings be held in abeyance until the likely enactment of the proposed legislation. [105]

F. Alaska Native Claims Settlement Act

1. Extinguishment of Claims

In sweeping language, Section 4 of the Alaska Native Claims Settlement Act purports to extinguish aboriginal claims as follows:

(a) All prior conveyances of public land and water areas in Alaska, or any interest therein, pursuant to Federal law, and all tentative approvals pursuant to Section 6(g) of the Alaska Statehood Act shall be regarded as an extinguishment of the aboriginal title thereto, *if any.*

(b) All aboriginal titles, *if any,* and claims of aboriginal title in Alaska based on use and occupancy, including submerged land underneath all water areas, both inland and offshore, and including any aboriginal hunting or fishing rights that may exist, are hereby extinguished.

(c) All claims against the United States, the State, and all other persons that are *based on* claims of aboriginal right, title, use or occupancy of land or water areas in Alaska, or that are based on any statute or treaty of the United States relating to Native use and occupancy, or that are based on the laws of any other nation, including any such claims that are pending before any Federal or State court or the Indian Claims Commission are hereby extinguished (emphasis added). [106]

2. Edwardsen v. Morton [107]

On October 5, 1971, certain Inupiat Eskimos and the Arctic Slope Native Association, in the person of Charles Edwardsen, Jr., filed suit against the then Secretary of the Interior, Rogers Morton, for breach of fiduciary duty, alleging failure to protect Arctic Slope Native lands against state possession and third-party trespass. Prior to this time, the secretary had made interim conveyances of North Slope lands to the state and allegedly participated in third-party trespass by permitting geologic exploration and blasting on those lands.

On April 19, 1973, the federal District Court in Washington, D.C. issued its decision. *Edwardsen v. Morton* was a summary judgment action in which the Secretary of the Interior argued that as a matter of law the Arctic Slope Natives had no aboriginal land rights prior to ANCSA and that if they did ANCSA extinguished all such rights. [108] The Natives argued that they had two sorts of claims based on aboriginal title both of which accrued prior to ANCSA and neither of which were extinguished by ANCSA. [109] Their first claim was for aboriginal possessory interests in the North Slope lands conveyed to the state under the Statehood Act. The second claim was for trespass damages to those same aboriginal lands.

Edwardsen is important to the question of Alaska Native aboriginal title, because it found under the historic principles of aboriginal title emanating from *Johnson v. M'Intosh* and *Worcester v. Georgia*[110] that:

> [P]laintiffs' rights based on aboriginal title are rights to undisturbed use and occupancy. These rights entitle the holders to protection against all manner of physical intrusions into their lands, but they do not include ownership of alienable interests in exploitable resources such as oil and gas. These use and occupancy rights can be extinguished only by the United States acting through Congress, and until they are thus extinguished they remain as an encumbrance on the fee regardless of who holds it (emphasis added). [111]

Thus, two years after the claims act a federal court of general jurisdiction found for the first time that Native lands in Alaska were historically and as a matter of law held under valid claims of aboriginal title. Having done so, the court had no difficulty in finding that the Secretary of the Interior had a legal duty to protect those aboriginal lands from trespass: [112]

> As to the alleged fiduciary obligation imposed on the federal government to protect the interests of Native Americans, a lengthy examination of cases cited by plaintiffs is unnecessary. Whether or not cases concerning Indian lands in the 'lower 48' are on point, it is clear from the Supreme Court's opinion in *Tee-Hit-Ton, supra* that federal officers are obligated to protect aboriginal lands 'against intrusion by third parties' until such time as Congress acts to extinguish possessory rights therein. It is difficult to see how transferring lands out of federal jurisdiction and control could be consistent with carrying out this *duty of protection* (emphasis added). [113]

The court further held that unlike their *possessory* claims (see note 112 above), plaintiff's trespass claims were not extinguished by section 4 of ANCSA. Based on legislative history, the court concluded that ANCSA was not intended to extinguish civil tort claims like trespass. Furthermore, the court held such claims were property under the Fifth Amendment and, therefore, could not be extinguished without additional compensation. [114]

After *Edwardsen,* the Secretary of the Interior had two choices. He could appeal *Edwardsen's* determination that Alaska Natives had aboriginal title and that prior to ANCSA he had had an obligation to protect it. Alternately, he could assume his obligation and sue the alleged trespassers[115] on behalf of the Natives. He chose the latter, recognizing in executive policy what *Edwardsen* decided as law: Alaska Natives have historically held their lands under valid claims of aboriginal title. Therefore, prior to ANCSA, the federal obligation to protect aboriginal title in Alaska appeared to have been exactly the same as the federal obligation to protect aboriginal title in the rest of the United States.

3. U.S. v. ARCO [116]

U.S. v. ARCO does not change this conclusion. *Edwardsen* compelled the Secretary of the Interior to sue the alleged trespassers of the Inupiat aboriginal lands.[117] *U.S. v. Alantic Richfield Company (ARCO)* is the Alaska District Court decision in that lawsuit. It held that sections 4(a) and 4(c) of ANCSA retroactively extinguished all claims "based on aboriginal title" including any claims derived from aboriginal title, such as trespass.[118] In so doing, *ARCO* disagreed with *Edwardsen's* conclusion that ANCSA did not extinguish "accrued" claims based on aboriginal title, but it specifically avoided deciding whether or not the Inupiats held their lands under aboriginal title prior to ANCSA.[119] Instead, the court relied on the claims act because:

> [It] was the first and only legislative action in which Congress considered and undertook to resolve the claims of Alaska Natives. The Treaty of Cession and Congressional legislation, including the Statehood Act, which preceded the Settlement Act, incidentally affected issues relating to Native land claims *but did not purport to resolve them* (emphasis added).[120]

Thus, although *ARCO* does not reaffirm *Edwardsen's* conclusion as to the existence of aboriginal title, it discounts *Miller's* earlier reliance on the Treaty of Cession as extinguishing such title. After ANCSA and *ARCO,* the existence of aboriginal title within the state is perhaps a moot point, but that is not important here. What is important is that in the basic legal sense, acknowledged in *Edwardsen,* Alaska Natives have historically held their lands under aboriginal title. In that fundamental respect, first acknowledged by John Marshall in the early years of American nationhood, Alaska Natives have had the same status under American law as all other Native Americans.

4. Other Aboriginal Claims

The Inupiat Eskimos pursued their claims for trespass compensation beyond *ARCO* to the U.S. Court of Claims and beyond the borders of Alaska to the sea ice and waters of the Beaufort and Chukchi Seas. After losing their claim in the Alaska District Court against the *ARCO* defendants, the Inupiat Community of the Arctic Slope (ICAS), a "recognized tribe of Eskimos inhabiting the Arctic on North Slope of Alaska,"[121] filed a suit in the court of claims against the United States alleging both damages for the third party trespasses and breaches of federal fiduciary duties which had permitted the trespasses to occur. As did the district and circuit courts in *ARCO*, the court of claims held that ANCSA extinguished aboriginal title retroactively (i.e., before the trespasses occurred) and that the right to recover damages for trespass to aboriginal title was a right which Congress could also extinguish without compensation along with the aboriginal title upon which the trespass claims rested.[122] Finally, the court of claims concluded that the United States could not be held liable for breaches of fiduciary duty in the absence of a specific statute permitting recovery of monetary damages from the government.[123] The U.S. Supreme Court's refusal to hear an appeal from this decision, seems to preclude recovery for similar claims based on aboriginal title arising in Alaska.

However, the Inupiats have also asserted aboriginal claims to large portions of the Beaufort and Chukchi Seas lying beyond the three-mile limit of the borders of Alaska.[124] The Alaska District Court has also rejected these claims, holding that the constitutional allocation of federal jurisdiction over foreign affairs, foreign commerce and national defense precludes assertion of aboriginal claims to waters and seabeds beyond the three-mile limit as areas in which the federal government exercises exclusive authority. Without a reversal of this decision on appeal, it is difficult to foresee any other claims based on aboriginal title which might be successfully asserted after the claims act. It follows that the federal government no longer has obligations to protect such rights in Alaska, but that does not mean the entire federal relationship to Natives is extinguished in Alaska. Were that the implication of the extinguishment of aboriginal title, it would mean there is no federal relationship to other Native Americans either.

Virtually all aboriginal titles in the United States have been extinguished in exchange for money and recognition of some permanent form of occupancy or property ownership. The federal government has gone further in Alaska and recognized fee title in ANCSA lands; as with any property, federal taking of such fee title lands will require compensation under the Fifth Amendment. Thus, even as to extinguishment and recognition of a compensable interest in their lands, Congress has treated Alaska Natives as comparable to other Native Americans whose legal claim to aboriginal title has never been questioned. Under American law, those Native Americans maintain a special relationship to the federal government; so do Alaska Natives.

Finally, although the federal government may no longer have obligations to Alaska Natives related directly to aboriginal title, that does not mean the government has no obligations arising under the claims act.

Neither does it mean it has no obligations arising from factors totally unrelated either to aboriginal land claims or land and resource matters in general.[125] Nor does it mean it has no responsibility for land, and resource, social or political obligations assumed prior to or following ANCSA. Succeeding chapters explore these possibilities.

VI. Conclusion

Considering all of the cases together, the most tenable legal conclusion is that prior to ANCSA Alaska Native title was of the same legal nature as original Indian title elsewhere in the United States. As such, the United States had the exclusive authority to extinguish it and the obligation to protect it from third-party trespass.

There have been three instances where the courts have been directly confronted with the question of federal authority or obligation to protect Native title in Alaska. In each case (Berrigan, Cadzow and Edwardsen) the Courts have upheld either the right or the obligation of the federal government to protect that title. Aboriginal title is the only legal theory from which such federal power and responsibility could be derived.

The validity of each of these cases is further enhanced by the court of claims decision in Tlingit and Haida Indians, which found that both the Tlingit and Haida Indians had valid claims of aboriginal title to almost all of southeast Alaska. When viewed in light of the Tlingit-Haida decision, the previous U.S. Supreme Court decisions in Tee-Hit-Ton and Kake gain added historical relevance. Furthermore, Tlingit-Haida confirms the existence of aboriginal title in southeast Alaska from 1867 through statehood, and neither Tee-Hit-Ton nor Kake cast doubt on that conclusion.

There is no reason to doubt that prior to ANCSA aboriginal title could have been demonstrated for substantially all Alaska Native communities. Even after ANCSA, Edwardsen v. Morton held that the Inupiat Eskimos had a demonstrable claim of aboriginal title to much of Alaska's North Slope. On that basis, the Secretary of the Interior was obligated to sue alleged trespassers to recover damages to the Inupiat aboriginal claims. Prior to that time, Secretary of Interior Stewart Udall was obliged to freeze state land selections in order to protect Alaska Native claims based on aboriginal possession. The Ninth Circuit upheld the potential validity of those claims in Alaska v. Udall.

In the context of these cases, the holdings in Heckman and Worthen Mills along with the holding and dicta in Miller are neither on point nor persuasive. In Berrigan and Cadzow the department of the Interior acted voluntarily to protect Alaskan Native aboriginal title. In Edwardsen, the Department was compelled to do so. These cases and the others discussed span nearly seventy years and comfirm that with respect to aboriginal title and the authority and obligations which arise out of it, the federal relationship to Alaska Natives has historically been the same as its relationship to other Native Americans under American law.

ANCSA itself confirms this conclusion. Whether or not Congress admitted the existence of aboriginal title in Alaska is irrelevant. The fact is that Congress exercised its authority to settle Alaska Native land claims in the same manner that it settled many previous aboriginal claims. It extinguished Native claims to large tracts of land in exchange for money and recognition of permanent rights to smaller tracts of land. In this respect ANCSA confirms that under American law, the federal relationship to Alaska Natives is the same as the federal relationship to Native Americans generally.

ENDNOTES

[1]See generally F. Cohen, *Handbook of Federal Indian Law* (Charlottesville, Va.: Michie Bobbs-Merril, 1982) at 486-493.

[2]See Cohen, above, at 53-57 and 486-487, n. 128.

[3]Worcester v. Georgia, 31 U.S. (6 Pet.) 515, 545-556 (1832).

[4]See Cohen, note 1, above, at 58-59.

[5]The North American experience is in sharp contrast to the South American. Spain conquered the Mexican Indian civilizations. The conquistadors reduced those Indian lands and resources to their own possession with little reliance on legal principles. See, e.g., Cohen, note 1, above, at 52, n. 17.

[6]It is well settled that aboriginal title is group or tribal title. By definition, an individual cannot have aboriginal title. See Cherokee Nation v. Hitchcock, 187 U.S. 294, 307 (1902). See also Johnson v. M'Intosh, 21 U.S. (8 Wheat.) 543 (1823) at 595, alluding to a possible theory behind tribal (as distinguished from individual) possession based on "group" discovery of unoccupied lands.

[7]Cohen, note 1, above, at 487-488.

[8]Prior to the first Trade and Intercourse Act of 1790 (1 Stat. at 138, 25 USC 177), the original 13 colonies also had authority to buy and sell aboriginal lands as permitted by the crown. Cohen, note 1, above, at 55-58 and 109-110.

[9]21 U.S. (8 Wheat.) 543 (1823).

[10]31 U.S. (6 Pet.) 515 (1832).

[11]*M'Intosh,* note 6, above, at 588-589.

[12]See Cohen, note 1, above, at 488-491.

[13]*Worcester,* note 3, above, at 539 and 557-558.

[14]Id. at 543-545.

[15]The aboriginal title in *Worcester* was also protected by treaties with the United States, but the absence of a treaty does not diminish the federal duty to protect against trespass. See Edwardsen v. Morton, 369 F. Supp. 1359 (D.C.D.C. 1973). See also Cohen, note 1, above, at 488.

[16]*M'Intosh* note 6, above, at 591.

[17]*Worcester,* note 3, above, at 551-552. The discussion at this point concerns a specific section of a treaty between the United States and the Cherokees. In that section, the United States obligates itself to protect Cherokee lands.

[18]Id. at 544.

[19]E.g., Tee-Hit-Ton v. U.S., 348 U.S. 272, 279 (1955), noting also that:
[Indian title] is not a property right but amounts to a right of occupancy which the sovereign grants and protects against intrusion by third parties but which right of occupancy may be terminated and such lands fully disposed of by the sovereign itself without any legally enforceable obligation to compensate the Indians.

[20]E.g., *Edwardsen v. Morton,* note 15, above. Secretary of the Interior breached duty of protection by issuing land use permits and blasting licenses for land held in aboriginal possession by Inupiat Eskimos on Alaska's North Slope. This case compelled the United States to sue the alleged trespassers of behalf of the Eskimos. See U.S. v. ARCO et al., 435 Supp. 1009 (D.C. AK. 1977); aff'd, 612 F. 2d 1132 (9th Cir. 1980); cert. den 449 U.S. 888 (1980). The court denied relief, holding that Section 4(b) of the Alaska Native Claims Settlement Act [43 USC 1603(b)] extinguished all claims "based on" aboriginal possession.

[21]Act of June 30, 1834, 4 Stat. 729. See generally 39 N. Dak. L. Rev. 50 (1963). See F. Prucha, *American Indian Policy in the Formative Years* (Lincoln: University of Nebraska, 1962) at 274.

[22]*"American State Papers" (Indian Affairs),* I (1832):142, 923-4. Cited in Joint Tribal Council of Passamaquoddy Tribe v. Morton, 388 F. Supp. 649, 661 (1975), aff'd 528 F.2d 370 (1st Cir. 1975)."

[23]14 Op. Atty. Gen. 290, 293 (1873).

[24]U.S. v. Seveloff, 1 Ak. Fed. Rpts. 64 (1872), dismissing prosecution for importing liquor into Alaska in violation of the Intercourse Act.

[25]Act of March 3, 1873, c. 227, 17 Stat. 530. See In re Carr, 1 AK. Fed. Rpts. 75 (1875), upholding applicability of 1873 statute to liquor importation offense but discharging defendant on other grounds.

[26]Waters v. Campell, 1 AK. Fed. Rpts. 91 (1876).

[27]Act of June 25, 1948, c. 645, 62 Stat. 757, as amended (18 USCA 1151), defining "Indian country" to include reservations, allotments and any dependent Indian communities.

[28]See Oneida Indian Nation v. County of Oneida, 414 U.S. 661 at 674, n. 9 (1974), holding that land alienation restrictions of the Intercourse Act were a basis for claims of unlawful taking of lands lying outside the area defined as "Indian country" in the 1834 act. See also Mohegan Tribe v. Connecticut, 638 F. 2d 612 (2nd Cir. 1980); cert. den. 450 U.S. 1028 (1981), Rehnquist, J. dissenting. The circuit court held specifically that the Intercourse Act's restrictions on alienation applied to all tribal land whether or not in Indian country. See generally Cohen at 29-30, note 1, above.

[29]Act of June 30, 1834, c. 161, sec. 12, 4 Stat. 730 (25 USCA 177).

[30]*M'Intosh,* note 6, above, at 587.

[31]See Cohen, note 1, above, at 492-493. See also 1 Op. Atty. Gen. 456 (1821).

[32]United States v. Santa Fe R. Co., 314 U.S. 339, 354 (1941).

[33]United States v. Gemmill, 535 F2d 1145, 1148 (9th Cir. 1976).

[34]Amendment V provides in part:
> No person shall...be deprived of life, liberty or property without due process of law; nor shall private property be taken for public use, without just compensation.

[35]*Tee-Hit-Ton,* note 19, above, at 278-279.

[36]See e.g., 5 Amer. Ind. L. Rev. 75, 113-122 (1977), for one such criticism.

[37]E.g., Act of June 19, 1935, 49 Stat. 388, conferring jurisdiction on the court of claims to enter judgment on behalf of the Tlingit and Haida Indians of Alaska for the prior loss of their aboriginal lands.

[38]See e.g., Tlingit and Haida Indians of Alaska v. U.S., 147 Ct. Cls. 315, 177 F. Supp. 452 (1959).

[39]See generally, Cohen, note 1, above, at 741-742.

[40]Treaty of March 30, 1867, 15 Stat. 539.

[41]See *Tlingit-Haida,* note 38, above, at 315, 387, and also D.H. Hunter, *The Alaska Treaty,* (Kingston, Ontario: Limestone, 1981, at 71 ff., describing these events.

[42]E.g., U.S. v. Alaska, 422 U.S. 184, 192, n. 13 (1975).

[43]See *Tlingit-Haida,* note 38, above, at 386-387. See also *The Alaska Treaty,* note 41, above, at 71 ff.

[44]*Tlingit-Haida,* note 38, above, at 386-387.

[45]See Johnson v. Pacific Coast S.S. Co. 2 Ak. Rpts. 224, 240 (D.C. Ak. 1904), characterizing Alaska Native occupancy as "in common".

[46]In re Minook, 2 Ak. Rpts. 200, 220-221 (D.C. Ak. 1904), so holding in the context of an Alaska Native citizenship petition.

[47]Act of June 2, 1924, ch. 233, 43 Stat. 253 [superseded in 1940 but carried forward at 8 USCA 1401(b)].

[48]See generally, Cohen, note 1, above, at 142-143 and 642-645, discussing the history and modern implications of Native American citizenship.

[49]See generally, *Minook,* note 46, above, at 213-219, for a complete discussion of the alleged basis for these distinctions in Russian colonial society. Senator Sumner, in his April 8, 1867 speech before the Senate also distinguished between those "under the direct government" of the Russian American Company and those outside its jurisdiction. See *The Alaska Treaty,* note 41, above, at 207. See also Atkinson v. Haldane, 569 P. 2d. 151 at 154 (Ak. 1977), discussing Art. III.

[50]See Elk v. Wilkins, 112 U.S. 94 at 103-104 (1884), discussing various citizenship provisions of treaties with Indian tribes contemporary with the 1867 Treaty of Cession. *Elk v. Wilkins* also held that mere abandonment of tribal relations was not sufficient for U.S. citizenship unless a specific congressional act permitted it. Id. at 106-107. See also Cohen, note 1, above, at 142.

[51]*The Alaska Treaty,* note 41, above, at 71, reprinting Seward's memorandum.

[52]Id. at 89, reprinting in translation de Stoeckl's Russian Foreign Office dispatch No. 10. In the memorandum de Stoeckl uses the terms "savage tribes" and "Indian tribes" interchangeably.

[53]Id. at 208, citing the report of Captian Lester A. Beardslee, U.S.N. (Senate Executive Document No. 71, 47th Cong., 1st Sess., Serial 1989), at 37.

[54]*Minook,* note 46, above, is the principal example of this sort of case. An alternate holding of *Minook* was that the plaintiff was a citizen because he had abandoned his tribal relations and was therefore a naturalized citizen under independent provisions of the 1887 General Allotment Act, 2 Ak. Rpts. at 222-224. Accord, Nagle v. U.S., 191 F. 141, 145-146 (9th Cir. 1911).

[55]Act of January 27, 1905, Ch. 277, Sec. 7, 33 Stat. 616.

[56]Davis v. Sitka School Board, 3 Ak. Rpts. 481 (D.C. Ak. 1908).

[57]U.S. v. Berrigan, 2 Ak. Rpts. 442 (D.C. Ak 1904) and U.S. v. Cadzow, 5 Ak. Rpts, 125 (D.C. Ak 1914).

[58]Sutter v. Heckman, 1 Ak. Rpts. 188 (D.C. Ak 1901), aff'd on other grounds, Heckman v. Sutter, 119 F. 83 (9th Cir. 1902), Worthen Lumber Mills v. Alaska-Juneau Gold Mining Company 229 F. 966 (9th Cir. 1916).

[59]159 F. 2d 997 (9th cir. 1947).

[60]*Tee-Hit-Ton,* note 19, above, at 272.

[61]Id. at 278.

[62]*Tlingit-Haida,* note 38, above.

[63]*Edwardsen,* note 20, above.

[64]Organic Act of May 17, 1884, c. 53, 23 Stat. 24, Sec. 8.

[65]*Heckman,* note 58, above, at 88.

[66]*Berrigan,* note 57, above, at 443-445.

[67]Id. at 447-448.

[68]Id. at 448-449. The acts included: Organic Act of May 17, 1884, c. 53, 23 Stat. 24 Sec. 8; Act of March 3, 1891, c. 561, 26 Stat. 1095 Sec. 14; Homestead Act of May 14, 1898, c. 299, 30 Stat. 412, Sec. 7; Act of June 6, 1900, c. 786, 31 Stat. 330 Sec. 27.

[69]Wickersham confuses section 8 of the 1884 Act on which *Heckman* relied with section 27 of the 1900 statute. The confusion is irrelevant because both sections provide that: "The Indians...shall not be disturbed in the possession of any lands actually in their use or occupation." See Berrigan, note 57, above, at 448 and 451. Compare Heckman, note 58, above, at 199.

[70]*Berrigan,* note 57, above, at 451.

[71]*Cadzow,* note 57, above, at 125-129.

[72]Id. at 133.

[73]Id. at 131-132.

[74]*Worthen Mills,* note 58, above, at 966, 969.

[75]*Berrigan,* at 448; *Cadzow,* at 131, note 57, above.

[76]*Berrigan* at 447-448 *Cadzow,* at 129-130, note 57, above.

[77]See also 37 L. D. 334, 336-337 (1908), holding that the 1884 Act did not permit Natives to alienate land.

[78]*Miller,* note 59, above, at 1005. See notes 34-38, above, and accompanying text regarding the compensability of "recognized" and "unrecognized" aboriginal title.

[79]*Miller,* note 59, above, at 1002.

[80]"Dictum," plural "dicta," are statements or conclusions in court opinions which do not speak to the specific question then being litigated. Dicta, because they do not address the specific question before the court, do not constitute precedent or authority for subsequent decisions. See Llewellyn, Karl, *The Bramble Bush* at 42.

[81]*Miller,* note 59, above, at 1002. The *Miller* dictum has been disapproved by the solicitor, 60 I.D. 142, 145 (M-35028 1948) and the U.S. Supreme Court (note 88, below).

[82]Id. at 1005.

[83]On remand, the Natives in *Miller* were held not to have established "use and occupancy" even under the 1884 act and were therefore held not to be entitled to compensation. U.S. v. 10.95 Acres of Land, 75 F. Supp. 841 (D.C. Ak. 1948).

[84]Not because it acknowledges individual Native land rights, but because it does so at the expense of aboriginal (tribal or group) title. The United States Supreme Court has upheld the rights of individual Indians to land they use and occupy as individuals even to the point of cancelling a federal patent which was inconsistent with such use and occupancy. Cramer v. U.S., 261 U.S. 219, 227 (1923), cancelling a railroad patent which was inconsistent with individual Indian occupancy established pursuant to a "well understood policy" which encouraged Indians to abandon nomadic habits and establish fixed homes.

[85]*Tee-Hit-Ton,* note 19, above, at 277. The Tee-Hit-Ton also relied on a provision similar to section 8 in section 27 of the Act of June 6, 1900.

[86]Id. at 278.

[87]Id.

[88]Id. at 283, n. 16, citing Hynes v. Grimes Packing Co., 337 U.S. 86, 106, n. 28 (1948).

[89]Id. at 284-285. The *Tee-Hit-Ton* decision is much criticized for its conclusion that "unrecognized" aboriginal title is not compensable. E.g., Henderson, J. Youngblood, *Unraveling the Riddle of Aboriginal Title,* 5 Amer. Ind. L. Rev. 75, 109-118 (1977).

[90]Id. at 274 "Only those (issues) pertinent to the petitioner's interest, *if any,* in the lands are here for review (emphasis added)."

[91]Id. at 294, Douglas J. dissenting. Without citing *Tee-Hit-Ton,* the Alaska District Court once again determined (relying on *Miller*) that the 1884 act recognized a right to compensation for use and occupancy, but held against the Native claimants because they failed to prove use and occupancy. U.S. v. Alaska, 201 F. Supp. 796 (D.C. Ak. 1962).

[92]There are other Alaska cases which touch aboriginal title issues, but they are not of major importance here. See U.S. v. Lynch, 7 Ak. Rpts. 568, 572 (D.C. Ak. 1927); Aleut Community of St Paul v. U.S., 480 F. 2d 831, 837 (Ct. Cls. 1973) and U.S. v. Libby, McNeill and Libby, 107 F. Supp. 697 (D.C. Ak. 1952).

[93]See e.g., Gruening, Ernest, *The State of Alaska,* (New York: Random House, 1968) at 380.

[94]Act of June 19, 1935, 49 Stat. 388, ch. 295 (as amended by Act of June 5, 1942, 56 Stat. 323 and Act of June 4, 1945, 59 Stat. 231).

[95]Tlingit and Haida Indians of Alaska v. U.S., 177 F. Supp. 452, 147 Ct. Cls. at 388-392 (1959). See 147 Ct. Cls. at 385-392 findings No. 58-62, for a description of the negotiations previously alluded to concerning the purpose of Art. VI of the treaty. Correspondence from Seward both before and after the treaty was signed confirms that Art. VI was not intended to extinguish aboriginal title. See also *The Alaska Treaty,* note 41, above. This decision only held that the Tlingits and Haidas had been deprived of their aboriginal lands. A later case decided the damages. Tlingit and Haida Indians of Alaska v. U.S., 389 F. 2d 778 (1968).

[96]177 F. Supp. at 463-64.

[97]The *Tlingit-Haida* holding as to the legal effect of the treaty does not lessen the burden of proving the factual existence and extent of aboriginal use and occupancy. To some extent the facts to be proven depend on the specific jurisdictional act. At a minimum, exclusive use and occupancy for a substantial period must be established and it must be shown to have been of a "tribal" or communal nature. E.g.,*Tlingit-Haida,* note 38, above, at 323-324 and 328-329.

[98]369 U.S. 60 (1962)

[99]Id. at 65.

[100]See State of Alaska v. Udall, 420 F. 2d 938 (9th Cir. 1969). See also *Edwardsen,* note 20, above, describing the Secretary's actions and the rationale behind them.

[101]Id. at 939-940.

[102]Id. at 940.

[103]Id. By this time the Secretary had formalized the freeze in Public Land Order No. 4582, January 17, 1969, "for the determination and protection of the rights of the Native Aleuts, Eskimos and Indians of Alaska," as cited in *Edwardsen,* note 20, above, at 1364, n. 11.

[104]*Berrigan,* note 57, above.

[105]*Udall,* note 100, above, at 940.

[106]43 U.S.C.A. 1603.

[107]*Edwardsen,* note 20, above.

[108]Id. at 1362.

[109]Id. at 1365.

[110]Id.

[111]Id. at 1373.

[112]Because aboriginal interests in land cannot be conveyed to private parties and because ANCSA extinguished plaintiff's possessory interests anyway, the court granted partial summary judgment to the secretary as to the possessory claims only. Id. at 1372 and 1378.

[113]Id. at 1375.

[114]Id. at 1379.

[115]The alleged trespassers included the State of Alaska and the oil and other commercial concerns who had used Arctic Slope lands prior to the claims act.

[116]U.S. v. ARCO, 435 F. Supp. 1009 (D.C. Ak. 1977); aff'd. 612 F2d. 1132 (9th Cir. 1980); cert. den. 499 U.S. 888 (1980).

[117]*Edwardsen,* note 20, above, at 1378-79. After *Edwardsen,* the Secretary entered into a stipulation with the plaintiffs requiring federal officials to investigate the trespass claims and to recommend that the Attorney General sue for trespass on the plaintiffs' behalf.

[118]*ARCO,* note 116, above, at 1022-29. See also *Paug-Vik v. Wards Cove Packing,* 633 P. 2d 1015 (Ak. 1981), holding that prior conveyance of water rights under 43 USCA extinguished aboriginal title to such rights under 4(c) of ANCSA [43 USCA 1603(c)].

[119]ARCO, above, at 1020.

[120]Id. at 1021.

[121]Inupiat Community of the Arctic Slope v. U.S. (ICAS I), 680 F.2d 122 (Ct. Cl. 1982), cert. den.____U.S.____, 51 U.S.L.W. 3339 (Nov. 2, 1982). ICAS is organized under section 16 of the Indian Reorganization Act (25 USCA 476).

[122]ICAS I, above, at 129.

[123]See U.S. v. Mitchell, 445 U.S. 535 (1980), requiring specific statutory authority both waiving sovereign immunity and providing a substantive right in order to recover monetary damages against the United States for alleged breaches of trust owed Native Americans. But see U.S. v. Mitchell (Mitchell II),____U.S.____, 51 U.S.L.W. 4999 at 5002 (1983), holding that 28 USCA 1491 waives federal sovereign immunity for all such claims and permitting recovery if a statute affords a substantive right.

[124]Inupiat Community of the Arctic Slope v. U.S. (ICAS II,), 548 F. Supp. 182 (D.C. Ak. 1982), appeal pending.

[125]See e.g., Aleut Community of St. Paul Island v. U.S., 480 F. 2d 831 (1973), obligations arising out of the special statutory treatment accorded the St. Paul Islanders.

CHAPTER THREE

RESERVATIONS

I. Introduction

On December 18, 1971, all Alaska Native reservations (with the exception of Metlakatla) were abolished by section 19 of the Alaska Native Claims Settlement Act (ANCSA). Until that day, the creation and management of Native reserves was the most significant and highly visible aspect of federal Native policy in Alaska. Reservations were the key issue in four of the five Alaska Native cases to reach the U. S. Supreme Court between 1916 *(Alaska Pacific Fisheries v. United States)*[1] and 1962 *(Metlakatla v. Egan).*[2] More than any single factor, federal reservation policies established the historical fact of the special relationship between the federal government and Alaska Natives.

A. *Alaska Pacific Fisheries v. United States*

This case established the reservation as a device to protect Alaska Natives and to improve their economic advantage. The case arose out of what were to become familiar circumstances—a contest between the U.S. Government and Alaska business interests, with control of a rich fishery resource at stake.

The Annette Island (Metlakatla) Reserve was established by an 1891 act of Congress.[3] In early April 1916, Alaska Pacific Fisheries, a California corporation, began to build a fishtrap off the coast of the reservation. In late April 1916, before the trap was complete, President Woodrow Wilson issued a proclamation reserving the waters within three thousand feet of the shore of the reserve "for the benefit of the Metlakatlans and such other Alaskan Natives as joined them or may join them in residence on these islands."[4]

The U. S. Department of Justice brought suit in trespass against Alaska Pacific Fisheries. In June 1916, the Alaska District Court held in favor of the United States and enjoined the trespass, citing both the presidential proclamation and the 1891 act;[5] the Ninth Circuit Court of Appeals affirmed the district court on the basis of the presidential proclamation alone.[6] The U. S. Supreme Court affirmed the Ninth Circuit solely on the 1891 statute and the congressional intent behind it. The Supreme Court held that the Metlakatla Reservation was not a private grant:

> But simply a setting apart (until otherwise provided by law), of designated public property for a recognized public purpose—that of *safeguarding and advancing dependent Indian people dwelling within the United States* (emphasis added).[7]

With this principle in mind, the Court deduced from the location of the reserve (an island three-fourths of which was rock and mountain) and the situation and needs of the Indians (fishermen and hunters who relied on the fishery surrounding the island for their support) that Congress intended to include the navigable water surrounding the Annette Islands in the original reservation grant. The Court bolstered this conclusion with the principle of liberal interpretation that is applied to statutes passed for the benefit of dependent Indian tribes or communities.[8]

B. General Principles

For purposes of future discussion, it is well to keep in mind that in 1918 the Alaska District Court in Juneau, the Ninth Circuit Court of Appeals in San Francisco and the U.S. Supreme Court in Washington, D.C., among them, recognized the following principles as applicable to Alaska Native reservations:

1. The president could establish executive order Indian reservations in Alaska;[9]
2. These reservations were created for the benefit and protection of Alaska Natives;
3. A liberal construction would be given to statutes passed on behalf of Alaska Native communities; and
4. The United States had standing in equity to sue trespassers on reserved lands or waters.

By the time of the *Alaska Pacific Fisheries* decision, various presidents had created a number of both large and small Alaska Native executive order reserves. Then in 1919, within a year after that decision, Congress prohibited formation of Indian reserves except by congressional enactment.[10] However, that did not prevent the president from withdrawing land by executive order for various "public purposes." Although reserves withdrawn under this authority were not legally "Indian" reserves, they could still be used for the "public purpose" of assisting Alaska Natives. Among the most significant of these reserves were those created under a 1925 act[11] permitting the Secretary of the Interior to establish a "vocational training system" for Alaska Natives. Finally, in 1936, the 1934 Indian Reorganization Act was modified and extended to Alaska.[12] Under this authority, the Secretary of the Interior created several, large Native reserves in the territory.[13]

Taken together, the history of Alaska Native reservations constitutes an eighty-year federal policy of protecting Alaska Native lands and resources. Prior to 1936, Alaskan reserves were generally small (sometimes less than an acre), although some were as large as several hundred thousand acres. These early reserves do not appear to be associated with any coherent federal policy of satisfying potential Alaska Native land claims.[14] Rather, they appear to attend programs operated by the Bureau of Education (i.e., education, reindeer herding, medical care, etc.), which either directly or indirectly were for the protection and benefit of Alaska Natives. None of these reservations were "Indian reservations" in the full legal sense of the term.

1. Indian Reservations

Indian reservations are created by treaty or congressional statute usually after the extinguishment of extensive aboriginal land claims. The exact nature of the reservation and the rights the Native tribe has in the reservation depend on the language used in the treaty or congressional statute.[15] Usually, the language in the treaty or statute effectively "disposes" of the land. That means the United States retains title to the fee, but the land is held in trust for the use and benefit of the Native occupants. Only Congress may thereafter completely dispose of reservation lands, but the Natives retain a compensable property interest which must be satisfied under the Fifth Amendment to the United States Constitution. As a practical matter, the existence of a compensable interest inhibits the United States from eliminating Indian reservations.

As noted in chapter 2, whether a Native tribe or community has a compensable interest in the land it occupies depends upon whether or not Congress has "recognized" the community's aboriginal right of occupancy or "aboriginal title." Unless Congress recognized the right of occupancy, Native Americans have no *permanent* and therefore no *compensable* interest in the land. Congressional recognition need not take any particular form but there must be "a definite intention by congressional action or authority to accord legal rights, not merely permissive occupation."[16] A congressional statute, agreement or treaty ratification is usually sufficient to recognize permanent and compensable rights to the land occupied.[17]

2. Executive Order Reservations

Executive order reservations on the other hand, are not so secure. They are sometimes characterized as "reservations at will." Like other such reserves (i.e., military reserves, petroleum reserves, etc.), they are created for a particular public purpose. It is easy to understand the public purpose behind a petroleum or military reservation. One is to conserve oil for future public use; the other supports national defense. In either case, it is not the people living on the reserve who are benefited, but the public at large. Executive order Indian reservations are sometimes characterized in the same manner. They are not created to benefit the people who reside on them so much as they are created to benefit the public at large by preventing the residents from becoming dependent on state or territorial public welfare.[18]

Unlike true "Indian" reservations, executive order reservations do not recognize permanent or compensable interests in lands.[19] It has been argued that certain federal statutes relating to leasing on executive order reservations do create a compensable interest, but that position has never been accepted by the Department of the Interior.[20] Instead, the so-called "Indian Leasing Laws" constitute a complex body of law which somewhat erratically regulate mineral and other leases on both executive order and "Indian" reservation lands.[21]

3. Summary

Prior to 1936 and the Indian Reorganization Act, there were four methods of creating Alaska Native reserves:

Treaty reserves—available until 1871, but none were created in Alaska.

Statutory reserves—only two were created in Alaska: Metlakatla in 1981 and Klukwan in 1957.[22]

Executive order Indian reserves—before 1919 approximately one hundred fifty of these were created in Alaska.[23]

Public purpose reserves—five of these were established between 1920 and 1933 by executive order, but because of the 1919 prohibition, they were not technically "Indian" reserves.

The *Alaska Pacific Fisheries* cases verified the authority of the president to create Alaska Native executive order Indian reserves, but Congress statutorily revoked that authority in 1919. Thereafter, the president made a few withdrawals for the "public purpose" of assisting the Alaska Natives. The most notable of these were the vocational education reserves authorized under a 1925 act. Finally, in 1936 the IRA was applied to Alaska. Under that authority, the Secretary of the Interior created several large Alaska Native reserves.

II. Development and Decline of the Alaska Reservation Policy

A. Eight Phases

Federal Alaska Native reservation policy can be divided into roughly eight phases spanning the years 1891 to 1971. They are as follows:

1. 1891-1919: Creation of the Metlakatla and the first executive order reserves
2. 1920-1933: Creation of "Public purpose" reserves

3. 1936-1940: Application of the IRA to Alaska and small reservation policy
4. 1940-1943: Adoption of large reservation policy and withdrawal of the Venetie and Karluk reserves
5. 1944-1949: Policy implementation, litigation and political opposition (Kake, Klawock and Hydaburg hearings, *Hynes v. Grimes Packing Company* and SJR-62)
6. 1949-1952: Policy defeated *(Hynes v. Grimes Packing Company* and *United States v. Libby, McNeill and Libby)*
7. 1952-1960: Dormancy (Termination Era)
8. 1960-1971: Restrictions and revocation (*Metlakatla* and *Kake v. Egan,* new Karluk policy and ANCSA)

B. 1891-1919—Metlakatla and the First Executive Order Reserves

1. Metlakatla

Metlakatla was the first of only two statutorily created Alaska Native reserves.[24] It is an anomaly on the Alaskan scene and came into existence just four years after Congress passed the General Allotment Act of 1887—designed to break up Indian reservations.[25] One can only speculate that the remoteness of Alaska along with the missionary zeal of William Duncan and his supporters were responsible for its creation.[26]

The U. S. Supreme Court has found that the language creating the Metlakatla Reserve is similar to that used in creating other statutory reservations; however, the reservation is unique because of the Interior Secretary's specified and continuing regulatory role.[27] Despite the unique circumstances of its creation, the purpose of the reservation appears well settled. In 1918, the U. S. Supreme Court held that the Metlakatla Reservation was established:

> to encourage, assist and protect the Indians in their effort to train themselves to habits of industry, become self-sustaining and advance in the ways of civilized life.[28]

The U. S. Supreme Court has confirmed its status in two opinions *(Alaska Pacific Fisheries* and *Metlakatla),* spanning nearly fifty years, as being similar to other reservations established for the benefit of Native Americans.[29]

2. The First Executive Order Reserves

Another missionary, Sheldon Jackson, preceded Duncan in Alaska, and his influence was responsible for many of the executive order reserves established in the early twentiety century. Jackson was appointed General Agent for Education in Alaska on April 31, 1885, to implement section 13 of the 1884 Organic Act.[30] Reverend Jackson had been a missionary in Alaska for several years prior to his appointment, and perhaps for that reason saw his educational responsibilities as including the general "betterment" of the Native population.

He introduced reindeer to the Alaska Natives and was instrumental in establishing federal reserves for reindeer herding. The reindeer and therefore the reserves were intended to benefit the Natives by providing a reliable source of food and opportunity for training in animal husbandry. He also established the first village schools. In time these became the focal point not only for "education" but also for medical services, assistance to the needy, reindeer herding, community development, law enforcement and other social welfare activities.

The U. S. Office of Education within the Department of the Interior continued the reservation policy Sheldon Jackson had begun. Between 1905 and 1919, the federal government established at least fourteen reserves for the same general purposes as attended the reindeer reserves. These reserves ranged in size from 17.21 acres (Chilkat Fisheries Reserve) to 316,000 acres (Norton Bay, Elim).[31]

Authority for creating these reserves was derived from both statutory and case law. A 1910 statute authorizing executive order land withdrawals is sometimes cited as specific authority for creating these reserves.[32] As noted previously, the *Alaska Pacific Fisheries* cases also affirmed that the president had such authority based on past practice and case precedent,[33] but in 1919 Congress prohibited the creation of executive order Native reservations without specific congressional authorization.[34] Thus only those executive order reserves created before 1919 could be characterized as "Indian" reserves without the specific approval of Congress.

The analysis of these first executive order reserves begins with Sheldon Jackson's reindeer reserves; they set the pattern and purpose for those which followed. We will briefly examine the weakness which permitted summary revocation of these reserves and the congressional action which corrected it. We will also discuss at some length the question of executive reserve leasing and the federal-Native relationships which grew out of the federal Indian leasing laws.

a. Reindeer Reserves

Sheldon Jackson imported the first reindeer from Russia in 1891.[35] In the early part of the twentieth century, various executive orders withdrew 1.25 million acres for reindeer reserves.[36] One of these withdrawals was the whole of St. Lawrence Island;[37] administrative proceedings relating to the ANCSA rights of St. Lawrence Island's Natives demonstrate the purpose of the reindeer reserves.

In order for the Native residents of St. Lawrence Island to acquire surface and subsurface rights to their land, Section 19 of ANCSA[38] required it to be shown that the St. Lawrence reserve was created "for Native use or for administration of Native affairs." The Department of the Interior apparently questioned whether the reserve was created for the benefit of the Natives or for the reindeer. Alaska Legal Services submitted a brief on behalf of the St. Lawrence Island Natives which the Department of the Interior (after review by the Solicitor) accepted as confirming that the reserve was established to support the reindeer for the benefit of the Natives.[39]

This brief, coupled with the department's acceptance of it, established that the St. Lawrence Reserve had two purposes:

1)   Preventing starvation of the Natives;
2)   Training Natives in the "civilizing arts" of animal husbandry.

This latter fact is particularly important, because it demonstrates that the Department of the Interior made similar use of the St. Lawrence Island reindeer as was made of horses and cattle among the Indian tribes of the "lower forty-eight." Of that it has been said:

> The purpose and object of the government in its dealings with these Indians, and in the relation that it maintains toward them and their property, is to encourage habits of industry and reward labor, and to encourage them to undertake the cultivation of the soil, the raising of stock, or engage in pastoral pursuits, enabling them to support themselves, and as a means of obtaining a livelihood.[40]

The solicitor for the Department of the Interior relied on this language in 1925 when he held that the Territory of Alaska could not impose a tax on reindeer controlled or killed by Alaska Natives. In answering the question of whether there was "anything in the government's relationship with (the Alaskan) Natives which prevents the application of the [tax] act to reindeer killed by them," the solicitor concluded that:

> [I]f the Territory has the power to levy and collect that tax, it might...very materially interfere with this instrumentality which the Government has adopted for the advancement of these natives. That act, in so far as it relates to reindeer killed by Natives is, consequently, repugnant to the Constitution and hence without effect.[41]

One thing seems clear from the Department's acceptance of the *St. Lawrence Brief* and the solicitor's 1925 opinion; at least as to the reindeer reserves, the federal relationship to Alaska Natives was very similar to its relationship with other Native Americans outside Alaska. In either case, the government's historical purpose has been to enable the Natives to "support themselves." To that end it has established various programs "for the advancement of these Natives." To ensure the success of such programs, the government has established methods to protect the Natives from local taxation and other forms of interference.[42] From its earliest involvement with Alaska Natives, the Department of the Interior pursued the same policies in Alaska as it did elsewhere, thereby confirming the similarity of its relationship to Native Americans here and in the continental United States.[43]

b. Reserve Revocation—Hydaburg and Klawock

The federal-Native relationship that might develop in conjunction with a reserve was always subject to one threat—summary revocation. Although Congress prohibited the creation of new executive order "Native" reserves in 1919, it did not thereby prevent the revocation of existing reserves. Because they were created by the executive, theoretically they could be destroyed by the executive.[44] In at least two Alaskan cases, the theory was put into practice.

In 1912, President Taft established a seventy-eight hundred-acre land and water reserve for "the use of the Hydah tribe of Indians and such of the Natives of Alaska as may settle within the limits of the reservation."[45] The reservation is the site of the present village of Hydaburg, which the Haida Indians had then newly established with the support of the Bureau of Education. Two years later President Wilson established a land reserve at Klawock for the "use of the U. S. Bureau of Education and of the Natives of indigenous Alaska race who may there reside."[46]

Contemporary correspondence establishes that both reserves were intended to protect the Natives from white encroachment on Native fishing sites.[47] The Hydaburg reserve was twelve square miles in area and included large bodies of water over which the Natives and the Federal Government had exclusive control.[48] In spite of the obvious value of these reserves and the explicit purpose of creating them to protect and benefit their Native occupants, Calvin Coolidge revoked both in 1926 and reduced them to school reserves of less than two acres each.[49]

The next year Congress prohibited any further revocations of executive order reserves in the Indian Leasing Act of 1927.[50] The 1927 act was in response to a number of Indian leasing questions which arose during the Harding and Coolidge administrations. Section 4 of the act prohibited:

> changes in the boundaries of reservations created by executive order, proclamation, or otherwise for the *use and occupation* of Indians...except by Act of Congress (emphasis added).[51]

By taking this action, Congress further solidified the federal-Native relationship established in the creation of previous executive order reserves.

c. Leasing of Executive Order Reserves—Tyonek and Elim

i. Introduction

These first executive order reserves were established with the express purpose of enabling their Native occupants to develop some means of self-support. A key factor in achieving that purpose was to make economic use of the lands and other resources available to the reserve. Leasing of reserve lands to process renewable resources (e.g., fish canneries and lumber mills) or to extract mineral resources (e.g., oil and gas) was the principal method used to establish economic self-support.

Leasing carried with it concepts of close government supervision of leasing negotiations and distribution of lease proceeds. In this respect it created what might in the narrowest sense of the term be called a federal "trust responsibility" to the Natives occupying the executive reserves. The government appears always to have been careful to restrict the scope of this responsibility to management of the leased lands and not expand it to the whole of the executive reserve. That does not mean that by statute, appropriations and executive action the government did not develop other responsibilities to Alaska Natives based on relationships more broadly defined than those of a land-related "trust." These are the topics of a later chapter.[52]

ii. Tyonek

The leasing question was a complex one in Alaska, and the Tyonek Reserve became the eventual focal point for its resolution. The Tyonek Reserve (also known as the Moquawkie Reserve) was established in 1915, for the "use of the U.S. Bureau of Education, subject to any existing right."[53] A 1923 solicitor's opinion found that the reserve's primary purpose was to enable the Bureau of Education to:

> maintain a school and otherwise *care for, support and advance* the interest of the aboriginal Natives who [inhabited] the village...(emphasis added).[54]

The Commissioner of Education requested this opinion to determine whether the Bureau of Education had authority to enter into a lease for operation of a cannery at Tyonek. In concluding that the Bureau had such authority, the solicitor found that:

> The fundamental consideration underlying this question is the fact that these natives are, in a very large sense at least, *dependent subjects of our Government* and in a state of tutelage; or in other words, they are *wards of the government* and under its guardianship and care. *The relations existing between them and the Government are very similar and in many respects,*

identical with those which have long existed between the Government and the aboriginal people residing within the territorial limits of the United States... (emphasis added).[55]

The solicitor found that the Tyonek Reserve was created for the same purposes as the U.S. Supreme Court found supporting the Annette Island Reserve:

to encourage, assist and protect the Indians in their efforts to train themselves to habits of industry, become self-sustaining and advance to the ways of civilized life.[56]

Based on these purposes and the public duty of the government toward the Tyonek Natives (as wards essentially), the solicitor concluded that the public purpose in creating the reserve was to protect the Natives and to permit the Bureau of Education to: "aid them in advancing toward civilized life and complete self-support."[57] The bureau was, therefore, authorized to use the reserve lands:

for any reasonable purpose which will advance the interest of the natives, provided it does not undertake to make such disposition [of the land] as will eventually embarrass the Government's title.[58]

The bureau, in short, was authorized to lease a portion of the reserve for a cannery to benefit the Natives. However, the opinion concluded, the cannery lease had to be directly negotiated by the Bureau of Education and the proceeds of the lease "disposed of for the benefit of the natives."[59] This last point is important because it established an essential principle of any "trust" relationship—that of benefiting the party for whom the trust was created. Even prior to the various leasing acts (later enacted to clarify the disposition of lease proceeds from executive order reserves), the Department of the Interior recognized its obligation to manage executive order reserve lands for the benefit of the Natives occupying the land.

The 1923 Tyonek opinion must be viewed in the context of the public land leasing policies of President Warren G. Harding's adminstration (1921-1923). Prior to that time, executive order reserves were treated like statutory or treaty reserves for leasing purposes. No land reserved for Indian occupancy could be leased without specific congressional action permitting it.[60] Contrary to this seemingly well-established principle, Harding's Secretary of the Interior, Albert Fall, began leasing executive order reserves for mineral exploration under the General Leasing Act of 1920.[61]

Section 1 of this act permitted the leasing of lands "owned by the United States" with certain specified exceptions. Executive order Indian reserves were not among the specified exceptions, and a 1922 solicitor's opinion determined that this omission permitted mineral leasing of executive order Indian reserves as lands "owned by the United States."[62] President Harding died in 1923, and Albert Fall was drummed out of office on corruption charges involving mineral leases on public lands. In 1924, Attorney General Harlan F. Stone issued an opinion to President Coolidge advising against further leasing of executive order reserves.[63]

Leasing of executive order reserves apparently ceased, because in 1925 bills were introduced in Congress to permit it to continue.[64] There was substantial opposition concerning the disposition of the royalty income from the proposed leases, because the pending legislation placed the lease income in trust for the Native occupants of the reserves. The view was frequently advanced in the hearings on these bills as well as the floor debate in both houses of Congress, that requiring income from the lease sales to be held in trust for the Natives occupying the reserves would recognize a compensable interest in the executive order reserves.

The act, which finally passed Congress in 1927, permitted only oil and gas leases on executive order reserves. It did require that all income from these leases be held in trust for the Natives occupying the reserves.[65]

This policy was said to be:

> in evident accord with equity and with the historical fact that the greater part of all the existing Indian reservation area has been created since 1871, the date when the treaty-making power with the Indian was ended.[66]

Thus, at least as to oil and gas, the 1927 act provided a "uniform policy" for such leases on executive order reserves.[67] The statute's clear implication is that as to the proceeds of oil and gas leases the federal government assumed a trust relationship to the Natives occupying the reserve which supported the lease. It seems unnecessarily metaphysical to argue that having gone this far the government does not also have a general trust responsibility toward executive reserve lands absent a specific statutorily authorized lease. On the other hand, the Department of the Interior has always been careful to confine the implications of this particular trust responsibility to the narrowest possible interpretation of the 1927 and subsequent leasing statutes. The department's reluctance might be the result of cautious adherence to a detailed congressional scheme regulating leases on executive order and other reserves.[68] It could also result from an abiding concern not to inadvertently confer compensability on executive order reserves.

Arguably, in passing the 1927 leasing act, Congress recognized compensable title on behalf of Natives occupying executive order reserves. The theory is that by requiring proceeds from leases on executive order reserves to be held in trust, Congress thereby recognized the equitable interest of the Natives in the reserves. If the lease proceeds are being held for the benefit of the Natives, it is pretty difficult to avoid the conclusion that the Natives are being "compensated" for a partial taking of the reserve. It follows that if the occupants must be compensated for a partial taking, they must also be compensated for a full taking if the executive order reserve were ever revoked. [69]

Whether for these reasons or not, the 1927 leasing act was not applied to Alaska until 1963. The delay may have been because Alaska was not a state at the time of the 1927 enactment (which permitted states to tax the production of oil and gas on reservations) or perhaps because a subsequent 1938 act arguably repealed the 1927 act and limited mineral leases to:

> unallotted lands within [an] Indian *reservation* or land *owned* by
> [a] tribe, group, or band of Indians...(emphasis added). [70]

If the 1938 act was applied to Tyonek (and therefore other Alaska executive order reserves), then the clear implication would be that those reserves were "owned" by the Natives occupying them. [71] In his 1963 "Tyonek decision" (70 I.D. 166) the solicitor avoided that conclusion and relied on the 1927 Mineral Leasing Act as establishing authority for oil and gas leases on Tyonek and other similar Alaska executive order reserves. In doing so, he also avoided the question of whether the 1927 act recognized the compensability of Alaska executive order reserves. [72]

By skirting these issues, the Tyonek decision narrowly applied the 1927 Mineral Leasing Act to pre-1919 Alaskan executive order reserves so that oil and gas leases would not be held to imply Native "ownership" of the reserve. In light of a 1955 Klukwan decision, [73] the Tyonek decision also implies that other types of mineral leases (i.e., coal, iron ore, etc.) were not possible without further statutory authorization.

iii. Elim Reserve

Following the Tyonek decision, the field solicitor in Juneau had occasion to analyze the BIA's leasing authority on another pre-1919, Alaskan, executive order reserve. Like Tyonek, Elim had been withdrawn as a reserve by President Wilson. The Elim reserve was specifically set aside:

> for the use of the United States Bureau of Education and of
> the Natives of indigenous Alaska race, subject to any valid ad-
> verse rights which may exist by prior inception. [74]

In 1966, the Elim village council requested a VISTA volunteer, David L. Spencer, to "investigate their mineral and extractive rights on the reserve." He wrote that the "BIA has done a small amount of lumbering [on the reserve] presumably under the sanction of the [executive] order." He also noted that the villagers' "uncomfortable feeling [is] that their only right is subsistence habitation." [75] In his reply, the field solicitor noted that under the 1963 Tyonek decision the Elim Reserve could clearly lease lands under the 1927 oil and gas leasing act similar to the leases then possible at Tyonek.[76] The field solicitor went on to state that for the Elim Natives to lease lands for other sorts of mineral exploration or to lease the land for lumbering or other business purposes would require a finding that the Elim Natives "owned" the land. With this in mind, the solicitor advised Mr. Spencer that "absent a change in existing leasing laws" he did not expect Elim to be in a "position either to lease the reservation for mining purposes (other than oil or gas) or to lease surface commercial rights...."[77]

In a letter of the same date to the BIA Area Director, however, the field solicitor indicated that another statute might (under proper interpretation) permit the commercial leasing or sale of timber on the Elim Reserve.[78] This letter alludes to another directive from the BIA central office of March 23, 1966, which "limits your actions regarding surface leasing on Indian reservations in Alaska."[79] The field solicitor concluded that although the central office restrictions applied to certain surface leases, he thought that there was authority for both oil and gas leases at Elim under the Tyonek decision and lumber leases under 25 USCA 407.

In a subsequent 1967 letter, the BIA Area Realty Officer informed the BIA Area Housing Office that the United States still held the title to the Elim Reserve but that the reserve had been withdrawn from the public domain for use of the Native people residing on it.

The area realty officer concluded:

> [T]his reserve is not a trust reservation like Annette Island. A trust reservation means that the title to the land is held in trust by the United States for a tribe, village or group of Indians, Eskimos, or Aleuts.[80]

3. Status of Pre-1919 Executive Order Reserves

The thirteen executive order reserves established prior to 1919 appear to be "Indian" reserves in the same sense as were executive order reserves in the "lower forty-eight." They were lands set apart for the benefit of allegedly dependent people. Reading together the solicitor's 1923 and 1963 Tyonek decisions, the leasing acts and the Elim correspondence, these reserves appear to share the following characteristics:

a. Leasing

Leasing on these reserves was possible under the limited statutory provisions of 25 USCA applicable to executive order Indian reserves. Applicable provisions include and appear limited to: 25 USCA 398 et. seq. (oil and gas leases). Additionally, the 1923 Tyonek opinion authorized the Secretary of the Interior to enter into business leases on behalf of the reserve occupants. Unlike oil and gas leases, proceeds from business leases were recovered to the U. S. Treasury and not held in trust for the Natives. The Natives, however, might receive "incidental" benefit from the lease such as employment.[81]

b. Compensability

Although a good argument can be made that the 1927 leasing act recognized an equitable and compensable interest in these reserves, the solicitor's office and BIA administrative personnel resisted that conclusion. No case has been found holding that the 1927 leasing act was a recognition of a compensable interest. ANCSA (Section 19) extinguished these reserves; therefore, the question of compensability is moot.

c. Trust Relationship

The statutory requirement that certain lease proceeds be held in trust for the reservation occupants created a trust responsibility between the federal government and the Natives; however, the government has always construed the responsibility narrowly, to exclude unleased reserve lands. Nevertheless, a trust responsibility clearly exists as to any such leaseholds or lease proceeds now held by the government on behalf of the occupants of the pre-1919 executive order reserves.[82]

d. Guardianship

An important implication arises from the department's denial of "trust" status to unleased executive reserve lands. The department has frequently restricted the scope of legally enforceable federal obligations to Natives to a narrow definition of the "trust responsibility" based on the management of "trust" lands and resources.[83] Yet, the 1923 Tyonek decision bases the department's authority to lease the cannery land not on the "trust" status of the land but on:

> The fundamental consideration...that these Natives are, in a very large sense at least, dependent subjects of our government...and under its guardianship and care.[84]

On the basis of this relationship, it was found that the Bureau of Education had authority to lease the land for any purpose which will "advance the interest of the Natives," provided that the government 1) negotiated the lease, and 2) disposed of the proceeds "for the benefit of the Natives."[85] Because the Natives were dependent on the government, the government had power to enter into the lease for their benefit. In a 1964 opinion, the solicitor reaffirmed the 1923 opinion and held that similar leases were permissible on post-1919 reserves providing the leases promoted the "interests of the Natives" and accomplished the "purpose of the withdrawal".[86]

The fact the government's obligations under these leases arose out of the government's guardian relationship implies that guardianship may be the source of other responsibilities as well. Like the lease obligations, these other responsibilities may not exist unless specifically assumed; however, once assumed they cannot be easily cast aside. We will further explore the implications of guardianship in chapter 6. It is important only to note here that at an early date the department recognized as to Alaska Natives both the authority and responsibility its guardianship imposes.

C. 1920-1933—"Public Purpose" Reserves

1. Introduction

It is necessary to unravel one final thread for a complete understanding of executive order reserves in Alaska. First recall that in 1919 Congress required that:

No public lands of the United States shall be withdrawn by Executive Order, proclamation, or otherwise, for or as an *Indian* reservation except by Act of Congress (emphasis added). [87]

The statute by its terms prohibited executive-created Indian reserves; therefore, by definition, no Indian reservation could be established after 1919 unless by act of Congress. However, the prohibition did not prevent the president from creating reserves for other "public purposes" under the continuing authority granted in 1910. [88] This authority was used after 1919 to reserve Alaskan lands and waters for the benefit of Alaska Natives, but the reserves created under this authority simply were not "Indian" reserves in the legal sense of the term. [89]

2. The Five Public Purpose Reserves

In 1925, Congress authorized the Secretary of the Interior to "establish a system of vocational training for the aboriginal native people of the Territory of Alaska." [90] Shortly thereafter (September 25, 1925) the White Mountain reserve was created, followed two years later by the Eklutna reserve, each in excess of a thousand acres. [91] Tetlin was established in 1930, and at 786,000 acres it is one of the largest of all Alaskan reserves. According to the terms of the excutive order creating it, Tetlin was:

temporarily withdrawn...to promote the interests of the natives by appropriate *vocational training* to encourage and assist them in restocking the country and protecting the furbearing animals, and to otherwise aid in the support of said natives... (emphasis added). [92]

In July of the same year, sixty-four hundred acres were withdrawn for the Point Hope Reserve "for the use of the Office of Education."[93] Finally Amaknak Island (110 acres) was withdrawn in 1933 "for the protection of the fishing rights of Alaska Natives."[94] Its purpose is unique.[95] It was also the last reserve created during the Hoover administration and the last Native reserve to be created in Alaska for the next ten years. By then there would be a new president, a new staff at the Department of the Interior and a new law.

3. Status of Public Purpose Reserves

As far as the federal-Native relationship goes, the most significant aspect of some of these reserves was that their "public purpose" was Native vocational education and support. That was particularly true of Tetlin, the largest. Arguably, the congressional act which permitted establishment of vocational education reserves constituted congressional recognition of an obligation to advance and support the interests of Alaska Natives. Such an obligation could not have been based on any sort of land-related "trust" responsibility because these reserves were not Indian "trust" lands in any sense of the term.

a. Leasing

A 1967 solicitor's opinion held that the Eklutna Reserve was not leasable under any of the Indian leasing laws because it was not an "Indian" reserve.[96] The reserve lands could be leased for any purpose consistent with the purpose of the reserve (e. g., vocational education) but the lease proceeds would be recovered directly to the U. S. Treasury and not held in trust for the Natives.[97]

b. Compensability

Similarly, because the 1919 act prohibits it, these reserves could not in any sense be characterized as "Indian" reservations. The 1927 Leasing Act's restrictions against revocation would therefore not apply.[98] Like any public purpose reserve, they could be revoked at will without any obligation to compensate the Native occupants.

c. Trust Responsibility

For these reasons, the secretary had no land-related trust responsibility as to these reserves.

d. Guardianship

It appears that the government had at least an obligation to ensure that the reserves were used for the beneficial purposes for which they were created.[99] Congress, by authorizing vocational education for Alaska Natives, arguably assumed responsibility for Native education on the basis of its guardianship over those Natives. The president, in authorizing reserves such as Tetlin, also assumed a similar obligation. The most significant factor in each circumstance is that the obligation does not arise out of a trust relationship to Native land, but a guardian relationship with Native people.

The obligation could be avoided by revoking the reserves, and ANCSA did that. But the point again is that at least in Alaska the government has historically assumed obligations to Natives in the absence of a trust responsibility to land. The implication is that other congressionally or executively recognized obligations based on the guardian relation exist which ANCSA did not specifically extinguish.

D. Application of the IRA to Alaska and the Small Reservation Policy

In 1934, another "new era" in Indian relations was ushered in with the Indian Reorganization Act.[100] Due to an unintentional error in drafting, the IRA was not immediately applicable in Alaska.[101] The IRA was amended in 1936 by what is sometimes called the "Alaska Reorganization Act."[102] This legislation not only applied the Indian Reorganization Act to Alaska, but also permitted creation of a new type of reservation. The new law was in two sections. The first section applied relevant sections of the 1934 IRA to Alaska and provided that:

> [G]roups of Indians in Alaska not heretofore recognized as bands or tribes, but having a common bond of occupation or, association, or residence within a well-defined neighborhood, community or rural district, may organize to adopt constitutions and bylaws and to receive charters of incorporation and Federal loans under Section 16, 17 and 10 of the Act of June 18, 1934 (the IRA).[103]

Section 2 permitted the Secretary of the Interior to designate as an Indian "reservation":

> any area of land which has been reserved for the use and occupancy of Indians or Eskimos by [the 1884 Organic Act, the 1891 Act creating Annette Islands reserve], or which has been heretofore reserved under any executive order and placed under the jurisdiction of the Department of the Interior or any Bureau thereof, together, with additional public lands adjacent thereto, within the Territory of Alaska, or any other public lands which are actually occupied by Indians or Eskimos within said Territory.[104]

Felix Cohen reportedly drafted the 1936 amendments, and they were supported by William L. Paul, Sr., on behalf of the Alaska Native Brotherhood, as well as Alaska delegate, Anthony J. Dimond.[105] In a letter to the House Indian Affairs Committee, Secretary Ickes described three reasons for authorizing the Secretary of the Interior to set aside reservations in Alaska:

1. To define Alaskan tribes by identifying particular groups with the land they occupied;

2. To stipulate geographical limits of jurisdiction so that Native communities in Alaska could set up systems of local government.

3. To enable the United States Government in part to fulfill its moral and legal obligations to protect the"economic rights"of Alaska Natives.[106]

Ickes expanded upon what he considered to be the source of the "moral and legal obligation" of the government by citing section 8 of the 1884 Organic Act and section 15 of the 1891 Timber Culture Act.[107] Secretary Ickes concluded from these acts that "lands which should have been, by virtue of these Acts, segregated for Natives of Alaska, have not been so segregated." Section 2 of the Alaska IRA amendments permitted the federal government to rectify this situation and protect Native interests in the future.[108]

During the first years of the IRA's application in Alaska, the Interior Department held that the Alaska amendments authorized only relatively small reservations associated with existing Native villages and townsites or based on strict proof of "actual" use and occupancy.[109] However, during the same period, delegate Dimond placed in the *Congressional Record* a 1935 letter he had written to William L. Paul, Sr. The letter stated that the Alaska amendments were intended to permit the creation of reserves in Alaska similar to the Annette Island reserve.[110] Presumably, Dimond was talking about fairly large reserves (Metlakatla was over eighty-six thousand acres in size) created for Native protection and benefit. It appears therefore, that even though the department initially doubted its authority to create large reserves under section 2 of the Alaska amendments, the Alaska delegate, who supported the legislation, believed the department had that authority.

E. 1940-1942—Reversal of Policy and Creation of the Venetie Reserve

In 1940 or 1941, Secretary Ickes began receiving appeals from Alaskan Native communities for protection from competitive non-Native interests.[111] On February 13, 1942, the Solicitor for the Department of the Interior, Nathan R. Margold, issued the so-called "Margold opinion" which supported protection of Alaska Native fishing rights under section 2 of the Alaska amendments.[112] The opinion permitted the creation of large reserves (including water) based on aboriginal use and occupancy. On May 20, 1943, 1,408,000 acres were withdrawn for the Venetie Reserve in northeast interior Alaska. Two days later 35,200 acres of land and water were withdrawn in southwest coastal Alaska for the Karluk fishing reserve.[113] These two reserves were the beginning of a new Alaska reservation policy.

F. 1944-1949—The IRA Reserves: A Policy That Failed

1. Introduction

As Secretary Ickes noted in his letter to the House Indian Affairs Committee, there were three land-related reasons to establish new reserves in Alaska. First, the Department of the Interior wanted to define tribal entities in Alaska and identify them with particular tracts of land. Second, the Department wanted to define geographic bounderies for tribal governments so that their territorial jurisdiction would be clear. Third, by establishing reserves the government wanted to protect the "economic rights" of Alaska Natives. The first two concerns relate to tribal recognition and tribal government and are discussed in chapters 9 and 10.

The third relates to the land-related obligations of the federal government which are the subject of this chapter. Protection of Native "economic rights" actually included two concerns. The first was identifying and protecting the geographic limits of aboriginal title. The second was providing a sufficient land and resource base to enable the Alaska Natives to become self-supporting. Efforts to satisfy these two distinguishable but related objectives shaped the department's Alaska reservation policy during the next five years (1944-1949). Ultimately, World War II pressures, territorial politics, bureaucratic conflict, Native mistrust and adverse court decisions defeated the policy. Nevertheless, congressional and executive efforts to implement the policy tend to confirm rather than deny the existence of the unique federal-Native relationship in Alaska.

2. Kake, Klawock and Hydaburg

Both Venetie and Karluk were created without any advance notice, but public outrage over this procedure caused the Interior Department to schedule hearings on the proposed creation of three fishing reserves in southeast Alaska. These reserves were to be for the benefit of the communities of Kake, Klawock and Hydaburg. In design, the reserves appeared to duplicate the Metlakatla, Annette Island Reservation.

Secretary Ickes appointed Richard H. Hanna, a former justice of the New Mexico Supreme Court, to preside over the hearings on the Kake, Klawock and Hydaburg claims. At stake were more than two million acres of land and the exclusive right to fish within three thousand feet of the shore. Judge Hanna held hearings in the affected villages as well as in Ketchikan and Seattle during September 1944. Hanna's opinion, released in the spring of 1945, found a much reduced land occupancy and no exclusive right of fishery.[114] Secretary Ickes overruled the finding, granting between seventy-seven and one hundred thousand acres to each of the three communities, and found an exclusive right of fishery based on the Margold opinion. Other proceedings continued through 1945; on January 11, 1946, Secretary Ickes issued his final opinion, confirming the land and waters to the villages.[115] Kake and Klawock both rejected the proffered reserves, and it was not until 1949 that Hydaburg accepted its reserve.

Felix Cohen visited each of the three communities prior to the hearings. He encountered open opposition to the proposed reserves within both the department's Fish and Wildlife Service[116] and the territorial government.[117] Cohen, in a memo to John Collier, Commissioner of Indian Affairs, suggested that:

> There is a great deal of popular confusion in Alaska as to the *significance of aboriginal rights and the relation of such rights to the utilization of Alaskan resources,* and this confusion should be cleared away at the earliest possible moment by a fair and comprehensive statement of the position of the Department. The proposed statement notes that the *policy of the Department today in Alaska is what the Interior Department policy always has been in Alaska and in the States,* namely to respect and protect aboriginal possession against private trespass or public domain disposition until such time as Congress has compensated the Indians for the relinquishment of such possessions as they do not need (emphasis added).[118]

It is clear from this passage that clarification and ultimate extinguishment of aboriginal title was one of the principal purposes behind the reservation policy.[119] The fact the proposed reserves included large bodies of water (with implied fishing rights) indicates that in clarifying the scope of aboriginal title the department also intended to confirm a sufficient resource base to the Natives to assure their economic self-support. As discussed previously, federal efforts to extinguish aboriginal title and provide for Native self-support are key elements in the historic federal-Native relationship. Cohen's memo also confirms that in both respects the department's Alaska policy was the same as it "always has been in Alaska and in the States."

3. Karluk

a. Introduction

The department's withdrawal of land for the Karluk Reserve was almost simultaneous with the hearings in southeast Alaska, and encountered similar opposition. This time the opposition came from the non-Native, commercial fish packing companies on Kodiak Island, and the department engineered a test case of its authority to create and preserve the IRA reserves. In theory it won the case in the U. S. Supreme Court, but as a practical matter it lost. In the final analysis, the department's bureaucratic inability to protect the reservations (rather than a true legal barrier) defeated the Alaska reservation policy.

b. The Reserve

Thirty-five thousand acres of land and water was withdrawn for the Karluk Reserve on May 22, 1943. A year and a day later the people of Karluk approved the reserve. [120] The weakness in the armor of the reservation policy gradually became apparent. While the reservation could be created by secretarial order and voter approval, it could not easily be protected against non-Native incursion if it contained valuable resources such as fish.

In the first place, the authority to create the reserves was in question. In the second, there was no clear criminal sanction which could be imposed for violating the reserve boundaries. The Alaska BIA superintendent forsaw the enforcement problem. On June 1, 1944, Don Foster, General Superintendent, Alaska Native Service, wrote a letter to William Zimmerman, Assistant Commissioner of Indian Affairs; in retrospect, it was prophetic. After noting that the Karluk election carried by a vote of forty-six to zero, Mr. Foster wrote:

> The question now arises, how are we to enforce the provisions of protection that the establishment of this reservation naturally carried?

In a footnote to Felix Cohen, Foster stated:

> It looks like the election in Karluk has really brought out into the open a problem that will confront us on the establishment of every reserve in Alaska where fishing rights are involved. [121]

The key problem was that the Bureau of Indian Affairs had no authority to enforce fishing regulations. The BIA could only enforce trespass actions for violations of reservation boundaries, but the Department of Justice was the federal agency which had to bring the trespass action, and all such actions had to be approved in Washington, D. C. It was a time-consuming and ineffective process; perhaps for that reason, the Department of the Interior reached for another enforcement method. Specifically, Interior sought to establish criminal sanctions for violating the fishing reserve; to impose those santions, it was necessary to adopt regulations under the 1924 White Act. [122]

The White Act was the chief means whereby the federal government enforced fish conservation measures in Alaska. Another agency (the Fish and Wildlife Service) of the Department of the Interior was responsible for enforcement of this act. Unfortunately for the reservation policy, the Fish and Wildlife Service was generally opposed to the creation of Native fishing reserves. [123] Nevertheless, some two years after establishing the Karluk Reserve, the Department of the Interior adopted a regulation under the White Act which compelled the Fish and Wildlife Service to protect the new reservation. [124]

The White Act permitted the establishment of fishing reserves for conservation purposes and the exclusion of all fishing within such reserves, but specifically prohibited establishment of "exclusive" fishing privileges for any class of people. [125] The regulation which Interior adopted to protect the Karluk Reserve appeared to violate the latter provision of the White Act by creating an exclusive fishing privilege for the Karluk Natives. Nevertheless, two officers from the Indian Service were deputized to the Fish and Wildlife Service to protect Karluk fishing rights during the 1946 fishing season. [126]

c. The Lawsuit

The Kodiak salmon packers filed suit *(Grimes Packing Co. v. Hynes)* to enjoin enforcement of the White Act regulation and challenged the department's authority to create large water reservations in Alaska. [127] Interior lost at both the district and circuit court levels and achieved only a partial win in the U. S. Supreme Court. Specifically, the Supreme Court approved the authority of the Secretary to create the Karluk reserve under the Alaska IRA, but denied his authority to enforce exclusive Native fishing on the reserve under the White Act.

The Supreme Court also cast doubt on the status of Alaska IRA reserves by comparing the Karluk Reserve to executive order reserves. [128] The packing company argued that in creating the Karluk Reserve the Secretary of the Interior was permanently withdrawing the waters within the reserve thereby permanently denying non-Native fishermen access to the valuable fishing ground. The Court implied that if the reserve were characterized as a "permanent" withdrawal, the Indian Reorganization Act would be strictly construed to determine whether Congress intended to grant the secretary permanent withdrawal authority. To avoid strict construction, Interior was compelled to argue that the IRA only granted the secretary temporary withdrawal authority. [129]

Characterizing the reserve as "temporary" implied it could be revoked without compensation to its occupants. On the other hand, so long as the reserve existed, the United States had clear authority and probably an obligation to protect it against trespass.[130] Insofar as the United States can and does protect reserved waters against trespass, it might be said to protect Native "fishing rights" in those waters, but as with executive order reserves, the temporary nature of the IRA reserve argues against the theory that the reserve itself was a recognition of compensable "fishing rights."[131]

Felix Cohen, no longer with the Interior Department, telegraphed Larry Ellanak, President of the Karluk Village Council, on June 3, 1949, to congratulate him on the *Grimes Packing* "victory." On June 11, he wrote Mr. Ellanak an eight-page, single-spaced, typewritten letter explaining what Karluk would have to do to enforce the Supreme Court decision. The length of the letter indicated the complexity of the situation. Although deciding in favor of the Department of the Interior and its authority to create the reserve, the Supreme Court effectively gutted the department's ability to protect the exclusive fishery—a major reason for creating the reserve in the first place. The only recourse was an action in trespass, based on adequate proof and agreed to by the United States Justice Department in Washington, D. C.[132]

d. The Aftermath

Even if the Grimes Packing decision had proved enforceable, it is unlikely that enough dedicated people remained in the Department of the Interior to carry out the policy. In March 1945, Commissioner Collier retired; in February 1946, Secretary Ickes resigned, and in January 1948, Felix Cohen did likewise. Secretary Ickes was replaced by Julius A. Krug who continued to pursue the reservation policy until he too resigned in November 1949. Finally, in early 1950, Don Foster, General Superintendent (Area Director) of the Alaska Native Service, also resigned. All of these people had been with the Department of the Interior since 1933 and the beginning of the Roosevelt administration. With them passed an era and a policy.

There was one final attempt to eliminate the Alaska IRA reserves. Senate Joint Resolution 162 was introduced in Congress to rescind "certain orders" of the Secretary of Interior establishing Indian reservations in the Territory of Alaska. The Senate report accompanying the resolution vigorously attacked the reservation policy. Significantly, Secretary Krug defended the policy on the grounds of aboriginal rights to the land and the duty of the United States to protect the economic basis of Native life:

> The reservations heretofore established and the proposed reservations are in *areas occupied and used by the Natives and their ancestors since time immemorial.* These lands constitute the *economic basis for Native life.* The exploitation and spoilation of some of the ancestral hunting and fishing and trapping

grounds of the Natives by non-Natives have already worked a hardship on many of the Natives. Unless they are *protected in their occupancy* of these ancestral areas and are permitted to establish their local governments, the virtual destruction of these people is almost sure to result (emphasis added). [133]

Senate Joint Resolution 162 was never adopted, but given what followed, it was a hollow victory.

In his June 11 letter to Lary Ellanak, Felix Cohen suggested that Ellanak and his people take several steps to protect the Karluk Reserve. These included marking the reservation fishing boundaries, enforcing a local licensing ordinance, identifying trespassers, suing them and hiring private attorneys if the Justice Department would not prosecute. Cohen's letter also makes it clear that the ability of the Bureau of Indian Affairs to assist the Karluk people might be limited by internal conflicts between the BIA and the Fish and Wildlife Service. On July 10, Larry Ellanak wrote to Cohen, telling him they had done as suggested and that at least one cannery (the Alaska Packers Association) was respecting the reservation. [134]

In late July 1949, Roy Peratrovich, a special officer with the Alaska Native Service, met with the Karluk Native Association and developed an ordinance with them to license non-Native fishermen on the reservation. Mr. Peratrovich indicated that the licensing system had achieved a measure of success among the nearby cannery operators although it was "yet too early to tell just how successful these fishing permits will be." [135]

The next year, Jack Jenkins, of the Alaska Native Service Anchorage office, reported that while the non-Native fishermen generally respected the Karluk fishing permits, there were serious violations of the reservation boundaries when seine boats drifted over the Native-operated beach seine nets, ripping them and releasing all the fish. [136] Both outgoing Area Director Foster and the new area director, Hugh Wade, made some effort that year to collect information on the Karluk trespasses for referral to the Attorney General in Washington, D. C.

The attempt was apparently unsuccessful, because in 1951 the teacher at Karluk, Warren Tiffany, wrote Area Director Wade indicating the situation in Karluk was deteriorating and there was little confidence among the Karluk people that either the Fish and Wildlife Service or the Bureau of Indian Affairs would assist them in protecting the fishing reserve. [137] In his reply, Director Wade indicated that a suit was pending over the legitimacy of the Hydaburg reservation which would determine whether or not the Karluk fishing reserve could be protected. [138] In May 1951, the United States did file suit against the Libby Packing Company for trespass on the Hydaburg Reserve. [139]

The suit was intended to enjoin the Libby Company from using a fishtrap on the Hydaburg Reserve, but it is not clear why the Justice Department chose to file suit on the Hydaburg rather than the Karluk Reserve. One explanation may be that trespass at Hydaburg was easier to prove since it involved only one fishtrap. Trespass at Karluk would have beenmore difficult to prove because it involved movable boats and depended on eyewitnesses to verify the violation. In any case, the Alaska District Court delivered the United States a complete defeat, and the decision was not appealed. The difficulty in protecting the Karluk Reserve under the *Grimes Packing* decision and the absolute defeat in the *Libby* case ended the reservation policy in Alaska for all practical purposes.[140] Of course, neither decision terminated valid reservations.[141] Only Congress could do that.

4. Status of IRA Reserves Prior to ANCSA

Grimes Packing and *Libby* cast a cloud of doubt over the status of the IRA Alaska reserves. A total of six such reserves were created under the act.[142] These included Venetie, at 1,408,000 acres the largest of all Alaskan reserves. Because of their unique origins under the IRA and, one suspects, as a result of the *Grimes Packing* and *Libby* decisions, they were treated cautiously amid doubts as to their authority and prerogatives.[143]

A 1968 memorandum issued by Hugh Wade, the Alaska Regional Solicitor, provides a comprehensive analysis of the status of these reserves.[144] The memorandum specifically applies its analysis to all the Alaska IRA reserves, but avoids any extension of the analysis to executive order reserves. Its analysis of IRA reserve land status may be summarized as follows:

a. Trust Responsibility

The IRA reserves:

> possess relatively broad powers for the local management of their affairs, under the department's usual *trust supervision* common to all reservations generally (emphasis added).[145]

The source of this broad local management authority appears to rest in the powers "granted" to the IRA village councils in their IRA constitutions bylaws and corporate charters. However, Akutan, as a traditional council occupying an IRA reserve, was said to have the necessary authority to "accomplish the same goals as the more formal [IRA councils]."[146]

Because of its broad governmental authority under the constitution and bylaws approved by the Secretary of Interior, the memorandum concludes that "the tribe, that is, the Native village of Karluk, possesses a substantial quantum of ownership control over reserve lands." It appears that this "ownership control" (acquired through the action of the secretary with the consent of the tribe) is the source of the broad trust supervision "common to reservations generally." In many respects this sort of agreement between the secretary and the tribe is analogous to the treaty agreements negotiated with the "lower 48" Native Americans prior to 1871. The Regional Solicitor found a general trust responsibility for the IRA reserves similar to the trust responsibility arising out of treaties. This conclusion is consistent with Felix Cohen's often quoted statement:

> The extension of the Wheeler-Howard Act to Alaska has removed the last significant difference between the position of the American Indian and that of the Alaska native. [147]

b. Leasing

Basing his analysis on the tribe's "substantial quantum of ownership control", the Regional Solicitor also found authority for the tribe to lease reservation lands and receive proceeds from those leases under the leasing statutes applicable to Indian reservations generally. The leasing statutes applicable to the IRA reserves included the following sections of 25 USCA as amended: 396a (mining), 398 (oil and gas), 407 (timber), and 415 (public, religious, educational, recreational and business).

c. Compensability

Recognizing the implications of *Grimes Packing,* the memorandum found that the IRA reserves did not create a compensable ownership interest on behalf of the Native occupants. The memorandum assumed that despite the IRA:

> Congress has retained the authority...to alter or abolish the status of the Karluk Reservation....without creating any liabilities for compensation to the individuals involved. [148]

5. Conclusion

At least as to the six Alaskan IRA reserves, it may be said that prior to ANCSA they, with the exception of Metlakatla and Klukwan, were the ones which most nearly approximated the true Indian reservations of the lower forty-eight states. Except for establishing a permanent, compensable ownership interest in the reserved lands, they established the same sort of trust relationship and leasing options "common to all reservations generally." As with both treaty and statutory reserves, they were authorized by Congress and had established their relationship to the federal government by mutual agreement.

With the exception of Metlakatla, and Klukwan, the relationship of the IRA reserves to the federal government, more than any other Alaskan reserves, grows out of the federal government's narrowly defined trust responsibility to Native lands. Yet, the fact remains that prior to ANCSA there were only two statutory reserves and six IRA reserves. In spite of that, the federal government maintained a substantial relationship with the other Native communities in Alaska absent a clearly defined, land-related trust responsibility. Again, the implication is there must be some independent (i.e., nontrust) basis for the relationship.

G. 1951-1960—Dormant Period

Following the *Libby* case, there was no serious attempt to enforce exclusive Native fishing or to create other Native reserves in Alaska.[149] Natives were permitted to use fishtraps under Department of the Interior regulations, but exclusive Native fishing rights were not enforced. In fact, the BIA Area Office in Juneau openly encouraged nonexclusive fishing during this nine-year period and encouraged the Secretary of Interior to continue nonsegregated fishing in order to maintain "good relations between Native and non-Native fishermen."[150]

H. 1960-1968—State vs. Federal Jurisdiction

In 1959, Alaska became a state. On April 17 of the same year the new state adopted a comprehensive fish and game code and shortly thereafter assumed complete control over natural resources.[151] As part of its fish management scheme, the state absolutely banned the use of fishtraps within its borders. The then governor, William Egan, informed the Native communities within the state that use of fishtraps, even with the permission of the Secretary of Interior, was illegal.

The Natives refused to give up the fishtraps; some were arrested, and two lawsuits were filed. The villages of Kake and Angoon joined together in one suit to enjoin the state's enforcement of the anti-fishtrap law *(Kake v. Egan)*. The Metlakatlans sued for an injunction on the same grounds *(Metlakatla v. Egan)*. Both Kake and Metlakatla argued that Alaska, under section 4 of the Statehood Act, disclaimed all right and title to:

> any lands or property (including fishing rights), the right or title to which may be held by any Indians, Eskimos, or Aleuts...or is held by the United States in trust for said Natives....

The United States, according to Section 4, retained "absolute jurisdiction and control" over such Native property.[152]

The only distinction between Metlakatla, and the Kake and Angoon communities was that Metlakatla was an Indian reservation created by an act of Congress and under the regulatory authority of the Secretary of Interior.[153] Neither Kake nor Angoon had been provided reservations nor was there any statutory authority for the Secretary of Interior to permit them to operate fishtraps contrary to state law.[154] With this distinction in mind, the Supreme Court held that state regulation of fishing at Kake and Angoon did not interfere with any Indian "property" right because regulation was only the exercise of the state's governmental authority over the fish resource.[155]

The Court finally concluded that while the people of Kake and Angoon might have aboriginal rights in fish, the state could regulate the exercise of these aboriginal rights in the absence of any federal law to the contrary. Thus, the deciding factor in each case was the extent to which the Indian communities had been brought under the protective principles of federal Indian law through the reservation system or pre-emptive federal legislation. Absent either a reservation or pre-emptive federal law, the Court concluded that the State of Alaska had jurisdiction over the activities of Natives on state waters and (by implication) lands. So long as it did not intrude on federally reserved water, the state could regulate aboriginal rights to fish:

> [E]ven on reservations state laws may be applied to Indians unless such application would interfere with reservation self-government or impair a right granted or reserved by federal law.
>
> * * * *
>
> But state regulation of off-reservation fishing certainly does not impinge on treaty-protected reservation self-government....Nor have appellants any fishing rights derived from federal laws.[156]

The Court confirmed federal and (by implication) Native control over the waters of the Annette Island Reservation.[157] In 1963, immediately following the Metlakatla decision, the Secretary of Interior promulgated regulations governing all fishing within the Annette Island reserve and commercial fishing within the Karluk Reserve.[158] The regulations are complete as to the Annette Island Reserve and in 1975 were amended in effect to permit the Metlakatla community, with the approval of the BIA Area Director, to regulate fishing within the reserve.[159]

The Karluk regulations, on the other hand, permitted fishing by non-Natives only insofar as "their fishing activities...do not restrict or interfere with fishing by [the] Natives."[160] In 1968-69 the village of Karluk requested that regulations be amended to permit the Karluk Natives greater control over access to their fishing reserve. The then Commissioner of Indian Affiars, Robert Bennett, proposed that the Department of the Interior adopt regulations for that purpose. The regulations were based on article 4 of the Karluk Constitution (giving the village power to stop trespass on its land or waters) and 18 USC 1165 (imposing criminal penalties for trespass on Indian lands).[161] The proposed regulations would have enabled the Secretary of Interior and the Karluk council to exercise jurisdiction over reservation waters concurrently with the state.[162] The regulations were never adopted.

In 1971, Karluk and all other reservations, with the exception of Metlakatla, were abolished by section 19 of the Alaska Native Claims Settlement Act. [163] Since any right to exclusive Native fishing at Karluk depended upon the water reservation originally granted in 1943, elimination of the reservation in section 19 probably eliminated any right of exclusive fishery otherwise available to the Karluk Natives.

III. Some Conclusions

A. Trust Responsibility to Land Before ANCSA

1. Five Types of Reserves

The federal trust responsibility to Indian lands must necessarily be founded on an identifiable body of lands. Prior to ANCSA, and except for those lands held under a claim of aboriginal title, [164] the trust responsibility in Alaska arose in conjunction with land reserved for Native use or occupancy. [165] As described herein, there appear to have been five distinct types of Alaskan reserves:

    a) Executive Order Reindeer Reserves
    b) Statutory Reserves (Metlakatla and Klukwan)
    c) Pre-1919 Executive Order Indian Reserves
    d) Post-1919 Executive Order Reserves
    e) IRA Reserves

The federal government, primarily through the Department of the Interior, most clearly acted in its full capacity as trustee of Native lands with respect to the IRA and statutory reserves. Oil and gas leases negotiated on behalf of pre-1919 executive order Indian reserves also involved the federal government in its full capacity as trustee of the lease proceeds under federal leasing statutes. Logically, this statutory responsibility might also extend to the reindeer reserves which, after ANCSA, were determined to have been established for "Native use."

The government assumed no trust responsibility as to nonleased lands on the pre-1919 reserves, nor did it assume a trust responsibility for the proceeds from leases, except those for oil and gas, on these reserves. The federal trust responsibility as to lands enclosed in post-1919 executive order reserves appears negligible, given the difficulty of finding an "ownership interest" on behalf of the Native occupants of such reserves.

2. Continuing Trust Responsibility

Insofar as ANCSA has not terminated federal responsibility for Native lands in Alaska, the trust responsibility must be assumed to continue. Termination of the federal-Native relationship must be clear from legislative language or history in order to be effective.[166] ANCSA revoked all reservations in Alaska (except Metlakatla) thereby eliminating a continuing trust responsibility founded solely on the reservation's existence. The Alaska Regional Solicitor has concluded in light of ANCSA's legislative history that the revocation of an IRA reserve also deprived the IRA governing council of the proceeds due from a lease of the previously reserved land.[167] Under current law all proceeds from such leases must be held in federal escrow for distribution to the "corporation or individual" receiving lands under ANCSA.[168]

3. Recovery for Breach of Trust

ANCSA extinguished all claims based on *aboriginal title* or any *statute or treaty* "relating to Native use and occupancy."[169] It seems likely that this language extinguishes claims arising out of federal laws relating to leasing on Indian reservations or for any other pre-ANCSA breach of trust responsibility incurred in the management of any Alaska reservation except Metlakatla.[170]

B. Trust Responsibility to Land After ANCSA

One commentator has noted that ANCSA has "fundamentally reduced" the federal trust responsibility to Native land in Alaska.[171] It is neither necessary nor wise to go beyond this generalization. ANCSA clearly disfavors creation of a "lengthy trusteeship,"[172] but the use of the qualifying adjective implies that a trusteeship of limited duration is permissible. Many ANCSA provisions are characteristic of previous federal-Native "trust" relationships. For example the Secretary of Interior is responsible for enrollment (section 5), stock is inalienable for twenty years (section 7(h)), the Secretary of the Interior was required to approve corporate charters (section 7(e)), etc.

The extent of these and other potential responsibilities has yet to be determined by the courts or assumed by the responsible federal agencies.[173] Clearly ANCSA does not favor expansion of a land and resource-related trust responsibility. That fact alone probably ensures a highly limited trusteeship and a continuing judicial reluctance to interpret the existence of a trusteeship unless ANCSA or subsequent acts of Congress reasonably imply it.[174]

C. Guardianship

Even prior to ANCSA, the federal government assumed only minimal (although highly specific) land-related trust responsibilities in Alaska. Nowhere is this fact more obvious than in the complexities surrounding the "trust" status of the various Alaska reserves. In this respect, the federal-Native relationship in Alaska appears to differ from the "trust relationship" the federal government has by treaty or agreement assumed with many Native communities in the contiguous United States. ANCSA appears to reduce the scope of these land-related responsibilities even further.

However, a distinction must be drawn between a narrow concept of trust related solely to disposition of property[175] and a broader concept of federal guardianship over Native Americans. More than any sing e activity or policy prior to ANCSA, the establishment of federal Native reserves manifests the exercise of that guardianship in Alaska. Without exception, each of the five types of reserves previously discussed were established for the purpose of benefiting Alaska Natives. The Department of the Interior has historically supported the existence and uses to be made of these reserves on the basis of its guardian relationship to Alaska Natives. On that basis the Solicitor has repeatedly concluded that:

> The fundamental consideration underlying this question is the fact that these natives are, in a very large sense at least, dependent subjects of our Government and in a state of tutelage; or in other words, they are wards of the Government and under its guardianship and care.

* * * *

> From the foregoing it is clear that no distinction has been or can be made between the Indians and other natives of Alaska so far as the laws and relations of the United States are concerned whether the Eskimos and other natives are of Indian origin or not as they are all wards of the Nation, and their status is in material respects similar to that of the Indians of the United States.[176]

As will be discussed more fully in chapter 6, the guardian-ward nature of the federal-Native relationship changed gradually over the years as it became increasingly obvious that the "ward" was in need of less guidance. Enlightened federal policy and Native American political strength translated this sociological fact into political reality through the Indian Self-Determination Act.[177] Alaska Natives were specifically included within the scope of this legislation and other similar enactments.[178] Thus, apart from purely land and resource obligations, the federal government has continued to include Alaska Natives within a core element of the general historical federal relationship derived from guardianship and the present relationship which appears largely defined in terms of various statutory services, programs, restrictions and benefits.[179]

ENDNOTES

[1]248 U.S. 78 (1918).

[2]Metlakatla Indian Community, Annette Island Reserve v. Egan, 369 U.S. 45 (1962).
Organized Village of Kake v. Egan, 369 U.S. 60 (1962) was the third case and a companion to Metlakatla.
Hynes v. Grimes Packing Co., 337 U.S. 86 (1949) was the fourth case.
Tee-Hit-Ton Band of Indians v. U.S., 348 U.S. 272 (1959) (compensability of aboriginal title) was the single exception to the reservation line of cases.

[3]Act of March 30, 1891, 25 Stat. 1101, 48 USC 358 (1970) provides:

> That until otherwise provided by law the body of lands known as Annette Islands, situated in Alexander Archipelago in southeastern Alaska, on the north side of Dixon's entrance, be, and the same is hereby set apart as a reservation for the use of the Metlakatla Indians, and those people known as the Metlakatlans who have recently emigrated from British Columbia to Alaska, and such other Alaskan Natives as may join them to be held and used by them in common, under such rules and regulations and subject to such restrictions, as may be prescribed from time to time by the Secretary of the Interior.

[4]39 Stat. 1777. The Presidential proclamation was specifically based on the fact that the Secretary of the Interior was planning to build a cannery on Annette Island to enable the Metlakatlans to support themselves. The extension of the reservation was said to be necessary for "supplying fish and other aquatic products" for the cannery. "Three thousand feet from shore" also became the guideline for fishery reserve boundaries established under the Indian Reorganization Act. See 56 I.D. 110 (1937).

[5]U.S. v. Alaska Pacific Fisheries, 5 Ak. Rpts. 484 (D.C. Ak. 1916).

[6]Alaska Pacific Fisheries v. U.S. 240 F. 274 (9th Cir. 1917).

[7]Alaska Pacific Fisheries v. U.S. 248 U.S. 78, 88 (1918), citations omitted.

[8]Id. at 88 and 89.

[9]Although the Supreme Court did not specifically affirm the authority of the President to reserve the Annette Island waters, neither did it disapprove the Ninth Circuit and District Court holdings that he had such authority. A previous Supreme Court decision (U.S. v. Midwest Oil Co., 236 U.S. 459, 471) affirms his authority as well. The Alaska District Court (5 Ak. Rpts. at 491-492), the Ninth Circuit (240 F. at 281) and the Solicitor (49 L.D. 592, 596 (1923)) have all affirmed the executive authority to create executive order Indian reserves in Alaska.

[10]Act of January 30, 1919, 41 Stat. 34, 43 USCA 150. The 1919 prohibition arguably did not affect the authority of the Secretary of Interior to make "temporary"

withdrawals if permitted by general legislation. In 1927 Congress specifically exempted temporary secretarial withdrawals from a futher restriction on executive authority to effect changes in the boundries of executive order reserves. Act of March 3, 1927, 44 Stat. 1347, 25 USCA 398d. The fact that the secretary could only make temporary withdrawals may have been a factor in the U.S. Supreme Court's later determination that IRA reserves were only "temporary" reserves. See *Grimes Packing*, note 2, above. The secretary's temporary withdrawal exemption was eliminated in the BLM Organic Act of October 21.1976, P.L. 94-579, Title VI. Sec. 704(a), 90 Stat. 2793.

[11]Act of February 25, 1925, Pub. No 468, 68th Cong. See also 53 L.D. 111 (1930).

[12]Act of May 1, 1936, 49 Stat. 1250, amending the Act of January 18, 1934, 48 Stat. 984, 25 USCA 461 et. seq., commonly known as the "Wheeler- Howard Act" or "Indian Reorganization Act" (IRA).

[13]Another less important Act of May 31, 1938 (52 Stat. 593, 48 USC 353a) permitted the secretary to withdraw up to 640 acres for Alaska Native school sites.

[14]See notes 115-118, below, and accompanying text regarding later policies which did address the land claims issue.

[15]See *Grimes Packing*, note 2, above, at 103; see also Sioux Tribe v. U.S., 316 U.S. 317 (1942).

[16]Tee-Hit-Ton Band of Indians v. U.S., 348 U.S. 272, 279 (1954) and *Grimes Packing*, note 2, above, at 101.
Tee-Hit-Ton is a leading (and much criticized) case on the "recognized" aboriginal title subject. Because it deals specifically with the question of aboriginal title in Alaska, more extensive analysis of its importance will be found under the "Aboriginal Title" discussion, chapter 2 above.

[17]E.g., *Sioux Tribe*, note 15, above, at 326.

[18]C.f. Id. at 324-325.

[19]Id. at 331.

[20]See *Tribal Property Interests in Executive Order Reservations: A Compensable Indian Right*, 69 Yale L.J. 627, (1960). But see 70 I.D. 166, 168 (1963).

[21]Congress passed the first leasing act on February 25, 1920 (41 Stat. 437). During the Harding administration this act was used (somewhat questionably) to lease executive order Indian reserves for oil exploration. See 34 Ops. Atty. Gen. 171 (May 27, 1924). Congress next passed the Indian Leasing Act of 1924 (Act of May 29, 1924, 43 Stat. 244, 25 USCA 398 et. seq.). This act did not clearly permit leasing of executive order reserves either. (See 70 I.D. 166, 168-169). In 1927 Congress amended the 1924 act to specifically permit oil and gas leasing on executive order reserves. (Act of March 3, 1927, 44 Stat. 1347, 25 USCA 398a). Leasing laws for other types of Indian lands are codified at 25 USCA 391 et. seq.
In 1941 the U.S. Supreme Court decided *Sioux Tribe*, note 15, above, which

held that executive order reserves were not recognitions of aboriginal title but merely temporary withdrawals which could be terminated by the executive or Congress at will. Id. at 331. That decision seems to place executive order reserves in a unique position. They are not trust lands in any general sense, but because of their separate treatment in the Indian leasing acts, they do not appear to be lands in the public domain either. Instead they are subject to specific acts of Congress which control leasing of executive reserve property.

[22]Klukwan was established as an executive order reserve on April 21, 1913 (E.O. 1764) and enlarged and confirmed by Congress in 1957, 71 Stat. 596. See also *Alaska Natives and the Land, Report of the Federal Field Committee,* (Washington, D.C.: GPO, 1968) at 444.

[23]Jones, Richard S., *Alaska Native Claims Settlement Act of 1971 (Public Law 92-203): History and Analysis,* (Washington, D.C.: Congressional Research Service, 1972) at 23 (citation omitted).

[24]Klukwan was the other. See note 22, above. Like Metlakatla, it was created in the midst of a period of adverse Federal-Indian relations. House Joint Resolution 103 was passed in 1954 favoring termination of the federal-Indian relationship. Three years later, Klukwan was confirmed a nearly nine hundred-acre reserve. One can only speculate that the fact U.S. Steel Corp. wanted an iron ore exploration lease over six hundred of these acres may have had something to do with favorable Congressional action. See *Natives and Land,* note 22, above, at 443. Confirmation of the Klukwan reservation appears to have been compelled by the Tribal Mineral Leasing Act of May 11, 1928, which permitted iron ore mineral leases only on "reservation lands or lands owned by [a] tribe." An executive order reserve was not a "reservation" (i.e., permanent withdrawal) and therefore could not be leased. See also 70 I.D. 166, 167 (1963).

[25]Act of February 8, 1887, 24 Stat. 388, 25 USC 331 et. seq. The General Allotment Act, sometimes called the "Dawes Act" after its chief sponsor, was seldom applied in Alaska because it only applied to "States or Territories" and Alaska did not become a Territory until 1912 (Act of August 24, 1912, 37 Stat. 512). In 1906, Congress passed the Alaska Allotment Act (Act of May 17, 1906, 34 Stat. 954). This Act permitted Alaska Natives to acquire up to 160 acres on nonmineral lands to be held in trust by the Federal Government. However, in 1965 the Solicitor issued an opinion holding that a non-Alaska American Indian could acquire an allotment under the Dawes Act in Alaska. (Clark v. Tabbytite, 72 I.D. 124 (1965)). Language in the *Tabbytite* opinion indicates that after 1912 and before 1971 the 1887 Allotment Act was applicable to Alaska Natives. See 72 I.D. 124 at 132. See also Nagle v. U.S., 191 F. 141 (1911) holding that the 1887 Act was applicable to Alaska Natives for purposes of establishing citizenship. Alaska allotments are discussed more fully in chapter 4, below. See also *Natives and Land,* note 22, above, at 451.

[26]William Duncan was an Anglican missionary to an important Tsimshian Indian community at Metlakatla in British Columbia. Because of a dispute with the Canadian Government over recognition of Tsimshian land claims, Duncan secured permission from President Grover Cleveland to move the community to the Annette Islands and did so in 1887. Four years later Congress reserved "the body of lands known as Annette Islands" for the Metlakatlans and "such other Alaska Natives as may join them." See *Metlakatla,* note 2, above, at 52.

[27]See *Metlakatla,* note 2, above, at 52-53. The fact the reservation was created "until otherwise provided by law" could argue against its permanence; on the other hand, the congressional debates surrounding the 1891 statute pretty clearly indicate an intention to create a permanent (therefore compensable) reservation. Id. at 53.

[28]*Alaska Pacific Fisheries,* note 1, above, at 89.

[29]The Alaska Supreme Court has recently done likewise. See Atkinson v. Haldane, 569 P.2d 151 (Ak. 1977) recognizing sovereign immunity of the Metlakatla community government.

[30]Act of May 17, 1884, Section 13, 23 Stat. 24 provided in pertinent part as follows:

> That the Secretary of the Interior shall make needful and proper provision for the education of the children of school age in the Territory of Alaska, without reference to race, until such time as permanent provision shall be made for the same....

[31]*Natives and Land,* note 22, above, at 445 lists the following executive order reserves created between 1905-1919.

Copper Center	15 February 1905	1,041.34 acres
Ft. Yukon	24 February 1914	75.00 acres
Kobuk River	21 November 1914	144,000.00 acres
Tyonek (Moquawkie)	27 February 1915	26,918.00 acres
Klukwan	2 August 1915	82.42 acres
Chilkat Fisheries	2 August 1915	17.21 acres
Yendistucky	25 May 1916	143.80 acres
Norton Bay (Elim)	3 January 1917	316,000.00 acres
Akiak	22 November 1917	1,373.06 acres
Mountain Village	22 November 1917	2,180.00 acres
Tatilek	22 November 1917	480.00 acres

Hydaburg (7,833.6 acres) and Klawock (230 acres) were also established as reserves on June 19, 1912 and April 21, 1914 respectively. Calvin Coolidge revoked both on April 17, 1926 and reduced them to school reserves of less than two acres each.

[32]Act of June 25, 1910, 36 Stat. 847:

> [T]he President may, at any time in his descretion, temporarily withdraw from settlement, location, sale, or entry any of the public lands of the United States including the District of Alaska and reserve the same for water-power sites, irrigation, classification of lands, or other public purposes to be specified in the orders or withdrawals, and such withdrawals, or reservations shall remain in force until revoked by him or by Act of Congress.

[33]Alaska Pacific Fisheries v. U.S., 240 F. 274, 281 (9th C.A. 1918) citing U.S. v. Midwest Oil Co., 236 U.S. 459, 471. See also U.S. v. Alaska Pacific Fisheries, 5 Alaska Rpts. 484, 491-492, (D.C. Ak. 1916) and 49 L.D. 592, 596 (1923). See note 9, above, and accompanying text.

[34]See note 10, above.

[35]E. g. Jackson, Sheldon, *Fifteenth Annual Report on Introduction of Domestic Reindeer into Alaska,* (Washington, D.C.: GPO, 1905) at 8.

[36]*Natives and Land,* note 22, above, at 444. William McKinley issued an executive order on March 30, 1901 creating two such reserves at Cape Denbigh (seventy-five square miles) and Unalakleet (one hundred square miles) (RG 75, Series 822, Executive Orders 1901-1902, National Archives, Washington, D.C.).

[37]Unnumbered executive order of January 7, 1903. Curiously, the order itself is not listed in any index of executive orders for the period nor has the order been microfilmed with the other 1903 orders. The BIA, Juneau Area Office does have a copy in its Gambell and Savoonga village files.

[38]43 USC 1618 (1972 supp.)

[39]Windahl, Ethan and William H. Timme, "Application of Section 19 of the Alaska Native Claims Settlement Act to the St. Lawrence Island Reserve," a brief to the U.S. Department of the Interior on behalf of the village corporations of Gambell and Savoonga (1973). See also letter of September 14, 1973, from Secretary Morton to Bering Straits Native Corporation accepting the argument in the brief and qualifying St. Lawrence Island under ANCSA. Both documents are on file with the Regional Solicitor's Office, Anchorage.

[40]231 F. 270, 277 (D.C.S.D. 1916).

[41]51 L.D. 155, 157 (1925).

[42]Even though the reserves have been abolished, the reindeer presumably are still protected from local taxation by operation of federal law. The 1925 Solicitor's opinion did not depend on the existence of the reserve for its holding, but on the possibility that local taxation could destroy the federal reindeer program. Since then, Congress has enacted special legislation putting the reindeer even more clearly under federal authority. See Act of September 1, 1937. 50 Stat. 900, 48 USCA 250 et. seq. The purpose of this Act was to "establish and maintain...a self- sustaining economy" for the Natives of Alaska by "acquiring and organizing...a reindeer industry or business" for the Natives. The Act restricts the sale of live Alaska deer to non-Natives and otherwise appears to pre-empt local governmental authority over the reindeer program. The legislation is still on the books and several Native organizations operate reindeer businesses under its authority. The further implications of this Act are discussed in Chapter Five, below.

[43]In addition to the reindeer reserves, between 1907 and 1930 the Bureau of Education established a number of executive order school reserves. Up to forty-two such reserves were authorized by an unnumbered executive order of May 4, 1907. An additional forty reserves were authorized by Executive Order No. 5289 (March 4, 1930). These orders authorized school reserves in specific villages, subject to survey and posting of the tracts in the named villages. It is difficult to determine the exact number of school reserves. They range in size from

three to forty acres (*Natives and Land*, note 22, above, at 443) and number between eighty and one hundred thirty-five (Jones at 23 citing a December 28, 1961 report to the secretary of Interior by a Task Force on Alaska Native Affairs).

[44]*Sioux Tribe*, note 15, above, at 331.

[45]E. O. No. 1555, June 19, 1912.

[46]E. O. No. 1920, April 21, 1914.

[47]See letter of May 11, 1912, from Acting Commissioner of Education to Secretary of Interior (RG 75, Alaska Div., Hydaburg-8, 1911-12 Nat. Arhcives, Washington, D.C.) concerning establishing the Hydaburg Reserve to "protect [the Natives] from the encroachments of white men on the village and fishing streams." This correspondence also favorably compares the advantages of the proposed Hydaburg Reserve to those then enjoyed by the Metlakatla Reserve.

[48]See letter of February 16, 1911, from Secretary of Interior to Commissioner of Education (RG 75, Alaska Div., "Natives (Reservations)" 1910-1911, Id.), noting that the executive clearly had authority to withdraw the total area for exclusive Native use. The attempt to include similar waters within the Klawock Reserve failed, because, according to the local Alaska forest officer, those waters included a bay frequented for many years by non-Native fishermen, and it would "hardly be justifiable to withdraw the bay from general use." Letter of June 7, 1913, from Acting Secretary of Agriculture to Secretary of Interior (RG 75, Ak. Div., Klawock 1912-1913, Id.)

[49]Unnumbered Executive Order, April 17, 1926.

[50]Act of March 3. 1927, 44 Stat. 1347, 25 USC, 398a et. seq. (1970) See also 69 Yale L.J., note 20, above, at 632.

[51]25 USC 398d (1970). Temporary withdrawals by the Secretary of Interior were exempted from this restriction until 1976 when that authority was also withdrawn by the BLM Organic Act of October 21, 1976, P.L. 94-579, Title VII, Section 704(a), 90 Stat. 2793. In any case, section 4 of the 1927 Leasing Act prohibited future revocations of then existing executive order Native reserves without congressional approval.

[52]See chapter 6, below.

[53]E. O. No. 2141, February 27, 1915.

[54]49 L. D. 592 (1923).

[55]Id. at 593.

[56]Id. at 596, citing *Alaska Pacific Fisheries*, note 1, above.

[57]Id. This is substantially the same purpose as was used two years later to prohibit territorial taxation of Native reindeer. See note 41, above, and accompanying text.

[58]Id. at 597.

[59]Id. The Comptroller General restricted this last conclusion to prohibit actual distribution of lease proceeds to the Natives. The rationale for doing so appears to be the lack of statutory authority for such distributions. See Op. Sol. M-36761, note 81, below, and accompanying text.

[60]See 34 Ops. Attys. Gen. 171 (No. 7579, 1924) at 172. The opinion notes that even though Harding's Secretary of Interior, Albert Fall, had (perhaps improperly) authorized the leasing of executive order Indian reserves for mineral exploration, he had placed the proceeds of those leases in U.S. Treasury accounts for the ultimate benefit of the Indians occupying the reserves. Id. at 174-175.

[61]Act of February 1920, 41 Stat. 437 as amended 30 USC 181 et. seq. (1970).

[62]49 L.D. 139, 144 (1922). See also 69 Yale L.J., note 20, above, at 631-632, n. 26.

[63]34 Ops. Attys. Gen. 171, note 60, above. Stone's opinion was overruled by a Utah Federal District Court in 1925. The court of appeals certified the district court opinion to the U.S. Supreme Court, but the issue was mooted by the passage of the 1927 Indian Mineral Leasing Act, which did permit leasing of executive order reserves for certain purposes. Act of March 3, 1927, 44 Stat. 1347, 25 USCA 398a et. seq. See 69 Yale L.J. at 632.

[64]See generally 69 Yale L.J., at 632-640 for a lucid discussion of the background and legislative history of the events summarized here.

[65]25 USC 398b (1970).

[66]S. Rep. No. 1240, at 4, H.R. Rep. No. 1791, at 3-4 cited in 70 I.D. 166 (1963) (Op. Sol. M-36652).

[67]Id. 70 I.S. 166, 169.

[68]See 25 USC 391 et. seq. (1970).

[69]See 69 Yale L.J., note 20, above, at 633, n. 35. The legislative history analyzed in this article indicates that Congress thought recognition of the compensability of executive order reserves would be the result of requiring that lease proceeds be held in trust. Id. 633-640.

[70]70 I.D., note 66, above, at 172-73.

[71]Id. If the reserves are "owned" it also follows that they are "compensable" as Fifth Amendment "property."

[72]Id. at 167.

[73]Id. citing unpublished Solicitor's memorandum of September 7, 1955, finding no authorization to lease lands of the Klukwan reserve for iron ore exploration without legislation fixing authority for such a lease. Significantly, Congress

shortly thereafter confirmed the Klukwan reserve by statute thereby recognizing its compensability. See note 24, above.

[74]E. O. 2508, January 3, 1917.

[75]Letter of October 31, 1966 from David Spencer to Richard Bradley, Field Solicitor, Juneau. (BIA files, Juneau, 307.3 Elim).

[76]Letter of October 31, 1966 from Bradley to Spencer citing 25 USCA 398a (i.e. the 1927 Leasing Act.) (BIA files, Id.)

[77]Letter Id. Citing Mineral Leasing Act 396a of May 11, 1938, c. 198, section 1, 52 Stat. 347 25 USCA and Indian Surface Leasing Act 25 USCA 415 of August 9, 1955, c. 615, section 1, 69 Stat. 539, as amended. Note: The 1955 Surface Leasing Act appears to restrict leasing in a manner not anticipated in the 1923 *Tyonek* opinion. See notes 53-59 above, and accompanying text.

[78]Letter of October 31, 1966 from Bradley to Area Director (BIA files, Juneau 307.3 Elim citing 25 USC 407, Act of June 25, 1910, c. 431, Section 7, 36 Stat. 857 as amended).

[79]Id. at 3.

[80]Letter of April 12, 1967 (BIA files, Juneau, 307.3 Elim).

[81]Op. Sol. M-36761, Leasability of Lands in the Vicinity of Eklutna, May 1, 1964 concludes that the 1923 *Tyonek* decision (49 L.D. 592) permitted such leasing under 5 USC 485 (1964) for uses which will "promote the purposes of withdrawal." Id. at 5-6. 25 USC 2 appears to provide similar authority. By 1967, however, the Comptroller General had determined that proceeds from business leases could not be held in trust for the reservation Natives. Id. See note 59 above.

[82]ANCSA, Section 4(c) extinguishes "all claims...based on claims of aboriginal right, title, use or occupancy...[or] on any statute or treaty of the United States relating to Native use and occupancy."
This seems broad enough to extinguish claims based on pre-1971 mismanagement of leases. The statutes authorizing the leases frequently "relate" to executive order reserves established for Native "use and occupancy." See 25 USC 398; see also U.S. v. ARCO, 435 F.Supp. 1009 (D.C. Ak. 1977) implying that ANCSA eliminated all conceivable "use and occupancy" claims.

[83]See *American Indian Policy Review Commission, Final Report,* Committee Print (Washington, D.C.: GPO, 1977) at 129-130 n. 29.

[84]See note 54, above, and accompanying text.

[85]But the Comptroller General later rejected the latter conclusion. See note 58, above.

[86]As recently as 1964, the Solicitor further approved the 1923 decision in support of authority to lease the Eklutna Reserve. See note 81, above.

[87]43 USC 150 (1970).

[88]See note 32, above. The authority also existed under case law. See note 33, above.

[89]They were as follows:

Name	Date Established	Size
White Mountain	25 September 1925	1,200 acres
Eklutna	5 December 1927	1,819 acres
Tetlin	10 June 1930	768,000 acres
Point Hope	8 July 1930	6,400 acres
Amaknak Island	23 February 1933	110 acres

Source: *Natives and Land,* note 22, above, at 445.

[90]Act of February 23, 1925, Pub. No. 468, 68th Cong.

[91]*Natives and Land,* note 22, above, at 444-445.

[92]E. O. No. 5365, June 10, 1930.
Immediate objections were raised over the size of the Tetlin reserve. See memorandum from Commissioner of Education to Burlew. October 23, 1930, (RG 75, Ak. Divl, "Executive Orders," Nat. Archives, Washington, D.C.).
Significantly, under the terms of the order creating it, the right to explore for and extract minerals on the reserve was retained by the United States under "such rules as the Secretary of Interior shall prescribe."
The Secretary of Interior applied the "general mining regulations" approved in an April 11, 1922, circular to the Tetlin Reserve. See letter from Secretary of Interior to the Commissioner, General Land Office, December 16, 1930 (RG 75, Ak. Div., Executive Orders, Id.)

[93]E. O. No. 5391, July 8, 1930.

[94]E. O. No. 6044, February 23, 1933.

[95]A probable justification under the "public purpose rubric" might be aboriginal fishing rights. Protecting aboriginal rights could conceivably be a public purpose, and it is hard to see how protecting the "fishing rights of Alaska Natives" could refer to anything but aboriginal rights.

[96]Op. Sol. M-36761. Leasability of Lands in the Vicinity of Eklutna, May 1, 1967. See note 81, above.

[97]The reserves were leasable under the general leasing statute (5 USC 4 and 5 (1964)), authorizing the Secretary to promote the purpose of any such reserve. The Secretary has similar authority under 25 USC 2, which permits him to regulate Native affairs.

[98]See note 51, above.

[99]See Op. Sol. M-36761 at note 81, above.

[100]Cited note 12, above.

[101]H. Rpt. 2244, 74C:2s, 3-5 (1936) Letter of Secretary Ickes to the House Committee on Indian Affairs. The 1934 Act did not apply Section 17 (25 USC 477) to Alaska. Section 17 was the only means whereby Native organizations could take advantage of IRA loan provisions of Section 10 (25 USC 470).

[102]Act of May 1, 1936, 49 Stat. 1250. Forrest J. Gerrard, former Assistant Secretary for Indian Affairs, uses the term "Alaska Reorganization Act" in an October 1976 report he prepared as a professional staff member to the Senate Committee on Interior and Insular Affairs. See Gerrard, Forrest J., "Congressional Responsibility for American Indian Policy: History, Current Issues and Future Goals," Unpublished Report to the Senate Interior and Insular Affairs Committee, October 1976 at 13. The term also appears in early Department of the Interior "Instructions" on the implementation of the 1936 Amendments in Alaska.

[103]Id. 25 USCA 473a

[104]25 USC 496 (1970) repealed by the BLM Organic Act of October 21, 1976, P.L. 94-579, Title VII, Section 704(a), 90 Stat. 2793.

[105]See Gruening, Ernest, *The State of Alaska* (New York: Random House, 1968) at 364 Re: Cohen's role. See H. Rpt. No. 2244, 74c:2s, 3 (1936) Re: support of Paul and Dimond.

[106]Id. H. Rpt No. 2244 at 4.

[107]Act of May 17, 1884, Section 8, 23 Stat. 24 provides in pertinent part:

> [T]he Indians or other persons in [Alaska] shall not be disturbed in the possession of any lands actually in their use or occupation or now claimed by them, but the terms under which such persons may acquire title to such lands is reserved for future legislation by Congress.

The Timber Culture Act of March 3, 1891, Section 14, 16 Stat. 1095, 1100 excluded from trade and manufacturing sites land "to which Natives of Alaska" have prior rights by virtue of actual occupation. Section 15 of this same Act established the Metlakatla Reservation. See note 3, above.
Additionally, and not noted by Secretary Ickes, the Act of June 6, 1900, Section 27, 31 Stat. 321 provides that "Indians or persons conducting schools or missions shall not be disturbed in the possession of any lands now actually in their use or occupation."

[108]H. Rpt. No. 2244, note 101, above, at 4.

[109]Internal memorandum for Secretary from Nathan R. Margold, September 14, 1937 (BIA files, Juneau 307.3 Tyonek). See also Op. Sol M-28987, 56 L.D. 110 (April 19, 1937).

[110]83 Cong. Rec. Pt. 9, 179-82 (1938).

[111]*N. Y. Times,* December 24, 1944. See also *The Evening Star,* December 25, 1944, B-6, Washington, D.C. (RG 348, Box 462, Folder 40-4d No. 1, Terr. Gov. Files, Federal Record Center (FRC) Seattle).

[112]Op. Sol. M-31634, February 13, 1942.

[113]*Natives and Land,* note 22, above, at 444.
The Venetie Reservation was created in order to protect the Native community from non-Native trappers competing for the fur resources. Letter of April 19, 1945, from E.L. Bartlett to Ickes (RG 348, Box 462, folder 40-4d No. 1 Terr. Gov. Files, FRC, Seattle.) The letter actually disputes the veracity of the alleged competition, but confirms non-Native competition was the stated justification for the reserve.

[114]Hearings on Claims of Natives of the Towns of Hydaburg, Klawock, and Kake, Alaska, Pursuant to the Provisions of Section 201.216 of the Regulations for Protection of the Commercial Fisheries of Alaska, Report of Presiding Chairman. (RG 348, Box 462, Folder 40-4d No. 1, Files of Terr. Gov., FRC Seattle.) Ernest Gruening also provides an account of these events in the *State of Alaska* note 105, above, at 368-369.

[115]Order and Opinion No. 123903, January 11, 1946 (RG 348, Id.).

[116]See July 10, 1944, memorandum from Cohen to Commissioner of Indian Affairs, at 2 (RG 348, Box 462 Folder 40-4d No. 1 Terr. Gov. Files, FRC Seattle.)

[117]Gruening, note 105, above, at 367-369 confirms his personal opposition to the policy. At the time of these events, Gruening was territorial governor of Alaska.

[118]July 10, 1944, memorandum, note 116, above, at 2. See also "Native Claims in Alaska," Unpublished Solicitor's Memorandum (March 25, 1947).

[119]Secretary Ickes realized that the department itself could not extinguish aboriginal title; only Congress could do that. See *New York Times,* December 24, 1944, signed article by Harold Ickes. It seems likely, however, that by establishing reserves the department would thereby define the shape of future congressional extinguishment.

[120]Letter from Superintendent Don Foster to Asst. Commissioner Zimmerman June 1, 1944 (BIA files, Juneau, 307.3 Karluk). Section 2 of the Alaska IRA Amendments required the Natives occupying the proposed reserve to approve its creation by majority vote of at least thirty percent of the adult residents.

[121]Id.

[122]Act of June 6, 1924, 43 Stat. 464 as amended 48 USC 221 et. seq. (1958).

[123]See note 116, above.

[124]Alaska Fisheries General Regulations, 50 CFR 208.23 (1946 Supp.).

[125]Section 1, 43 Stat. 464, as amended 48 USC 222 (1958). Irving L. Paul, Sr. provides an interesting sidelight on this White Act provision. At the 1946 Alaska Native Brotherhood Convention, he claimed credit for the equal fishing provisions which later deprived the Karluk Reserve and still later the village of Kake of their exclusive fishery. (RG 348, Box 462 Folder 40-4d No. 1 "ANB and ANS" Terr. Gov. Files, ERC, Seattle).

[126]*Grimes Packing,* note 2, above, at 98.

[127]67 F. Supp 43 (D.C. Ak. 1946) aff'd Hynes v. Grimes Packing, 165 F. 2d 323 (9th Cir. 1947).

[128]See *Grimes Packing,* note 2, above, at 103-08. The Karluk reserve is specifically compared to the noncompensable executive order reserves which *Sioux Tribe,* note 15, above, distinguished from compensable treaty or statutory reserves. See notes 17-19, above, and accompanying text.

[129]*Grimes Packing,* note 2, above, at 116 and 122 respectively.

[130]The Act of March 3, 1893, 27 Stat. 631, 25 USC 175 (1970) as amended permits the United States Attorney to represent "reservations or allotted Indians" in "all suits at law and equity." The Act of July 12, 1966, 74 Stat. 469, 18 USC 1165 (1976) makes it a criminal offense to "willfully and knowingly" trespass on lands "reserved for Indian use, for the purpose of hunting, trapping or fishing thereon." Insofar as the U.S. Attorney is required to enforce the law, he would be required to prosecute for trespass.

[131]It is therefore unlikely that IRA or executive order reserves recognized "fishing rights" in the same sense as do treaty or other congressionally recognized reserves. E.g., U.S. v. Winans, 198 U.S. 337, 381 (1904) So long as the reserves existed, fishing or other exclusive uses could be protected on a federal trespass theory. Revocation of the reserves eliminated the Federal remedies available on that theory.

[132]Telegram and letter of Cohen to Ellanak of June 3 and 11, 1946, respectively (BIA files, Juneau, 307.3 Karluk).

[133]S. Rpt. 1366, 80C:2s, 20 (1948).

[134]C.f. Letter of August 1, 1949, from Cohen to Ellanak (BIA files, Juneau, 307.3 Karluk).

[135]Memorandum of August 3, 1949, from Peratrovich to Foster (BIA files, Id.).

[136]Letter form Jenkins to Acting Area Director June 21, 1950 (BIA files Id.).

[137]Letter of June 13, 1951, from Tiffany to Wade (BIA files, Id.).

[138]Letter, June 26, 1951, from Wade to Tiffany (BIA files, Id.) In view of the

Grimes Packing decision, one must question the accuracy of Mr. Wade's statement. Clearly, *Grimes Packing* established the legitimacy of the Karluk reserve. Perhaps Wade, as a new Area Director, was simply unfamiliar with the litigation surrounding the Karluk reserve. Perhaps he felt, politically or otherwise, he needed a "win" in Hydaburg to enable him to pursue a vigorous Karluk enforcement policy. The past conceals the reason.

[139]U.S. v. Libby, McNeil and Libby 107 F. Supp. 697 (1952).

[140]See Gruening, note 105, above, at 379-81.

[141]*Libby,* note 139, above, did hold the Hydaburg reserve was not legally established and therefore void.

[142]See *Alaska Native Management Report,* vol. 2, No. 9 (May 15, 1973) at 5.

Name	Size in Acres
Karluk	35,200
Akutan	72,000
Diomede	3,000
Unalakleet	870
Wales	21,000
	(includes 14,000 acres of water)
Venetie	1,408,000

When surveyed under ANCSA, Venetie was determined to be 1,800,000 acres in size.

[143]See memorandum from Regional Solicitor, Anchorage, to Anchorage Superintendent, BIA, "Native Village of Karluk and the [R]eservation at Karluk," January 22, 1968. On file with the Regional Solicitor, Anchorage.

[144]Id. The memorandum was in response to a series of questions which Alex Brown, Chairman of the Karluk Village Council. had asked the Anchorage BIA Superintendent concerning the legal status of the Karluk Reserve.

[145]Id. at 2.

[146]Id. another possible interpretation of the IRA is that the IRA constitution, bylaws and charter function as an agreement between the federal Government and the Native community affirming and reserving the inherent authority of the Native community to govern itself. The required ratification of the IRA reservation by community vote may constitute a similar sort of agreement. Thus the traditional council on an IRA reserve occupies substantially the same position as the more formally organized body.

[147]F. Cohen, *Handbook of Federal Indian Law,* (Washington, D.C.: U.S. Govt. Printing Off., 1942; New York: AMS Press, reprint 1972) at 406.

[148]Mem. Reg. Sol, note 143, above, at 5.
It is difficult to see why the same logic would not apply to the pre-1919 executive order reserves as well. By separating the compensable ownership interest from

the remaining "substantial quantum of ownership control," pre-1919 executive order reserves seem to be in the same position as the IRA reserves. The significant difference is that the executive order reserves were not (for the most part) the product of an agreement between the tribe and the government.

[149]Klukwan is an exception to this statement. See notes 22 and 24, above. See also *Natives and Land,* note 22, above, at 443 and 446, noting that although ninety petitions for IRA reserves were prepared in 1950 "no action" was taken to confirm them.

[150]Letter of April 26, 1960, form Area Director Jack Hawkins to Theodore F. Stevens, Assistant to the Secretary of Interior (BIA files, note 132, above).

[151]*Metlakatla,* note 2, above, at 45, 47 (1962).

[152]Section 4, 72 Stat. 339 (1958) amended by 73 Stat. 141 (1959). See note 2, above, for full case citations to *Kake* and *Metlakatla.*

[153]*Metlakatla,* note 2, above, at 59.

[154]*Kake,* note 2, above, at 62. Inexplicably (to this writer) the Interior Department attempted to permit exclusive Native fishing at Kake and Angoon through regulations again adopted under the White Act (43 Stat. 464 as amended 48 USC 221-228). The U.S. Supreme Court once again rejected the White Act regulations for substantially the same reasons as in *Grimes Packing,* note 2, above. See notes 122-128, above, and accompanying text.

[155]*Kake,* note 2, above, at 69.

[156]Id. at 75-76.

[157]*Metlakatla,* note 2, above, at 59.

[158]25 C.F.R. Pt. 88 (1963).

[159]25 C.F.R. 88.3, above, and conversation of August 22, 1977, with Wallace Leask, Mayor, Metlakatla.

[160]25 C.F.R. 88.5(b), above.

[161]See note 130, above.

[162]Letter of April 29, 1969, from Commissioner Bennett to Secretary of Interior (BIA files, Juneau, 307.3 Karluk).

[163]Act of December 18, 1971, P.L. 92-203, 85 Stat. 688, 43 USC 1601 et. seq. Section 19 provides in pertinent part:

> Sec. 19(a) Notwithstanding any other provision of law, and except where inconsistent with the provisions of this Act, the various reserves set aside by legislation or by Executive or Secretarial Order for Native use or for Administration of Native affairs, including those created under the Act of May 31, 1938, (52 Stat. 593), are hereby

revoked subject to any valid existing rights of non-Natives. This section shall not apply to the Annette Island Reserve established by the Act of March 3, 1891 (26 Stat. 1101), and no person enrolled in the Metlakatla Indian community of the Annette Island Reserve shall be eligible for benefits under this Act.

[164]See Chapter 2, above.

[165]Management of allotment and townsites may also activate the federal trust responsibility, but the responsibility as it relates to these is the topic of Chapter 4, below.

[166]C.f. Menominee Tribe of Indians v. U.S., 391 U.S. 404 (1968).

[167]Op. Reg. Sol. (Alaska) "Entitlement of the Akutan Village Council to Rental Proceeds from Ls. Na. E00C14200079" (Nov. 2, 1978).

[168]Id. Sec. 1411, P.L. 96-487, 94 Stat. 2497 (ANILCA).

[169]ANCSA Sec. 4(c), 43 USC 1603(c).

[170]The fact section 2 of the Alaska IRA Amendments authorized reservations on a "use and occupancy" or "actually occupied" theory would likely bar recovery under the broad language of ANCSA 4(c). Similarly, the fact the 1927 Leasing Act (25 USCA 398 et. Seq.) applied to executive order reserves established on the basis of "use and occupancy" (25 USCA 398) appears to bar claims under the "treaty or statute" language of ANCSA 4(c).

[171]Price, Monroe E., *Region Village Relations under the Alaska Native Claims Settlement Act,* 5 UCLA-Alaska Law Review 58, 61 (1975).

[172]ANCSA Sec. 2(b), 43 USC 1601(b).

[173]In 1974, the solicitor held that ANCSA was a "unique" piece of legislation and not enacted for the benefit of Natives. He characterized it as a "public land statute" and therefore refused to interpret its provisions liberally to benefit the Natives (Op. Sol. M-36876, 81 I.D. 316 (1974). However the courts have consistently interpreted ANCSA as Native legislation entitled to liberal construction.

[174]E.g., Koniag Inc. v. Kleppe, 405 F. Supp. 1360, 1373 (D.C.D.C. 1975), aff'd. in part rev'd. in part *sub nom* Koniag v. Andrus, 580 F. 2d 601 (D.C. Cir. 1978); cert. den. 419 U.S. 1052, acknowledging a generalized "trust responsibility" to determine ANCSA eligibility fairly. Compare Cape Fox Corp. v. U.S., 456 F. Supp. 784 (D.C. Ak. 1978); rev'd. on jurisdictional grounds 646 F. 2d 399 (9th Cir. 1981), holding that there is no trust responsibility for the administration of ANCSA lands prior to conveyance.

[175]A.W. Scott *The Law of Trusts* (Boston: Little, Brown and Co., 1967) at 34-41 (sec. 2).

[176]53 I.D. 593, 604-605 (1932), citing 49 L.D. 592 (1923).

[177]Indian Education and Self-Determination Act of January 4, 1975, P.L. 93-638, 25 USC 450a et. seq. (1974 Supp.).

[178]E.g., Indian Financing Act of April 12, 1974, 88 Stat. 77, 25 USC 1451 et. seq. (1975 Supp.). Indian Health Care Improvement Act of September 30, 1976, 90 Stat. 1401, 25 USCA 1601 et. seq.

[179]This aspect of the relationship is discussed more fully in chapters, 6 and 10, below.

CHAPTER FOUR

NATIVE ALLOTMENTS AND TOWNSITES

I. Generally

Although both were repealed in the 1970's, the 1906 Alaska Native Allotment Act and the 1926 Alaska Native Townsite Act (ANTA) subsequently became the focus of many lawsuits and at least one legislative effort to clarify the land rights of Alaska Natives. Unlike ANCSA, both these statutes were primarily intended to define individual Alaska Native land titles rather than group or corporate rights. They also differ from ANCSA in that they incorporate concepts of restricted title and federal oversight of Native land rights common to the administration of Native lands elsewhere in the United States. Additionally, the federal courts have consistently interpreted restricted Alaska allotment and townsite lands to be subject to specific federal "trust responsibilities". Thus, to a degree never determined prior to their repeal, these two statutes have become afterwards one focus of unique federal responsibilities to Alaska Natives. Enforcement of these responsibilities owed Native individuals has, however, repeatedly complicated or delayed the conveyance of lands to Native owned or ANCSA corporations.

The allotment act has added substantially to the difficulty and uncertainty of making the land distributions required under both ANCSA and the Alaska Statehood Act. For example, lawsuits brought under the allotment act successfully established due process rights of Alaska Natives to factual hearings prior to being denied allotments. This result was initially interpreted to require the Interior Department to reinstate some one thousand allotment applications which had been denied and closed over the years without such hearings. When they were originally denied, these applications were removed from federal land records, which permitted others to select and even receive title to the same lands originally applied for as allotments. If lands previously conveyed to others are now determined to be subject to valid Native allotment applications, the courts have also held that the federal government has a trust responsibility to bring another lawsuit to recover the land for the allotment applicant. Besides this rather significant difficulty, the Interior Department was also faced with the prospect of literally hundreds of hearings to adjudicate many allotments which were still pending.

The whole affair became so confusing, time consuming and inequitable that Congress passed a law in 1980 intended to give statutory approval to most of the some eight thousand pending allotments without any factual hearings. It was not immediately clear, however, whether the new law did anything more than substitute one set of legal difficulties for another.

The Alaska Native Townsite Act engendered additional confusion in the administration of ANCSA, but for other reasons. Unlike the allotment act, ANCSA did not specifically repeal ANTA. Subsequent legislation did so in 1976, but by then others (including many non-Natives) had laid claim to townsite lots available, under one interpretation of the townsite act, to any occupant. The problem was that under one interpretation of ANCSA some of these same lands might be deemed to have been withdrawn for ANCSA village corporations on December 18, 1971. If that is held to be true, then anyone who began occupancy of such townsite lands after that date will be dispossessed by the ANCSA corporation's superior legal rights. Until the dispute is resolved, the land status in some one hundred Alaska Native villages is subject to substantial doubt.

It is a bit ironic that these two early, previously ignored statutes, designed to afford individual Alaska Natives land title, should now be the focus of so much controversy due in part to the settlement of Alaska Native communal land claims. It is even more ironic that the controversy surrounds two statutes which have been repealed. Nonetheless, it is also significant that the federal government has been held to the responsibility of a trustee in the administration of lands conveyed under both statutes. And, in spite of their repeal, the Alaska Native Allotment and Townsite Acts are likely to remain vital indefinitely in terms of their influence on other Alaska land rights and continuing federal responsibilities to Alaska Natives.

II. Allotments

A. Allotment Policies

1. Alaska Use and Occupancy

Early attempts to protect Alaska Native use and occupancy[1] give some insight into the motivation behind the Alaska Allotment Act. Beginning with the Treaty of Cession,[2] Congress repeatedly protected Alaska Native possessory rights to the lands they occupied. A typical provision, from the 1884 Alaska Organic Act, stated in part:

> [T]he Indians or other persons in said district shall not be disturbed in the possession of any lands actually in their use or occupation or now claimed by them, but the terms under which such persons may acquire title to such lands is reserved for future legislation by Congress.[3]

Liberal interpretations of occupancy expanded the meaning of "actual use and occupancy"; thus, use of trails and access to water and to river harbors were also protected.[4] Judicial decisions upheld the possessory rights under these statutes while expanding the scope of Native "title."

> The prohibition contained in the act of 1884 against the disturbance of the use or possession of any Indian or other person

of any land in Alaska claimed by them is sufficiently general and comprehensive to include tidelands as well as lands above the high water mark.[5]

Two Alaska cases also stressed the need to consider the communal aspects of Native life in extending protection to village lands.[6] Finally, *U.S. v. Berrigan*[7] expanded the scope of federal responsibility to include protections against attempts to relieve Natives of their land by contract. More importantly, the court held the Natives of Alaska to be wards of the government; thus, the United States, not the individual Indian, was the proper party to maintain an action for trespass on Native land.[8]

As a practical matter, mere statutory recognition of Native property rights was inadequate to protect Native lands from encroachment. Furthermore, the early statutes offered no opportunity for Natives to obtain individual title to land. The Alaska Native Allotment Act[9] was, in part, a congressional response to this situation; it provided Alaska Natives with an opportunity to obtain individual title to land. The purpose of the legislation, expressed in a General Land Office report submitted to the Senate Committee on Public Lands, was to extend "to the Natives of Alaska the rights, privileges and benefits conferred by the public land laws upon citizens of the United States."[10]

2. Allotment Policies Generally

Although the 1906 Alaska Native Allotment Act and the earlier 1887 General Allotment Act,[11] differ substantially in purpose and procedure, it helps to understand the 1906 Alaska act to compare it with the earlier 1887 act. Both were to some extent the product of reform-minded politicians and missionaries, but each was adopted in a different historical period in response to different political circumstances. They differed in their effect as well. The General Allotment Act is usually credited with a terrible erosion of the Native American land base; whereas, the Alaska allotment act seems now to offer the promise of a significant increase in Alaska Native land ownership.

A basic premise underlying the General Allotment Act was that individual ownership of land was an indispensable requirement of "civilization."[12] Theodore Roosevelt illustrated this point in a 1901 Congressional message, describing the 1887 act as "a mighty pulverizing engine to break up the tribal mass" whereby "some sixty thousand Indians have already become citizens of the United States."[13] Demands of westward moving settlers and railroads for Native reservation lands were more pragmatic concerns.[14] These factors were summarized in a 1934 report of the House Committee on Indian Affairs:

> In conclusion, let it be said that allotment was first of all a method of destroying the reservation and opening up Indian lands; it was secondly a method of bringing security and civili-

zation to the Indian. Philanthropists and landseekers alike agreed on the first purpose, while the philanthropists were alone in espousing the second. Considering the power of those landseeking interests and their support by the friends of the Indian, one finds inescapable the conclusion that the allotment system was established as a humane and progressive method of making way for "westward movement."[15]

From these philosophies and realities, a law of land distribution developed having little relation to traditional Indian communal land ownership.

The General Allotment Act, as subsequently amended, did the following: (1) granted tracts of 40 acres (irrigated), 80 acres (agriculture) or 160 acres (grazing) to individual Natives; (2) made the grants from reservation lands or from the public domain if the allottee did not reside on a reservation; (3) provided that the U.S. retain title to the allotted lands (prohibiting alienation or encumbrance) until an initial trust period expired; and (4) granted citizenship to those Indians who either voluntarily lived apart from the tribe (adopting the habits of "civilized" life) or who occupied their allotment on the date the trust period expired.[16]

The consequences of the 1887 act were disastrous. According to former BIA chief counsel, Theodore H. Haas, the acreage granted was usually insufficient for an economic unit, and fractionalization, due to intestate division after the allottee's death, added to the difficulty.[17] As predicted by Senator Henry M. Teller, a former Secretary of Interior (1882-1885) and an outspoken critic of the act, most allottees soon lost their land at bargain prices.[18] In less than fifty years, some 90 million acres, or two-thirds of the Indian land base of 1887, and generally the most productive, was lost; approximately 90 thousand Indians were left landless.[19]

From its inception, the most frequently mentioned source of Indian objection to the allotment act was the disastrous effect individual ownership of land had on tribal government, unity and culture. The 1887 appeal of the Indian organized International Council of Indian Territory is typical:

> Like other people, the Indian needs at least the germ of political identity, some governmental organization of his own, however crude, to which his pride and manhood may cling and claim allegiance, in order to make true progress in the affairs of life. This peculiarity in the Indian character is elsewhere called patriotism, and the wise and patient fashioning and guidance of which alone will successfully solve the question of civilization. Preclude him from this and he has little else to live for. The law to which objection is urged does this by enablng any member of a tribe to become a member of some other body politic by electing and taking to himself a quantity of land which at the present time is the common property of all.[20]

3. Alaska Allotment Policy

When Congress did extend the allotment philosophy to Alaska, factors influencing the General Allotment Act were found generally inapplicable. According to one Interior Department Solicitor, the relatively few white settlers in early Alaska did not compete with traditional Native land use.[21] Freedom from settlement pressure allowed Alaska Natives to continue their traditional land uses free from the restrictions of allotment laws.[22] Furthermore, in the early days between 1867 and about 1900 it was repeatedly held (without much explanation) that Alaska Natives did not bear the same relation to the federal government as did other Native Americans.[23] Thus, it appeared that allotment laws, applicable to other Native Americans, were inapplicable to Alaska Natives.[24]

The several reports and studies before Congress in 1906 give a fairly detailed and accurate account of the varied conditions of the Alaska Natives. The Department of the Interior received reports in 1903[25] from J. W. Witten, a law clerk acting as special inspector, and from Brigadier General Frederick Funston, documenting Alaska Native afflictions. The next year the Senate Committee on Territories conducted extensive hearings in Alaska to compile data for future legislation. The committee noted the "demoralizing influence" of white men, particularly gold seekers.[26] At the request of President Theodore Roosevelt, retired Navy Lieutenant G. T. Emmons submitted his "Report on the Condition and Needs of the Natives of Alaska" to the Senate in 1905.[27] Congress also received a report from the General Land Office[28] which relied on the previously cited material and proposed a bill to grant individual title to the Natives.

The Land Office report reaffirmed the predominant theme behind the allotment policy (i.e., the necessity of breaking down Indian social structures, culture and religion to create a property-owning citizen).

> *The laws enacted to empower American Indians to acquire lands from the Government for his individual use have proven, perhaps, the wisest and most effectual means of disrupting tribal relations and bringing them into a civilized condition;* and it is not seen why the giving of similar rights to the Natives of Alaska would not have much (the same) or greater beneficial effect, since they are by nature a more energetic, industrious and frugal people than the American Indians (emphasis added).[29]

Emmons, on the other hand, emphasizes the importance of granting property rights purely as a matter of equity to give Alaska Natives:

> the right to acquire, hold, and dispose of all real and personal property upon the same terms and conditions as is given to other inhabitants. Discrimination is neither reasonable nor calculated to encourage them in self-improvement.[30]

The 1887 act, when granting lands to individuals, affirmed the belief that farming was the best way to "civilize" Indians. Given the Native American heritage of communal land use and subsistence hunting and fishing, it now seems incredible to think that Indians would willingly adapt to such a drastic switch in livelihood. Nevertheless, it is interesting to note that the House Committee on Public Lands believed agriculture could also play a role in Alaska's allotment act.

> It will be observed that the lands to be allotted under the provisions of this bill are to be nonmineral in character, which necessarily implies that they are to be *agricultural* lands (emphasis added).[31]

Obviously, the House authors had no firsthand knowledge of Alaska geography. It is fortunate, therefore, that the Senate took the lead in adapting Native allotment policy to Alaska Native cultures.

The courts have held that the purpose of the Alaska Native Allotment Act was to permit Natives to perfect legal title to the lands they used and occupied.[32] It was obvious to Congress that unless the Natives had legal title, miners, settlers and other non-Natives could trespass, even expropriate, Native lands with impunity by purporting to perfect independent title under other federal laws.[33] Given their ignorance of legal procedures and the distance of most Native lands from a court, it was predictable that Natives could not retain land holdings through the slender thread of protection offered by aboriginal possessory rights.

The Alaska allotment act's legislative history also confirms that Congress believed that traditional reservation policies did not suit the seminomadic lifestyles practiced by the majority of Alaska's Natives and that contact with encroaching white settlements brought grief to Natives through disease, liquor and unfair game laws.[34] Both Emmons and Witten stressed the diversity of Native cultures,[35] and the Interior Department Solicitor has held that Congress recognized a need for flexibility in administering allotments to various groups and chose the secretary of the interior to mitigate the harshness of any rigid legislative plan.[36] The interior secretary's Alaska allotment authority is exercised by two bureaus, the Bureau of Land Management (BLM) and the Bureau of Indian Affairs (BIA) whose roles in the administration of Alaska allotments are examined below.

4. Guardianship

Many of the reports Congress had before it in 1906 also suggest that the government should assume a comprehensive supervisory role over the social welfare of Alaska's Native population. Witten's report noted the spread of epidemics and a corresponding lack of hospital care, the ravages of alcohol, poor diets and starvation, as well as inequitable fish and game laws. He recommended legislation to establish government guidance over Natives.[37] The Senate investigating committee concurred when advising that responsibility for Native welfare should be assumed by government agents.[38] The Emmons report on Alaska conditions discussed the American Fur Company's perpetuation of a paternal system of employing Native hunters and fishermen and looking after their welfare—which also kept them thoroughly dependent.[39]

Eskimos were in want of schools, hospitals, rigid enforcement of liquor laws and realistic game laws but particularly needed "a system of careful supervision, instruction and advice to lead them toward self-support."[40] *In re Sah Quah*[41] said the Natives were "practically in a state of pupilage...similar to that of a ward to a guardian," and the 1906 General Land Office Report said it was the "plain duty which our government owes to them as guardian" to aid Natives in every possible manner to develop.[42] These official declarations tend to establish the origins of the U. S. government's relationship to Alaska Natives in a context separate and distinct from the land-related trust responsibilities subsequently embodied in the 1906 Alaska Native Allotment Act. In that respect, the history leading up to the enactment of the allotment act tends to confirm that by the beginning of the twentieth century the federal government equated the status of Alaska Natives with that of Native Americans generally.

B. Substantive Provisions of the Native Allotment Act

The operative section of the 1906 act provides that:

> The Secretary of the Interior is hereby authorized and empowered, in his discretion and under such rules as he may prescribe, to allot not to exceed one hundred and sixty acres of nonmineral land in the district, of Alaska to any Indian or Eskimo of full or mixed blood who resides in and is a Native of said district, and who is head of a family or twenty-one years of age, and the land so alloted shall be deemed the homestead of the allottee and his heirs in perpetuity, and *shall be inalienable and nontaxable until otherwise provided by Congress.* Any person qualified for an allotment as aforesaid shall have the preference right to secure by allotment the nonmineral land occupied by him not exceeding 160 acres (emphasis added).[43]

Compared to the General Allotment Act, the 1906 Alaska Act makes qualification appear simple. To obtain a preference right to a maximum of 160 acres of nonmineral land the applicant had only to 1)reside in Alaska, 2) be an Alaska Native, 3) be 21 or head of a family, and 4) meet whatever incidental requirements the secretary might lawfully prescribe. Upon Department of the Interior approval, the applicant and his heirs received a perpetual "homestead"; however, the land could not be alienated or taxed until otherwise provided by Congress.

Then, in a multifaceted 1956 amendment, Congress did authorize the conveyance of allotments by deed, vesting *complete* title in the purchaser, upon approval of the secretary.[44] Other important changes included the right to select lands valuable for coal, oil and gas, provided mineral interests were reserved to the United States.[45] Aleuts were also afforded status equal to Indians and Eskimos and granted the opportunity to apply for allotments.

The apparent codification of existing departmental regulations provided the final changes. First, lands in a national forest could be allotted if founded on occupancy predating establishment of the forest or if the national forest land was valuable for agriculture or grazing purposes.[46] Second, the 1956 amendments legislatively ratified a 1935 administrative rule requiring five years' use and occupancy[47] before an application could be granted.

Section 18(a) of ANCSA repealed the Alaska Allotment Act, but with a savings clause preserving any allotment application that was "pending before the Department of the Interior" on December 18, 1971, ANCSA's effective date. Although there is no definitive calculation of the number of allotments "pending" in 1971, reliable estimates range up to seven thousand.[48] Accurately calculating the total number has been complicated by continuing legal controversies.

There is also no guarantee that all those who had pending allotment applications will be awarded land. Interior Department policies in the early 1970's disfavored awarding allotments where the extent of a Native's use and occupancy could not be established by clear physical evidence. Since traditional Native land uses (hunting, fishing and gathering) did not leave much such evidence, the effect of the policy was to eliminate or sharply reduce the size of many allotments.[49] The Interior Department also adopted several restrictive legal interpretations which purported to limit allotment entitlement on a variety of grounds. All of these obstacles to obtaining an allotment were initially supported by a broad view within the department of the secretary's discretion to grant (or deny) an allotment application.

The restrictive use and occupancy requirements eventually gave way to more liberal views as did many of the legal interpretations; moreover, the secretary's discretion was sharply limited by the courts. Nevertheless, the prospect of adjudicating the entitlement of some seven thousand Natives to allotments promised to keep Native (and other) land rights in limbo for decades. Then in 1980 Congress, with some exceptions, granted wholesale legislative approval to most of the "pending" allotment applications. This was intended to eliminate the bureaucratic necessity of individually adjudicating most of the allotments, but, as was arguably permitted under the law, the State of Alaska initially protested approval of some six thousand of these applications. To make matters worse, there was also renewed debate about what constituted a "pending" application. These events are examined more fully below.

C. Changing Alaska Allotment Policies

1. Introduction

The Alaska Native Allotment Act was primarily intended to afford individual Alaska Natives the opportunity to perfect legal title to the lands they used and occupied.[50] However, the act was not self-executing; rather it required people who were often illiterate and unfamiliar with bureaucratic procedures and technical legal requirements to file a written application with an often distant government office and to establish their use and occupancy by legally sufficient proofs. Moreover, the government agencies responsible for implementing the act took an initially passive role and in the years immediately preceeding the act's repeal, often interpreted their responsibility as requiring a rigorous testing of each application's legal and factual sufficiency.[51] The act's implementation became further confused in the 1960's and 1970's by shifting administrative interpretations of the legal and factual criteria by which allotment applications were to be judged. Later judicial determinations held that some of these criteria were erroneous and an abuse of agency discretion.

The Alaska Allotment Act has spawned at least eight (often very technical) legal issues, only some of which have been judicially laid to rest. Those which remain lie like little booby traps beneath the ground of federal land policy in Alaska. The factual question of what constitutes "use and occupancy" sufficient to qualify for an allotment under the Interior Department's regulations[52] has been another area of fertile debate. Until judicially reversed as an abuse of due process, the Interior Department took the view that it had nearly unfettered discretion to determine these factual issues. The Interior Department has abandoned many of the more restrictive policies either voluntarily or under judicial decree, but the policy shifts have left uncertainty in their wake, because allotments rejected under earlier regimes (and removed from the records) may now have to be reinstated.

The situation has perhaps become more confused since the 1980 passage of the Alaska National Interest Lands Conservation Act (ANILCA)[53] Section 905[54] of that act eliminates all the legal and factual criteria for the approval of many allotments pending before the Department of the Interior "on or before" December 18, 1971. Three years after the passage of ANILCA it was still not clear which allotments were excepted from its provisions and the extent to which allotments rejected before December 18, 1971 might still be considered to have been pending "on or before" that date. These legal, factual, due process and ANILCA issues are discussed more fully below.

2. Legal Issues

a. Preference Right

It is well established that the Alaska Allotment Act entitles Alaska Natives to a "preference right" to an allotment based on their use and occupancy of land.[55] In practical terms this means that if an Alaska Native occupies a tract of land, he or she has a preferred right to file for title to the land under the allotment act. A third party who files for the land while the Native still occupies it can obtain no rights to the land. However, it has been administratively determined in a case involving competing individual claims to the same land that in order to maintain the preference right prior to filing an allotment application, there must be sufficient physical evidence of the Native's occupancy to put a third party on notice. Alternatively, the Native can establish and maintain the preference right in the absence of physical evidence of occupancy by filing an allotment application.[56]

b. Ancestral Use

Among other things, the 1956 amendments to the Alaska allotment act permitted Natives to acquire lands in national forests if the application for the allotment was "founded on occupancy of the land prior to the establishment of the particular forest."[57] It was not clear from the language whether "founded on occupancy" meant founded on the applicant's personal occupancy or founded on prior Native occupancy generally. The Tongass National Forest in southeast Alaska was the principal forest affected by this amendment. It had been established in a series of withdrawals in the early twentieth century. Obviously, if the 1956 amendments were construed to apply only to *personal* occupancy begun before the early twentieth century, precious few Alaska Natives would be alive in 1956 to claim the benefit of these later amendments.

The government, with some earlier unreported exceptions, interpreted this provision to require the applicant's personal occupancy prior to the establishment of the forest. In 1977, a Native named Albert Shields, Sr. filed a lawsuit on behalf of himself and approximately two hundred other applicants, claiming he and the others were entitled to allotments in the Tongass and Chugach National Forests because their ancestors had occupied the lands for which they had applied prior to the establishment of the forests. The courts rejected these claims and instead adopted the government's interpretation of the statute.[58]

Ancestral use also became an issue in a 1982 case involving allotments located within the boundries of federal wildlife refuges (another form of federal land withdrawal). Although no question of statutory interpretation is involved here, under the terms of the allotment act and its implementing regulations, Natives may only obtain title to land which was "vacant, unappropriated and unreserved" at the time Native occupancy commenced.[59] In many cases, the federal withdrawals which removed the lands from the "vacant, unappropriated and unreserved" category go back many years. Since Natives did not begin applying for allotments in significant numbers until the 1960's, it can be inferred that in many cases the personal occupancy of the applicant did not commence until after the lands were withdrawn for some federal purpose. Thus, in these cases, ancestral use and occupancy may be the only basis on which the necessary Native occupancy can be established. Although this case was decided against the Natives on similar grounds as was the *Shields* lawsuit, the Natives have raised new arguments and presented different facts which might yield a different result on appeal.[60]

c. Five-Year Prior Rule

The regulations implementing the 1906 Alaska Allotment Act and later the 1956 amendments to it required the allotment applicant to "make satisfactory proof of substantially continuous use and occupancy of the land for a period of five years."[61] For many years the Department of the Interior interpreted this requirement to mean that the five years of use and occupancy had to be completed while the land was also "vacant, unappropriated and unreserved." In other words, if a Native commenced occupancy of a tract of land in 1900, but the land was withdrawn for some other federal purpose in 1904, the Native allotment would be denied because the required use and occupancy had not been completed "five years prior" to the later withdrawal. Natives brought a lawsuit challenging this interpretation, but before the lawsuit could be decided the secretary of the interior reversed the rule.[62] Allotments which were rejected on the basis of the old rule were subsequently reinstated on the Interior Department records.[63]

d. Statutory Life

If an allotment applicant failed to make the necessary proof of five years' occupancy within six years after the date of the allotment application, the Interior Department would routinely close the file and reject the allotment. Prior to doing so, the department would send the applicant a letter requesting his or her proof of occupancy, but in the absence of a response the file would be closed. The Interior Department considers the six years requirement to prove use and occupancy to be the "statutory life" of an allotment application. In other words, if the applicant does not make the required proof of five years use and occupancy within six years, the application is automatically presumed to die. It is not clear whether this presumption is justified, and the question has lead to repeated litigation.[64]

e. Married Woman Rule

The Alaska Allotment Act permitted allotments to be made only to the "head of a family" or to Natives over twenty-one years of age.[65] The Interior Department originally presumed that a married woman could not qualify for an allotment under the first criterion, because she was not the head of a household; her spouse was presumed to hold that distinction. The department subsequently changed its position so that a married woman could obtain an allotment so long as she was 21 years of age.[66] Applications denied under the prior rule were subsequently reinstated.

f. Mineral Waiver.

The allotment act prohibited allotments on lands which had potential value for mineral extraction, but the 1956 amendments permitted allotments on lands which were valuable for coal, oil or gas so long as those minerals were reserved to the United States under applicable law.[67] If the lands were found to be valuable for these minerals, the Interior Department sent the applicant a request to waive his right to the minerals (a "mineral waiver"). However, if the applicant did not respond to the request, the file was closed and the application rejected. On later analysis, the Interior Department concluded that it was not necessary to request the waiver and that the coal, oil or gas could be reserved to the United States under the authority of existing law whether the applicant waived the rights or not.[68]

This policy shift naturally raises the question of whether the applications of the Natives who failed to provide the mineral waivers should now be reinstated. Although it had reversed its previous policy, as of 1983 the department still took the position that such applications need not be reinstated. There is some question whether the position is legally supportable.

g. Relinquishments

Allotment applicants may voluntarily relinquish their applications, but there is a question about the scope of the government's responsibility to ensure that any relinquishment is knowing, voluntary and in the allotment applicant's best interest. An allotment applicant might be motivated to relinquish his or her claim under a variety of circumstances. For example, if the lands applied for conflict with the claim of a village corporation entitled to lands under ANCSA, the corporation might agree to convey other lands to which the corporation may be entitled to the applicant, in exchange for the applicant's relinquishment of the allotment application for the land in the village selection. In other cases, allotment applicants might be motivated to relinquish part of their application in order to settle third party claims challenging the applicant's entitlement to the land.

In any such case, however, there is always a question of whether the allotment applicant is being treated fairly and not acting under duress or other undue pressure. It is also the established policy of the Interior Department to enable Alaska Natives to acquire title to the lands they use and occupy and to protect those lands from encroachment.[69] It seems to follow that this policy requires the department to take some independent steps to ensure that relinquishments do not, in effect, deprive Alaska Natives of their land entitlement under the allotment act.

To this end, the Bureau of Indian Affairs (BIA), has an internal policy requiring independent BIA investigation and approval of all relinquishments.[70] It is not clear, however, that the policy has always been strictly followed or that the BIA has always been able to make fully informed judgements on the sufficiency of the relinquishments. Rumors persist that substantial numbers of allotment applications have been improperly relinquished. If true, lawsuits could quite probably require the reinstatement of improperly relinquished allotment applications.

h. Missing Allotment Applications

According to regulations first published in 1964, the BIA was required to certify each allotment application to ensure that the applicant was Native, that the applicant occupied the lands and that the claim did not infringe on other Native claims.[71] The regulations presupposed a more active BIA role in the allotment program, including assisting Natives in making applications.[72] However, due to inadequate funding, the BIA was unable to meet this added burden, so it began to rely on non-bureau personnel to perform the BIA certification duties. Moreover, it became apparent in 1969 or 1970 that the settlement of Alaska Native land claims would likely mean repeal of the Alaska Allotment Act. This gave impetus to a coordinated drive among several agencies, aided by the BIA, to assist Natives in filing allotment applications.

Using the combined resources of the Alaska Legal Services Corporation (ALSC), the Rural Alaska Community Action Program (RurAl CAP), the Alaska Federation of Natives (AFN) and the BIA, the drive produced some 8,500 applications in the space of 16 months. The drive began with a meeting in June 1970 at which the participating agencies agreed on their respective roles. In the ensuing drive, the BIA (with the assistance of the BLM) trained ALSC and RurAl CAP volunteers in the requirements of the allotment act. RurAl CAP prepared the applications in the field and forwarded them to the BIA for certification and delivery to the BLM.[73] Unfortunately in the rush, between three hundred to five hundred applications were "lost." Many of these were collected by RurAl CAP volunteers but never delivered to the BIA; they were discovered several years later in villages and RurAL CAP offices throughout Alaska.

The discovery resulted in a lawsuit in part on the theory that the RurAl CAP volunteers were acting as agents of the BIA and that their receipt of the allotment applications constituted receipt of the applications by the Interior Department. The court never decided the issue, because the Interior Department and plaintiffs agreed to a settlement at a preliminary stage of the litigation. Under the terms of the settlement, about five hundred allotment applications will be reinstated.[74]

3. Factual Issues: Use and Occupancy Criteria

Recall that under the terms of the Alaska Allotment Act the Secretary of the Interior was permitted to grant allotments "in his discretion and under such rules as he may prescribe". One of the major requirements of the secretary's regulations was that an allotment applicant must establish five years' "substantially continuous use and occupancy" of the applied for lands.[75] As further elaborated in the regulations, the use and occupancy must also be "substantial actual possession and use of the land, at least potentially exclusive of others, and not merely intermittent use."[76]

The use and occupancy criteria, even as elaborated in the regulations, were open to further administrative interpretation, particularly as to the type of use and occupancy which would qualify. For example, if "substantial actual possession and use" were interpreted to mean "intensive, physical possession and use," then seasonal occupation of a fish camp might be sufficient occupancy for an allotment to only the land immediately surrounding the camp. The result, typcially, would be the reduction of a 160 acre claim to a five acre tract, and indeed that was the effect of early twentieth century Interior Department interpretations.[77]

This restrictive interpretation was reemphasized in unpublished internal memoranda in the early 1960's which equated the criteria for Alaska Native use and occupancy to the criteria used under other federal laws to adjudicate the land rights of non-Natives. For example, under other laws non-Natives could claim up to five acres for a headquarters site, ten acres for a homesite or 160 acres for a homestead.[78] Analogizing Alaska Native use and occupancy to the use and occupancy requirements of these acts translated into five acres for a fish camp or subsistence hunting site, ten acres for a principal place of residence and the full 160 acres only if the land were "intensively used or improved" such as for farming or industry.[79] Largely as a result of this policy, the average land grant to an Alaska Native allotee fell to forty-six acres in the early 1960's; during the same period of time, non-Natives applying for land under the Alaska Homestead Act received and average of 124 acres.[80]

In 1964, however, the Interior Department Solicitor reexamined the use and occupancy criteria and concluded that the Alaska allotment act was intended to give credit for more typical types of Alaska Native use and occupancy such as fishing, berry picking and hunting. He also concluded that, given the semi-nomadic way of Native life, it was permissible for the 160 acre entitlement of any individual to be spread among several parcels.[81] These criteria were more liberal than those previously employed, but as discussed earlier there were relatively few allotment applications pending before the Interior Department until the allotment drive in 1970-71. Following the drive, the department was faced with some seven thousand applications, and pressure began to build within the federal bureaucracy to limit allotment awards and size. [82]

Following the passage of ANCSA, the Interior Department adhered initially to liberal use and occupancy requirements characterized by the absence of any requirement that applicants demonstrate signs of physical use. In early 1973, however, at the suggestion of the BLM Alaska State Office, the department reversed itself and, among other things, required applicants to demonstrate substantial physical evidence such as fishwheels, campsites, docks and trails. Two months later, however, the BLM suspended these guidelines in the face of massive Native criticism and subsequently abandoned the physical evidence requirements if the applicant could provide corroborating testimony of use and occupancy. [83]

Thus, by 1973, the policies adopted in 1962 requiring intensive, physical possession and use had been jettisoned and replaced by criteria which were more favorable to the type of use Alaska Natives typically made of land as well as less rigid requirements of proof. Nonetheless, the repeated shifts in the use and occupancy criteria no doubt generated substantial confusion among Natives subject to the policy. Nor were allotments rejected or reduced in size under the earlier policy necessarily redetermined under the later, more liberal criteria. Even more important, however, throughout this period the department took an expansive view of the scope of its discretion under the allotment act, to the point of denying allotments without opportunity for full factual hearings or even adequate notice. It took a judicial decision, but it was later held to be a denial of due process to reject allotments under these circumstances.

4. Allotment Due Process

The Fifth Amendment to the U.S. Constitution requres, among other things, that persons may not be deprived of a "property" right without due process of law. Notice and an opportunity for a fair and impartial hearing are fundamental requirements of due process, but persons are not entitled to them if what they stand to lose at the hands of government does not constitute "property". Since the allotment act, by its terms, authorized the secretary to grant allotments "in his discretion," the Interior Department took the position for many years that Alaska Natives had no "property" interest in obtaining an allotment. Under this view, whether the Secretary granted an allotment or not was purely a matter of choice (discretion), and receiving an allotment was therefore a "privilege" rather than a right.

During the nineteenth and early twentieth centuries, the courts had developed a fairly clear distinction between rights (entitled to due process) and privileges (which were not). But by the 1960's and early 1970's the U. S. Supreme Court had "fully and finally rejected the wooden distinction between 'rights' and 'privileges' that once seemed to govern the applicability of procedural due process rights."[84] Shortly thereafter, a dispute arose in Alaska over whether the procedures the Interior Department used to deny Alaska Native allotments conformed to due process. The Interior Department argued that its procedures were sufficient because receiving an allotment was a privilege; therefore, denial of an allotment did not require procedural due process.

An Alaska Native, named Sarah Pence, had been denied her allotment, as had several hundred others. These denials were based on the BLM's factual conclusion that the Natives had not used and occupied the land as required under the allotment regulations, discussed earlier. That conclusion was usually based on a physical examination of the land from a helicopter at low altitude. If no evidence of use and occupancy were found, the applicant was advised of the deficiency by letter and given additional time to submit other evidence to substantiate use and occupancy. If the applicant failed to respond or the evidence was deemed insufficient, the BLM rejected the application and so advised the applicant by letter. The applicant then had thirty days to appeal the decision to the Interior Department's Board of Land Appeals (IBLA). After filing the appeal, the applicant could then request an oral factual hearing, but (because an allotment was deemed a privilege), IBLA took the position that it had no obligation to provide such a hearing.[85]

Sarah Pence filed a lawsuit to compel the Interior Department to provide hearings before denying any allotment. The lower court agreed with the government,[86] but the Ninth Circuit reversed on appeal and ordered the government to provide the requested hearings.[87] In doing so, the court concluded that entitlement to an allotment was a "sufficient property interest" to warrant procedural due process. As a result, the Interior Department has had to reopen 221 allotment applications previously rejected for factual reasons without opportunity for a hearing.[88] There was further litigation over the precise nature of the procedures to be followed in conducting the hearings; Native interests contended that the usual Interior Department hearing procedures were not suitable, given Native cultural and language differences. The courts rejected these arguments unless it could be shown that the department's normal procedures prejudiced Natives,[89] but the need for the hearings was substantially reduced in 1980 with the passage of the Alaska National Interest Land Conservation Act (ANILCA).

In 1982, however, the IBLA cast doubts on the propriety of reopening many of the *Pence* allotments. In an appeal known as *Mary Olympic,*[90] IBLA ruled that any allotment which had been finally rejected by the Department *prior* to December 18, 1971, may not be reopened if the allotment applicant (Mary Olympic's father) had failed to file a timely appeal or request for reconsideration of the rejection. In this case, the allotment application mistakenly described other land than that which the applicant was occupying. BLM asked the applicant for a new land description in 1967, but he died before he could comply. Shortly thereafter, his application was rejected for failure to describe the land he was claiming, and the applicant's heirs did not appeal or ask for reconsideration.

Since neither the heirs nor the applicant contended that he had used and occupied the land applied for, he was deemed not to have been denied a hearing and therefore not entitled to have the application reinstated under the court's decision in *Pence I*.[91] Since the rejection and failure to appeal all occurred *prior* to 1971, IBLA held that ANCSA's savings clause preserving allotments "pending on" December 18, 1971 did not apply to an allotment finally rejected before 1971. Conversely, IBLA has held in a case called *Frederick Howard* that an allotment rejected *after* December 18, 1971, was (by definition) "pending on" December 18, 1971 and so protected by the ANCSA savings clause. Whether the applicant appealed the rejection or not was held irrelevant.[92]

5. Effects of ANILCA[93]

a. Generally

Section 905[94] of ANILCA attempts to reduce the likelihood of literally thousands of use and occupancy hearings by legislatively approving many allotments without such hearings. ANILCA also reduces the importance of determining whether allotments are "nonmineral" in character and permits allotment applicants to amend the land descriptions in their applications to more accurately reflect their original intent as well as giving the Secretary of the Interior broad powers to adjust land descriptions to eliminate conflicts among applications. Section 905 also authorizes allotments located in powersite withdrawals and in the National Petroleum Reserve—Alaska (NPRA) even if the applicant cannot prove that use and occupancy was established prior to these withdrawals. Finally, it requires that any other rights individuals may have to the land applied for as an allotment be adjudicated prior to granting the allotment. If those rights are found to be valid, then the allotment is required to be made "subject to" those rights.

b. Legislative Approval

Until ANILCA, the major obstacle to the rapid approval of many pending allotments was the use and occupancy requirement imposed by the regulations implementing the allotment act. Whether use and occupancy was established by physical evidence or the testimony of others, it took a substantial amount of time for the BLM to investigate each allotment. Then, if there was a dispute about the extent of the applicant's use, an administrative appeal was likely to follow, consuming more time and energy, before the fate of the application could be adjudicated. In the meantime state and Native corporation conveyances could not be finalized until potentially conflicting allotments had been adjudicated. ANILCA attempts to cut through this thicket by granting legislative approval to large numbers of allotments, thus reducing the need for factual investigations and hearings on use and occupancy questions.

Briefly, section 905 provides for legislative approval (on the 180th day following the effective date of the act) of all allotment applications "which were pending before the Department of the Interior *on or before* December 18, 1971" (emphasis added).[95] However, there are four major exceptions to the blanket approval, some of which are fraught with legal issues. In addition, some three years after ANILCA it was not entirely clear what constituted an application which was "pending...on or before" December 18, 1971. Each of these issues is discussed more fully below.

c. The Exceptions

Allotment applications covering lands which were affected by any of four factors were excepted from legislative approval and will have to be adjudicated, for the most part, under the normal procedures required under the allotment act. The lands subject to these exceptions are: (1) lands which within 180 days after ANILCA's effective date, the secretary determined valuable for minerals (other than coal, oil or gas); these lands are subject to adjudication of their mineral status only; (2) lands within a national park or which have been "validly selected," temporarily approved ("TA'd") or patented to the state, unless those lands had been withdrawn for village corporation selection under ANCSA; (3) lands subject to Native corporation, state or private protest under specified circumstances; and (4) lands which an applicant has "knowingly and voluntarily" relinquished.[96]

The most controversial of the exceptions is that relating to state protests;[97] it imposes specific requirements on the exercise of the protest right. First, all protests had to be filed with the Interior Department within 180 days of ANILCA's effective date. Second, protests could only be filed if the allotment application was for lands which were "necessary" for access to lands owned by the United States, the state or one of its political subdivisions or to public waters used for transportation. Furthermore, the state had to specify the facts demonstrating the necessity of the lands for access and that there was no reasonable alternative access. The state filed six thousand protests on the 180th day following the enactment of ANILCA, most of which did not appear to meet the requirements of specificity required under the law.[98] By mid-1983, however, the state had abandoned all but about fourteen hundred of its protests and many of those remaining were still under review.[99]

d. "Pending On or Before"

Section 905 applies only to allotment applications which were "pending" before the Interior Department "on or before December 18, 1971". Read literally, this phrase could mean that any allotment application filed prior to December 18, 1971 was, by definition, "pending before" December 18, 1971. The question of what was a pending application in 1971 is further confused by the IBLA's decisions in *Mary Olympic* and *Frederick Howard,* discussed above. *Mary Olympic* construed the language in ANCSA ("pending on") and not ANILCA ("pending on or before") because the allotment at issue was within one of the exceptions to ANILCA's legislative approval. *Frederick Howard* involved a legislatively approved allotment, but whether the allotment was pending "before" December 18, 1971 was not critical since the allotment was clearly pending "on" that date. Therefore, it is yet to be decided what "or before" really means in the case of an allotment to be legislatively approved under ANILCA. [100]

e. Allotment Minerals

In section 905(a)(2), Congress apparently ratified the Interior Department practice of reserving any coal, oil and gas under an allotment found valuable for those resources to the United States. More significantly, however, this provision also defined sand and gravel as being "non-mineral" and required the Interior Department to identify all allotments which were valuable for other minerals within 180 days. These last two provisions, in effect, sharply reduced in importance the requirement under the allotment act that allotments be allowed only on "non-mineral" lands.

f. Petroleum Reserve and Powersite Lands

Prior to ANILCA, allotments, by the terms of the allotment act, could only be had on "vacant, unappropriated and unreserved" lands. A number of complex questions had arisen over conflicts between various federal withdrawals and the claims of allotment applicants. The applicants frequently contended that their occupancy predated the withdrawals or that the withdrawals themselves permitted new Native occupancy. The government, on the other hand, generally took the position that the withdrawals precluded new Native occupancy and that, at least for the older withdrawals, few Natives had initiated valid occupancy prior to the withdrawal. Nowhere were these problems more acute than within the National Petroleum Reserve—Alaska (NPRA, formerly Naval Petroleum Reserve No. 4) and the numerous powersite withdrawals which peppered the state.

Although the NPRA and powersite lands are treated somewhat differently in different subsections of section 905, [101] ANILCA legislatively changed them from occupied, appropriated or reserved lands to lands which were "vacant, unappropriated and unreserved" for purposes of the allotment act. Allotments within the NPRA were specifically included with all the other allotments located on "unreserved" lands which were legislatively approved under ANILCA. Allotments within the powersite withdrawals were subject to legislative approval only under certain circumstances, however. For example, allotments within currently licensed or operating powersites were not to be legislatively approved. Similarly, if the allotment applicant commenced use and occupancy of the powersite lands after they had been withdrawn for a powersite, then the allotment was made subject to a 20-year right of reentry in favor of the United States.

g. Boundary Adjustments

ANILCA provides for the adjustment of allotment boundaries under two circumstances: (1) unilaterally by the Interior Department if the land descriptions of two or more allotment applications conflict and (2) by the allotment applicant if the application does not reflect his or her true intent at the time of application. [102] The Interior Department's adjustments must be consistent with the prior use of the land and beneficial to the affected parties "to the extent practicable." Most importantly, however, the Interior Department's decision is shielded from judicial review unless it decreases an allotment by thirty percent or more ar excludes an applicant's improvements. This seems to be a limited legislative exception to the due process types of limitations imposed on the Interior Secretary's discretion under *Pence I.*

An allotment applicant's amendment of his or her land description operates to permit legislative approval of the amended land description only, but also affords anybody who may have another claim to the lands covered by the amended description sixty days to protest the amendment. Thus, an allotment applicant who wants to amend an application runs the risk that by doing so the application may lose its prior legislative approval. On the other hand, if the original application is within one of the exceptions to legislative approval, it might then be possible to amend it in such a way as to take it out of the exception. Finally, the Interior Department can require that all allotment applications in any particular area be amended by a certain date in order to facilitate survey of all the allotments in the area.

h. Other Conflicting Entries

It should be noted that the Interior Department's authority to adjust boundaries, discussed above, is confined to conflicts between two or more *allotment* applicants. It cannot be used, apparently, to resolve conflicts between allotment applicants and other individual applicants for rights to the public lands (e.g., mining claims or homesteads). Resolving these conflicts appears to be the purpose of section 905(e) which requires the Interior Department to identify and adjudicate other recorded land entries in conflict with an allotment application prior to granting an allotment. Somewhat ambiguously, section 905(e) requires only that any allotment approved under ANILCA which conflicts with another valid, individual entry shall be made "subject to" the conflicting entry. Thus it appears possible for an allotment applicant to have legal title to an allotment which is subject to the right of another to use the land. [103] By its terms, however, this provision does not apply to the entries of Native corporations, the state or other allotment applicants which are covered under other provisons of section 905.

D. From Trust to Restricted Status

1. General

The concept of a "trust," unique to the English common law, developed out of efforts to avoid some of the limitations on feudal land in early England.[104] A trust relationship in the strict sense of the term always involves the disposition of property between two types of owners—legal and equitable. The legal owner holds the legal title to the property but only for the benefit of the equitable owner. The equitable owner has the full right to use and occupy the property and do anything with it except sell or lease it; powers of sale and lease are part of the legal title which belongs solely to the legal owner.

In this strict sense of "trust", the United States assumes a "trust relationship" with Native Americans whenever it retains the legal title to Native lands and accords the Native a permanent right of occupancy and use (i.e., an equitable interest). This is the usual basis of the trust relationship between the federal government and Native American tribes on treaty or statutory reserves.[105] The same narrow trust relationship exists between the federal government and Native allottees under the 1887 General Allotment Act, so long as the government has not granted a fee patent to the allotee.[106]

"Trust land" is, therefore, land (or an interest in land) which is held between the United States as legal owner and the Native tribe or individual as equitable owner. "Restricted lands" are theoretically distinguished from trust lands, because both the legal and equitable title are held by the Native owner; however, the ability of the owner or others to affect the title is restricted by federal statutes and regulations.[107] In most circumstances, the U.S. Supreme Court has found the distinction between trust and restricted title to be unimportant in determining the benefits and burdens imposed on restricted or trust lands.

One leading case held that administrative practice and congressional appropriations supporting it required the probate of both trust and restricted allotments to be determined by the Secretary of the Interior;[108] two later cases held that Oklahoma's estate tax could be imposed alike on restricted[109] and trust lands.[110] In determining federal obligations over Native lands, the Supreme Court has generally relied on the specific statute or regulation at issue rather than abstract ideas of restriction and trust;[111] In most cases, the practical outcome is similar for both trust and restricted property;[112] nevertheless, some statutes imply that trust lands might be afforded more protection than restricted lands.[113] Other statutes, however, may afford more flexibility to restricted property owners in dealings with their land.[114]

2. Restricted Status in Alaska

a. General

For seventy-five years the Interior Department officially interpreted the Alaska Allotment Act to authorize trust allotments only.[115] Then in 1980, the IBLA overruled the department's earlier precedent and held that Alaska Native allotments were held in restricted title.[116] The basis for the decision was the actual language of the documents which conveyed allotments as "the homestead of the allottee and his heirs in perpetuity." The IBLA also relied on an Interior Department regulation[117] which, pursuant to the 1956 amendments to the allotment act, authorized the *allottee*, with the approval of the Secretary of the Interior, to convey the *complete title* to the land by deed to another free of any restrictions against alienation and taxation. Since the allottee was authorized to convey the full title and since the department appeared to convey a "homestead" to the "allottee and his heirs in perpetuity," the IBLA concluded that the allottee also held the legal title to the allotment, subject to statutory restrictions against alienation and taxation.[118]

b. Fee Patent Issue

The 1980 IBLA decision had one immediate and positive result; it permitted Alaska Native allottees to obtain fee patents to their allotments in their own names. Originally the 1906 allotment act prohibited any sale or transfer of an Alaska allotment other than by inheritance, but the 1956 amendments did permit Natives to sell their allotments with the approval of the Secretary of the Interior.[119] If the sale was to a non-Native, the effect was to remove the restrictions against alienation and taxation, but there was no legal authority for an Alaska Native to have the restrictions removed without selling the land. The only authority which could be used in Alaska applied only to restricted allotments and permitted the Secretary of the Interior to remove restrictions against alienation by granting a "certificate of competency" upon the allottee's application.[120] Thus, redefining the status of Alaska allotments also redefined the Interior Department's ability to remove Alaskan allotment restrictions against alienation.[121]

c. Other Administrative Matters

Because most of the federal statutes dealing with the administration of allotments apply alike to restricted and trust allotments, Alaska allotments are subject to many of the same statutory protections and limitations imposed on allotments elsewhere. For example, the general right-of-way,[122] probate[123] and leasing[124] statutes are all applicable to Alaska allotments. Similarly, the provisions of law imposing restrictions on taxation and alienation on fee lands purchased with the proceeds from the sale of nontaxable restricted lands, have also been held to apply to pro ceeds from Alaska Native allotments.[125] So Alaska Natives can sell their allotments and reinvest the proceeds in unrestricted, taxable lands which will then become restricted and tax exempt. In general, administrative determinations tend to clarify the legal status of Alaska Native allotments and to treat them in all significant respects as other restricted Native American lands are treated elsewhere.[126]

E. Allotment Administration

1. Generally

The Bureaus of Land Management (BLM) and Indian Affairs (BIA) are the two agencies within the Interior Department responsible for the administration of the Alaska Native Allotment Act. The BLM is primarily responsible for adjudicating the applicant's entitlement to an allotment, while the BIA is responsible for administering the land after it is conveyed to the Native and so long as it remains in restricted status. The legislative approval of many allotments under ANILCA will, in the long run, significantly reduce the BLM's adjudicative role while at the same time substantially increase the BIA's responsibilities.

Initial processing of an allotment application begins with the BIA's certification of the application, but investigation, adjudication, survey and conveyance of the allotment are the BLM's responsibility. Though coexisting within the Department of the Interior, their differing statutory authorities and philosophies have frequently put the two bureaus in conflict with each other. One must manage all Indian affairs and matters arising from Indian relations,[127] while the other is charged with protecting more general government and public interests in federal lands.[128]

2. BLM's Role

a. Processing Allotment Applications

The allotment application was required by regulation to be filed with the appropriate Alaska BLM office having jurisdiction over the lands.[129] However, since the BIA also had to certify that the applicant was a Native and certain other matters,[130] the applications were frequently submitted to the BIA first for certification after which the BIA was to file the application with the BLM. Thereafter, the applicant or the BIA had six years to make "satisfactory proof" that the land had been used and occupied for a substantially continuous period of five years.[131] In the absence of clear physical evidence, this was typically a form or affidavit, completed by three persons knowledgeable of the facts, which was submitted by the BIA or the applicant's lawyer.

Once an application was filed with BLM, the agency adjudicated the applicant's entitlement to an allotment. It was this phase of the administrative process which section 905 of ANILCA eliminated for all those allotments qualified for legislative approval. BLM, of course, still has the task of determining which allotments were legislatively approved. Allotment applications not legislatively approved under ANILCA are adjudicated according to BLM's regulations and procedures described below.

On receipt, the application is referred to "preadjudication" for serialization and preliminary examination to insure all qualifications have been met. If deficient, the application is returned to the BIA or the applicant for curative action. An accepted form is submitted to the Alaska BLM's land records department to be noted on the public lands status plats, thereby providing public notice of the segregation. This makes the occupied plot unavailable for subsequent application (except for State of Alaska or ANCSA corporation top filing). [132]

During preadjudication, the status of the land is reviewed to determine if, as required by the 1956 amendments, the land is "vacant, unappropriated and unreserved"; [133] although, under ANILCA this requirement is eliminated or modified for lands within the NPRA or a powersite withdrawal. Under the long-standing regulations and current court decisions, adjudicated allotment applicants must satisfy a five-year use and occupancy requirement either prior to or subsequent to application. [134] Furthermore, in order to establish a preference right to state land selections, the applicant must demonstrate that occupancy began some time prior to the date of the state's selection application. [135] Applications within most federal withdrawals must also be for occupancy commenced prior to the withdrawal. [136] Applications are no longer subject to screening to determine if they are valuable for minerals unless they were so determined within the 180 day time limits of section 905(a)(3) of ANILCA.

After preadjudication, the application is scheduled for a field examination. A field examination may also be scheduled for allotments approved under ANILCA as a means of checking boundaries prior to survey. Thirty days before the examination, the applicant and appropriate ANCSA corporations are notified. The applicant or his designee is requested to accompany the examiner, and interpreters are used if there is a language barrier. BLM realty specialists are responsible for doing the field examination and preparing a report of their findings. One of the principal problems facing a realty specialist is verifying use and occupancy where the land is often covered by snow over half the year and the claimed use of fishing, hunting or berry picking leaves little or no physical evidence of occupation. Frequently, under these circumstances, witness verification of the applicant's use and occupancy is the only possible proof.

The results of the field examination are reported to the BLM's land law examiners who, in a process called "final adjudication", make a preliminary finding of acceptance or rejection of the claim. If the application is rejected, the applicant has thirty days to appeal the decision and is entitled to a hearing if there are factual issues in dispute.[137] If the allotment is granted, the applicant receives an "administrative approval" of his application pending a land survey. The survey (which can take many years to work into BLM's survey schedule) establishes the legal boundries of the allotment. After survey, the BLM issues a conveyance instrument called a "Native Allotment" which, as provided in the allotment act, grants the "allottee and his heirs" a "homestead...in perpetuity" which is restricted against taxation or alienation.[138]

b. Erroneously Conveyed Allotments

Owing to the uncertainty of Native use and occupancy and shifting allotment policies, lands have sometimes been mistakenly conveyed to another—usually the State of Alaska. Unfortunately for the allotment applicant, it is also well-established that once the Interior Department conveys land it loses all jurisdiction to retract the conveyance, even if the conveyance was due to fraud or mistake.[139] Under this doctrine, a federal lawsuit brought by the United States is the only way to cancel the erroneous patent and recover the land.

It was against this background in 1976 that Ethel Aguilar, on behalf of herself and other Alaska Natives, sought to compel the United States to recover the land she had applied for but which had been patented to the State of Alaska. The United States contended that it had no jurisdiction to recover the land, but the Alaska Federal District Court held that since Natives had a preference right under the allotment act to lands they used and occupied, the United States had a trust responsibility to investigate the legitimacy of her claim. If her claim to the land could be established, the court held that the United States also had an obligation to bring a lawsuit to recover the land.[140]

In early 1983, the representatives of the allotment applicants and the United States stipulated to court approved procedures requiring the government to investigate erroneously conveyed allotments.[141] Under these procedures, the Alaska BLM office is required to review all allotment applications on lands conveyed to the state. If an application is determined to be legally defective, then it will be rejected without an administrative hearing. However, if it is found defective for some factual reason (e.g., failure to establish use and occupancy), then the BLM must schedule a hearing for the applicant and any other party which might be adversely affected by the applicant's claim. If the application is found valid (either with or without a hearing), then the case will be referred to the U.S. Department of Justice, which has the final administrative decision of whether to bring a lawsuit to cancel the erroneous patent.

3. BIA's Role

a. General

Most BIA responsibilities in Alaska are directed through the Juneau Area Office, headed by an area director. The Juneau Area Office is composed of several functional divisions, branches and offices, among them one responsible for the BIA's realty program.[142] The area office realty staff typically includes a director, one or more realty specialists, a land law examiner and an appraiser as well as secretarial support. The area realty staff insures that all regulations and laws have been followed by reviewing virtually every action taken at lower bureaucratic levels. All papers requiring approval or a decision by the area director are funneled through the area realty staff. Additionally, the area office interacts with other government agencies (e.g., BLM, Housing and Urban Development, or Economic Development Administration) when it comes to other land related federal Native programs in Alaska.

Local BIA realty programs are currently located in five agency offices located in Juneau, Anchorage, Fairbanks, Bethel and Nome. These agencies are charged with directly assisting the BIA's Native clientele and are headed by superintendents who are assisted by realty officers and specialists. When necessary, the area office assists the agency realty staffs with appraisals, training and the like. In all agencies some or all of the agency realty program has now been contracted out to regional tribal organizations under the Indian Self-Determination Act (P.L. 93-638).[143]

Thus, the BIA agency office or a tribal contractor is typically the first point of contact for a Native allottee with a question related to the administration of allotted land. The agency or contractor provides counseling and advice regarding sales, leases or grants of rights-of-way related to allotments and also investigates all trespass claims.[144] However, the actual responsibility for approving a sale or lease or granting a right-of-way generally remains with the area director and is not contractible to a tribal organization.[145] Unlike most other area offices, however, the Juneau Area Office does not maintain land records relating to Alaska Native allotments. This role has been delegated to the agencies, but in actual practice the BIA has always used the Alaska state recording system to record the titles of Native allotments.[146]

b. Pending and Approved Allotments

For many years there was substantial confusion about BIA authority over applied for allotments, because the land was theoretically under the BLM's jurisdiction until it was actually conveyed to an allottee. Upon the filing of an allotment application, the BLM characterized the allotment as "pending"; upon administrative approval it was termed an "approved" allotment; and upon conveyance it became "certified." For many years the lands covered by the allotment application were considered to be within the BLM's jurisdiction so long as the application was either pending or approved. That turned out to have sometimes serious consequences for the allotment applicant, even though the Interior Department had an obligation to protect Alaska Native use and occupancy. [147]

Although the practice has now been discontinued, pending and approved Alaska allotments were sometimes treated like public lands, especially when it came to federal executive actions affecting those lands. [148] Thus, there are reports that the BLM has permitted the extraction of sand and gravel from pending allotments even though the practice seems to be prohibited under BLM's regulations. [149] Similarly, rights-of-way on "Indian lands" are to be granted only by the BIA, [150] but "Indian lands" is nowhere clearly defined to mean pending or approved Alaska Native allotments.

The situation became more acute during the construction of the Transalaska Pipeline in the mid-1970's. Oil companies, working against construction deadlines, sometimes needed to acquire rights-of-way across pending or approved Native allotments, but it was not clear whether a grant only from the BLM would protect the companies against later claims of trespass once the land was conveyed to the Native applicant. The companies resorted to a hybrid procedure involving a right-of-way grant from the allotment applicant with the "non-objection" of the BIA. In at least one such case, the practice resulted in prolonged litigation when the allottee refused to consent to the right-of-way after he received conveyance of the allotment. [151]

The impasse was at least partially resolved in 1979 by a memorandum of understanding (MOU) between the BLM State Director and the BIA Area Director, spelling out their respective agencies' responsibilities over pending and approved allotments. [152] Under the terms of the MOU, BIA is to have full authority over approved allotments to grant less than fee interests (e.i., sales were not originally permitted) and to protect against trespass. Both agencies are to coordinate the granting of less than fee interests on pending allotments, but the BLM retains trespass abatement authority on these lands. [153] The Assistant Stcretary for Indian Affairs has subsequently determined that approved allotments can also be sold under BIA procedures prior to survey. [154]

III. Native Townsites

A. Townsite Administration

Like the 1906 allotment act, the 1926 Alaska Native Townsite Act (ANTA)[155] provided an opportunity for individual Alaska Natives to obtain "title" to lands in the public domain. [156] However, federal administration of the townsite act has been plagued by bureaucratic and statutory confusion. Initially, the Interior Department may have assumed that section 3 was a separate scheme for the establishment of exclusively Native towns,[157] but in 1938 it adopted a regulation permitting non-Natives to get townsite deeds in Native villages as well.[158] From at least 1938 to 1959, ANTA townsites appear to have been administered in substantially the same way and according to the same regulations as townsites under the 1891 act, which granted citizens (usually non-Natives) the right to establish townsites in Alaska.[159]

Under the 1891 townsite act,[160] the Secretary of the Interior was required to name a trustee to designate public lands in Alaska as townsites for the "several use and benefit" of townsite occupants. According to the published regulations, the occupants of a proposed townsite applied for the BLM State Director to survey the town's exterior boundaries.[161] Once the exterior boundaries were surveyed, the residents petitioned the Secretary of the Interior to designate a trustee to supervise the subdivision of the townsite.[162] The federal government then issued the trustee a patent for the proposed townsite land, thereby permitting the trustee to "enter" those lands and withdraw them from the public domain.[163] As a matter of practice, the original occupants then obtained a subdivisional survey for the occupied portion of the townsite and deeds to their individual lots within the subdivided plat. The townsite trustee held any remaining unsubdivided lands in trust for future occupants until such time as they might petition to have the land subdivided into lots.

The costs of subdividing (i.e., survey) were prorated against the lots, and right of occupancy was determined as of the date of the subdivisional survey.[164] After paying the assessed fees, the occupants of each lot received their deeds from the trustee, and the unoccupied lots were sold at public auction. Any remaining unsold lots were deeded to the municipality. Because the first subdivision did not usually use up all the unsubdivided land in the townsite, the trustee would repeat the process for the unsubdivided lands until the whole townsite was subdivided and all the lots either individually acquired or deeded to the municipality.[165] When that was accomplished, the trustee could close out his trust.

Section 4 of ANTA[166] permitted the secretary to adopt regulations to implement the act, but except for deed applications and fee payments, he adopted no such regulations. Instead, he applied the procedures used under the 1891 act to the establishment and disposition of Native townsites.[167] These procedures made no clear distinction between Natives and non-Natives in townsite administration. Prior to 1959, it was possible for both Natives and non-Natives to be deeded lots within the subdivided portion and to occupy land in the unsubdivided portion of the same townsite. Under pre-1959 townsite administration, the major differences between Natives and non-Natives were that Natives were not required to pay survey fees and were issued a deed which restricted their ability to convey their property. The property was also statutorily protected from taxation, execution on a debt or contract, liabilities of the patentee and claims of adverse occupancy or prescription.[168] If a lot was vacant after subdivision, the trustee prior to 1959 could either sell it at auction or, if the municipality had a corporate charter, deed it to the municipality. Vacant, subdivided lots could not be simply occupied by individuals after the date of the subdivision.

Then in 1959, the Interior Solicitor issued the first of the so-called *Saxman* opinions.[169] The opinion stated that section 3 of the 1926 act authorized the trustee to convey vacant subdivided lots of a Native townsite only to *Natives*. The trustee was prohibited from disposing of any vacant Native townsite lots "to white purchasers by competitive bidding...or otherwise."[170] A subsequent opinion prohibited the trustee from conveying unoccupied Native townsite lots to the municipality as well.[171]

These opinions had the practical effect of protecting predominantly Native communities from non-Native encroachment. The townsite trustee had no alternative but to retain unoccupied lots in trust until they could be occupied and deeded to individual Natives.[172] Inconsistently, however, the trustee still permitted both Natives and non-Natives to occupy vacant *unsubdivided* land within the exterior townsite boundaries.[173]

The trustee's authority to permit non-Natives to occupy the unsubdivided portion of a Native townsite was finally challenged in 1974 by the predominately Native City of Klawock. In *Klawock v. Gustafson,* the Alaska Federal District Court affirmed the right of non-Natives to occupy unsubdivided lands and went on to overrule the reasoning of the *Saxman* opinions and held:

> There is no basis in the statute or legislative history for special treatment of townsites that are predominantly Native beyond the statutory provision for restricted deeds and prohibitions of charges for liens on Native-owned lots for the owner's debts.[174]

The *Klawock* decision required that administration of Native townsites be according to the methods used prior to the *Saxman* opinions. Following the decision, however, the pressure by non-Natives on Native communities became even greater. In 1976 the unsubdivided townsite lands were the only federal lands in Alaska then available merely for the cost of occupying and improving them.[175] This made them especially attractive in light of the then expanding non-Native population and an acute shortage of available land.

ANCSA did not clearly resolve the status of unoccupied land in pending Native townsites in Native communities. Section 14(c) of ANCSA[176] provides an alternative means for municipalities and individuals to acquire lands in villages. However, some 106 townsites established under ANTA were not clearly eliminated either by ANCSA or the subsequent repeal of the Native Townsite Act in 1976 by the Federal Land Policy Management Act (FLPMA).[177] The federal townsite trustee administers the ANTA townsites and a state trustee administers the ANCSA municipal lands; often these include lands in the same villages. Non- Natives may still be able to establish new occupancy rights under ANTA on the same types of lands for which ANCSA supposedly prohibited occupancy rights as of December 18, 1971. These problems add confusion to the ANCSA settlement and create conflict over lands within the core of many ANCSA villages, all of which seems inconsistent with the general intent of the claims settlement.

This background raises the major questions surrounding "townsite" administration in Alaska. Specifically, these include:

1. The nature of federal obligations to Natives under ANTA.

2. Native occupancy rights under ANTA.

3. The effect of ANCSA and FLPMA on ANTA.

B. Federal Obligations

1. Two Agencies

Similar to the administration of allotments, federal administration of the 1926 townsite act is divided between the two federal agencies, BLM and BIA. The BLM employs the townsite trustee who is responsible for withdrawing, surveying and deeding townsite lands. The BIA area director, along with area and agency realty staff, handles land management matters for the Native owners of restricted townsite lots. Although both the townsite trustee and the BIA have "trust" responsibilities toward the Native occupants, these responsibilities appear legally different in kind.

2. Townsite Trustee's Obligations

Under current judicial interpretation, the townsite trustee is a federal employee who holds land in trust for Native and non-Native "inhabitants"[178] of a particular townsite. Until he issues a deed to each townsite occupant, he holds the legal title to property in which the occupant has an equitable interest, but at least after the *Klawock* decision his trust responsibilities do not appear to include protection of predominately Native towns from non-Native residence and ownership of land. On the other hand, he has been held to "strict fiduciary standards" in implementing ANTA for individual Native benefit. [179]

The trustee's role relates bact to an 1867 "lower forty-eight" townsite act[180] which provided that a county judge could hold townsite land in trust, do the survey and establish the rights of occupants. Presumably because there were no "county judges" in Alaska, Congress permitted the Secretary of the Interior to appoint a trustee to administer the 1891 Alaska Townsite Act. Although the secretary initially appointed private citizens to the trusteeship, in time the townsite trustee became a federal employee.

Under the 1891 act, the trustee was specifically required to approximate the procedures of the 1867 act "as near as may be" and to reach:

The same results...as though the entry had been made by a county judge and the disposal of lots in such townsite and the proceeds of the sale thereof had been prescribed by the legislative authority of a State or Territory. [181]

Because Natives were excluded from the 1891 act, Congress enacted the 1926 Native Townsite Act. The *Saxman* opinions indicated that the trustee had more responsibilities for Native townsites than for non-Native townsites, because he had to hold vacant subdivided lots until settled on by Natives. [182] As previously discussed, the implication from the *Saxman* opinions was that the trustee had an obligation to protect Native townsites from non-Native encroachment; however the *Klawock* decision overruled the *Saxman* opinions. [183] Unless there is a different legal interpretation in the future, there can be only one conclusion. ANTA does not require the townsite trustee to protect Native townsites from non-Native encroachment, [184] but it does require careful administration of ANTA to benefit Native occupants of townsites. [185]

3. The BIA's Obligations

It is important to recall that under the 1926 townsite act a Native occupant received a "deed" or "patent" to the occupied lot. This language indicates that the Native occupant received full legal and equitable title to his or her approved lot (subject to certain restrictions). As noted earlier, the difference between the legal and equitable (beneficial) title to property is the distinguishing feature of a property-related trust responsibility. [186] Because townsite lots are deeded to the occupant, they convey full title and therefore do not establish a federal-Native "trust responsibility" in the narrow sense of the term. That does not mean the federal government, particularly the BIA, cannot have other equally binding obligations to Alaska Native townsite owners. It can and it does.

These obligations arise in part because Native townsite deeds normally are restricted to prevent the owner from selling the lot. Prior to 1948, all Native townsite deeds were inalienable except on approval of the Interior Secretary; then ANTA was amended to permit the owner to obtain an unrestricted deed by petitioning the secretary for a determination that the owner was competent to manage his or her own affairs. [187] Initially, the Interior Department required that any proposed sale of Native townsite property be reviewed by the Commissioner of Indian Affairs, [188] but current regulations require only the BIA Area Director's approval for sale of restricted townsite lots [189] or issuance of unrestricted deeds. [190] These restrictions, necessitated by the statutory inalienability of the land, quite naturally require Native owners of restricted lands to rely on the BIA for advice in the sale or other disposition of their lands.

Moreover, as restricted lands, Native townsite lots are afforded a variety of BIA services under a number of specific federal statutes and regulations applicable to restricted Indian lands.[191]

The necessity for these services appears founded on the statutory requirement that the townsite remain inalienable.[192] Moreover, Native reliance on the services probably creates enforceable federal obligations even though there is no "trust responsibility" arising out of the restrictions on the property alone. At least so long as the BIA provides these services or obtains congressional funding to do so, it has an obligation to provide the services equally to all owners of inalienable townsites.[193] It is also clear that the federal obligations arising out of specific statutes authorizing these services are "fiduciary obligations" in the strict sense.[194]

C. Issues in Townsite Administration

1. Introduction

The issues inherent in the administration of the 1926 Alaska Native Townsite Act remained virtually dormant until the mid-1970's. Then with the implementation of ANCSA and increased attention to village land rights there came an explosion of litigation. Although there are several lawsuits, there are two main issues: (1) whether ANTA permits only Native occupancy and (2) the effect of ANCSA and FLPMA on ANTA.

2. Native Occupancy Rights

a. General

Recall that Alaska Native occupancy rights were theoretically protected from encroachment by section 8 of the 1884 Organic Act, but the terms under which Natives could acquire title to the lands they occupied were "reserved for future legislation by Congress."[195] Initially, the Interior Department permitted Natives to acquire townsite lands under the 1891 Townsite Act,[196] but subsequent Interior Department decisions prohibited lands occupied by Natives from being included in lands withdrawn as townsites under the 1891 act.[197] Subsequent regulations adopted in 1904 again permitted both Natives and whites to acquire lands under the 1891 act,[198] but these too were amended in 1908 to preclude Natives from acquiring title.[199] In doing so the Interior Department concluded that the 1884 Organic Act was intended to protect Native occupancy rights by retaining title to the land in government ownership. Permitting Natives to acquire title under the 1891 act would have given them unencumbered title and was held to be contrary to the usual policy of restricting the sale of Native owned lands.[200]

As discussed earlier, section 1 of ANTA permitted Natives living in predominately white towns to acquire title to Native occupied lands, while section 3 permitted the Interior Secretary to withdraw lands "oc-cupied by...Natives of Alaska, as a town or village" which the townsite trustee was then to convey to the individual Native occupants.[201] Thus ANTA permitted Natives living in white communities to acquire townsite lots by restricted deed and arguably permitted the setting aside of other lands exclusively for Native communities. However, from 1938 to 1959 townsites were administered similarly under both sections of the 1926 act.[202] The so-called *Saxman* opinions changed these procedures in 1959 and seemed to require that lands administered under section 3 be held exclusively for Native occupancy.[203] Then in 1976 the *Saxman* opinions were judicially reversed, and all the ANTA townsites were seemingly opened to non-Native occupancy.[204] ANCSA and the 1976 repeal of the townsite act both cast doubt on this conclusion.

b. The *Saxman* Opinions

Recall that under the usual requirements of Alaska townsite admin-istration, the residents of the proposed townsite would petition for a townsite. The lands for the townsite were then withdrawn, surveyed and patented to the trustee. Occupants would then petition for a subdivisional survey of their lots and would receive deeds for lots based on the survey. When the lands were subdivided, there would usually be lots within each subdivision which were not occupied. The regulations permitted such lots to be sold either to the highest bidder or for "fair value" to a govern-ment agency; any lots remaining could be deeded to the municipality. Typically in Alaska, not all of the lands withdrawn would be surveyed; those that were not remained "unsubdivided" until future occupants petitioned for a survey. Until 1959, these were the procedures used to administer both Native and non-Native townsites.[205]

The first *Saxman* opinion concluded that section 3 of the 1926 act required the trustee to dispose of the lots "to *Native* occupants of a *Na-tive* town or village" (emphasis added), which precluded sales of unoc-cupied, subdivided lands in Native townsites to non-Natives by competi-tive bid. The opinion implied further that the trustee could fulfill the trust by deeding the lands in the subdivided portion to Natives whose occu-pancy began *after* the subdivisional survey.[206] Although the *Saxman* opin-ion suggested that the townsite regulations ought to be revised to reflect its conclusions, the regulations were never revised. A subsequent sol-icitor's opinion concluded on the basis of the *Saxman* opinion that unoc-cupied subdivided lands in Native townsites could not be deeded to municipalities either.[207] Thus, under the *Saxman* opinions, subdivided lots in Native townsites could be disposed of only to individual Native oc-cupants.

c. *Klawock v. Gustafson.*

The *Saxman* opinions limited the trustee's options when it came to disposition of the subdivided lots, but the trustee apparently interpreted them not to prohibit non-Native occupancy of the unsubdivided portion of a Native townsite. Non-Natives occupying such lands could then request a subdivisional survey and receive deeds to the lands they occupied, thus establishing non-Native occupancy of what under the rationale of the *Saxman* opinions were lands supposedly held for exclusive Native occupancy. The situation came to a head in the southeast Alaskan Native community of Klawock. The State of Alaska and individual non-Natives had occupied parcels in the unsubdivided portion of the Klawock townsite and constructed substantial improvements. Following subdivisional survey, the occupants applied for and were awarded deeds over the protests of the City of Klawock, which claimed, among other things, that under section 3 of ANTA only Natives could occupy lands in Native townsites.

The city appealed the trustee's award of the deeds administratively, but lost;[208] on judicial review, the Alaska Federal District Court rejected the reasoning of the *Saxman* opinions and concluded that the "Native" townsites administered under section 3 of ANTA were to be administered according to the same regulations as non-Native townsites under the 1891 act. In reaching its decision the court concluded that the 1926 act:

> was primarily concerned not with establishing Native towns, but with issuing deeds to individual Alaskan Natives for the parcels they occupied within townsites on federal land in Alaska.[209]

d. Effects of *Klawock v. Gustafson*

Like a stone dropped into a quiet pool, *Klawock v. Gustafson* has sent ripples to the far shores of Alaska townsite administration. First, by overruling the *Saxman* opinions, it cast doubt on the land rights of individuals who commenced occupancy after subdivisional survey. Second, it affirmed at least initially, the right of non-Natives to establish occupancy on unsubdivided lands in Native townsites. Third, it was interpreted administratively to permit municipalities in Native townsites to acquire unoccupied subdivided and (later) unsubdivided lands. This administrative interpretation led to a successful claim for attorney fees by Klawock's lawyers to which all Native townsites in the state had to contribute.

i. Native Occupancy After Subdivision

Under the townsite regulations, the date of the subdivisional survey is the crucial date for the determination of an occupant's claim to a lot.[210] Under the first *Saxman* opinion, however, Natives could establish occupancy after the subdivisional survey. In rejecting this aspect of the *Saxman* opinion, the *Klawock* decision implies that Native occupants after the subdivision who have not received their deeds may never receive them. Since there were no such occupants before the court, they were not considered in the decision and their status is in doubt.

ii. Non-Native Occupancy

At the time of the *Klawock* decision (1976) there was relatively little land available in Alaska which people could acquire merely by occupying it. Most lands were tied-up by ANCSA or state selections or the national and public interest withdrawals under sections 17(d)(1) and (2) of ANCSA. The court's decision kept open some sixty-four hundred acres[211] of unsubdivided townsite lands for acquisition by occupancy. The seeming availability of these lands for inexpensive settlement resulted in a non-Native land rush of fairly serious proportions in once isolated, culturally homogeneous villages.[212] Subsequently, the Interior Department's Alaska Regional Solicitor concluded that the Federal Land Policy Management Act (FLPMA), which repealed ANTA some 21 days before the *Klawock* decision, also prevented new occupancy of unsubdivided townsite lands.[213] In 1983, the issue was still in litigation.[214]

iii. Municipal Land Rights

Following the *Klawock* decision, the Interior Department was asked again to examine the right of a municipality to lands under the 1926 act. In 1977 the Interior Department's Alaska Regional Solicitor concluded that since the proceeds of any sale of subdivided lots went to the municipality, the municipality could, in effect, outbid any purchaser.[215] The townsite trustee subsequently advised occupants of unsubdivided lands that unless their occupancy predated the 1976 repeal of the 1926 act, the municipalities would be entitled to receive all the unsubdivided lands as well.[216] The entitlement of the municipalities to the unoccupied, subdivided lands seems clear,[217] but it is less clear as to the unsubdivided lands.[218]

iv. Attorney Fees

One of the truly unanticipated results of the *Klawock* decision was that every Native townsite in the state was required to contribute a portion of the value of the lands within each townsite to the payment of the City of Klawock's attorney's fees. The federal appeals court held that as a direct result of the lawsuit each Native community became entitled to lands to which they were not previously entitled under the *Saxman* opinions. Since each of these communities benefited from the efforts of the attorneys on behalf of Klawock, the court held that the lands the communities were to receive constituted a "common fund" for the payment of the attorney fees.[219] Ultimately the federal district court confirmed an award of $176,000 in fees which the affected communities paid in proportion to the amount of land they were due to receive as a result of the *Klawock* litigation.[220]

3. Effects of ANCSA and FLPMA

a. General

The Alaska Native Claims Settlement Act (ANCSA)[221] and the Federal Land Policy Management Act (FLPMA)[222] are unrelated statutes, but both have been claimed to affect the scope of rights under ANTA. Read one way, ANCSA can be interpreted to withdraw for ANCSA corporation selection unsubdivided ANTA townsite lands located in Native villages. FLPMA, on the other hand, specifically repealed ANTA on October 21, 1976, but it is not yet clear what effect the repeal had on persons who attempted to establish townsite occupancy on unsubdivided lands after the date of repeal. Since the effects of both ANCSA and FLPMA are "subject to valid existing rights," whether and under what circumstances the federal townsites constitute such rights has become the focus of the debate. In addition to these issues, ANCSA also established a separate scheme of municipal land entitlements and townsite administration which went beyond the federal townsite laws.

b. ANCSA

Among other things, secton 11(a)(1) of ANCSA automatically withdraws for ANCSA corporation selection all "public lands" within the "core" township(s) enclosing a Native village.[223] "Public lands" are defined in ANCSA to mean "all Federal lands and interests therein" in Alaska,[224] which might well include land withdrawn for townsites but not yet subdivided or occupied by individuals. The Ninth Circuit Court of Appeals has held that this might be sufficient to automatically withdraw for ANCSA selection all vacant, unsubdivided townsite lands.[225] If this interpretation is correct, it means that the unoccupied, unsubdivided lands in the core townships will have to be conveyed to Native corporations under ANCSA instead of to individuals or municipalities under ANTA.

However, the ANCSA 11(a)(1) withdrawals are all "subject to valid existing rights;" therefore, the question is at what point the rights of the townsite trustee and the townsite occupants and the municipality become "valid" as to the ANCSA withdrawals. It is generally assumed that if the rights were "vested" before December 18, 1971, then they were both "valid" and "existing" at the time ANCSA became law. Given the procedures for administering the townsites, however, it is not at all clear whose rights were vested and when. For example, it can be argued that a community's application for a townsite segregates the entire tract applied for and establishes a vested right in the individuals and the community to eventually receive it.[226] One unreported decision of the Alaska Federal District Court has gone so far as to uphold the claim of the City of Barrow to unoccupied, subdivided townsite lands as a "valid existing right" predating the ANCSA withdrawals,[227] but merely surveying the land and patenting it to the townsite trustee might also vest such rights.[228] On the other hand, it can also be argued that there are no vested rights prior to occupancy and a subdivisional survey of occupied lots.[229] If that is true, then there may be no "valid existing rights" to lands which were unoccupied and unsubdivided on December 18, 1971. As of mid-1983, these issues were in some stage of litigation in at least two cases.[230]

c. FLPMA

Section 703(a) of FLPMA specifically repeals the townsite provisions of both the 1891 and 1926 acts, but section 701 prevents termination of any "land use right or authorization" and preserves all land "withdrawals, reservations, classifications and designations" in effect as of the date of the repeal. It has been held administratively that the effect of the repeal was to prevent all new occupancy of townsite lands after October 21, 1976.[231] On the other hand, it can also be argued that repeal of the townsite laws only prevents the establishment of new townsites, but does not affect the administration of already existing ones.[232] This issue is also in litigation.[233]

d. ANCSA Municipal Lands

Section 14(c) of ANCSA appears to be an alternative to the subsequently repealed Alaska townsite laws. As now amended, it requires each village corporation to deed to local residents, businesses and nonprofit organizations the surface estate of those village lands they occupied as of December 18, 1971.[234] As originally enacted, a minimum of 1,280 acres of the remaining surface estate also had to be conveyed to the incorporated municipality or to the state in trust for any future municipality, but 1980 amendments to ANCSA now permit village corporations to negotiate lower municipal grants with the state or affected municipalities.[235]

These provisions permit more flexibility in the administration of municipal lands than is possible under the Alaska townsite laws, but they may also impose yet another bureaucratic layer on those unincorporated communities in townsites administered by the federal townsite trustee. As things now stand in these communities, the federal townsite trustee will continue to administer the unoccupied or unsubdivided lands until the entire townsite is subdivided and all the unoccupied lands are either sold or deeded to a yet to be formed municipality.[236] In the meantime, the state municipal lands trustee will also administer the lands reserved for municipal purposes under 14(c) of ANCSA. Of the two schemes, ANCSA is more flexible, because the state trustee, in consultation with the community, has better control over new occupancy and land use.

The federal trustee, in contrast, is limited by regulations which only permit him to award lots based on occupancy, sell unoccupied, subdivided lands and deed unoccupied lands to incorporated municipalities. Depending on the outcome of pending litigation, these limitations could stymie any coordinated community planning with continued piecemeal subdivisions of land and uncontrolled occupancy tied only to the date of the next subdivisional survey. If, for example, the townsite trustee is determined to have continuing authority to administer townsites even after ANTA's 1976 repeal, incorporated communities wishing to plan for rational land use may find themselves responding instead to the demands of land speculators and the haphazard occupancy of those who wish to stake their claim to an acre of rural Alaska. Congress repealed ANTA because ANCSA had made it "obsolete," but as discussed above, it is not at all clear that the repeal resolved any of the problems associated with the old act.[237] Perhaps the continuing lawsuits will.

4. Miscellaneous Issues

There are numerous opportunities for error in any procedurally complex, bureaucratic land withdrawal and conveyance scheme. The 1926 townsite act is no exception. In at least one instance too much land was identified for possible inclusion in a townsite and erroneously patented to the townsite trustee. Although the trustee protested the error, procedures were perhaps not then available to correct the patent. Individuals occupied the excess lands and an ANCSA village corporation also selected it. When petitioned to subdivide the land and deed the lots, the trustee refused. On appeal, the IBLA concluded that the excess lands had not even been included in the survey of the designated "townsite" and had therefore been erroneously patented to the trustee. The occupant's claims were rejected and the village land selection affirmed.[238]

It has also been held, however, that the trustee has a fiduciary obligation to administer ANTA for the benefit of Native occupants of townsite lots. The responsibility is based in part on the restricted status of the lands conveyed to Natives under the act as well as the general special responsibility of the federal government to Natives.[239] The precise responsibilities of the trustee are likely to depend on the facts of any particular case, but it seems likely to include a duty to take special care to ensure that those claiming occupancy of Native townsite lots are in fact the persons entitled to them.

IV. Jurisdictional Issues

A. General

The restricted titles of Alaska Native allotments and townsite lots carry certain jurisdictional implications with them. First, they are subject to certain federal statutes applicable to restricted lands governing probate and the granting of rights of way, leases and similar interests. These effectively preclude state courts from exercising jurisdiction to decide disputes arising over these matters on allotment and townsite lands. Other federal statutes grant special authority to the federal courts to adjudicate disputes about allotment entitlements and specifically preclude state jurisdiction. Nontheless, these jurisdictional niceties are sometimes not fully appreciated in Alaska; this has led to litigation testing the precise scope of state authority on a variety of issues.

B. Federal Court Jurisdiction

The federal courts have exclusive jurisdiction under 25 USCA 345 and 346[240] to adjudicate "the right of any person, in whole or in part of Indian blood or descent, to any allotment of land under any law or treaty." In all such suits the United States must be named initially as a defendant,[241] but others may be named also,[242] and it has been held that the statute affords jurisdiction to decide disputes involving both the issuance of allotments and the interests of Natives in their allotments after they are acquired.[243] The statute applies to both trust and restricted lands[244] and has been applied to Alaska townsite and allotment lands in several circumstances.[245]

Prior to the enactment of this statute neither state nor federal courts had jurisdiction over allotment disputes. The United States was an indispensable party to most such disputes because of the trust or restricted status of the allotted lands, but had not waived its immunity from suit, so it was impossible for a court to acquire jurisdiction over all the parties necessary to resolve most allotment disputes. Only the Secretary of the Interior had authority to resolve such disputes.[246] The statute is a limited waiver of federal sovereign immunity for federal jurisdictional purposes, but it does not permit state courts to adjudicate disputes involving the title, ownership or possession of an allotment.

C. Effect of P.L. 280

Under P.L. 280,[247] some states, including Alaska, now have general jurisdiction to adjudicate "causes of action" arising in "Indian country" (which includes allotments).[248] However, P.L. 280 itself excludes from such jurisdiction any authority to "adjudicate, in probate proceedings or otherwise, the ownership or right to possession of [trust or restricted] property or any interest therein." Moreover, nothing in P.L. 280 is intended to "authorize the alienation, encumbrance or taxation" of trust or restricted lands or the regulation of such lands in a manner "inconsistent with any Federal treaty, agreement, or statute or with any regulation made pursuant thereto."[249]

1. Civil Disputes

Thus, in the civil arena, P.L. 280 has been construed as a fairly limited grant of state jurisdiction only to *adjudicate* disputes,[250] and to preclude local taxation,[251] zoning or other regulation[252] of restricted Indian lands. The Alaska Supreme Court has also consistently interpreted P.L. 280 to prohibit state court adjudication of disputes involving restricted or trust property.[253] Nonetheless, disputes frequently arise about the jurisdiction of Alaska state courts over restricted allotment and townsite lands, particularly in domestic relations matters. In a typical divorce, the allottee's spouse will claim to have contributed during the marriage to the improvement of the allotted land. Under these circumstances (especially if there are children involved), the lower courts have attempted to indirectly apportion the benefit of the allotment between the parties.

For example, in one case the superior court ordered the allottee to will the allotment to the children of the marriage.[254] In another, ironically involving the same land, the court in effect ordered separate maintenance of the spouse and children on the allotment.[255] In yet another instance, the lower court ordered the "value" of the allotment included in the calculation of the property division.[256] No case presenting the question of the scope of Alaska state court jurisdiction to indirectly apportion the benefit of an allotment has yet been reported, but under the meager authority now available, it does not seem likely that a court would have such jurisdiction if it in any way authorized the "alienation [or] encumbrance" of the land or constituted an adjudicaiton of "ownership or right to possession...or any interest" in the allotment.[257]

2. Criminal Disputes

As applied to Alaska, P.L. 280 affords the state broad jurisdiction to enforce its criminal laws with the "same force and effect" within Indian country as elsewhere in the state.[258] As with civil jurisdiction, however, enforcement of criminal laws cannot authorize the "alienation, encumbrance or taxation" of trust or restricted property, nor may it become an excuse for the adjudication of "ownership or right ot possession...or any interest" in an Alaska allotment.[259] In practical terms, though, criminal prosecutions do not generally involve issues which will touch on any of those matters prohibited under P.L. 280, so the state's criminal jurisdiction of alloted and townsite lands is relatively unfettered.

One potential area of doubt, however, centers on the distinction between criminal (prohibitory) and regulatory (permissive) laws. It has been held, for example, that where gambling is permitted under state regulation, laws punishing gambling violations as crimes are not "criminal" for purposes of a state's P.L. 280 criminal jurisdiction.[260] As a result, tribes have been permitted to continue gambling operations in Indian country even though they did not comply with state regulations. Following this line of reasoning, it is possible to conclude that other regulatory schemes which impose "criminal" penalties may also be excluded from the state's P. L. 280 allotment and townsite jurisdiction. [261]

D. Probate

A comprehensive statutory scheme places the probate of restricted allotment and townsite lands, such as those found in Alaska, within the exclusive jurisdiction of the Secretary of the Interior. [262] A statute enacted in 1910 requires the secretary to determine the heirs of any allottee who dies intestate; the same statute also permits allottees to devise (bequeath) their restricted or trust lands by will, with the approval of the Secretary of the Interior. [263] Both provisions apply to restricted and trust lands, [264] and have been applied in Alaska for many years. [265] If there are no heirs, public domain allotments (such as those in Alaska) escheat (revert) to the United States. [266]

Restricted and trust lands are probated under Interior Department regulations promulgated under the authority of the 1910 act. [267] Under these regulations, the appropriate BIA agency superintendent acts as executor or administrator of the estate. [268] He initiates the probate by forwarding information about the estate to an administrative law judge. [269] The judge notifies interested parties, holds a hearing and determines the heirs, or devisees, as well as the disposition of creditors' claims and any attorneys' fees. [270] Any person "aggrieved" by the decision has sixty days to request a rehearing, [271] but all decisions of the IBIA are final for Board of Indian Appeals (IBIA). [272] The decisons of the IBIA are final for the Interior Department but may be reviewed in federal court. [273] Review of intestacy cases is limited to issues unrelated to the determination of heirs, because, under the 1910 act, the secretary's decision is "final and conclusive" on that point. [274] The scope of review is broader for testacy cases, and the secretary's discretion to disapprove a will is somewhat limited and also subject to judicial review. [275]

E. Federal Income Tax

Native Americans, like most United States residents are generally subject to the federal income tax, but the courts have carved out an exception for income "derived directly" from allotted lands. [276] Although that case arose on trust land held under the terms of the 1887 General Allotment Act, the lower courts and the Internal Revenue Service have applied the ruling generally to most allotments and to income traced "directly" to the land. [277] The exemption also applies to all types of income whether it is capital gains or ordinary income, but the exemption has been denied if the income is not derived from the land. Thus, the U.S. Supreme Court has held that the interest or other reinvestment income earned on tax exempt income is not itself exempt from tax. [278] Similarly, the lower courts have held that rental from cattle grazing on trust or restricted lands is not tax exempt, presumably because the tax had no direct effect on the land. [279] Somewhat analogously, the lower courts have held that income derived from improvements located on an allotment is not tax exempt. [280] The suggestion in these cases is that income from a business located on an allotment is separable from the income which could be allocated to the land alone. [281]

F. Condemnation

There is no general prohibition against federal condemnation of individual trust or restricted lands, but state condemnation is available only under the authority of federal law. [282] It has also been held (in a case arising on an 1887 trust allotment in Alaska) that condemnation under this authority must be by judicial action and may not be had less directly by "inverse condemnation." [283] The Secretary of the Interior also has authority under several statutes to grant rights of way across allotments for fair compensation, with or without the consent of the landowner, [284] but has interpreted his authority under the more recent of these statutes to require the consent of the allottee for all rights of way. [285] It has been contended that these authorities also preclude state condemnations without the consent of the secretary and the Native owner, but thus far the lower courts have rejected that argument. [286]

V. Conclusion

It is more than a little ironic that the 1926 Alaska Native Townsite Act, which Congress has termed "obsolete," and the Alaska Native Allotment Act, which was only "passively" administered for many years, should now be the focus of so much litigation. The court decisons resulting from this litigation emphasize the continuing responsibilities of the federal government which have evolved from these two enactments. These responsibilities have been characterized as those of a fiduciary or trustee for Native lands. So, although the Alaska Native Allotment and Townsite Acts have both been repealed, the lands conveyed under them will likely remain an important focal point of the federal "trust responsibility" in Alaska.

Both acts convey lands subject to federal restrictions against alienation and taxation; since 1932 these restrictions have been held sufficient to entitle Alaska Natives to the full range of federal protection and services afforded restricted Native lands elsewhere. [287] Thus, restricted Alaska allotments and townsite lots are probated through the Interior Department, may only be alienated according to federal statutory and regulatory requirements, and are not generally subject to state taxation or regulation. As with restricted lands elsewhere, it has been repeatedly held in Alaska that the federal government has a fiduciary responsibility to administer these lands for the benefit of Alaska Natives. [288]

These responsibilities are derived from the federal restrictions imposed on the allotments and townsite lots and from numerous specific statutes regulating allotment use.[289] Under these restrictions and statutes, the allottees and restricted lot owners must rely on the government to protect their title and to provide competent advice regarding land use and ownership decisions. As the U.S. Supreme Court has said in the context of another statute:

> From their [the Indians] very weakness and helplessness, *so largely due to the course of dealing of the Federal Government with them...* there arises the duty of protection, and with it the power (emphasis added).[290]

Alaska allotments and restricted townsite lots are not, in the strict sense of the term, "trust" lands. Nonetheless, the statutory limitations imposed on them along with the comprehensive statutory and regulatory framework in which they are administered has drawn the federal government and some seven thousand or more Native landowners into a "course of dealing" which compels the Natives to rely on the government for protection and advice. If this is not a "trust" relationship in the strict property sense of the term, it is a close enough approximation to impose "fiduciary" obligations on the government. Native reliance on the relationship, coupled with the government's "overriding duty of fairness" when dealing with the Natives also compel this conclusion.[291]

ENDNOTES

[1]See generally, chapter 2, above, "Aboriginal Title."

[2]15 Stat. 539, 542 (1867).

[3]Act of May 17, 1884, 23 Stat. 24, 26. For a discussion of related laws and administrative action, see F. Cohen, *Handbook of Indian Law* (Washington, D.C.: G.P.O., 1942; reprint New York: AMS, 1972), at 411-412.

[4]See Cohen, above, at 412, n. 172. See also 71 I.D. 342, 349 (1964).

[5]Heckman v. Sutter, 119 F. 83, 89 (9th Cir. 1902), aff'd on reconsideration 128 F. 393 (9th Cir. 1904).

[6]Johnson v. Pacific Coast ss. Co. 2 Ak. Rpts. 224, 240 (D. Ak. 1904), U.S. v. Lynch, 7 Ak. Rpts. 568, 572-573 (D.C. Ak. 1927). See also U.S. v. Cadzow, 5 Ak. Rpts, 125 (D.C. Ak. 1905).

[7]2 Ak. Rpts. 442 (1905).

[8]See also *U.S. v. Cadzow* and *U.S. v. Lynch,* note 6, above.

[9]Act of May 17, 1906, 34 Stat. 197 (formerly codified at 43 USC 270-1 [1970]), repealed with savings clause under the Alaska Native Claims Settlement Act, P.L. 92-203, Sec. 18, 45 Stat. 710 (43 USCA 1617).

[10]S. Doc. No. 101, 59th Cong. 1st Sess. (1906).

[11]Act of Feb. 8, 1887, 24 Stat. 388, (codified as amended in par at 25 USCA 348-349), also called the "Dawes Act" after its chief sponsor. See also Act of June 25, 1910, 26 Stat. 855, in effect amending the General Allotment Act as it relates to allotments on the public domain (codified as amended in part at 25 USCA 336).

[12]*Allotment of Land to Alaska Natives,* 71 I.D. 340, 347 (m-3662 Sep. 21, 1964), citing an 1876 report from the Commissioner of Indian Affairs. F. Cohen, *Handbook of Federal Indian Law* (Charlottesville, Va.: Michie Bobbs-Merril, 1982 ed.), at 127-138, discussing the history of federal allotment policies.

[13]35 Cong. Rec. Part 1, 90 (57th Cong. 1sr Sess., 1901) F. Prucha, ed. *Americanizing the American Indian: Writings by the "Friends of the Indian" 1880-1900* (Cambridge: Harvard University, 1973), focuses on the ultimate goal of the allotment policy as total assimilation of Indians:

> The aim was to do away with tribalism, with communal ownership of land, with concentration of Indians on reservations, with the segregation of Indians from association with good white citizens, with Indian cultural patterns, with Native languages, with Indian religious rites and practices—in short, with anything that deviated from the norms of civilization as practiced and proclaimed by the white reformers' themes. Id. at 7-8.

[14]D.S. Otis, *The Dawes Act and the Allotment of Indian Lands,* (Norman: University of Oklahoma, 1973) at 83.

[15]Hearing on HR 7902 before the House Committee on Indian Affairs (73rd Cong. 2d. Sess. 1934) at 439-40, cited in 71 I.D. 340, 348 (1964).

[16]25 USCA 331 et seq.

[17]Haas, "The Legal Aspects of Indian Affairs from 1887-1957," *Annals,* May 1957, at 12-22. The problem still plagues allotment administration everywhere, including Alaska.

[18]Id. at 16.

[19]Dept. Interior, *Report of the Commissioner of Indian Affairs* (1933). Some 60 million of these acres were disposed of as "surplus lands" not needed for allotments of particular reservations. See generally, Cohen, note 12, above, at 138.

[20]Cited in D.S. Otis, note 14, above, at 94-95. The minority opinion on the 1887 act also focused on this point. The opposition was based upon the experimental nature of the act and the obvious conflict between communal ownership and a scheme for civilization based upon individual property.

> We are free to admit that the two civilizations so different throughout, cannot well coexist, or flourish together. One must, in time give

way to the other, and the weak must in the end be supplanted by the strong. But it cannot be violently wrenched out of place and cast aside. Nations cannot be made to change their habits and methods and modes of thought in a day. To bring the Indian to look at things from our standpoint, is a work requiring time, patience and the skill as well as the benign spirit of Christian statesmanship.

See also *The Problem of Indian Administration,* L. Meriam, Technical Director, (Baltimore: Johns Hopkins, 1928); and Otis, note 14, above, at 124-155, discussing the negative effects of the allotment process. H. Rep. No. 1576, 46th Cong. 2d Sess. 7-10 (1879-1880).

[21]71 I.D., note 12, above, at 348. The solicitor is the chief legal counsel for the Interior Department.

[22]Id. citing a 1903 report on Alaska by J.W. Witten, discussed in text accompanying note 25.

[23]See *Leasing Lands within Reservations Created for the Benefit of the Natives of Alaska,* 49 L.D. 592, 594 (May 18, 1923), for examples.

[24]But see Nagle v. U.S. 191 F. 141 (9th Cir. 1911) holding that the 1887 allotment act did apply to Alaska for purposes of determining Indian citizenship. The court reasoned that Article III of the 1867 Treaty of Purchase made federal Indian laws applicable to Alaska Natives and that the Act of March 3, 1871, (16 Stat. 544, 566), prohibiting future Indian treaties, instituted a policy of dealing with Indians by statute rather than treaty. On that basis, the court concluded that the 1887 allotment act was a federal Indian law applicable to Alaska Natives. Accord, In re Minook, 2 Ak. Rpts. 200 (D.C. Ak. 1904) Contra. In re Incorporation of Haines Mission, 3 Ak. Rpts. 588 (D.C. Ak. 1908). See also Pence v. Kleppe, 529 F. 2d 135, 140 (9th Cir 1976), noting that when Congress passed the 1906 Alaska Native Allotment Act, there was doubt that the 1887 allotment act applied to Alaska, because early cases had held that Alaska Natives were not within the definition of "Indian" as used in the 1887 act. *Pence* holds that "Indian" means "the aborigines of America" and that Alaska Natives are therefore included under a statute granting federal jurisdiction over Native allotment claims.
The logical conclusion to be drawn from these cases is that, prior to 1911, lower court cases implied there was a difference between the status of Alaska Natives and "lower forty-eight" Natives. After the *Nagle* decision, their status in many respects was held to be similar. *Pence* if recent evidence of their continued similarity.

[25]Rep. of the Secretary of Interior (1903) at 269-279.

[26]S. Rep. No. 282, 58th Cong. 2d. Sess. (1904).

[27]S. Doc. No. 106, 58th Cong. 3rd Sess. (1905).

[28]See S. Doc. No. 101, note 10, above.

[29]Id. at 6.

[30]S. Doc. No. 106, note 27, above.

[31]H.R. Rep. 3295, 59th Cong., 1st Sess. (1906).

[32]U.S. v. Atlantic Richfield Co., 435 F. Supp. 1009, 1015 (D. Ak. 1977), aff'd 612 F. 2d 1132 (9th Cir. 1980), cert. den. 449 U.S. 888 (1910).

[33]S. Doc. No. 101, note 10, above; H.R. Rep. 3295, note 31, above.

[34]Witten, note 22, above, at 279; S. Doc. No. 106, note 27 above, at 3; S. Doc. No. 101, note 10, above, at 8, 131, 163.

[35]S. Doc. No. 106, note 27, above, at 2.

> The Native people of Alaska comprising four ethnic stocks living under varied conditions of country, climate, pursuits, and food supply, differ essentially from one another, and consequently demand somewhat different treatment according to their several needs.

[36]71 I.D., note 12, above, at 354.

[37]Witten, note 22, above, at 5-16.

[38]S. Rep. No. 282, note 26, above, at 28 (1904).

[39]Witten, note 22, above, at 5.

[40]Id. at 8 and 14.

[41]31 Fed. 327, 329 (1886).

[42]S. Doc. No. 101, note 10, above, at 6.

[43]Act of May 17, 1906; 34 Stat. 197.

[44]Act of August 2, 1956, 20 Stat. 954 (formerly codified at 43 USC 270-1 [1970]). Incredibly, although the 1956 Amendments permitted the Native allottee to convey the land in fee simple (even to another Native), it did not permit the *original* Native allotee to obtain a fee simple "patent" to the land."

[45]Id. Equity demanded extension of this right to allotments because it was previously granted to homesteads by the Act of March 8, 1922 (codified at 43 USCA 270-11, repealed effective Oct. 21, 1986).

[46]Formerly codified at 43 USC 270-2 (1970)

[47]Formerly codified at 43 USC 270-3 (1970). See 55 I.D. 282, 285 (1935); See also 43 CFR 67.13 (1938 ed.), 43 CFR 2561.2 (1976 ed.). Discussed in Eluska v. Andrus, 587 F. 2d 996, 998 (9th Cir. 1978) and Shields v. U.S., 698 F. 2d 987, (9th Cir. 1983); cert. den. 52 USLW 3262 (1983).

[48]"Native Allotment Briefing Paper", Bureau of Land Management, Alaska State Office (June 17, 1983).

[49]See Frank St. Clair, 52 L.D. 597 (1929), use of land for fishing sufficient occupancy to qualify for an allotment. Compare with Frank St. Clair, 53 L.D. 194 (1930), amount of land actually used for fishing held to reduce allotment from 160 to 9.36 acres.

[50]*U.S. v. Atlantic Richfield Co.,* note 32, above, at 1015. See also, S. Rep. No. 495, 92d Cong., 1st Sess. at 91 (1971).

[51]Barr v. U.S., unpublished Slip Op. No. A 76-160 Civil (D. Ak. Jan. 18, 1980) at 5-6.

[52]43 CFR Subpart 2561 (1982).

[53]P.L. 96-487, 94 Stat. 2371 (Dec. 2, 1980).

[54]Id. Sec. 905, 94 Stat. 2435 (43 USCA 1634).

[55]E.g., Aguilar v. U.S. (Aguilar II), 474 F. Supp. 840 (D. Ak. 1979), preference right held sufficient to require federal government to recover land for Native applicant if erroneously conveyed to another. See also, Yakutat & Southern Railway v. Setuck Harry, Heir of Setuck Jim, 48 L.D. 362, 364 (1921); Frank St. Clair, 52 L.D. 597, 598 (1929).

[56]U.S. v. Flynn, 53 IBLA 208, 237-238, 88 I.D. 373, 389-390 (1981). Accord U.S. v. 10.95 Acres of Land, 75 F. Supp. 841, 844 (D. Ak. 1948). Regarding requirements of physical occupancy, see also U.S. v. Alaska, 201 F. Supp. 796 (D. Ak. 1962); Kittie Cleogeuh, 28 L.D. 427 (1899); A. S. Wadleigh, 13 L.D. 120 (1891); Herbert H. Hilscher, 67 I.D. 410, 416 (1960). Discussed also in Mary Olympic (On Reconsideration), 65 IBLA 26 at 30-31 (June 22, 1982). However it is arguable whether the same requirements of evidence of physical occupancy would apply where the competing claim (e.g., a state land selection) was not initiated in reliance on the absence of such evidence. See generally, *Aguilar II,* note 55, above at 843-845, discussing Native preference rights in the context of state land selections.

[57]Formerly codified at 43 USC 270-2 (1970).

[58]*Shields v. U.S.,* note 47, above.

[59]Formerly codified at 43 USC 270-1 (1970). See also 43 CFR 2561.0-3 (1982).

[60]Akootchook v. Watt, Slip Op. No. F-82-4 Civil (D. Ak. Aug. 5, 1983), on appeal, Akootchook v. Watt No. 83-4181 (9th Cir. 1983).

[61]43 CFR 2561.2(a) (1982). See also, *Shields v. U.S.,* note 47, above, stating in dicta that the five-year occupancy requirement applies to allotments outside national forests.

[62]S.O. 3040 (May 25, 1979). See also, Solicitor's Opinion, Recision of the 'Five-Year-Prior Rule' for Alaska Native Allotments (April 26, 1979).

[63]Forty three allotments have been reinstated due to the recision of the five-year-prior rule, January 17, 1984, interview with Alaska Regional Solicitor.

[64]Olympic v. U.S., Civil No. A 82-396 Civil (D. Ak. Sep. 30, 1982). See also, Mary Olympic, 47 IBLA 58 (April 14, 1980); on reconsideration, 65 IBLA 26 (June 22, 1982), rejecting allotment application where applicant failed to prove five years' use and occupancy prior to his death in 1967. Compare with Frederic Howard, 67 IBLA 157 (Sep. 27, 1982), accepting allotment application for approval where rejection for failure to prove use and occupancy occurred *after* December 18, 1971; therefore, allotment was deemed to be pending "on or before" Dec. 18, 1971 and subject to automatic approval under section 905 of ANILCA, discussed below.

[65]Formerly codified at 43 USC 270-1 (1970). See also 43 CFR 2561.0-3 (1982).

[66]"Native Land Allotments in Alaska," Memorandum from Acting Regional Solicitor to State director, BLM, Anchorage and Area, Director, BIA, Juneau (April 29, 1965).

[67]Formerly codified at 43 USC 270-1. See also 43 CFR 2561.0-3. See also Act of March 8, 1922, 42 Stat. 415 [43 USC 270-11, (repealed effective Oct. 21, 1986)], permitting reservations of coal, oil and gas to the United States.

[68]Of the 687 allotment files closed prior to ANCSA, 459 were rejected on grounds of statutory life or failure to file a mineral waiver. Of the remaining 228, 221 were originally reopened under *Pence I,* but recent IBLA decisions throw doubt on the legality of all but 80 of those reopenings, see note 100, below. Interview with John M. Allen, Alaska Regional Solicitor (Dec. 15, 1982). See also notes 86 et seq., below, and accompanying text.

[69]43 CFR 2561.0-2 (1982). See also 43 USCA 1634 (a)(6) exempting allotment applications which have been "knowingly and voluntarily relinquished" from ANILCA's statutory approval provisions.

[70]Juneau BIA Area Director Memorandum, "Procedure for Filing Requests for Reinstatement of Relinquished Native Allotment Applications" (August 16, 1983).

[71]43 CFR 2561.1(d)(1982).

[72]*Barr v. U.S.,* note 51, above, at 6-7.

[73]Id. 7-8. See also 1985 USCCAAN 5070 at 5181-5182.

[74]Barr v. U.S., A 76-160 Civil, "Order Approving Settlement" (Oct. 1, 1982).

[75]43 CFR 2561.2 (1982).

[76]43 CFR 2561.0-5(a) (1982).

[77]E.g., *Frank St. Clair,* note 49, above.

[78]43 USCA 687a, headquarters and homesites (repealed effective Oct. 21, 1981); 43 USC 270 (1976), homesteads (repealed effective Oct. 21, 1976).

[79]Unpublished memorandum from Robert Coffman, Chief of Lands and Minerals, Department of the Interior, to BLM Anchorage and Fairbanks district managers (June 7, 1962), cited in D. Case, *The Special Relationship of Alaska Natives to the Federal Government,* (Anchorage: Alaska Native Foundation, 1982), at 56.

[80]Public Land Statistics 1962-1971, BLM, Alaska.

[81]71 I.D. 344-354 (1964).

[82]Case, note 79, above, at 56.

[83]Id. at 57.

[84]Board of Regents v. Roth, 408 U.S. 564 at 571 (1972).

[85]There were also practical reasons for not allowing hearings; the administrative cost of possibly several thousand such hearings have been substantial.

[86]Pence v. Kleppe, 391 F. Supp. 1021 (D. AK. 1975).

[87]Pence v. Kleppe (Pence I), 529 F. 2d 135 (9th Cir. 1976).

[88]Interview with Acting Chief, Allotment Section, BLM Alaska State Office (Jan. 27, 1984). See also notes 68, above, and 100, below.

[89]Pence v. Andrus (Pence II), 586 F.2d 733 (9th Cir. 1978).

[90]Mary Olympic (On Reconsideration), 65 IBLA 26 at 27 (June 22, 1982).

[91]Id. at 35. The IBLA's decision has been appealed to federal court, Olympic v. U.S., A82-396 Cir. (D. Ak., filed Sep. 30, 1982).

[92]Frederick Howard, 67 IBLA 157 (Sep. 30, 1982).

[93]Act of Dec. 2, 1980, P.L. 96-487, 94 Stat. 2371 (codified in scattered parts of 16 and 43 U.S. Code).

[94]Sec. 905 Stat. 2371 (43USCA 1634); see generally, S. Rep. No. 413, 96th Cong., 1st Sess. 238 (1979), reprinted in 1980 USCCAAN 5182.

[95]Sec. 905 (a) (1).

[96]Sec. 905 (a) (3), (4), (5) and (6), respectively.

[97]Sec. 905(a)(5)(B).

[98]C.f. Henrietta Roberts Vaden, 70 IBLA 171 (1983).

[99]Personal interview with Robert D. Arnold, Deputy Commissioner, Alaska Department of Natural Resources (June 10, 1983).

[100]See *Mary Olympic* and *Frederick Howard,* notes 90-93 above and accompanying text. See also 1980 USCCAAN 5020 at 5182, for the legislative history of the "on or before" language in sec. 905.

[101]Sec. 905(a)(1), NPR-A; sec. 905(d), powersites. Prior to passage of ANILCA, some of the lands covered by allotment applications within NPR-A were reportedly conveyed to the Barrow ANCSA village corporation as a part of its ANCSA entitlement. The status of the allotment applications covered by those conveyances is apparently an unresolved issue. Personal interview with Department of the Interior, Alaska Regional Solicitor (Feb. 2, 1984).

[102]Sec. 905(b) and (c), respectively. *Mary Olympic,* see notes 90 and 91, above, held that the right to amend an application was personal to an allotment applicant and could not be exercized by the applicant's heirs. This conclusion casts a cloud over many allotment applications since the applicants are often elderly and many of the land descriptions in the applications are rumored to be inaccurate.

[103]The allotment, however, would not likely survive if the valid, conflicting interest was also a fee interest (e.g., a homestead) for the same land. On the other hand, the allotment would probably survive if the conflicting interest was less than a fee interest (e.g., an easement). See Arnold v. Morton, 526 F. 2d 1101 (9th Cir. 1976), discussing the meaning of "subject to" clauses in federal withdrawals. See also, 43 CFR 2650.3- 1(a), excluding fee interests but including less than fee interests in ANCSA conveyances under sections 14(g) and 22(b) of ANCSA. Accord Ak. Reg. Sol. Memo, "Legislative Approval of Native Allotments," (Mar. 10, 1981) at 7 and Ak. Reg. Sol. Memo, " Right-of-way On A Native Allotment" (Dec. 22, 1983) at 3-5.

[104]A.W. Scott *The Law of Trusts* (Boston: Little, Brown and Co., 1967 at 3-26 (sec. 1).

[105]See e.g., Seminole Nation v. U.S., 316 U.S. 286 (1942).

[106]Act of February 8, 1887, note 11 above. See also U.S. v. Rickert, 188 U.S. 432 (1902), denying authority to the State of South Dakota to tax permanent improvements or personal property on allotments because of the trust status of the land. But see, U.S. v. Mitchell (Mitchell I), 445 U.S. 535, 542 (1980), describing the nature of the "limited trust" under the General Allotment Act. See also U.S. v. Mitchell (Mitchell II), 51 USLW 4999 (1983), describing the scope of the trust responsibility under other statutes specifically regulating allotment administration.

[107]See 25 CFR 152.1(d) defining "trust land" for allotments, and 25 CFR 152.1(c) defining "restricted land" for allotments. Townsites under the Alaska Native Townsite Act (formerly codified at 43 USC 733 [1970]) are also restricted lands.

[108]U.S. v. Bowling, 256 U.S. 484 (1921).

[109]Oklahoma Tax Commission v. U.S., 319 U.S. 598 (1943).

[110]West v. Oklahoma Tax Commission, 334 U.S. 717 (1948).

[111]E.g., U.S. v. Bowling, note 108, above; see generally, Cohen (1982), note 12, above, at 605-638 and *Mitchell I* and *II,* note 106, above.

[112]See e.g., 25 CFR 162, 1(b) and 131.1 et seq., relating to leasing.

[113]See e.g., 25 USCA 202, prohibiting inducement of an Indian to execute an instrument purporting to convey trust land and imposing criminal penalties.

[114]Act of June 25, 1910, c.431, sec.1, 36 Stat. 855, as amended (25 USCA 372), permitting certificates of competency to remove restrictions against alienation upon a restricted allottee's application. See also 25 CFR Part 152. Compare with Act of May 8, 1906, c. 2348, 34 Stat. 182 (25 USCA 349), permitting the Secretary of the Interior to issue fee patents unilaterally under the General Allotment Act of 1887.

[115]Charlie George, 44 L.D. 113 (1915); Frank St. Clair, 52 L.D. 597, 601 (1929). See also Worthen Lumber Mills v. Alaska Juneau Gold Mining Co., 229 F. 966 (9th Cir. 1916).

[116]State of Alaska, 45 IBLA 318 (1980).

[117]43 CFR 2561.3 (1979).

[118]*State of Alaska,* note 116, above, at 322. Curiously, however, sec. 905 (a)(1) of ANILCA requires the Secretary of the Interior to issue a "trust certificate" for a legislatively approved allotment.

[119]Formerly codified at 43 USC 270-1 (1970).

[120]Act of June 25, 1910, note 114, above. See Assoc. Sol. Indian Affairs Memo, "Administrative appeal of Nels W. Nelson, Jr. (Mar. 2, 1981). Compare with Op. Ak. Reg. Sol., "Certificates of Competency" (Jan. 16, 1975), prohibiting application of 25 USCA 372 because Alaska allotments were then considered trust lands.

[121]It is perhaps not clear that removing the restrictions against alienation under 25 USCA 372 also removes the restrictions against taxation imposed under the terms of the Alaska Allotment Act. See Choate v. Trapp, 224 U.S. 665, 673 (1912), tax exemption held to be a separate property right which survived congressional elimination of restrictions against alienation.

[122]25 USCA 311 et seq.; see also 25 CFR Part 169 (1982).

[123]25 USCA 373 et seq.; see also 43 CFR Subpart D (1982).

[124]25 USCA 391 et seq.; see also 25 CFR Part 162 (1982).

[125]Op. Ak. Reg. Sol., Katherine Koskoff—Applicability of 25 USCA sec. 409a (1970) to Sale of Native Land Allotment (Feb. 7, 1975). See 25 USCA 409a.

[126]E.g., Frank St. Clair, 52 L.D. 597, 600 (1929).

[127]See 725 USCA 2.

[128]See Federal Land Policy and Management of 1976, P.L. 94-579, 90 Stat. 2743 (43 USCA 1701 et seq.).

[129]43 CFR 2561.1(a).

[130]43 CFR 2561.1(d).

[131]43 CFR 2561.2

[132]43 CFR 2091.1(a), 2091.6-5 (ANSCA corporation top filing); sec. 906(e) of ANILCA (State top filing).

[133]Formerly codified at 43 USC 270-1 (1970).

[134]43 CFR 2561-2; See also *Shields v. U.S.*, note 47, above.

[135]*Aguilar II,* note 55, above; Archie Wheeler, 1 IBLA 139 (1970); Lucy Ahvakana, 3 IBLA 341 (1971); John Nusunginya, 28 IBLA 83 (1976).

[136]43 CFR 2561.0-8(c). See also S.O. No. 3040 (May 25, 1979), recinding the "five-year-prior" rule, and George Kostrometinoff, 26 L.D. 104 (1898).

[137]43 CFR 4.411. See also, *Pence I*, note 87, above.

[138]BLM procedures were furnished by the Alaska BLM State Office Division of Conveyance Management. See generally, State of Alaska, 45 IBLA 318 (1980). See also BLM Alaska State Office, *Conveyance News,* Vol. 6, No. 2 (May/June 1983), discussing the then current status of BLM allotment processing, procedures and issues. It is commonly reported that survey of all allotments will take fifty to seventy years.

[139]Germania Iron Co. v. U.S., 165 U.S. 379, 383 (1897); see also, e.g., State of Alaska, 45 IBLA 328 (1980).

[140]*Aguilar II,* note 55, above, discussed also in State of Alaska, 45 IBLA 328, 333-334 (1980), Burski concurring.

[141]Aguilar v. U.S., A76-271 Civil, Stipulated Procedures for Implementation of Order (Feb. 7, 1983).

[142]The precise names for each of these divisions, branches and offices have changed over the years, but their functions remain substantially the same.

[143]Act of Jan. 4, 1975, 88 Stat. 2203 (25 USCA 450 et seq.).

[144]See generally, 25 CFR Part 152 (sales), Part 162 (leasing and permitting) and Part 169 (rights-of-way).

[145]These responsibilities are delegated from the Commissioner of Indian Affairs to the BIA Area Directors in BIA Manual (BIAM) 10 BIAM 3 (Jan. 20, 1975). See also 39 Fed. Reg. (No. 173) 32166 (Sep. 5, 1974), regarding delegations to the Commissioner (now the Assistant Secretary), of Indian Affairs. The title of Commissioner was changed to Assistant Secretary in 209 Interior Department Manual (DM) 8.1. See also 25 CFR 271.32(d), regarding contractible realty programs which do not constitute trust responsibilities.

[146]See 25 CFR 150.5(b).

[147]See 43 CFR 2091.6-3, 2091.6-5 and 2561.0-2. See also Pacific Steam Whaling, 26 L.D. 558 (1898), trade and manufacturing site denied if it would encroach on a Native village; accord, Baranof Island, 36 L.D. 261 (1908), Johnson v. Pacific Coast S.S., 2 Ak. Rpts. 224 (D. Ak. 1904).

[148]Compare Charley Clattoo, 48 L.D. 435 (1920), approval of allotment prevented withdrawal of townsite covering same land, and U.S. v. Lynch, 7 Ak. Rpts. 568 (D. Ak. 1927), Natives in possession under 1884 Organic Act could not be dispossessed by court or Secretary of the Interior, with Herman Joseph, 21 IBLA 199 (July 30, 1975), allotment application did not preclude subsequent powersite withdrawal. See also Russian American Co. v. U.S., 199 U.S. 570 (1905), occupancy begun after 1884 does not prevent later federal withdrawal; Alaska Commerical Co., 39 L.D. 597 (1911), rev'd on reconsideration 41 L.D. 75 (1912) occupancy prior to 1884 affords a priority of continued occupancy as against a later federal withdrawal.

[149]43 CFR 3600.0-3(c), prohibiting disposal of mineral materials on "Indian lands."

[150]43 CFR 2802.1-6.

[151]State of Alaska v. Juneau Area Director, 9 IBIA 126, 88 I.D. 1020 (1981); see also Heffle v. Alaska, 633 P.2d 264 (Ak. 1981).

[152]Memorandum of Understanding (MOU) between the Bureau of Land Management (BLM) and the Bureau of Indian Affairs (BIA) on division of responsibilities for Native allotments, BLM Agreement No. AK-950-AG9-323 (1979).

[153]However, a delegation from the Acting Deputy Commissioner of Indian Affairs to the Juneau Area Director purports to delegate joint authority to the BIA Area Director for trespass abatement under 43 CFR 2561.0-2.

[154]Letter from Assistant Secretary-Indian Affairs to James Vollentine (Dec. 2, 1983).

[155]Act of May 25, 1926, 44 Stat. 629, [formerly codified at 43 USC 733 et seq. (1970)].

[156]See Cohen (1942), note 3, above, at 412.

[157]Secs. 1 and 3, 44 Stat. 629, respectively [formerly codified at 43 USC 733 and 735 (1970)]. See note 155, above.

[158]Compare 51 L.D. 501, 502 (1926); 52 L.D. 65-66 (1927), Native villages only, with 56 L.D. 569, 571 (1938), permitting non-Native deeds in Native villages.

[159]City of Klawock v. Gustafson, Slip Op. No. K 74-2 (D.C. Ak. November 11, 1976) at 14, discussed in Klawock v. Gustafson, 585 F. 2d 428 (9th Cir. 1978), See also 37 L.D. 334, holding that Alaska Natives could not acquire title under the 1891 Act. Compare 43 CFR 2564.0-4(b), relating to the establishment of "Native townsites" with 43 CFR 2565.1, relating to the establishment of "non-Native townsites."

[160]Act of March 3, 1891, Sec. 11, 26 Stat. 1095, 1099, 43 USC 732 (1970).

[161]See 43 CFR 2565.1(a). But see 43 CFR 2564.0-4(b) and 2564.3, relating to "Native townsites." It is still not clear whether the townsite trustee precisely followed the 1891 procedures when it came to "Native townsites." The size of the townsites was limited to between 160-640 acres depending on the population, see 43 CFR 2565.1(c), but townsites range in size from 10.73 acres (Kodiak) to 805.17 acres (Barrow).

[162]43 CFR 2565.1(b).

[163]43 CFR 2565.1(c). "Withdrawal" and "entry" are now considered to occur at the time the petition is filed. Source: Townsite Trustee, phone conversation (May 11, 1974). Under established precedent, the effect of "entry" by the townsite trustee was to vest the ultimate right to the land in the occupants and the community. McCloskey v. Pacific Const. Co., 160 F. 794, 798 (9th Cir. 1908).

[164]43 CFR 2565.3(c).

[165]See Klawock, note 159 above, at 15, where these procedures are explained.

[166]Formerly codified at 43 USC 736 (1970).

[167]Klawock, note 159, above, at 14. See also 43 CFR 2564.0-3 et seq.

[168]Formerly codified at 43 USC 733 (1970).

[169]"Disposal of Lots in Saxman, Alaska," 66 I.D. 212, 2 Op. Sol. on Ind. Affairs 1857 (M-36563, May 11, 1959). The opinion held that Section 3 of the 1926 act (formerly codified at 43 USC 735 [1970]) did not permit the trustee to collect the prorated survey fee from Native occupants.

[170]66 I.D. at 214.

[171]See Op. of Acting Field Solicitor, Juneau, (August 31, 1960), cited in Klawock, note 159, above, at 16.

[172]In practical terms, the trustee had to leave the unoccupied lots open to Native occupancy even after the subdivision was completed. This was not specifically permitted by the regulations, which required that the unoccupied lots either be

sold to private parties or deeded to the municipality. *Klawock,* note 159 above, at 16. See also 43 CFR 2565.5 and 2565.7.

[173]*Klawock,* note 159, above, at 16-17.

[174]Id. at 17-18. The court also held that these restrictions were sufficient to prevent Natives from being assessed for the costs of the subdivisional services.

[175]Under Interior Department regulations, unoccupied, subdivided lots can only be 1) sold at auction (43 CFR 2565.5[a]), 2) sold to a federal, state or local government agency (43 CFR 2565.5[b]) or 3) deeded to the municipality (43 CFR 2565.7). The Alaska Regional Solicitor has held that if the city formally objects to the sale (43 CFR 2565.5[b][3]), the trustee does not hae to attempt to sell the unoccupied lots before deeding them to the city. Op. Ak. Reg. Sol., "Disposal of Unoccupied Lots in Alaska Townsites" (February 8, 1977).

[176]43 USCA 1613(c).

[177]Act of October 21, 1976, 90 Stat. 2744, 43 USCA 1701 et seq.

[178]See *Klawock,* note 159, above, at 17 and 19.

[179]Carlo v. Gustafson, 512 F. Supp. 833, 838 (D. AK. 1981).

[180]Act of March 2, 1867, Ch. 177, 14 Stat. 541, R.S. 2387 (formerly codified at 43 USC 718 [1970]).

[181]Formerly codified at 43 USC 732 (1970).

[182]*Klawock,* note 159, above, at 16-17. See also 66 I.D. note 169, above, at 215.

[183]See note 159, above. See also *Carlo v. Gustafson,* note 179, above, Ruth B. Sandvik, 26 IBLA 97 (July 9, 1976), and City of Klawock v. Andrew, 24 IBLA 85, 83 I.D. 47 (1976).

[184]Following the *Klawock* decision, the townsite trustee publicly announced that "unsubdivided lands in some patented townsites are available to both Native and non-Natives alike to stake and build upon." Unnumbered Bulletin, "Unsubdivided Townsite Lands" (June 14, 1971).

[185]*Carlo v. Gustafson,* note 179 above.

[186]*Scott on Trusts,* note 104, above, at 3-4.

[187]Act of February 26, 1948. 62 Stat. 35, (formerly codified at 43 USC 737 [1970]).

[188]Circular No. 1082a, 56 I.D. 569, 570 (1938). See also 25 CFR 121, 22(a) and 45 CFR 2564.5 et seq., relating to BIA approval for transfer of restricted lands.

[189]43 CFR 2564.5.

[190]43 CFR 2564.6 and 2564.7. These restrictions do not, of course, grow out of the lack of complete title in the owner. They are based on statutory prohibitions, not a deficiency in the owner's title. The situation is analogous to a person's being legally determined to be incompetent to manage his or her own; affairs. Such a person may have complete title to property, but is deprived by a court of the authority to deal with the property. Title to restricted lands is in this respect different from title to either trust or aboriginal lands. In either of the latter cases, the United States holds the legal title and the Natives have an equitable interest. In either case, the federal government also has a trust responsibility to protect the lands from encroachment. Note: The Juneau Area Director has delegated his authority to issue unrestricted deeds to agency superintendents.

[191]E.g., 25 CFR Pt. 152 (sale of restricted lands), Pt. 162 (leases and permits on restricted lands), Pt. 169 (rights-of-way over Indian lands) and 43 CFR 4,200 et seq. (probate). See also the associated statutes cited in the regulations.

[192]C.f. Cohen (1942), note 3, above, at 110, nn. 260 and 261 and accompanying text.

[193]C.f. Ruiz v. Morton, 415 U.S. 199, 236 (1973), applying this principle in the context of BIA general assistance benefits.

[194]*Mitchell II,* note 106, above, at 5004-5005.

[195]See note 3, above.

[196]*Non-Mineral Entries in Alaska,* 12 L.D. 583, 595-596 (1981).

[197]Kittie Cleogeuh, 28 L.D. 427 (May 22, 1899). Accord, Louis Greenbaum, 26 L.D. 512 (April 13, 1898); Pacific Steam Whaling Co., 26 L.D. 558 (April 22, 1898); John G. Brady, 28 L.D. 535 (June 23, 1899), all relating to protection of Native occupancy from disposition under sections 12-14 of the 1891 act.

[198]33 L.D. 163, 167-8 (Aug. 1, 1904).

[199]37 L.D. 337 (Dec. 29, 1908).

[200]The non-citizen status of Natives was also sometimes advanced as a reason that the 1891 act could not be applied to them. In 1923 the Interior Department adopted regulations permitting citizen Natives to acquire lots under the 1891 act (50 L.D. 27, 46). The General Citizenship Act of 1924 (8 USCA 1401) seemingly eliminated this obstacle for non-citizen Natives as well, but Congress nonetheless enacted ANTA two years later.

[201]See note 157, above, and accompanying text.

[202]See notes 158 and 159, above, and accompanying text.

[203]See note 169, above, and accompanying text.

[204]See notes 174 and 175, above, and accompanying text.

[205]See generally, *Klawock v. Gustafson,* note 159, above, at 15 and 43 CFR subparts 2564 and 2565.

[206]66 I.D., note 169, above, at 215.

[207]Discussed in *Klawock v. Gustafson,* note 159, above, at 16.

[208]*City of Klawock v. Andrew,* note 183, above.

[209]*Klawock v. Gustafson,* note 159, above, at 12.

[210]43 CFR 2565.3(c); see also, e.g., *City of Klawock v. Andrew,* note 183, above.

[211]Statistics from BLM State Office, Townsite Trustee.

[212]See, e.g., AFN Convention Resolution No. 77-8, Native Townsites—Claims in Unsubdivided Townsite Tracts, summarized in *1977 AFN Convention Report* at 29 (Jan. 4, 1978).

[213]Op. Ak. Reg. Sol., "Effect of Repeal of Townsite Laws on Occupants who entered after Oct. 21, 1976" (Feb. 20, 1980).

[214]E.g., Royal Harris, 45 IBLA 87 (Jan. 17, 1980), on appeal Royal Harris v. Andrus, A 80-174 Cir. (D. Ak. 1980).

[215]Op. Ak. Reg. Sol., (Feb 8, 1977), note 175, above; see also 43 CFR 2565.5(b)(3), requiring city approval of any sale and 2565.7, regarding disposition of proceeds of sales.

[216]Discussed in *Royal Harris,* note 214, above, at 88.

[217]See *Klawock v. Gustafson,* note 159, above.

[218]See *Royal Harris,* note 214, above, at 93, Burski dissenting.

[219]*Klawock v. Gustafson,* note 159, above.

[220]Interview with John M. Allen, Ak. Regional Solicitor (Dec. 15, 1982).

[221]Act of Dec. 18, 1971, P.L. 92-203, 85 Stat. 688 (43 USCA 1601 et seq.).

[222]Act of Oct. 21, 1976, P.L. 94-579, 90 Stat. 2743 (43 USCA 1701 et seq.).

[223]43 USCA 1610(a)(1)(A).

[224]43 USCA 1602(e).

[225]Aleknagik Natives Ltd. v. Andrus, 648 F. 2d 496 (9th Cir. 1980; on rehearing, 648 F. 2d 505 (9th Cir. 1981).

[226]C.f. 43 CFR 2091.4. See also 43 CFR 2565.1(a) and Op. Ak. Reg. Sol., "Effect of Repeal of Townsite Laws on Occupants who entered after October 21, 1976" (Feb. 20, 1979) at 3; see also, McCloskey v. Pacific Coast Co., 160 F. 794, 798 (9th Cir. 1908).

[227]City of Barrow v. Gustafson, A 80-333 Civil Slip Op. (D.C. Ak. Aug. 27, 1981).

[228]See 43 CFR 2565.1(c).

[229]C.f. *Aleknagik v. Andrus,* note 225, above, at 506. See also 43 Cfr 2565.3(c), tying entitlement to lots to occupancy as of the date of the subdivisional survey.

[230]Aleknagik Natives Ltd. v. Watt, A77-200 (D. Ak. Filed: Sep. 27, 1977); Unalashka Corp. v. City of Unalashka, A 81-435 (D. Ak. 1981).

[231]*Royal Harris,* note 214, above.

[232]Id. at 97, Burski dissenting.

[233]Id. It is also an issue in *Aleknagik v. Watt,* note 230, above.

[234]43 USCA 1613(c)(1).

[235]43 USCA 1613(c)(3).

[236]The trustee cannot deed unoccupied lots to a community until it is incorporated, 43 CFR 2565.7.

[237]H. Rpt. No. 94-1163 at 26, reprinted in 1976 USCCAAN 6175, at 6200.

[238]Stephen Kenyon (On Reconsideration), 65 IBLA 44 (June 23, 1982), on appeal sub nom, Ouzinkie Native Corp. v. Andrus, A80-196 Civ. (D. Ak. 1980).

[239]*Carlo v. Gustafson,* note 179, above.

[240]Act of Aug. 15, 1894, ch. 290, 28 Stat.305, as amended. Also codified in part at 28 USCA 1353. See generally Cohen (1982), note 12, above, at 313-316.

[241]This requirement was added in 1901; prior to that time the United States was not a necessary party. Hy-Yu-Tse-Mil-Kin v. Smith, 194 U.S. 401, 413 (1904).

[242]E.g., McKay v. Kalyton, 204 U.S. 458 (1907). Whether the United States is an "indispensable" or merely a "necessary" party may depend on the circumstances, particularly whether the dispute involves ultimate ownership of the land. See Cohen (1982), note 12, above, at 315, n. 273.

[243]E.g. Scholder v. U.S., 428 F.2d 1123, 1129 (9th Cir 1970), cert. den. 400 U.S. 942.

[244]*McKay v. Kalyton,* note 242, above, trust lands; Heckman v. U.S., 224 U.S. 413, 441 (1911), restricted lands. See also Arenas v. U.S., 322 U.S. 4129 (1943); U.S. v. Payne, 264 U.S. 446 (1924).

[245]Alaska v. Agli, 472 F. Supp. 70 (D. Ak. 1979), 25 USCA 1353 grants exclusive jurisdiction to federal courts to determine entitlements to allotments; Pence v. Kleppe (Pence I), 529 F.2d 135 (9th Cir. 1976), federal jurisdiction to determine initial entitlement to allotment; Carlo v. Gustafson, note 179, above, restricted townsite treated as an allotment for purposes of 25 USCA 345.

[246]*McKay v. Kalyton,* note 242, above, at 468 (citation omitted).

[247]P.L. 83-280, Act of Aug. 15, 1953, ch. 505, 67 Stat. 588, now codified as amended in scattered parts of 18 and 28 USCA. See 28 USCA 1360 (mandatory civil jurisdiction), applied to Alaska, Act of Aug. 8, 1958, P.L. 85-615, 72 Stat. 545. Other provisions of P.L. 280 not related to Alaska were repealed and substantially reenacted as part of the 1968 Indian Civil Rights Act, P.L. 90-284, Title IV, Apr. 11, 1968, 82 Stat. 78 (25 USCA 1321-1326).

[248]"Indian country" is now defined at 18 USCA 1151 to include reservations, allotments and dependent Indian communities.

[249]28 USCA 1360(b).

[250]See generally Bryan v. Itasca County, 426 U.S. 373 (1976), regarding the limitations of P.L. 280 jurisdiction. See also C. Goldberg, *Public Law 280: The Limits of State Jurisdiction Over Reservation Indians,* 22 *UCLA L. Rev.* 535 (1975).

[251]People of South Naknek v. Bristol Bay Borough, 466 F.Supp. 870 (D. Ak. 1979), local government precluded from taxing restricted townsite lots and permanent improvements (fixtures), but permitted to tax personal property located on allotment.

[252]Santa Rosa Band of Indians v. Kings County, 532 F.2d 655 (9th Cir. 1975), cert. den. 429 U.S. 1038, upholding 25 CFR 1.4 which prohibits state or local regulation of the use of trust and restricted lands except with the authorization of the Secretary of the Interior. See also Applicability of Health and Sanitation Laws of the State of California on Indian Reservations, 2 Op. Sol. on Ind. Aff. 1986 (M-36768 Feb. 7, 1969); 58 I.D. 42 (1942). The numerous federal statutes and regulations governing the lease, sale, etc. of restricted lands are also likely to preempt state or local regulation of these lands. C.f. White Mountain Apache Tribe v. Broker, 448 U.S. 136 (1980). See also notes 122-126, above, and accompanying text.

[253]Heffle v. Alaska, 633 P.2d 264 (Ak. 1981), state courts have no jurisdiction over allotments; therefore, state court injunction against barricading disputed right-of-way held improper. See also, c.f. Ollestead v. Native Village of Tyonek, 560 P.2d 31 (Ak. 1977), cert. den. 434 U.S. 938, state courts have no jurisdiction to adjudicate entitlement to tribal trust property; Calista v. Mann (Ak. 1977), state adjudication of restricted ANCSA stock prohibited except as permitted under ANCSA.

[254]Schade v. Schade, No. 67-55 (Third Judicial Dist., Ak. Superior Ct. Order dated Dec. 20, 1967).

[255]Schade v. Schade 3KO 80-385 (Ak. Superior Ct. order dated Jan. 20, 1981), permitting ex-spouse and children to remain on ex-husbands allotment pending further action in the case.

[256]Wilson v. Wilson, 3 AN-76-4251 civil (Ak. Superior Ct, order dated March 29, 1978. The Assistant Secretary for Indian Affairs subsequently refused to permit sale of the allotment to satisfy the divorce judgement; See "In the matter of the application for sale of Native allotment by Noel B. Wilson," Memorandum from Assistant Secretary (Sep. 14, 1978). The federal bankruptcy court subsequently excluded the value of the allotment from Wilson's bankruptcy estate on the strength of government arguments that the State court had no authority to include it in the divorce award (D.Ak. Bankruptcy Ct. No. 3-79-00310. But see Sheppard v. Sheppard, 655 P.2d 895 (Ida. Dec. 16, 1982), upholding award of value spouse contributed to purchase of trust property; accord Fisher v. Fisher, 656 P. 2d 129 (Ida. Dec. 30, 1982). But see *Sheppard v. Sheppard*, above, at 923-924, Bistline, J. dissenting.

[257]*McKay v. Kalyton*, note 242, above, at 469 prohibiting indirect state court adjudication of allotment possession. See also In re Humboldt Fir, Inc., 426 F. Supp. 292, 296 (N.D. Cal. 1977), prohibiting application of *any* state law to dispute involving trust or restricted property.

[258]18 USCA 1162(a).

[259]18 USCA 1162(b).

[260]Compare Seminole Tribe of Indians v. Butterworth, 658 F.2d 310 (5th Cir. Oct. 5, 1981), cert. den. 455 U.S. 1020, gambling held regulatory; with U.S. v. Marcyes, 557 F.2d 1361 (9th Cir. 1977), sale of fireworks held prohibited under state law and, therefore, a criminal violation within the meaning of the Assimilative Crimes Act (18 USCA 13).

[261]It may be significant, however, that Alaska allotments and townsites are located "off-reservation." C.f. Mescalero Apache Tribe v. Jones, 411 U.S. 145, 148-149 (1973), discussed in New Mexico v. Mescalero Apache Tribe, U.S. , 72 L. Ed. 2d at 621, n. 18 (1983), regarding off-reservation state jurisdiction.

[262]See generally Cohen (1982), note 12, above, at 633-638.

[263]Act of 1910, ch. 431, 36 Stat. 855. (25 USCA 372), determination of intestate heirs; (25 USCA 373), disposal of allotments by will.

[264]*U.S. v. Bowling*, note108, above. The implementing regulations also treat restricted and trust property the same. 43 CFR 4.201(m) (1982).

[265]*Authority of the Secretary of the Interior to Dispose of Reindeer Belonging to Estates of Deceased Natives of Alaska*, 54 I.D. 15 at 19; reprinted as Regulation of Reindeer Owned by Alaska Natives in 1 Op. So. on Ind. Aff. 320 at 322 (M-27127 Jul. 26, 1932).

[266]25 USCA 373b.

[267]43 CFR Part 4 subpart D (1982).

[268]See 43 CFR 4.210 and 4.270 (1982).

[269]If the estate has a cash value of less than $1,000, the agency superintendent may determine the heirs and distribute the assets, 43 CFR 4.271 (1982).

[270]There is some question whether creditors' claims may be paid out of the assets of a restricted or trust estate. See Cohen (1982), note 12, above, at 637, n. 41.

[271]43 CFR 4.241 (1982).

[272]43 CFR 4.310-.323 (1982).

[273]Tooahnippah v. Hickel, 397 U.S. 598, 605-07 (1970)

[274]See Cohen (1982), note 12, above, at 638, n. 48.

[275]*Tooahnippah v. Hickel,* note 273, above.

[276]Squire v. Capoeman, 351 U.S. 1 (1956).

[277]See generally Cohen (1982), note 12, above, at 391-399 and at 394, n. 38.

[278]Superintendent of Five Civilized Tribes v. Commissioner, 295 U.S. 418 (1935).

[279]U.S. v. Anderson, 625 F.2d 910 (9th Cir. 1980), cert. den. 450 U.S. 920. See generally Cohen (1982), note 12, above, at 395.

[280]E.g., Critzer v. U.S., 597 F.2d 708 (Ct. Cl. 1979), cert. den. 444 U.S. 920 (1970), income from motel, restaurant and gift shop not tax exempt.

[281]Allotments and income from allotments have also been held exempt from federal estate taxes; the same principles seem applicable to exempt them from gift taxes as well. Cohen (1982), note 12, above, at 398-399.

[282]Act of Mar. 3, 1910, ch. 832, sec. 3, 31 Stat. 1084 (25 USCA 357).

[283]U.S. v. Clarke, 445 U.S. 253 (1980).

[284]Compare Act of Feb. 5, 1948, ch. 45, 62 Stat. 17 (25 USCA 323- 328), which requires consent, with various rights of way permitted without consent under earlier statutes codified at 25 USCA 311-322a.

[285]See 25 CFR Part 169 (1982). See generally Cohen (1982), note 12 above, at 626-627.

[286]Yellowfish v. City of Stillwater, 691 F.2d 926 (10th Cir. 1982), cert. den. 51 USLW 3825.

[287]See 54 I.D. 15, 19, note 265 above.

[288]Aguilar II, note 55, above, allotments; Carlo v. Gustafson, note 179, above, townsite lots.

[289]Mitchell II, note 106, above.

[290]U.S. v. Kagama, 118 U.S. 375, 384 (1886), upholding the constitutionality of the federal Indian "Major Crimes" Act on the basis of Native American "dependency."

[291]E.g. Morton v. Ruiz, 415 U.S. 199 at 236 (1972), acknowledging such a duty in the context of the BIA general assistance welfare program. See also note 106, above, at 5005.

PART III

FEDERAL
HUMAN SERVICE
OBLIGATIONS

CHAPTER FIVE

HISTORY OF NATIVE SERVICES
IN ALASKA

I. Overview

Except for fur traders, gunrunners and whalers, the first American contacts with Alaska Natives were through the military and the missionaries.[1] The military introduced "hoocheeno"[2] and the missionaries brought religion. Along with religion came education of one sort or another. Of the missionaries, Sheldon Jackson of Sitka and William Duncan of Metlakatla are probably the best known, and in their respective spheres, the two that had the greatest impact. Of the two, Sheldon Jackson is more important, because, under the 1884 Organic Act,[3] he became the Alaska Agent for the United States Office (later Bureau) of Education.

A. Bureau of Education—1884 to 1931

Sheldon Jackson, both as a missionary and as a government official, concentrated much of his energy on Alaska Natives. He expanded the scope of "education" to include other activities related to Native health, economic, educational and community development needs. In doing so, he and those who followed him incorporated these activities into the federal government's Alaska Native program. The various Alaskan reserves became one important aspect of that program.

1. Reserves

These reserves were created for various specific purposes and by various means. As discussed in chapter 3, between 1903 and 1933 approximately 150 such reserves were created by executive order. These reserves were generally for the benefit of the Natives in one respect or another but were established for a variety of specific purposes. These included:

Economic Development—The earliest such reserves (1901-1906) were for the St. Lawrence Island and other reindeer reserves. Between 1912-1933 others were created for fishing and fish processing. These included the Tyonek and the early Hydaburg and Klawock reserves, as well as the Chilkat and Amaknak fishing reserves. The Hydaburg reserve (1912) also supported a Native lumber mill. In 1930 the large Tetlin reserve was established to protect Native fur trading.

Education—These reserves were established between 1902 and 1936 and included approximately eighty school reserves as well as the vocational educational reserves of Tetlin, Eklutna, White Mountain and Pt. Hope.

Community Development—Established between 1912 and 1915, these reserves include the first Hydaburg and Klawock reserves as well as Klukwan.

Health—The Klukwan sanitarium reserve of 1915 is the prime example.

2. Legislation and Appropriations

From 1884 to 1931, Congress made repeated appropriations to the Office of Education for its expanding activities among Alaska's Natives. The reindeer appropriations were the first of these[4] and were especially significant, because the Comptroller of Treasury had earlier held that the Secretary of Interior was not authorized to spend money for the benefit of Alaska Natives absent congressional authorization.[5] Thus, congressional appropriations, such as those for reindeer, constitute congressional approval of the expanding federal-Native relationship in Alaska.[6]

The Nelson Act of 1905[7] was the next significant development. Section 7 of this act provided for separate education of "uncivilized" Indians and Eskimos under the direction of the Secretary of the Interior. Non-Natives and "civilized" people of mixed blood were to be educated in schools established by the towns of the territory.[8] Full-blooded Natives could only attend Native schools. The appropriations under the Nelson Act committed the Secretary of Interior "to provide for the education and *support* of the Eskimos, Indians and other Natives of Alaska" (emphasis added). Furthermore, the 1908 appropriation act gave the Commissioner of Education wide discretion to spend the appropriations:

> in conformity with such conditions, rules and regulations, as to conduct and methods of instruction and *expenditure of money,* as may from time to time be *recommended by him* and approved by the Secretary of Interior (emphasis added).[9]

All subsequent appropriations up to at least 1931 contained similar broad authority for continued federal "support" of Alaska Natives.[10] These appropriations were the principal legal authority for the expanding scope of Alaska Native programs under the federal Office of Education.

B. Bureau of Indian Affairs—1931 to Present

In 1931, the Alaskan responsibilities of the Office of Education were transferred to the Bureau of Indian Affairs.[11] Under the authority of the Snyder Act[12] the BIA extended the federal government's service responsibilities to Alaska Natives. As discussed previously in chapter 3, the Interior Department's reservation policies were also expanded under the Alaska amendments to the Indian Reorganization Act, and the department attempted to create fishing reserves and other large reserves for the economic support of Alaska Natives throughout the territory. By 1932, it appeared obvious to the Department of the Interior Solicitor that congressional acts and appropriations for the benefit of Alaska Natives, as well as the court decisions relating to them, placed Alaska Natives in substantially the same position as other Native Americans.

> [I]t is clear that *no distinction* has been or can be made between the Indians and other Natives of Alaska *so far as the laws and relations of the United States are concerned* whether the Eskimos and other natives are of Indian origin or not, as *they are all wards of the Nation, and their status is in material* respects similar to that of the Indians of the United States (emphasis added). [13]

Similarly, and after an extensive review of the cases, Delegate Dimond concluded in a 1935 letter to William L. Paul:

> These appropriations [for the education and medical welfare of the Alaska Natives] can be based only upon the theory that the government, and therefore Congress, does owe a *special duty* to the Natives of Alaska, which is *not owed to other citizens of the Territory* (emphasis added). [14]

II. Education

A. History of Education in Alaska

1. Background

Under Russian rule, small Greek Orthodox Church schools provided educational services in several Russian-American settlements. In 1785, Gregory Ivanovich Shelekhov established the first such school at Three Saints Bay on Kodiak Island. The Russian-American Company established other schools in connection with its trading posts; however, due to financial difficulties, the company schools were discontinued prior to the transfer of Alaska to the United States. [15] Upon cession of the territory to the United States, Russia closed many of its schools and withdrew many priests and teachers, although the last Russian church school did not close until 1916. [16] During the first seventeen years following the Alaska purchase, the United States made no provision for education in the territory; however, in addition to the few remaining Russian church schools, the Presbyterian Church maintained Native mission schools in southeast Alaska. [17]

2. 1884 Organic Act

From 1877 to 1883, Sheldon Jackson, then Superintendent of Presbyterian Missions in Alaska, delivered a series of lectures on Alaska throughout the United States, calling for enactment of legislation and appropriation of funds for educational purposes in the territory.[18] On May 17, 1884, Congress passed the first Alaska Organic Act. Section 13 appropriated $25,000 and required the Secretary of the Interior to use as much of the money as was necessary to:

> make needful and proper provisions for the education of the children of school age in the Territory of Alaska, *without reference to race,* until such time as permanent provisions shall be made for the same…(emphasis added)[19]

The act also provided for the continuance of mission schools by permitting missionary stations, previously established "among the Indian tribes," to occupy up to 640 acres of land.[20] On July 4, 1885, fifteen thousand dollars was appropriated for the support of education in Alaska;[21] in the same year, the U.S. Commissioner of Education (Department of the Interior) appointed Sheldon Jackson as General Agent for Education in Alaska.[22]

3. Subsequent Legislation

The Act of June 6, 1900, "An Act making further provisions for a civil government for Alaska, and for other purposes," again provided for the education of Native and non-Native children in the territory. Section 28 required that:

> The Secretary of the Interior shall make needful and proper provisions and regulations for the education of the children of school age in the district of Alaska, without reference to race, and their compulsory attendance at school, until such time as permanent provisions shall be made for the same.[23]

The 1900 act also protected the occupants of schools or missions in the territory "in the possession of any lands now actually in their use or occupancy," and reaffirmed the 640-acre grants to missionary stations provided for in the 1884 Organic Act.[24]

4. Missionary Schools

From 1887 to 1895, missionary stations supported most of the schools in the territory. Because the federal Office of Education budgets during this period were inadequate to meet the needs of Alaska's many remote villages, the Office of Education contracted with missionary societies to maintain schools in the vicinity of the missions. This allowed the school system to be extended more rapidly than could have been done through government efforts alone. [25]

Thus, in 1885 a school was established at Bethel by contract with the Moravian Church. In 1886, contracts were let to various Catholic, and Protestant, churches for schools in the valleys of the Yukon and Nushagak Rivers, and in 1890 schools were established at Point Barrow, Point Hope and Cape Prince of Wales through contracts with Presbyterian, Episcopal and Congregational missionary societies. [26] A report made by Governor Swineford in 1888, stated that religious denominations were responsible for support of 28 of 43 schools in the Territory of Alaska; [27] however, in 1896 the federal government began to phase out the mission school subsidies. [28] Although several missions maintained important boarding schools, they gradually turned the day school program over to the federal government.

5. Dual System of Education (The Nelson Act)

Both the 1884 Organic Act and the Act of June 6, 1900, provided for education "without reference to race." However, on January 27, 1905, Congress enacted legislation which marked a turning point in the history of Alaskan education. The 1905 act, commonly known as the Nelson Act, established a dual system of education in the territory.

The Nelson Act provided that any community outside of an incorporated town, having a school population of 20 "white children and children of mixed blood who lead a civilized life," could petition the clerk of the court for establishment of a school district. It also required the incorporated communities to establish school districts. For Native children it provided that:

> the education of the Eskimos and Indians in Alaska shall remain under the direction and control of the Secretary of the Interior, and school for and among the Eskimos and Indians of Alaska shall be provided for by an annual appropriation, and the Eskimo and Indian children of Alaska shall have the same right to be admitted to any Indian boarding school as the Indian children in the States or Territories of the United States. [29]

Under the Nelson Act, the territorial governor was responsible for funding the education of white children and children of mixed blood living "civilized" lives in both incorporated and unincorporated school districts, but each district had administrative control over its own schools. The Bureau of Education assumed full responsibility for education of any "uncivilized Alaska Natives;"[30] this was a new link in the federal relationship to Alaska Natives.

6. "Civilization" Issue

The Nelson Act required Alaskan communities to provide schools only for those Native children of "mixed blood" who led "civilized" lives. In 1908, the Alaska Federal District Court discussed the statutory meaning for the term "civilization" in *Davis v. Sitka School Board.*[31] The case involved a petition for a writ of mandamus requiring the Sitka school board to admit children of mixed blood to a white school. The court found, in denying the petition, that "civilization" required the Natives not only to adopt the white man's style of living, but also to cease associating with other Natives.[32] The court approved the dual school system, relying on the authority of the federal government, through the Secretary of the Interior, to deal with Indian Affairs.

> But whatever the method adopted by the government in its dealings with the aboriginal inhabitants of this continent, it has always regarded him (sic) as of a benighted race, in a state of pupilage, a ward of the nation, needing care, control, protection and education and until comparatively recent years incapable of citizenship....*Nor is the status of the Alaska Native materially different from that of the red men of the United States.* The Aboriginal tribes of Alaska and their descendants are, then, the wards of the nation as truly as are those inhabiting the states with which the government since its organization has had to deal (emphasis added).[33]

7. Territorial Control

In 1917 the Alaska Territorial Legislature was granted control of the school system. The statute empowered the legislature to establish and maintain schools for "white and colored children and children of mixed blood who lead a civilized life."[34] Construing this statute in the case of *Jones v. Ellis,*[35] the court held that a child of mixed blood who led a civilized life and resided within city limits, had a legal right to attend city schools despite the existence of Indian schools in the city which she could also attend. However, this decision did not solve the dual system problem. Although mixed-blood Natives leading a "civilized life" had a right to attend territorial schools, outside of major population centers the burden of most Native education fell upon the federal government, first through the Bureau of Education and later the Bureau of Indian Affairs.

8. Summary

The Organic Act of 1884 required the Secretary of Interior to establish a system of education in Alaska "without reference to race"; the nondiscriminatory nature of that system was reaffirmed by the Act of June 6, 1900. However, in 1905 the Nelson Act created a dual school system, providing schools for "white children and children of mixed blood who lead a civilized life" and separate schools for all other Natives. In 1917, the territorial legislature was given the power to control schools, at which time the Alaska Department of Education was established, but Native education remained largely under the federal Bureau of Education. Finally, the BIA replaced the Bureau of Education in 1931. From that time until well after statehood, the Bureau of Indian Affairs had nearly exclusive control over Native education in Alaska.[36]

B. Current Status of Education in Alaska

1. Missionary Schools

Beginning in 1896, missionary day schools were gradually phased out and replaced by federal day schools.[37] Several mission boarding schools were maintained and established after 1896, most of which have since closed.[38]

2. BIA Schools

As a practical matter, after 1931 the Bureau of Indian Affairs was responsible for the education of most Alaska Natives. BIA schools were supported entirely from federal funds appropriated under the Snyder Act.[39] Such schools were to provide education for Native children who did not have access to public schools; eligible students were those in kindergarten through 12th grade who were at least one-fourth Native. Even Natives who did have access to public schools were sometimes accepted to BIA boarding schools on the basis of special social and psychological need.[40]

A federal statute permits the transfer of Indian schools to state or local authorities, and the Bureau of Indian Affairs has adopted a policy of gradual elimination of its direct educational functions throughout the United States.[41] This policy began as early as 1930 in Alaska with federal legislation intended to permit the Secretary of Interior to contract with territorial school boards for the education of "nontaxpaying Natives."[42] However, this legislation was not effective, because it did not provide enough money to the territorial schools to take care of the new Native enrollment. In fact, during the 1930's approximately 19 "all-Native" schools were transferred from the territory back to the BIA.[43] In 1934, the Johnson-O'Malley Act[44] was passed to provide a means of transferring the education of Native children from the federal government to state and local school systems,[45] but it was not until 1952 that Alaska entered into its first Johnson-O'Malley (JOM) contract.[46] Prior to statehood (between 1942 and 1954), about 46 schools were transferred from federal to territorial control, but these transfers ceased until after Statehood because of the territory's inablility to assume the cost.[47]

3. Statehood, Self-Determination and School Transfers

The Alaska Constitution requires the state to "maintain a system of public schools open to all the children of the state."[48] Federal policy encourages Indians to attend state public schools unless they have special educational or social needs.[49] The result was that by 1984 the Mt. Edgecumbe boarding school and all but 10 of the BIA day schools were to be transferred from federal to state control. Although official policy has favored federal school transfers since 1930, policy has been subject to a number of practical political considerations over the years.

Prior to statehood, school transfer policy was based on population shifts, the need for integration of Native children and antidiscrimination laws. After Alaska became a state, opponents of the dual system claimed it was also in conflict with the Alaska Constitution.[50] During the 1960's a cooperative effort evolved between the BIA and the state to transfer BIA schools to state·administration. In 1962, the BIA and the state signed an "agreement of understanding on educational policies." This called for the gradual consolidation of state and BIA operated schools into a single state school system. The agreement stated in part:[51]

> 4. It is the mutual goal of the State and Federal Governments to establish for all people in Alaska a single system of public elementary and secondary education.

> 5. All public schools in the State of Alaska should ultimately be included in the State educational system notwithstanding that Federal financial participation will remain essential for some time...

By 1977, however, there was growing opposition in Native communities to the federal-state school transfer policy. The philosophy behind the 1975 Indian Self-Determination Act[52] encouraged the exercise of community control over BIA-operated schools and offered an alternative to state-supervised schools. Perhaps motivated by this philosophy, the then BIA Juneau Area Director wrote the Alaska State Commissioner of Education in January 1977 to advise that in the future the BIA would require village concurrence before agreeing to a school transfer. The area director stated that the BIA was not opposed to further school transfers, but that the policy shift was a recognition:[53]

> of a third and very important entity, the village people, who we feel should be directly involved in the decisions regarding transfer of schools in their communities.

The comprehensive restructuring of the BIA educational program under the 1978 federal education amendments[54] further increased federal incentives favoring community control of BIA day schools, including the hiring and firing of teachers and the design of curriculum.[55] There were also financial difficulties in transferring the schools, because most required substantial modernization in order to conform to state health and safety criteria.[56] Thus, when the federal government first attempted to force a wholesale transfer of all the Alaska BIA schools by 1983, the state had little incentive to cooperate, especially in the face of community opposition.

The numbers of schools transferred over the years seems to reflect the shifting influence of these political considerations. For example, 28 schools were tranferred in the four years between 1967 and 1970, reflecting implementation of the 1962 BIA-state transfer agreement.[57] Nevertheless, as of 1974 there were still 51 BIA day schools in operation,[58] and in the next eight years only 14 of these were transferred.[59] The slower pace probably reflects, at least in part, the effect of BIA's village consent requirement. Then in 1982 17 schools were transferred due to a congressional funding cut;[60] at village request, one other school was transferred in 1983.[61] In 1982, the BIA dropped the self-imposed requirement for village consent to future school transfers and proposed the transfer of Mt. Edgecumbe and "a portion" of the remaining day schools during 1983-84.[62] The state assumed control of Mt. Edgecumbe in 1983, although its future operation remained in doubt, and the BIA announced that 9 of the remaining 19 day schools would be closed in 1984.[63] Five of the remaining 10 day schools were contracted out to Native governments under the Self-Determination Act,[64] but it seemed likely that with the elimination of the village consent requirement all the remaining day schools would be transferred to the State by 1985.[65]

4. Regional Educational Attendance Areas (REAA's)

a. Background

The Alaska Constitution provides for the education of Alaskan children by directing the legislature to establish and maintain a public school system. Pursuant to this provision, the legislature enacted Title 14 of the Alaska Statutes. Title 14 originally established the Alaska State-Operated School System (ASOSS) to administer those schools located outside the boundaries of incorporated municipalities.

In 1975, a suit was brought against ASOSS on behalf of twenty-eight secondary school-age Alaska Natives to compel the state to provide secondary school in plaintiffs' communities of residence.[66] At the time of the suit, commonly known as the "Molly Hootch case," there were no public secondary schools in the plaintiffs' rural western Alaska villages. Rural Native students were given the option of attending state-operated regional schools, Bureau of Indian Affairs boarding schools, or participating in state-funded correspondence studies.[67]

The plaintiffs' argument was based on two claims: first, that the State-Operated School System denied the right of education guaranteed by the Alaska Constitution and statutes; and second, that the system constituted a denial of equal protection by enforcing racial and geographic discrimination. The Alaska Supreme Court held that the right to an education under the State Constitution did not include the right to attend secondary school in one's community of residence. Since the State Constitution did not require uniformity in the school system, differences in the manner of providing education were acceptable so long as they were not violative of equal protection. The court, therefore, remanded the case to the trial court for determination of the equal protection issue. "Molly Hootch" finally resulted in a settlement, whereby the State of Alaska conceded past discrimination and agreed to open up new rural schools. In 1976, the people of Alaska approved a $59 million bond issue, in part to build rural Alaskan schools.

b. Statutory Provisions

In response to the *Hootch* case and public opinion, the legislature abolished the State-Operated School System in 1975 and established 21 Regional Educational Attendance Areas (REAA's).[68] The new law permits three types of districts in the state school system.

1. First-class cities in the unorganized borough constitute city school districts.[69]
2. Organized boroughs constitute a borough school district.[70]
3. Areas outside an organized borough or first class city are divided into REAA's.[71]

c. Effect of REAA's

Creation of the REAA's substantially decentralized education in rural Alaska. It is not immediately clear, however, whether the dispersion of educational policy making will permeate through each REAA to individual villages. Although every community with a school is supposed to have a community school committee, the powers of the committees appear advisory only.[72] Policy making therefore tends to accrue to the regional school board which is often removed from the villages within its jurisdiction by distance and difficult conditions of travel. On the other hand, the REAA school boards have substantial flexibility in dividing their respective regions into sections to ensure board representation of even small communities.[73] In all likelihood, as they demonstrate the capability to deliver quality education, the REAA's or their successors will replace the few remaining BIA day schools with state-supervised facilities. That, however, does not imply that federal responsibilities for Alaska Native education will necessarily cease. There are two significant sources of federal support for Native education in state facilities.

C. Federal Support for State Education

1. Johnson-O'Malley Act

The Johnson-O'Malley Act (JOM)[74] of 1934 was part of the New Deal legislation of the 1930's; it provides for federal-state cooperation in Indian education throughout the United States. It allows for the distribution of federal Indian education funds through a contract system under which the recipient school provides educational services in accordance with standards established by the Secretary of the Interior.[75] The Secretary of the Interior is authorized to contract with any state, territory, political subdivision, university, college, school or any other appropriate institution, for the education of Indians.[76]

From its beginning in the 1930's, debate about the JOM program has focused on the "supplemental" nature of the aid provided. The program was originally based on the concept that education was a state responsibility and that Indian children, as state citizens, were entitled to the same *basic* education as other citizens. Accordingly, states saw JOM funds as "supplemental" to state basic education budgets to enable states to assume responsibility for "basic" Indian education needs. However, annual JOM appropriations consistently reflected broader supplemental purposes beyond mere "basic" education.[77] Over the years, JOM funds were appropriated to supplement basic Indian education with programs aimed at unique Native cultural, linguistic and other needs. Largely for financial reasons, Alaska originally used JOM funds only to supplement the state's basic education budget; more recent policy changes, however, have made the Alaska JOM program more truly supplemental to Alaska Native needs.

2. JOM in Alaska

During the early 1970's, JOM funds were used primarily to support the state's boarding home program, which brought Natives from villages without high schools into larger Alaska towns. The additional costs of this program were considered beyond the normal costs of school operation and therefore to be "supplemental" educational needs. During this period, the State Department of Education served as the prime contractor for JOM funds.[78]

In March 1973, state officials and the Alaska Federation of Natives (AFN) met to discuss the possibility of greater Native control over JOM funds. AFN regarded the boarding home program as a "basic", rather than a "supplemental" education program, and claimed the state had misappropriated JOM funds by putting them into the state general fund instead of specific JOM programs. To remedy these problems, the state and AFN agreed to the transfer of the JOM program to AFN administration. Accordingly, in fiscal 1974, $1.4 million in JOM funds went to AFN for redistribution to subcontractors; the remaining $4.3 million in JOM funds went to the state boarding home program.[79] In fiscal 1975, the first year that AFN became prime contractor, no JOM funds were used for the state boarding home program.[80]

According to AFN administrators, the inexperience of some subcontractors was one of the greatest difficulties AFN encountered in its administration of the JOM program. Since no technical assistance or monitoring was included in the contract terms, it was extremely difficult to keep track of expenditures. AFN, as prime contractor, was held legally liable for any misappropriation of funds. These fiscal problems, as well as demands for local community control, led to voluntary termination of AFN as sole administrator of the JOM program. After 1975, control of JOM funds was transferred back to BIA, with the understanding that the programs would be decentralized and contracted out to smaller regional nonprofit and village Native organizations. The 1975 amendments to the Johnson-O'Malley Act further mandated this result.[81]

3. Indian Education Act (IEA) of 1972

The Indian Education Act[82] is intended to provide programs which meet the special educational needs of Indian students.[83] It was passed in response to national concern over the generally low quality of Indian education everywhere. The act provides financial assistance to local educational agencies, federal schools and Indian organizations for developing programs designed to improve educational opportunities for Indian students.[84]

IEA programs operate simultaneously with other federal programs in Alaska, such as the Johnson-O'Malley Act and Title I of the Elementary and Secondary Education Act (ESEA).[85] This allows for a more comprehensive system of specialized programs for Native students. Although there is some overlapping among the federal programs, each provides different services to different student populations. For example, IEA programs serve children of one-sixteenth or more Native blood, whereas JOM serves those of one-fourth or more. Title I ESEA programs are intended for all disadvantaged students and so do not necessarily meet the unique needs of Native children; IEA funding permits added flexibility.[86]

4. Indian Self-Determination and Education Assistance Act

The Johnson-O'Malley Act was amended in 1975 by Title II of the Indian Self-Determination and Education Assistance Act.[87] Consistent with maintenance of the federal trust responsibility and the unique federal-Indian relationship,[88] the education assistance provisions of the act are specifically intended to upgrade Indian education and support the right of Indian citizens to control their own educational activities.[89]

The Title II amendments added three new sections to the JOM Act. The first requires prospective contractors to submit plans which meet minimum conditions. The second requires school districts affected by

JOM contracts, where the school board is not comprised of a majority of Indians, to cooperate with an Indian parents' committee. The last section authorizes JOM funding for school programs attended by Native students in federal dormitories.[90]

Title I of the Self-Determination Act permits "tribal organizations" to assume control over the planning or operation of nearly any service which the BIA or the Department of Health, Education and Welfare provide for Natives. This could include control over part or all the operations of a BIA school or administration of any JOM program. ANCSA villages and regional and village corporations are defined as "Indian tribes" whose "governing bodies" can request the BIA to contract with "tribal organizations" for these services.[91] As noted earlier, however, by 1984 only 10 BIA operated schools were available for tribal contracting in Alaska. Of these, only 5 were contracted to Native governments in 1983.

D. Conclusion

Education was the first federal Native program to be extended to Alaska. Native schools originally were part of a larger congressional committment to educate the residents of the territory "without regard to race." However, these early schools were frequently mission schools, often serving wholly Native communities under federal contract, and in 1905 the Nelson Act made official what by that time had become a dual system of education. In 1931, the BIA assumed control of the schools from the federal Bureau of Education, and from that time to the present has operated Native schools and other Native education programs under the authority of the Snyder Act, other more specific legislation, and related regulations. For many years, the federal government has pursued a policy of transferring BIA schools to state control. Federal legislation specifically authorized the Secretary of the Interior to convey these schools to state or local school authorities when the federal Indian school is no longer needed for educational purposes.[92] The decentralization of the state school system and the rapid construction of village schools throughout rural Alaska, coupled with federal spending cuts, make it appear likely that direct federal funding of Alaska Native schools will soon be a thing of the past. Nevertheless, the Johnson-O'Malley and other acts related to Indian education continue in Alaska as a substantial part of a national program of support for Native education.

III. Economic Development

A. Introduction

Promoting Native American economic self-sufficiency has been a part of federal Indian policy at least since the General Allotment Act of 1887. That particular effort, perhaps well-intended, had disastrous consequences, because many Indians sold their individual allotments (See chapter 4, above). In 1934, Congress prohibited future allotments on reservations by passing the Indian Reorganization Act (IRA).[93] Among other things, the IRA also permitted Native Americans to organize tribal business enterprises and to obtain loans from a revolving loan fund in order to finance those businesses.[94] In 1974, the IRA loan fund was consolidated with other similar funds under the Indian Financing Act. Three years earlier, ANCSA had also provided Alaska Natives with a substantial amount of land and money, in part to promote Alaska Native economic development.

In addition to these statutory programs, federal officials have administratively supported Alaska Native economic development since the the turn of the century. They have done so on the strength of continued congressional appropriations for the "education and *support*" of Alaska Natives. From the reindeer program at the turn of the century to ANCSA in 1971, there have been at least four economic development programs targeted for Alaska Natives.

B. Reindeer

Sheldon Jackson imported the first reindeer to Alaska in 1891.[95] His original purpose was to prevent starvation of the Natives due to the rapid depletion of the whale, walrus, seal, fish and other aquatic resources which sustained them.[96] Congress made the first federal reindeer appropriation in 1893,[97] and by 1910 there were approximately 27,000 reindeer located at thirty stations scattered from Point Barrow to the Aleutian Islands and from the Bering Straits to the upper Yukon River.[98] By 1911, in addition to supplying food, the deer had become "the most important feature of the industrial work of the Bureau of Education among the Natives of northern and western Alaska."[99] During this period, the herds increased in size by thirty to fifty percent per year,[100] until by 1914 they numbered some 57,800 animals.[101] Of these, approximately 37,800 were in small herds owned by individual Native families.[102] The government and mission deer were both associated with schools; these deer were maintained by the Natives, but were part of the "equipment for industrial training."[103] In other words, they were used for vocational education to eliminate the need for nomadic hunting and to establish Natives in a commercial enterprise. The program was phenomenally successful, but its very success led to its downfall.

From the beginning, the Office of Education carefully restricted the sale and slaughter of female deer. Female deer could be owned by the government or the Natives, but the missions were prohibited from selling them to non-Natives without government approval.[104] In 1914, a Nome trader, Gudbrand Lomen, bought a herd of deer from a Lapp herder;[105] in 1916 he also bought the Teller Mission herd. The United States sued Lomen, alleging that the government's contract with the mission prevented the sale of deer to him.[106] The government lost. Thereafter, Lomen and others acquired many of the Native-owned deer and consolidated the small herds into more economically efficient large ones.

Perhaps in response to the competition, the government consolidated the remaining Native herds into large "unit" herds, issued shares of stock to the former Native owners (one share for each deer) and hired the former owners as herders.[107] In 1936, against violent Native opposition, the village herds were merged into large holding companies, and close herding of the reindeer was suspended.[108] A disastrous decline of the herds followed, accompanied by racial tension between the Eskimo and white herders.[109] By this time, the Nome gold rush had played out, and the non-Native reindeer corporations could find no market for reindeer meat outside Alaska. Their business began to fail.[110]

To remedy the situation, Congress passed the Alaska Reindeer Act in 1937, which authorized and directed the Secretary of the Interior to purchase non-Native-owned reindeer and reindeer equipment and to place it in trust for the Natives.[111] After a period of study, $720,000 was appropriated in 1939 to repurchase the reindeer; by June 1940, reacquisition was nearly complete.[112]

Alaska's Delegate Dimond drafted the legislation; his remarks in the House debates confirm Congress' commitment to establish the reindeer as a self-supporting Native economic enterprise:

> I am not coming here to ask you to take care of [the Eskimos] today or tomorrow. I am asking you to assist them in setting up a system which will enable them to take care of themselves and their children for the next hundred years....We are setting up a business establishment that they can operate and their children can operate after them.[113]

To ensure that the reindeer were never again acquired by non-Native interests, Congress prohibited any but Natives from owning any live deer and the alienation of any "stock or other interest in any [Native] corporation...engaged in...the reindeer industry or business."[114] It was also Congress' intent that the reindeer economy should be developed according to Native values; the reindeer enterprises were to be operated by Natives in "their native way, on native lands".[115]

Significantly, the House Report recommending passage of the Alaska Reindeer Act also noted:

> The Natives of Alaska, including Eskimos, are held to have essentially the *same status* as the Indians of the United States. The Federal Government has recognized and acknowledged this responsibility through *appropriations* for their support, education and medical treatment as well as by the introduction and distribution of reindeer. It is likewise the *responsibility* of the Federal Government to look after the social and economic welfare of the Natives (emphasis added).[116]

It is clear from this passage and from the House debates on the act that Congress passed the reindeer act in recognition of a federal responsibility to promote the economic welfare of Alaska's Natives. By the mid-1970's there were still some eighteen privately owned Native herds (30,000 deer) in Alaska.[117] The reindeer act is still valid law, and at least one ANCSA regional corporation is involved in reindeer herding.

In 1975, the BIA loaned NANA Regional Corporation nine hundred reindeer; the next year NANA purchased two thousand deer from private herders.[118] With these deer, NANA has begun a commercial reindeer program in northwest Alaska. As was intended by the reindeer act, the NANA program is intended to be a profit-making enterprise which can be adapted to the lifestyle of NANA's shareholders. Reindeer meat is generally sold locally, although there is a limited market in Alaska's larger cities. Hides are either sent outside Alaska to be tanned and sold or sold raw locally. Velvet antlers are the other major byproduct. They are sold in the orient as an aphrodisiac.[119] Through enterprises such as these, the reindeer act continues to emphasize the "responsibility of the federal government to look after the social and economic welfare of the Natives."

C. The Hydaburg Model Village

In 1905, a Haida Indian leader wrote Sheldon Jackson requesting that he use his influence to obtain land for the Haidas, free from the encroachment of whites. Nothing came of the request until 1911 when the town councils of Klinkquan and Howkan voted to obtain government assistance in building a new town near the site of the old village of Sukwan (the site of the present community of Hydaburg). The Haida Indians wished to establish a new town so they could own their own sawmill, stores, fish, business and property and establish a modern industrial training school.[120]

With the active assistance of the Office of Education, the Haidas completed the move in 1911 and by 1912 had constructed a sawmill and were producing lumber for their own use and for sale to nearby canneries. To establish the mill, thirty-eight residents of the new village subscribed to 81.5 shares of the stock at $10 per share and formed the Hydaburg Lumber Company. The Hydaburg village store contributed another $1,800 for a total cash deposit of $2,615.

The Hydaburg Lumber Company then entered into a contract with the Department of the Interior, whereby, the department provided the machinery for the sawmill plus an industrial teacher to assist in setting up and teaching the resident workers how to run the mill. In return, the Hydaburg Lumber Company agreed to pay $200 per year rent, erect the mill buildings and install the machinery. The contract provided that the mill could be purchased on or before January 1, 1915, and that the money paid for rental would apply fully to the purchase price. It was anticipated that at least part of the mill's income would be from government lumber purchases to construct the Hydaburg school and other government buildings.[121]

The contract was very liberal and gave the Haidas complete freedom in the operation of the mill; the money spent for the purchase of machinery and the industrial education teacher came solely from Office of Education funds. It was also understood that should the Hydaburg people be unable to pay for the mill within the contract period, the Commissioner of Education would use his "discretion to extend the time."[122] Ownership of the mill was to be retained by the United States "for a few years, if necessary, permanently,"[123] Apparently to further assure Hydaburg's economic success, a substantial area of land and water was withdrawn as a reserve in 1912.[124] Similar withdrawals were made shortly thereafter for Klawock and Klukwan—two other reserves established for substantially the same purposes as Hydaburg.

These reserves demonstrate the role of federal executive agencies in the development of the federal-Native relationship in Alaska. Operating under congressional appropriations for the "education and *support*" of Alaska Natives, officials of the Office of Education actively supported Native efforts to improve their economic position. These were not acts of pure charity, because, as the Hydaburg lumber contract demonstrates, the Natives also committed their relatively meager financial resources to these economic enterprises. Long before Congress, in passing the Alaska Reindeer Act, specifically recognized the "responsibility of the federal government to look after the social and economic welfare of the Natives," federal officials accepted that responsibility by their support of enterprises like the Hydaburg model village. Congress also tacitly recognized this responsibility through continued appropriations for the "education and *support*" of Alaska Natives.

D. Fish Canneries

Following the Hydaburg experience, the Bureau of Education attempted to establish salmon canneries as another means of improving Alaska Native economic conditions.[125] As noted in the previous chapter, the Interior Department Solicitor justified the new activity on the basis of the guardian-ward relationship between the United States government and the Alaska Natives.[126] In a parallel development, the Ninth Court of Appeals Circuit held, based on this special relationship, that the Annette Island Packing Company, which owned and operated a cannery at Metlakatla, was exempt from territorial taxation.[127]

Until 1965, the Bureau of Indian Affairs, under section 10 of the Indian Reorganization Act, also loaned money to the IRA chartered corporations at Hydaburg, Kake, Klawock and Metlakatla to construct and operate fish canneries.[128] In the 1960's, and particularly after the U. S. Supreme Court decision in *Kake v. Egan*,[129] these canneries began to suffer severe financial losses. They fell behind in repayment of the IRA loans, and the Hydaburg and Klawock cannery operations were consolidated, allegedly for more efficient operation. In 1974, the Hydaburg Cooperative Association sued the United States for breach of fiduciary duty in its handling of the cannery consolidation and in failing to make the cannery profitable.

Following years of litigation, the lawsuit finally arrived before the United States Court of Claims. There the United States moved for summary judgement on the grounds that it owed no special duty of trust to the cooperative association either because the cannery was located on trust lands (acquired under section 5 of the IRA) or because it was financed with federal loans (advanced under section 10 of the IRA). The Court of Claims agreed, holding that the government had only a creditor relationship with the association under the IRA and therefore no special duty to ensure that the borrowed funds were administered in a way best calculated to make the cannery profitable. [130]

The Hydaburg lawsuit illustrates one of the probable limits of the federal trust responsibility to Native Americans. The federal courts have rather consistently held that unless there is a specific statute imposing a responsibility on the United States, the government is generally shielded from a lawsuit for money damages by the doctrine of sovereign immunity. [131] The U.S. Supreme Court has applied the doctrine in the field of Indian affairs to prevent the recovery of money damages for alleged breaches of trust unless a specific statute imposes a clear responsibility on the federal government from which it can be concluded that Congress intended to waive the immunity of the United States. [132] The limitation does not mean, however, that damages can only be had for loss of property. All that is required is that Congress has adopted a statute accepting some particular responsibility the breach of which causes money damages. [133] Nor does it mean that other (non-monetary) relief, such as an injunction, cannot be had where monetary relief is not appropriate. [134]

E. ANCSA and The Indian Financing Act

In recent years the Federal Government has passed major legislation, intended to improve Native American economic potential. [135] The Alaska Native Claims Settlement Act itself is one such piece of legislation; the Indian Financing Act of 1974 is another. Brief descriptions of the economic development aspects of these acts and their influence on the federal-Native relationship follow.

1. ANCSA

Although the claims settlement act was passed to resolve Alaska Native land claims, section 2(b) of the act affirms that the settlement was to be "accomplished rapidly, with certainty, in conformity with the real *economic* and social needs of the Natives..." (emphasis added). The House Report accompanying the bill that became ANCSA states that the amount of land and money to be confirmed to the Natives under the act was not based on the probable extent of aboriginal title but on the assets necessary for economic development. As to land, the report states that:

In determining the amount of land to be granted to the Natives, the committee took into consideration the land needed for ordinary village sites and village expansion, the land needed for a subsistence hunting and fishing economy by many of the Natives, and the land needed by the Natives as a *form of capital for economic development.*

The 40 million acres is a generous grant by almost any standard.

The acreage occupied by villages and needed for normal village expansion is less than 1 million acres. While some of the remaining 39 million acres may be selected by the Natives because of its subsistence use, most of it will be selected for its *economic potential.* The land selected is not required to be related to prior use and occupancy, which is the basis for a claim of aboriginal title (emphasis added).

As to money the Report states that:

The $925 million figure is an arbitrary one. It is not intended to be related to the value of the lands claimed by the Natives under the doctrine of aboriginal title.

The figure chosen by the committee, $925 million over half of which will come from the state, is based on the following considerations: the extreme poverty and underprivileged status of the Natives generally, and the need for adequate resources to permit the Natives to *help themselves economically.* The Natives constitute about one-fifth of the total population of the State, but they are almost completely *lacking in the capital* needed to compete with the non-Native population and to raise their standard of living through their own efforts. *The money grant in this bill is intended to provide that capital* (emphasis added). [136]

This language demonstrates that Congress chose principles of economic development and capital formation as the means to gauge the size of the Alaska Native claims settlement. In this respect, ANCSA also conforms to the historic federal policy of promoting Native self-sufficiency and the more recently defined policy of Native self-determination. This is an important point, because it brings ANCSA within the mainstream of national Indian policy generally and historic Alaska Native policy specifically, as is confirmed by subsequent legislation.

2. Indian Financing Act of 1974

The Indian Financing Act of 1974[137] is one such piece of legislation.

It is intended to:

> provide capital on a reimbursable basis to help develop and uti-
> lize Indian resources, both physical and human, to a point
> where the Indians will fully exercise responsibility for the utili-
> zation and management of their own resources and where
> they will enjoy a standard of living from their own productive
> efforts comparable to that enjoyed by non-Indians in neighbor-
> ing communities. [138]

The act consolidates previous revolving loan funds into a single $50 million fund to provide direct federal loans to Native organizations and individuals. [139] Titles II and III authorize a new Indian loan guaranty and insurance fund to enable Native organizations and individuals to obtain private financing otherwise unavailable to them. [140] Three $20 million appropriations in FY 1975, 1976 and 1977 were expected to generate up to $200 million in private loans for Native business enterprises. [141] Title IV provides direct grants up to fifty thousand dollars to Indian tribes who wish to set up small businesses, [142] and Title V requires, along with any grant or loan, that the Interior Secretary provide "competent management and technical assistance consistent with the nature of the enterprise being funded."[143]

As with most "Indian" legislation, [144] Alaska Native villages and "Native groups…as defined in the Alaska Native Claims Settlement Act" are eligible for benefits under the financing act. [145] It is also significant that "reservations" are defined as including "land held by incorporated Native groups, regional corporations and village corporations under ANCSA."[146] That is significant because "reservations" are specifically recognized in the act's legislative history as being among those areas of the nation most in need of the type of economic assistance that the act provides. [147]

> One of the most serious problems on the Indian reservations
> is the inadequate availability of financial resources to permit
> the Indian people to develop their own resources and poten-
> tial.…
>
> On every reservation today there is almost a total lack of an
> economic community. If the long sought goal of Indian self-suf-
> ficiency is to be reached, such financial assistance must be
> provided or facilitated.

Considerations such as these demonstrate the similarity between the federal government's relationship to Alaska Natives and its relationship to Native Americans generally. Such legislation also demonstrates the continuing congressional commitment to Alaska Native economic development and self-sufficiency.

F. Conclusion

At least since the reindeer appropriations at the turn of the century, the United States has had a consistent policy of advancing the economic development of the Alaska Natives. ANCSA and subsequent legislation, such as the Indian Financing Act, continue this policy in significant respects. While implementation of these policies, in the advance of loans for example, has been held to create a creditor-debtor relationship rather than a trust responsibility, that is not a distinction unique to Alaska Natives. Rather the application to Alaska Natives of economic development policies applicable to Native Americans generally illustrates the parallels between the treatment of Alaska Natives and other Native Americans. Statutes passed to satisfy the historic and continuing economic development needs of Native Americans, while they may not necessarily create a trust relationship, do maintain a special relationship between Native Americans and the federal government.

IV. Welfare Benefits and Services

A. Introduction

In a study called *Alaska Natives and the Land,*[148] before ANCSA, and in the *2(c) Report*[149] required by ANCSA, Alaska Natives were confirmed to be among the most disadvantaged people in the nation. The findings of the *2(c) Report* are typical:

> Three out of eight Native families are below the official poverty line. (If we took account of the high prices in Alaska, probably half of the Natives would be found to be living in poverty.) Poverty among Alaska Natives is four times as prevalent as in the U. S. population, and more than eight times as prevalent as among Alaska non-Natives.[150]

Testimony surrounding the claims act frequently described the educational,[151] health, social and economic disadvantages[152] of the Alaska Natives. These were not new problems; in fact, they were very old. The federal government had long recognized them and enacted legislation and appropriated funds in response to them. Federal education and economic development programs were both intended to improve the material condition of Alaska Natives. Federal Native welfare services have a similar history; they began with the Bureau of Education's response to the destitution of the Natives living near government schools.

B. Copper Center and Vicinity—1907-1910

The government's first response to Native destitution was at Copper Center and other points along the old military telegraph line.[153] This line extended from Haines and Valdez north to Eagle and from Copper Center west along the Tanana and Yukon rivers to St. Michael on the Bering Sea. Military posts were located along the line at Haines (Fort Seward), Copper Center/Tonsina (Ft. Liscum), Eagle (Ft. Egbert) and Tanana (Ft. Gibbon). [154] Telegraph stations were also established at communities along the line.

From 1907 to approximately 1910, military personnel at the forts were responsible for issuing food supplies to destitute Natives. In 1907, five thousand dollars was set aside from Bureau of Education appropriations for direct relief of Alaska Native destitution. By an order of April 24, 1907, the Secretary of War dictated the method for distribution of the "destitution supplies." Prior to issuing any supplies, post commanders had to advise the Commissioner of Education directly by wire of the cost of supplies to be issued. The Commissioner would then approve the distribution in Washington, D. C., and telegraph the approval to the appropriate commander. This was to insure that expenditures did not exceed the five thousand dollars set aside. Once the supplies were distributed, the Bureau of Education merely transferred funds from its appropriations to the War Department's "Subsistence of the Army" appropriations. [155]

In 1908, a Bureau of Education teacher, Mrs. H. S. Atkins, was placed at Copper Center and assumed responsibility for food distribution. She was given careful instructions not to distribute food to able-bodied Natives unless they would perform work for the government school; the Bureau of Education wished to avoid creating a "pauperized, dependent set of Natives at Copper Center." [156] The bureau apparently became disenchanted with Mrs. Atkins' ability to distribute the food as requested and shortly thereafter transferred her. For a time the military resumed distribution of the foodstuffs, but in 1910 the newly appointed Superintendent of Education, Northern District, took over the program. [157] Destitution relief remained the Bureau of Education's responsibility until 1931 when federal jurisdiction over Alaska Native affairs was transferred to the BIA.

C. The Snyder Act

The Copper Valley destitution relief program indicates the importance of appropriations legislation in the formulation of Indian policy. Merely by obtaining an appropriation for "education and support" for the Natives in Alaska, the Bureau of Education could set aside monies from that appropriation for various sorts of programs. For many years appropriation legislation was the principle means Congress used to shape (however unreliably) national Indian policy. [158]

Until 1921, the scope and purpose of BIA programs were, like Bureau of Education programs, largely shaped by individual congressional appropriations. In 1921, Representative Snyder of New York introduced HR 7848 in an attempt to regain House control of Indian appropriations. It was to become the Snyder Act of 1921. [159] The Snyder Act only applies to the BIA; therefore, it did not initially affect activities of the Bureau of Education in Alaska. However, the transfer of the Bureau of Education's Alaska activities to the Bureau of Indian Affairs in 1931 brought Alaska Native programs under the authority of the Snyder Act. [160]

The scope and purpose of the Snyder Act have only recently come under judicial scrutiny. The act is an extremely broad authorization of appropriations "for the benefit, care and assistance of Indians throughout the United States." Although the BIA attempts to restrict its "benefit, care and assistance" only to Indians living "on or near" a reservation, realities in Alaska required the bureau to expand the scope of its activities to include all Alaska and to treat all of Alaska as a "reservation."

The scope of the bureau's service jurisdiction under the Snyder Act has been a subject of congressional inquiry from the mid-1960's to the present. [161] In 1971, then Commissioner of Indian Affairs, Louis R. Bruce, testified before the House Subcommittee on Interior Appropriations and defined the BIA's concept of its service jurisdiction as follows:

> The service population of the Bureau of Indian Affairs is usually defined to include, according to Title 18 of the United States Code, those Indians who (a) live on trust land under the jurisdiction of the United States Government, (b) are dependent Indian communities within the borders of the United States, whether within the original or subsequently acquired territory thereof— [162]

At this point, Representative Julia Butler Hanson, the Subcommittee Chair, interrupted and stated that the last provision "affects the State of Alaska particularly." Mr. Bruce then continued:

> Yes; [or] whether within the limits of a state and, (c) all Indian allotments, Indian titles of which have not been extinguished, including rights-of-way, running through the same.

Mr. Bruce went on to note that the service population in Alaska was approximately 56,800 Aleuts, Eskimos and Indians (i.e., the entire then known Native population). Simply put, there is no equivalent of the "on or near the reservation" requirement for Alaska Natives. Because Alaska Natives were not generally confined to reservations, the federal government has historically acknowledged a broader service obligation to them. [163]

Until 1981, the Bureau of Indian Affairs had shown no tendency to withdraw from its expansive view of its Alaskan obligations. In 1977, for example, it issued new regulations governing eligibility for general assistance, child welfare assistance, miscellaneous assistance and family and community services. [164] The regulations restricted eligibility to those Native Americans living "on or near reservations", [165] but, as defined in the regulations, reservations specifically included "Alaska Native regions established pursuant to the Alaska Native Claims Settlement Act.[166] Similarly, the 1978 Indian Child Welfare Act (ICWA) and the regulations implementing it extend grant eligibility for Indian child welfare programs to Alaska Natives regardless of their reservation status.[167]

Then, in 1981, the bureau proposed the wholesale elimination of the Alaska general assistance program by eliminating its funding from the BIA's 1982 fiscal year appropriations. Congress appeared to comply, but when the bureau actually tried to terminate the program, individual welfare recipients and Native contractors sued to prevent it. Although the Natives lost in the Alaska Federal District Court, the Ninth Circuit reversed a year later on appeal and enjoined termination of the program.[168] The appellate court concluded that it was not clear Congress intended to terminate the program in the absence of comparable state benefits. The future of the BIA general assistance program in Alaska was thus not clear as of mid-1983, but the federal government continued to fund several other Native welfare programs in Alaska, most notably under the Indian Child Welfare Act.[169]

D. BIA Social Service Programs

1. Introduction

The BIA operates or funds several social service programs in Alaska under the primary authority of the Snyder Act.[170] The regulations promulgated in 1977 distinguish between two types of welfare programs—financial assistance and social services.[171] Financial assistance programs provide cash to needy Natives; social service programs (called "family and community services") rely on "the social work skills of casework, group work or community development to solve social problems involving children, adults or communities."[172] Family and community services are frequently provided in association with financial assistance. The Indian Child Welfare Act (ICWA) provides grants to Indian tribes and organizations for Indian child and family programs.

There are three types of financial assistance available from the BIA child welfare assistance, miscellaneous assistance and general assistance. Child welfare assistance payments provide for foster care or other nonmedical, special care for Native children who are away from home as well as other services not available to such children under the general assistance program or from the state.[173] Miscellaneous assistance is a catch-all program primarily used to provide burial services, emergency food or disaster relief or "other financial needs...related to assistance for needy Indians."[174]

2. General Assistance

At least until 1982, the general assistance program was the most important of the BIA financial assistance programs in terms of both total budget and numbers of Native people served.[175] Total expenditures of general assistance were in excess of $4 million in fiscal years 1973, 1974 and 1977.[176] During FY '75 and FY '76 (periods of peak pipeline employment) expenditures dropped below that level, but by FY 1981 estimates for a fully funded program were almost $10 million.[177] On the other hand, child welfare budgets in FY '72, FY '73 and FY '74 averaged less than $1 million, and miscellaneous assistance budgets during the same period were between forty and fifty thousand dollars.[178] These expenditure and budget levels reflect the relative caseloads for each type of assistance. During FY '74, for example, general assistance was granted in 4,037 cases (benefiting 13,160 individuals) while child welfare payments went to only 457 cases and miscellaneous assistance to an estimated 287 cases.[179]

General Assistance, like all BIA social welfare programs, is only provided when "assistance or services are not available or not being provided by state, local or other agencies."[180] It might be characterized in this respect as a "gap filling" program, to be continued only until such time as state or other agencies assume its role; however, such a description conceals the real importance of the program. As one study notes:

> the only income maintenance program...oriented to the special circumstances of Natives is the general assistance program of the BIA social services, which exclusively serves Natives. This program addresses precisely the need ignored by the other income maintenance programs.[181]

BIA general assistance is a noncategorical aid program for needy Natives; its principal advantage is that it fulfills real Native needs without requiring Native beneficiaries to fit into eligibility "categories."[182] By contrast, other federal and state "public assistance" programs are based on the assumption that need stems from some underlying problem beyond the control of the needy individual. Eligibility for these programs requires that the individual, in addition to being needy, fit into a particular problem category.

Thus, Supplemental Security Income (SSI) is only available to the needy who are blind, aged or disabled;[183] Aid to Families with Dependent Children (AFDC) is only available to needy families deprived of parental support when the parent having the duty of support (usually the father) is "absent from the home."[184] Somewhat similarly, unemployment insurance is only available to those who have been employed for significant periods each year, and the level of unemployment benefits is tied to the amount earned during periods of employment. Many Alaskan Natives are, therefore, ineligible for unemployment insurance benefits because they are only employed in nonmonetary subsistence activities or short-term, low-paying jobs.[185]

a. Specific Advantages

Unlike any of these programs, BIA general assistance requires Alaska Native applicants to meet only three need-related criteria.[186] First, they must have "resources" insufficient to meet their "need."[187] Second, they must not be eligible for or receiving SSI, AFDC or "other public assistance."[188] Third, they must reside in areas where "comparable general assistance is not being provided to all residents on the same basis from a state, country or local public jurisdiction."[189]

BIA regulations specifically exclude from general assistance eligibility those Natives who are eligible for SSI or "other public assistance."[190] Although this excludes Native families who are eligible for AFDC, that is not usually detrimental to Natives, because those who are eligible for AFDC receive the same level of assistance from the state as they would from the BIA, except for statutory maximums in some instances. Furthermore, the regulations still permit the BIA to provide general assistance to Natives who have applied for AFDC, pending receipt of the first AFDC payment.

Even more important, BIA general assistance is available to a large category of needy Native families who are not eligible for AFDC because neither parent is "absent from the home." This is particularly important, inasmuch as many Native families, even with both parents in the home, are needy because of chronic unemployment or underemployment. That is particularly true in rural Alaska, which has a dearth of income-producing jobs.[191] Without BIA general assistance, these families would be eligible only for the state General Relief (GR) program. Unfortunately, the state GR program is limited to emergency aid, provides substantially less aid than BIA general assistance and provides no direct cash assistance.[192] If forced to rely on state GR, parents of these families would either be unable to meet their cash needs or be forced to separate in order to meet AFDC categorical requirements. General assistance permits Natives to avoid this problem, thereby preserving Native family unity and social stability.

BIA general assistance is also available to single or married adults without children. The amount of adult assistance is determined according to the state's need schedule for its Adult Public Assistance (APA) program, which includes Old Age Assistance (OAA), Aid to the Disabled (AD) and Aid to the Blind (AB). Under the APA schedule, single adults in 1977 were entitled to assistance of up to $334 per month.[193]

A non-Native individual who does not fit into one of the APA categories, is only eligible for state General Relief. However, the funding restrictions on the state GR program mean that it is unable to meet even approximate levels of real need. On the other hand, BIA general assistance has in the past always had sufficient funds to meet the needs of adult Native applicants.

b. Attempts to Terminate General Assistance

The BIA general assistance program has been available to Alaska Natives since 1939,[194] but in 1981 the bureau attempted to eliminate the program by representing to Congress that the state was willing to enact and fund a "comparable" program. In retrospect those representations appear at best to have been wishful thinking. Unlike the federal government, the state could probably not constitutionally limit a non-categorical assistance program to Natives alone. If it were to fund such a program for Natives, it would have to do the same for all its needy citizens, and the cost would likely be several times the estimated $10 million annual cost of the BIA program. Not surprisingly, the state failed to fulfill the bureau's congressional representations.

In early 1981, faced with imminent termination of the program, Natives representing some thirty four hundred BIA general assistance beneficiaries, sued to enjoin the Secretary of the Interior from cutting off their benefits. In granting the injunction on appeal, the circuit court concluded that the Interior Department had not met its heavy burden of showing that Congress had acquiesced in the department's decision to terminate the general assistance program. Instead the court found that Congress, based on the department's representations, might well have intended to cut the program's appropriation only if the state funded a comparable replacement.[195] The decision illustrates a judicial reluctance to read congressional appropriations as terminating Native programs unless the intent behind the appropriation is unequivocal.

3. BIA Social Service Contracting

National policy since about 1971 has favored the contracting of BIA services with Native American tribes or organizations. The 1974 *2(c) Report* noted that the BIA had been contracting for social services under the Buy Indian Act[196] at least since 1971, but that the program had remained "small scale in Alaska." At that time there were ten such contracts in effect, most of which were limited to providing general assistance and emergency child welfare services.[197] The Buy Indian Act, however, was a very limited vehicle for government contracting since it merely permitted the Secretary of the Interior to employ "Indian labor" and purchase the "products of Indian industry" and did not clearly authorize the contracting of entire programs to Native tribes and organizations. The Self-Determination Act[198] overcame these difficulties and resulted in a significant increase in the scope of Alaska Native social service contracting. As of 1975, approximately fifty percent of all BIA social service programs had been contracted to Native organizations.[199]

4. Indian Child Welfare Grants

The Indian Child Welfare Act (ICWA) authorizes a variety of grants to Indian tribes and organizations to improve their response to the social needs of their families and children.[200] As with the general assistance program, these grants are funded out of Snyder Act appropriations.[201] The regulations implementing the grant program impose very rigid time requirements on the BIA's processing of grant applications and require the BIA to tell the applicant of any deficiencies in the application prior to its rejection.[202] Generally the funding for these grants has been limited and the competition keen among Indian tribes and organizations. In Alaska, the BIA has also had difficulty meeting the time requirements for processing applications.[203] Nevertheless, for those tribes and organizations lucky enough to get them, the grants have provided an important source of funding for badly needed social service programs aimed specifically at strengthening Native families.

E. Conclusion

Since at least the turn of the century, the federal government has provided an increasing variety of social welfare services to Alaska Natives because of their status as Natives. Although the BIA attempted to eliminate the long-established general assistance program in 1981, it was not clear in 1983 that the attempt would stand up in court. Even if the general assistance program were to be eliminated, however, it would not eliminate the ICWA grant program and the other social service programs, many of which are now contracted to Alaska Native tribes and organizations under the Self-Determination Act.

V. General Conclusions

The long history of federal educational, economic development and social welfare services for Alaska Natives goes back to the beginning of the twentieth century. There is some evidence, beginning in the 1980's, that the federal executive branch is attempting to sharply restrict these human services, particularly in the fields of education and welfare payments. On the other hand, beginning with ANCSA, the federal government's committment to Alaska Native economic development appears stronger and more likely to bear fruit than at any time in the past. Even in the fields of education and social services, the elimination of federal Native schools and general assistance would not eliminate other less direct support programs available under the Johnson-O'Malley, Indian Education, Self-Determination and Indian Child Welfare Acts.

ANCSA itself does not imply a reduction of the long-standing federal committment to Alaska Native human services either, but the claims act did require an early analysis of the various programs provided to Alaska Natives,[204] and a later report (due in 1985) on the "status of the Natives."[205] As with any ongoing political process, there is always the risk it will end in policies which are to the disadvantage of an under-represented minority. Nevertheless, it appears that repeated opportunities will arise to subject the federal government's human service committment to Alaska Natives to political scrutiny.

ENDNOTES

[1]Sheldon Jackson, *Thirteenth Annual Report on the Introduction of Domestic Reindeer into Alaska, 1903,* (Washington, D.C.: GPO, 1904), at 165, n. 6. Hereafter "Reindeer Report (1903)," etc.

[2]Ernest Gruening, *The State of Alaska,* (New York: Random House, 1968), at 36. The military initially attempted (1867 and 1870) to interdict the liquor trade between whites and Alaska Natives in the belief that Alaska was "Indian country" under the 1834 Trade and Intercourse Act (Id. at 35, n. 6); subsequent court decisions held it was not. See U. S. v. Seveloff, 1 Ak. Rpts. 64 (1872). In 1873 Congress specifically applied the liquor control sections of the Intercourse Act to Alaska, and prosecutions under the amended act were upheld. *In re Carr,* 1 Ak. Rpts. 75 (1875). However, prohibitions against trading other merchandise with Indians did not apply. Waters v. Campbell, 1 Ak. Fed. Rpts. 91 (1876). The probable result was free trade in molasses—the principal ingredient of "hoochenoo" (Gruening at 41). See also Clarence C. Hulley, *Alaska Past and Present,* (Portland, Or.: Binfords and Mort, (1970) at 233. The federal definition of "Indian country" was revised and codified in 1948 to include the lands of any reservation, allotment or "dependent Indian community." See 18 USC 1151. The new federal definition seems to undercut the vitality of the holding of *Waters v. Campbell,* above.

Perhaps in response to the 1873 Trade and Intercourse Act amendments, the Secretary of Interior, Columbus Delano, requested that Congress appropriate money for an Alaska Indian agent. Congress refused, but Delano appointed Frederick S. Hall as a special Alaska agent anyway. That was in April 1873, but the Comptroller of the Treasury decided the Bureau of Indian Affairs was not authorized to use Bureau funds in Alaska. The Alaska Agency was therefore abolished in November 1873; by that time it was winter and Hall was living at St. Michael on the western Alaska coast. He did not receive word of the agency's demise until May 1874. See staff files "Ref. 8-RG75-1A Bureau of Indian Affairs Copy for Alaska Guide June 30, 1967"at 2-3 on file with the Federal Archives and Records Center (FARC), Seattle. The referenced file is part of an early draft compilation of federal records relating to Alaska prepared by the National Archives and Records Source (NARS), Washington, D. C.; see also George S. Ulibarri, *Documenting Alaska History* (Fairbanks, Ak: University of Alaska, 1982), at 245-246.

The Alaska Natives, along with the rest of Alaska's residents, remained under Army "control" until 1877. The Army was then withdrawn, and until 1879 the Collector of Customs was the only U. S. Government official in Alaska. In 1879, the Navy took over and remained until the 1884 Organic Act established the first civil government and authorized a General Agent for the Office (later Bureau) of Education in Alaska. See generally Gruening, above, at 36-43.

[3]Act of May 17, 1884, 23 Stat. 24, 27. Section 13 authorized the Secretary of Interior to make "needful and proper" provisions for the education of school age children in the territory "without reference to race until such time as permanent provisions shall be made for the same."

[4]$6,000 was appropriated in 1894 to support Dr. Jackson's reindeer program. See *Reindeer Report, 1903, note 1, above, at 166. See note 94, below.*

[5]See note 2, above.

[6]*See U. S. v. Sandoval, 231 U. S. 28, 47 (1913). See also F. Cohen, Handbook of Federal Indian Law* (Washington, D.C.: G.P.O., 1942; reprint New York: AMS, 1972), at 88, regarding the role of appropriations as manifestations of federal Indian policies.

[7]Act of March 30, 1905, 33 Stat. 1156.

[8]See David H. Getches, *Law and Alaska Native Eduction* (Fairbanks, Ak.: Center for Northern Educational Research, University of Alaska, 1977) at 4.

[9]Act of May 27, 1908, 35 Stat. 317, 351, cited in 53 L.D. 593, 598 (1932).

[10]53 L.D., note 9, above, at 598.

[11]Secretarial Order No. 494, March 14, 1931.

[12]Act of November 2, 1921, 42 Stat. 208 (25 USC 13). This is the principle authorizing legislation for most BIA activities.

[13]53 L. D., note 9, above, at 605. See also U. S. v. Berrigan, 2 Ak. Rpts. 442 (1905); Alaska Pacific Fisheries v. U. S., 248 U. S. 78 (1918).

[14]83 Cong. Rec. Pt. 9, 180, 75th Congress, 3rd session (1938). Significantly, this letter was written in 1935 during the time when Congress was considering the advisability of extending the IRA to Alaska. In 1936 Congress passed the Alaska amendments (49 Stat. 1205) applying the IRA to Alaska.

[15]William R. Marsh, *North to the Future: Alaska Department of Education, 1785-1967* (Juneau: State of Alaska Department of Education,, 1967), at 8.

[16]Getches, note 8, above, at 3.

[17]Id.

[18]*North to the Future,* note 15, above, at 10.

[19]Act of May 17, 1884, 23 Stat. 24, 17.

[20]Id. Section 8, 23 Stat. at 26.

[21]Act of July 4, 1884, 23 Stat. 75, 91, cited in F. Cohen (1942), note 6, above, at 407.

[22]*North to the Future,* note 15, above, at 17.

[23]Act of June 6, 1900, Sec. 28, 31 Stat. 300.

[24]Id. Sec. 27.

[25]*North to the Future,* note 15, above, at 17. See also H.D. Anderson and W.C. Eells, *Alaska Natives, A Survey of Their Sociological and Educational Status*

(Stanford: Stanford University Press, 1935) at 391.

[26]*North to the Future,* note 15, above, at 17.

[27]Id. at 14. Report of Governor Swineford, 1888, from *Biennial Report of Commissioner of Education,* June 30, 1920.

[28]Getches, note 8, above, at 4.

[29]Act of January 27, 1905, 33 Stat. 616, 619.

[30]The previous education provisions in the acts of May 17, 1884 and June 6, 1900, were superseded by the 1905 act. The Organic Act of 1912, creating the Territory of Alaska, expressly reserved from the legislature the power to alter, amend, modify, or repeal the Nelson Act of 1905. See Act of August 24, 1912, 27 Stat. 512. See also Getches, note 8, above, at 4-5.

[31]3 Ak. Rpts., 481 (1908).

[32]Id. at 493-494. See also Getches, note 8, above, at 5.

[33]Id. at 485.

[34]Act of March 3, 1917, 39 Stat. 1131. The Alaska Department of Education was established at this time.

[35]8 Ak. Rpts. 146 (1929).

[36]Anderson and Eells, note 25, above, at 215.

[37]See note 28, above, and accompanying text.

[38]Phone conversation with Anchorage Catholic Archdiocese, August 9, 1977.

[39]25 USC 13, note 12 above.

[40]*2(c) Report, Federal Programs and Alaska Natives,* "Task II, Part B, Section 2," at 3. See also 25 USC 282 et seq. and 25 CFR 31.0 et seq. regarding federal schools for Indians.

[41]*North to the Future,* note 15, above, at 75. See also 25 USCA 293(a) (1970), authorizing conveyance of federal schools to state or local authorities.

[42]Act of May 14, 1930, ch. 273, 46 Stat. 279, 231, cited in note 8, above, at 6.

[43]Id.

[44]Act of April 16, 1934, 48 Stat. 596 (codified as amended at 25 USC 452-457).

[45]Getches, note 8, above, at 7.

[46]Id.

[47]Id. at 7-8. See generally, F. Cohen, *Handbook of Federal Indian Law* (Charlottesville, Va.: Michie Bobbs-Merrill, 1982 ed.), at 762-763.

[48]Alaska Const. Art. VIII, Sec. 1.

[49]Cohen (1982), note 47, above, at 681.

[50]*North to the Future,* note 15, above, at 76.

[51]Id. at 77, 138, "Memorandum of General Agreement, State of Alaska- Bureau of Indian Affairs, March 1, 1962".

[52]Act of January 4, 1975, P.L. 93-638, 88 Stat. 2203 (25 USCA 450 et seq.).

[53]Remarks of Clarence Antioquia delivered to the Association of Village Council Presidents Convention, Bethel, Alaska, January 29, 1977. These remarks also described a breakdown in negotiations with the state concerning the fiscal, logistic and construction requirements to be satisfied prior to any school transfer.

[54]P.L. 95-561, Title XI, Nov. 1, 1978, 92 Stat. 2316 (25 USCA 2001 et seq.)

[55]See, e.g., 25 USCA 2010, requiring the BIA to "facilitate Indian control of Indian affairs in all matters relating to education"; 25 USCA 2011, relating to qualifications and appointments of educational personnel, and 25 USCA 2013, relating to policies and procedures. These provisions are implemented by regulations in 25 CFR Parts 32 and 38 (1982).

[56]*2(c) Report,* note 40, above, "Task II, Part B, Section 2," at 1.

[57]Getches, note 8, above at 8.

[58]*2(c) Report,* note 40, above, "Task II, Part A, Sec. 1," at 7-9. These schools served approximately 6,041 children (thirty-four percent of all the children living in rural Native villages) at a yearly cost of $11,476,900. Id. at 4. Although the pace of school transfers slowed in the next eight years, by FY 1981 there were only about three thousand Native children in BIA schools. However, BIA school expenditures had increased to $13,540,000. James E. Hawkins, *A Preliminary Profile of Federal Programs Provided to Alaska Natives,* (Washington, D.C.: Assistant Secretary of Indian Affairs 1982), at 5 and 19.

[59]47 Fed. Reg. 8409 (Friday, Feb. 26, 1982), proposing the transfer at the remaining seventy-seven day schools.

[60]E.g., Ak. Reg. Sol. memo, "Transfer of BIA School Sites in Alaska" (May 14, 1982).

[61]The village was Tuntutuliak, personal phone conversation with senior BIA Office of Education official, Juneau, Alaska, June 3, 1983.

[62]48 Fed. Reg. 37967 (Aug. 27, 1982).

[63]*Tundra Times* May 18, 1983, at 1, and *Tundra Drums* Dec. 29, 1983, at 8.

[64]Akiachak, Akiak, Chefornak, Chevak and Tuluksak were the contract schools, personal phone conversation, note 61, above.

[65]*Tundra Drums,* note 63, above.

[66]Hootch v. Alaska State-Operated School System, 536 P. 2d 793 (1975).

[67]See generally Getches, note 8, above at 21-22.

[68]124 SLA 1975, codified at AS 14.08.011 et seq. See generally, G. McBeath, *The Dynamics of Alaska Native Self-Government* (Lanham, Md.: University Press of America, 1980) at 69.

[69]AS 14.12.010.

[70]AS 14.13.020.

[71]AS 14.08.031(d).

[72]Getches, note 8, above, at 29. See also McBeath, note 68, above, at 70.

[73]Getches, note 8, above, at 29.

[74]Act of April 16, 1934. 48 Stat. 586 as amended by Act of June 4, 1936, 49 Stat. 1958; as amended by the Indian Education Assistance Act, P.L. 93-638, Act of January 4, 1975 88 Stat. 2213 (25 USCA 452-457).

[75]Cohen (1942), note 6, above, at 241.

[76]25 USCA 452.

[77]Getches, note 8, above, at 13-16, regarding the changing meaning of "supplemental" in the Alaska JOM program.

[78]*2(c) Report,* note 40, above, "Task II, Part B, Sec. 2, JOM Programs," at 1.

[79]Information gathered from talks with Gordon Jackson and Frank Berry, former Directors of the AFN/JOM program, August 10, 1977. In March 1973, the State Board of Education passed a resolution stating they no longer wished to be the prime JOM contractor and urged the BIA to seek more Native input as to the disposition of JOM funds. See Hawkins, note 58, above, at 5, regarding funding levels. By FY 1980 JOM funding levels in Alaska had risen to $7 million, Id.

[80]*2(c) Report,* note 40, above, "Task II, Part B, Sec. 2, JOM program," at 2. Also Frank Berry interview, note 79, above.

[81]25 USCA 455-457 (Indian Education Assistance Act); See notes 82-88, below, and accompanying text.

[82]Indian Education Act of June 23, 1972, 86 Stat. 335 (20 USCA 241aa et seq.). Regulations are contained in 45 CFR Part 187. See generally Cohen (1982), note 47, above at 692-693.

[83]These programs are supplemental to JOM and state-funded programs and permit grant funds for pilot programs, planning projects and equipment to meet the special educational needs of Indian children. (20 USCA 241cc) In Alaska these programs have included cultural heritage, land claims and bilingual-bicultural classes as well as counseling services. See Getches, note 8, above, at 19.

[84]*2(c) Report,* note 40, above, "Task II, Part B, Sec. 2" at 1.

[85]Title I of the Elementary and Secondary Education Assistance Act (ESEA) of April 11, 1965, P.L. 89-10, 79 Stat. 27, 20 USCA 241a et seq. provides the basic funding for improving the educational opportunity of poverty-stricken families. Since its enactment, rural Alaska has been one of the pricipal beneficiaries. But see Getches, note 8, above, at 17, describing the administrative shortcoming of ESEA.

[86]The IEA was amended in 1974 to extend through 1978 and in 1978 to extend through 1983, Nov. 1, 1978 P.L. 95-561, Title XI, 92 Stat. 2328.

[87]Indian Self-Determination and Education Assistance Act of January 4, 1975, P.L. 93-638, 88 Stat. 2206 (25 USCA 450 et seq.).

[88]1974 United States Congressional and Administrative News (USCAAN) at 7781.

[89]Id. at 7782.

[90]25 USCA 455-457.

[91]Id. 450b(b) See also, e.g., 25 CFR 273.21 (1982), describing the role of tribal "governing bodies" in JOM contracting.

[92]See note 41, above.

[93]25 USCA 461. Sec. 462 also extended the trust status of existing allotments indefinitely.

[94]25 USCA 70.

[95]*Reindeer Report* (1905) at 8, see note 1, above.

[96]*Reindeer Report* (1896) at 18; see note 1, above. Commercial exploitation was frequently alleged as the cause of the depleted resources. Id. at 126 et seq.

[97]*Reindeer Report* (1905) at 8; see note 1, above.

[98]Reindeer Report (RG 75, Entry 806, Ak. Div. Files [Reindeer] 1911- 1912), Nat. Archives, Wash., D. C.

[99]Letter of April 3, 1911, from the Acting Secretary of the Interior to Senator George Chamberlain (RG 75, Id., Reindeer [General] 1910-11).

[100]See *Reindeer Report (1905)* at 9; see note 1, above.

[101]*The Eskimo,* C.L. Andrews, ed., (Microfilm M-939, No. 273. Terr. Gov. Files 40-04c "Natives," Archives Branch, Federal Archives and Records Center (FARC), Seattle.

[102]Id.

[103]Reindeer Report (1905) at 9; see note 1, above.

[104]Id.

[105]Sheldon Jackson also "imported" Laplanders to teach herding principles to the Natives. *Reindeer Report* (1896) at 17-18; see note 1, above.

[106]U.S. v Lomen & Co., 8 Ak. Rpts. 1, 4-5 (D.C. Ak. 1921).

[107]*The Eskimo,* note 101, above. See also 7:2 (April 1940) and 8:3-4 (Oct. 1941): 1-8.

[108]Froelich G. Rainey, "Memorandum Concerning Control and Ownership of Native Reindeer in Arctic Alaska," unpublished memorandum, Files of Terr. Gov. ca. 1939 (M-939, No. 273, File 40-04 "Native Misc.," FARC, Seattle).

[109]Id. See also note 95 above. The speculated causes for decline of the herds included the following:
1. Suspension of close herding permitted the domestic deer to assimilate into wild caribou herds.
2. Consolidation of small family herds into large unit herds and stock companies was not compatible with Eskimo cultural values and also eliminated pride in family herd ownership.
3. Range depletion, wolf predation, disease and human overkilling.
4. Another theory was that the Natives exaggerated the original herd sizes to obtain more stock certificates in the newly formed stock companies.

[110]81 Cong. Rec. 9470-9493, 75th Cong., 1st session (1937), Debates on the Alaska Reindeer Act.

[111]Act of September 1, 1937, 25 USCA 500 et seq.

[112]Letter of June 24, 1940, from Secretary Ickes to Representative Taylor, (Terr. Gov. Files 40-04b "Natives," M-939, No. 273, FARC, Seattle).

[113]81 Cong. Rec., note 110, above, at 9486.

[114]25 USC 500i. The prohibition against stock alienation is broad and absolute. Arguably, if a reindeer enterprise is entwined in the other activity of an ANCSA village or regional corporation, the Reindeer Act's nonalienation provisions could

apply to all of that corporation's stock. That could conceivably prevent alienation of that corporation's ANCSA stock to non-Natives even after 1991. See 43 USC 1606(h) and 1607(c). The Interior Department has only adopted minimal regulations implementing the reindeer act. Among other things they fail to describe the conditions under which reindeer products may legally be transferred to non-Natives under 25 USCA 500i. See 25 CFR Part 243 (1982).

[115]81 Cong. Rec., note 110, above, at 9480 (1937), remarks of Rep. Green.

[116]H.R. Rep. No. 1188 at 1 (1937).

[117]*Juneau Area Activities Report 1975-1976,* BIA, Juneau Area Office Report at 35.

[118]Phone conversation with Nick Landis, Planner, NANA Corp. February 21, 1978.

[119]*1975-1976 Area Report,* note 117, above, at 35.

[120]Letter of July 1, 1912, from Chas. W. Hawksworth to Commissioner of Education (RG 75, Entry 806, Alaska Div. Files. Hydaburg-8 1911-12, Nat. Archives, Wash., D.C.).

[121]Contract Between Hydaburg Lumber Co. and Department of the Interior (RG 75 Id.).

[122]Letter of January 5, 1912, from Chief, Alaska Division to Hawksworth (RG 75 Id.)

[123]Telegram of September 12, 1911, from Chief Ak. Div. to Bureau of Education, D.C. (RG 75 Id.).

[124]E.O. No. 1555, June 19, 1912. See generally "Reservations," chapter 3, above.

[125]By 1917, Metlakatla had established both a lumber mill and a cannery. It is unclear whether these enterprises were supported by the Bureau of Education or private funds, but in 1917 the Secretary of the Interior leased land on the reserve to the Annette Island Packing Co. to construct and operate a cannery. The lease also granted exclusive rights to the packing company to operate fish traps on the reserve. In exchange for these concessions, the packing Company was required:

> to purchase all piling lumber and material possible from the Indians at market values, to employ the Indians in connection with the erection of traps and buildings so far as possible, to cooperate with the Commercial Company of the Indians in every way possible, to employ Native labor, as far as possible, in the manufacture of cans and salmon packing, and to purchase from the Indians all requisite box shooks and lumber at market prices.

Territory of Alaska v. Annette Island Packing Co., 289 F. 671, 672-73 (9th Cir. 1923)."

[126]49 L. D. 592 (1923).

[127]*Annette Island Packing,* note 125, above, at 674-75. The holding is also based on the now discredited "federal instrumentality" doctrine, see Mescalero Apache v. New Mexico, 411 U.S. 145, 155 (1973), but could also be sustained on the basis of the reservation. C.f. McClenahan v. Arizona, 411 U.S. 164 (1973) or pre-emption of state law, Metlakatla v. Egan, 369 U.S. at 56 & 59 (1962).

[128]Section 10 (25 USCA 470) provides in pertinent part:

> There is authorized to be appropriated...$20,000,000 to be established as a revolving loan fund from which the Secretary...may make loans to Indian chartered corporations for the purpose of promoting the economic development of such tribes and of their members...

The corporations were chartered under Sec. 17 of the IRA (25 USCA 477).

[129]Kake v. Egan, 369 U.S. 60 (1962) permitted the State to enforce its fish trap law which eliminated the Kake fish traps. Without the fish traps, it is unlikely the Kake cannery could acquire sufficient fish for profitable operation. Today, Metlakatla is the only place in Alaska permitted to use fish traps; their cannery is the only IRA cannery still in operation.

[130]Hydaburg Cooperative Association v. U.S., 667 F. 2d 64 (Ct. Cls. 1981).

[131]U.C. v. Testan, 424 U.S. 392 (1976); U.S. v. Mitchell (Mitchell II), 51 USLW 4999 (1983), upholding money damage award against U.S. because federal statutes established responsibility for the management of allotted forest lands.

[132]U.S. v. Mitchell (Mitchell I), 445 U.S. 535, 546 (1980), "narrow" trust under the General Allotment Act held sufficient to establish federal liability.

[133]The case of Aleut Community of St. Paul Island v. United States, 480 F. 2nd 831 (Ct. Cls. 1973) expands on this point. The case involved a cause of action under the "fair and honorable dealings" clause of the Indian Claims Commission Act (25 USC 70 et seq.) The Court of Claims held that in both an 1870 and a 1910 act:

> The United States recognized the dependence of the Native population of St. Paul Island on the right to kill seals. These statutes are also a clear pronouncement of a special relationship undertaken by the government towards the well-being of the Natives of the Islands. Id. at 840.

This principle is important because it establishes that Native claims for breach of fiduciary duty can arise out of circumstances not involving trust property. In this case, the potential federal duty was based on congressional recognition of a specific need. Compare Gila River Pima-Maricopa Band of Indians v. U.S., 427 F. 2d 1194 (Ct. Cls. 1970) holding that no fiduciary obligation exists in the absence of some statute, executive order or treaty "creating a guardian-ward-type relationship."

Breach of "fair and honorable dealings" was a unique cause of action under the Claims Commission Act. [25 USC 70a(5)]. Although such a cause may not survive the termination of the Claims Commission (on September 30, 1978, pursuant to per 25 USC 70v), the described principle might be applicable in other contexts.

[134]E.g. Morton v. Ruiz, 415 U.S. 199 (1973), prohibiting the BIA from denying general assistance welfare benefits to off-reservation Natives in the absence of proper regulations and notice. See also Eric V. Secretary of U.S Dept. of Housing and Urban Development, 464 F. Supp. 44 (D.C. AK. 1978), federal government has a trust responsibility under the Bartlett Housing Act to build adequate houses for Alaska Natives. Accord, Koniag v. Kleppe, 405 F. Supp. 1360, 1370 (D.D.C. 1975), requiring additional due process for Alaska Native villages denied ANCSA eligibility, in part because sec. 2(b) of ANCSA requires "maximum participation by Natives in decisions affecting their rights and property".

[135]This discussion focuses on programs administered through the Department of the Interior, but other federal agencies share responsibility under other statutes. For example, the Department of Health and Human Services supports various projects to promote Native American economic and social self-sufficiency under the Native American Programs Act of 1974 (USCA 2991 et seq.). See generally Richard S. Jones, *Federal Programs of Assistance to American Indians,* Report to the Senate Select Committee on Indian Affairs, 9th Cong., 2d Sess. (Dec. 1982), and Hawkins, note 58, above.

[136]H. Rpt. No. 92-523, reprinted in 1971 USCAAN 2192, 2195-2196 (September 28, 1971). See also Aleut Corp. v. Arctic Slope Regional Corp., 421 F. Supp. 862 (D.C. Ak.1976), regarding the economic development thrust of ANCSA.

[137]Act of April 12, 1974, P.L. 93-262, 88 Stat. 77, (25 USCA 1451 et seq.)

[138]25 USCA 1451.

[139]Id. 1461 et seq.

[140]Id. 1481 et seq.

[141]1974 USCAAN 2873, 2875.

[142]25 USCA 1561 et seq.

[143]Id. 1541.

[144]E.g., The Native American Programs Act of 1974 (42 USCA 2991 et seq.)

[145]25 USCA 452(c), defining "Tribe."

[146]Id., (d) defining "Reservation."

[147]1974 USCAAN at 2874.

[148]*Natives and the Land,* Federal Field Committee for Development Planning in Alaska, (Washington, D.C.: GPO, 1968), at 14

> Considered in comparison to the total population of the State, Alaska's Natives constitute a disproportionate ratio of those receiving welfare payments.

[149]*2(c) Report,* note 40, above, "Intro. & Summary, Part C, Sec. 5," 1-6.

[150]Id. Sec. 1, 1.

[151]E.g., Hearings on H.R. 13142 and H.R. 10193, House Sub-committee on Indian Affairs, Committee on Interior and Insular Affairs, 91st Cong., 1st Sess., Part I. Serial No. 91-8 (August 4-6 and September 9, 1969) at 147-151, letter and accompanying documents from Keith Miller, Governor of Alaska, to Wayne Aspinall, Chairman, Committee on Interior and Insular Affairs.

[152]E.g., Id. Part II, Serial No. 91-8 (October 17-18, 1969) at 506- 507, testimony of Emil Notti, President, Alaska Federation of Natives.

[153]Sheldon Jackson's reindeer program also responded to Native destitution, but, unlike the Copper Center program, the reindeer were intended to relieve destitution through the development of a Native-owned industry rather than through direct issues of food and clothing.

[154]Map of Alaska, Department of the Interior, Bureau of Education, 1910 (RG 75, Entry 806, Box 1 "Natives (Destitution)" 1907-09, Nat. Archives, Washington, D.C.)

[155]Letter from Commissioner of Education to Commander, Ft. Liscum, May 12, 1908. See also Communication (No. 49766-182 BK.) February 7, 1908, from Commissary General, War Dept. to Secretary of War (RG 75, Id.).
The supplies issued at Tonsina and Copper Center in April 1908 included:

> 979 lbs. Bacon
> 400 lbs. Flour
> 100 lbs. Hard Bread
> 14 lbs. Baking Powder
> 30 lbs. Rice
> 12 lbs. Evaporated Apples
> 70 lbs. Sugar

Memo from Commissary Officer to Adjutant, Ft. Liscum April 2, 1908 (RG 75, Id.)

[156]Letter from Commissioner to Atkins, February 10, 1908, (RG 75, Id.)

[157]See RG 75, Id., Box 10, for memos and requests from military posts for reimbursements extending through 1909. See also telegram from Acting Commissioner to Commander, Ft. Egbert January 11, 1910, advising that the new Superintendent of Education for the Northern District would assume responsibility for destitution relief (RG 75, Id. Box 21).

[158]Cohen (1942), note 6, above, at 88. Recall also that the termination of Indian treaty making was required by the appropriations act of March 3, 1871 (15 Stat. 544, 566, 25 USCA 71). Appropriations still play a policy-making role in Indian matters. See Morton v. Ruiz, 415 U.S. 199 (1972) for a modern example.

[159]Act of November 2, 1921, 42 Stat. 208, 25 USCA 13, Representative Snyder was the chairman of the House Indian Affairs Committee. The previous year the Indian Affairs Committe had been stripped of its appropriations jurisdiction; thereafter, all Indian appropriations were funneled through the House Appropriations Committee. Absent the guiding hand of the Indian Affairs Committee, these appropriations became subject to "point of order" objections on the floor of the House whenever a congressman wished to block a particular appropriation. Invariably the "point of order" was that the appropriation was not authorized by specific legislation. The Snyder Act is the "specific legislation" intended to remedy the problem for the entire range of general BIA programs. See 61 Cong. Rec. 4683-84. Remarks of Mr. Snyder. See also *Scope of the Snyder Act of November 2, 1921*, Op. Sol. M-36857 (February 22, 1973).

[160]See note 11, above, and accompanying text regarding authority for the 1931 transfer.

[161]See generally *Morton v. Ruiz*, note 134, above, at 212-230.

[162]Appropriations for 1972: Hearings before the House Subcommittee on Department of the Interior and Related Agencies of the House Committee on Appropriations, 92d Congress, 1st Sess., March 19, 1971, Part 2, at 1095. (July 1971 Mo. Cat. Entry 10658).

[163]See *Morton v. Ruiz*, note 134, above, at 212-213. Oklahoma Natives have historically been afforded similar special treatment.

[164]25 CFR 20.2 (1982) "Purpose," 42 Fed. Reg. 6558, 6570, February 2, 1977.

[165]Id. at 20.20 "General."

[166]Id. at 20.1(v) "Definitions."

[167]P.L. 95-608, Nov. 8, 1978, 92 Stat. 3069 (25 USCA 1901 et seq.) at 25 USCA 1932-1934, relating to off-reservation child welfare grant programs. See also 25 CFR Part 23 (1983) at 23.2(d)(3), defining off-reservation service eligibility.

[168]Wilson v. Watt, 703 F.2d 395, (9th Cir. 1983).

[169]Alaska Native health programs are beyond the scope of this discussion, but their history appears similar to that of the education, economic development and social services programs. Health programs began about 1906 with contracts between the Bureau of Education and local Alaskan hospitals and medical professionals. By the early 1920's, the Bureau of Education had constructed five Native hospitals throughout Alaska; in 1931, these were all turned over to the BIA. In 1954, an Act of Congress transferred responsibility for Indian health care from the BIA to the Surgeon General of the United States Public Health Service

(42 USCA 201 et seq., as amended). In 1966, all functions of the Surgeon General were transferred to the Secretary of Health, Education and Welfare (1966 Reorg. Plan No. 3, 31 Fed. Reg. 8855, 80 Stat. 610). The present-day Indian Health Service appears to derive its authority from both the 1954 Act and the Snyder Act of 1921. See generally Lewis v. Weinberger, 415 F. Supp. 652 (D.C. N. Mex. 1976) for an analysis of the history and present responsibilities of the Indian Health Service.

[170]In FY 1980 total expenditures of the Indian Health Service in Alaska amounted to $74,687,000 or about $1,220 per Native person in Alaska. *Hawkins*, note 58, above, at 6. The Johnson-O'Malley Act (25 USCA 452 et seq.), Indian Child Welfare Act (25 USCA 1901 et seq.) and the Self-Determination Act (25 USCA 450 et seq.), as well as annual appropriations, provide additional statutory authority for various BIA Programs amounting in FY 1981 to a total expenditure of $34,375,000 in Alaska. Other agencies spend even more, particularly in the field of housing loans. For example, in FY 1981 the Department of Housing and Urban development budgeted $167,837,000 in support of its various Indian housing loan and subsidy programs in Alaska. Hawkins, note 58, above at 7 and 22. See also, Alaska Chapter, Associated General Contractors of America v. Pierce, 694 F. 2d 1162 (9th Cir. 1980), Indian preference in HUD housing contracts. The Department of Agriculture also provides loans for land acquisition by tribes and their members through the Farmers Home Administration under 25 USCA 488 et seq. See also generally Jones, note 135, above, regarding other federal assistance to American Indians.

[171]25 (CFR Pt. 20 (42 Fed. Reg. 6568, February 2, 1977).

[172]25 CFR 20.1(k) and 20.24 (1982).

[173]Id. 20.1(h) and 20.22. Most child welfare services for Native children are now provided by the state. *Juneau Area Report 1975-76*, note 117, above, at 47.

[174]Id. 20.1(g) and 20.23. In the Anchorage BIA Agency, miscellaneous assistance is mostly devoted to burial payments. These can include travel and food for potlatch services as well as other direct burial expenses. Source: Ella Craig, Supervisory Social Worker, Anchorage Agency, interview, February 10, 1978.

[175]*2(c) Report,* note 40, above, "Task II, Part B, Sec. 5, Bureau of Indian Affairs, Social Service Program" at 5 and 7.

[176]Actual grant costs for General Assistance are as follows in $1,000:

FY'73	FY'74	FY'75	FY'76	FY'77	FY'78 est.
4,593	4,182	3,462	3,297	4,055	4,500

Source: Telegram from BIA Area Social Services to Anchorage Agency Social Services, February 13, 1978 and May 16, 1978 Juneau Area Office phone conversation.

[177]S. Rep. No. 166, 97th Cong., 1st Sess. at 39 (1981), cited in *Wilson v. Watt,* note 168, above, at 402-403.

[178]*2(c) Report,* note 40, above, "Task II, Part B, Sec. 5, BIA Social Service Program" at 5. As noted previously (note 173, above), most child welfare assistance is now provided by the state.

[179]Data extrapolated from *2(c) Report,* note 40, above, "Task II, Part A, Sec. 4" at 2, and "Part B, Sec. 5, BIA Social Service Programs" at 7. It is interesting to note that in 1982 there were significantly fewer general assistance recipients (3,400), yet the anticipated cost was dramatically higher ($10,000,000). See *Wilson v. Watt,* note 168, above, at 401-402. The $10,000,000 figure seems high because the FY 81 combined social service budget was only $6,983,000. See Hawkins, note 58, above, at 19.

[180]25 CFR 20.3, "Policy."

[181]*2(c) Report,* note 40, above, "Task II, Part A, Sec. 4," at 3.

[182]C.f. 25 CFR 20.21.

[183]P.L. 92-603, See generally *2(c) Report,* note 40, above, "Task II, Part B, Sec. 5, Supplemental Security Income Program" at 1-15.

[184]See *2(c) Report,* Id., "Public Assistance and Food Stamp Programs" at 3, note 12.

[185]See *2(c) Report,* Id., "Unemployment Insurance Program" at 1-3. Natives are also eligible for food stamp benefits, but that is another form of noncategorical assistance based on need only. *2(c) Report,* Id., "Public Assistance and Food Stamp programs" at 3-4.

[186]In addition to being needy, Alaska Native applicants must also be one-quarter or more Native blood (25 CFR 20.20(a) (1)) and accept available employment for which they are able and qualified. [25 CFR 20.21(d)].

[187]Id. 20.21(a), "Resources" means available services or income not excluded by federal statute [Id. 20.1(w)]. "Need" means the deficit between "resources" and the money necessary to meet basic or special living costs as determined by the state under the federal Social Security Act (Id. 20.1[s]).

[188]Id. 20.21(b) "Public Assistance" means assistance programs provided under Title IV of the Social Security Act. (Id. 20.1[t]) AFDC is the most important of these.

[189]Id. 20.21(c).

[190]25 CFR 20.21(b).

[191]*2(c) Report,* note 40, above, "Intro. & Summary, Part C, Sec. 5" at 1.

[192]*Wilson v. Watt,* note 168, above, at 397.

[193]Source: Juneau BIA Area Office memorandum, "Standards for BIA Social Services, Financial Assistance (Reviewed 12/16/77)" The maximum level of as-

sistance varies with the recipient's housing costs. One hundred dollars additional is allowed for each additional eligible adult after the first two.

[194]*Wilson v. Watt,* note 168, above, at 398.

[195]Id. at 402-403.

[196]Act of June 25, 1910, sec. 23, 36 Stat. 861, 25 USCA 47.

[197]*2(c) Report,* note 40, above, "Task II, Part A., Sec. 4" at 6-7. BIA Juneau Area personnel state that the Area Office has been contracting under the Buy Indian Act at least since 1968.

[198]25 USCA 450 et seq.

[199]*Juneau Area Report (1975-76),* note 117, above, at 47.

[200]25 USCA 1932-1934.

[201]25 USCA 1933(b).

[202]25 CFR 23.29 to 23.34.

[203]Aleutian-Pribilof Islands Association v. Acting Deputy Assistant Secretary Indian Affairs (Operations) 9 IBIA 254, 89 I.D. 196 (1982).

[204]P.L. 92-203, sec. 2(c), 85 Stat. 688 (43 USCA 1601[c]).

[205]Id. sec. 23, 85 Stat. 715 (43 USCA 1622).

CHAPTER SIX

NATIVE ENTITLEMENT TO SERVICES

I. Introduction

A. Three Legal Theories

At least three related legal theories support the existence of a federal obligation to provide Native education, economic development, welfare assistance and other human services. Those three theories are based on the concepts of 1) statutory entitlement, 2) due process, and 3) guardianship. Statutory entitlement and due process are expanding concepts in what, for lack of a better term, might be called the field of "welfare law."[1] Beginning in 1969, the courts have generally interpreted statutory entitlements and the due process procedures associated with them to be a source of government obligations to provide welfare benefits for the general population.

Guardianship, on the other hand, is a colonial doctrine historically applied in the field of Indian law to support the authority of the federal government to enact numerous statutes governing Native affairs, including statutes providing for Native welfare. It is an ethnocentric doctrine which, up until the mid-twentieth century, often justified colonial domination of aboriginal people.[2] During the nineteenth century, the federal courts translated the doctrine into an article of domestic law supporting the plenary authority of Congress over Indian policy.[3] During the twentieth century, however, the courts have transformed the doctrine into a source of federal obligations to Natives based on a "special relationship" or "trust responsibility."[4]

B. Authority and Obligation

It is especially important to distinguish between the *authority* of the executive branch to provide services to Natives and its *obligation* to do so. Although Congress may legislatively grant administrative officers authority to provide Native services, until recently that did not appear to mean that an officer's authority was limited by specific obligations as to whom, where or how he would grant or deny those services. Indeed the Secretary of the Interior and the Commissioner of Indian Affairs have long had such wide discretion in the "management of all Indian Affairs and of all matters arising out of Indian relations"[5] that their obligation to provide services has, at times, appeared only as compelling as their willingness to do so. Their discretion was especially broad in the field of welfare benefits, which have historically been viewed as "privileges" rather than "rights." Until the late 1960's, the "right-privilege" distinction was one legal dividing line between broad and limited administrative discretion.[6]

On the other hand, many Native programs and services were more like rights than privileges, because they were historically connected to treaties or agreements between the Natives and the federal government. In exchange for Native land, the government consented by treaty or (agreement) to hold relatively large sums of money in trust for the Natives from whom the land had been purchased. With the principal and interest from these funds, the United States, according to the wishes of the Natives, paid for food, clothing, livestock and tools, as well as blacksmiths, teachers, physicians and others who provided various Native services. Because these so-called treaty or tribal funds were in payment for Native land, they were not mere gratuities but contractual rights to which the Natives were lawfully entitled.

When these tribal and treaty funds were exhausted, and in time many were, the government continued these services because they were essential to Native survival. The difference was that now the appropriations to pay for such services were no longer required by treaty or other agreements. Therefore, they were often characterized as "gratuity appropriations" and the services as mere privileges which the government had the authority, but no longer an obligation, to provide.[7] The recent demise of the "right-privilege" distinction changes all of that and imposes in its stead statutory entitlements protected by certain due process principles.

The application of statutory entitlement and due process theories to Native social welfare laws is especially important to Alaska Natives because the federal government has negotiated no treaties and few if any other agreements with them on which a federal obligation to provide human services could be based. However, as we have seen in chapter 5, the government has long exercised its guardianship authority over Alaska Natives. Under that authority, these Natives have acquired the same statutory entitlement to education, economic development, welfare and other human services which the federal government provides by statute to other Native Americans. The balance of this chapter discusses in more detail the federal government's continuing authority and the scope of its obligations to provide these services.

II. Sources of Federal Authority To Provide Human Services

A. Generally

Federal authority over Native Americans springs from several, sometimes ill-defined, sources. Chief Justice Marshall noted in *Worcester v. Georgia* that the Constitution:

> confers on congress the powers of war and peace, of making treaties, and of regulating commerce with the foreign nations, and among the several states, and with the Indian tribes. These powers comprehend all that is required for the regulation of our intercourse with the Indians.[8]

In addition to the war, treaty and commerce powers, Felix Cohen has noted that the power to admit new states and to establish post roads, inferior courts and uniform rules of naturalization have all been used to support the authority of Congress to enact "Indian" legislation.[9] He concluded that whatever the source of federal power over Native Americans:

> the powers mentioned by Chief Justice Marshall proved to be so extensive that in fact the Federal Government's powers over Indian affairs are as wide as State powers over non-Indians, and therefore one is practically justified in characterizing such Federal power as "plenary."[10]

B. Guardianship as a Source of Federal Authority

Federal guardianship over Native Americans is nowhere mentioned in the Constitution as one of the powers conferred on the federal government. Nevertheless, Cohen notes that;

> [w]hile the decisions of the courts may be explained on the basis of express constitutional powers, the language used in some cases seems to indicate that the decisions were influenced by a consideration of the peculiar relationship between Indians and the Federal Government.[11]

That peculiar relationship has been described variously as including a "distinctive obligation of trust"[12] or "trust responsibility."[13] However, it was Chief Justice Marshall in *Cherokee Nation v. Georgia* who first described the relationship as resembling that of "a ward to his guardian."[14] The guardianship aspect of this relationship was crucial to Marshall's determination that, for purposes of original Supreme Court jurisdiction, the Cherokee Nation did not have the status of a "foreign state" under the Constitution.

> [The Cherokees] occupy a territory to which we assert a title independent of their will, which must take effect in point of possession, when their right of possession ceases. *Meanwhile, they are in a state of pupilage; their relation to the United States resembles that of a ward to his guardian.* They look to our government for protection; rely upon its kindness and its power; appeal to it for relief to their wants; and address the president as their great father....These considerations go far to support the opinion, that the framers of our Constitution had not the Indian tribes in view, when they opened the courts of the Union to controversies between a state or the citizens thereof and foreign states (emphasis added).[15]

Marshall appears to be drawing a subtle connection here between the Native American "right of possession" to the lands the Cherokee occupied and the "state of pupilage" which described relationship of the Cherokee people to the United States. "Meanwhile [so long as the Cherokee occupied their territory,]...their relation to the United States resembles that of a ward to his guardian."

For the next forty years following *Cherokee Nation,* the United States continued to regulate its relationships with Native people and their lands through treaties. In 1871, Congress prohibited future Indian treaties,[16] but that did not eliminate the guardianship theory of the authority of the United States over Native Americans. In *U.S. v. Kagama* (1886), the U.S. Supreme Court once again examined Marshall's decisions in *Cherokee Nation* and *Worcester.* A unanimous court concluded that:

> In the opinions in these cases they [Native Americans] are spoken of as "wards of the nation," "pupils," as local dependent communities. In this spirit the United States has conducted its relations to them from its organization to this time. But, after an experience of a hundred years of the treaty-making system of government, Congress has determined upon a new departure—to govern them by acts of Congress.[17]

Kagama involved a challenge to the then recently enacted "Major Crimes Act"[18] which among other things subjected Indians committing certain crimes against Indians on reservations within a state to federal prosecution. An Indian (Kagama) accused of murdering another Indian on a reservation in California challenged the authority of Congress to pass such a law. Kagama's argument appears to have been that the United States had no such authority over a politically distinct Indian tribe such as the one of which he was a member.

Having determined that Congress was now governing Native Americans by statute rather than treaty, the *Kagama* court concluded that Congress also had authority to pass statutes subjecting Native Americans to federal criminal jurisdiction, because:

> These Indian tribes *are* the wards of the nation. They are communities *dependent* on the United States. Dependent largely for their daily food....From their very weakness, and helplessness, so largely due to the course of dealing of the Federal Government with them and the treaties in which it has been promised, there arises the duty of protection, and with it the power. This has always been recognized by the Executive and by Congress, and by this court, whenever the question has arisen.

* * * *

The power of the General Government over these remnants of a race once powerful, now weak and diminished in numbers, is necessary to their protection, as well as to the safety of those among whom they dwell. It must exist in that government, because it never has existed anywhere else, because the theatre of its exercise is within the geographical limits of the United States, because it has never been denied, and because it alone can enforce its laws on all the tribes (emphasis in original).[19]

Beginning in 1913, the U.S. Supreme Court further extended the scope of federal authority over Native Americans to include nonreservation lands of New Mexico Pueblos Indians. In three cases spanning 20 years, Mr. Justice Van Devanter held that on the basis of federal guardianship, the United States had broad authority to protect the Pueblo Indians and their real and personal property. These cases reversed an 1876 Supreme Court opinion *(U.S. v. Joseph).*[20] *Joseph* held that the United States had no authority to protect Pueblo lands from non-Native encroachment, because the United States had relinquished all title to the Pueblo lands by an earlier act of Congress.[21] *Joseph* overlooks the fact the Pueblo Indians were still in possession of their lands and at least for that reason still under control of the federal guardian. Van Devanter's Pueblo decisions (corrected) this error.

U.S. v. Sandoval[22] was the first of the Van Devanter opinions. It involved a prosecution under the Indian liquor laws, which prohibited the introduction of liquor into "Indian country." The defendant argued that Congress had no authority to regulate liquor on the Pueblo lands because 1) the Pueblo Indians were citizens, and 2) they owned their lands in fee simple. Their personal status as citizens and the fee simple nature of their land title, it was contended, placed them under state not federal jurisdiction.

In rejecting these arguments, a unanimous court held that neither the citizenship, if any, of the Indians nor the status of their lands prohibited the United States from enacting laws for their protection. The guardianship authority relied on in *Kagama* was the rationale for this conclusion.

[L]ong continued legislative and executive usage and an unbroken current of judicial decisions have attributed to the United States as a superior and civilized nation the power and the duty of exercising a fostering care and protection over all dependent Indian communities within its borders, whether within its original territory or territory subsequently acquired, and whether within or without the limits of a State.

* * * *

Considering the reasons which underlie the authority of Congress to prohibit the introduction of liquor into the Indian country at all, it seems plain that this authority is sufficiently comprehensive to enable Congress to apply the prohibition to the lands of the Pueblos.[23]

In 1925 the Supreme Court applied these same principles in *U.S. v. Candelaria*[24] to sustain a suit by the United States to remove non-Indians from the lands of the Laguna Pueblo. The United States based its suit in *Candelaria* on the theory that the Pueblo Indians were "wards of the United States" and that the government therefore had both the authority and duty under the Indian Non-Intercourse Act to protect them in the "ownership and enjoyment of their lands."[25] The Supreme Court unanimously agreed.

Finally, in 1933 the Supreme Court held in *U.S. v. Chavez*[26] that the so-called Assimilative Crimes Act[27] applied to the New Mexico Pueblos. This act made crimes committed by non-Indians against Indians in "Indian country" punishable in federal court. The question was whether the Pueblos constituted "Indian country" for purposes of the Assimilative Crimes Act. It was argued that they did not, because the Pueblo lands were owned in fee simple. After reviewing both *Sandoval* and *Candelaria,* the Court once again held unanimously that the people of the Pueblos were:

Indian wards of the United States; that the lands owned and occupied by them under their ancient grant are Indian country...that the United States, in virtue of its guardianship, has full power to punish crimes committed within the limits of the Pueblo lands by or against their property—even though, where the offense is against an Indian or his property, the offender be not an Indian....[28]

C. Guardianship in Alaska

By the late nineteenth and early twentieth centuries, the theory of federal guardianship appears to have been well developed as a concept supporting broad federal authority over Indian affairs. Development of the guardianship concept coincided with the extension of Native American human service programs to Alaska under the U.S. Office of Education. Congress was by that time governing Native affairs solely by statute. It had approved no treaties with Alaska Natives; therefore, federal authority over Alaska Native affairs could not be justified by the treaty-making power. Furthermore, it may have strained credibility to use federal constitutional authority over Indian commerce as a justification for Native education and social welfare programs.[29]

In any case, Felix Cohen has noted that one established source of federal power over Alaska Natives is congressional authority to:

> ...enact any legislation it deems proper for the benefit and protection of the Natives of Alaska, because they are wards of the United States in the sense that they are subject to the plenary power of Congress over Indian affairs (footnote omitted).[30]

Although Congress had the authority to enact legislation to benefit and protect Alaska Natives, it did not do so until the Organic Act of 1884. The omission resulted in early court, Attorney General and Department of the Interior opinions distinguishing the status of Alaska Native from that of Native Americans in general.[31] However, early twentieth century Alaska cases held that federal guardianship was the source of federal authority to protect Alaska Native lands.[32] Then in 1918, the U.S. Supreme Court handed down its landmark decision in *Alaska Pacific Fisheries v. U.S.*[33]

The case centered on the authority of the United States to statutorily reserve the Annette Islands (and surrounding waters) for the Metlakatla Indians. Mr. Justice Van Devanter, again writing for a unanimous court, held that:

> The reservation was not in the nature of a private grant, but simply a setting apart, "until otherwise provided by law," of designated public property for a recognized public purpose— that of safeguarding and advancing a dependent Indian people dwelling within the United States. See *United States v. Kagama*, 118 U.S. 275, 279, *et seq.*

> * * * *

> The purpose of creating the reservation was to encourage, assist and protect the Indians in their effort to train themselves to habits of industry, become self-sustaining and advance to the ways of civilized life.[34]

Subsequent solicitor's opinions exhaustively discussed the status of Alaska Natives and the source of federal authority over them. In a 1923 opinion, the solicitor determined that the Secretary of the Interior had authority to enter into a cannery lease on the Tyonek Reserve on the basis of federal guardianship. After describing early congressional neglect of Alaska Natives, the solicitor stated that:

> Later, however, Congress began to directly recognize these natives as being, to a very considerable extent at least, under our Government's guardianship and enacted laws which pro-

tected them in the possession of the lands they occupied; made provision for the allotment of lands to them in severalty, similar to those made to the American Indians; gave them special hunting, fishing and other particular privileges to enable them to support themselves, and supplied them with reindeer and instructions as to their propagation. Congress has also supplied funds to give these natives medical and hospital treatment and finally made and is still making extensive appropriations to defray the expenses of both their education and *their support.*

* * * *

From this it will be seen that these natives are now unquestionably considered and treated as being under the guardianship and protection of the Federal Government, at least to such an extent as to bring them within the spirit, if not within the exact letter, of the laws relative to American Indians... (emphasis in original).[35]

Ten years later, and after an even more exhaustive review of the laws, cases and decisions relating to Alaska Natives, the solicitor once again concluded that:

From the foregoing it is clear that no distinction has been or can be made between the Indians and other natives of Alaska so far as the laws and relations of the United States are concerned whether the Eskimos and other natives are of Indian origin or not as they are all wards of the Nation, and their status is in material respects similar to that of the Indians of the United States. It follows that the natives of Alaska, as referred to in the treaty of March 30, 1867, between the United States and Russia, are entitled to the benefits of and are subject to the general laws and regulations governing the Indians of the United States....[36]

"Guardianship" from that day to the present continues to be the theoretical source of federal plenary authority over Alaska Native social services.

D. The Snyder Act

This act[37] is the statutory authority for the BIA's broad range of human service programs. It provides in pertinent part:

The Bureau of Indian Affairs, under the supervision of the Secretary of the Interior, shall direct, supervise, and expend such moneys as Congress may from time to time appropriate, for the benefit, care, and assistance of the Indians throughout the United States for the following purposes:

General support and civilization, including education.
For relief of distress and conservation of health.
For industrial assistance and advancement and general administration of Indian property.
And for general and incidental expenses in connection with the administration of Indian affairs.

In 1931, the act became applicable to Alaska when the functions of the Bureau of Education were transferred to the BIA; appropriations since that time have always included funds for BIA's Alaska Native human service programs.

The Snyder Act was passed in response to a political problem that arose in the House of Representatives when the House Indian Affairs Committee was stripped of its appropriations jurisdiction. The Chairman of the Indian Affairs Committee and sponsor of the Snyder Act, Representative Snyder of New York, generalized the purposes of the Act in these terms:

It may seem strange to some of the membership that I am here advocating the passage of this bill [the Snyder Act] because of the fact that I raised most of the points of order upon it when it was under consideration in the House. But I want to say, that I have just one desire as a member of this body, and that is to expedite good legislation. I do not care to be a party to impeding proper legislation, and I do not care what committee has the making of the appropriation. I want it arranged so that the legislation regarding these appropriations can be carried on in this House and not in the body at the other end of the Capitol.... This House ought to have the right to say what appropriations shall be made for [the Indian] service, and if this present bill is enacted, it will have that right.... Therefore, on behalf of good order and good legislation, I hope this bill will pass, so that either the Indian appropriation committee or the present appropriation committee will be given the right to authorize appropriations for the various activities of this bureau without being subject to points of order and in a regular and orderly way.[38]

Thus the purpose of the legislation was to eliminate points of order and restore to the House its full function as a decision-maker in Indian affairs.

In the House debate on the bill, Congressman Kelly of Pennsylvania spoke first in its favor. His testimony is long and highly critical of the bureau, but it is clear that Congressman Kelly recognized the legal authority for the legislation lay in Congress' theoretical guardianship over Native Americans.

> [N]o failure or maladministration in government service can reflect so directly upon the Nation as in our relations with the American Indians. They are wards of the Nation, not of any State or community. They are disenfranchised and inarticulate, forced to look to Washington for every need. [39]

Congressman Kelly went on to describe the history of federal Indian policy noting that between 1789 and 1849:

> the "reservation" plan was adopted and the Indians in the Eastern States were moved to western territory and segregated there. *The government assumed the guardianship of the persons of the Indians, and also acquired through treaties and laws, the complete control of their property.* [40]

Others who spoke in favor of the bill either praised or critized the BIA and discussed the purposes to be achieved by federal Indian policies. None indicated that the bill would terminate federal guardianship, although many expressed the belief that such was the ultimate goal of these policies. [41] The Snyder Act debates as a whole indicate that the purpose behind the legislation was to return to the House its full measure of control over federal Indian policy. However, not even those who were opposed to the bill denied that the source of congressional authority to enact the measure was the federal government's "guardianship" over the persons and property of Native Americans. Congressman Kelly's remarks specifically affirm it.

E. Conclusion

Chief Justice Marshall, in *Cherokee Nation v. Georgia,* was the first to compare the relationship of Native Americans and the federal government to that of a ward and its guardian. He also implied that this relationship was sustained at least so long as the Natives retained the right to possession of their lands. In *U.S. v. Kagama* (1886), the U.S. Supreme Court held that federal guardianship over Natives could be exercised by statute even though, as in that case, there were no treaties permitting the United States to extend its criminal laws to Indian reservations. In the New Mexico Pueblo cases, Justice Van Devanter determined that federal guardianship did not depend on the citizenship or status of Native land titles, but was largely a matter of congressional determination. Beginning in the early 20th century, these principles were applied to Alaska

Natives as authority for federal human service programs benefiting them. From then until now, "guardianship" has been recognized by the courts and the Interior Department as the theoretical source of federal authority to provide Alaska Native human service programs.

III. Federal Social Service Obligations

A. Executive Obligations

As noted initially, a clear distinction must be drawn between the authority and obligation to provide Native human services. However, because obligations logically spring from limitations on authority, we must also keep in mind the relative limitations of congressional and executive authority over Indian affairs.

As noted earlier, congressional authority over Indian affairs is plenary;[42] it is limited, however, by principles of rationality[43] and specific constitutional restrictions such as the Bill of Rights.[44] Executive authority, on the other hand, extends only as far as the congressional statutes granting it may permit. Felix Cohen has described the relationship between congressional and executive authority as follows:

> [Executive] power is dependent upon and supplementary to the legislative power....[It] is important to distinguish between the problem of whether Congress possesses the authority to pass certain legislation and the problem of whether Congress has vested its power in an administrative office or department.

> "We have no officers in this government (citation omitted) from the President down to the most subordinate agent, who does not hold office under the law, with prescribed duties and limited authority."[45]

It is from this "limited authority" that executive obligations to provide human services spring.

However, congressional "guardianship" authority is so broad and so much of that authority was delegated to the Secretary of the Interior that until recently the secretary had few practical obligations to provide Native services. Federal "guardianship" differs in this respect from the obligations of guardianship under private law. As Cohen has also noted:

> There is thus not only an important difference but indeed a striking contrast between the use of the wardship concept in relation to Indian tribes and the use of the concept in private law. In private law, a guardian is subject to rigid court control in the administration of the ward's affairs and property. In con-

stitutional law the guardianship relation has generally been invoked as a reason for *relaxing* court control over the action of the "guardian" (emphasis in original).[46]

Although Cohen is speaking here of "relaxed court control" over congressional actions, the same principle applies if executive action is lawfully committed to the broad discretion of administrative officers. Ultimately, the question of whether an administrative officer, such as the Secretary of the Interior, has an obligation to provide statutorily allowed Native services comes down to a determination of whether the officer has the discretion *not* to provide such services. Two doctrines emerged in the 1970's as restrictions on administrative discretion in the field of human services: 1) due process and 2) statutory entitlement.

B. Due Process

1. Right-Privilege Doctrine

Due process limitations on administrative discretion frequently arise in the context of administrative adjudications denying or terminating statutorily conferred benefits. One commentator in the field of administrative law has noted that:

> The essence of justice is largely procedural. Time and again, thoughtful judges have emphasized this truth. Mr. Justice Douglas: "It is not without significance that most of the provisions of the Bill of Rights are procedural. It is procedure that spells much of the difference between rule by law and rule by whim or caprice. Steadfast adherence to strict procedural safeguards is our main assurance that there will be equal justice under law." Mr. Justice Jackson: "Procedural fairness and regularity are of the indispensable essence of liberty." Mr. Justice Frankfurter: "The history of liberty has largely been the history of procedural safeguards (footnotes omitted)."[47]

However, both this commentator and the courts acknowledge that the amount and type of procedure or "process" which is "due" in a particular administrative adjudication depends on the nature of both the private and governmental interests affected by the administrative action.[48] Prior to the U.S. Supreme Court's welfare decisions of the late 1960's, and early 1970's, welfare benefits under state administered federal welfare programs were frequently characterized as mere "privileges" or "gratuities." As such, administrative termination of such benefits was frequently held not to require those due process hearing procedures afforded more substantial "rights."[49]

In 1970, the Supreme Court's landmark decision of *Goldberg v. Kelly*[50] eliminated the "right-privilege" distinction for termination of welfare benefits. Subsequent decisions applied due process restrictions to the exercise of administrative discretion in other contexts. Then in 1972, the Supreme Court said that it had "fully and finally rejected the wooden distinction between 'rights' and 'privileges' that once seemed to govern the applicability of due process rights" in administrative adjudications. [51]

It is not necessary to discuss here the specific notice, hearing and other procedures which the BIA might be required to use in administrative adjudications related to its various human service programs. Recent Indian legislation specifically describes the procedures to be followed in granting or denying the benefits those laws provide. [52] The secretary has also promulgated regulations describing the procedures to be followed in granting or denying benefits under most such recent legislation. [53] Other regulations specifically provide new procedures to be followed in the denial of benefits under existing legislation, such as the Snyder Act. [54]

2. General Requirements

In cases where there are neither statutory or regulatory guidelines, the procedures to be followed in granting or denying benefits will be measured against the relative importance of the private and governmental interests involved. In recent cases, the result has been limitation of the secretary's discretion to deny benefits; two Ninth Circuit cases illustrate the point.

a. *Pence v. Kleppe.*

Although it does not involve a direct human service benefit, *Pence v. Kleppe*[55] contains a comprehensive discussion of general administrative due process requirements. The Interior Secretary argued in *Pence* that he could deny Alaska Native allotments without a hearing or much other procedure, because the 1906 Allotment Act[56] permitted him to make allotments "in his discretion and under such rules as he may prescribe."[57] By thus permitting him to make allotments in his discretion, the secretary argued that Congress had precluded judicial review of his allotment procedures.

The court rejected that claim in part on two principles. It concluded first that "statutes passed for the benefit of dependent Indian tribes and communities are to be liberally construed in favor of the Indians."[58] On that basis it determined second that:

> [a] permissive statutory scheme...is not by itself to be read
> as a Congressional Command precluding judicial review. The
> question is whether nonreviewability can be fairly inferred
> from the overall statutory scheme [citation omitted].[59]

Under these two principles, arbitrary denials of most Native statutory benefits would be entitled to judicial review unless a federal statute specifically required nonreviewability.

The secretary also argued that the Native allotment applicant in *Pence* was not entitled to due process in the denial of her allotment, because the allotment was a "privilege" not a "right." In rejecting that claim, the court noted that the U.S. Supreme Court had rejected the right-privilege doctrine.

> Instead, the Court has adopted the test of whether the person claiming a violation of due process had a sufficient "property interest" in the government benefit denied by the agency.[60]

What constitutes a "sufficient property interest" for due process purposes is not clearly defined, but relying on a recent U.S. Supreme Court opinion, the *Pence* Court concluded that:

> "To have a property interest in a benefit, a person clearly must have more than an abstract need or desire for it. He must have more than a unilateral expectation of it. He must, instead, have a legitimate claim of entitlement to it. It is a purpose of the ancient institution of property to protect those claims upon which people rely in their daily lives, reliance that must not be arbitrarily undermined."[61]

Whether Native human services and programs include such legally protected "property interests" will generally depend on the statutes and appropriations establishing the entitlement (and the legislative purpose behind those enactments). If the legislation creates an entitlement or reliance on the particular benefit or program, then the benefits of that program cannot be arbitrarily denied to Natives who may be entitled to them. Some due process is required.

However, determining that denial of an allotment required due process was only the first step. The final question in *Pence* was what process was due. Relying on the Supreme Court's decision in *Goldberg v. Kelly,* the Ninth Circuit noted that:

> "the extent to which procedural due process must be afforded the recipient is influenced by the extent to which he may be 'condemned to suffer grievous loss,' (citation omitted) and depends upon whether the recipient's interest in avoiding that loss outweighs the governmental interest in summary adjudication (citation omitted)."[62]

Balancing the private recipient's interest in the allotment against the government's convenience, the *Pence* court concluded that, at a minimum, allotment applicants:

> whose claims are to be rejected must be notified of the specific reasons for the proposed rejection, allowed to submit written

evidence to the contrary, and, if they request, granted an opportunity for an oral hearing before the trier of fact where evidence and testimony of favorable witnesses may be submitted before a decision is reached to reject an application for an allotment....[63]

These general principles appear to apply just as easily to any Native human service program where there is 1) a "property interest" or reliance on the benefits conferred by the program and where 2) denial of that interest or reliance would result in a "grievous loss."

b. *Fox v. Morton.*

Prior to *Pence,* the Ninth Circuit decided another case which involved due process procedural rights in the context of a federal Native welfare program. The issue in *Fox v. Morton*[64] was whether participants in a Tribal Work Experience Program (TWEP) were entitled to a due process hearing before their termination from the program. The unusual aspect of this case is that the TWEP participants were terminated, not because they were determined ineligible for the program, but because the local BIA office ordered termination of the program for lack of funds.[65]

The TWEP project was part of the BIA General Assistance Program authorized under the Snyder Act. Because the Snyder Act is legislation intended to benefit Indians, the *Fox* court held that programs administered under the Snyder Act must be liberally construed in favor of the Natives benefiting from such programs.[66] Relying on the then recent Supreme Court decision in *Morton v. Ruiz,*[67] the Ninth Circuit determined that the government's "overriding duty of fairness" when dealing with Native Americans, along with the due process requirements of *Goldberg v. Kelly* meant that BIA's:

> Summary termination of TWEP deprived appellants of due process rights which could have been secured by a properly conducted evidentiary hearing. At such hearing all factors could have been aired, including both appellants' eligibility for the program and the government's interest in terminating it.[68]

One authority on administrative law criticizes this result noting that:

> An evidentiary hearing on the question whether to continue or to terminate such a program would be a procedural monstrosity! The Ninth Circuit lost its bearings, forgetting that the purpose of a trial is to resolve issues of specific fact, not to determine a broad question of policy as to what programs for Indians should be continued or terminated.[69]

On the other hand, the Self-Determination Act as a matter of national policy assures

> maximum Indian participation in the direction of educational as well as other federal services to Indian communities so as to render such services more responsive to the needs and desires of those communities.[70]

Relying in part on a similar policy statement in section 2(b) of ANCSA, the Washington, D.C., District Court imposed certain due process requirements on the Secretary of the Interior when making ANCSA village eligibility determinations.[71] By analogy, the "maximum Indian participation" policy of the Self-Determination Act also supports the due process requirements in *Fox*. Thus, a program termination decision without Indian involvement could justify a public hearing to determine the legitimacy of the decision.

Considerations such as these, along with the Government's "overriding duty of fairness," when dealing with Native Americans appear to attach additional due process obligations to the administration of BIA human service programs. *Fox v. Morton* is still good law, and it specifically holds that both policy decisions terminating a BIA human service program and individual entitlements to that program are subject to a due process hearing prior to termination.

c. Conclusion

Although *Fox v. Morton* might be criticized from an administrative law standpoint, it appears to have validity in the context of Indian law. The "overridding duty of fairness" and the policies of the Self-Determination Act certainly require as much (and perhaps more) due process in the administration of Native American human service programs as in non-Native programs.

C. Statutory Entitlement

1. General

No matter what the scope of executive authority, it is clear that it must be exercised consistent with the provisions and intent of the statute delegating the authority.[72] Thus, when Native individuals or communities are statutorily entitled to what we have termed "human services," they can only be denied those services if it is consistent with the statute to do so. Furthermore, when an executive officer exercises his authority to deny such services to all or a part of the general Native population, it is also clear that the officer must follow certain procedures in order to validly do so. These general statutory and procedural requirements limit executive discretion, thereby imposing obligations toward Natives on the executive officer—usually the Secretary of the Interior or a subordinate.

On the other hand, two statutes have, since 1832, given the secretary broad authority to make rules implementing Indian legislation.[73] This includes both the authority to make law in the form of "legislative" rules and to define the meaning of ambiguous statutes through "interpretive" rules.[74] Legislative rules, so long as they are consistent with the provisions and intent of the statute and are validly adopted, have "the force of law." Interpretive rules, on the other hand, are entitled to "great weight" in a court's interpretation of a statute provided, among other things, such rules are consistent with each other and are within the administrative agency's area of expertise. Two recent cases (one Ninth Circuit and one U.S. Supreme Court) discuss the restrictions these principles place on the executive's ability to limit Native entitlement to statutory benefits.

2. *Rockbridge v. Lincoln*

This case imposes a significant limitation on the most frequently exercised form of administrative discretion: the decision *not* to act.[75] In *Rockbridge,* representatives of the Navajo Nation sued to compel the local BIA area director to adopt "adequate rules and regulations" governing traders on the Navajo Reservation. A statute provided that:

> The Commissioner of Indian Affairs shall have the sole power and authority to appoint traders to the Indian tribes and to make such rules and regulations as he may deem just and proper specifying the kind and quantity of goods and the prices at which such goods shall be sold to the Indians.[76]

The area director contended that this language gave him the "sole power and authority" to determine whether or *not* to adopt *any* regulations. In other words, that Congress had given the area director (through the Commissioner of Indian Affairs) complete discretion permitting him to do nothing if he so chose.

The Arizona Federal District Court agreed that the area director's discretion was a bar to court review of his failure to act. The Ninth Circuit reversed on appeal holding that the statute:

> does not mean that the Commissioner has unbridled discretion to refuse to regulate, but rather that he shall exercise discretion in deciding what regulations to promulgate....[77]

In reaching this conclusion, the court focused not only on the history of this particular statute, but on the "legal relationship between the United States and the Indians." It concluded on the basis of well established precedent that the relationship "resembles that of a ward to its guardian." The court also noted that those who represent the government "in dealings with the Indians should...be judged by the most exacting fiduciary standards."[78]

These principles, coupled with the congressional intent of the statute (i.e., to protect the Navajos from sharp trading practices), led the court to conclude that the statute was:

> passed with a specific objective in mind and that lawfulness of the Commissioner's exercise of discretion—his decisions to regulate or not to regulate in any particular instance, as well as the particular mode of regulation chosen—is to be determined by reference to these objectives.[79]

This was probably sufficient to require the area director to adopt *some* trading regulations. But the *Rockbridge* Court went on to say that a then recent Supreme Court opinion and the Federal Administrative Procedure Act[80] permitted further judicial oversight:

> [S]crutiny of the facts does not end, however, with the determination that the Secretary has acted within the scope of his statutory authority. [The Administrative Procedure Act] requires a finding that the actual [regulation] was not 'arbitrary, capricious, or an abuse of discretion, or otherwise not in accordance with law.' (citation omitted) To make this finding the court must consider whether the decision was based on consideration of the relevant factors and whether there has been a clear error of judgement.[81]

These principles are sufficient to establish that even the broad grants of discretion so common to much "Indian" legislation are not sufficient to permit the secretary or his delegates to escape their obligation to adopt regulations appropriate to each statutory program they operate. Failure to adopt regulations governing area or agency programs should be carefully considered to determine whether continued inaction is consistent with the legislative purpose of such programs.[82]

3. Morton v. Ruiz.

This 1974 U.S. Supreme Court decision[83] illustrates two important principles relating to the exercise of administrative discretion. First, administrative decisions must be consistent with the purposes of the statutes and appropriations which authorize them. Second, such judgements must be made in a lawful manner under the Federal Administrative Procedure Act. As the Supreme Court said in *Ruiz:*

The power of an administrative agency to administer a congressionally created and funded program necessarily requires the formulation of policy and the making of rules to fill any gap left, implicitly or explicitly, by Congress. In the area of Indian affairs, the Executive has long been empowered to promulgate rules and policies, and the power has been given explicitly to the Secretary and his delegates at the BIA. This agency power to make rules that affect substantial individual rights and obligations carries with it the responsibility not only to remain consistent with the governing legislation (citations omitted) but also to employ procedures that conform to law (citations and footnotes omitted). [84]

The issue in *Ruiz* was whether two Papago Indians were eligible for BIA general assistance even though they did not live on a reservation. The court found that Congress had consistently appropriated money on the secretary's representations that BIA programs were provided to all Indians living "on or near" a reservation. The Papago plaintiffs in *Ruiz* apparently argued that they lived near the reservation and were logically indistinguishable from other Natives living "on or near" reservations who did receive assistance. [85] The court agreed but noted that fact alone would not be sufficient to deny the secretary authority to deny the plaintiffs general assistance.

The deciding factor in the case was the method the secretary had used to deny assistance. The plaintiffs had a hearing on their denial, so this was not a due process problem. [86] Rather, the decision to deny assistance was based on a now superseded portion of the BIA manual, purporting to limit assistance only to those Native Americans living "on reservations" (except in Alaska or Oklahoma).

The problem was that this restriction, although it affected a large number of potential beneficiaries, had never been published in the Federal Register according to the requirements of the Administrative Procedure Act. [87] That was important, the court said, because:

The Administrative Procedure Act was adopted to provide,...that administrative policies affecting individual rights and obligations be promulgated pursuant to certain stated procedures so as to avoid the inherently arbitrary nature of unpublished *ad hoc* determinations (citation omitted). [88]

Furthermore, the act required in part that:

Each [Federal] Agency shall separately state and currently publish in the Federal Register for the guidance of the public—

* * * *

(D) substantive rules of general applicability adopted as au-thorized by law, and statements of general policy or interpre-tations of general applicability formulated and adopted by the agency...[89]

Because the secretary had chosen not to treat "this extremely significant eligibility requirement, affecting the rights of needy Indians" according to the requirements of the Administrative Prodecure Act, the court con-cluded that the "on reservation" requirement was "ineffective so far as extinguishing rights of those otherwise within the class of beneficiaries contemplated by Congress.... "[90]

One authority on administrative law criticizes *Ruiz* as unnecessarily complicating the administrative process.[91] This commentator notes that administrative agencies have always made policy decisions in *ad hoc* (i.e., individual) decisions and that such decisions are a necessary part of the administrative process. The criticism misses the point of *Ruiz;* "state-ments of general policy or interpretations of general applicability" must be published in the Federal Register in order to be valid. Publication of the *Ruiz* eligibility requirement was especially important, because that requirement was "extremely significant" and affected "the rights of needy Indians."

IV. Beyond Due Process and Statutory Entitlement

Several of the foregoing cases appear to enhance federal statutory obligations to Natives by tying those obligations to a legally unique fed-eral-Native relationship. Additionally, at least one recent federal circuit court has suggested that the relationship itself may be the source of fed-eral human service obligations. These two approaches are discussed below.

A. The *Ruiz* Approach

It is significant that the Supreme Court in *Ruiz* tied the Interior Sec-retary's statutory obligations to the nature of the federal-Native relation-ship.

The overriding duty of our Federal Government to deal fairly with Indians wherever located has been recognized by this court on many occasions (citations omitted).

Particularly here, where the BIA has continually represented to Congress, when seeking funds, that Indians living near re-servations are within the service area, it is essential that the legitimate expectation of these needy Indians not be extin-gushed by what amounts to an unpublished *ad hoc* determina-tion of the agency that was not promulgated in accordance with its own procedures, to say nothing of those of the Administrative Procedure Act. The denial of benefits to these respondents under such circumstances is inconsistent with "the distinctive obligation of trust incumbent upon the Government in its dealings with these dependent and sometimes exploited people" (citations omitted).

Before benefits may be denied to these otherwise entitled Indians, the BIA must first promulgate eligibility requirements according to established procedures.[92]

This reasoning is similar to that in *Rockbridge,* where the court also focused on the "legal relationship between the United States and the Indians"[93] in determining the BIA area director's obigation to adopt trading regulations. Similar reasoning was used in *Fox v. Morton,* where it was determined that a due process hearing before termination of TWEP participants was required, in part because of the government's "overriding duty of fairness."[94] Thus, these cases indicate that the guardianship or special relationship may combine with normal principles of administrative due process and statutory entitlement to create special obligations of fairness and rule-making in the administration of statutory Native programs.

B. The *White v. Califano* Approach.

White v. Califano[95] affirms a previous decision of the South Dakota Federal District Court *(White v. Matthews)*[96] in which that court found there was federal jurisdiction over a lawsuit to compel the Secretary of Health, Education and Welfare to provide hospitalization for a mentally ill Native woman. *Matthews* held that the federal district court had jurisdiction in part because of the "trust responsibility" of the United States to Native Americans. The Court did not seem to base its conclusion on the existence of any statutory obligation to provide hospitalization.[97]

In *White v. Califano,* the same court affirmed the "trust responsibility" as the basis for its jurisdiction, but also held that the 1976 Indian Health Care Improvement Act[98] constituted congressional "recognition" of that responsibility. The court cited section 3 of that act in which Congress declared:

that it is the policy of this nation, in fulfillment of its special responsibilities and legal obligations to the American Indian people, to meet the national goal of providing the highest possible health status to Indians and provide existing Indian health services with all resources necessary to effect that policy.[99]

On the basis of this statutory provision, the *Califano* court concluded that:

The Congress in 1976 stated that the federal government had a responsibility to provide health care for Indians. Therefore, when we say that the trust responsibility requires a certain course of action, *we do not refer to a relationship that exists only in the abstract, but rather to a congressionally recognized duty to provide services* for a particular category of human needs. The trust responsibility, as recognized and defined by statute, is the ground upon which federal defendants' duties rest in this case (emphasis added).

* * * *

When the Congress legislates for Indians only, something more than a statutory entitlement is involved. Congress is acting upon the premise that a special relationship is involved, and is acting to meet the obligations inherent in that relationship....We have, therefore, read and construed the Indian Health Care Improvement Act as a manifestation of what Congress thinks the trust responsibility requires of federal officials, with whatever funds are available, when they try to meet Indian health needs. [100]

On this rationale the court found that:

(I)t is difficult to conceive how congress could appropriate *any* money specifically for health care for Indians and intend to ignore the most wretched human condition requiring health care, *i.e.,* insanity. What is more conceivable is that congressmen...assumed that...where necessary, federal officials would act [to provide health care] (emphasis in original). [101]

Plaintiff's need for care was so obvious, that once the *Califano* court found federal officials had the duty to provide *some* care, it concluded that plaintiff could not be fairly denied hospitalization.

C. *Ruiz-Califano* and the Transformation of "Guardianship"

Both *Ruiz* and *Califano* reached the same result, although by slightly different routes. *Ruiz* (as well as *Fox* and *Rockbridge*) first determined that Native plaintiffs had a statutory entitlement and then that the "unique legal relationship" placed a special obligation on administrative officials to satisfy that entitlement. *Califano* held that the federal obligation to provide health care was found in the "unique legal relationship" itself. When congress legislated on the basis of that relationship (i.e., for Natives only), then it gave statutory "recognition" to the obligations inherent in the relationship. In *Califano,* those "inherent" obligations meant that "more than a statutory entitlement is involved" in such legislation and that "where necessary, federal officials would act" to provide health care to Natives.

Ruiz and its progeny, *Fox,* imply that the "unique legal relationship" requires special observance of fairness and due process concepts when limiting or altering Native entitlement to human service benefits and programs. *Rockbridge* (a pre-*Ruiz* case) implies that the "legal relationship between the United States and the Indians" can require the executive branch to act even where a statute appears to grant broad discretion not to act.

Earlier cases focused on the legal relationship (frequently characterized as a "guardianship") as a source of federal *authority* over Indian affairs.[102] However, these recent cases illustrate that the Supreme Court and lower federal courts are now interpreting that legal relationship as also imposing federal executive *obligations* to scrupulously interpret and apply Native human service statutes to the best advantage of their Native beneficiaries.

V. Conclusion

A. Describing the "Legal Relationship"

Any discussion of the federal obligation to provide Native human services, encounters a number of semantic barriers. In the foregoing discussion, we have tried to get behind those barriers by concentrating on the use the courts have made of the "unique legal relationship" concept without concentrating on the words used to describe that concept. For the sake of consistency (and because it is the term historically used to describe the Alaska Native relationship), we have frequently used the term "guardianship" to describe the total "unique legal relationship." However, this term is largely of historical importance.

As Felix Cohen has noted, courts have used "guardianship" in several different respects;[103] we have used "guardianship" here as shorthand for "subject to the plenary power of Congress."[104] That plenary power, however described, gives Congress extremely broad authority to legislate on behalf of Native Americans. Whether Natives are subject to that power because of "guardianship" or some other concept is irrelevant. The point is Natives are subject to plenary power so long as Congress desires to make them subject to it.[105]

"Trust responsibility," like "guardianship," is merely another phrase used to describe the "unique legal relationship." However, using the word "trust" to describe human service obligations creates legal, semantic problems. In the strict, legal sense of the term, "trust" denotes a legal relationship involving property.[106] This explains the logical tendency for lawyers to connect the concept of a "trust responsibility" to some sort of underlying property relationship. In *White v. Califano,* the South Dakota District Court got around this problem by equating "trust responsibility" to the "unique legal relationship."[107] The court then reasoned that Congress had "recognized" the health care obligations inherent in that relationship by passing the 1976 Indian Health Care Improvement Act.

If we must use a single phrase to describe the relationship of the federal government to Native Americans, perhaps the one the *Califano* Court chose is the most useful. However, whether that relationship is described as resembling "that of a ward to its guardian,"[108] a "distinctive obligation of trust,"[109] an "overriding duty of fairness,"[110] or a "trust responsibility" is of little consequence. What is most important is the existence of the general "unique legal relationship" and the specific action Congress has taken to recognize and define that relationship.

B. Authority and Obligation

We have concentrated in this discussion on the interplay between federal authority and federal obligations in the context of Native human service benefits and programs. What we will now call the "unique legal relationship" appears from early and recent court decisions to be the source of both that authority and those obligations. The early cases, beginning with *Kagama,* concentrate on the limits of federal authority and conclude that the legal relationship is the source of federal authority to enact criminal and protective legislation applicable to Native Americans. Taken together, these cases provide broad authority for the exercise of federal power in the field of Indian affairs.

Largely because the issues have changed, recent cases have held that the legal relationship is also the source of federal executive obligations. These obligations have never been found to exist in the absence of *some* statute giving them congressional shape and meaning,[111] but in the context of such statutes, the legal relationship has been held to impose special obligations of rule-making *(Ruiz* and *Rockbridge),* due process *(Fox),* and health care *(Califano).* Taken together, these cases demonstrate that the legal relationship can also be used to cut and shape executive power so that it is exercised for statutorily authorized Native benefit.

It seems possible that this transition from authority to obligation was made possible by the demise of the so-called right-privilege doctrine. Prior to that, Native human service programs (unless they were tied to a treaty or other agreement) were legally characterized as "gratuities"— mere privileges.[112] Because they were privileges, bureaucrats were seldom subject to due process requirements or court review of their actions in administering these programs. This principle appeared to apply to both Native and non-Native social service programs and would be especially applicable in Alaska where Native social service programs were never associated with treaty obligations and seldom, if ever, with other agreements.

By 1972, the U.S. Supreme Court had rejected the "wooden distinction" between rights and privileges and adopted a balancing test which focused on the beneficiary's "property interest" or "reliance" on the entitlement conferred under federal statutory programs.[113] In the context of this new form of property interest or "entitlement" the Supreme Court found in *Ruiz* that the Interior Secretary had an obligation to publish general assistance eligibility requirements in the Federal Register. The secretary's obligation to do so was enhanced by the legal relationship (i.e., "distinctive obligation of trust") between the federal government and the Natives. Similarly, the South Dakota Federal District Court has found that, if it is statutorily recognized, the legal relationship requires the executive branch to provide health care for mentally ill Natives.

The real importance of the "unique legal relationship," therefore, does not appear to lie in any abstract characterization of that relationship as a "trust responsibility," "guardianship", or other vague generality. Rather, the importance of the relationship is the extent to which it can be said to impose legal obligations on executive officers to act for the benefit of Native Americans. No Supreme Court case has held that such obligations do not exist outside federal statutes, but *Ruiz,* several Ninth Circuit cases and *Califano* have found that such obligations do exist in association with several federal human service statutes. Administrators of federal Native programs should, therefore, carefully examine their obligations under such statutory programs to ensure that they are met in compliance with the "unique legal relationship."

C. ANCSA and Federal Obligation

The federal government's authority to provide benefits and programs to Alaska Natives has never depended on the status of Native lands. Few reservations were ever created in Alaska (only one exists now), but the United States has always defined its social service jurisdiction as including *all* Alaska Natives.[114] Justice Van Devanter's decisions in *Sandoval, Candelaria* and *Chavez*[115] also confirm that federal authority over Native Americans does not depend on the status of their lands. In each of those cases, federal authority was founded on the legal relationship (there called "guardianship") between the government and the Natives; the Interior Department Solicitor and the courts have long recognized a similar source of federal authority over Alaska Natives. The relevant question then is whether ANCSA terminated federal authority to provide human services to those Natives.

To ask the question is to answer it. ANCSA is first of all Native *land* claims legislation; it does not purport to affect federal human service programs. Furthermore, subsequent federal Native legislation has always included Alaska Natives within its scope.[116] Finally, it seems well settled that if the federal government is going to terminate its relationship with Native Americans, it must do so clearly for the termination to be effective.[117] It is clear that ANCSA itself does not terminate that relationship with respect to human services.

ANCSA's only references to Native "social" needs or programs are found in sections 2(b) and 2(c) of the Claims Act:

Sec. 2. Congress finds and declares that

(b) the settlement should be accomplished rapidly, with certainty, in comformity with the real economic and social needs of Natives...with maximum participation by Natives in decisions affecting their rights and property....

(c) [T]he Secretary is authorized and directed, together with other appropriate agencies of the United States Government, to make a study of all Federal programs primarily designed to benefit Native people and to report back to the Congress with his recommendations for the future management and operation of these programs within three years of the date of enactment of this Act.

Section 2(b) requires that the settlement conform to the *"real economic and social needs of the Natives"* and that the Natives participate in decisions affecting their rights. To say that other language in this section somehow authorizes the termination of Alaska Native benefits and programs without Native participation would be contrary to the clear language of the congressional policy statement.

Section 2(c) deals specifically with the future of Alaska Native human service programs. Far from terminating them, it directs the Secretary of Interior to study "all Federal programs" benefiting Native people and to report back to Congress with recommendations for the *"future management and operation"* (emphasis added) of those programs. Again the plain language of this clause implies that there will be a "future" for such programs. [118]

Of course, Congress could terminate these programs at any time it thought appropriate, [119] and beginning in 1981, initiated perhaps the first steps to do so with the closure of BIA day schools and an attempt to cut off appropriations for BIA general assistance welfare benefits. [120] As of 1984, the closure of the BIA schools appeared all but certain, but the termination of general assistance was more problematic. [121] It is not clear whether these cut-backs are merely the first of a trend or relatively isolated efforts to trim federal expenditures. In any event it is clear that ANCSA does not mandate termination of any federal services.

Significantly, a claims settlement bill adopted by the Senate in 1970 did specifically require termination of welfare and education programs within five years. [122] The bill died with that Congress, and when ANCSA was enacted the next year it did not require any specific termination of services. Moreover, every subsequent piece of federal Indian welfare legislation enacted since 1971 has incorporated Alaska Natives fully within its scope of entitlement.[123] Just as importantly, federal expenditures for Alaska Native programs showed general (and often dramatic) increases at least between 1970 and 1980.[124] Beginning in 1981, there have been some significant cuts in these expenditures,[125] but these cuts can more properly be attributed to budget reduction policies adopted in 1981 rather than to requirements of ANCSA.

The entitlement of Alaska Natives to federal services remains a congressional prerogative but one which, under the philosophy of self-determination and ANCSA in particular, should be exercised with the "maximum participation of Natives" and "in conformity with the real economic and social needs of Natives." It is always difficult, of course, to determine the extent to which Congress and the nation will remain committed to this philosophy.

ENDNOTES

[1]Goldberg v. Kelly, 297 U.S. 254 (1969) is the landmark case which clearly establishes due process rights to statutory entitlements.

[2]See generally, A. H. Snow, *The Question of Aboriginies in the Law and Practice of Nations,* (Northbrook, Ill.: Metro Books, 1972), at 24-37.
M.F. Lindley, *The Acquisition and Government of Backward Territory in International Law,* (New York: Negro University, 1926; reprinted in 1969), at 328-336.
Felix Cohen also discusses the colonial origins of the guardianship doctrine in "The Spanish Origin of Indian Rights," *The Legal Conscience,* (New Haven: Yale University, 1960, reprinted Archon, 1970) at 245-247. See also G. Bennett, "Aboriginal Rights in International Law," *Occasional Paper No. 37* (Royal Anthropological Institute, 1978), at 7-11.

[3]U.S. v. Kagama, 118 U.S. 375, 384 (1886) is the germinal case. It held that the Indian Major Crimes Act (18 USCA 1153, 3242) was constitutional based on the "necessity" of federal guardianship. See also U.S. v. Sandoval, 231 U.S., 45-46 (1913), liquor prohibition of Pueblo Indian lands; U.S. v. Candelaria, 271 U.S. 432, 439 (1925), protection of Pueblo Indian lands; U.S. v. Chavez, 290 U.S. 354, 362 (1933), federal prosecution for larceny on Pueblo Indian property.

[4]Seminole Nation v. U.S., 316 U.S. 286 (1942) is seemingly the first case to impose monetary damages against the federal government because of a breach of "the distinctive obligation of trust incimbent upon the Government in its dealings with these dependent and sometimes exploited people."

[5]25 USCA 2, derived from Acts of July 9, 1832 (4 Stat. 564) and July 27, 1898 (15 Stat. 228). See also 25 USCA 9 (1970), authority of the president to prescribe Indian regulations.

[6]See generally Kenneth Culp Davis, *Administrative Law Treatise;* (St. Paul, Minn.: West Publishing 1958 [1976 Supp.] [Vol. 1, 7.00-1]). Hereafter 1 Davis 7.00-1 (1976 Supp.), etc.

[7]See F. Cohen, *Handbook of Federal Indian Law* 1942 ed. (Washington, D.C.: G.P.O., reprinted New York: AMS, 1972) at 237.

[8]31 U.S. (6 Pet.) 350, 379 (1832).

[9]Cohen, note 7, above, at 90.

[10]Id. at 91.

[11]Id. at 90, citing *U.S. v. Kagama,* note 3, above; Perrin v. U.S., 2232 U.S. 478, 486 (1914); Gritts v. Fisher, 224 U.S. 640, 642-643 (1912); U.S. v. Thomas, 151 U.S. 577, 585 (1894), and U.S. v. McGowan, 301 U.S. 535, 538 (1938), stating that "Congress alone has the right to determine the manner in which the country's guardianship...shall be carried out...."

[12]Seminole Nation v. U.S., 316 U.S. 286, 296 (1942).

[13]See e.g., White v. Matthews; 420 F. Supp. 882, 887 (D.C.S.D. 1976).

[14]Cherokee Nation v. Georgia, 30 U.S. (5 Pet) 1, 12 (1831).

[15]Id.

[16]25 USCA 71 derived from Act of March 3, 1871, 16 Stat. 566.

[17]*Kagama,* note 3, above.

[18]18USCA 1153, derived from Act of March 3, 1885, 23 Stat. 385.

[19]*Kagama,* note 3, above, at 383-385. The *Kagama* court also specifically rejected the more specific commerce clause constitutional rationale as a basis of federal authority to enact criminal laws relating to Native Americans. Id. at 378-379.

[20]94 U.S. 614 (1876).

[21]Id. at 616.

[22]231 U.S. 28 (1913).

[23]Id. at 46 and 48.

[24]271 U.S. 432 (1925).

[25]Id. at 437.

[26]U.S. v. Chavez 290 U.S. 357 (1933).

[27]18 USCA 1152, derived from 25 USC 217 (1940).

[28]*Chavez,* note 26, above, at 378-379.

[29]C.f. *Kagama* note 2, above, at 378-379, rejecting commerce clause reasoning as authority for Congress to enact criminal laws relating to Indians in Indian country.

[30]Cohen, note 7, above, at 403.

[31]Id. at 414. See also 49 L.D. 592, 594-595 (1923), citing earlier opinions.

[32]See U.S. v. Berrigan, 2 Ak. Rpts. 442 (D.C. Ak. 1904); U.S. v. Cadzow, 5 Ak. Rpts. 125 (D.C. Ak. 1914).

[33]248 U.S. 78 (1918).

[34]Id. at 88 and 89.

[35]49 L.D. 592, 594 and 595 (1923).

[36]53 I.D. 593, 605 (1933). See also 54 I.D. 15 and 39.

[37]Act of November 2, 1921, 42 Stat. 208, 25 USCA 13.

[38]61 Cong. Rec. 4683-84, 67th Cong.; 1st sess. (1921).

[39]Id. at 4660.

[40]Id.

[41]E.g., Remarks of Representative Carter (Okla.) Id. at 4672.

[42]See notes 10 and 30, above, and accompanying text.

[43]See Sandoval, note 22, above, at 46. See also Delaware Tribal Business Comm. v. Weeks, 430 U.S. 73, 85 (1977), requiring that federal power be "tied rationally to the fulfillment of Congress' unique obligations toward the Indians...." (citation omitted).

[44]See Cohen, note 7, above, at 91. See also U.S. v. Sioux Nation, 448 U.S. 371 (1980), compensation required for the taking of Indian reserved lands.

[45]Id. at 100, citing The Floyd Acceptances, 7 Wall. 666 (1868).

[46]Id. at 171.

[47]Davis, note 6, above, at 7.20 (1958).

[48]E.g., Goldberg v. Kelly, 397 U.S. 254, 263 (1970).

[49]C.f. Davis, note 6, above, at 7.12-1 (1970 Supp.).

[50]397 U.S. 254 (1970).

[51]Board of Regents v. Roth, 408 U.S. 564, 571 (1972).

[52]See e.g., 25 USC 450f, conditions under which the Secretary may decline to contract under the Self-Determination Act.

[53]See e.g., 25 CFR 93.1 et seq. Loan Guaranties, Insurance and Interest Subsidies under the Indian Financing Act. See also, 25 CFR 271.1 et seq. Contracts under the Indian Self-Determination Act.

[54]E.g., 25 CFR 20.30. Hearings and Appeals in the denial of Financial Assistance or Social Services under the Snyder Act.

[55]Pence v. Kleppe 529 F. 2d 135 (9th Cir., 1976).

[56]43 USC 270-1 through 270-3 (1970), repealed by 43 USCA 1617, discussed in chapter 4, above.

[57]*Pence,* note 55, above, at 137.

[58]Id. at 140.

[59]Id.

[60]Id. at 141.

[61]Id., citing Board of Regents v. Roth, 408 U.S. at 577 (1972).

[62]Id. at 142.

[63]Id. at 143.

[64]Fox v. Morton 505 F. 2d 254 (1974).

[65]Id. at 256, Gray, J. dissenting.

[66]Id. at 255.

[67]415 U.S. 199 (1974).

[68]*Fox,* note 64, above, at 256.

[69]1 Davis 7.00-11, note 6, above, at 275 (1976 Supp.).

[70]25 USCA 450a(a).

[71]Koniag v. Kleppe, 405 F. Supp. 1360, 1370 (D.C. D.C. 1975).

[72]See e.g., Morton v. Ruiz 415 U.S. 199 (1973), holding that denial of BIA general assistance to Indians living "near" a reservation violated the intent of the general assistance appropriations. See also Wilson v. Watt, 703 F. 2d 395 (9th Cir., 1983), granting a preliminary injunction against the termination of BIA general assistance in Alaska prior to the implementation of a "comparable" state

program when Congress intended that the BIA program be terminated only if the State provided "comparable" assistance.

[73]25 USCA and 25 USCA 9.

[74]See 1 Davis, note 6, above, at 5.03 (1958) for an explanation of the distinction between "legislative" and "interpretive" rules. The distinction is not important for the BIA; 25 USCA 9 and 25 USCA 2 have long granted it general authority to adopt both sorts of rules in the field of "Indian affairs."

[75]Rockbridge v. Lincoln, 449 F. 2d 567 (9th Cir., 1971). Davis notes that "inaction decisions may be ten or twenty times as frequent as action decisions." 1 Davis, note 6, above, at 91 (1958).

[76]25 USCA 261.

[77]*Rockbridge,* note 75, above, at 571.

[78]Id. at 570, citing cases.

[79]Id. at 572.

[80]5 USCA 706(2)(A).

[81]*Rockbridge,* note 75, above, at 572.

[82]The same principle has been applied in Alaska to require the Secretary of Health and Human Services to adopt regulations implementing the Indian Preference Provisions of 25 USCA Sec. 472., Preston v. Schweiker, 555 F. Supp. 886 (D. Ak. 1983).

[83]Morton v. Ruiz, 415 U.S. 199 (1974). See also Lewis v. Weinberger, 415 F. Supp. 652 (D.N.M. 1976), entitlement to off-reservation health care.

[84]*Ruiz,* note 83, above, at 231-232.

[85]Id. generally at 209-229.

[86]Id. at 204-205.

[87]5 USCA 551 et seq.

[88]*Ruiz,* note 83, above, at 232.

[89]5 USCA 552(a)(1)(D), cited in *Ruiz,* note 83, above, at 232-233.

[90]*Ruiz,* note 83, above, at 236.

[91]See 1 Davis, note 6, above, at 6.13-1 (1958).

[92]*Ruiz,* note 83, above, at 236.

[93]See *Rockbridge,* note 78, above and accompanying text.

[94]See notes 67 and 68 above and accompanying text.

[95]White v. Califano 437 F. Supp. 543 (D.C. S.D. 1977) aff'd. sub nom White v. Matthews, 420 F. Supp. 882 (D.C. S.D. 1976), aff'd. per curiam 581 F. 2d 697 (8th Cir. 1978).

[96]*White v. Matthews,* note 95, above.

[97]Id. at 887, discussing the "trust responsibility" as "[m]ore compelling than cites to certain Federal statutes."

[98]Act of September 30, 1976, 90 Stat 1400, 25 USCA 1601 et seq.

[99]25 USCA 1602.

[100]*Califano,* note 95, above, at 557.

[101]Id. at 558. Note: Budgetary restrictions could legitimately limit executive obligations, but in this case the court found such limits could not extend to "the most wretched human condition requiring health care, i.e., insanity."

[102]See e.g., *Kagama, Sandoval, Candelaria* and *Chavez* at note 3, above, and accompanying text.

[103]Cohen, note 7, above, at 169-173. Cohen actually discusses the uses made of the "wardship" concept, but the difference between "wardship" and "guardianship" is insubstantial.

[104]Id. at 170-171.

[105]See e.g., *U.S. v. Sandoval,* note 3, above, at 46, citing Tiger v. Western Investment Co., 221 U.S. 286, 315 (1911).

[106]A.W. Scott, *Law of Trusts,* Vol. 1 (Boston: Little, Brown and Co., 1967), at 3-4.

[107]*Califano,* note 95, above, 437 F. Supp. at 557, n.9.

[108]*Cherokee Nation v. Georgia,* note 14, above, at 12 (1831). See also *Rockbridge v. Lincoln,* note 75, above, at 570.

[109]*Morton v. Ruiz,* note 83, above, at 236, citing Seminole Nation v. U.S., 316 U.S. 286 (1942).

[110]*Fox v. Morton,* note 64, above, at 256.

[111]See generally, Gila River Pima-Maricopa Indian Community v. U.S., 427 F. 2d 1194, 1198 (Ct. Cls. 1970).

[112]See e.g., Cohen, note 7, above, at 237-238.

[113]C.f. *Pence v. Kleppe,* note 55, above, at 141.

[114]See *Ruiz,* note 83, above, at 212.

[115]See notes 22-28 above, and accompanying text.

[116]See 25 USC 450 et seq. (Self-Determination Act of 1975); 25 USC 1601 et seq. (Indian Health Care Improvement Act of 1976); 25 USC 1451 et seq. (Indian Fianacing Act of 1974); 25 USCA 1901 et seq. (Indian Child Welfare Act of 1978).

[117]See Menominee Tribe v. U.S. 391 U.S. 404 (1968).

[118]The Secretary of the Interior submitted the comprehensive *2(c) Report* to Congress in 1975, but the report specifically declined to make recommendations. "Introduction and Summary" *2(c) Report: Federal Programs and Alaska Natives* (Anchorage: Robert R. Nathan, c. 1975), at vii. The letters transmitting the report to Congress indicates that recommendations will be made at a later date. Letters from Interior Secretary Morton to House Speaker Albert and Senate President Rockefeller (April 22, 1975). No recommendations have ever been submitted, and it appears unlikely that the requirement could be judicially enforced. C.f. 13th Regional Corporation v. Department of the Interior, 654 F. 2d 758 (D.C. Cir. 1980), denying relief for failure to include non-resident Natives in the 2(c) study because plaintiffs waited too long to sue.

[119]C.f. *Sandoval,* note 3, above, at 46.

[120]See generally, chapter 5, above.

[121]Wilson v. Watt, 703 F. 2d 395 (9th Cir. 1983), discussed in chapter 5, above.

[122]Section 4(b)(1) of S. 1830 directed the Secretary of the Interior together with other U.S. government agencies to:

> ...initiate a study and to develop programs for the orderly transition of educational, health, welfare and other responsibilities for the Alaska Native people from the United States to the State of Alaska. Within five years from the date of enactment of this Act, the United States shall cease to provide services to any citizen of Alaska solely on the basis of racial or ethnic background.

Health care and Johnson-O'Malley education programs were specifically excepted from the termination. The termination provision was vigorously debated, but its opponents were unsuccessful in amending it. See 116 Cong. Rec. 24216 et seq. (July 14, 1970).

[123]See note 116, above.

[124]For example between 1970 and 1980 BIA expenditures in Alaska went from $12,242,000 to $333,410,000. Source James E. Hawkins, "A Preliminary Profile of Federal Programs Provided to Alaska Natives" (circa 1981). This report was prepared for the Interior Department's Assistant Secretary for Indian Affairs as a preliminary description of the number and scope of federal and state programs benefiting Alaska Natives. The data has substantial gaps because for most agencies (except the BIA) there was no information on 1970 budget levels.

The 1980 budget levels for some agencies appear substantial (e.g., Indian Health Service, $74,687,000; HUD Indian Housing Program, $228,201,000). The report cautions, however, that it is not a complete inventory and that no such inventory exists. It further notes that:

> The number and diversity of federal programs being provided to Alaska Natives give little indication of their well being....[and that] care must be taken to insure that inflated state and federal contributions to Alaska Natives do not obscure major economic and social problems. Id. at 11 (unnumbered).

[125]HUD Indian Housing expenditures dropped from $228,201,000 in 1980 to $163,295,000 in 1981; Indian Health Service dropped from $74,687,000 to $73,111,000; BIA expenditures increased from $33,410,000 to $34,375,000, but that included over $20.5 million for school operations ($13,546,000) and general assistance ($6,983,000).

PART IV

THE FEDERAL
OBLIGATION TO
PROTECT SUBSISTENCE

CHAPTER SEVEN

SUBSISTENCE IN ALASKA

I. Protecting Subsistence Generally

A. Introduction

Protecting their subsistence way of life is among the most pressing concerns of Alaska's Natives. They are not unique among Native American people in their desire to maintain their subsistence livelihood; subsistence has been a consistent and fundamental issue in past conflicts between the aboriginal and immigrant American cultures. Frequently, these conflicts have arisen from commercial exploitation of resources used for subsistence or of the environment which supports those resources. Recent urbanization in Alaska and the transformation of hunting and fishing into a sport for many Alaskans have added another element to this competition which has made it politically difficult to define "subsistence" to popular satisfaction. The 1982 ballot measure to repeal Alaska's subsistence priority in favor of "consumptive use" indicates that the debate is not dead, [1] but the adoption in 1980 of a federal subsistence law, [2] coupled with the defeat of the repeal initiative, may substantially moot the debate's political relevance. [3] Nevertheless, it is important to have some understanding of the various ways in which the term "subsistence" is used and the historic role the concept plays in federal Indian law before discussing the Alaskan situation.

B. "Subsistence"

Recent federal legislation identifies at least three elements in the subsistence concept: (a) continued economic or physical reliance, (b) cultural or social value and (c) custom or tradition. [4]

1. Economic or Physical Reliance

It seems obvious that subsistence uses must, at the very least, include "sustenance": hunting, fishing or gathering for the primary purpose of acquiring food. In that respect, subsistence is necessary from both individual and community economic and physical standpoints. This is especially true in Alaska, where those communities and persons relying on the subsistence way of life do in fact depend on renewable resources for a substantial portion of their nutrition. [5] This is not only a matter of choice but of necessity imposed by a combination of factors, including great distance from other food sources, chronic regional unemployment and resulting lack of cash to exchange for imported food. Thus, nutrition, location, and a weak position in the cash economy combine to make rural communities physically and economically reliant on subsistence uses of resources.

2. Cultural or Social Value[6]

For Natives engaged in subsistence uses, the very acts of hunting, fishing, and gathering, coupled with the seasonal cycle of these activities and the sharing and celebrations which accompany them are intricately woven into the fabric of their social, psychological and religious life.[7] Actions and events which interfere with subsistence inevitably cut across the whole cloth of Native culture. Understandably, Natives perceive threats to subsistence as threats to their cultural survival; history has proven their concern to be well founded. One of the chief causes of Indian decimation during the 19th century was the loss of the hunting grounds and the game on which the Indian tribes subsisted.[8]

3. Tradition or Custom

The third element in the subsistence concept, at least as it is defined in federal legislation,[9] is closely related to ideas of cultural or social values. Tradition and custom imply that a certain degree of permanence or at least only gradual evolution is characteristic of those values.

It is unrealistic to require cultural or social values to remain forever fixed; indeed change is common to all societies. For example, some resource uses, such as fur trapping, have taken on a commercial significance which has become a part of the overall cultural or social value of the resource. However, when it comes to resource preservation, it is important that resources harvested for subsistence not become commercially exploited. Thus, while concepts of tradition or custom do not prohibit evolution of subsistence cultural or social values, they allow only limited transformation into commercial enterprise.

C. Subsistence Protection Alternatives

Prior to 1871, aboriginal people in the continental United States bargained to preserve their subsistence uses through treaties. More recently these concerns have manifested themselves in legislation protecting the subsistence ways of rural Alaska Natives. Alaska Native cultural existence is so intimately bound to subsistence that, if Alaska Natives are to continue their cultural distinction within American society, their rural subsistence uses must be accorded continued legal protection. Native Americans have historically had three alternatives for protection of resources used for subsistence: (a) reservations, (b) off-reservation treaty rights and (c) other federal pre-emptive legislation.

1. Reservations

Nineteenth century Indian treaties and agreements usually confined the aboriginal people to reservations, which were reduced areas of the lands they had held aboriginally. If the reservations were large enough and game still plentiful, it was possible for Natives to live according to their cultural traditions. Generally, the reservations were not adequate for these purposes, however, so subsistence culture inevitably declined. Nevertheless, some reservations, either because they included unique resources such as a bountiful lake[10] or because the traditional needs of the people centered on agricultural production[11] have perhaps been sufficient to protect Native cultural values.

Generally, federal treaties, statutes or agreements implicitly protect reservation subsistence uses.[12] Because state laws are not generally permitted to infringe on reservation tribal self-government,[13] one might assume that tribes have exclusive control also over reservation fish and wildlife resources. Recent cases, however, have tended to balance perceived federal, state and tribal interests. For example, it appears that a state acting under a court order can regulate on-reservation fish or wildlife harvest if it is necessary for "conservation" purposes.[14] Additionally, it has been held that a state has exclusive jurisdiction over non-Indian fishing on non-Indian fee lands within a reservation.[15] But tribal control of both non-member and member hunting and fishing on reservation trust or restricted lands is still insulated from state interference, especially when the relative tribal, federal and state interests balance in favor of the tribe.[16]

2. Off Reservation Rights

In addition to reservation hunting, fishing and gathering rights, some Native tribes have been guaranteed similar off-reservation rights. The 1855 treaties with the Natives living in Washington Territory guaranteed them the right to off-reservation fishing:

> at all usual and accustomed places, in common with citizens of the Territory and [to erect] temporary buildings for curing [fish]; together with the privilege of hunting, gathering roots and berries, and pasturing their horses and cattle upon open and unclaimed land....[17]

The U.S. Supreme Court has recognized that off-reservation fishing rights guaranteed by this language were:

> a part of larger rights possessed by the Indians, upon the exercise of which there was not a shadow of impediment, and which were not less necessary to the existence of the Indians than the atmosphere they breathed.[18]

Of these guaranteed rights, the Supreme Court differentiated between those which were exclusive (within the boundaries of the reservation) and those which were off-reservation and held "in common with citizens of the Territory." These off-reservation rights were not exclusive, because other citizens of the Territory were also entitled to fish, but the Indians retained a perpetual right to cross even the private lands of citizens to fish at "all usual and accustomed places."[19] More recent decisions have held that the "in common" language of the treaties entitles the treaty tribes to up to fifty percent of the available fish resources.[20] However, other decisions imply that these rights may be subject to state control if that is "necessary" for "conservation" purposes.[21]

Although it is clear the state cannot condition off-reservation hunting, fishing and gathering rights on the purchase of a state license,[22] it can regulate manner, size of take, and commercial fishing for conservation purposes, so long as such regulations do not discriminate against the Indians *(Puyallup I)*.[23] The Supreme Court has since held *(Puyallup II)* that a regulation which permitted sports fishing for steelhead but prohibited Native steel-head net fishing was discriminatory as to the Natives and therefore barred.[24] Most recently, however, *(Puyallup III)* the U.S. Supreme Court held that off-reservation fishing can be regulated by the state if necessary for conservation.[25] To summarize the Washington State situation, the Supreme Court has recognized that at least under some cicumstances the states can regulate treaty-protected, off-reservation fishing for conservation purposes so long as the regulation does not "discriminate" against the Indians.

3. Other Forms of Preemption

Because ANCSA purports to abolish all Alaska reservations (except Metlakatla), and Alaska Natives have no off-reservation, treaty-protected hunting, fishing or gathering rights, other forms of federal statutory protection have become increasingly important. Given the recent inroads of state jurisdiction for "conservation" purposes, even on reservation lands, these other forms of protection might afford Alaska Natives protection similar to that of a traditional reservation system.

In the case of Metlakatla, the 1891 statute establishing the reservation has proven to be a more substantial barrier to the exercise of state jurisdiction than might the usual limitations imposed by the reservation alone. In addition to withdrawing the land for the reservation, the statute also required that the reserve be used "under such rules and regulations, and subject to such restrictions, as may be prescribed from time to time by the Secretary of the Interior."[26] In *Metlakatla v. Egan,* the U.S. Supreme Court held that this statutory provision prevented the state from exercising any jurisdiction over fishing on the Metlakatla reserve.[27] In the companion case of *Kake v. Egan,* however, the Supreme Court held that the state could prohibit off-reservation Native fishing if Native fishing methods (i.e., fish traps) were inconsistent with state law.[28] The absence of Alaska reservations and the scope of the state's off-reservation political authority have made it even more important to preserve and develop other federal preemptions protecting Native subsistence.

II. Federal Preemption in Alaska

A. General

The United States Constitution and federal treaties and statutes adopted pursuant to it are the supreme law of the land;[29] they preempt any contrary state laws.[30] Since the beginning of the twentieth century, the United States has adopted a number of treaties and statutes aimed primarily at protecting migratory wildlife, but these enactments have also provided some guarantees of continued Alaska Native subsistence.[31] The most recent statutes and treaties (and recent amendments to previous ones) have broadened these protection to include similarly situated non-Natives as well. Thus, recent legal trends are away from exclusive Native protections toward inclusion of others to the extent they participate in subsistence uses. In one sense these trends represent a diminution of Native rights, but in another they represent incorporation of Native values into non-Native culture. In either case, it is clear that each of these enactments preempts inconsistent state laws affecting uniquely Native rights. Significantly, courts have also held that this preemption is based on the exercise of a federal "trust responsibility" to protect Native communities and subsistence culture.

B. Preemptive Treaties

International treaties governing wildlife resources offer excellent opportunites to protect Native subsistence uses. The United States has adopted several such treaties and enacted specific statutes to implement them. Several of these treaties are potentially adverse to Native subsistence uses because, among other things, they inject international political considerations into decisions of whether, when and how the United States should act to protect those uses. On the other hand, Alaska Natives have also proven adept at injecting themselves into and influencing international political events in favor of their subsistence interests.[32] Political skill, therefore, may prove a guarantee of those interests separate from specific, subsistence-oriented treaty provisions.

There are seven specific wildlife treaties, implemented by four correlative statutes, which relate specifically to Alaska Native subsistence:

1. Migratory Bird Treaty with Great Britain (as signatory for Canada) (1916)

2. Migratory Bird Treaty with Mexico (1937)

3. Migratory Bird Treaty with Japan (1974)

4. Migratory Bird Treaty with the Soviet Union (1976)
   (Each of the Migratory Bird Treaties is implemented by the Migratory Bird Treaty Act of 1918.)[33]

5. Fur Seal Convention (1957)
    (Implemented by the Fur Seal Act of 1966.)[34]

6. International Whaling Convention (1946)
    (Implemented by the Whaling Convention Act of 1950.)[35]

7. Polar Bear Convention (1976)
    (Implemented by the Marine Mammal Protection Act of 1972.[36]

With the exception of the Whaling Convention, each of these treaties provides specific, though sometimes ineffective, exceptions for Alaska Native subsistence. Each of the treaties can be classified generally as a "conservation" measure which pledges the signatory nations to undertake wildlife conservation measures within the general framework of each agreement.

1. Migratory Bird Treaties

The four migratory bird treaties now in force were adopted over a period of sixty years. Because there have been substantial policy changes, the conservation provisions of the earlier treaties are inconsistent with the subsistence exemptions in the most recent treaties with Japan and the Soviet Union. Indeed, the federal government's subsistence policy has apparently been developing so rapidly that the subsistence provisions of the 1974 Japanese treaty are inconsistent with those of the Soviet treaty adopted four years later. Because each treaty affects substantially the same bird species, the more restrictive provisions of the earlier treaties limit the more liberal provisions of the latest treaty.[37]

a. British/Canadian Treaty

The 1916 treaty with Great Britain (as signatory for Canada) requires a "close[d] season on migratory game birds...between March 10 and September 1" and that hunting during the remaining six months be restricted to no more than three and one-half months. A very limited exception is provided for Alaska "Eskimos and Indians" to take *non-game* birds restricted to "auks, auklets, guillemots, murres and puffins and their eggs for food and their skins for clothing."[38] With some exceptions, closing the hunting season between March 10 and September 1 eliminates the possibility of hunting migratory game birds in arctic Alaska. The birds simply do not arrive in the arctic before April and are gone by October and are therefore not legally available in the areas and at the times when they are traditionally hunted. The problem is particularly acute for coastal Eskimo communities in the spring.

b. Mexican Treaty

The Mexican treaty provides no specific exception for Native hunting and limits migratory game bird hunting to four months out of the year with a closed season for wild ducks between March 10 to September 1.[39] Again, closing the season on ducks between March 10 and September 1 substantially diminishes the possibility of legally hunting ducks in arctic Alaska; the British/Canadian treaty continues to control the other migratory bird species. The Mexican treaty thus permits Mexicans to hunt migratory game birds (other than ducks) during any four months of the year, but the British/Canadian treaty continues to restrict Alaskan game bird hunting.

c. Japanese Treaty

The 1974 Japanese treaty provides a clear exception permitting "Eskimos [and] Indians...[to hunt] for their own food and clothing."[40] This exception is narrowly drawn to include only people of aboriginal descent; however, the Soviet treaty, adopted in 1978, appears to broaden the exception to all "indigenous inhabitants."

d. Soviet Treaty

Article II of the Soviet treaty generally prohibits the hunting and sale of migratory birds except for scientific or educational purposes and during hunting seasons as required by other provisions of the treaty. As to "indigenous inhabitants" the treaty further permits:

> the taking of migratory birds and the collection of their eggs by the indigenous inhabitants of...the State of Alaska for their own nutritional and other essential needs...during seasons established [in accordance with the treaty].[41]

Congress amended the Migratory Bird Treaty Act in 1978 to permit the Secretary of the Interior to adopt regulations permitting subsistence hunting of migratory birds in Alaska in line with the Soviet treaty.[42] However, the legislative history of the amendment makes it clear that the secretary's authority to adopt such regulations depends on the renegotiation of the earlier inconsistent treaties.[43] Accordingly, regulations promulgated in 1982 permitted migratory game bird hunting only between September 1 and January 22, with further limitations depending on the species.[44] Thus, even though the Soviet treaty exception is broad enough to exempt all Alaskan subsistence hunting, and Congress has passed a law permitting the secretary to liberalize the regulations, the restrictive provisions of the earlier treaties prevent him from doing so. Until the earlier treaties are renegotiated, they will remain a barrier to any meaningful migratory game bird subsistence protection.

2. Fur Seal Convention

The 1957 convention prohibits pelagic (open sea) hunting of the North Pacific fur seal (except for very restricted Native taking) and establishes an exclusive harvesting and profit sharing arrangement among the four signatory nations (the United States, Japan, the Soviet Union and Canada). The convention also establishes the North Pacific Fur Seal Commission which is authorized, among other things, to study ways to permit pelagic sealing without decimating the fur seal population[45] Although the convention is officially described as an "interim" treaty, it has been renewed repeatedly,[46] presumably because it is not feasible to permit pelagic sealing without renewed destruction of the fur seal population. The 1980 protocol extended the convention to October 14, 1984, unless otherwise agreed among the parties.

The 1976 and 1980 amendments both indicate a growing federal interest in the economic effect of the fur seal harvest on the Native residents of the Pribilof Islands. The 1976 amendments added provisions to article V of the convention requiring the Fur Seal Commission to give consideration to the effect of any reduction in the fur seal harvest on the "subsistence needs" of the Pribilof Natives. In ratifying the 1980 extension, the U.S. Senate went beyond "subsistence needs" to specify that any changes in the level of the fur seal harvest should "be consistent with the development of stable, diversified and enduring economy for the Aleut residents of the Pribilof Islands", including increasing Aleut control over the harvest itself.[47]

Subchapter I of the 1966 Fur Seal Act[48] implements the prohibition, research and harvest provisions of the convention. Subchapter II goes on to establish a special reservation on the Pribilof Islands for the management and protection of fur seals and other wildlife. Other provisions authorize the Secretary of Commerce to provide the Pribilof Island Natives with food, fuel, shelter, transportation, education and other "facilities, services and equipment as he deems necessary" with or without compensation. Still other provisions provide for education, health care and federal administration of a municipal townsite.[49]

These provisions obviously establish a special relationship between the federal government and the Pribilof Island Natives.[50] Recently, however, the U.S. Department of Commerce, the federal agency responsible for the administration of the Fur Seal Act, has advocated termination of the federal role on the islands because, among other things, the fur seal harvest is no longer profitable enough to support its cost. Legislation was enacted in 1982 to terminate direct federal involvement in the harvest,[51] but the language accompanying the 1980 convention protocol indicates that termination of direct involvement is not intended to be at the cost of the Pribilof Island Aleut economy. Conceivably, it could result in greater Native control of the harvest itself.

3. International Whaling Convention

This convention provides for the regulation of whaling among thirty-nine signatory nations and establishes the International Whaling Commission (IWC). The IWC is empowered to adopt certain resolutions "and other provisions regulating the taking of whales." These resolutions become binding on the signatory nations unless an affected nation objects within ninety days after the date of the resolution. [52]

Perhaps owing to the provisons of an earlier whaling convention, the IWC had never adopted a resolution restricting aboriginal whaling. [53] Indeed, by its explicit terms, even the current convention may not apply to aboriginal whaling. [54] Nevertheless, in 1977, the IWC adopted a resolution placing a total ban on bowhead whale hunting. [55] The ban posed a particularly severe threat to Inupiat whaling communities. (See chapter 8) The Secretary of the Interior, recognizing that he had to "face [his] trust responsibilities" recommended that the federal government object to the ban. [56] The Departments of Commerce and State supported the ban, so the United States did not object.

The Inupiat sued the Secretary of State to force him to object, but the court refused to grant the injunction, holding that it would be an unwarranted judicial interference with the conduct of foreign affairs. [57] The Inupiat filed another suit, this time against the Secretary of Commerce, arguing that neither the whaling convention nor the act implementing it authorized limitations on aboriginal whaling. On appeal, the court held that the implementing act, not the treaty, was the "law of the land" and that the district court might have authority to decide issues raised under the statute. [58] Although this case has not been decided on the merits, it does indicate that aboriginal people may have judicial remedies even in cases where their interests clash with the international interests of the United States.

The Inupiat also responded politically to the threatened whaling ban by forming the Alaska Eskimo Whaling Commission (AEWC). The AEWC was formed with the support of the North Slope Borough government and represents each of the nine affected whaling villages. [59] Working in cooperation with the AEWC, the federal government convinced the IWC to replace the 1977 ban with a limited bowhead harvest quota. [60] In subsequent years, the AEWC and the federal government were able to wrest slightly better quotas out of the IWC. [61] In the meantime, the AEWC, backed by the North Slope Borough, persuaded the State of Alaska and a group of ten oil companies to underwrite a study of the bowhead whale population. [62] This study and others financed directly through the North Slope Borough succeeded in establishing a generally agreed upon population estimate of 3,800 whales, or about 3,000 more than the estimate which led to the initial IWC ban. [63] Other studies were aimed at improving whaling methods to reduce the number of animals struck but not landed. [64]

These combined efforts appeared to culminate at the IWC's 1982 meeting, where the commission established separate management principles and procedures to govern aboriginal subsistence whaling. The U.S. IWC Commissioner said that:

> These principles and procedures formally recognize the distinction between commercial and aboriginal subsistence whaling and codify the IWC's practice of attempting, where necessary, to strike a proper balance between the needs of aboriginal people who depend on limited whaling to meet subsistence, cultural, and nutritional needs and the conservation needs of the affected whales. [65]

Finally, the IWC agreed to establish a standing subcommittee to review aboriginal subsistence whaling and to advise the commission on these matters in much the same way as the commission's scientific committee does on other matters.

These developments over the last six years, coupled with the continued cooperation between the AEWC and the federal government, may represent the first time since before the American Revolution that American aboriginal people have participated in international negotiations directly affecting their aboriginal rights. [66] The AEWC has a cooperative agreement with the Department of Commerce for continued bowhead whale management and its representatives have participated as part of the official American delegation to the IWC meetings following the 1977 ban. [67] In general, the relationship between the AEWC and the federal government approaches that of partnership for the joint management of resources used for subsistence and is some evidence of federal acceptance of a "trust responsibility" to manage those resources for subsistence purposes. The relationship is also consistent with the federal government's policy of Native self-determination.

4. Polar Bear Convention

The 1976 Polar Bear Convention among Canada, Denmark, Norway, the Soviet Union and the United States prohibits the taking of polar bear except for certain purposes, including takings:

> by local people using traditional methods in the exercise of their traditional rights and in accordance with the laws of that Party;
> or
> wherever polar bears have or might have been subject to taking by traditional means by its nationals. [68]

Although these provisions might be open to some limiting interpretations, they do correspond to the recent amendments to the Marine Mammal Protection Act, permitting "rural Alaska residents" to take marine mammals for non-wasteful subsistence purposes.[69] In this respect, the treaty language and the implementing legislation closely parallel the use of the term "indigenous inhabitants" in the contemporary Soviet Migratory Bird Treaty and its implementing legislation.

5. Conclusion

If there is a general trend among the various conservation treaties related to Alaska Native subsistence, it is to expand the scope of the subsistence exceptions to apply to all subsistence uses by all participants. For example, the early migratory bird treaties permit only Native taking of certain specified non-game species, while the most recent Soviet treaty permits "indigenous inhabitants" to take any birds for "nutritional and other essential needs."[70] Similarly, the recent polar bear convention permits takings by "local people" and "nationals" using "traditional methods...in accordance with the laws of [each] Party." Coupled with the current subsistence requirements of the Marine Mammal Protection Act, these provisions also seem to extend to all subsistence uses and participants.

The fur seal and whaling conventions are less clearly part of this trend, but that may be due to the relative isolation of the Pribilof Islands on the one hand and the still uniquely aboriginal nature of subsistence whaling on the other. The almost exclusive Native population of the Pribilof Islands coupled with the general prohibition against pelagic sealing ensures that only Pribilof Islanders have any opportunity to take seals at sea.[71] The continued federal monopoly on the fur seal harvest, coupled with environmentalist opposition to any harvest, also tend to preclude any movement to expand currently limited subsistence uses.[72] The whaling convention, of course, does not prohibit subsistence whaling, but the recently announced IWC principles and procedures focus only on "aboriginal" subsistence whaling. Presumably, the IWC could later expand these limits to include others engaged in subsistence whaling, should that ever become necessary. In the meantime, the apparently exclusively aboriginal nature of subsistence whaling precludes the necessity of further expanding the limits.

Viewed narrowly, treaties protecting other than aboriginal subsistence interests may be seen as diluting historically unique economic systems and aboriginal hunting and fishing rights. On the other hand, such treaties might also be viewed as protecting the unique cultural values traditionally associated with those rights. In this light, the more recent treaties may be the first attempts to actually incorporate aboriginal cultural values into American society. If this is the beginning of a trend, it is carried further in recent domestic conservation laws applicable to endangered species, marine mammals and Alaska subsistence generally. Similar to the history of the treaties, earlier legislation focuses on subsistence as an aboriginal right, but the latest enactments tend to protect subsistence as both an economic system and as a cultural value. In any case, the effect of the federal law is to preempt inconsistent state laws on the same subject.

C. Preemptive Statutes

There are four major federal statutes which preempt Alaska State law and include specific subsistence provisions. [73] These are the Reindeer Industry Act of 1937, [74] the Marine Mammal Protection Act of 1972, [75] the Endangered Species Act of 1973 [76] and the Alaska National Interest Lands Conservation Act (ANILCA) of 1980. [77] The Reindeer Industry Act is unique among these, because it attempts to substitute federally sponsored economic development activity (i.e., reindeer herding) for Native subsistence. The more recent statutes aim to protect both Native and non-Native subsistence harvests of *wild* renewable resources and in that respect may be part of a trend affording federal protection to Native subsistence values, generally.

1. Reindeer Industry Act

The reindeer act was intended to provide a "means of subsistence" for Alaska Natives, but it was to achieve that goal by establishing a reindeer herding industry under Native control. [78] The legislation was in response to non-Native competition in the reindeer industry and the resulting bad feeling generated between Native and non-Native herders. [79] It aimed to correct this situation by directing the Secretary of the Interior to acquire all non-Native owned deer, to distribute them to Natives and to prevent future alienation of deer to non-Natives. It also established a revolving loan fund to finance the reindeer business and permitted the Secretary of the Interior to delegate his administrative authority over the deer to Native organizations. [80]

On its face, the reindeer act seems designed more to promote American business values than Native cultural and economic values; however, the extended House debate demonstrates that Congress understood its broader cultural implications. Representative Green of Florida, floor manager of the bill, said that:

> The purpose of this bill is to try to help [the Eskimo] survive in his native way, in his native land without being destroyed by white encroachment.

> * * * *

> Its motives are the best. It is for the purpose of protecting the native Eskimo of Alaska in his own rights there, that the white man may not continue to encroach upon him and shove him to the North Pole and into the Pacific Ocean. (Applause). [81]

Congress also recognized that the act was an acknowledgment of federal responsibility for Alaska's Natives and that this responsibility was the same as was owed to other American aboriginal people:

> The natives of Alaska, including the Eskimo, are held to have practically the same status as the Indians of the United States. The Federal Government has recognized this responsibility. It is likewise the responsibility of the Federal Government to protect and look after the social and future economic welfare of these natives. [82]

Finally, Representative (later Speaker of the House) John McCormack of Massachusetts emphasized that the Alaska Natives should not be subject to the same hardships as were visited on the American Indian:

> Certainly none of us want to see conditions exist in Alaska that have existed with reference to the American Indians. A disgrace in the pages of American history has been the manner in which we have in the past allowed the American Indian, a ward of our country, to be capitalized and exploited.
>
> The Alaskan native is in the same situation. They (sic) are wards of the Federal Government. The purpose of this bill is to protect our wards in Alaska and to prevent the scandalous situation [from] existing in the future with reference to Alaska that the pages of American history are filled with in relation to the American Indian. [83]

Opposition to the reindeer act was vocal but aimed largely at the $2 million appropriation attached to it. [84] None of the opposition disagreed with the intent of the legislation, the status of the Natives or the authority of the federal government to promote their "social and future economic welfare." The bill passed the House by a two to one margin; [85] it is still good law.

The reindeer act is important for several reasons. In the first place, its stated purpose is to provide for Native subsistence. The House debate reveals that its broader intent is to help the Alaska Native "survive in his native way, in his native land." Thus, the act is perhaps an early demonstration of congressional concern for the protection of Alaska Native culture.

Second, the act is evidence of congressional acceptance of its responsibility for Alaska Native "social and future economic welfare." It puts Congress on record as recognizing the same relationship with Alaska Natives as exists between the federal government and other Native Americans. Legislation since the reindeer act, including ANCSA and ANILCA, forms a continuous pattern of congressional efforts to promote Alaska Native cultural and economic well-being.

Finally, the Reindeer Act is the first example of federal preemptive legislation designed specifically to address Alaska Native subsistence uses. This is more than merely historically interesting; it became a pattern for the future. Although recent legislation extends the scope of federal subsistence protections to include certain non-Natives, Native cultural values clearly remain within the scope of these protections.

2. Endangered Species Act (ESA)

As reenacted in 1973, the ESA provides a means to conserve the ecosystems upon which endangered and threatened species depend and to develop conservation programs for those species. It also permits the United States to take other steps to fulfill the various international wildlife agreements to which it is a party.[86] "Endangered species" is defined as:

> Any species which is in danger of extinction throughout all or a significant portion of its range...[87]

"Threatened species" is defined as:

> Any species which is likely to become an endangered species within the foreseeable future throughout all or a significant portion of its range.[88]

Depending on whether the species is plant or animal and in the case of animals depending on the type of animal, the Secretaries of the Interior, Commerce or Agriculture are required to determine, "on the basis of the best scientific and commercial data available" and after consultation with various interested parties, whether a species is "endangered" or "threatened."[89] If the species is determined to be either endangered or threatened, then the appropriate secretary can promulgate regulations controlling its "taking" (i.e., importation, hunting, etc.)[90] The act also preempts state laws or regulations governing endangered species but only if such laws or regulations either permit what is prohibited or prohibit what is authorized under the ESA.[91]

a. Subsistence Exception

The ESA excepts Native and non-Native subsistence uses from its restrictions as follows:

> This [Act] shall not apply with respect to the taking of any endangered species or threatened species, or the importation of any such species taken pursuant to this section, by—
>
> (A) any Indian, Aleut, or Eskimo who is an Alaskan Native who resides in Alaska; or

(B) any non-native permanent resident of an Alaskan native village;

if such taking is primarily for subsistence purposes. [92]

So long as the taking is not "accomplished in a wasteful manner," the exception also permits sale of "authentic Native articles or handicrafts and clothing" in interstate commerce. The exception further defines "subsistence" as including the selling of any:

edible portion of fish or wildlife in native villages and towns in Alaska for native consumption within native villages or towns....[93]

Thus, the exception applies generally to both Natives and non-Natives living in Alaskan villages who use fish and wildlife for consumption, handicrafts or other "subsistence" purposes. [94]

The exception also permits the appropriate secretary to make regulations for subsistence use of endangered or threatened species if the secretary determines:

That any species of fish or wildlife which is subject to taking under the provisions of this (exception) is an endangered species or threatened species, *and* that such taking *materially and negatively* affects the threatened or endangered species... (emphasis added). [95]

b. Legal Significance.

Several of the provisions described above are important for subsistence values. First, the ESA defines "endangered" and "threatened" species and sets up a regulatory scheme for the appropriate secretary to determine when a particular species becomes endangered or threatened. [96] After determining that a species qualifies, the secretary may then carefully regulate future taking and importation of that species. State laws are preempted and void if they permit activity prohibited or prohibit activity authorized under the ESA.

Second, the subsistence exception includes a separate regulatory scheme for subsistence taking. If subsistence uses do not "materially and negatively" affect the species, then such uses are not subject to regulation. Even if there is such an effect, subsistence can be allowed under appropriate regulation. In effect, the exception permits subsistence use of even endangered or threatened species. The regulations controlling such use would be developed under federal administrative and political processes with which the state would also have to comply. That fact may ultimately give Alaskans reliant on subsistence uses more influence over the shape of the regulatory scheme than they might have over state regulations drafted without federal oversight.

Finally, the ESA and similar environmental legislation have been held to describe the scope of the federal government's "trust responsibility" to Alaska Natives. The North Slope Borough brought a law suit to prevent a federal oil and gas lease sale in the Beaufort Sea. Although the appellate court permitted the sale, the decision does make it clear that the ESA and other similar legislation impose requirements on the government to give careful attention to the subsistence needs of Alaska Natives in decisions likely to adversely affect resources used for subsistence.[97]

3. Marine Mammal Protection Act (MMPA)

Although the MMPA's primary goal is to ensure the well-being of marine mammals,[98] it has also been held to protect Alaska Native subsistence values as well.[99] These two, not necessarily inconsistent, goals are expressed in the form of a moratorium on marine mammal taking and imports[100] and a broad (but not unlimited) exception to the moratorium for Alaska Native subsistence uses.[101] As amended in 1981, the MMPA prohibits enforcement of all state laws relating to the taking of marine mammals, but requires the federal government to transfer enforcement back to states meeting certain requirements.[102] Additionally, the 1981 amendments require the state of Alaska to incorporate detailed marine mammal subsistence protections into its fish and game statutes and regulations as a prerequisite for return of jurisdiction.[103] The required protections are similar (but not the same) as the subsistence protections required for other wildlife under the Alaska National Interest Lands Conservation Act (ANILCA). That means, among other things, that the present federal, exclusively Native, subsistence exemption will become a broader based subsistence protection for "rural Alaska residents" if jurisdiction is returned to the state.

a. Moratorium

The act provides for a moratorium on all taking and importation of marine mammals or their parts because, among other things, there is a lack of knowledge about the size of marine mammal populations.[104] Recognizing that the moratorium was a drastic measure which could adversely affect certain classes of people, Congress permitted three initial exemptions from the general prohibition; the Alaska Native exemption is one of them.[105] Recent amendments have liberalized the authority of government agencies administering the act to grant additional exemptions for limited periods of time for certain unintentional takings of marine mammals under special circumstances.[106]

b. Native Exemption

The MMPA permits "any Indian, Aleut or Eskimo who dwells on the coast of the North Pacific Ocean or the Arctic Ocean" to take marine mammals in a non-wasteful manner for "subsistence purposes" or to create "authentic Native"handicrafts or clothing. The federal government, however, can regulate even Native taking of any marine mammal species which becomes "depleted."[107] As originally enacted, there was some question whether the Native exemption applied if the State of Alaska attempted to resume jurisdiction over marine mammals. In the mid-1970's, state petitioned for the return of management authority over walrus and included provisions in its regulations which had the effect of prohibiting Native walrus hunting in some geographic areas. One of those was the coastal region near the southwestern Alaskan community of Togiak.

When the Department of the Interior issued regulations purporting to transfer walrus jurisdiction to the state, the people of Togiak filed a lawsuit.[108] They contended that the MMPA's Native exemption preempted any state regulation of Native marine mammal hunting and that the regulations were therefore invalid. The court agreed, in part because it found the Native exemption to be an exercise of federal authority in the field of Indian affairs and an outgrowth of the federal government's unique responsibilities toward Native Americans:

> These various responsibilities impose fiduciary duties upon the United States, including the duties so to regulate as to protect the subsistence resources of Indian communities and to preserve such communities as distinct cultural entities against interference by the States. It is presumably to implement these various powers and duties that Congress adopted the Native exemption from the general moratorium established by the MMPA, and an abandonment of those responsibilities should not be lightly presumed (citations ommited).[109]

Following the lawsuit, the federal government withdrew its regulations, and the state abandoned its plans to assume jurisdiction over walrus and other marine mammals. Congress, however, amended the law in 1981, to permit the state to resume marine mammal jurisdiction so long as it provided marine mammal subsistence protections for "rural Alaska residents."

c. State Management

It is clear from the 1981 MMPA amendments that the federal, exclusively Native exemption is subject to the state's future resumption of marine mammal management.[110] It is equally clear, however, that state management must include federally approved subsistence protections for the predominately Native residents of rural Alaska.[111] It is clear from the House Committee report on the amendments that Native subsistence is the focus of both the exemption and of any federally approved state management regime.

The Committee believes that the issue of subsistence taking must be addressed in Alaska's management program, given the importance of that take to persons dependent upon subsistence taking and given the history of court cases surrounding the authority of the state to regulate subsistence taking by Alaskan Natives. If management of a marine mammal species is returned to the State of Alaska, Native takings should be blended into the overall state regulatory regime. *It should be emphasized that [this bill] submits Native taking to state regulation only as part of a state mangement program which has been approved by the [federal government] and only for so long as that program is in effect* (emphasis added). [112]

Although the state may obtain management authority over all subsistence taking of marine mammals, state management of Native subsistence is still subject to federal oversight, and an exclusive Native exemption can be reinstituted if the state regime falls out of compliance with the federally approved subsistence protections. Moreover, even the federal government's authority to permit "incidental" taking of marine mammals must be consistent with the availability of the species for Alaska subsistence. [113]

Finally, the subsistence protection is clearly described in both the legislation and its history as including a priority over any other consumptive use. That means before any other consumptive use of marine mammals can be allowed, it must first be determined that it "will have no significant adverse impact upon subsistence uses of the species." Furthermore, the law also requires that the regulation of other consumptive uses (e.g., sport hunting) provide economic opportunities (e.g., employment as guides) for residents of rural coastal villages who make subsistence uses of marine mammals. [114] The House report also emphasizes that "all subsistence uses of a species [must] be satisfied before the state may authorize any non-subsistence taking." [115]

What emerges from these detailed limitations on state marine mammal management is a continuing federal concern for protection of Alaska Native villages and their subsistence cultures. Although Native subsistence is to be "blended" into any state regulatory regime, it is clearly also to be protected by that regime even to the point of affording additional economic opportunities to rural residents. Furthermore, if the state should ever abandon the federally required subsistence protections, then the exclusive Native exemption will replace it. Thus the ultimate federal protection of an exclusive Native right is held in abeyance only so long as the state adheres to a federally approved substitute. This amounts to a continuing federal commitment to what the courts have characterized as a "trust responsibility" to preserve Native communities "as distinct cultural entities." [116]

D. Trust Responsibility for Subsistence

The emergence of a judicially recognized, federal "trust responsibility" to protect Alaska Native subsistence culture and economy is an important by product of the various subsistence exemptions found in fed eral conservation treaties and statutes. The responsibility has its greatest force when federal law preempts state attempts to regulate subsistence activities.[117] The responsibility appears to have slightly less force when it conflicts with other federal domestic responsibilities, such as offshore leasing.[118] Finally, the doctrine has been held insufficient to warrant direct judicial interference with federal foreign policy interests.[119]

The doctrine first emerged in *People of Togiak v. U.S.*, discussed earlier. There the court interpreted ambiguous provisions of the MMPA in light of the long history of Alaska Native subsistence exemptions in federal treaties and statutes, and concluded that the federal government could not authorize the State of Alaska to regulate marine mammals. Doing so, the court said, would require an unwarranted presumption that the federal government had abandoned its responsibility to preserve Native subsistence values.[120] Although Congress subsequently amended the MMPA to permit the state to exercise jurisdiction, it is clear that state authority is not to be asserted at the expense of Native village subsistence culture for economy.

The doctrine next emerged in a lawsuit brought by the North Slope Borough challenging a proposed federal oil and gas lease sale in the Beaufort Sea. The lower court held that the responsible federal agency had not obtained an adequate "biological opinion" prior to making the lease decision as required under the Endangered Species Act. Failure to do so, the court said, was a breach of the federal trust responsibility imposed by the Native exemption under the ESA.[121] On appeal, the circuit court held that the federal government's responsibilities to Natives were met when the federal leasing agency had both "acted responsibly" toward the environment and given "purposeful attention" to the interests of the Natives; it concluded the agency had done both in this case.[122]

Thus, when pitted against often competing public interests of the United States, the federal trust responsibility emerges as an important but not overriding consideration. When pitted directly against the international interests of the United States, however, the responsibility has been held insufficient to warrant court intervention to compel the Secretary of State to object to an International Whaling Commission ban on Native subsistence whaling.[123] Later cases arising out of the same circumstances indicate that the responsibility may have more force in the context of domestic statutes implementing treaties rather than the treaties themselves.[124]

Although the federal trust responsibility doctrine related to Alaska Native subsistence is still developing, it is emerging as a judicially recognized statutory responsibility arising out of a continuous history of Native subsistence exemptions in various conservation treaties and statutes.

The doctrine appears to have its greatest strength in the context of federal domestic statutes limiting state authority to regulate subsistence hunting and fishing. In this respect its effect is not unlike similar federal limitations on state authority over off-reservation hunting and fishing arising out of treaties in the lower forty-eight states. Alaska Native off-reservation subsistence uses under recent enactments are not generally exclusive rights, but are exercised in common with other similarly situated (i.e., rural) Alaska residents. Alaska Native off-reservation hunting and fishing rights are perhaps in some sense diminished because other rural residents share in authorized subsistence uses. However, they are also protected from state interference by federal preemptive laws. The most comprehensive of these laws grew out of the policies of the Alaska Native Claims Settlement Act (ANCSA) and are implemented under Title VIII of the Alaska National Interest Lands Conservation Act of 1980 (ANILCA).

III. Subsistence and ANCSA

A. Introduction

In general, self-government, land claims, and subsistence are three interests which Native Americans have always tried to preserve. ANCSA addressed the land claims of Alaska Natives and extinguished their subsistence claims, seemingly without compensation. However, in the conference report accompanying ANCSA, Congress expressed the clear intention that Alaska Native subsistence (hunting and fishing) interests should be protected by the Secretary of the Interior and the State of Alaska. Neither the secretary nor the state lived up to these congressional expectations, so it became increasingly obvious that other steps were necessary to adequately protect Alaska Native subsistence. Fortunately, the seeds of the political compromise required to achieve this goal were buried in the provisions of Section 17(d) (2) of ANCSA. In December of 1980, those seeds and that compromise became Title VIII of the Alaska National Interest Lands Conservation Act (ANILCA). Before discussing ANILCA, however, it is important to understand precisely what ANCSA did to Alaska Native hunting and fishing rights.

B. The Effect of ANCSA

It is reasonably clear from ANCSA's legislative history that subsistence was one of the key elements which the Natives and Congress intended to protect through the land claims settlement. The first AFN draft bill emphasized subsistence protection, as did Emil Notti's supporting memorandum.[125] The final Senate version of the land claims bill (S. 35) included elaborate provisions protecting Native subsistence.[126] Furthermore, ANCSA itself anticipated that village land selections would be available for subsistence uses[127] and that these lands would be managed by each village corporation "for and on behalf of" the Native village.[128]

Section 4(b) of ANCSA (43 U.S.C. 1603[b]) purports to extinguish "any aboriginal hunting or fishing rights that may exist," and the specific subsistence provisions of S. 35 were not adopted in the final version of the act. Nevertheless, the conference committee report which accompanied the claims act makes it clear that Congress viewed neither the purported extinguishment of hunting and fishing rights nor the absence of specific subsistence provisions as the end of Alaska Native subsistence interests. The report notes in this regard:

> The Conference Committee after careful consideration believes that *all Native interests in subsistence resource land can and will be protected* by the Secretary through the exercise of his existing withdrawal authority. The Secretary could, for example, withdraw appropriate lands and classify them in a manner which would protect Native subsistence needs and requirements by closing appropriate lands to entry by *nonresidents* when subsistence resources for these lands are in short supply or otherwise threatened. *The Conference Committee expects both the Secretary and the State to take any action necessary to protect the subsistence needs of the Native* (emphasis added).[129]

C. Problems With State Protection

It was the clear intent and expectation of Congress that both the Secretary of the Interior and the State of Alaska would "take any action necessary to protect the subsistence needs of the Native." Nevertheless, some nine years later it was compellingly clear that neither the state nor the secretary were likely to protect subsistence in the manner Congress had contemplated. Neither the secretary nor the state had withdrawn any lands for subsistence uses, let alone established any sort of hunting and fishing preferences to limit *nonresident* access to resources needed by *local* subsistence users. Although as early as 1973 the Alaska Department and Boards of Fish and Game adopted a policy giving subsistence the "highest priority among beneficial uses,"[130] in reality the priority received only lip service when it came to the tough questions of excluding nonresidents from a local resource. Subsequent state statutes defined "subsistence" for various purposes,[131] established a separate "subsistence section" (now a division) in the Department of Fish and Game,[132] and even delegated authority to the Game Board to establish subsistence hunting areas and provide for subsistence uses,[133] but none of these policies, statutes or authorities were sufficient to overcome several real and imagined legal, political and economic issues confronting the state when it came to implementing a true subsistence priority for *local* subsistence uses.

1. Legal Issues

Article VIII of the state constitution establishes the basic principles for wildlife management in Alaska. Through its subsections, Article VIII grants broad power to the Alaska legislature to provide for the "utilization, development, and conservation" of Alaska's natural resources "for the maximum benefit of its people."[134] Section 4 of the same article permits the legislature to manage these resources "subject to preferences among beneficial uses." It is important to note that under other provisions of Article VIII, the Alaska Supreme Court has approved state regulations providing for different treatment of various "user groups," including those who use resources for subsistence. [135]

On the other hand, there were arguably *state* constitutional problems with "Native only" state subsistence protections. Article I, sections 1 and 3 of the Alaska Constitution together prohibit separate treatment of state citizens on the basis of race or color. Arguably, because the state did not have the same historic political relationship with Alaska Natives as the federal government, any state discrimination in favor of Natives only might have been "racial" and, therefore, prohibited under the state constitution. Furthermore, state distinctions based only on *Native* subsistence cultural values might also have run into the same obstacle, since it is logically difficult to discriminate in favor of Native culture without also discriminating in favor of Native race. So, even though the state might have been constitutionally able to discriminate in favor of subsistence uses, in the absence of any overriding federal subsistence law, there were several legal questions about the state's ability to protect Alaska Native subsistence culture. There were also several practical political issues.

2. Political Issues

At least until 1983, it was a fact of Alaska political life that the state's Department of Fish and Game was dominated by non-Native urban, sports and commercial hunting fishing interests. [136] As one observer noted in 1978:

> Fish and game management in Alaska is controlled by a seven-member board of fish and board of game. Both boards are dominated by white, urban Alaskans with little allegiance to and slight knowledge of the subsistence way of life. They also have no responsibility for the overall socioeconomic effects of their policies. [137]

Until relatively recently, the Boards of Fisheries and Game made wildlife management policy in splendid isolation from the rural, predominately Native populations, which were most heavily affected by that policy. That was of little consequence when urban hunting and fishing pressure was as low as it was from Alaska's pre-pipeline urban population, but during the pipeline boom Anchorage was America's third fastest growing city. Between 1965-1975 the number of resident hunting and fishing licenses exploded from 68,000 to 119,300.[138] Behind these statistics was the growing power of Alaska's sporting interests.

Rural (predominately Native) Alaskans were in no position to challenge this trend without federal assistance. The prospect of reapportionment of the Alaska legislature promised a significant cut in rural representation. Furthermore, rural Alaskans were isolated from the Alaska fish and game administrative structure by distance and urban indifference. During this time, at least one federal administrative law judge found that: "Persuasive testimony received from Native areas (of Alaska) mandates that the state take steps to make participation [in game management policy] more meaningful to those areas."[139] The Governor, Jay Hammond, also acknowledged that there is "some justification" for the rural perception that state fish and game management is biased in favor of urban sport uses.[140]

Given the unequal strength of the rural/subsistence and urban/sports and commercial interests, it was virtually certain that even if the state had been legally able to protect Native subsistence, it would be politically incapable of doing so. It was in this context that former Secretary of the Interior, Stewart Udall, advised AFN in a 1978 memorandum that:

> (T)here can be no subsistence program worth the paper it is written on unless the Congress uses its power under the U.S. Constitution and grants such rights to the Alaska Natives.[141]

Even Governor Hammond reached a similar conclusion when he acknowledged that:

> The allocation of resources to competitive consumers is a difficult problem at best. Thus, I would hope this congress establishes the priority of subsistence use where there is a conflict on national interest lands. I believe this is a legitimate subject for legislation, and hope that this principle, which has been state policy for some time, is enacted into federal law.[142]

3. Economic Issues

The political problem was made worse by the federal grant scheme which funded most of the state's fish and game management program. Until the passage of ANILCA the Alaska Department of Fish and Game was substantially financed by two federal grant programs: Pittman-Robertson (game)[143] and Dingell-Johnson (fish).[144] Funds for these federal grants are generated by federal taxes on ammunition and guns, but were available to the state only under a matching formula. State matching money came from the sale of hunting and fishing licenses and game tags; the more licenses and tags sold, the larger federal contribution to the department's budget.[145]

Although a substantial number of rural people were eligible for twenty-five-cent licenses based on economic need,[146] it was probable that many did not purchase these licenses at all because it simply was not worth the trouble. In any case twenty-five-cent licenses were unlikely to generate much revenue for the fish and game department. Consequently, urban Alaskans accounted for most of the state's Pittman-Robertson, Dingell-Johnson matching funds. Understandably, the concerns of urban Alaskans became the practical focus of the department's policy, even though its announced policy favored subsistence uses.[147] Rural Alaskans simply did not have the "buying power" to gain the department's attention. Federal legislation was at least partially to blame for this situation, and it appeared that federal legislation was the only way to change it.

D. ANILCA

The Alaska National Interest Lands Conservation Act (ANILCA)[148] is, among other things, a massive land withdrawal and classification scheme whose seeds were sown in sections 17(d)(1) and (2) (43 U.S.C.A. 1616[d][1] and [2]) of ANCSA. Section 17(d)(1), automatically withdrew all unreserved public lands for ninety days and permitted the Secretary of the Interior to classify such lands for any authorized purpose in order to protect the "public interest" in those lands. Section 17(d)(2) directed the secretary to withdraw up to 80 million acres for possible inclusion in the National Parks, Forests, Wildlife Refuges or Wild and Scenic Rivers systems. Lands withdrawn under 17(d)(2) came to be called "national interest" lands.

The secretary had nine months to make the (d)(2) withdrawals and two years to make recommendations to Congress for the disposition of those lands. Congress had an additional five years to act on the secretary's recommendations. In short, ANCSA set a clock ticking which gave the federal government seven years to decide on the inclusion of up to 80 million acres of Alaska lands in traditionally restrictive public lands classifications. The secretary withdrew 79.3 million acres under 17(d)(2) for "national interests" and 60 million additional acres under 17(d)(1) for possible "public interests." About 140 million acres were thus withdrawn for possible inclusion in several restrictive federal land management schemes.[149]

The secretary made his final d-2 recommendations in December 1973, which gave Congress until December 1978 to permanently classify the lands in one of the restrictive federal land management systems. It was obvious toward the end of 1978 that Congress was not going to be able to pass the necessary legislation, so the Secretary of the Interior, Cecil Andrus, exercised his "emergency" withdrawal authority under the Federal Lands Policy and Management Act[150] to set aside 110 million acres in temporary three-year withdrawals. Shortly thereafter, President Carter exercised his authority under the Antiquities Act[151] to designate an additional 56 million acres as national monuments—a very restrictive land classification.

Although the state filed a lawsuit to overturn these federal actions,[152] their practical effect was to indefinitely delay congressional action on the d-2 question and to preclude further development on nearly one-half the lands in Alaska.[153] This set the stage for the next two years of political debate over the fate of much of the public land in Alaska. During the course of this debate, Alaska Natives and other Alaska subsistence advocates were able to trade their support for ANILCA's environmentally oriented land classifications for environmentalist support of ANILCA's Title VIII subsistence provisions.

By its terms, Title VIII of ANILCA is intended to carry out the subsistence related policies and fulfill the purposes of ANCSA. In this respect, it is in some sense a "settlement" of the Alaska Native aboriginal hunting and fishing claims seemingly extinguished in ANCSA. Unlike previous such settlements, however, ANILCA does not afford Alaska Natives off-reservation or other exclusive rights to hunt and fish because of their membership in a particular tribe. Instead, bowing to present day political reality, ANILCA established subsistence protections for most rural Alaska residents—Native and non-Native. Nevertheless, it is quite clear from the congressional findings in Title VIII that ANILCA is also federal legislation enacted for the benefit of Native Americans and is intended in significant part to protect Alaska Native "physical, economic, traditional and cultural existence."

ANILCA also seems to be a comprehensive approach to the legal, political and economic issues which plagued the state's subsistence policy. Its "Findings" provide the legal justification for federal protection of Native subsistence culture (and non-Native subsistence "society"). Its administrative scheme requires the state to provide for the subsistence uses of rural Alaska residents with a priority for those uses and a "system of local advisory committees and regional advisory councils." It also restricts the authority of the Alaska Fish and Game Boards to make policy contrary to the recommendations of the advisory councils with respect to subsistence uses. Finally, the law provides for federal funding for up to fifty percent of the cost of the advisory committee/council administrative structure. Beyond these essentials, Title VIII also provides for federal oversight and judicial enforcement of state and federal compliance with its provisions. It also provides for subsistence use of public lands restrictively classified as parks or park monuments and full consideration of the impact any future disposition of public lands might have on the subsistence value of those lands.

1. The Legal Issues

Section 801 of ANILCA (16 U.S.C.A. 3111) invokes the historic federal authority over Native affairs to protect Native "physical, economic, traditional, and cultural existence."[154] Because the relationship of the federal government to Native Americans is a political one, federal law can reach out to protect Native cultural values without running afoul of the U.S. Constitution's prohibitions against racial discrimination.[155] Furthermore, as the "supreme law of the land,"[156] federal legislation based on this relationship preempts contrary provisions of Alaska's Constitution or other laws.[157] Therefore, the umbrella of federal law reinforces the state's ability to manage fish and game resources in substantial part for the benefit of Native subsistence culture.

However, ANILCA goes even further, because it *requires* the state to manage fish and game resources according to *federal* subsistence requirements as the price to be paid for the right of managing fish and game on federal (public) lands.[158] From the state's standpoint, the result is a substantial incentive to conform its policy and procedures to the federal requirements in order to maintain its statewide fish and game management authority. The result, from the rural point of view, is an improvement in the policies and procedures the state must follow in implementing its own subsistence program. There are three sections in Title VIII which, taken together, virtually compel the state to manage its fish and game resources in a way that protects subsistence uses by rural Alaska residents. These are: a. Section 803 (Subsistence Uses Definition), b. Section 804 (Subsistence Preference) and c. Section 805(d) (State Compliance). By May 1982, the state had conformed its laws to the federal requirements either by regulation or regulatory interpretation of prior state subsistence statutes.

a. Section 803 (Subsistence Uses Definition)

Section 803 (16 U.S.C.A. 3113) defines "subsistence uses" as:

the customary and traditional uses by *rural Alaska residents* of wild, renewable resources for direct personal or family consumption as food, shelter, fuel, clothing, tools, or transportation; for the making and selling of handicraft articles out of nonedible byproducts of fish and wildlife resources taken for personal or family consumption; for barter, or sharing for personal family consumption; and for *customary trade* (emphasis added).

The section further defines "family" and "barter,"[159] and, with two significant exceptions, is the same as the parallel state section of definitions for all these terms.[160]

Unlike the state statutory definition, "subsistence uses" under the ANILCA scheme are restricted to "rural Alaska residents."[161] The state statutory definition of "subsistence uses," found in AS 16.05 940(26), is not similarly restricted, although it has been interpreted in state fish and game regulations as applying only to rural residents. The omission of "rural residents" from the state definition was apparently a drafting error which arose out of the state's efforts in 1978 to enact subsistence legislation identical to the ANILCA subsistence provisions in the bill then being considered by the U.S. Congress. The original ANILCA definition was not limited to "rural residents" either, an oversight which was corrected prior to final passage. By that time, however, the state had already adopted its definition which omitted "rural residents."[162] In order to conform the state and federal definitions, the Alaska fish and game boards adopted regulations in 1982 restricting "subsistence uses" to "rural residents·" This regulatory approach also appears consistent with the federal law which pretty clearly contemplates that the state rulemaking will be part of "dynamic process for the regulation of subsistence resources and other uses."[163]

The treatment of "customary trade" in the federal definition was the other point at which the state and federal subsistence schemes differed. Under the state definition "customary trade" (along with barter and sharing) had to be for "personal or family consumption." Under Title VIII, only barter and sharing are required to be for personal or family consumption; "customary trade" is not linked to any particular purpose. This would seem to leave open the possibility that some forms of trade (e.g., fur trade) can be classified as a "subsistence use" even though they might involve money and commerce. However, it is clear from ANILCA's legislative history that customary trade cannot result in the "establishment of significant commercial enterprises," which suggests that at least the form of such trade must pre-exist ANILCA (i.e., be customary or long established).[164]

b. Section 804 (Subsistence Preference)

Section 804 (16 U.S.C.A. 3114) establishes the ANILCA subsistence preference in the following terms:

> Except as otherwise provided in this Act and other Federal laws, the taking on *public lands* of fish and wildlife for *non-wasteful* subsistence uses shall be accorded priority over the taking *on such lands* of fish and wildlife for other purposes. Whenever it is necessary to restrict the taking of populations of fish and wildlife on such lands for subsistence uses in order *to protect the continued viability* of such populations, or *to con-*

tinue such uses, such priority shall be implemented through appropriate limitations based on the application of the following criteria (emphasis added)

    (1)   customary and direct dependence upon the populations as the mainstay of livelihood;

    (2)   local residency; and

    (3)   the availability of alternative resources (emphasis added).

The preference contains at least two important qualifications. First, it applies only to subsistence uses on federal "public lands" as that term is defined in ANILCA. Second, it only limits non-subsistence uses when it is necessary to restrict the taking of fish and wildlife either to "protect the continued viability" of the resource or to permit continued subsistence uses.[165]

i. "Public Lands"

As defined in section 102 of ANILCA, "public lands" include only "lands, waters, and interests therein" the title to which (after December 2, 1980) "is in the United States." State selections which have been tentatively approved, Native corporation selections made under ANCSA which have not been conveyed and the lands of the former reserves mentioned in section 19(b) of ANCSA (43 U.S.C.A. 1618[b]) are all specifically excluded from this definition.[166] This all means that the ANILCA subsistence preferences apply only to renewable resource use on lands or waters or "interests" in lands or waters "owned" by the federal government. The preference does not necessarily apply to state or private lands (including lands owned by Native corporations) unless the state incorporates the preference into state law.

ii. Priority

Under both the state and federal schemes, a true subsistence "priority" (e. g., when limits are imposed on non-subsistence uses but not on subsistence uses) is required only when all uses cannot be accomodated.[167] But under either scheme, it is also important for the fish and game boards to give specific consideration to subsistence uses in each rule they make, even if no true priority is necessary. If the boards do not specifically consider (on the record) the relationship of the rules to subsistence uses, then the boards may expose the rules they do adopt to claims that they do not take subsistence uses into account. Moreover, unless they are consistently careful in their rule-making, it is likely that the boards will fail to implement a true priority in circumstances where it is warrented.

Both the state's implementing regulations and the legislative history of section 804 seem to require the fish and game boards to give specific consideration to the effect of their rules on subsistence uses "on an ongoing basis," even when no priority is required.[168] On the other hand, it is also clear under both the state and federal schemes that non-subsistence uses are not to be restricted unless it is necessary either to preserve the resource or to protect subsistence uses.[169]

c. Section 805(d) (State Compliance)

Although it is part of ANILCA's larger political solution, discussed below, Section 805(d) (16 U.S.C.A. 3115[d]) is crucial to statewide implementation of the federal subsistence definition and preference as well. Section 805(d) required the state, through "laws of general applicability" to implement the ANILCA subsistence definition and preference on federal public lands by December 2, 1981. Failure to do so would have transferred management of those lands to the federal government, thus depriving the state of a substantial amount of its fish and game management authority. The state went a few months past the deadline, but the boards of fish and game did adopt general regulations in July 1982 which appear to fully incorporate the federal subsistence definition and preference.[170]

2. The Political Issues

Section 805 of ANILCA also incorporates the structure of the state's already established system of regional advisory councils and subsidiary advisory committees, but, at least as to the "public lands," it went much further than the state's scheme and vested the advisory councils with real influence over subsistence policy making. ANILCA also established a formal link between the advisory councils and the Secretary of the Interior and provided for judicial enforcement of its provisions. Although the state did not have to follow ANILCA's administrative requirements in the management of fish and game on state or private lands, if it did not comply with ANILCA's provisions on federal public lands, it would be prevented from managing the resources of those lands. The result was that the state, in order to maintain statewide fish and game management authority, agreed to exercise its authority in compliance with ANILCA's administrative scheme on federal public lands. The practical effect was to require the state to manage these resources according to the same policies on state and private lands as well.

a. The Advisory Committeees and Councils

Section 805(a) of ANILCA requires the Secretary of the Interior to establish at least six "subsistence resource regions" in the State of Alaska and regional advisory councils in each region as well as subsidiary advisory committees. The councils, with the assistance of the local committees, are given the power to review and evaluate the Interior Secretary's subsistence management proposals and to provide forums for interested people to express their opinions and recommendations on any matter related to subsistence. The councils are also allowed to encourage local and regional participation in subsistence decisions and are permitted to prepare an annual report to the secretary on a variety of matters related to implementing ANILCA's subsistence scheme. The Secretary of the Interior is also required to assign "adequate qualified staff" to the advisory councils. But most importantly he is required to accept any council's subsistence management recommendation unless it: (1) is not supported by substantial evidence, (2) violates recognized principles of fish and wildlfife conservation, or (3) would be detrimental to subsistence needs.

b. State Compliance

As elaborate as these requirements appear, they are secondary to ANILCA's real intent, which was to encourage the state to incorporate meaningful local and regional participation in state fish and game board *subsistence* decisions.[171] Although the state had a statute (AS 16.05.260) permitting the fish and game boards to establish "advisory committees," the committees were in fact merely advisory and had little influence on fish and game policy. Section 805(d) required the state to incorporate the federal role assigned the advisory councils and committees, including the requirement that no council recommendation be rejected unless it: (1) was not supported by substantial evidence, (2) violated recognized principles of fish and wildlife conservation or (3) would be detrimental to subsistence needs. By May 1982, the Alaska Boards of Fish and Game had adopted regulations substantially incorporating these requirements.[172]

c. Monitoring and Enforcement

Sections 806 (16 U.S.C.A. 3116) and 807 (16 U.S.C.A. 3117) provide, respectively, for federal monitoring and judicial enforcement of both state and federal implementation of ANILCA. Section 806 merely provides for an annual report to Congress, but section 807 provides a direct federal judicial remedy for "local residents and other persons and organizations aggrieved" by a failure of either the state or the secretary to provide for the subsistence protections established under section 804 as made applicable to the state under section 805(d). This gives any person or group (e.g., village, non-profit corporation, etc.) access to federal court; the only significant limitation is the exhaustion of any available federal or state administrative remedies. Significantly, the law also provides for the award of court costs and attorneys fees to prevailing plaintiffs. Except for costs and attorney fees, however, equitable (non-monetary) remedies are the only federal remedies available.[173]

3. The Economic Issue

Section 805(e) provides for federal reimbursement for up to fifty percent (up to $5 million annually) of the state's cost of implementing the regional advisory committee and council scheme. If fully funded, this provision promises to substantially equalize the economic influence of subsistence interests within the Alaska fish and game administrative structure.

E. Federal Land Use and Subsistence

In addition to subsistence on the "public lands," ANILCA also includes specific provisions for the regulation of subsistence within lands restrictively classified as "parks" or "park monuments." Secs. 808 and 816 (43 U.S.C.A. 3118 and 3126). Another provision requires that most future federal land use decisions take into account their effect on subsistence sec. 810 (16 U.S.C.A. 3120). Other provisions permit the Secretary of the Interior to negotiate cooperative agreements (sec. 809 [43 U.S.C.A.3119]), and require "reasonable access" to resources used for subsistence on the public lands (sec. 811 [43 U.S.C.A. 3121]). Each of these provisions affects public land use decisions in Alaska in a manner not found elsewhere in the United States. Of these provisions, those relating to subsistence in parks and park monuments and imposing subsistence considerations in public land use decisions seem most important.

1. Subsistence in Parks and Monuments

Under sec. 808, a "subsistence resources commission" was to be appointed for each park or park monument in the State.[174] The governor of Alaska and the regional advisory council within whose jurisdiction the park or park monument lies were each to appoint three members to each commission. By mid-1982 these commissions were to "devise and recommend" a subsistence hunting program within the park or monument which, after consultation and public hearing, the Interior Secretary was to "promptly implement" unless it: (1) violated recognized principles of wildlife conservation, (2) threatened the conservation of healthy wildlife populations, (3) was contrary to the purposes for which the park or monument was established, or (4) would be detrimental to local subsistence needs.

Until the subsistence hunting program could be implemented, the Secretary of the Interior was directed to permit subsistence uses in the parks and monuments by "local residents" in accordance with the provisions of ANILCA and other applicable federal and state law. Six months after passage of ANILCA, the National Park Service promulgated regulations further defining who would be considered a "local rural resident" and establishing procedures for setting up "resident zones" in each of the parks or monuments. The regulations also define "subsistence uses."[175]

Briefly, a "resident zone" is any area within or areas or communities near a park or monument with "significant concentrations of rural residents who (without using aircraft) have customarily and traditionally engaged in subsistence uses" within the park or monument. A "local rural resident" is someone who makes a permanent home in a resident zone. Subsistence uses are defined the same as in sec. 803 of ANILCA, except "customary trade" is limited generally to fur trading for cash. Under other provisions, subsistence fishing and trapping as well as the non-commercial use of timber and other plant material are permitted in parks and monuments.[176]

On the other hand, sec. 816 of ANILCA permits the secretary to close any particular park or monument to uses either "temporarily" or in case of an "emergency." Temporary closures are permitted if "necessary" for reasons of: (1) public safety, (2) administration, or (3) to assure the continued viability of a particular fish or wildlife population. Emergency closures are permitted only if necessary to assure public safety or continued viability of a particular fish or wildlife population. The regulations implementing sec. 816 permit temporary closures "so long as reasonably necessary to achieve the purposes of the closure."[177] Emergency closures, on the other hand, are limited by the statute to only sixty days. Thus, temporary closures can in fact be indefinite closures and are possible for the rather vague and undefined reasons of "administration."

2. Federal Land Use Decisions

Section 810 imposes significant, though mainly procedural, restrictions on future dispositions (i.e., leases, permits, withdrawals, etc.) of public lands in Alaska. Under this provision, all such future decisions (with the exception of those necessary for state and ANCSA corporation conveyances) must take into account their effect on subsistence. Prior to any such disposition, the federal agency managing the lands must evaluate the effect of the disposition on subsistence and alternatives available to reduce or eliminate the need to make the disposition. If the disposition will "significantly restrict subsistence uses," then it cannot be accomplished until the agency: (1) gives notice to the state and the affected local committees and regional councils, (2) gives notice and holds a hearing near the lands being disposed of, and (3) determines essentially that restriction of subsistence is necessary, that the least possible amount of land will be affected and that reasonable steps will be taken to lessen the adverse effects on subsistence. Nonetheless, it must be emphasized that these requirements are mostly procedural. If the agency follows the procedure and still reasonably concludes that the disposition is appropriate, then the lands can be disposed of even if there is an adverse effect on subsistence.[178]

IV. Subsistence Management Today

A. Introduction

After years of political maneuvering and ultimately federal statutory intervention, Alaska seems on the verge of implementing a workable subsistence management system. It has three key elements: (1) a subsistence use definition focused on "rural residents" and protections which take into account Native culture (among other things), (2) locally oriented policy making, and (3) a subsistence research and evaluation division in the department of fish and game. These elements evolved over several years in the form of state policies, statutes and regulations, but at least as to the first and second, took their present form in fish and game regulations adopted in 1982.

B. Subsistence Definition and Protections

At least since 1978, the Alaska Boards of Fish (A.S. 16.05.251[b]) and Game (A.S. 16.05.255[b]) have been under statutory directives to adopt regulations permitting the taking of fish and game for "subsistence uses." As noted earlier, however, the state statutory definition of "subsistence uses" (A.S. 16.05.940[26]) was not necessarily tied to rural residency. The definition, instead focused on "customary and traditional uses in Alaska" of fish and game for "personal or family consumption." The new regulations (5 AAC 99.010 *et seq.*), while seemingly within the scope of the state statutory definition, make it clear that subsistence uses are:

> customary and traditional uses of fish or game resources by rural Alaska residents for food, shelter, fuel, clothing, tools, transportation, making of handicrafts, customary trade, barter and sharing. 5 AAC 99.010(a)(2)

The regulations further establish eight separate criteria for identifying "customary and traditional subsistence uses by rural Alaska residents," (5 AAC 99.010[b]). These criteria consider, significantly, whether the use includes a pattern of community sharing including customary trade with "limited exchanges for cash" (99.010[b][7]) as well as whether the use of fish and game "provides substantial economic, *cultural,* social, and nutritional elements of the subsistence user's life," (99.010[b][8]) (emphasis added). Once the fish and game boards have identified these subsistence uses for a particular area and determined the approximate amount of fish and game necessary to supply those uses, the regulations *require* the boards to adopt regulations providing the opportunity for adequate subsistence use of the resource (99.010.[d]). After they have established subsistence regulations, the boards are then permitted to adopt regulations for non-subsistence use, so long as that use does not adversely affect the management of fish and game on a sustained yield basis or jeopardize subsistence uses, (99.010[e]).

Subsistence uses may also be restricted under the regulations if those uses would jeopardize the sustained yield of a fish or game population or continuation of subsistence uses, but then only if restriction of non-subsistence uses will not resolve the problem and then only according to the criteria established in section 804 of ANILCA. In general, the regulations conform to the subsistence definition and protections established in sections 803 and 804 of ANILCA and apply those criteria to all fish and game management in the state.

C. Policy Making

The Alaska Fisheries and Game Boards are by statute (A.S. 16.05.221 et seq.) the state's fish and game policy-making and regulatory bodies. As discussed earlier, however, the boards were for many years (and for many reasons) somewhat unresponsive to rural subsistence interests. The administrative scheme established under ANILCA and the state's response to it may have substantially resolved this problem. The regional advisory committees and councils required under ANILCA and the positive policy-making and regulatory role they can now play appear to be the key. In 1982, the fish and game boards adopted comprehensive, revised regulations (5 AAC 96.010 et seq.), which (at least) in theory incorporated ANILCA's committee/council structure into the state subsistence policy-making and regulatory system. It is not yet clear, however, whether the new administrative structure is adequately funded to do its job.

1. Committees and Councils

Although Alaska has had a system of fish and game advisory committees at least since statehood, it was only relatively recently that the state substantially funded the committees. In 1975, the statute authorizing the committees (A.S. 16.05.260) was substantially revised, and in 1979 the fish and game boards, acting under that statute, established a system of regional fish and game advisory councils. However, it was not until after the passage of ANILCA that the boards devised definite geographic jurisdictions for the regional councils and clarified their roles in regulations. See 5 AAC 96.200 et seq. as amended June 2, 1982.

As presently constituted, six regional advisory councils have been established, one for each "fish and game resource management region" (96.210 and .220). Some seventy local advisory committees have been set up within the six combined resource regions; one member from each of the local committees also sits as a member of the corresponding regional advisory council (96.080[a]). The committees are composed of from five to fifteen people "representative of fish and game user groups" within the geographic area which the committee serves (96.030). By regulation the committees are the "primary forums" for obtaining fish and game management recommendations from local residents (96.080[b]), and the advisory councils are, among other things, required to assist their respective committees so as to obtain "the greatest possible participation" in fish and game decisions (96.250[b]). Both the councils and the committees can make independent recommendations to the fish and game boards (96.610[d]), but the councils are instructed to attempt to negotiate compromises between conflicting recommendations of their local committees (96.610(d)[2]).

2. Timing and Procedure

The regulations provide a detailed time frame for interaction of the advisory committees and councils with the fish and game boards (5 AAC 96.600 *et seq.*) and permit the boards to limit the portions of existing fish and game regulations which are open to change and subject to committee or council recommendations (96.610[b]). The regulations establish four phases for the consideration of fish and game regulations, with the exact deadlines for each phase to be set by the respective boards in advance. In phase 1 the boards request proposals for changes to specific regulations; in phase 2 the board staffs compile all proposals received from the committees and councils and send them out to all affected committees and councils for review; in phase 3 the committees and councils review all the proposals and provide their recommendations; and in phase 4 the boards hold public hearings in all the proposals, review the committee and council recommendations along with staff reports from the department of fish and game, and adopt regulations.

The boards are under no *general* requirement to adopt the recommendations of either the local committees or regional councils, but under sec. 805(d) of ANILCA and (96.610[e]) of the regulations the boards *are* required to adopt a *regional councils* recommendations related to *subsistence use* within its region unless the appropriate board determines in writing that the recommendations:

(1) are not supported by substantial evidence presented during the course of the board's administrative proceedings;

(2) violate recognized principles of fish and wildlife conservation; or

(3) would be detrimental to the satisfaction of subsistence needs.

Thus, it seems likely that *subsistence use* recommendations from regional advisory councils might carry more weight with a reluctant fish or game board than would the recommendations of an advisory committee. There is some concern, however, that, even though ANILCA requires it and the federal government at least partially reimburses the expense, the state has not yet funded the necessary staffs to permit the regional councils to adequately consult with local committees and develop effective recommendations. [179]

D. Subsistence Division

For many years, one of the major obstacles to effective subsistence fish and game management in Alaska was the absence of any professional staff within the department of fish and game dedicated to subsistence use research. It was difficult, even risky, for the fish and game boards to make subsistence policy decisions in this vacuum. In at least a partial answer to this deficiency, the legislature established...what is now the subsistence division... within the department of fish and game in 1978 Among other things, the division is required to compile data and conduct studies on "all aspects" of the role of subsistence hunting and fishing in the lives of Alaska residents, and to assist the department and boards of fish and game in determining "what uses of fish and game, as well as *which users* and what methods, should be termed subsistence uses, users, and methods." The subsistence division is also authorized to evaluate the impact of state and federal laws on subsistence and make recommendations to correct deficiencies. In short, the subsistence division has a broad mandate to provide a wide variety of information necessary to implement subsistence policy in Alaska. [180]

V. Possibilities for Tribal Control

A. Introduction

Whether a tribe has authority to control fishing and hunting is a question of the tribe's "jurisdiction" or the scope of its governmental power. However, the scope of this power today is not only a matter of a tribe's inherent power to govern its members and its lands. Frequently the tribe is caught in a web of competing tribal, state and federal interests. Usually, in the case of fish and game matters, the jurisdictional dispute is between a state and a tribe, and there are three jurisdictional possibilities: (1) exclusive tribal jurisdiction, (2) exclusive state jurisdiction, or (3) concurrent tribal and state jurisdiction. The outcome frequently seems to depend on two factors: (1) whether the person being regulated is an Indian or not and (2) whether the land is within a reservation or otherwise protected by federal law. In the hard cases (i.e., involving non-Indians on a reservation or Indians unprotected by federal law) the courts are likely to look at a broader range of interests in order to strike a balance between the tribe and the state.

In general, in the absence of any reservation or a federal law protecting tribal hunting and fishing rights off the reservation, the exercise of *exclusive* tribal jurisdiction is unlikely. The U.S. Supreme Court has even permitted limited (i.e., "reasonable and necessary") state conservation regulations both on and off the reservation in the case of treaty protected fishing rights.[181] More recently, in *White Mountain Apache Tribe v. Bracker,*[182] the Supreme Court suggested the following three-prong test for evaluating competing state and tribal interests:

(1) Whether there is a comprehensive federal regulatory scheme which leaves no room for state regulation;

(2) Whether permitting state regulation would obstruct federal policies relating to profitability and management of Indian enterprises;

(3) Whether functions and services provided by the state justify state taxation or regulation.

B. Exclusive Tribal Jurisdiction

Except for Metlakatla, there are no reservations or federally protected exclusive fishing rights in Alaska; therefore, at least for now, the *Bracker* criteria are perhaps the best guidelines for determining the circumstances under which exclusive tribal regulation might be possible in Alaska. The prospect seems unlikely. ANILCA is the most comprehensive federal regulatory scheme, and it seems to favor state jurisdiction so long as the state complies with its requirements.

Of course, the state has been prohibited from regulating fishing on the Metlakatla Reservation when, among other things, such regulation would interfere with the purpose of the reservation.[183] On the other hand, in *Organized Village of Kake v. Egan,* the state, in the absence of a reservation, was permitted to control Indian fishing even when that had a serious economic impact on a tribally owned fish cannery.[184] Finally, the state at present provides the vast bulk of intrastate fish and game management services. It seems unlikely under these circumstances (in the absence of federal preemption) that Alaska Native tribes could exercise exclusive jurisdiction.

C. Exclusive State Jurisdiction

The U. S. Supreme Court has upheld exclusive state jurisdiction to regulate non-Indian fishing on lands owned by non-Indians even within the boundries of an Indian reservation.[185] Although this case might be limited to its facts, it is certainly an indication that states may have exclusive jurisdiction over non-Indian hunting and fishing under these circumstances. It is even clearer that Alaska would also have exclusive jurisdiction over non-Natives on such lands outside any reservation. However, that does not answer the question of state jurisdiction over Natives and non-Natives on tribally owned or occupied lands.

D. Concurrent Jurisdiction

There is authority for tribal concurrent jurisdiction over Indians on ceded lands of a former reservation.[186] Most of these cases involve Indian tribes terminated in the 1950's whose original treaties included specific protections for hunting and fishing rights which were not affected by the termination. There were only two reservations in Alaska which were statutorily established and might, therefore, be entitled to similar treatment.[187] Metlakatla is one of these and Klukwan (Chilkat Indian Village) is the other.[188] All the other reserves were "temporary" in nature and therefore extinguished without compensation under section 19 of ANCSA (43 U.S.C.A. 1618) as were aboriginal hunting and fishing rights under section 4(b) (43 U.S.C.A. 1603[b]).[189]

One circuit court, however, has held that land of a former reservation held as allotments or in trust status is still subject to Indian reserved hunting and fishing rights, but not state jurisdiction, because the lands were "Indian country."[190] The same court in a subsequent review of the same case indicated, but did not decide, that it might be possible that even ceded land of the former reserve now held as public lands would be subject to concurrent state and tribal jurisdiction.[191] The concept of "Indian country" might therefore provide a means of defining Alaska tribal jurisdiction over hunting and fishing. The term is defined by federal statute as including any reservation, allotment or "dependent Indian community."[192]

Historically, Indian country has been those lands which were occupied by tribal Indians and subject to either tribal or federal jurisdiction.[193] What constitutes a reservation or an allotment is easily understood, but the "dependent Indian community" concept is ambiguous. As defined by the U.S. Supreme Court, however, the term includes "any unceded lands owned or occupied by a...tribe of Indians."[194] The term was applied to Alaska Natives living on the Tyonek reservation in 1959 in a case which upheld the exclusive jurisdiction of the tribe in a criminal matter not covered by federal law.[195] More recently the Alaska Federal District Court has upheld the jurisdiction of an Alaska Native village (tribal) government to adjudicate ownership of tribal property located on tribally owned land.[196] These cases suggest that, at least on tribally owned land, Alaska Native villages may have jurisdiction to regulate other matters as well—perhaps including fish and game. On the other hand, the criteria previously discussed, the absence of reservations or tribal trust lands in Alaska and the comprehensive management scheme of ANILCA all suggest that such jurisdiction would be concurrent with the state.[197]

E. Lacey Act Amendments

The Lacey Act was originally enacted in 1900; it was one of the first federal attempts to outlaw interstate traffic in wildlife taken in violation of state laws. It was amended in 1981 to simplify its enforcement and administration.[198] Significantly, the amendments extend the scope of the law to include the transportation, sale, or other disposition of fish, wildlife or plants taken or possessed in violation of "any Indian tribal law."[199] "Indian tribal law" is defined as:

> any regulation of, or other rule of conduct enforceable by, any Indian tribe, band, or group but only to the extent that the regulation or rule applies within Indian country as defined in (18 USCA 1151).[200]

The amendments provide for civil and criminal penalties as well as forfeitures for violations of its provisions. The amendments also permit federal enforcement agencies to negotiate agreements with Indian tribes to use tribal personnel, services and facilities for enforcement purposes.[201] Finally, the new legislation specifies that it is not intended to modify either the rights or privileges of Indian tribes or communities under other federal laws or the authorities of state or tribal governments on "reservations."[202]

In general, the recent amendments enhance the already existing powers of Indian tribes over "Indian country" by affording federal enforcement to restrict the transportation, sale or other disposition of wildlife taken in violation of Indian tribal law. Thus, violation of a tribal law coupled with a federally prohibited activity such as transportation will bring federal enforcement agencies to bear on any offender of tribal law. In Alaska, it is especially significant that the geographic scope of the tribe's jurisdiction under these amendments may not be confined to a reservation, but is presumed to include allotments and any "dependent Indian community" as defined in 18 USCA 1151.[203] Moreover, there is no requirement that the tribe's law be "consistent" with any state law on the same subject as is the case under PL 280.[204] Even though these amendments do not delegate federal fish and wildlife enforcement authority to Indian tribes, they do equate the authorities of tribes in "Indian country" with those of the states elsewhere and provide federal support for tribal enforcement efforts.

VI. Conclusions

To some extent, federal treaties and statutes have protected Alaska Native subsistence interests for many years. Earlier enactments afforded minimal exemptions, often limited to specific species or wildlife taken by primitive hunting methods. In all likelihood more realistic forms of protection were unnecessary because there was little real conflict over the exercise of aboriginal hunting and fishing rights. However, Alaska statehood, the enactment of ANCSA and the relatively rapid development of the new state exacerbated these conflicts. The federal response has not been the abandonment of Native subsistence values, but the protection of those values in the form of exemptions from recent wildlife conservation treaties and statutes. Moreover, the state has been virtually compelled under ANILCA to adopt statewide subsistence protections, structured in significant part to protect Native subsistence interests.

Although the umbrella of federal protection now shelters both Natives and non-Natives, that fact does not entail a diminishment of Native values so much as an acknowledgement that in Alaska significant numbers of non-Natives now share those values by their participation in the subsistance economy. Nor do recent federal enactments necessarily preclude the possibility of some tribal control of subsistence hunting and fishing. In fact, recent amendments to the Lacey Act imply that, even in Alaska, tribal fish and game management may receive additional support through federal enforcement. Particularly when faced with competing state interests, the courts have also concluded that this long and continuing history of federal protection constitutes statutory acceptance of a trust responsibility for the maintenance of subsistence culture.

ENDNOTES

[1]Ballot Measure No. 7, Personal Consumption of Fish and Game, would have repealed the state's existing subsistence management program and enacted a replacement scheme which, among other things, would have required that fish and wildlife resources be "equally available to personal consumption users" and would have prohibited the state boards of fish and game from imposing distinctions based on factors employed since statehood: "economic status, land ownership, local residency, past use or past dependence on the resource, or lack of alternative resources."

Alaskan voters rejected the measure by a vote of 111,770 to 79,679. State of Alaska Official Returns by Election Pricinct, General Election, November 2, 1982 at 47.

[2]Title VIII, Alaska National Interest Lands Conservation Act (ANILCA) of Dec. 2, 1980, P.L. 96-487 (94 Stat. 2371, 2422, 16 U.S.C. 3111 et seq.) discussed below.

[3]Supporters of Ballot Measure No. 7 filed suit to block implementation of the state subsistence law on constitutional grounds (McDowell v. Collinsworth, (3AN-83-1592 civil).

[4]See secs. 801(1) and 803 of ANILCA (16 U.S.C. 3111(1) and 3113), congressional findings and definition of "subsistence," respectively.

The Alaska Supreme Court has also acknowledged the cultural differences among Alaska's Native (predominantly rural) population as including:

> ...economies which rely on hunting, fishing and gathering activities, strong kinship bonds, isolation from those parts of Alaska that approximate mainstream America, different seasonal activity patterns, concepts of time and scheduling, which, in accordance with other cultural divergences, may be quite different from those of mainstream America, and finally, very limited participation in the cash economy.

Alvarado v. State, 486 P.2d 891, 894 (Ak. 1971), jury selection for trial of a Native defendant must include fair cross section of the community in which the crime allegedly occurred.

[5]Those opposed to subsistence advocate no distinction among "personal consumptive uses" on any grounds. Current state regulations treat "personal use" which does not qualify as "subsistence" and is neither sports or commercial as a separate use category under a separate regulatory scheme. See 5 AAC 77.001-015.

[6]Sec. 801(1) of ANILCA apparently distinguishes between Native "cultural existence" and non-Native "social existence," but treats both as values to be protected under a federal subsistence definition which includes only "rural Alaskan residents" under sec. 803 (codified at 16 U.S.C. 3111(1) and 3113, respectively).

[7]See e.g., Camerino, Vicki, *Subsistence in Alaska and the Effect of H.R. 39,* 3 American Indian Law Journal, No. 12 (December 1976) at 16. See generally, *Does One Way of Life Have to Die So Another Can Live? A Report on Subsistence and the Conservation of the Yupik Life-Style,* Art Davidson, ed. (Anchorage: Yupiktak Bista (1974).

[8]Robert D. Arnold, *Alaska Native Land Claims* (Anchorage: Alaska Native Foundation, 197660 at 28-30.

[9]E.g., secs. 801(1) and 803 of ANILCA (16 U.S.C. 3111[1] and 3113, respectively).

[10]C.f. Pyramid Lake Paiute Tribe of Indians v. Morton, 354 F.Supp. 252, 254-255 (D.D.C. 1973), recognizing that the purpose of the Pyramid Lake Reservation included: "the maintenance and preservation of Pyramid Lake and the maintenance of the lower reaches of the Truckee [River] as a natural spawning ground for fish and other purposes beneficial and satisfying to the needs of the Tribe."

[11]The Navajo Reservation is perhaps one example.

[12]Alaska Pacific Fisheries v. U. S., 248 U.S. 78 (1918), statutory reserve including certain islands held sufficient to reserve exclusive Native fishery. Cf. Menominee Tribe v. U.S., 391 U.S. 404 (1968), reserved hunting and fishing not extinguished by termination statute; Kimball v. Callahan, 493 F.2d 564 (9th Cir.), cert. denied 419 U.S. 1019 (1974), treaty hunting and fishing not extinguished by termination statute. See generally F. Cohen, *Handbook of Federal Indian Law,* 1982 ed. (Charlottesville, Va.: Michie Bobbs-Merrill, 1982) at 449-450.

[13]E.g., Williams v. Lee, 358 U.S. 217, 220 (1959).

[14]Antoine v. Washington, 420 U.S. 194, 207 (1975), implying "reasonable and necessary" state conservation regulations; Puyallup Tribe v. Department of Game (Puyallup III), 433 U.S. 165 (1977), permitting state conservation regulation of tribal members under court order.

[15]Montana v. U.S., 450 U.S. 544, 564 (1981).

[16]E.g., New Mexico v. Mescalero Apache Tribe,____U.S.____, 76 L. Ed. 2d 611 (1983).

[17]Article III of the Yakima Treaty (12 Stat. 951), cited in U.S. v. Winans, 198 U.S. 371, 378 (1905). See also U.S. v. Michigan, 471 F. Supp. 192 (W.D. Mich. 1979); aff'd. in pertinent part and remanded, 653 F.2d 277 (6th Cir. 1981); modified, 8 Ind. L. Rep. 2132 (6th Cir. 1981); on remand, 520 F.Supp. 207 (W.D. Mich. 1981); tribal fishing regulations approved,____F. Supp.____, 9 Ind. L. Rep. 3050 (W.D. Mich. 1982). The net effect of the Michigan cases appears to be to uphold exclusive off-reservation treaty fishing rights and to enjoin enforcement of more restrictive state fishing regulations in favor of tribal fishing regulations.

[18]*U.S. v. Winans,* note 17, above, at 381.

[19]Id.

[20]U.S. v. Washington, 384 F. Supp. 312 (W.D. Wash. 1974); aff'd. 520 F. 2d 676 (9th Cir. 1975); cert. den. 423 U.S. 1086. Accord, Washington v. Washington State Passanger Fishing Vessel Association, 443 U.S. 658 (1979).

[21]*Antoine v. Washington* and *Puyallup III,* note 14, above.

[22]Tulee v. Washington, 315 U.S. 863 (1942).

[23]Puyallup Tribe v. Department of Game (Puyallup I), 391 U.S. 392 (1968).

[24]Washington Game Department v. Puyallup Tribe (Puyallup II), 414 U.S. 44 (1973).

[25]*Puyallup III,* note 14, above. See also, Johnson, Ralph W., *The States Versus Indian Off-Reservation Fishing: A United States Supreme Court Error,* 47 Wash. L. Rev. 207, for a lucid explanation of the confusion behind "conservation" and regulating a fishery resource in order to "spread the catch" among all users and

"allocating" the catch among different user classes. Professor Johnson's point is that the Supreme Court should recognize the Indian treaty right to exclusive control of the fishery off the reservation, thereby compelling Congress to set up a regulatory scheme. *Puyallup III* forecloses that possibility and goes one step further by permitting state regulation on the reservation as well.

[26]26 Stat. 1101, 25 USCA 495.

[27]Metlakatla v. Egan, 369 U.S. 552 (1962).

[28]Kake v. Egan, 369 U.S. 60 (1962). *Kake* is also often cited as authority for the application of state laws to Indians on the reservation "unless such application would interfere with reservation self-government or impair a right granted or reserved by Federal law." Id. at 75. Recent cases seem inexplicably disinclined to treat fish and game management as an aspect of "reservation self-government." See e.g. *Puyallup III,* note 14, above.

[29]Art. VI, cl. 2, U.S. Const.

[30]Missouri v. Holland, 252 U.S. 416 (1920), holding that the Migratory Bird Treaty of 1916 and the federal laws enacted to implement it preempted Missouri's game laws.

[31]See generally, F. Cohen, note 12, above, at 757-761.

[32]For example, the response of the Inupiat Eskimos to the 1977 attempts of the International Whaling Commission (IWC) to prohibit Inupiat whaling under the terms of the Whaling Convention was to establish the Alaska Eskimo Whaling Commission (AEWC). The AEWC negotiated a management role with the federal government in the bowhead whale harvest and has since participated actively in the formulation of U.S. policy before the IWC. See e.g., Stan Jones, "Eskimos Aim to Better Efficiency Strike Average," *Fairbanks Daily News-Miner,* Friday, Feb 11, 1983, at 1 and 6.

[33]Act of July 3, 1918, c. 128, 40 Stat. 755 as amended (16 USCA 703 et seq.)

[34]Act of November 2, 1966, P.L. 89-702, 80 Stat. 1091 (16 USC 1151 et seq.)

[35]Act of August 9, 1950, c. 653, 64 Stat. 421, as amended (16 USCA 916 et seq.)

[36]Act of October 21, 1972, 86 Stat. 1027, as amended (16 USCA 1361 et seq.)

[37]The United States is reportedly attempting to renegotiate the provisions of the three earlier treaties to bring them into line with the Soviet treaty. S. Rpt. No. 95-1175 (Aug. 31, 1978) at 6 (reprinted at 1978 USCCAAN 7641, 7645), accompanying recent amendments to the Migratory Bird Treaty Act (PL 95-616).

[38]Art. II, Treaty of December 7, 1916; 39 Stat. 1702; TS 628. See also, 54 I.D. 517, holding that the same treaty prohibits Native hunting on the Swinomish Indian Reserve in Washington State.

[39]Art. II(c) and (d), Treaty of March 15, 1937; 50 Stat. 1311; TS 912; supplemented March 10, 1972 (23 UST 260; TIAS 7302) to add additional species.

[40]Art. III(1)(e), Treaty of Sep. 19, 1974; 25 UST 3329; TIAS 7990, as amended to add species.

[41]Art. II 1(c), Treaty of Oct. 13, 1978; 29 UST 4647; TIAS 9073.

[42]PL 95-616, sec. 3(h), Act of Nov. 8, 1978, 92 Stat. 3112 (16 USC 712).

[43]S. Rpt. No. 95-1175 (Aug. 31, 1978) at 6 (reprinted in 1978 USCCAAN 7641 at 7645. The Senate Report notes specifically that the term "indigenous inhabitants" as used in the negotiation of the Soviet treaty is intended to include "both Native and non-Native peoples who have legitimate subsistence hunting needs. The Canadian treaty was amended by protocol in 1979, but by 1983 the United States and Canada were still formulating a joint management agreement. See 48 Fed. Reg. (No. 48) 10101-10103 (Thursday, March 10, 1983)."

[44]50 CFR 20.102; see also, 47 Fed. Reg. (No. 168) 38248 (Monday, Aug. 30, 1982), establishing 1982-83 seasons and bag limits in Alaska. The regulations do permit Eskimos and Indians to "take, possess, and transport, in any manner and at any time, auks, auklets, guillemots, murres, and puffins" in accordance with the British/Canadian treaty. 50 CFR 20.132(a) (October 1, 1982).

[45]Interim Convention on Conservation of North Pacific Fur Seals, Oct. 14, 1957; 8 UST 2284; TIAS 3948, replacing the terminated convention of Dec. 15, 1911, 37 Stat. 1542, TS 564. Art. II describes the general goals of fur seal research under the treaty; Art. III prohibits pelagic sealing, except for limited research purposes; Art. V established the North Pacific Fur Seal Commission and describes its duties; Art. VII exempts "Indians, Ainos (sic), Aleuts, or Eskimos" living near fur seal inhabited oceans from the treaty restrictions so long as they use only traditional [i.e., primitive] means to harvest seals at sea and are not employed by or contracted to deliver fur seal pelts to others; Art. IX establishes harvest and profit sharing arrangements.

[46]Amended and extended, Oct. 8, 1963 (15 UST 316; TIAS 5558); extended, Sep. 3, 1969 (20 UST 2992; TIAS 6774); amended and extended, May 7, 1976 (27 UST 3371; TIAS 8368); extended with statements of intent, Oct. 14, 1980 (TIAS 10020).

[47]Protocol Amending the Interim Convention of February 9, 1957, as amended and extended (Oct. 14, 1980; TIAS 10020) at 2.

[48]PL 89-702, Title I, secs. 101-109 (16 USCA 1151-1159).

[49]PL 89-702, Title II, secs. 201-208 (16 USCA 1161-1168). Sec. 201 established the special reservation; sec. 203 provided for facilities, services and equipment deemed necessary; sec. 204 provided for agreement with state to provide education; sec. 205 provided for medical care from the Public Health Service; sec. 206 provided for administration of the townsite, including restrictions on individual Native property.

[50]Breach of similar provisions of a predecessor statute were held sufficient to attach federal liability for breach of "fair and honorable dealings" under the Indian Claims Commission Act. See Aleut Community of St. Paul Island v. U.S., 480 F.2d 831 (Ct. Cls. 1973).

[51]Fur Seal Act Amendments of 1983, Act of Oct. 14, 1983, P.L. 98-129.

[52]Convention for the Regulation of Whaling, entered into force Nov. 10, 1948 (62 Stat. 1716; TIAS 1849); amended effective May 4, 1959 (10 UST 952; TIAS 4228).

[53]See also Convention for the Regulation of Whaling, entered into force Jan. 16, 1935 (49 Stat. 3079; TS 880). Unlike the present convention, the earlier version had a specific exemption for aboriginal whaling if limited to primitive methods. See also, Hopson v. Kreps, 462 F.Supp. 1374 (D. Ak. 1979); rev'd. on other grounds, 622 F.2d 1375 (9th Cir. 1980), discussing past IWC aboriginal whaling policies. See generally, *Case of the Bowhead Whale,* 3 American Indian Law Journal No. 12 (Dec. 1977) at 23.

[54]See also, Hopson v. Kreps, 622 F.2d 1375, 1381-1382 (9th Cir. 1980), holding that a court could decide whether the domestic statute implementing the whaling convention permitted review of regulations adopted under that statute even though the terms of the treaty itself might not be subject to review.

[55]*Washington Post,* October 8, 1977, at A-8, referring to a unanimous vote at the June 1977 IWC meeting to ban bowhead whaling, with the United States abstaining.

[57]Adams v. Vance, 570 F.2d 950 (D.C. Cir. 1977).

[58]Hopson v. Kreps, note 54, above, at 1381-1382.

[59]Wales, Kivalina, Point Hope, Wainwright, Barrow, Nuiqsut, Kaktovik, Gambell and Savoonga, as reported in the *Fairbanks Daily News-Miner* note 32, above), at 1. Gambell and Savoonga are Siberian Yupik villages situated on St. Lawrence Island.

[60]"Whaling Puzzle," Editorial, *Anchorage Daily News,* Dec. 23, 1977, citing statement by Eben Hopson, North Slope Borough Mayor.

[61]For example, the quota was set at 45 whales landed or 65 struck during the combined 1981, 1982 and 1983 seasons, *Fairbanks Daily News-Miner,* Feb. 8, 1983 at 5.

[62]Id. See also, "New Study: Bowhead Population Greater," *Alaska Offshore,* SOHIO Petroleum Co., Nov. 1982, at 7 and *Fairbanks Daily News-Miner,* note 32, above, at 6.

[63]*Fairbanks Daily News-Miner,* note 32, above, at 1 and 6. See generally, G. McBeath, *North Slope Borough Government and Policymaking,* (Fairbanks: ISER, University of Alaska, 1981 at 79-81, regarding the Borough's continuing role as an "intercessor institution" in matters related to subsistence and Native culture.

[64]*Fairbanks Daily News-Miner,* id.

[65]Testimony of John V. Byrne, Administrator, National Oceanic and Atmospheric Administration and U.S. Commissioner, International Whaling Commission, before the Subcommittee on Human Rights and International Organizations, Committee on Foreign Affairs, U.S. House of Representatives (Sep. 16, 1982).

[66]D. Jones, *License for Empire: Colonialism by Treaty in Early America,* (Chicago: University of Chicago Press, 1982) at 1-5. See also E. Spicer, *A Short History of the Indians of the United States,* (New York: Van Nostrand, 1969) at 11-44.

[67]*Anchorage Daily News,* note 60, above.

[68]Convention for the Conservation of Polar Pears, entered into force Nov. 1, 1976 (27 UST 3918; TIAS 8409), Art. I prohibits the taking of polar bears except for the "scientific," "conservation," emergency or "traditional" purposes permitted under Art. III.

[69]Act of Oct. 21, 1972, 86 Stat. 1027, PL 92-522, as amended (16 USCA 1361 et seq.), discussed below.

[70]Art II 1(c), Treaty of Oct. 13, 1978 (29 UST 4647; TIAS 9073).

[71]Native pelagic sealing is restricted by both the fur seal treaty and the implimenting legislation (16 USCA 1152) to the most primitive means. For all practical purposes, limitation to these methods precludes even Native pelagic sealing.

[72]The statement of intent accompanying the Senate's June 11, 1981 ratification of the October 14, 1980, extension (reprinted in TIAS 10020) anticipates that future treaty amendments will attempt to bring the fur seal convention into line with the Marine Mammal Protection Act. Presumably, that means expanding the treaty exceptions to correspond with the act's subsistence provisions.

[73]The Walrus Protection Act of Aug. 18, 1941, 55 Stat. 632 (48 USC 248 et seq. [1958 id.]), is perhaps another. See People of Togiak v. U.S., 470 F. Supp. 423, 427, n. 9 (D.C.D.C. 1979), discussing but not deciding whether the Walrus Protection Act has been repealed. It is also possible that the more recent and comprehensive Marine Mammal Protection Act repealed the Walrus Protection Act by implication, but implied repeals are not favored—especially in the field of Indian law. E.g., *Menominee Tribe v. U.S.,* note 12, above, Menominee hunting and fishing rights not extinguished by implication upon termination of the Menominee reservation.

[74]Act of Sept. 1, 1937, 50 Stat. 900 (25 USCA 500 et seq.)

[75]Act of Oct. 21, 1972, 86 Stat. 1027, PL 92-522, as amended (16 USCA 1531 et seq.)

[76]Act of Dec. 28, 1973, 87 Stat. 885, PL 93-205, as amended (16 USCA 1531 et seq.)

[77]Act of Dec. 2, 1980, 94 Stat. 2371, 2422; Title VIII, PL 96-487 (16 USCA 3111 et seq.)

[78]25 USCA 500.

[79]See generally 81 Cong. Rec. 9470-9493, 75th Cong., 1st Sess. (1937).

[80]25 USCA 500a, acquisition of non-Native deer; 25 USCA 500g, distribution of deer; 25 USCA 500i, prevents future alienation to non-Natives, 25 USCA 500e, revolving loan fund, and 25 USCA 500h, delegation of administrative authority to Native organizations.

[81]81 Cong. Rec., note 79 above, at 9480-9481.

[82]Id. at 9485, remarks of Rep. Englebright (Calif.).

[83]Id. at 9489.

[84]Id. at 9489, remarks of Rep. Rich. (Penna.)

[85]Id. at 9492-9493.

[86]16 USCA 1531(b).

[87]Id. 1532(4).

[88]Id. (15).

[89]Id. 1533.

[90]Id. (f).

[91]Id. 1535(f). See generally, H. J. Justin & Sons, Inc. v. Brown, 519 F. Supp. 1383 (D.C. Cal. 1981).

[92]Id. 1539(e)(1). Non-Natives who are "not primarily dependent upon the taking of fish and wildlife for consumption or for the creation and sale of authentic Native articles of handicrafts and clothing" are not protected by the exception even though they may live in a Native village.

[93]Id. 1539(e)(3)(i).

[94]Non-Natives living in Native villages or towns are limited in some ways that Natives are not. See note 92, above. It is also unclear whether non-Natives living in such villages can buy edible animal parts of endangered species, since sales of edible parts may be limited to "native consumption" under 16 USCA 1539(e)(3)(i).

[95]Id. 1539(4).

[96]Id. See also 50 CFR 17.11 listing endangered and threatened species.

[97]North Slope Borough v. Andrus, 642 F. 2d 589 (D. C. Cir. 1980).

[98]Committee for Humane Legislation, Inc. v. Richardson, 414 F. Supp. 297, 309 (D.C.D.C. 1976); aff'd. 540 F. 2d 1141, 1148 (D.C. Cir. 1976). "Marine mammals" are defined as "any mammal which is...morphologically adapted to the marine environment...or primarily inhabits the marine environment" and includes sea otters, walrus, seals, whales and polar bears, 16 USCA 1362(5).

[99]People of Togiak v. U.S., note 73, above, at 426.

[100]16 USCA 1371(a).

[101]Id. 1371(b).

[102]Id. 1379(b) and (c).

[103]Id. 1379(f).

[104]Id. 1361(3). Other reasons include the danger of marine mammal extinction, restoration of marine mammals to their optimum sustainable population and their international esthetic, recreational and economic significance. 16 USCA 1361 (1), (2) and (6) respectively.

[105]Other exceptions included an initial two-year exception following passage of the act to permit taking of marine mammals incidental to commercial fishing operations (16 USC 1371 [a][2] [1972 supp.]) and a hardship exemption for up to one year following enactment (16 USCA 1371[c]).

[106]The major exceptions are for incidental takings during commercial fishing operations (16 USCA 1371[a][4]) and other non-fishing activities (16 USCA 1371[a][5]) if the particular marine mammal species involved is not "depleted."

[107]16 USCA 1371(b), "depleted" is defined in 1362(1) and relates to "optimum sustainable population," as defined in 1362(8). Under 1379(i), the federal government can also require Natives to mark, tag and report marine mammals taken under the exemption even if there is no "depletion."

[108]People of Togiak v. U.S., note 99, above.

[109]Id. at 428.

[110]16 USCA 1371(b).

[111]16 USCA 1371(b) and (f).

[112]H. Rpt. No. 97-228 (Sept. 16, 1981) at 28; 1981 USCCAAN 1458, 1478. No Senate Report was submitted with these amendments.

[113]16 USCA 1371(a)(5)(A)(i).

[114]Id. 1379(f)(1)(B).

[115]H. Rpt. No. 97-228, note 112, above. The House Report also notes that the MMPA subsistence definition is similar to and "intended to operate in the same manner" as the ANILCA subsistence priority (discussed below.), but unlike ANILCA, the MMPA priority does not include "customary trade" as a subsistence activity. Cryptically, the House Report says that: "The removal of customary trade from the subsistence use definition is not intended to diminish the Committee's recognition of the importance of customary trade of marine mammals in many rural Alaska villages."

[116]*People of Togiak v. U.S.*, note 99, above, at 428.

[117]Id.

[118]North Slope Borough v. Andrus, 486 F.Supp. 332 (D.C.D.C. 1980); rev'd in part, 642 F.2d 589 (D.C. Cir. 1980).

[119]Adams v. Vance, 570 F.2d 950 (D.C. Cir. 1977).

[120]*People of Togiak*, note 99, above, at 427 and 428.

[121]*North Slope Borough v. Andrus*, note 118, above, at 486 F. Supp. 344.

[122]*North Slope Borough v. Andrus*, note 118, above at 642 F.2d 612.

[123]*See Adams v. Vance*, note 119, above. See also Nevada v. U.S.,_____U.S. ——, 51 USLW 4974 at 4982 (June 24, 1983), regarding the limits on the trust responsibility in the presence of congressionally authorized conflicts of interest.

[124]See *Hopson v. Kreps*, note 54, above, at 1381-1382.

[125]See Hearings on H.R. 13142 and H.R.10123, House Committee on Interior and Insular Affairs, Subcommittee on Indian Affairs, August 4-6 and September 9, 1969, at 51 (AFN Memorandum of June 20, 1969) and at 55 (AFN draft bill). Section 2(a)(5) of the AFN draft bill stated that among the act's purposes would be the settlement of land claims by providing for:

> (5) Protection of Native subsistence hunting, fishing, trapping and gathering rights and, where it is within the power of the Federal Government, measures for the conservation of subsistence biotic resources.

Emil Notti was the first President of the Alaska Federation of Natives, Inc.

[126]E.g., Section 15(f) of S. 35 provided for selection of five to sixty acres as campsites for the "harvesting of fish, wildlife, berries, fuel or other products of the land" on public lands outside of those selected under the act and in federal parks, refuges or national forests. Section 15(j) permitted issuance of multiple use permits on federal refuges for the purposes described in 15(f).

[127]See e.g., H. Rpt. No. 92-523, accompanying the Alaska Native Claims Settlement Act (reprinted in 1971 USCCAAN 2192 at 2195).

[128]"Native village" is defined in Sec. 3(c) of ANCSA (43 U.S.C. 1602 [c]) as "any tribe, band, clan, group, village, community, or association in Alaska...composed of twenty-five or more Natives."

"Village Corporation" is defined in Sec. 3(j) (43 U.S.C. 1602[j]) as "an Alaska Native Village Corporation organized under the laws of the State of Alaska...to hold, invest, manage and/or distribute lands, property, funds, and other rights and assets for and on behalf of a Native village in accordance with the terms of [ANCSA]."

These definitions suggest that the "village corporation" may have an obligation to manage ANCSA lands "for and on behalf of" the political community which constitutes the "Native village." So, if the community which constitutes the Native village wants the village corporation to manage its lands to maximize subsistence resources instead of economic profit, it is possible the village corporation may have an obligation to do so even if other shareholders outside the community object.

[129]S. Rpt. 92-581, 92nd Cong.; 1st Sess., December 14, 1971 at 37.

[130]Commissioner, Alaska Department of Fish and Game and Alaska Board of Fish and Game, "Policy Statement on Subsistence Utilization of Fish and Game," May 4, 1973.

[131]E.g., A.S. 16.05.940(17) (subsistence fishing); A.S. 16.05.257(h)(1) (subsistence hunting); A.S. 16.05.940(26) (subsistence uses); A.S. 16.05.251(b) and .255(b) requiring the boards of fish and game to provide for subsistence uses. See generally, "History and Implementation of Ch. 151 SLA 1978, The State's Subsistence Law," Draft Report Alaska House of Representatives Special Committee on Subsistence (May 15, 1981).

[132]AS 16.05.090(c) and .094 (describing the duties of the section).

[133]A.S. 16.05.257.

[134]Alaska Const., Art. VIII, sec. 2.

[135]Kenai Penninsula Fishermen's Cooperative Assoc. v. State, 628 P.2d 897, 904 (Ak. 1981) upholding fishing regulations under Art. VII secs. 2 and 15, but voiding regulations adopted by improper procedures. The Alaska Attorney General has also concluded that other provisions of the Alaska Constitution (i.e. Art. VIII, sec. 3, "common use" and sec. 15, prohibiting exclusive fisheries) do not require a different result. Op. Ak. Atty. Gen., "Subsistence law: real and perceived problems" (File No. 166-448-83, Feb. 25, 1983).

[136]See e. g., Mitchell, Don, "Alaska Native Subsistence and H.R. 39," Rural Alaska Community Action Program, unpublished memorandum, July 10, 1978, at 2-6. See also, 3 Amer. Ind. L.J. No. 12 (Dec. 1977) at 22.

[137]Mitchell note 136, above, at 2.

[138]Id.

[139]Recommended Decision Concerning Resumption of State Management Over Nine Species of Marine Mammals (MMPA Docket No. WASH 76-1, June 30, 1977) at 74.

[140]Testimony of Governor Jay Hammond before the House Subcommittee on General Oversight and Alaska Lands, 95th Cong.: 1st Sess., Fairbanks, Alaska, August 20, 1977 (cited in Mitchell, note 136, above, at 5).

[141]Udall, Stewart L., "The Alaska Natives and Their Subsistence Rights: A Discussion of the Constitutional Questions," Unpublished Memorandum to the Alaska Federation of Natives, July 1977, at 6-8.

[142]Cited in Mitchell, note 136, above, at 6.

[143]16 USCA 669.

[144]16 USCA 777.

[145]Mitchell, note 136, above, at 2. See also, A.S. 16.05.100 and .110, which implements this funding scheme.

[146]A.S. 16.05.340(a)(5)

[147]Mitchell, note 136, above, at 2. See also note 130, above, and accompanying text.

[148]Act of Dec. 2, 1980, P.L. 96-487, Title VIII, 94 Stat. 2371, 2422 (16 U.S.C.A. 3111 *et seq.*).

[149]The 17(d)(1) and (2) withdrawals were the result of a political compromise between environmental, business, state and Native interests necessary for passage of ANCSA. See generally, R. Arnold, *Alaska Native Land Claims,* (Anchorage: Alaska Native Foundation, 1978) at 266-269). See also S. Rpt. No. 96-413 (Energy and Natural Resources Committee, Nov. 14, 1979) at 129-134, reprinted in 1980 U.S. Code Congressional and Administrative News (USCCAAN) 5070 at 5073-5078. There is a discrepancy between the Senate Report and Arnold as to the amount of land withdrawn in the "national interest" under 17(d)(2). The 79.3 million acre figure is the one cited in the Senate Report.

[150]Federal Lands Policy and Management Act (FLPMA) of Oct. 21, 1976, Sec. 204(e), P.L. 94-579, 90 Stat. 2744, 43 U.S.C.A. 1701 *et seq.*

[151]Act of June 8, 1906, 34 Stat. 225, 16 U.S.C.A. 431.

[152]Alaska v. Carter, A78-291 (D. Ak. 1978) (dismissed after passage of ANILCA).

[153]See generally, S. Rpt. 96-413, note 149, above, in 1980 USCCAAN at 5076-5078 for a discussion of these events.

[154]Sec. 801. The Congress finds and declares that—

> (1) the continuation of the opportunity for subsistence uses by rural residents of Alaska, including both Natives and non-Natives, on the public lands and by Alaska Natives on Native lands is essential to Native physical, economic, traditional, and cultural existence and to non-Native physical, economic, traditional, and social existence;
>
> * * * *
>
> (4) in order to fulfill the policies and purposes of the Alaska Native Claims Settlement Act and as a matter of equity, it is necessary for the Congress to invoke its constitutional authority over Native affairs and its constitutional authority under the property clause and the commerce clause to protect and provide the opportunity for continued subsistence uses on the public lands by Native and non-Native rural residents....

[155]U.S. Const., Amend. XIV. See Brown v. Board of Education, 347 U.S. 483 (1954), prohibiting racial segregation in education. Compare Morton v. Mancari, 417 U.S. 535 (1974), upholding Indian preferential employment practices.

[156]U.S. Const., Art. VI, cl. 2.

[157]See e.g., Missouri v. Holland, 252 U.S. 416 (1920)

[158]Denying the state the authority to manage fish and game resources on federal public lands would, of course, substantially impair the state's ability to manage these resources on state or private lands, since animals do not respect artificial, human, land boundaries.

[159](1) "family" means all persons related by blood, marriage, or adoption, or any person living within the household on a permanent basis; and(2) "barter" means the exchange of fish or wildlife or their parts, taken for subsistence uses—

> (A)for other fish or game or their parts; or
>
> (B)for other food or for nonedible items other than money if the exchange is of a limited and noncommercial nature.

[160]AS 16.05.940

> (26) "subsistence uses" means the customary and traditional uses in Alaska of wild renewable resources for direct personal or family consumption as food, shelter, fuel, clothing, tools, or transportation, for the making and selling of handicraft articles out of nonedible by-products of fish and wildlife resources taken for personal or family consumption, and for the customary trade, barter or sharing for personal or family consumption....

The terms "family" and "barter" are defined in the state statute in the same terms as in ANILCA. See note 159, above.

[161]See generally, Sen. Rept. (Energy and Natural Resources Committee) No. 96-413 (Nov. 14, 1979) at 233 (Reprinted in 1980 USCCAAN at 5177), discussing the reasons for limiting subsistence uses to "rural" residents.

¹⁶²Personal communication from Don Mitchell (May 1983). See also S. Rept. 96-413, above, at 268 (1980 USCCAAN at 5212, discussing the relationship between the state and federal definitions.

¹⁶³Id. at 269 (1980 USCCAAN at 5213).

¹⁶⁴Sen. Rept., note 161, above, at 233-234 (1980 USCCAAN at 5177-5178). The term "uses" also appears to include other forms and purposes of taking wildlife other than hunting and fishing for food. The state incorporated "customary trade" as one of the regulatory criteria for identifying" subsistence uses in 5 AAC 99.010(b)(7).

¹⁶⁵Subsistence use must also be "nonwasteful" as provided in section 804, although the term is not further defined.

¹⁶⁶See section 102(l), (2) and (3) (16 U.S.C.A. 3102[1], [2] and [3]), defining "land," "Federal land" and "public lands," respectively.

¹⁶⁷AS 16.05.251(b) (fish) and AS 16.05.255(b) (game). See also section 804 of ANILCA.

¹⁶⁸S. Rept. 96-413, note 161, above, in 1980 USCCAAN generally at 5213 and also at 5354-5355, the additional views of Senators Metzenbaum, Matsunaga, and Tsongas, noting that the preference is to be applied "on an ongoing basis" and not just when there is a threat to the resource. Compare also 5 AAC 99.010(d) with .010(e), requiring regulations "that provide an opportunity... for subsistence" but leaving it to board discretion whether to adopt regulations providing for non-subsistence uses.

¹⁶⁹S. Rpt. 96-413, note 161, above, at 233, and 235 and 269 (1980 USCCAAN at 5177, 5179 and 5213), discussing, respectively, the reasons for the addition of "rural resident" to the section 803 subsistence definition, the provisions limiting restrictions on non-subsistence taking in section 815(3) and the nature of the preference under section 804. See also, Op. Ak. Atty. Gen., "Subsistence law: real and perceived problems" (File No. 166-448-83, Feb. 25, 1983) at 12, concluding that the "priority becomes active if it is necessary to restrict the taking of fish and game." Compare, H. Rpt. No. 97-228 (Sep. 16, 1981) at 28 (1981 USCCAAN at 1478), comparing the ANILCA priority to the similar subsistence priority established under the 1981 amendments to the Marine Mammal Protection Act.

¹⁷⁰5 AAC 99.010 et seq. Approved pursuant to section 805 (d) of ANILCA by Secretary of the Interior Watt (letter of May 14, 1982).

¹⁷¹See S. Rpt. No. 96-413 note 161, above, in 1980 USCCAAN at 5178.

¹⁷²5 AAC 96.010 et seq.

¹⁷³Of course, state judicial remedies are also available; ANILCA does not require exclusive federal remedies. See generally, State v. Tanana Valley Sportsmen's Association, 582 P. 2d 854 (Ak. 1978), striking down improperly

promulgated (oral) permit system; Frank v. State, 604 P.2d 1068 (Ak. 1979), upholding Native taking of moose contrary to state season if for religious (potlatch) purposes.

[174]ANILCA establishes or expands nine parks and four park monuments in Alaska. See secs. 201 and 202 (94 Stat. 2377-2382).

[175]36 CFR Part 13 at sec. 13.42.

[176]Id. secs. 13.47, 13.48 and 13.49 respectively.

[177]Id. sec. 13.50.

[178]S. Rpt. 96-413, note 161, above, at 1980 USCCAAN 5178.

[179]Local Committees Assume New Significance on Issues," *Fairbanks Daily News-Miner,* Nov. 30, 1982, at 1 and 5. Section 805(e) requires the Secretary of the Interior to reimburse the state for up to fifty percent of the annual costs for establishing and maintaining the committee/council structure.

[180]A.S. 16.05.090; the duties of the subsistence division are spelled out in A.S. 16.05.094.

[181]E.g., Antoine v. Washington, 420 U.S. 194, 207 (1975).

[182]448 U.S. 136 (1980). Although *Bracker* involved state taxation of a federally regulated timber sale, the Ninth Circuit discussed and applied the Supreme Court's criteria in White Mountain Apache Tribe v. Arizona, 649 F.2d 1274 (9th Cir. 1981), a hunting and fishing regulation case. See also New Mexico v. Mescalero Apache Tribe,____U.S.____, 76 L. Ed. 2d 611 (1983), upholding exclusive tribal hunting and fishing jurisdiction on the reservation.

[183]Metlakatla v. Egan, 369 U.S. 552 (1962).

[184]369 U.S. 60 (1962). The communities of Kake and Metlakatla are both Alaska Native communities located in southeast Alaska. At the time of this litigation, both had profitable cannery operations which were largely dependent on fish traps for economical operation. Today Metlakatla is the only operational tribal cannery in Southeast Alaska and the only place in the state where taking salmon by trap is still allowed.

[185]Montana v. U.S., 450 U.S. 544.

[186]Menominee Tribe v. U.S., 391 U.S. 404 (1968); and Kimball v. Callahan, 493 F. 2d 564 (9th Cir.) cert. den., 419 U.S. 1019 (1974) and 590 F. 2d 768 (9th Cir.) cert. den., 444 U.S. 826 (1979), involving the Menominee and Klamath tribes, respectively, are the best known cases.

[187]Native American hunting and fishing rights which are unrecognized in a treaty, statute or agreement can be extinguished without compensation, F. Cohen, note 12, above, at 467-468. Except for Metlakatla and Klukwan, all the reserva-

tions in Alaska were created either by executive order or under the 1936 amendments applying the Indian Reorganization Act to Alaska. The U.S. Supreme Court has held that reservations created under either method are "temporary" and not subject to compensation upon extinguishment. See Sioux Tribe v. U.S., 316 U.S. 317 (1942) and Hynes v. Grimes Packing Co., 337 U.S. 86 (1949), respectively. See generally, D. Case, *The Special Relationship of Alaska Natives to the Federal Government,* (Anchorage: Alaska Native Foundation, 1978), at 31-43, discussing the pre-ANCSA Alaska reservations.

[188]Metlakatla was created by the Act of March 30, 1891, 25 Stat. 1101, 48 U.S.C. 358 (1970); Klukwan was enlarged and confirmed by Congress in 1957, 71 Stat. 596.

[189]Although the extinguishment of rights under ANCSA is extremely broad (43 USCA 1603), it is arguable that the abolition of the reserves (43 USCA 1618) does not specifically include reserved hunting and fishing rights. Even though all but two of those reserves were "temporary", it is certainly clear that even these included hunting and fishing rights. E.g., Hynes v. Grimes Packing Co., 337 U.S. 86 (1949), fishing rights on the Karluk IRA reserve. The U.S. Supreme Court has held that similar rights survive the termination of a reservation absent explicit extinguishment. *Menominee Tribe v. U.S.,* note 186, above. But see, U.S. v. Atlantic Richfield Co., 435 F. Supp. 1009 (D. Ak. 1977); aff'd, 612 F.2d 1132 (9th Cir. 1980); cert. denied, 449 U.S. 888 (1980), construing the broad extinguishment of claims under section 4(c) of ANCSA (43 USCA 1603[c]).

[190]Cheyenne-Arapaho Tribes v. Oklahoma, 618 F.2d 665 (10th Cir. 1980).

[191]Cheyenne-Arapaho Tribes v. Oklahoma, 681 F.2d 705 (10th Cir. 1982).

[192]18 U.S.C.A. sec. 1151. Although the term is defined in a criminal statute, it has been held applicable generally in civil matters as well. DeCoteau v. District County Court, 420 U.S. 425, 427 n.2 (1975), See also Moe v. Confederated Salish & Kootenai Tribes, 425 U.S. 463, 478-479 (1976).

[193]See generally, F. Cohen, note 12, above, at 27-46.

[194]U.S. v. Chavez, 290 U.S. 357 (1933).

[195]In Re McCord, 151 F. Supp. 132 (D.C. Ak. 1957).

[196]Johnson v. Chilkat Indian Village, 457 F. Supp. 384 (D.C. Ak. 1978).

[197]P.L. 280 (Act of August 15, 1953, 67 Stat. 588, now codified as amended to include Alaska in 18 U.S.C.A. 1162 and 28 U.S.C.A. 1360), transfers federal jurisdiction to adjudicate criminal and civil matters to the State, but provides that in civil matters:

> (c) Any tribal ordinance or custom heretofore or hereafter adopted by an Indian tribe, band or community in the exercise of any authority which it may possess shall, if not inconsistent with any applicable

civil law of the State, be given full force and effect in the determination of civil causes of action pursuant to this section. 28 U.S.C.A. 1360(c).

It is possible that in the absence of reservations this provision is also an expression of tribal-state concurrent jurisdiction.

[198]Act of Nov. 16, 1981, PL 97-79, 95 Stat. 1073 (16 USCA 3371 et seq.). See also, S. Rpt. 97-123 (May 21, 1981), explaining the purpose of the amendments (1981 USCCAAN 1748).

[199]16 USCA 3372.

[200]Id. 3371(c).

[201]Id. 3373 (penalties); 3374 (forfeiture), and 3375 (enforcement). See New Mexico v. Mescalero Apache Tribe,____U.S.____, 76 L. Ed. 2d 611, 51 USLW 4741, 4745 and 4746 (1983), discussing enhancement of tribal law under the Lacey Act.

[202]Id. 3378(c)(2) and (3). It is perhaps significant that the statute only disclaims modification of state or tribal authority on "reservations" and not "Indian country" generally since "Indian tribal law" is defined in terms of Indian country and not just reservations. See notes 199 and 200, above, and accompanying text.

[203] The Department of the Interior has concluded for other federal statutory purposes that Alaska Native villages and ANCSA lands constitute "dependent Indian communities." See discussion of "Indian country" in chapter 10, below.

[204]See note 197, above.

PART V

NATIVE SELF–GOVERNMENT

CHAPTER EIGHT

TRADITIONAL ALASKA NATIVE SOCIETIES

I. Introduction

Anthropological studies of the political systems of Alaska Native societies at and immediately following contact are rare at least; their absence represents a major gap in the literature. However, the absence of written material should not imply that the traditional societies were devoid of political structures and processes. All Alaska Native traditional societies had political systems (structures and processes) which governed their members and controlled individual behavior. These arrangements, like those in many other Native American societies, operated successfully in the absence of specialized political institutions or centralized state governments. Ideological beliefs and customary laws defining interpersonal relationships and spiritual relationships to the environment and wildlife created a tacit, yet powerful, sanction system which contributed to the maintenance of social order. Mechanisms for identifying a society's territory and political autonomy and for regulating external relationships with other societies existed in all culture groups.

As used here, "traditional" refers to the form of culture at the time of European contact. This chapter is based on data from early historical sources and information from Alaska Natives. The focus is on social and political systems in the five major culture areas of the state: (1) Southeast Alaskan Indians; (2) Athabaskans; (3) Aleuts; (4) Northwest Alaskan Inupiat Eskimos; and, (5) Southwest Alaskan Yupik Eskimos. Social and political systems in all human societies are closely related to economic systems; therefore, subsistence systems, including harvesting activities, distribution and exchange systems, settlement patterns, and associated land use are described to set the context for discussions of society and polity. Early changes subsequent to historical contact with westerners in each culture area are also discussed.

Because very detailed knowledge of traditional political systems is not always available, local variations in cultural patterns cannot be fully described. References cited, however, can be consulted for a more complete picture than can be described in this broad review. Much of the information presented here on traditional society (as well as changes during the early contact period) is the result of relatively recent anthropological studies. Some of these studies document the continuing persistence of many elements and forms of the traditional cultures as well as adaptation to changes created by contact with non-Natives. External challenges to Native village life have often been met by innovative responses or by incorporating western elements into traditional patterns.[1] A fuller understanding of Alaska Native village histories and cultures seems vital to an understanding of past successes and failures of the federal-Native relationship and to future improvement of that relationship for the benefit of all. This chapter is a modest contribution to that understanding.

II. Southeast Alaskan Indians

A. Subsistence

At contact in the last quarter of the eighteenth century, about ten thousand Tlingit Indians densely populated the coasts of southeast Alaska from Cape Fox to Yakutat Bay.[2] In the eighteenth and nineteenth centuries the Tlingit expanded to the Northwest into an area formerly occupied by the Eyak-speaking Indians whose territory thus became more restricted in the vicinity of the mouth of the Copper River.[3] Apparently in the latter half of the eighteenth century, Haida Indians from the Queen Charlotte Islands moved into Tlingit territory, inhabiting the southern portion of Prince of Wales Island.[4] Still later, in 1887, a group of Tsimshian Indians migrated from British Columbia to Tlingit territory on Annette Island, establishing New Metlakatla under the leadership of the Anglican missionary, William Duncan. In 1891, the island was made a reservation by act of Congress.[5]

The environment of southeast Alaska contained abundant and diverse resources in its coastal areas of dense western hemlock, Sitka spruce forests. The overwhelming orientation of southeast subsistence economies was to the sea, and the focus was on five species of salmon that annually migrate up freshwater streams to spawn. Other fish, such as cod, halibut, herring, eulachon, and shellfish were important supplements. Small sea mammals (principally seal and sea otter) and sea lion were exploited, particularly when other resources were scarce.[6]

Land resources also contributed to the diet. Black bear, black-tailed deer, mountain goat, porcupine, hare, and marmot were regularly hunted. In addition, in the mountains and in interior regions, moose, caribou, mountain sheep, and brown bear were taken. The forest provided many species of berries as well as a variety of greens and a number of fur-bearing animals that were hunted and trapped for their pelts. Wood products supplied raw materials for nearly all aspects of material culture (houses, dishes, containers, boats, totem poles).

Settlements in southeast Alaska were along shorelines and rivers. Each regional group, known as a *kwaan,* had one or more main winter settlements with large, permanent dwellings. Mainland Tlingit settlements were at the mouths of or along streams that contained salmon nearly year-round. Tlingits moved from these places to fish camps in May to harvest eulachon and render their oil. Some of the largest villages were on major river systems which also functioned as important trade routes to the interior; main island settlements were associated with deep-sea fishing. Families moved to salmon fishing camps in the summer (July), returning to the winter village in November. In areas where salmon was not as abundant, the inhabitants occupied spring sealing camps (generally in March) until summer salmon fishing began.[7]

B. Social and Political Organization

Throughout southeast Alaska, Indian society was organized by a matrilineal family system. The largest family group of all four societies was a collection of exogamous matrilineal clans (unilineal groups of relatives tracing descent from common ancestors through the mother). Among the Eyak, Tlingit, and Haida, the clans were grouped into moieties. Tsimshian clans were organized into four large groups (phratries). Tlingit society is described here as representative of general southeast Indian culture.[8]

At contact, the Tlingit were divided between two large moieties— Raven and Wolf (the designation Eagle replaced Wolf in the historic period). Each contained over twenty *naa* (matrilineal clans).[9] These social groupings functioned to formally regulate the institution of marriage and to define ceremonial activities. Clans from opposite moieties often formed alliances. Clans and their local divisions, which were made up of one or more *hit* housegroups or houses, figured prominently in Tlingit political organization. In addition to membership in a moiety and a clan which was determined by the matrilineal descent system, each Tlingit also belonged to one of about eighteen to twenty *kwaan,* large territorial groups. Since clans and moieties were exogamous groups, each kwaan, like each housegroup, always had members from each moiety and from at least two clans. Most clans were affiliated with one kwaan; with some of the larger found in more than one such territorial group.[10]

Each kwaan had one to several permanent winter villages, a well-defined territory, and a local linguistic identity name, such as Chilkat kwaan (Haines and Klukwan), Auke kwaan (Juneau). While demographic estimates are highly variable, the evidence suggests that the population of many kwaans was substantial. For example, the Hoonah people numbered between five hundred and nine hundred. Within these territories, clans and houses lawfully owned specific hunting, fishing, and ceremonial gathering sites. Sites which were prominent in clan history were also owned. They defended their property militarily when necessary. Clan leaders, with consent of other clan members, could sell clan-owned land. This included not only "land" but associated resources and offshore waters and their resources.[11]

Clans and houses, functioning as property-owning units in society, also owned diverse kinds of material and non-material items, such as rights to certain names, titles, "crests" (which were material representations of events associated with family history), dances, and ceremonial objects. Property rights were recounted in clan histories to sanction their association with a particular house or clan. "Property relationships among the Tlingit, while formed by economic considerations, are made binding by the legal sanctions of their social organization and the religious sanctions embodied in their belief system."[12]

Each village contained local divisions of clans whose housegroups were composed of individuals sharing a large wooden plank house. House populations ranged from about ten to forty people, and were formed around a core of matrilineally related men, such as brothers and their sisters' sons, and their respective spouses and children. Wives, nonetheless, maintained loyalty to their own clans.

The housegroup was the basic economic unit in society, with members having specialized skills.[13] Men in each housegroup had rights to specified portions of land through their clan membership. Other clan members were expected to ask permission to use these areas if such a need arose. The housegroup itself owned valuable commodities that its members used, such as large canoes, ceremonial objects, and utensils. Inheritance rules and marriage rules functioned to maintain and accumulate all forms of property within the housegroup. Housegroup members also harvested resources together and provided food and goods that were consumed communally within the house. Individuals had their own property, such as clothes and tools, but the economic security of the housegroup figured above individual interests. Housegroups were also units for purposes of resolving disputes, and they often initiated potlatches or feasts.

Social rank was an important feature of Tlingit society, cross-cutting family affiliation.[14] Houses within a local clan division were ranked, as were local clans themselves. Ranking was based on a group's relative success in accumulating and displaying wealth within a competitive social and economic context; potlatches provided an arena for such competition. Members of the highest ranked clans had considerable social prestige and constituted a "noble" class. However, rigidly defined classes in the sense of a "caste" system did not exist. The ranking system was disputed continually and required validation at potlatches.

Leading housegroups (the nobles) in the leading local division of a clan were usually closely related. This was accomplished through marriage arrangements that paired them as spouse-givers and spouse-receivers. Social and ceremonial obligations, such as those connected with housebuilding and funerals provided the framework for interaction between paired (and other) houses in different clans in opposite moieties. Local clans sometimes cooperated in tasks benefiting the whole village, such as clearing trails, and defending the village against invaders. However, one's loyalties were primarily to one's own clan and were "class"-oriented. Loyalty to one's own clan and the desire to maintain or achieve high status for one's family housegroup functioned to produce a leading house in each moiety in each village. Other houses and their respective clans were also graded. The institution of slavery was another major feature of Tlingit society. Slaves were not considered clan members, but were treated as property; they were usually taken as prisoners of war or purchased from other groups, mainly through southern trade.

Generally, the eldest male in a housegroup was its ceremonial leader and represented the house to other houses in the clan. *Hit s'aati* (housekeepers) of ranking houses were recognized as nobles or *aan Yadi*; (rich men); they were important in clan ceremony and might call other housekeepers together to discuss clan disputes. Dispute resolution within a clan and between clans was the prerogative of clan leaders and decisions were final. "In Tlingit law the clan is the ultimate source of political power."[15]

Political organization among the Haida and Tsimshian was similar to that of the Tlingit, with local clan divisions acting as political units. However, sometime before contact certain Tsimshian groups in Canada developed the institution of the village chief, who was the head of a dominant, wealthy clan in a village.[16] It is also reported that a "moiety chief" acted as the single political leader for one Eyak village, which contained two moiety leaders. But Tlingit and Eyak villages also had a "peacemaker," who settled disputes. His position was marked by possession of a special paddle.[17] In summary, with the exception of some Tsimshian villages, the basic political units among southeast Alaskan Indian societies were the local clan division and house group, each of which possessed self-governing, autonomous powers.

C. Early Contact Government

Early contacts with English, Spanish, American, and Russian explorers in the latter half of the eighteenth century were not unfriendly; the Tlingit engaged in profitable trading with the newcomers who were competing with one another for the Indian trade.[18] In marked contrast, Tlingit contacts with Russians at the end of the century were hostile due to Russian attemps colonize in Tlingit territory; for example, Tlingits destroyed the Russian forts at Yakutat and at Sitka. Although the Russians were eventually successful in negotiating to establish settlements in Tlingit territory, the major effects of Russian presence were changes in the Tlingit material culture. Russian efforts to Christianize the Tlingit were not very successful, and they never succeeded in establishing political control over local populations.[18] The wealth and local prestige of Tlingit leaders was enhanced by their role as "middlemen" in the fur trade between Europeans on the coast and the interior Athabaskan fur trappers.[19] Ceremonial activity became more elaborate with the addition of this newfound wealth. However this same period also saw a substantial population loss, especially due to a smallpox epidemic in the region between 1836 and 1840; it is estimated that one-half of the Tlingit population at or near Sitka was lost.[20]

Later Tlingit contacts with Americans, like those with the Russians, were not friendly. However, local populations soon became impressed with the military strength and technological weaponry of Americans. For example, the Americans destroyed thirty-five Indian houses as well as canoes and two forts in 1869 in reprisal for the alleged murder of two white men.[21] The destruction of Angoon in 1882 due to a disagreement over the death of two Indians further established American power in the area.[22]

Changes during the early American period, especially in the 1870's and 1880's were rapid. They were directly related to non-Native population expansion connected with the development of commercial fisheries, mining, and the timber industry. "The year 1878 stands as an important turning point, for in that year the first fish canneries were established in Alaska (at Klawock and Sitka) as well as the first full-fledged gold camp (at Windham Bay or "Shuck"). The first in a series of new American settlements also appeared in 1878 with the establishment of a Presbyterian mission station at the site of the present town of Haines."[23]

Commercial economic activities, accompanied by new settlements, such as Juneau (1880) and Ketchikan (1888), encroached seriously on Tlingit and Haida lands and economic systems. In some areas, their subsistence base was quickly shattered due to loss of hunting areas, salmon streams and the depletion of salmon stocks with the introduction of fish traps. In many areas, however, the Native economy continued to be centered on fishing. Wage employment, especially work in the canneries or mines, became more common, and a mixed cash-subsistence based economy developed which has persisted in some areas until today.

Another consequence of economic change was increasing concentration of settlements. This process which took place within kwaans was part of an earlier trend that became intensified during the early American period. Factors leading to concentration included population reduction, destruction of the resource base in some areas, external pressure from non-Natives (missionaries and government), the economic advantages of living near white settlements, and more efficient boats, permitting considerable travel from a central place.[24] People who tended to stay within their *kwaan* territories retained their group cohesiveness; a survey in 1946 indicated remarkable cultural vitality for such groups since the earliest available records.[25]

Missionary schools also were a major source of change in southeastern Alaska; most communities had a school by 1890.[26] American missionary efforts in Alaska, led by the Presbyterian Sheldon Jackson in the last decades of the 19th century, were extraordinary in their zeal and devastating in their effects on Native language and culture,[27] which were viewed by American missionaries and government officials as detrimental to the acculturation of Natives into American society. By the end of the century, most Indians had been converted, and gradually these came to view schools as a major avenue to self-determination, as discussed below.

Although economic and religious changes were very apparent by 1900, the clan organization remained intact. Clan leaders were important throughout the latter half of the nineteenth century as the contact points with agents of the American government. For example, in 1879, a U.S. Naval Commander solicited the help of two Tlingit clan leaders to form a council of chiefs to act as a judicial body responsible for local Indians.[28] Similarily, in 1890, a Tlingit clan leader was hired by a local factory to keep order among its employees and in the nearby villages.[29] Many clan leaders cooperated with whites primarily because they were concerned about the deteriorating economic situation of the Indian societies. Hence, some of the strongest supporters of the American government and the missionaries were important clan leaders who believed change was inevitable and that education offered through the church was a prerequisite to future survival. This principle is amply demonstrated by the decision of several Haida villages (with the urging of the federal Bureau of Education) to form a municipality (Hydaburg) in 1911 to improve their educational opportunities.[30]

Through participation in church clubs, Indians learned parliamentary prodedures and the principles of elective government. The Tsimshian in New Metlakatla came to Alaska in 1887 with a basic understanding of Western representative government as taught to them by their missionary leader, William Duncan. Consequently the new town had a council and elected policemen, firemen, and churchmen, although elected Native officials reportedly served subject to Duncan's approval.[31] Many Tlingit villages organized municipal governments under the Organized Village Act of 1910. The Alaska Native Brotherhood was established in 1912 with nine Tlingit and one Tsimshian member. Its stance was pro-change to be accomplished by education, attainment of citizenship, and modification of traditional customs.[32] The popularity of the organization, which was joined by nearly all Tlingit and Haida men, illustrates the magnitude of the change during the previous forty years by the very fact that a non-kinship based voluntary organization could assume a major political role, cross-cutting traditional social divisions and affiliations. The organization, along with the associated Alaska Native Sisterhood, still plays a significant social and political role in southeast Alaskan communities. (See chapter 9)

In recent years, well-known Alaska Native leaders from southeast Alaska such as the late William Paul, Sr., the first Alaska Native elected to the territorial legislature, have applauded the early emphasis on education in the region by pointing out that the first Alaska Native nurses, teachers, lawyers and legislators came from southeast Alaska. Accomplishments within white society, however, have not detracted from many basic Tlingit beliefs. As William Paul, Sr. noted, "Tlingits are their own governors, which is the purest democracy. Their link to their origins is one of respect; indeed that is the basis of Tlingit law."[33]

III. Northern Athabaskan Indians

A. Subsistence

At contact, Northern Athabaskan-speaking Indians occupied nearly all of interior Alaska, making this language group the most widespread in terms of total land area in the state.[34] Although population estimates are not reliable, Northern Athabaskans in Alaska probably did not exceed a total of around thirteen thousand people spread over a wide area.[35] First contact varied greaty from place to place. For example, some Tanaina groups, had direct contact by the late nineteenth century; others, like some Koyukon people, had little direct contact until the time of the gold rush at the beginning of this century. All, however, had indirect contact through Western trade goods long before they met many white people.[36]

The environment in the interior boreal forest is harsh; it did not lavishly support people whose subsistence was based on hunting, fishing, and gathering. A basic feature of the ecology is that resources are concentrated in habitats that are not uniformly distributed in the forest. Another feature of the ecology is cyclic fluctuations in population size of major resources. In fact, one investigator has determined that of the nineteen resources regularly used in one area, six are characterized by wide shifts in availability and another ten by moderate shifts.[37] Hence, the total population of a species and the numbers of different species available over time commonly show dramatic fluctuations. From historic data it is also known that the distribution of some resources changed. As a result, human populations were widely dispersed and highly mobile, with an estimated population density ranging from 1 to 1.4 persons per 100 square miles.[38] Through the use of strategic hunting, fishing, and gathering, people carefully scheduled their movements in order to harvest fish and game when species populations were together in large numbers and most accessible.[39] Although the culture was adapted to these uncertain ecological features, embodying alternative subsistence strategies, periods of scarcity were not unknown. Relative to other areas of Alaska, the subsistence quest in the boreal forest was a sometimes marginal system requiring intimate knowledge of the environment and flexibility.

With the exception of some of the Tanaina in the Cook Inlet region, who had direct access to marine mammals and shellfish, and the Ingalik along the lower Yukon River, who occasionally obtained sea mammals and could subsist on large salmon harvests, Northern Athabaskan societies depended on a large number of interior forest animal and fish species. For example, the Koyukon Indians in the Koyukuk River region regularly harvested ten species of mammals and over thirty species of birds.[40] Large game, such as moose, black and brown bear, caribou, and Dall sheep were important whenever available, as well as smaller mammals such as hare, beaver, muskrat, and porcupine, and birds (especially waterfowl, grouse and ptarmigan). In most areas, beaver and muskrat played substantial roles in the economy for both food and clothing. Hare, grouse, and ptarmigan, all of which have sharp fluctuations in abundance, often assumed critical importance in the absence of larger mammals. At least nine species of fur bearers, such as wolf, wolverine, marten, and mink were also trapped. Fish were a major resource everywhere; in addition to anadromous salmon and whitefish, the Athabaskans harvested at least ten other species when available, including blackfish from the lakes during hard times in the Northern areas.[41]

Settlement patterns varied considerably and reflected the quantity and distribution of resources in an area. Similar to other Pacific rim societies, Athabaskans in the Cook Inlet area were relatively sedentary, occupying winter villages and summer fish camps. Inland riverine groups, such as those of the Ahtna along the Copper River, were more mobile using winter villages, spring camps, and summer fish camps. The most mobile societies were northern interior groups, whose constant food quest required multiple settlements, including a winter settlement and numerous other task-specific seasonal camps throughout the year. The largest settlements (about one hundred people) were on the coast in the Cook Inlet area; the smallest (no more than about sixty-five) people were in the interior in areas lacking salmon. [42]

B. Social and Political Organization

Although the nature of Northern Athabaskan social and political organization has been debated in anthropology for many years, it seems clear that the basic social and political unit throughout the area was the band. Band societies were made up primarily of persons related by blood and marriage. Local band organization also defined both a linguistic community and a subsistence-use area with well known boundaries. In most areas, band territory was open to all members of the band for subsistence activities; however, in at least two regions, use rights to parts of a band territory were controlled by particular families, although this may be an artifact of the early fur trade era (1850-1880). "Among the Koyukun, beaver houses and ponds, muskrat swamps, fishing locations, bear hibernation holes, certain big game territories where hunting corrals were built, berrying grounds adjacent to fish camps and some bird hunting areas were privately held."[43] Even in these cases, use rights of land seem not to have been permanent; vacation of a site opened it for others. And ownership of an artifact such as a fish trap carried with it the obligation of providing for others. There are also reports of family control through matrilineal clans of hunting and fishing areas for the Cook Inlet Tanaina. [44]

Band territory was ordinarily closed to other groups unless permission was granted for use. For example, among the Ahtna, "a stranger speaking an alien tongue and lacking a proper introduction risked being killed on sight."[45] However, in many cases, long-term arrangements existed between adjacent bands that permitted exploitation of a resource (especially caribou) in an area other than one's own if that resource was lacking in a person's home area. [46]

Each band had at least one named major settlement where the society congregated, especially in mid-winter for social and ceremonial activity. Often this settlement was associated with a nearby named landmark. For example, in the Tanana River region and the Copper River area, major band settlements were located near hills that were "honored in potlatch songs and oratory as the 'grandfather's face' of the village people."[47] Family organization in most areas was matrilineal, and clan organization cross-cut band boundaries.[48] So, although an individual belonged to a particular band society, he or she also had numerous clan relatives in other bands. This assured welcome when an individual went to a strange village; upon indication of a visitor's clan, village members of the same clan would provide food, shelter and protection. In some areas, such as Copper River, clans were grouped in a dual division (a moiety organization) like that described earlier for Tlingit society. It functioned to define reciprocal duties and obligations between two different but cooperating social groups within band society. Moieties and clans defined one's relatives as well as those individuals a person could not marry. They also functioned to organize labor and duties at times of life crises, especially death. In areas with matrilineal clans, the basic principles of dual structure appear to underlie the social organization, even when a moiety structure is ill-defined.

Each major band settlement had a "chief" who was its recognized leader. Although the term "chief" is used in the literature, aboriginally this individual is more properly referred to as an authority which more closely fits the meaning of the Athabaskan term *kkuskkaa* used for this person throughout the area.[50] Chiefs were expected to be wise and generous, and often had supernatural (shamanistic) powers, expressing important Athabaskan ideals. Their authority was also derived from their economic success as demonstrated to the society through gift-giving at potlatches. Although the support of a large family or one's clan was important in achieving and maintaining recognition as a leader, unlike ranked societies, leadership did not automatically pass through family lines, but rather was based on demonstrated ability. However, in most, if not all, areas leadership tended to be associated with certain families, chiefly succession ultimately depending on individual qualities and on the voluntary cooperation of band members.

Leadership was more formal and elaborate among the Southern Athabaskan ranked societies of the Ahtna and Tanaina.[51] Chiefs could command the labor of their followers as well as of their slaves received in trade or war; their families also constituted a privileged group of high rank. Chiefs were also at the center of a trading and sharing network, which channelled resources to them for redistribution within society.

Within all Athabaskan band societies social control was primarily a family matter, although leaders played a role in internal dispute resolution and occasionally acted as negotiators with chiefs from other societies. Among the Ahtna, the chief was responsible for enforcing the traditional 'law' within his own settlement and for defending his people in legitimate grievances involving other groups. Deliberate murder and theft of food were punishable by death, and a chief might order the execution of a troublemaker unless he escaped to relatives in a distant place.[52] Among the lower Yukon Ingalik, meetings of all men and female elders were held to discuss transgressors and banishment or death were possible penalties.[53] Murder in all Northern Athabaskan societies was punishable by death but, unlike the Ahtna, most groups made the decision to execute and the delivery of punishment the responsibility of a family group. Although the degree of political control exercised on a community level reported for the more sedentary Ahtna and Ingalik groups are unusual in Athabaskan culture, leaders everywhere functioned to maintain peace within the society.

Social control was achieved by a number of informal sometimes subtle mechanisms. Children were taught that their words would travel far and, therefore, they should think carefully before speaking. Social avoidance mechanisms also acted to prevent confrontation or disharmony among closely related people. When two individuals had a problem, their families could simply move elsewhere to let time render the conflict less important. [54]

Throughout interior Alaska, local Northern Athabaskan bands were joined in loose regional groupings created by marriage and trading. These larger groups generally circumscribed a marriage universe from which spouses were sought, a language community containing loosely related dialects, and social boundaries, within which war did not usually occur. Interestingly, in the upper Yukon-Porcupine River area, the more nomadic Kutchin regional groups appear to have functioned somewhat differently. People from local bands would regularly join together for temporary economic or ritual activities, as well as for war, thus suggesting that the regional society was more important than in other Athabaskan areas of Alaska. Recognized leaders, however, were associated with local groups as in other areas. [55]

C. Early Contact Government

By 1850, most Northern Athabaskans in Alaska had experienced some form of contact, at least through trade. Yet in some places sustained contact did not begin until the late nineteenth or early twentieth century. People were drawn into the fur trade system, and a settling-in around trading posts and missions eventually led to the development of predominantly all-Native villages with more or less sedentary populations throughout the year. Although in some areas the process of centralization was not complete until the 1940's, with portions of local bands still living primarily away from the new settlements, in the late nineteenth and early twentieth centuries, the number of traditional settlements in all areas diminished due to disease, which everywhere took its toll, and to the process of village centralization. However, traditional cultural/linguistic boundaries were maintained, particularly with regard to resource harvesting.

During the Russian period (?-1867), trading company managers and Russian Orthodox priests in the Tanaina area appointed traditional leaders (*qeshqa* or "rich man") as chiefs, who they gave the title, *tayen,* (locally called *duyeg*), as they had done elsewhere along the Pacific rim. Sources indicate that the "chief " had no power unless he was also a successful traditional leader, and the Indians always made a sharp linguistic distinction between the two roles, as they still do today.[56]

The introduction of the fur trade during the Russian and early American (1867-1880) periods served to strengthen the traditional institution of "rich man" to the point that in some areas individuals were able to extend their influence to societies other than their own. This was accomplished through successful manipulation of trading relationships, setting up a network controlled by the chief who established himself as the middleman between the white traders and Native trappers. Later, however, the proliferation of trading posts in the late nineteenth century increased individual accessibility to European traders and immediately reduced the power of the trading chief. At about the same time, community leadership roles were weakened in some areas when the band societies, which had been dominated by a major family (clan in some areas) and its affinal (in-law) relatives, changed to a composite of several major families.

Although in some areas elected chiefs and councils were introduced early in the century by territorial officials or by church representatives,[57] traditional leadership is still recognized in Athabaskan societies. In 1915, traditional chiefs from the lower Tanana River region met with Judge Wickersham in Fairbanks to discuss land claims, and educational and employment issues.[58] As a result of the meeting, the political organization of at least one community, Nenana, was altered by the introduction of an elected chief and council.[59] During a community meeting in Nenana following the Fairbanks meeting, young men who had been to Fairbanks with the chiefs told the community the whites wanted an elected chief and council. The traditional chief rose and pointed out he had always been their chief and objected to the idea. After considerable discussion, it was agreed that a "working chief" would be elected to represent the community but that he would in no way displace the traditional chief. This incident also dates the beginning of an elected "traditional council" in this portion of the river. Data on the contact history of political organization in other Athabaskan communities are lacking. However, the case study of Nenana is probably not unlike the sequence of events in other similar communities. In interior Alaska today, traditional leaders, who do not always occupy formal positions on elected councils, receive widespread local and regional recognition and are referred to locally as "chiefs."

IV. Aleuts

A. Subsistence

At the time of sustained Russian contact beginning in 1744, Aleut populations were distributed along the western portion of the Alaska Peninsula, and on every major island having adequate fresh water throughout the Aleutian chain to Attu. The population of the Aleutian Islands was about sixteen thousand at contact.[60] The population density reflects the wealth of natural resources available to hunting and gathering populations in the region.

Aleut subsistence was based on marine resources, many of which were obtained by the development of a complex technology related to open sea kayak hunting. The harvest of 1) resident and migratory sea mammals, especially fur seals, sea otters, sea lions, and whales; 2) deep sea fish such as halibut and cod; 3) sea urchins, octopus, and seaweeds from reef systems at low tide and shellfish from tidal pools; and 4) many kinds of birds and eggs all contributed to a substantial and reliable economic base and allowed an accumulation of surplus. Although land resources (fuel for heat, grasses for weaving, and a few food plants) were used, sustenance ultimately depended on marine resources which provided not only food but most raw materials for clothing, houses, and tools.[61]

The settlement pattern included long-established, stable winter and summer settlements and seasonally used camps. Winter villages were situated on the Bering Sea side of the islands along the shoreline, at places near food sources, good landing beaches, and fresh water, on narrow necks of land with access to two water bodies, which provided an escape route in the event of attack.[62] The optimal environmental conditions for traditional settlements were in the eastern Aleutians (Andreanof and Fox Islands), where well-protected coastlines existed with reefs and bays providing significant resources. About three-fifths of the population was clustered here and on the Alaska Peninsula at the time of contact.[63]

B. Social and Political Organization

Data on aspects of traditionl Aleut culture, other than subsistence, are somewhat incomplete. However, ethnohistoric research provides some broad outlines of Aleut social and political organization. Each island society had permanent, named villages, occupied winter and summer, and families might occupy seasonal subsistence sites.[64] An average winter village in the eastern Aleutians contained large communal houses, occupied by related families, as well as smaller residences. Summer dwellings tended to be smaller, perhaps housing an individual nuclear (often polygynous) family. Village size ranged up to two hundred to three hundred persons. Single family dwellings in winter and summer villages were more common in the western Aleutians, where villages averaged about sixty persons.[65] Each village had a specified territory; its boundaries were carefully scrutinized daily by a scanning system employing permanent look-out stations from which invaders could be spotted. The territory was a resource use area which excluded other Aleut groups unless they received permission from the resident society.[66]

Information on family organization from early sources is particularly confusing and sometimes contradictory. Family relationships traced through the mother apparently were very important, as evidenced by the significance of the mother's brother in the historic family system. Some sources suggest the existence of a clan organization but others do not.[67] Whether the uncertainties about family structure derive from incomplete or inaccurate reporting, or whether the family system was undergoing a transition at the time of contact has not been fully resolved.

Social ranking was an important organizational principle in the society, as it was with other traditional Alaskan societies of the North Pacific rim,[68] and early sources speak of an Aleut "class system." Analyses of available data, however, suggests a two-class system of "free" Aleuts and slaves, primarily war captives.[69] Each village had a dominant family that claimed status due to its wealth and local history. This family provided the village leader, or chief, with authority to organize economic activities, settle internal disputes, lead in time of war, and direct the protection of group boundaries.[70] In the more populous eastern Aleutians, several villages were affiliated with an overall leader, chosen from among the leaders of individual villages. His "sole function, as far as we know, was to declare war and establish peace."[71]

Village chiefs represented their villages and were the formal links between local groups. Alliances between villages were established by marriage and trade, especially between the families of leaders, and were maintained by ceremonial feasting ("potlatches"). Apparently, some villages or island societies established long-term peaceful relationships while maintaining equally long-lasting hostilities with others.

Dispute resolution within a society in the eastern Aleutians was directed primarily at reestablishing social harmony rather than imposing a punishment. However, for some crimes, such as murder or theft, group sanctions were applied. Penalties could be severe and the repeat offender might be put to death by decision of the village chief and other elders, respected for the wisdom associated with their age. In the smaller populations of the western Aleutians, family rather than community resolution of internal village conflict was the rule.[72]

In addition to the formal structure of political control, Aleut culture, like other traditional cultures, contained many informal mechanisms of social control that promoted peace within a village society. Every individual operated within a broad circle of well-known people encountered in everyday life, and the social system defined categories of people based on age, sex, kinship, and prestige to whom very specific codes of behavior and reciprocal obligations applied. Families tacitly controlled the behavior of their members through the enactment of cultural conventions. The institution of feuding, (the practice of the victim's family assuming responsibility for taking revenge in kind on an offender from another family) both created and resolved conflict between families, but also served to restrict individual behavior. Aleut communication patterns also tended to avoid personal confrontations. "Aleuts followed two rules in this respect: (1) if they had nothing worthwhile to say about someone or something, they said nothing; and (2) if they had nothing to say, they said nothing."[73] Potentially disruptive situations in the economic sphere, both within and between villages, were avoided by the institution of "polite barter" for trade, employing an intermediary who worked out the exchange. Finally, religious as well as secular ideological beliefs outlined penalties for transgressions. Disregard for valued beliefs led to shame and public sanction in the form of loss of esteem or severe chastisement. [74]

In sum, while the Aleuts evolved an effective system of formal internal self-government through their village and island social and political structures, many other aspects of the culture channeled individual behavior toward cooperation and maintenance of smoothly funtioning society. As William S. Laughlin described it:

> The architects of Aleutian culture designed a series of patterns for living that provided law without lawyers and leaders without elections. The codes for conduct were drilled into each individual. Like Swiss watches, each Aleut had his own mainspring. With proper oiling, occasional resetting, and daily winding, he performed as his cultural preceptors had designed him to perform. [75]

C. Early Contact Government

Substantial changes occurred in the Aleutians during the Russian period (1744-1867), the most significant of which was the reduction of the population to about one-fifth its former size in the first 75 years, primarily due to introduced infectious diseases. [76] Many Aleuts were also slain in the early years. The Russian mercantile policy was designed to utilize Aleuts to hunt sea otters along the entire Prince William Sound area and into Southeast Alaska. Aleuts were also used for warfare with the Tlingit who resisted Russian expansion into their territories. To capitalize on the abundant fur seal population in the Pribilof Islands, Aleuts, primarily from Atka and Unalaska were forced to re-settle, occupying these islands permanently for the first time. Elsewhere, settlements were consolidated and moved to the mouths of rivers, households were reduced to nuclear family dwellings, and warfare was prohibited. [77]

Village chieftainship was supported by the Russians since they required the cooperation of a local leader in the organization of local labor. Initially, family relationship to traditional chiefs was a disadvantage since, during the early contact period, relatives from dominant families were taken as hostages to be returned at the completion of hunting activities. Later in the period, however, relatives of chiefs taken as hostages were sometimes sent to Russia for education; some of these individuals eventually returned to act as mediators between the Russians and Aleuts. [78] Russian managers, in general, claimed the right to appoint and remove chiefs and denied them a role in local conflict resolution if a Russian or Creole (part-Russian, part-Native) was involved. [79]

According to one analysis, by 1830 conditions had stabilized under the Russian American Company and the Russian Orthodox Church.

> The Aleuts in Company employ received salaries; indepen-
> dent villages were paid for their furs in accordance with an es-
> tablished schedule of payments; social advancement was pos-
> sible; Aleuts and Creoles—that is persons who could claim at
> least one Russian ancestor—occupied managerial, decision-
> making positions....Soon the clergy numbered several Aleuts
> in its ranks,...Several Aleuts became paramedics or assistant
> physicians.[80]

In summary, during the Russian period, decimation of the Aleut population along with major changes in the areas of technology, settlement pattern, family organization, and religion seriously disrupted cultural continuity. However, some basic institutions of Aleut culture survived as did the language; in fact, Aleut literacy developed and flourished under the guidance of the Russian Orthodox priests.[81] At the close of the period a new cultural tradition had emerged, incorporating aspects of Russian and traditional Aleut heritages.

As with the early Russian period, the early American period (1867-1910) was characterized by uncontrolled commercial exploitation of marine mammals, particularly whales, seals and sea otters. The total (otter and seal) harvest between 1867 and 1890 exceeded that of Russian commerce of the previous 125 years, resulting in the near extinction of both species. This situation was checked in 1911 by a treaty among the United States, Russia, Canada and Japan, regulating the harvest of both the sea otter and fur seal.[82]

The continued disruption of Aleut life was exacerbated during World War II with the removal of most of the islands' populations in 1942 to southeast Alaska. Only about one-half of the refugees returned to the islands after the war. Those who did found that most traditional Aleut villages had been destroyed. For example, American forces had bombed Attu in attempting to retake the village from the Japanese and had burned Atka to prevent its occupation. Government officials discouraged the resettlement of some of the smaller or more remote islands, such as Attu, Biroka and Kashega because of administrative problems in delivering educational and other services.[83] Hence, today many villages in the Aleutians represent new societies containing a mix of descendants from formerly distinct Aleut island groups. Many leaders and elders died in southeast Alaska leaving the societies without access to traditional knowledge and values. "Survivors were hard put to pass on even basic survival skills—trapping, weaving, and sewing—to a generation of uprooted youngsters."[84]

Today, Aleuts control most of the private land in the islands, and supported by surviving village elders who provide traditional authority, a new young leadership struggles to provide the means to maintain village life within the context of uncertain economic conditions. As Larry Merculieff, president of the St. Paul village corporation in the Pribilofs, comments—"Aleuts have lived under the harshest of conditions in the most trying of circumstances for 10,000 years, and they have confidence in their abilities to survive in a new world of their own making."[85]

V. North Alaskan Inupiat Eskimos

A. Subsistence

Prior to contact, north Alaskan societies who referred to themselves as Inupiat—the "real people," inhabited and utilized the coastal region and portions of the interior in north Alaska from Barter Island near the Alaska-Canada border to the northern shore of Norton Sound. According to conservative estimates, more than six thousand people occupied this vast area in the mid-nineteenth century.[86] After contact (about 1850 for most of the region), Inupiaq populations in Alaska expanded south around Norton Sound to Unalakleet and north and east to Canada.

North Alaska is far from uniform in the distribution of wildlife resources. Ecological variations contributed to the development of many distinctive social patterns and annual cycles. Annual harvest cycles were adapted to the "relative abundance of animals and their migratory patterns. Environmental conditions, including wind, current, snow and all the movement of sea ice also affected hunting patterns."[87]

Everywhere, the Inupiat intensively harvested most available resources for food and raw materials for clothing, tools, housing, and fuel. The predominant orientation was to the sea and rivers. Nearly all societies relied on the harvesting of large or small sea mammals, fish and waterfowl. All societies hunted caribou, the skins of which were especially suitable for arctic winter clothing. In some inland areas, caribou hunting dominated the subsistence system. Three patterns broadly define Inupiat subsistence orientations. The following description reviews the characteristics of each of these patterns, but it does not represent an exhaustive discussion of the known characteristics of each type.

1. Large Sea Mammal Hunters

Large sea mammal hunters depended primarily on the harvest of the bowhead whale and/or the Pacific walrus during their migrations. The largest settlements in north Alaska were associated with large sea mammal hunting. Islands in the Bering Strait (such as King and Diomede islands) and mainland promontories (such as Cape Prince of Wales, Point Hope, and Point Barrow) provided locations with direct access to the migration routes of large marine mammals. These major resources were supplemented by a range of other wildlife resources, which varied in each area. For example, the people of Point Hope hunted bowhead whale, walrus, and beluga. In addition, they regularly hunted "three species of seal, caribou, eight species of fur-bearing animals, polar and grizzly bear, fourteen species of fish, twenty-five species of birds, and twelve species of invertebrates".[88] In the most northern coastal areas bowhead whale hunting was traditionally the most prestigeous hunting activity and was associated with a highly complex technology integrated into an elaborate ceremonial life. On some of the Bering Strait islands, the Pacific walrus was the primary resource and was central to social and cultural activities.[89]

2. Small Sea Mammal Hunters and Fishers

Small sea mammal hunters and fishers (such as those on the Seward Peninsula area at Teller and Shishmaref, farther north along the northern shore of Kotzebue Sound and the Lower Noatak River, and south along Norton Sound) relied primarily on seals, fish, and caribou, with the relative importance of other resources depended on local environments. For example, sealing which occurred nearly year-round was a primary economic activity for Shishmaref society. In contrast, the Kotzebue Sound people spent most of the fall and winter fishing and hunting caribou and small game, sealing in spring on the ice, and hunting beluga in the sound after breakup.

3. Inland Caribou Hunters

Inland Inupiat relied heavily on winter caribou hunting, with secondary reliance on several species of salmon and whitefish and sea mammals, such as seal and beluga. Some societies on the Seward Peninsula and some farther north in the Utukok River drainage and the Upper Noatak region were also dependent on caribou. They also relied heavily on fish and small game. Sea mammals were more important in the first two areas than in the Upper Noatak region, where hunters pursued only beluga in Kotzebue Sound.

In addition to sea and land animals, berries, roots, and greens provided supplements to the diet. Although their relative abundance in the total annual dietary intake was low, some were important sources of vitamin C and other nutrients. They also provided welcome variation in the diet and a source of food when major migratory species were unavailable or available only in small numbers. Major migratory species were only available seasonally, demanding specialized cooperative hunting patterns and highly specific patterns of movement to maximize harvest efforts. Some important food resources, such as caribou and salmon and small game can vary considerably in abundance year to year. Variable weather and sea ice conditions can also severely restrict human access to food resources such as sea mammals. These variations created periods of scarcity and sometimes famine.

A major change in north Alaska occurred between 1850 and 1860 when the caribou population began to decline, apparently the result of a long- term population cycle. In addition, the commercial whalers, who began to remain in the Arctic throughout the winter, started utilizing caribou as a source of fresh meat. Between 1890 and 1920, "the herds became nearly extinct."[90] Societies which were primarily dependent on caribou were severely affected. The dwindling caribou population, and the declining Inupiaq population which resulted from disease and the decimation of marine resources by whaling fleets contributed to major population shifts. Many north Alaskan Inupiaq groups were forced to move to the coastal regions during the last decades of the nineteenth century.

Settlement patterns vary, since they were controlled by the many and various annual cycles. Generally, however, each group had a major settlement ("home village") with permanent (or semi-permanent) dwellings and a *qarigi* or "men's house." The village was the focus for social activity and identity. Typically, it was located in an area of high resource productivity. For example, settlements in the Point Hope area were usually situated within about five miles of major resource areas.[91] Nearby permanent settlements of smaller size were socially linked with a larger main settlement. Seasonal settlements, such as fish or caribou hunting camps, were common to all areas. Human concentrations at any locality were dependent on a fresh water supply and access to food resources. Spirits which inhabited specific sites also affected habitation of some areas.[92]

Settlement size, controlled by the availability of local resources, ranged from about thirty to sixty people.[93] Some major settlements with access to large sea mammals were larger. Point Hope, with its estimated population of six hundred in 1800, was apparently one of the largest in North Alaska.[94]

B. Social and Political Organization

Anthropological knowledge of traditional Inupiaq social and political organization were substantially changed and reinterpreted following the refinement of political anthropology and the dramatic increase in social scientific research in the years following the settlement of Alaska Native land claims.[95] In addition, many researchers incorporated much oral history, previously overlooked.

During the traditional period, north Alaska contained at least twenty-five distinct Inupiat societies which were autonomous socio-political entities. Each occupied a territory with well-defined boundaries. The Inupiaq term for this social unit, *nunatqatigiit,* meaning "people who are related to one another through their common ownership of land,"[96] emphasizes the territorial basis of the social grouping of traditional populations. "The collective land ownership and utilization was comparable to the ownership exercised by the citizens of nation-states in other parts of the world over their own territories."[97]

These locally named societies were distinguished by dialect differences, variances in clothing styles, distinctive annual subsistence cycles, and extensive kinship networks. The kinship systems were maintained by contracting most marriages between members of the same group. Each society had a group identity that emphasized its superiority over others. "The members of each society thought of their country as being better than that of their neighbors, and of themselves as being more intelligent, stronger, faster, and better looking, and as superior providers, dancers, story tellers, and lovers."[98]

The boundaries of these sociopolitical units were well known and, not coincidentally, fell along areas of low resource potential.[99] Geographic boundaries were also sharp social boundaries. They circumscribed a society within which an extensive set of social relationships were governed by codes of behavior that did not apply to members of other societies. However, movement out of one's territory for subsistence or trade purposes occurred in nearly all societal units.[100] Such movement usually was in summer, occurring when it was known that the foreign area was not occupied by its users and in strict accord with long-lasting agreements between the groups. Violation of these agreements could lead to armed conflict between societies. The institutions of partnerships and co-marriage (a permanent relationship between two married pairs) between members of different socieities created alliances across societal boundaries. They functioned to extend access to additional resources and to reduce potential conflict.[101] Large groups of people (at times over two thousand) from different societies gathered regularly under peaceful conditions for summer trade fairs, such as those held at Wales, Sheshalik on Kotzebue Sound, at Point Spencer, and later in the nineteenth century, at Unalakleet and Barter Island. In summary, while territorial boundaries were carefully maintained, several mechanisms facilitated interaction across boundaries (inter-societal relationships) without hostility.

The large, local, bilaterally extended family was the basic organizational unit of these societies. In major population centers, such as Wales, Point Hope, or Barrow, the families contained about fifty people and occasionally more than one hundred;[102] elsewhere they were considerably smaller. Large settlements, such as Point Hope, would contain a number of local families, whereas a smaller settlement might be a single local family unit. Local families (composed of couples, their offspring, and other relatives) typically occupied several households in close proximity to one another at the winter settlement.

In a large settlement, dwellings of local families would be concentrated in "neighborhoods", each with its own *qarigi*. Local extended families were self-sufficient economic and political units, each with a leader or *umialik*. Within a regional society, local extended families were linked by blood and marriage ties. These relationships established social obligations and a context for peaceful social interaction. Economic distribution and exchange between families was negotiated by family leaders.[103] Membership in a skin boat crew formed for large marine mammal hunting created important linkages between men in a community. Such crews and their *umialik* (boat captain) were a focus of economic and social interaction in large coastal settlements.[104] As a rule, membership was kin-based.[105]

Large local families and their leader were responsible for the behavior of their members. In coastal communities, umialiks played a major role in social and political control because of their economic status and personal influence. Within all settlements, local family governance, as well as feuding, friendships, and partnerships functioned as mechanisms of social control. Members from different local families also cooperated in subsistence activities (especially during time of potential famine), in defense, and sometimes in aggression against another society.

Secular institutions operated within an ideological system created by religious beliefs which carefully defined a person's relationship with the environment and with spiritual beings. The institution of shamanism, for example, was strongly developed in these societies, serving as a check on individual behavior and as an integrating mechanism since different local families would occasionally employ the same shaman. This could result "...in a complex pattern of taboos which was specific to each society. Thus even in the realm of magic, each society constituted an entity whose constituent parts were integrated with one another, but more or less clearly demarcated from all its neighbors."[106]

C. Early Contact Government

By 1850, most north Alaskan Inupiat were in contact with non-Natives. Like all other Alaska Natives, they experienced severe population reductions due to introduced diseases. Estimates suggest the population was reduced by fifty percent during the second half of the nineteenth century.[107] In addition, societies had to adjust to a significantly depleted resource base. The Western Brooks caribou herd, mentioned above, from some 300,000 animals in 1850 to about 10,000 to 15,000 in 1900. Bowhead whale and walrus populations were substantially reduced at the same time as a result of commercial whaling activities. These factors prompted formation of new settlement patterns and social groupings. Within the first decade of the twentieth century, populations also began to concentrate at sites with mission schools and trading posts. Some schools and trading posts were established in traditional settlements. The trend toward population concentration at service centers was complete by World War II, but seasonal movements for fishing, hunting, and trapping have continued.

Local family organization continued to be important, although individuals gradually participated more often in non-kin associations, such as schools.[108] The new settlements, while structurally different from those at the beginning of the century, (since they now contained members from previously distinct societies) were still organized on the earlier principles of local extended family relationships.

At the close of the nineteenth century, north Alaskan Inupiat communities were characterized by traditional patterns of self-government with family leaders exercising influential roles in community decision-making and dispute resolution.[109] Village councils were political creations of teachers, missionaries, and representatives of the federal government, particularly those employed by the Bureau of Indian Affairs. The Point Hope Council, one of the earliest in far northern Alaska, was begun in 1920 by the Episcopal Church. This council, later incorporated as an Indian Reorganization Act (IRA) council in 1940, acted as a "rule-making and law-enforcing body...."[110] While the structural form of the council was western, traditional leadership patterns prevailed. Disputes were most often settled according to traditional customary law. Council members are described as having considerable prestige, and it can probably be assumed that they were local family heads. Continuity with the past was emphasized by decisions based primarily on precedent; these "...decisions always reflect[ed] the desire to maintain peace and order in the village."[111]

VI. Southwest Alaskan Yupik

A. Subsistence

Prior to contact, some twenty thousand Yupik people inhabited the coasts, adjacent islands, and inland regions of southwest Alaska and the coasts and islands on the north Pacific rim in south Alaska.[112] Their nearly continuous coastal distribution from the northern shores of Norton Sound to the mouth of the Copper River was broken only by the Aleuts on the western end of the Alaska Peninsula and the Tanaina Athabaskan Indians at Cook Inlet.

Western contact with the southwest Alaskan Yupik, who referred to themselves as *Yupuiit* (the "real people"), was uneven, beginning in the late Russian period along the south coast. Russian penetration north of the Alaska Peninsula began in 1818 with the establishment of a post on the Nushagak River. The first post in the interior on the Kuskokwim River was established in 1832, followed the next year by the founding of Fort St. Michael on the shores of Norton Sound. However, much of the west Alaska Yupik population was not directly contacted until the late nineteenth century with the missionary activity of the Moravians who settled on the Kuskokwim in 1885 and the Catholics who visited Nelson Island in 1888.[113] Much of the west coast remained very isolated until the 1940's due to the shallowness of its offshore waters, which discouraged white whalers and traders, and to its lack of exploitable mineral resources.

The Yupik area, like that of the Inupiat in North Alaska, varies considerably in the local availability of food and raw materials; the annual cycles, like those of their northern neighbors, were likewise highly variable. However, the climate in this region is not nearly as rigorous as that farther north, and the resource base did not require as much long distance mobility during the annual subsistence cycle. Indeed, Yupik societies along the North Pacific rim inhabited the richest environment available to Eskimo populations anywhere; their economic base was similar to that of the Aleuts and North Pacific rim Indian societies. As a consequence, the highest population densities of Alaskan Eskimos were found in the areas of Kodiak Island and Prince William Sound.[114]

South of Norton Sound, migrating salmon played an important role in the subsistence economies of most Yupik societies. Subsistence patterns are most easily placed in two large categories—those characteristic of the coast and those of the large rivers. Coastal populations relied heavily on small sea mammals, with varying emphasis also on whales, walrus, salmon, herring, smelt, and other non-salmon species, as well as caribou. Salmon, on the other hand, was the staple of riverine communities, supplemented by other fish, caribou, small land mammals, and small sea mammals in the lower reaches of the large rivers. Migratory waterfowl were important everywhere. Four patterns summarize the highly diverse subsistence adaptations in the Yupik area.

1. Bering Sea Whale Hunters

The economy of the Bering Sea whale hunters on St. Lawrence Island, similar to the Inupiaq large sea mammal hunters in the Bering Strait, was strongly focused on migrating bowhead whale and walrus, both of which were intensively harvested in spring and fall.

2. Pacific Coast Whalers

Pacific Coast whalers, such as those on Kodiak Island, were able to exploit the open sea year-round from kayaks. Like the Aleuts, they hunted whale, seal, and sea otter. In addition, harvests of salmon provided important winter stores of dry fish. Also in this area, deep sea fishing for halibut and cod, the collection of shellfish, and the hunting of land animals supplemented a rich and diverse economic base.

3. Small Sea Mammal Hunters and Fishers

Small sea mammal hunters and fishers, such as those along the southwest coast of Alaska, relied heavily on spring and fall seal harvests. In some places, like Nunivak Island and the Kuskokwim Bay area, walrus were also an important source of food and raw materials.[115] Summer salmon fishing and a spring herring harvest supplemented sea mammal hunting. On Nelson Island, the herring harvest provided a main staple for winter food stores,[116] whereas in other areas, salmon provided this staple. A wide variety of other fish, such as cod, capelin, sculpin, flounder, rock fish, whitefish, blackfish, burbot, sheefish, pike, needlefish, char, smelt, and grayling were also used when available. In general, the more northerly groups along the Bering Sea coast relied less on winter and early spring fishing and more heavily on the storage of sea mammals products and salmon. Most societies had access to caribou, and all harvested small mammals such as hare, fox, beaver, otter, mink as well as ptarmigan and waterfowl.

4. Intensive Salmon Fishers

Intensive salmon fishers, such as those along the major rivers like the Yukon, Kuskokwim, and Nushagak (including inland villages that moved to a major river during summer) relied primarily on salmon and other fish for sustenance.[117] Four or five species of salmon, depending on availability, were harvested in the summer, providing ample quantities of fresh and stored food for the year. Harvests of sheefish (Yukon River) or smelt (both Yukon and Kuskokwim rivers) also provided important early summer food. In most areas, whitefish, blackfish, sheefish, pike, burbot were taken from fall through spring. A contemporary study[118] of Yukon delta communities demonstrates the significance of fall (before freeze-up) harvesting of whitefish, sheefish, and saffron cod in the overall economy of the area. In the lower portions of the Yukon and Kuskokwim rivers, seal and beluga were taken, as were fall and spring caribou where available. Small mammals (hare, beaver, muskrats) ptarmigan and waterfowl were harvested as supplements. Mink, land otter, fox, and lynx provided fur in some areas.

B. Settlement Patterns

Settlement patterns of Yupik groups varied since all were adjusted to local environments. Coastal and riverine societies usually occupied at least four locales, one of which was the main winter settlement. Summer fish camps were usually very close to or at the main settlement (riverine and south Alaska coastal communities). Fall and spring camps were also established for specialized harvesting activities. At least one exception to this pattern occurred in the Black River area in western Alaska where people spent most of the winter in scattered tundra camps away from the coast. Here major in-gatherings occurred briefly in winter for social and ceremonial activity. People also gathered at the mouth of the river in summer for fishing.[119]

Main settlements in the southern Yupik area were the largest and inhabited for the longest continuous periods of time (nine months). Although data are scarce and little analysis has been done, it appears that major coastal settlements probably did not exceed three hundred people (though some may have been larger). Riverine communities usually contained fewer than one hundred individuals although settlement size could vary considerably from small family settlements (about ten people in one house) to populous villages (the largest about three hundred people).[120]

In all areas major settlements were quite stable, persisting for many years; however, riverine and some coastal villages occasionally had to relocate due to river erosion or flooding.

C. Social and Political Organization

While recent anthropological research in the Yupik region has expanded our understanding of traditional subsistence patterns, there has been very little analysis of social and political organization. This general description draws on the currently available literature as well as some recently completed anthropological field work.

Without doubt, Yupik societies were organized very much like those of the Inupiaq, and the Yupik area contained a fairly large (as yet, undetermined) number of societies that functioned as autonomous social and political units. Each had its own well-defined territory. A Yupik word for this social unit, *nunakutellriit,* which literally means "those that share an area," emphasizes its territorial nature. [121] The term even today is applied to people who live in and use the resources of a particular village.

Each society had at least one major settlement which was the focus for a major subsistence activity as well as social and ceremonial activities, a homebase. This community was characterized by a continuity in personnel over a long period of time. Social boundaries defined a marriage universe and parents sought spouses for their children from within their own local group. Like Inupiaq societies, members of one society were differentiated from those of other societies by speech patterns, clothing details, annual cycles, and ceremonial life.

Inter-group marriage and trading partnerships created alliances between individuals in separate social groups. Most societies apparently participated in long-term alliances with neighboring groups for purposes of both offense and defense. Ceremonial occasions which involved members from different societies created the opportunity for each to demonstrate its strength. For example, it is said that a function of "potlatches" was to allow a group to show how "healthy" it was. [122] Such arrangements reinforced a sense of local identity and expressed the autonomous nature of Yupik societies as self-governing and distinct units.

Each individual in Yupik society typically was a member of a large, local, bilaterally extended family with a structure similar to that of the Inupiaq family. Since these families and their functions in maintaining order within society have already been described above, they are not discussed here except to note that families had considerable power over the behavior of their members. Exceptions to this form of social organization have been noted for St. Lawrence Island, [123] where the society constituted of a number of patrilineal clans, and Nunivak Island, [124] where social organization appears to have been transitional between a patrilineal clan system and a bilateral organization. In these societies, the concept of family was defined somewhat differently, yet in all it operated as the keystone of social and political organization.

The social structure of a west Alaska Yupik community commonly contained domestic households, made up of related women and their children, and one or more *qasgiq* ("men's house") where men lived, worked, taught and directed the community's political and ceremonial life. A young boy joined men in the qasgiq between the ages of five and ten and would sustain the social and residential relationships created with these men for the rest of his life, unless he left his village. At marriage, a man was expected to join the qasgiq of his wife's father, which might well have been his own.[125] (In north Alaska, men also belonged to a men's house [qarigi], as noted above, but they did not live there. In spite of this important difference, the men's house was the center of political, social, educational and religious activities, and the domain of adult males, in both Inupiaq and Yupik communities.). Participation in a men's house provided male elders the opportunity to scrutinize and comment on the behavior of other males. They could also direct the socialization of young men into the conventions and expectations of adult male Yupik life. Yupik elders today say the "man with no ears" *(ciutailnguq),* who did not hear the advice of older men, would experience strong social pressures to conform.[126]

Available data suggest that in a small Yupik community where membership in a qasgiq was made up primarily of men related by blood and marriage, the oldest male was respected as a leader. In larger communities, several men, representing local families, functioned as leaders and decision-makers. In the ranked Yupik societies in south Alaska, such as those on Kodiak Island and in the Prince William Sound area, leadership was more formally defined and was apparently inherited. Early sources report that the office of chieftainship was inherited by sons or nephews on Kodiak Island.[127] In the Prince William Sound area each community had a chief and an assistant chief.[128] In spite of the prestige associated with these positions, the scope of a chief's political power was limited to persuasion, but like other Yupik leaders, a chief was respected for his success and wisdom; hence his advice was rarely disputed. Although they represented their villages to other villages and led in decision-making in their own communities, these leaders did not have the formal power of dispute resolution between local families, which were responsible for managing their own affairs.

In addition to the formal structure of leadership and social control based in the family and qasgiq organizations, public sanction was also vested in gossip, ridicule songs, and joking partnerships which permitted criticism without retribution. The institution of feuding, and the numerous moral guidelines for life contained in the traditional ideological belief system further functioned to maintain a high degree of social control within Yupik society in all areas.[129]

D. Early Contact Government

Yupik societies in the North Pacific rim area experienced severe population reduction and major changes in their culture during the Russian period. The managers of the Russian American Company altered political organization on Kodiak Island as well as in the Aleutians and Cook Inlet (Tanaina) areas. By the beginning of the nineteenth century, it is reported that chieftainships, which had been hereditary institutions, were now controlled by managers of the trading company, who claimed the right to nominate chiefs. [130]

Political organization along the Kuskokwim River and in west Alaska was not altered by the Russians since they recruited traditional leaders to employ. "These individuals were given silver medals, called 'United Russia,' with the Tsar's picture on one side, a certificate designating the leader as a person of authority recognized by the company, and occasional incentive gifts."[131] In spite of these efforts, Russian activities north of the Alaska Peninsula were restricted compared to those to the south. Comparatively speaking, their effect on Yup'ik culture, exclusive of the Pacific rim societies, was minimal except for sporadic Christian proselitizing and increased fur trading. [132]

Major changes occurred late in the nineteenth century and early in the twentieth due to the establishment of Moravian and Catholic missions and schools along the Kuskokwim and lower Yukon respectively. At about the same time (1901-1902) most of western Alaska experienced a severe measles and influenza epidemic, called the "Great Sickness" by local people;[133] it reduced the population by about one-fourth. In some areas, entire villages were depopulated and there was considerable reorganization of sociopolitical units.

Research indicates that many settlements after this time were composed of large numbers of migrants from other villages that could no longer be sustained due to local population loss. [134] Wars ceased but territorial boundaries for subsistence and ceremonial activity were still sharply defined, and villages used new mechanisms to highlight their individual (and superior) identities. As in the past, this identity was most relevant in social relationships, with members of other village societies. Within the new villages, traditional principles of social organization structured social relationships and local families continued as major social and political institutions. However, the disappearance of the *qasgiq,* due to missionary coercion, introduced a degree of political disorganization at a time when other major changes were occurring. In larger traditional communities with more than one major local family, the *qasgiq* had provided a setting where elder male heads of large families could discuss matters of community concern and exert control over younger men in the community. Without the *qasgiq,* it is possible that local family organization became even stronger since many local families were remnants of formerly distinct social groups, who now became co-residents in a new social group in a new social environment.

The strength of traditional political arrangements within a Yupik community is illustrated by the history of "chieftainship" in relation to the introduction of an elected village coucil as reported for Napaskiak, a Kuskokwim River community. [135] In 1906, an elder from a large local extended family was appointed by a Russian Orthodox priest as the village "chief." The chief's duties were religious, and he was expected to promote the new religion in the community, arrange meetings for the priest, and protect church property. The position was maintained and continued to be associated with the head of a large extended family. Although Bureau of Indian Affairs representatives encouraged the village to establish an Indian Reorganization Act (IRA) council in 1939, it was not until 1945 that an elected council was actually formed. The "chief," established by the church, was given a seat on this council, and at some point in time that position also became an elected one. An investigator in the community in the 1950's reported that there was considerable confusion in the village about the duties of these various political organizations. "The head of the village is thought by some community members to be the chief (the original position), by others to be the head of the Brotherhood (a religious organization), and by still others to be the village council collectively."[136] One may deduce from these data that local families throughout this time period continued to exert traditional control through their elders and not through the introduced western political structure.

As noted earlier, contact and subsequent changes have been uneven in the Yup'ik area. Although there is practically no information available for the contact history for most of the villages in the region, what is available suggests that the persistence of traditional political arrangements during much of this time period, like that documented for Napaskiak, was not unusual.

VII. Summary

All Alaska Native societies based their economies on hunting, fishing, and gathering wild resources; they were subsistence foragers. Environmental and wildlife variation contributed to the development of various cooperative hunting efforts and distribution and exchange systems, annual harvest cycles and settlement patterns. Societies along the Alaska Pacific rim generally had large, stable settlements made possible by rich resources. Permanent communities also developed on the west coast in a few choice locations with access to large marine mammals. In contrast, interior settlements tended to be small and semi-permanent. Local groups moved often in response to wildlife availability, and to fluctuations in resource cycles.

In spite of geographic variation in the quantity and reliability of food supplies and raw materials, each Alaskan society was associated with a identifiable resource use area that would be defended from intrusion. Land ownership and use, in general, were collective; local societies operated as cooperative groups with regard to resource uses within their respective territories. In southeast Alaska, however, specific house group and local clan divisions claimed use areas within the larger socially defined territory (kwaan), which was associated with multiple clans. Territorial boundaries in some areas, such as north Alaska, were important social boundaries as well. Marriage within a society was prefered, and entry into the group was governed by rules specifying appropriate avenues for interaction. In other areas, such as interior Alaska, the small size and mobility of local groups encouraged more interaction with neighboring groups. Marriage was often contracted with a person from a group other than onc's own. In spite of the more diverse internal composition of interior societies, local group identity was strong and maintained by numerous mechanisms, one of the most important which was common use of a particular land area and its associated resources.

Each socio-territorial group was self-governing and autonomous. The family structure of each society was also the economic unit. Family elders exercised the most direct control over members, although family form varied from bilaterally extended local families in Inupiat and Yup'ik society to rigidly defined clans in some Indian societies. Dispute resolution was often a family or clan matter. Leaders also functioned as managers and decision-makers in society, sometimes mediating conflict between individuals, families or clans. Leaders were usually heads of large, extended families, which insured support from their members. They were also most often wealthy individuals, an achievement reflecting their spiritual as well as material successes as well as their ability to promote cooperative efforts. Leadership was more formally defined in the ranked societies of the Pacific rim. Family and clan affiliation, as well as considerable wealth, contributed to this status. Everywhere, however, leaders led through their status personal appeal rather than coercive force and received respect because of their widely recognized wisdom.

Social control was also accomplished through multiple informal mechanisms such as communication patterns and behavioral norms that avoided personal conflict. Gossip, social ostracism, and elaborate spiritual ideologies that closely defined interpersonal and spiritual relationships regulated behavior. Individual conflicts were reduced by the potential involvement of families or clans in the conflicts. The family or clan was also held responsible for individual members, which often served to dictate their behavior.

Leaders functioned as intermediaries between societies, especially during trading and ceremonial occasions. Marriages often linked the families of leaders in Pacific rim societies, and everywhere they functioned to link non-kin across local social boundaries. Ceremony, such as potlatches or other exchange feasts, also provided a context for intersocietal interaction. At such times people could interact peacefully, and sociopolitical arrangements were made or reinforced (or disrupted). Conflicts that involved large numbers of people in a society with individuals in another group could lead to war. A state of war was never sustained for a long time; hostilities would be forgiven but not forgotten and became an important part of local histories.

In summary, Alaska Native societies were self-governing autonomous socio-territorial groups. Family structures (local families, clans) were multi-purpose institutions, organizing economy, polity, and religion within a society. Sociopolitical organizations functioned to manage people and resource uses in a fashion designed to insure survival, diminish competition over resources, and reduce group conflict.

Changes in Alaska Native societies due to contact with expanding non-Native populations have followed roughly the same sequence in all areas. The time periods of major changes vary, reflecting historic circumstance, but everywhere the effects of contact were felt by 1850. Changes in traditional technology were followed by changes in economy and settlement pattern, encouraged primarily by the commercial exploitation of resources, such as the fur trade, commercial whaling and fishing, by compulsary western education, and by major population reductions due to disease. In some areas, such as the Aleutians, changes were violently initiated and enforced; in others, change was gradual and reflected local, more voluntary adaptations.

Mixed cash-subsistence economies developed and persist in many areas of Alaska today. Continuities in subsistence patterns have been accompanied by continuity in family structures. Local families in Inupiaq, Yupik and Aleut societies continue to exert considerable influence over members and set the context for social interaction in the village. Clan organization has continued to be important in ceremony in some Athabaskan communities. In southeast Alaska, clans still provide a framework for social affiliation, traditional property rights, and ceremony. On the surface traditional religion has been replaced by Christianity although many traditional beliefs co-exist with the newer ideologies; older beliefs are especially important in wild resource use activities and spiritual relationships to the environment and wildlife. New political institutions, such as city councils, reflecting the specialized nature of polity in western society have also been introduced. However, traditional leaders and customary laws continue to influence local decisions.

This brief overview has not comprehensively explored the dynamics of change and tradition in Alaska Native societies. Today, they are a complex mix of traditional and introduced institutions. Village society has shown considerable persistence and resilience; populations have rebounded to their former levels since the 1950's when better health care became available. In rural Alaska committment to a subsistence mode of production, distribution and exchange, based on the harvesting of wild resources is strong. Retention of land ownership, adverse impacts from development activities on the environment, and wildlife and subsistence limitations are vital concerns of Alaska Natives; today they are a major focus for contemporary political struggles between Native communities and state and federal bureaucracies.

ENDNOTES

[1]See e.g. Anne Shinkwin and Martha Case, *Modern Foragers: Wild Resource Use in Nenana Village, Alaska,* Alaska Department of Fish and Game, Division of Subsistence Technical Paper 91A (1984), Linda J. Ellanna, *Bering Strait Insular Eskimo: A Diachronic Study of Economy and Population Structure,* Alaska Department of Fish and Game, Division of Subsistence, Technical Paper 77 (1983). Priscilla R. Kari, *Land Use and Economy of Lime Village,* Alaska Department of Fish and Game, Division of Subsistence, Technical Paper 80 (1983). Robert J. Wolfe, *Norton Sound/Yukon Delta Sociocultural Systems Baseline Analysis,* Alaska Department of Fish and Game, Division of Subsistence, Technical Paper 59 (1981).

[2]George W. Rogers, *Alaska in Transition: The Southeast Region* (Baltimore: Johns Hopkins 1960) at 181.

[3]Kaj Birket-Smith and Frederica deLaguna, *Eyak Indians of the Copper River Delta, Alaska* (Copenhagen: Leven and Monksgaard, 1938).

[4]Philip Drucker, *Cultures of the North Pacific Coast* (New York: Chandler, 1965), Chapter 5.

[5]Viola E. Garfield and Paul S. Wingert, *The Tsimshian Indians and Their Arts* (Seattle: University of Washington, 1966).

[6]Kalervo Oberg, *The Social Economy of the Tlingit Indians* (Seattle: University of Washington, 1973). This excellent source is heavily relied on in following discussions.

[7]Id.

[8]Id. Some sources refer to Tlingit moieties as phratries. In early historic time, a dual organization was central to social and ceremonial activity, and this author, like most anthropologists, prefers the use of the term "moiety" which refers specifically to a dual division of society.

[9]Id. Oberg reports twenty-seven Raven clans and twenty-three Wolf/Eagle clans. According to William Paul, a Tlingit author, an additional clan in the Raven moiety apparently can marry either Raven or Wolf but belongs to the Raven Moiety, (see: Wilson Duff in Oberg, note 6, above, at ix).

[10]Frederica deLaguna, *Matrilineal Kin Groups in Northwestern North America,* Proceedings: Northern Athapaskan Conference, 1971, Canadian Ethnology Service, Paper No. 27, Vol. 1 (1975).

[11]Id. Frederica deLaguna, "Aboriginal Tlingit Sociopolitical Organization," in *The Development of Political Organization,* ed. E. Tooker, The American Ethnological Society, Washington, D.C. (1979 Proceedings, publ. 1983) at 79. See also, deLaguna, *Under Mount Saint Elias: the History and Culture of the Yakutat Tlingit,* Smithsonian Contribution's to Anthropology, Vol. 7, Part 1

(1972) at 119. See also, Walter R. Goldschmidt, and Theodore Haas, "Possessory Rights of the Natives of Southeastern Alaska," A Report to the Commissioner of Indian Affairs, (Mimeographed), Washington, D.C.

[12]Oberg, note 6, above, at 64.

[13]Id. at 29-38.

[14]Id. at 4; deLaguna (1983), note 11, above, at 74-75.

[15]Oberg, note 6, above, at 48-49. The U.S. Court of Claims has also judicially recognized this fact. See Tlingit and Haida Indians of Alaska v. U.S., 177 F. Supp. 452 (Ct. Cl. 1959).

[16]Garfield, note 5, above, at 33.

[17]Birket-Smith, note 3, above, at 130. The advent of one "moiety chief" for an entire village may have been a result of Russian influence which tended to establish a single village leader with whom the Russian-American Company dealt.

[18]deLaguna (1972), note 11, above, at 107-208.

[19]Drucker, note 4, above, at 189-222. See also Wendell H. Oswalt, "The Tlingit," In *This Land Was Theirs* (New York: John Wiley and Sons, 1966) at 325. See also, Catharine McClellan, "Culture Contacts in the Early Historic Period Northwestern North America," *Arctic Anthropology,* 2(1964):2:3-15.

[20]Rogers, note 2, above, at 195.

[21]Frederica deLaguna, *The Story of A Tlingit Community: A Problem in Relationship Between Archaeological, Ethnological, and Historical Methods,* Smithsonian Institution, Bureau of American Ethnology, Bulletin 172 (Washington: Government Printing Office, 1960) at 161.

[22]Id. at 162-172.

[23]Id. at 198.

[24]Oswalt (1966), note 19, above, at 328.

[25]Goldschmidt, note 11 above, at 34.

[26]Drucker, note 9, above, at 189-222.

[27]Id.; See also Michael E. Krauss, *Alaska Native Languages: Past, Present and Future,* Alaska Native Language Center, Research Papers, No. 4, University of Alaska, Fairbanks, (1980).

[28]deLaguna (1960), note 21, above, at 161.

[29]Id. at 175.

[30]Drucker, note 4, above, at 222-224.

[31]Garfield, note 5, above, at 8.

[32]Drucker, note 4, above, at 189-222.

[33]Paul, William, Sr., "My Family Came to Claim This Land," *Alaska Geographic,* 6(1979):3:235.

[34]Richard K. Nelson, *Athapaskan Subsistence Adaptations in Alaska,* Senri Ethnological Studies 4, National Museum of Ethnology, Osaka, Japan (1980) at 205-232.

[35]This total is based on estimates from a series of articles on Northern Athabaskan groups published recently in the *Handbook of North American Indians,* Vol. 6, Subarctic (Washington: Smithsonian Institution, 1981).

[36]See e.g., June Helm, et al., *The Contact History of the Subarctic Athapaskans: An Overview,* Proceedings: Northern Athapaskan Conference, 1971, Canadian Ethnology Service, Paper No. 27. Vol. 1 (1975).

[37]Nelson, note 34, above, at 223.

[38]Edward H. Hosley, Environment and Culture in the Alaska Plateau, *Handbook of North American Indians,* Vol. 6, Subarctic, (Washington: Smithsonian Institution, 1981) at 534.

[39]Nelson H.H. Graburn, and B. Stephen Strong, *Circumpolar Peoples: An Anthropological Perspective* (Pacific Palisades, California: Goodyear, 1973) at 61-78.

[40]Id. at 215.

[41]Id. at 211-213.

[42]Id. at 75-76.

[43]A. McFadyen Clark, "Koyukon," *Handbook of North American Indians,* Vol. 6, Subarctic, (Washington: Smithsonian Institution, 1981) at 585.

[44]Joan B. Townsend, "Tanaina," *Handbook of North American Indians,* Vol. 6, Subarctic, (Washington: Smithsonian Institution, 1981) at 632.

[45]Frederica deLaguna and Catharine McClellan, "Ahtna," *Handbook of North American Indians,* Vol. 6, Subarctic (Washington: Smithsonian Institution, 1981) at 644.

[46]Clark, note 43, above, at 584. Also, Marie-Francoise Guedon, *People of Tetlin, Why Are You Singing?* National Museum of Man, Ethnology Division, Mercury Series, Paper 9, Ottawa (1964).

[47]deLaguna (1975), note 10, above, at 91.

[48]Id.

[49]Id. at 133.

[50]James Arthur Fall, "Patterns of Upper Inlet Tanaina Leadership, 1741-1918," Ph.D. dissertation, University of Wisconsin, Madison (1981). See also Clark, note 43, above; also Guedon, note 46, above.

[51]deLaguna (1981), note 45, above. See also Townsend (1981), note 44, above.

[52]deLaguna (1981), note 45, above, at 657.

[53]Jeanne H. Snow, "Ingalik," *Handbook of North American Indians,* Vol. 6, Subarctic (Washington: Smithsonian Institution, 1981) at 606.

[54]Eliza Jones, Alaska Native Language Center, University of Alaska, Fairbanks, personal communication, June 1984.

[55]Richard Slobodin, "Kutchin," *Handbook of North American Indians,* Vol. 6, Subarctic (Washington: Smithsonian Institution, 1981).

[56]Fall, note 50, above, at 255-257.

[57]For example, Clark, note 43, above, at 585.

[58]Stanton H. Patty, "A Conference with the Tanana Chiefs: A Memorable Gathering at Fairbanks in the Summer of 1915," *Alaska Journal,* 1(1971):2:2-18.

[59]Shinkwin and Case, note 1, above.

[60]William S. Laughlin, , *Aleuts: Survivors of the Bering Land Bridge* (New York: Hall, Rinehart, and Winston, 1980) at 23.

[61]Laughlin, note 60, above, at 20.

[62]Henry B. Collins, et al., *The Aleutian Islands: Their People and Natural History,* Smithsonian Institution War Background Studies, No. 21 (Washington: Government Printing Office, 1945).

[63]Laughlin, note 60, above, at 10.

[64]Lydia Black, "Early History," *Alaska Geographic: The Aleutians,* 7(1980):33:82-89, 92-105.

[65]Id. at 87.

[66]Id.

[67]Margaret Lantis, *The Aleut Social System, 1750-1810, from Early Historical Sources,* Ethnohistory in Southwestern Alaska and the Southern Yukon, Studies in Anthropology, No. 7, The University Press of Kentucky, Lexington (1970), Part 2.

[68]Joan Townsend, "Ranked Societies of the Alaskan Pacific Rim," Senri Ethnological Studies 4, National Museum of Ethnology, Osaka, Japan (1980) at 123-156.

[69]Id.

[70]Lantis (1970), note 67, above, at 251-252.

[71]Black, note 64, above, at 88.

[72]Lantis (1970), note 67, above, at 260-262.

[73]Laughlin, note 60, above, at 61.

[74]Lantis (1970), note 67, above, at 258.

[75]Laughlin, note 60, above, at 58.

[76]Lantis (1970), note 67, above, at 277.

[77]Lantis (1970), note 67, above, at 179-189.

[78]Black, note 64, above, at 94.

[79]Dorothy Jones, *A Century of Servitude: Pribilof Aleuts Under U.S. Rule* (Lanlam, Maryland: University Press of America, 1980) at 5.

[80]Black, note 64, above, at 103.

[81]Krauss, note 27, above, at 16.

[82]Lael Morgan, ed., *Alaska Geographic: The Aleutians,* 7(1980):3:110-113.

[83]Id. at 162, 164.

[84]Id. at 162.

[85]Larry Merculieff, "Traditional Living in a Modern Society," *Alaska Geographic: Islands of the Seals, the Pribilofs,* 9(1982):3:106.

[86]Wendell H. Oswalt, *Alaskan Eskimos* (San Francisco: Chandler, 1967).

[87]Ernest S. Burch, Jr., "Traditional Eskimo Societies in Northwest Alaska," Senri Ethnological Studies 4, National Museum of Ethnology, Osaka, Japan (1980) at 275. An excellent summary of annual cycles is at 285-295.

[88]Ernest S. Burch, Jr., *The Traditional Eskimo Hunters of Point Hope, Alaska: 1800-1975,* ([n.p.]: North Slope Borough, Alaska 1981), at 8.

[89]Ellanna.

[90]Ernest S. Burch, Jr., "The Caribou/Wild Reindeer as a Human Resource," *American Antiquity,* 37(1972:3:356.

[91]Burch (1981), note 88, above, at 37.

[92]Id.

[93]Burch (1980), note 87, above, at 265.

[94]Burch (1981), note 88, above, at 44.

[95]Ernest S. Burch, Jr., *Eskimo Kinsmen: Changing Family Relationships in Northwest Alaska* (San Francisco: West Publishing Company, 1975). See also Burch (1980, 1981) notes 87, 88, above; Dorothy Jean Ray, *The Tribes of Bering Strait, 1650-1898* (Seattle: University of Washington Press, 1975).

[96]Burch 1981, note 88, above, at 11.

[97]Id.

[98]Burch (1980), note 87, above, at 278. See also Ray, note 95, above, at 105-106.

[99]Id. at 276.

[100]Id.

[101]Ernest S. Burch, Jr. and Thomas C. Correll, "Alliance and Conflict: Inter-regional Relations in North Alaska," *Alliance in Eskimo Society,* ed. D.L. Guemple, Proceedings of the American Ethnological Society, 1971, Supplement (Seattle: University of Washington Press, 1972) at 17-39.

[102]Burch (1980), note 87, above, 1980 at 263.

[103]Id. at 266-269.

[104]Ellana, note 1, above.

[105]Burch (1980), note 87, above, 1980 at 271.

[106]Id. at 272.

[107]Ernest S. Burch, Jr., "Indians and Eskimos in North Alaska, 1816- 1977: A Study in changing Ethnic Relations." *Arctic Anthropology,* 16(1979):2:123-151.

[108]Id.

[109]Ray, note 95, above, at 246-249; John Murdoch, "Ethnological Results of the Point Barrow Expedition," *Ninth Annual Report of the Bureau of American Ethnology, 1887-1888* (1892).

[110]James W. VanStone, *Point Hope: An Eskimo Village in Transition* (Seattle: University of Washington 1962) at 102-105.

[111]Van Stone (1962), note 110, above, at 103.

[112]Oswalt (1967), note 86, above, at 4-9. Three Yupik languages are found in Alaska "Siberian Yupik" is spoken on St. Lawrence Island, "Central Yupik," widespread in western Alaska, having three dialect areas (Bristol Bay, Kuskokwim, Yukon). "Alutiig" or Pacific Gulf Yupik (also called Suk, Sugpiaq, Sugcestun) has two dialects (Chugach and Koniaq). See Krauss, note 27, above.

[113]Wendall H. Oswalt, *Mission of Change in Alaska* (San Marino, California: The Huntington Library, 1963). Ann Fienup-Riordan, *The Nelson Island Eskimo: Social Structure and Ritual Distribution* (Anchorage: Alaska Pacific University Press, 1983) at 9.

[114]Oswalt (1967), note 86, above, at 114.

[115]Margaret Lantis, "The Social Culture of the Nunivak Eskimo," *Transactions of the American Philosophical Society,* n.s., Vol. 35, Part 3, (1946), at 153-323.

[116]Fienup-Riordan, note 113, above, at 94.

[117]See, for example, Oswalt (1966), note 19, above, at 81-140.

[118]Robert James Wolfe, "Food Production in a Western Eskimo Population," Ph.D. dissertation, University of California, Los Angeles, 1979.

[119]Anne D. Shinkwin and Mary Pete, fieldnotes, 1983.

[120]Oswalt (1966), note 19, above, at 90. See also Lavrentii Alekseevich Zagoskin, *Lieutenant Zagoskin's Travels in Russian America, 1842-1844* (Toronto: University of Toronto Press, 1967), who reports a coastal settlement in the Yukon Delta area said to contain 250 people prior to introduced disease, at 281.

[121]Shinkwin and Pete, note 119, above.

[122]Id.

[123]Charles C. Hughes, *An Eskimo Village in the Modern World* (Ithaca, New York: Cornell University 1960).

[124]Lantis (1946), note 115, above.

[125]Id.

[126]Shinkwin and Pete, note 119, above.

[127]G.L. Davydov *Two Voyages to Russian America, 1802-1807,* ed. Richard A. Pierce, Materials for the Study of Alaska History, No. 10 (Kingston, Ontario: The Limestone Press, 1977) at 190.

[128]Kaj Birket-Smith *The Chugach Eskimo,* (Copenhagen: Nationalmuseets Skrifter, Etnografisk Raekke, 6. 1953).

[129]Lantis (1946), note 115, above; Oswalt (1966), note 19, above.

[130]Davydov, note 127, above, at 190.

[131]James W. VanStone, *Eskimos of the Nushagak River: An Ethnographic History,* (Seattle: University of Washington Press, 1967) at 54-55.

[132]Oswalt (1963a), note 113, above, at 106-107.

[133]Robert J. Wolfe, "Alaska's Great Sickness, 1900: An Epidemic of Measles and Influenza in a Virgin Soil Population," Proceedings of the American Philosophical Society, Vol. 126, No. 2 (1982).

[134]Shinkwin and Pete, note 119, above.

[135]Wendell H. Oswalt, *Napaskiak: An Alaskan Eskimo Community* (Tucson: The University of Arizona Press, 1963).

[136]Id. at 66.

CHAPTER NINE

MODERN ALASKA NATIVE
GOVERNMENTS AND ORGANIZATIONS

I. Introduction

Even a casual observer will be impressed by the number of both unrelated and interrelated Native governments, corporations and associations representing modern Alaska Native interests. There are federally
recognized traditional and IRA governments, state organized municipal
governments, IRA and ANCSA corporations, nonprofit development
corporations, and regional Native associations, as well as fish and game
advisory boards and REAA school boards, to name only a few. Those
entities chartered under state law are frequently "Native" only because
their resident populations, memberships or shareholders happen to be
Native. Some of those chartered by the federal government, such as the
IRA governments and corporations, are exclusively "Native" because
federal law requires it; as a consequence, they enjoy a special relationship with the United States government. Other organizations, particularly the ANCSA village and regional corporations and regional associations occupy a conceptual space someplace between state-chartered and
federally recognized "Native" entities.

Perhaps the only valid generalization to be made about this complex
"nonsystem" is that it manifests an extraordinary amount of formal organization.[1] Formalization has resulted not only from federal Native programs (most notably under the IRA and ANCSA) but also from territorial
and state laws (which encouraged incorporation of remote villages) and
Native organizing efforts to achieve settlements of land and other grievances. It is difficult to discuss such a bewildering institutional array in
any particular order or ranking.[2] Instead I will distinguish among major
types of organizations and in the process compare, through case studies,
major variations within some of those types.

It is possible to describe any human organization in terms of its function, and that is the approach taken here. Of course, the categories chosen are no more immutable than those of the next mind which cares to
survey the field, but they do seem to represent separate functions which
have had real impact on Alaska Native social, economic and political life.
Functionally then, Alaska Natives seem to be organized into four distinguishable sorts of entities: 1) governments, 2) economic profit corporations, 3) nonprofit development and service corporations and 4) multi-re-
gional political organizations.[3]

As to each of these, the federal and state governments must choose
either to interact or not interact on any of a number of levels. For example, the Alaska Department of Public Safety may contract with a nonprofit
Native corporation under the state's Village Public Safety Officer (VPSO)

program to provide village criminal justice and other public safety services. The federal government may contract through the BIA with the same organization to improve tribal government services to the same villages under the Self-Determination Act. Each agency may contract for completely unrelated reasons and often to achieve unrelated goals. That is not necessarily bad policy, because it permits the Native association to choose from both Native-oriented and non-Native-oriented programs to achieve its own overall goals. Moreover, the fact the programs are not effectively coordinated among state and federal agencies may mean that the local Native contractor exercises effective control among several programs. Some commentators have concluded that such diffusions of service and government control "may be the most effective approach to the complex problems of rural Alaska."[4]

II. Governmental Organizations

A. Generally

There are two types of "Native" governments in Alaska, those which are chartered under State law and those recognized under federal law. The former are "Native" in fact only and do not have any legal status guaranteeing they will remain ethnically Native. Federally recognized governments, on the other hand, are exclusively Native either because of their inherently sovereign status or because of specific statutory or administrative recognition and support. There appear to be at least three types of federally recognized Native governments: 1) traditional governing councils, 2) IRA governing councils, and 3) the Tlingit and Haida Central Council.

B. Territorial and State Municipalities

Several Alaska Native communities, particularly in Southeast Alaska, were organized as municipalities prior to statehood. A 1915 territorial act permitted "Indian villages" to organize as units of local government. However, their powers were limited along racial lines (i.e., they had no jurisdiction "over the property of white residents") and the act was repealed in 1929. Native communities were later incorporated under territorial laws governing formation of local governments.[6]

As of 1980, some 120 predominantly Native communities were organized under Title 29 of the Alaska Statutes, the laws of state municipal incorporation.[7] Alaska municipalities are constitutionally[8] and statutorily invested with very broad general[9] and regulatory[10] powers; it has been suggested that these powers are sufficient to permit predominately Native communities to govern themselves by traditional means within broad due process limits.[11] However, as the American Indian Policy Review

Commission has pointed out, organization of a Native community under state law offers no guarantee that the government will remain "Native."[12] As the ethnic composition of a community changes, constitutional equal protection principles will require that all residents be permitted equal representation in state organized local governments.

Beginning in 1963, federal and state policymakers encouraged the incorporation of Alaska Native communities under state law.[13] Frequently, access to revenue sharing or installation of a village electric generator were the incentives for municipal incorporation, but little management assistance was initially given villages to help them master the obligations accompanying the benefits of municipal incorporation.

C. Traditional and IRA Governments

1. General

The federal government has recognized two types of Native governments in Alaska—traditional and IRA. Traditional governments are those mechanisms of social control which were discussed in chapter eight above. Although modified over time by western influence, traditional governments still exist in many remote Alaska Native villages. There were 210 Native villages recognized initially under ANCSA, of these approximately 120 are organized as municipalities under state law, and of those 120 approximately 70 also have organized IRA councils.[14] That leaves approximately 90 Alaska Native communities which are governed solely by traditional village councils.

Alaska Native IRA governments have been authorized since 1934 under section 16 of the Indian Reorganization Act.[15] Although officials and previous studies seldom agree on the exact number of IRA governments in Alaska,[16] a survey done for the present study revealed that twenty-four communities organized under the IRA in the late 1930's, forty in the 1940's, five in the 1950's, and two in 1971. That is a total of 71 IRA governments; however, many of these may not have been operational for many years owing to the confusion surrounding their status.[17] This was particularly true where, as in most cases, the community was also organized as a municipality under state law.[18]

2. Traditional Governments

As is the case with any traditional Native government, traditional Alaska Native governments have inherent governmental authority unless the federal government has specifically deprived them of it.[19] Unless modified by Congress, inherent powers of internal self-government allow Indian tribes to:

Adopt and operate under a form of government of the Indians' choosing, to define conditions of tribal membership, to regulate domestic relations of members, to prescribe rules of inheritance, to levy taxes, to regulate property within the jurisdiction of the tribe, to control the conduct of members by municipal legislation, and to administer justice.[20]

However, because Alaska is a "P.L. 280 state," the exclusive authority of traditional governments to exercise some of these powers may be something of a moot point. P.L. 83-280 is a federal statute granting certain states some measure of civil and criminal jurisdiction over Native Americans and their lands. The law was applied to Alaska in 1958. As a consequence, state government—with specific exceptions—appears to have some jurisdiction over many of those matters normally within the exclusive jurisdiction of traditional Native governments.[21]

Of course, the exercise of state jurisdiction does not prevent the federal government from recognizing traditional Native governments for purposes of federal Native programs and services. Most villages recognized as eligible for ANCSA benefits have also been specifically recognized for other federal services and programs by being included in the annual list of "Indian Tribal Entities Recognized and Eligible to Receive Services From the United States Bureau of Indian Affairs." These same villages are included in the Internal Revenue Service list of "tribal governments" eligible for benefits under the Tribal Tax Status Act of 1982.[22] However, twelve ANCSA villages with traditional councils are inexplicably excluded from these lists,[23] as are four non-ANCSA communities governed by traditional councils, all of which have long received BIA services.[24]

The Department of the Interior has recognized traditional governments for Native program and service purposes for many years prior to ANCSA. When it recognized traditional Alaska Native communities, the Bureau of Indian Affairs usually requested them to adopt a simple constitution and bylaws. The primary purpose in doing so was to assure that the bureau was dealing with a government which truly represented the Native people of the community and that it would not later be confronted with another group within the same village demanding equal recognition.[25] Adoption of a constitution and bylaws does not appear to be a requirement for recognition, but administratively the BIA has been reluctant to deal with a community not formally organized under these organic documents.[26]

Constitutions of traditional villages are patterned after IRA constitutions in some respects. For example, a traditional constitution must be approved by a majority vote in an election wherein at least thirty percent of those eligible participate.[27] Under a typical constitution, the traditional government has broad power

to do all things for the common good which it has done or has had the right to do in the past and which are not against Federal and State laws *as may apply* (emphasis added).[28]

Other powers include authority to deal with the federal and state governments and to levy "dues, fees and assessments for community purposes." These provisions were specifically written to preserve the community's inherent governmental authority.[29]

3. IRA Governments

Section 16 of the 1934 Indian Reorganization Act permits "[a]ny Indian tribe or tribes, residing on the same reservation" to organize for its common welfare by adopting an appropriate constitution and bylaws.[30] Because there were few reservations in Alaska, the IRA was amended in 1936 to permit Alaska Natives to organize on the basis of "a common bond of occupation, or association, or residence."[31] As noted earlier, seventy-one communities have adopted constitutions and bylaws under this provision of IRA.

A Native community does not appear to surrender any of its inherent powers of self-government by adopting an IRA constitution. Section 16 provides in part that:

> In addition to all powers vested in any Indian tribe or tribal council by existing law, the constitution adopted by said tribe shall also vest in such tribe or its tribal council the following rights and powers: To employ legal counsel...; to prevent the sale, disposition, lease, or encumbrance of tribal lands... without the consent of the tribe; and to negotiate with the Federal, State and local Governments.

The Interior Department Solicitor has interpreted "all powers vested...by existing law" to include all those powers of inherent sovereignty previously mentioned which are appropriate to Native governments generally.[32] However, as noted earlier, those inherent powers may be somewhat limited by the application of P.L. 280 to Alaska. Nevertheless, the tribes certainly retain the power to determine their membership, and the IRA as applied to Alaska implies that any community organized under the IRA will always be "recognized" as eligible for federal Native programs and services.[33] Thus, members of an Alaska IRA community or "tribe" will always be eligible for federal programs and services provided to Natives because of their status as Natives.

Currently, all Natives in Alaska appear to be eligible for those programs and services,[34] but there is concern among some that this will not always be so. Some believe eligibility for federal programs may be administratively restricted to those who can point to some sort of "tribal" membership. In Alaska that might mean being either a shareholder in a Native village or regional corporation or a member of some other "recognized" tribal entity.[35] It is apparent that many Natives born after the enactment of ANCSA will not become Native corporation shareholders for many years, if at all. Therefore, membership in an IRA (or traditional) community may be the only way in which individual Natives will be able to maintain a clear relationship with the federal government should current broad criteria for Alaska Native eligibility be reduced or eliminated.

Community membership under the most recently adopted IRA constitutions is determined by the tribal governing body, with any denial being appealable to the Commissioner of Indian Affairs. Membership under these same constitutions also requires at least one-fourth Indian blood quantum,[36] but earlier IRA Constitutions typically do not include either blood quantum requirements or appeal remedies. Instead, initial membership is determined according to a census list "made according to the Instructions of the Secretary of the Interior for organization in Alaska." Under these constitutions, children of members automatically became members; any other membership questions were determined by the governing council according to its own rules.[37] In addition to the the original "Instructions" (issued on December 22, 1937), the Interior Department adopted regulations in 1981 governing IRA organizational procedures.[38] However, neither the regulations not the earlier "Instructions" specify criteria for determining membership; it is therefore difficult to determine what, if any, policy considerations are responsible for the more restrictive membership provisions of the more recent constitutions.[39]

As previously mentioned, Alaska IRA governments have for many years been eclipsed by the organization of state-incorporated municipalities. Beginning in 1963, the BIA even encouraged IRA decline by supporting state municipal incorporation,[40] but the Self-Determination Act[41] has seemingly eliminated that trend, because IRA (and tradtional) village governments now have first priority for federal contracting and grants under that act.[42] However, access to federal funding in some cases has placed the IRA (and traditional) councils in competition with state-chartered city governments when it comes to community planning and service delivery within the same village. On the other hand, several commentators have suggested that "concurrent government," drawing on both "tribal" and state municipal forms of government may be the most effective way to govern rural Alaska villages.[43]

Many Native non-profit associations now have village or tribal government improvement programs which provide assistance to villages in the drafting or amendment of IRA constitutions as well as training and information on the application of federal law to the exercise of tribal self-government.[44] NANA Regional Corporation also relies on the IRA's to fulfill the approval requirements of section 14(f) ANCSA. Under 1976 amendments to ANCSA, NANA has merged all of its village corporations into the regional corporation. One of the statutory requirements for doing so was that a "separate entity" be conveyed the right to "withhold consent to mineral exploration, development, or removal within the boundaries of the Native village." The IRA governing bodies have been designated to perform that function in the NANA region.[45]

Most IRA councils are found in unincorporated villages, where they are the primary form of government.[46] Even in some of the state's larger municipalities, however, IRA councils have operated substantial social service programs. For example, in Sitka, the Sitka Community Association operates a tribal court and a variety of other programs employing a staff of about one hundred.[47] The Ketchikan Indian Corporation IRA operates a number of cultural, educational, vocational, health and community service programs out of a federally financed Native center located within the city of Ketchikan.[48] The Kotzebue IRA has managed welfare assistance programs.[49] Even in small communities, some IRA's have been able to attract substantial community development funds, but most rural Alaska IRA's have not been extremely active, primarily due to limited funds.[50]

The funding limits have been particularly noticeable (since) the 1981 federal budget cuts, especially in light of the corresponding increase in state-funded support for state chartered municipalities. The state legislature has from time to time adopted legislation to pass substantial revenues to unincorporated communities and even specifically to IRA chartered governments,[51] but at least up to 1984, the state executive branch, led by the restrictive interpretations of the attorney general, had interpreted the state constitution and these statutes narrowly to substantially restrict the funding which might otherwise have been available to IRA (and traditional) councils from state sources.[52]

In spite of these difficulties, the early 1980's has seen a remarkable resurgence of interest in the IRA in Alaska. By 1981 some thirty new applications had been filed with the Interior Department.[53] A few ANCSA village corporations (particularly on former reserves) have also transferred lands received under the claims act to IRA governments, and the IRAs have then made various jurisdictional assertions over those lands. In at least one case (Klukwan) the Alaska Federal District Court has upheld the IRA's authority to adjudicate the ownership of culturally important artifacts.[54] In another case the IRA government has asserted authority to exclude non-members from ANCSA village corporation lands;[55] still another community has apparently voted to dissolve its state-chartered municipal government and be governed solely under the IRA.[56] Each of these actions seems aimed in one way or another to protect the cultural integrity of the Native community by asserting the inherent political authority of a tribal government.

By 1984 it was difficult to predict to what extent IRA (or traditional) governing councils would become entrenched as effective governing bodies in rural and other communities. On the one hand, they seemed to offer the possibility of effective Native political control over their own communities, or at least over Native concerns in those communities. On the other hand, they are beset by limited funding, unresolved legal issues, a sometimes hostile state administration and the ambivalent policies of the Interior Department. Nonetheless, in the case of the regional corporation NANA, the IRA's have been used to implement the village consent requirements of ANCSA. And perhaps even more importantly, the IRA (or other form of tribal government) is seen by many Natives as a means of avoiding some of the perceived pitfalls of the claims settlement and of preserving their separate identity as a people.[57]

D. Tlingit and Haida Central Council

1. History and Purpose

The Tlingit and Haida Central Council is unique among Alaska Native governments. Its roots are in the Alaska Native Brotherhood (ANB) and Sisterhood (ANS).[58] The Brotherhood and Sisterhood were formed in 1912 and 1915, respectively, by Indians from throughout southeastern Alaska to encourage "progress" among the Tlingit and Haida Indians.[59]

The 1929 ANB convention authorized Tlingit-Haida action against the United States for some 20 million acres of land in southeastern Alaska—including the Tongass National Forest, Glacier Bay National Monument, and the Annette Island Indian Reservation—to which the Tlingits and Haidas claimed aboriginal title. In 1935, Congress passed a special jurisdictional act permitting the Tlingits and Haidas to file suit;[60] it was subsequently determined that the ANB's nonexclusive nature (its membership included non-Natives and Natives other than Tlingits and Haidas) cast doubt on its legal ability to press the suit. ANB therefore established a separate entity, which subsequently became the Central Council, as a legal base for purposes of pressing the lawsuit.[61]

By the terms of its constitution, the Central Council is the "general and supreme governing body of the [Tlingit and Haida] Tribes," and promotes their welfare and exercises other powers accruing to it through its federally recognized sovereignty.[62] As such, it concluded the Tlingit-Haida land suit and in 1968 became legal recipient of a $7.5 million judgment award.[63] Whether the Central Council was a recognized Indian tribe was a matter of some debate several years ago, but subsequent judicial and administrative decisions have consistently recognized the council's status as a tribal government.[64]

2. Organizational Structure

The Central Council's constitution, together with its Rules of Election, are the organic documents of the Tlingit and Haida Indians. The Council's constitutionally stated function is to:

> secure, preserve and exercise the sovereign rights, powers, privileges and immunities of the [Tlingit and Haida] Tribes and all such other rights, powers, privileges, and immunities as the Tribes shall possess or be granted, to maintain a roll of and promote the welfare of the members of the Tribes, and to legislate for and govern the Tribes and the members.[65]

According to its constitution, the Central Council:

shall possess sovereign and plenary power to legislate for and to govern, conduct and manage the affairs and property of the Tribes, including, [in part] without limitation, the following:

* * * *

b. To acquire and dispose of property, real and personal, by any and all means, for such consideration and upon such terms as it shall decide;

c. To negotiate and enter into contracts with persons and entities of every kind and description, public, and private;

* * * *

e. To employ qualified persons to render professional and technical services as needed;

* * * *

g. To consult with and advise any and all persons, officers and entities, public and private, concerning subjects and matters affecting the interests of the Tribes....[66]

The Central Council also has the authority to "charter... subordinate groups or entities to perform governmental or proprietary functions for the Tribes and their members...." and maintains strict control over the waiver of its tribal sovereign immunity.[67] Many of these powers appear similar to those exercised by tribes organized under the IRA, discussed previously, but unlike some powers of the IRA councils, none of the Central Council's constitutional powers (including the power to amend its constitution) appear subject to the approval of the Secretary of the Interior.[68] The Central Council's electoral procedures are, however, governed by a comprehensive set of election rules the amendment of which does require the approval of the Secretary of the Interior.[69]

As of 1984, the Central Council was composed of delegates from twenty-one Tlingit and Haida communities designated in accordance with the Council's constitution and rules of election.[70] Each community elects one delegate to the Central Council for each one hundred persons or fraction thereof registered on the official Central Council community voting list. The delegate serves for two years; alternates are elected to insure there is representation at the annual Central Council General Assembly.[71] Delegate elections are held every even-numbered year at least forty-five days prior to the meeting of the General Assembly of all delegates which meets annually in Juneau, generally on the first Thursday in October.[72] Only enrolled members of the Tlingit and Haida Tribes who are at least eighteen years of age and are properly registered on a community voting list are eligible to vote for delegates.[73]

The officers of the Central Council (a president and six vice-presidents) are elected every even-numbered year from among the delegates to the annual General Assembly. These officers form the executive committee, which exercises all the powers of the Central Council between assemblies.[74] The executive committee may also call special assemblies, but cannot alter actions taken by the Central Council at an assembly.[75] The president serves as the chief executive officer of the general government of the Tlingit and Haida Indians of Alaska and is generally responsible for the conduct of all tribal business; however, the president has broad authority to delegate his authority to others. The six vice-presidents have no specified duties, but are required to assist the president "as called upon to do so."[76]

3. Recognition

a. Tlingit-Haida Judgment Legislation

Although the Central Council has been operating under its organic documents for more than a decade, with the full knowledge and approval of the Secretary of the Interior, it is still not recognized for all purposes as the *only* governing body of the Tlingit and Haida Indians. Several federal statutes appear to recognize the Central Council's general governmental authority, but prior recognition of IRA governing councils throughout southeast Alaska raises practical obstacles to the exercise of that authority. Nonetheless, as noted earlier, it is now clear that the Tlingit and Haida Central Council is recognized as *one* of the tribes in southeast Alaska. Furthermore, in terms of the scope of its programs and the assertion of governing authority, the Central Council appears more and more to be assuming the role and function of a regional tribe.

The Central Council traces its history as a recognized tribe to the 1935 jurisdictional act which authorized the Tlingit and Haida Indians to sue the United States to determine their aboriginal claims to much of southeast Alaska. Although the act referred to a "central committee" which would compile a tribal membership role,[77] it defined neither how such a committee would be established nor the extent of its powers. In 1959, the Court of Claims held that the Tlingit and Haida Indians were entitled to compensation for United States' taking of their aboriginal lands and waters.[78] The amount of compensation was left for a later hearing, but the 1959 decision implied that the Tlingit and Haida Indians would receive a substantial judgment. On the other hand, the confusion over the Central Council's status created confusion about the use to which the anticipated judgment money would be put.[79]

In 1965, Congress sought to remedy this situation by passing legislation which "recognized" the existing Central Council of the Tlingit and

Haida Indians, providing the Secretary of Interior approved the council's methods of electing its members. This same legislation, subject to future congressional approval, permitted the Central Council to prepare plans for use of the anticipated judgment fund. [80]

In 1968, the Court of Claims held that the Tlingit and Haida Indians were entitled to $7.5 million for the previous taking of their aboriginal lands. [81] Bills providing for the use and disposition of the judgment fund were introduced in both houses of Congress in 1969; in 1970 legislation passed, authorizing the Tlingit and Haida Central Council to manage the judgment fund for the benefit of the Tlingit and Haida Indians. [82] In 1971, the Tlingit and Haida Central Council was acknowledged in ANCSA as an "existing Native association"[83] and authorized to name the five incorporators for what is now the Sealaska Regional Corporation. [84]

Based on this long legislative history and at least one recent court decision, [85] it seems clear that Congress has recognized the Tlingit and Haida Central Council as "the governing body" of the Tlingit and Haida tribes. Both the House and Senate Reports on the 1970 act state without limitation that the 1965 act recognized the Central Council in this capacity. [86] However, the Department of the Interior has always resisted the conclusion that the Central Council is now the *only* recognized Indian tribe of Tlingit or Haida Indians, instead the department has always considered the Central Council as but one recognized tribe among many in southeast Alaska[87] Although the Central Council's constitution was amended in 1983 to assert its authority as "the general and supreme legislature and governing body of the Tribes," the prior organization of IRA tribal governments in southeast Alaska villages might well limit the governing authority of the Central Council with respect to those IRA governments.

b. Self-Determination Act

Even though it may not be the only Tlingit and Haida "tribe" in southeast Alaska, the Central Council also has a history of tribal recognition first under the BIA's "Indian involvement" program[88] and later under the 1975 Self-Determination Act. [89] Under the Indian involvement program, the Central Council contracted the social service programs of the BIA's southeast agency for some six years, presumably on the theory that it was a tribe. [90] It is also recognized as both a "tribal organization" and a "tribe" under the Self-Determination Act. [91]

Under the Self-Determination Act, a "tribe" includes "any organized group or community...recognized as eligible for the special programs and services provided by the United States to Indians because of their status as Indians." A "tribal organization" is, among other things, "the recognized governing body of any Indian tribe."[92] The Self-Determination Act permits "tribal organizations" to contract for BIA services to more than one "tribe" only if each tribe so served approves the contract. [93] Thus, even though the Central Council's constitution asserts it is the "general and supreme legislature and governing body" of the Tlingit and Haida Indians, the Interior Department interprets the Self-Determination Act to require that the other southeast "tribes" it serves approve any BIA contract with the Central Council.

At least three separate entities appear to qualify as "tribes" under the Self-Determination Act: ANCSA regional corporations, ANCSA village corporations and "recognized" Native communities.[94] It is theoretically possible that approvals from each of these previously recognized "tribes" would be required before the Central Council could contract for services to them or the communities identified with them. However, the BIA has apparently established a first priority for IRA or traditional councils when it comes to these approvals.[95] In the absence of such councils, approvals from the appropriate ANCSA village or regional corporation would be required.[96]

c. Conclusion

The Tlingit and Haida Central Council has long been federally recognized for purposes of administering the proceeds of the Tlingit-Haida judgment. It has also been recognized for purposes of BIA "Native involvement" contracting prior to the Self-Determination Act. It is presently recognized as both a "tribe" and a "tribal organization" for self-determination contracting. However, none of these specific forms of recognition may overcome the prior recognitions of other "tribes" in southeast Alaska which, in the language of the Self-Determination Act, are "recognized as eligible for the special programs and services provided by the United States to Indians because of their status as Indians." While the Tlingit and Haida Central Council, established under the Tlingit and Haida Judgement Act, may be the governing body of one of those recognized tribes, that does not necessarily eliminate other "tribes" such as ANCSA regional and village corporations and other recognized Native communities such as those governed by IRA or traditional councils.

4. Present Activity

a. Subsidiary Corporations

Like the nonprofit Alaska Native associations discussed below, the Central Council receives and manages both state and federal grants. Unlike most of those associations, however, the Central Council administers several of these grants through "auxillary affiliated organizations" in order to better serve its constituents and to simplify the qualifying procedures for federal funding.[97] As of 1983, its auxiliary affiliates included the following:

i. Housing and Electrical Authority—Organized to receive funds

from the state and federal governments to provide housing and electricity for Tlingit and Haida communities.

ii. Credit Union—The Central Council sponsors a branch of the Fedalaska Federal Credit Union in Juneau.

iii. Fisheries Development Corporation—Set up to receive funds from the state and federal governments to research, rehabilitate and provide for the development of fish hatcheries within Tlingit and Haida communities. Using a $2.5 million loan from the State of Alaska, the corporation completed its first hatchery in 1982 located at Sandy Bay, forty miles south of Sitka on the west coast of Baranof Island.[98]

b. Direct Programs

Other federal and state programs are operated directly through the Central Council. In 1983, these included the following:

i. Human Services Programs—With BIA Self-Determination Act funding, supplemented by a grant from the state, the Central Council operated a social service advocacy and counseling service for elders. It also operated a head start program serving approximately 115 low and middle income children under a combination of state and federal funding. Other federally funded education programs under the Johnson O'Malley Act operated in seven southeast communities. The Central Council also administered a $267,000 federal grant under the Indian Child Welfare Act to fund tribal participation in child custody court proceedings affecting tribal members and the children of tribal members. This was supplemented by $127,000 from the state legislature to recruit and develop tribal foster and adoptive homes.[99]

ii. Education and Training Programs—These included several vocational education and employment training programs funded by grants from the federal Department of Labor and BIA self-determination contracts. The Central Council also provided supplemental funding under its College Student Assistance Program to some 345 students. The Central Council also administered the state funded Village Public Safety Officer (VPSO) program which provided for the training and supervision of thirteen officers in twelve southeast communities.[100]

iii. Community Services and Natural Resources—The Central Council has administered the BIA funded Housing Improvement Program (HIP) throughout southeast Alaska since 1971. As the name implies, this program is aimed at the improvement of existing but substandard housing, with highest priority accorded to housing for the elderly. During 1983, the Central Council also appropriated ten thousand dollars from the income from its trust fund to supplement emergency and other assistance provided its elders. This was also the fourth consecutive year it administered a federal block grant to provide supplements to low income families to meet home heating and utility costs.[101] The Central

Council also provides real estate services to individual owners of restricted allotment and townsite lands in southeast Alaska and employs
a forester to provide technical assistance to southeast Alaska timber-
owning ANCSA village and urban corporations.[102] Both programs are
funded under BIA self-determination contracts.

5. Conclusion

Of all the "existing Native associations" acknowledged in ANCSA,
the Tlingit-Haida Central Council appears to operate the largest volume
of governmental service programs. Through these programs, it provides
the Tlingit and Haida Indians of southeast Alaska many of the services
they would ordinarily receive from a state-organized regional government. However, its governmental functions are in at least potential conflict with the governmental functions of previously recognized "tribes."
This appears to be especially true of those Native communities in southeast Alaska served by IRA governing councils.

Although the Tlingit and Haida Indian Tribes established under the
special judgment act also appear to be "a tribe" under the Self-Determination Act, that does not eliminate the legal and political significance of
other "tribes" recognized either administratively or under the IRA or
ANCSA. Even identifying the Central Council as the supreme governing
body of the Tlingit and Haida Indians does not mean that the Central
council can contract under the Self-Determination Act without first obtaining the approval of the communities previously recognized as "tribes"
under the IRA, ANCSA or other law.

In many ways, the IRA councils and the Central Council resemble
a federal system of government. The analogy is not exact, because the
Central Council and the IRA councils draw their authority from separate
statutes and different organic documents. However, it seems clear that
in some respects, particularly in matters related to management of the
judgment fund, the Central Council has supreme authority. In other matters, not specifically delegated to it or not arising out of its administration
of the judgment fund, the Central Council apparently must accede to the
wishes of local, previously established tribal governing bodies. Whether
there are good reasons for this particular division of authority is beyond
the scope of this discussion. However, it is suggested that answering
that question (or rather the many questions within it) may be useful in
determining the proper scope of the Tlingit and Haida Central Council's
governing authority in southeast Alaska.

III. Economic Profit Corporations

A. Generally

Corporate organization is not new to Native Alaska. As far back as
the late 1920's there are reports that reindeer herders in western Alaska

were organized into "stock" companies and given one share for each head of deer contributed to the corporate herd. These corporations were of doubtful success and appear to have been forced on the Natives.[103] Beginning in 1936, corporations were routinely organized under Section 17 of the Indian Reorganization Act.[104] Typically, whenever an Alaskan Native community organized under the IRA, it did so both as a government (under section 16) and as a federally chartered corporation (under section 17).[105] However, Alaska Natives could also organize as cooperative economic enterprises under section 16 even if they did not, strictly speaking, function as governments.[106] Finally, and most recently, Alaska Natives were required to organize as village and regional corporations in order to receive benefits under the Alaska Native Claims Settlement Act.

The following discussion will briefly consider the function and purpose of the IRA and regional ANCSA corporations as manifested in their organic documents. This will not be a detailed analysis of each organization, but is intended only to identify gross comparisons and contrasts among them.

B. IRA Corporations

As applied to Alaska, the IRA permitted organization of federally chartered village businesses and federally chartered cooperative associations. The distinction between the two appears to lie in whether the common bond between the members was one of residence or only of occupation or association.[107] It will be recalled that, as applied to Alaska, the IRA permitted organization of Natives on the basis of any one of these common bonds.[108] IRA organic documents reflect this distinction.

1. Village Businesses

It appears that whenever a village was organized as an IRA government under section 16, it was also granted an IRA business charter under section 17. Moreover, the granting of the business charter appears to have been contingent on the village first agreeing to the governmental constitution and bylaws.[109] All members of the village under the constitution were also members of the corporation; thus, in many remote villages today the IRA governing council manages the village store,[110] even when it may exercise few other true governmental functions.

The federal corporate charters are typically broad in purpose, being granted "to enable the village and its members to do various kinds of business for their good."[111] The powers of the corporation are also broad, but do not include authority to sell or mortgage reserved land or to lease such land without approval of the Interior Secretary. The exercise of such broad powers may offer one particular danger—especially if IRA villages receive self-determination grants or contracts in their governmental capacity. Unless the IRA governing council's business and self-determination activities are separate, the council could inadvertently waive its sovereign immunity through the "sue or be sued" clause of its corporate charter.[112] If its self-determination funds are not otherwise protected, they might then be reached by a creditor to satisfy business liabilities.

2. Cooperative Associations

Unlike village businesses, cooperative associations appear to be organized more on the basis of common occupation or association rather than on strict geographic residence. For example, while members of the Tonuak Indian Credit Association in Dillingham resided in "convenient proximity to one another," they "voluntarily associate[d] together to promote [their] social welfare in the economic field by forming a local nonprofit cooperative association with capital stock." The purpose of the cooperative was to:

> carry on the business of borrowing money from the United States or from other sources and relending it to members for their economic improvement...[113]

The Hydaburg Cooperative Association, on the other hand, was organized by "a group of Indians having a common bond of occupation in the fish industry."[114] The purpose of this cooperative was to promote the welfare of its members "through the development and operation of economics [sic] and social enterprises." Membership was open to Indian residents of Hydaburg "who are engaging or intend immediately to engage in the fish industry," and "Hydaburg" was defined as including even the "areas usually frequented by the inhabitants" of the village and its surrounding lands.[115]

The Hydaburg cooperative was established under a "Constitution and Bylaws" which established a council as the cooperative's managing body. The constitution also included a "Bill of Rights" which provided in part that:

> The Council shall not restrict or in any way abridge the right of the members of the Association guaranteed under the Constitution of the United States....[116]

Thus, it seems this cooperative also had some characteristics of a local government, but it does not seem to have had all the powers of an IRA government council. The powers of the Hydaburg Association related primarily to economic matters.[117]

By contrast, the powers of an IRA village governing council included the power:

> To do all things for the common good which it has done or has had the right to do in the past and which are not against Federal law and such Territorial law as may apply.[118]

As noted earlier, governments organized under section 16 of the IRA have been held by the Interior Department Solicitor to have all the inherent powers of any Native government. Unlike the Hydaburg cooperative's constitution, IRA village government constitutions appear to preserve those inherent powers and to separate them from the governing council's managerial powers under its business charter.

C. ANCSA Corporations

There is, of course, little real comparison between the regional or village corporations established under ANCSA and Native corporations established under previous legislation. As an incident of their formation, the ANCSA corporations became entitled to substantial monetary and real property benefits; IRA cooperatives and village businesses, by contrast, only had access to a revolving loan fund[119] and other comparatively minor benefits. The ANCSA corporations are also authorized under federal law,[120] but are required to be formed according to Alaska state laws.[121] Previous Native corporations were strictly federal creations, and as a practical matter had only limited access to money markets and business development programs apart from federal Native programs.

ANCSA corporations, because they are incorporated under state law, appear to have all the powers permitted by the Alaska Business Corporation Act unless specifically limited by ANCSA. As a result they have access to both public and private capital markets as well as to "Native" business development programs such as the Indian Financing Act.[122] On the other hand, as state-incorporated enterprises. ANCSA corporations are exposed to the increased risks of the marketplace with limited federal protection in the event of corporate failure.

This dual federal-state status poses interesting questions about the future of the federal relationship to Alaska Natives. In 1991, the stock in the regional and village corporations becomes alienable,[123] and non-Native stockholders become eligible to acquire and vote shares in corporate director elections.[124] Presumably, that will permit non-Natives to participate in or even control corporate decision making. It is not clear under present legislation at what point corporations formed under ANCSA will cease to be recognized Native entities. For example, the Self-Determination Act recognizes ANCSA village and regional corporations as "tribes" and implies their "governing bodies" can obtain self-determination contracts so long as they permit the "maximum participation" of Natives in their affairs.[125] At what point does Native participation become less than "maximum"?

Clearly, if all the stock were acquired by non-Natives, then the corporation would no longer be "distinctly Native" and, under U.S. Supreme Court decisions, would no longer be eligible for federal Native programs.[126] But what is the result if a bare majority of non-Native stockholders technically controls the corporation, but elects a majority Native board, or conversely, if a bare majority of Native stockholders elects a majority non-Native board? Does the Native eligibility of the corporation change chameleon-like with the blood-quantum of its shareholders or directors? Who makes the determination of what is and is not "Native" and by what rules? Do these questions imply that the federal relationship to ANCSA corporations will be gradually terminated? Would termination of the relationship to ANCSA corporations have a negative political "spin-off" effect on the eligibility of IRA governments, businesses, cooperatives, and individual Natives for social welfare, economic development, education and other Native human service programs?

Perhaps it is important to keep in mind that ANCSA is land claims legislation. Its stated purpose is to settle Alaska Native claims "rapidly, with certainty," but the settlement was also to be accomplished "in comformity with the real economic and social needs of Natives."[127] Although the land and money confirmed under the act will indirectly satisfy some of those needs, it seems clear that ANCSA was not intended to terminate Native social and economic programs so long as those were necessary to meet "real" Native needs. Apparently Congress felt there was some necessity for those programs, because it requested a thorough survey of them and the secretary's recommendations for their future.[128]

Nor are ANCSA profit corporations legally capable of meeting the social needs of their shareholders. In the first place, at least for the regional corporations, ANCSA requires them to be profit-making enterprises.[129] Furthermore, the for-profit corporations simply cannot afford, as a practical matter, to use their thus far limited capital to meet the sometimes desperate needs of their shareholders. The ultimate price of doing so could be corporate bankruptcy. Second, the Alaska Business Corporation Act may require profit corporations to use their best efforts to make a profit; failure to do so could result in shareholder suits for breach of corporate responsibility.[130] Finally, some corporate organizers, or their lawyers, have drafted their articles of incorporation so as to limit corporate purposes to promoting the "economic development" of regional and village shareholders and corporations.[131]

These considerations imply that individual or community eligibility for Native social and economic programs is not logically tied to participation in the claims settlement act. The practical and legal inability of ANCSA corporations to provide those programs dictates that, so long as there are "real economic and social needs," the federal government should continue to provide such services to all Alaska Natives. As a matter of sound policy, ANCSA village and regional profit corporations should not become the *de facto* justification for the elimination of Alaska Native social and economic programs.

IV. Nonprofit Development and Service Corporations

A. Background

It is questionable whether there ever would have been an effective settlement of Alaska Native land claims had it not been for the regional Native associations formed in the late 1960's which pursued claims. However, it is also unlikely that these regional associations would have been as effective had it not been for the coincidental infusion of funds from the federal Office of Economic Opportunity (OEO). OEO was the implementing agency for the Economic Opportunity Act of 1964;[132] its purpose was to eliminate poverty in part by:

> strengthening…community capabilities for planning and coordinating the Federal, State and other assistance related to the elimination of poverty.[133]

The Economic Opportunity Act provided for community action agencies and programs, prescribed their structure and authorized financial assistance to assist the rural poor in becoming self-sufficient. The "community action agency" was intended to be a catalyst for change rather than a direct service agency; it was supposed to give people the skills necessary to obtain needed government services. In Alaska, the action agency was a federally recognized, state-incorporated, nonprofit organization, formerly called the Alaska State Community Action Program (ASCAP), but now known as the Rural Alaska Community Action Program (RurAL CAP).[134] Because of the relatively high level of poverty in rural Alaska the state was designated an OEO "target area" in 1966,[135] and RurAL CAP began to organize regional community development corporations to implement the OEO program throughout rural Alaska.

Almost simultaneously, Alaska Natives had begun to organize regionally to obtain a resolution of their land claims.[136] In 1966, they founded the Alaska Federation of Natives (AFN) and within five years had obtained the claims settlement. Because the majority of Alaska Natives lived in rural Alaska, those people who were seeking the land settlement were the same people who were to benefit from the Community Action Program. Indirectly, RurAL CAP made it possible for the members of the regional land associations to pursue the settlement by scheduling the meetings of its regional development corporations to coincide with the land association meetings and by funding travel and per diem for the attendees.[137] For all practical purposes, the corporations and the associations represented the same constituencies; thus a meeting of one easily became a meeting of both.

After the passage of the claims act in 1971, the ANCSA regional profit corporations assumed responsibility for the management of the money and land received under the act. The corresponding regional Native associations turned their concern to the service delivery and community development problems which still plagued rural Alaskans and would not realistically be solved by the claims act benefits. These concerns frequently duplicated the concerns of the RurAL CAP development corporations; as a result, the regional Native associations in many cases merged with or assumed the responsibilities of the development corporations.

This process was given added incentive in 1973 when RurAL CAP was threatened with termination by the expiration of the federal OEO program.[138] RurAL CAP's response was to encourage the Native regional nonprofit associations to assume responsibility for their own administration and programs and to obtain the grants and contracts necessary to maintain their regional programs, independent of RurAL CAP financial and administrative assistance. As a result, RurAL CAP now has few regional development corporations dependent on it for administrative and program support. Instead, it contracts with several regional "structures" for a variety of purposes related to its overall development and advocacy goals.[139] Most, if not all, of the the regional nonprofit Native associations have now become financially and administratively independent from RurAL CAP, although they may still share common development and advocacy interests.

For purposes of the federal-Native relationship, it is important to note that RurAL CAP's regional development corporations were only *de facto* Native organizations. They established no special relationship between their memberships and the federal government; they were part of a federal poverty program which only incidentally assisted Alaska Natives. The Native associations, on the other hand, restricted their membership to Natives only and most still appear to do so. The twelve Native non-profit associations are also acknowledged in section 7 of the claims act as "existing Native associations" and have been administratively determined to be "tribal organizations" eligible for grants and contracts under the Indian Self-Determination Act.[110]

Although the nonprofit Native associations have never been recognized as "Indian tribes,"[141] their present status under the Self-Determination Act implies a more formal federal relationship than was previously possible. Because the nonprofit associations are also performing the services characteristic of regional governments, it is beginning to appear that they are taking on the functional characteristics of regional "tribal" governments. On the other hand, their independent governmental status may be more apparent than real, their true function being merely that of a conduit for federal and state governmental programs.[142] The following case studies explore the history, function and legal status of three regional nonprofit associations in more detail.[143]

These three nonprofits have many characteristics in common but also some significant differences. The Tanana Chiefs Conference (TCC) can trace its history back to the traditional governing councils of the Athabascan Indians, while Maniilaq and the Bristol Bay Native Association (BBNA) have more recent histories. Maniilaq traces itself back to an earlier northwest Alaska Inupiat organization; after ANCSA it merged with a RurAL CAP development corporation to form the present nonprofit corporation. BBNA had a less formal organization until well after ANCSA and later merged with a previously existing RurAL CAP development corporation. All three provide significant services to Natives living in the regions they serve and appear, under certain federal statutes, to be either potential or actual repositories for the federal-Native relationship.

B. Tanana Chiefs Conference

1. History and Purpose

The Tanana Chiefs Conference (TCC or Dena' Nena' Henash) is the historic successor to the traditional consultive and governing assembly of the Athabascan people of interior Alaska and has a long history dating back to 1912. In 1962, it was reorganized to deal primarily with "land rights and other problems."[144] The main reason for its reorganization was the Statehood Act of 1958, section 6 of which gave the state the right to select 102,500,000 acres of land. This placed much pressure on the Athabascan villages because the state was selecting lands that villages traditionally used for hunting, trapping, and fishing.[145]

The present-day Tanana Chiefs Conference is a non-profit organization incorporated in 1971 under the laws of Alaska. As stated in its Articles of Incorporation, its purposes are:

a) To secure to the Alaska Native people of the region of the Tanana Chiefs Conference the rights and benefits to which they are entitled under the laws of the United States and the State of Alaska.

b) To enlighten the public towards a better understanding of the Native people of Alaska.

c) To preserve the customs, folklore, art and culture values of the Native people of the region of the Tanana Chiefs Conference.

d) To seek an equitable adjustment and settlement of Native affairs and the land claims of the Native People of said region.

e) To promote the common welfare of the Natives of Alaska and their physical, economic, and social well-being.

f) To foster continued loyalty and allegiance of the Natives of Alaska to the United States and the State of Alaska.

g) To promote pride on the part of the Natives of Alaska in their heritages and traditions.

h) To discourage and overcome racial prejudice.

i) To promote good government. [146]

2. Organizational Structure

a. Membership

The corporation has one class of members—Alaska Native villages. To be eligible for TCC membership, a village must be:

> An Alaska Native Village located in the geographic areas as described in the Alaska Native Claims Settlement Act of 1971 represented or claimed by the people of Dena' Nena' Henash (Tanana Chiefs Conference, Inc.). [147]

Additionally, the Fairbanks Native Association, the Tok Native Association and the Native villages of Tok and Fairbanks are recognized as TCC member villages. New membership is determined by a two-thirds majority vote of the TCC board of directors. [148]

b. Board of Directors

Each member village is entitled to elect one director to the TCC board of directors, and each director is entitled to one vote on the board. [149] There are forty-two member villages. [150] The full board meets at least once a year (usually in March), and each director is subject to annual election. [151] The general management of the corporation between meetings is in the hands of an "Executive Board of Directors" composed of the TCC president, vice president, secretary/treasurer and one representative each from each of the six TCC "Subregional Advisory Board Committees." [152]

c. Subregional Advisory Board Committees

The TCC service area comprises the central geographic region of Alaska, roughly the same as the Doyon region established under ANCSA. It is an immense, sparsely populated geographic region of 235,000 square miles (thirty-seven percent of Alaska's land mass) with few roads. Therefore, for administrative and service delivery purposes, TCC has divided the region into six geographically described subregions. [153] Each subregion has a central office through which TCC programs are administered to the member villages within the subregion. [154] In addition, the members of the TCC board of directors from the villages within each subregion constitute an advisory committee for that subregion. Each such committee selects one director to serve on the TCC executive board. The advisory committees are intended to advise the executive board "on the affairs of the corporation which affect the delivery of services to the respective subregions."[155] Since the advisory committees also select the memebers of the governing executive board, it seems likely that the executive board would also be responsible to subregional service needs and concerns.

d. Officers

The principal TCC officers are a president, vice-president, and secretary/treasurer; the board has the authority to elect or appoint other officers as necessary. If a board member is elected as an officer, the affected village must elect a replacement.[156] The president is elected every three years and is the chief executive officer in charge of administration; he also presides over all board and executive board meetings. The vice-president performs the functions of the president in his absence or his inability or refusal to act. The board has authority to elect a treasurer, but in practice the offices of secretary and treasurer are usually combined.[157] Unlike the president, the vice-president and secretary/treasurer are elected every two years.[158] The Tanana Chiefs Conference also has a lifetime traditional chief elected by the board of directors. The position is considered to be the "highest honor that can be bestowed upon a Native by the Tanana Chiefs Conference."[159]

3. Recognition

Tanana Chiefs is eligible for federal Native programs, because its member villages are recognized under ANCSA and other legislation as eligible for those programs. For example, its member villages are eligible for ANCSA benefits under 43 USCA 1610; these same villages are recognized as "tribes" under both the Indian Self-Determination Act and Indian Financing Act.[160] TCC appears to be among those entities defined as a tribal or Indian "organization" under both those acts, because it is either controlled, sanctioned, established, recognized or chartered by such "tribes."[161] TCC's eligibility for federal Native programs can therefore be characterized as dependent on the statutory recognition of its member villages or "tribes." Unlike the Tlingit and Haida Central Council, previously discussed, the Tanana Chiefs Conference is not itself recognized as a tribe, but from its organizational structure it might best be characterized as a tribal consortium.

4. Present Activities

Like the Tlingit and Haida Central Council, previously discussed, the Tanana Chiefs Conference operates a large variety and volume of federal and state funded programs.[162] In 1979-80, TCC administered some $6 million in programs;[163] by 1983-84, the total had climbed to some $10 million.[164] The subregional organizations seem to be the key to the effective and responsive delivery of a rather diverse and broad range of programs to a widely dispersed population. While Tanana Chiefs Conference has grown substantially in the past few years, it seems significant that it has also substantially decentralized its administration. In 1978, TCC employed approximately 150 personnel, 100 were located in a central office in Fairbanks and approximately 50 were stationed at various rural sites. By 1984, the organization had grown by fifty percent to about 225 personnel, but only 90 of those were located in Fairbanks; the remaining 135 were distributed throughout the six subregions.[165]

All TCC programs are under the supervision of a "program director" who coordinates services delivered through the subregions and manages four central office support divisions: (1) Health Services, (2) Education and Employment, (3) Community and Natural Resources and (4) Family Services.[166] The central office maintains a support staff in each of these divisions, and each subregion maintains a program delivery staff, depending on the programs being provided by the particular subregion. Each subregional director reports directly to the TCC program director as do the directors of each of the central office divisions, but the subregional directors are not under the administrative control of the central office support divisions. The organizational structure seems designed to preserve subregional autonomy to actually deliver the programs while at the same time providing technical support from a central pool of expertise. It is possible to give some idea of the scope of TCC's programs by briefly describing them.

a. Health Services

Unlike some regions, TCC maintains direct control of its health services program; these services are not controlled by a separately chartered "health corporation."[167] This division provides "patient care services" through some thirty village health aides stationed in villages throughout the region and at five subregional health centers each staffed by a health outreach worker.[168] The division also provides health education support and a mental health program. It also operates a patient hostel in Fairbanks for village people or their families who have to remain in Fairbanks for extended hospitalization or health care.

b. Education and Employment

Among other things, this division acts as a liason between employers and the regional work force served by TCC. Its personnel match up job orders with job applicants and can assist eligible Natives with employment related expenses. Programs administered by this division also provide vocational education and higher education assistance in the form of supplemental grants to help meet student living expenses.[169]

c. Community and Natural Resources

This is the largest TCC division in terms of the number and variety of programs. These include specifically: wildlife and parks, realty, forestry, agriculture, and community resources (including village public safety officers, village government, housing and energy). Wildlife and parks personnel focus most of their attention on subsistence issues; the realty staff provide property management services and advice to restricted allotment and townsite property owners. Forestry and agriculture are relatively small programs providing limited assistance to timber owners and small gardening projects. [170]

This division also puts substantial emphasis on the development of "community resources." For example, through the state Department of Public Safety, it coordinates the employment and training of sixteen village public safety officers in fourteen villages throughout the region. TCC also employs an attorney to advise village governments and assist them in dealing with the state and federal agencies which affect them. This includes advice on the relative merits of tribal and state- chartered municipal forms of government as well as the design of IRA constitutions and the review of city and tribal ordinances. [171] It is often necessary to combine funds available from more than one source for differing purposes in order to achieve a single goal. For example, by 1983, TCC's BIA-funded housing improvement program had been substantially reduced by federal budget cuts, but one-time federal funding available through the Department of Labor was used to provide labor and materials for new housing construction in at least two villages. [172] It is doubtful that the federal agencies themselves could have combined their resources so effectively to fill this apparent need.

d. Family Services

This division focuses primarily on child welfare concerns, including the development of Native foster homes and intervention on behalf of villages in state child custody proceedings under the Indian Child Welfare Act. [173] This division also coordinates the head start programs in four TCC villages which provide pre-school development programs for three-to-five-year-olds.

5. Conclusion

Because TCC does operate several programs which provide government-like services, it might be considered a "quasi-governmental" organization. Its village governmental services, housing, health and family service programs can all be characterized as government services, because they are similar to the services provided by federal, state, tribal and other local governments to their citizens. On the other hand, TCC does not appear to exercise jurisdiction over territory, pass laws or possess other attributes of Indian sovereignty. Although there is perhaps no clear reason for not doing so, the federal government has never recognized Tanana Chiefs as a tribe, eligible in its own right for federal programs available to Natives solely because of their status as Natives.[174]

Nevertheless, the Secretary of the Interior ackowledges TCC to be a tribal or Indian organization for the purpose of receiving grants, contracts and benefits under the Indian Financing Act and the Self-Determination Act. Eligibility for these programs brings TCC within the scope of the general federal-Native relationship by virtue of its relationship to recognized tribes. Given this status, its other governmental functions and the nature of its membership, TCC can logically be described as a federally recognized "tribal consortium" which performs governmental services for its Native village members.

C. Maniilaq Association

1. History and Purpose

The Maniilaq Association was organized in 1963 as the Northwest Alaska Native Association (NANA) in response to the land claims issue. Previously, its members were active in the Inupiat Paitot, an association that organized in 1961 around the issues of land and subsistence rights. The later dissolution of Inupiat Paitot was the beginning of many Native associations in Eskimo Alaska.

NANA was incorporated as a nonprofit corporation in 1967 to advocate for a land claims settlement. This was at the same time that the Office of Economic Opportunity (OEO), through the Alaska State Community Action Program (ASCAP), began to develop an outreach mechanism to serve the poor and disadvantaged throughout the state. At that time there was no social service delivery system in rural Alaska. To implement the OEO "War on Poverty" programs, the Northwest Eskimos organized the Kikiktagruk Area Community Development Corporation. The purpose of organization, according to its bylaws, was "to handle Federal, State and private funds for the overall economic, social and educational development of the people of the region."[175] OEO money funded the development corporation for these purposes and also permitted it to assist in the land claims drive. Direction for Kikiktugruk came from a board of directors "elected annually by a method approved by the Village Council in each Village"[176] within the northwest area.

Thus, for several years prior to ANCSA, NANA and Kikiktugruk were the two "Native" organizations serving the northwest Alaska region. NANA was locally organized for Native land claims advocacy; Kikiktagruk was organized for antipoverty purposes as part of the federal War on Poverty program. Of the two, only NANA was limited to Native membership; Kikiktagruk was a "Native" organization because it served a region populated almost exclusively by Natives. It did not have a restricted membership, nor was it organized as a tribal government or for any particular "Native" purpose.[177]

However, it is probable that both organizations assisted each other. They both served the same people, and settlement of the land claims issue was obviously crucial to the "overall economic, social and educational development of the people of the region." Pursuant to section 7(d) of ANCSA, a new entity, also called NANA, organized and incorporated as the profit corporation now known as the NANA Regional Corporation. To avoid confusion over their similar names and different functions, the nonprofit Northwest Alaska Native Association changed its name to "Mauneluk Association," which translates roughly into "no money" and reflects the corporation's nonprofit nature. (In 1981, the spelling was changed to the more traditional "Maniilaq," which was also the name of a traditional nineteenth century Inupiaq prophet, who lived in the region of the upper Kobuk River.)[178] To avoid duplication, the Kikiktagruk Area Community Development Corporation dissolved in 1972, and Maniilaq assumed all functions of that corporation. In the meantime, the Kotzebue Area Health Corporation was separately incorporated. Again to avoid costly duplication, the Health Corporation merged with Maniilaq in 1975. Today the Maniilaq Association is the nonprofit Native association for northwest Alaska.

According to its Articles of Incorporation, Maniilaq is organized to:

(a) promote the economic, social, educational and personal well-being of the people of the northwestern region of Alaska,

(b) assist the people and communities of the northwestern Alaska region to plan and implement means of furthering all institutions and activities pertinent to the economic, social, educational, cultural and personal well-being of the people of the northwestern region of Alaska;

(c) make loans to, invest in, and provide grants to commercial and nonprofit enterprises to further the economic, educational, social, cultural and personal well-being of the people of the northwestern region of Alaska;

(d) assist in and arrange for delivery of social, community, cultural, educational, medical, job training and other services and activities to further the economic, social, educational, cultural, and personal well-being of the people of the northwestern region of Alaska.[179]

2. Organizational Structure and Officers

According to its bylaws, Maniilaq Association is controlled by a board of directors. The board consists of one representative each from the villages of Ambler, Buckland, Deering, Kiana, Kivalina, Kobuk, Kotzebue, Noatak, Noorvik, Selawik, and Shungnak. Each director is appointed by the tribal government of each village, and all directors serve for one year "or until the tribal government represented appoints a successor...."[180] Officers are elected or appointed by the board every two years and consist of a board chairman, president, treasurer, assistant treasurer, secretary, and assistant secretary. The board chairman presides over all board meetings and is responsible for seeing that the board directs Maniilaq's policy decisions. The president serves as the chief executive officer and is responsible for Maniilaq's day to day operations.[181]

3. Recognition

Maniilaq now administers grants and contracts for several federal Native programs; the tribal governments of its member villages have authorized it to do so under the Self-Determination Act. Although Maniilaq is not recognized as a "tribe" under either the Self-Determination Act or the Indian Financing Act, it appears to be a tribal or Native "organization" under both, because it is established, controlled, sanctioned, recognized or chartered by the recognized tribal governments of its member Native villages.[182] Thus, Maniilaq is eligible for federal Native programs because its member "tribes" have delegated their own eligibility to it for various purposes. This derivative recognition appears to draw Maniilaq within the framework of the general federal-Native relationship.

Maniilaq has encouraged the revitalization of tribal government in its member villages by organizing them under the provisions of the Indian Reorganization Act. Ten of Maniilaq's eleven member villages have been so organized under Self-Determination Act tribal government improvement grants.[183] As noted earlier, NANA Regional Corporation has also designated these governments to exercise the village consent rights for subsurface development under section 14(f) (43 USCA 1613) of ANCSA.

4. Present Activities

As of 1983, Maniilaq employed a staff of approximately 120 people, responsible for some thirty-four separate programs administered through four program divisions. Maniilaq's programs have grown steadily over the last five years. In 1978, the corporation administered about $2.5 million in programs funded from state, federal and other sources. By 1983, the total had grown to over $6 million, with 53.4 percent of that coming from state sources, 28.9 percent from federal sources and 17.7 percent from private foundations and other sources.[184] These programs cover an impressive range including operation of both a senior citizens' home and a youth group home. They include not only a community health practitioner program in each village but also a unique traditional medicine program. Maniilaq is also a major focus for the Inupiat Ilitqusiat (or "Spirit") program and is primarily responsible for the development and monitoring of the NANA regional strategy plan. The Maniilaq programs are discussed in broad outline below, categorized by Maniilaq's four program divisions.

a. Senior Citizens Division

This division operates the Kotzebue Senior Citizens' Cultural Center with funding provided by the Alaska Department of Administration. The center provides a permanent residence for sixteen elders, with room kept available for transient residents. In addition, the center also provides evening meals to nonresident elders seven days a week and home delivers meals to elders in Kotzebue when requested. The center also provides nursing, transportation and laundry services and facilities to elders in Kotzebue and a region-wide telephone counseling service. It also hosts the annual elders' conference and is a general focus for Native cultural activity in Kotzebue. [185]

b. Health Services Division

The community health practitioner program is the heart of Maniilaq's Health Services Division. [186] Like many of the division's other programs, it is funded from a combination of state and federal sources. The health practitioner program operates a clinic in each of Maniilaq's eleven villages with support and training provided by Maniilaq's central staff. Each clinic is staffed by one or two primary health practioners and one alternate. Some practitioners have been working in the health field for twenty years. The practitioners dispense medication and provide immunizations, physical examinations, emergency care, health screening and counseling; during 1983 they had over 24,200 patient contacts. [187] The community clinics and practitioners are also key links in delivering Maniilaq's public health, health education, maternal and child health and emergency medical programs, to name just a few. [188]

Inupiat Ilitqusiat and Health Education are two complementary programs which perhaps deserve special attention. Both grew out of an awareness, beginning in about 1980, that medical dependency rather than self-care had become the expected norm. [189] These two programs are intended to promote health sufficiency by drawing on the knowledge of both Inupiat and western cultures. Inupiat Ilitqusiat promotes certain Inupiat values as a means of reaffirming individual identity and thus reducing the high incidence of alcohol, drug abuse, suicide and other destructive behavior among the Inupiat of northwest Alaska. The Health Education program concentrates on direct education to promote good health practices such as prenatal care and dental hygiene and to reduce such hazards as smoking and hypertension. [190]

c. Human Services Division

This division operates a variety of social service programs ranging from various types of welfare payments, to a women's shelter, to mental health and alcoholism programs. These are funded primarily by State of Alaska grants and contracts.[191] The Human Services Division also operates the Maniilaq group home, which was opened in 1982 to provide a safe, calm, structured living environment for children who are in state custody or who require temporary shelter in an emergency. The overall goal of the program is to reunite children with their families. The home can accomodate up to eight children at a time and is served by a staff of nine. During 1983 it provided ten children with long term care (three months to one year) and forty-eight children with short term shelter.[192]

d. Regional Services Division

Among other things, this division is responsible for monitoring the NANA regional strategy plan and coastal resource development. It also includes the Employment and Education, Housing, Economic Development, and Housing and Tribal Government Services programs.[193] The Regional Strategy Planning and Coastal Management programs are both key planning efforts to manage the rate of development in the northwest arctic.[194]

The Regional Strategy Planning program is funded by a combination of Maniilaq administrative funds and a contract with the Alaska Department of Community and Regional Affairs. In conjunction with local communities, the program has prepared local plans to meet community, as well as region-wide priorities. At both the local and regional levels, the plans cover issues of land use, physical facilities, economic development, health, social services, and cultural concerns. Local IRA and city councils are included in joint action to develop and implement local plans, and there are annual village and region-wide conferences to revise plans and evaluate achievements. Maniilaq's central staff monitors developments in the region and coordinates with the various state, federal and private organizations active in the region to achieve the local and regional goals established through this comprehensive planning process.[195]

The purpose of the Coastal Management program is to develop a land and water use plan for the state, Native and private lands in the NANA region and to influence the use made of federal lands within the region.[196] Although the program is funded through Maniilaq by the state and is staffed by Maniilaq personnel, it has a separate board (the NANA Coastal Resource Service Area Board), authorized under the state Coastal Management Act.[197] Under this act, each coastal resource area board is required to produce a land and water use plan implemented through the state's land and water permit system under state law. The policies established by the district board are therefore binding on state agencies and have some influence on the use made of adjacent federal lands. This planning and permit system is the primary means for realizing the land planning goals established as a part of the NANA regional strategy plan discussed above. [198]

Maniilaq's Tribal Government Services program is funded by the federal Department of Health and Social Services Administration for Native Americans. The program is designed to provide assistance and support to villages interested in preserving and strengthening Native forms of government. [199] It is staffed by an attorney and a paralegal assistant who educate IRA and traditional councils within the region in their rights under the law. The program provides workshops aimed at improving the application of traditional justice concepts and village control of local offenders by sharing the results of staff examination of tribal courts. The program also focuses on improving application of the Indian Child Welfare Act, by providing legal assistance and community education. [200]

5. Conclusion

The Maniilaq Association provides many of the services to the citizens of northwest Alaska that are usually reserved for regional local governments. These include Maniilaq's regional health, social services and regional planning functions. In these respects it might be considered at least a governmental entity in function if not in law.

The Secretary of Interior continues to recognize Maniilaq as a Native "organization" through the various contracts and grants he approves for Maniilaq's many strictly Native programs. However, it seems clear that the tribal governments of its member villages are the only true "Native" governments in the NANA region, a fact implicit in Maniilaq's Tribal Government Services program. Maniilaq's recognition under the Self-Determination Act is the direct result of requests from these Native governments for the Department of the Interior to contract with Maniilaq under the Self-Determination Act.

Finally, even though Maniilaq is directly controlled by the tribal governments of its eleven member villages, its Articles of Incorporation indicate that it provides services to *all* the people of the NANA region. Although it is a "tribal organization" under the Self-Determination Act and Indian Financing Act, and is completely controlled by the Native governing councils of its member villages, it is incorporated under the laws of the state to serve both the Natives and non-Natives of the NANA region. This appears to be unique among Alaska Native nonprofit regional associations.

D. Bristol Bay Native Association

1. History and Purpose

The Bristol Bay Native Association (BBNA) was formed in 1966, primarily to seek a settlement of the Alaska Native land claims issue. It was informally organized, and received no financial assistance until 1968, when the Alaska State Community Action Program (ASCAP) sent delegates to testify at land claims hearings and to attend the Alaska Federation of Natives convention. Financial assistance from the Rural Alaska Community Action Program (RurAL CAP, formerly ASCAP) increased when the RurAL CAP board decided to develop and expand their outreach capability by incorporating regional development corporations throughout the Alaska unorganized borough (all of Alaska not included within the boundaries of regional local governments).

At a meeting in Dillingham, Alaska, on March 23, 1969, representatives from most communities in the Bristol Bay area incorporated the Bristol Bay Area Development Corporation (BBDC). The core administration of the development corporation was funded by RurAL CAP. BBDC's purpose, according to its original articles of incorporation and bylaws, was "to develop the region served and the villages thereof by administering and seeking Federal, State and private funds for the economic, social, and educational betterment of the people of the region."[201]

Membership in the corporation was open to the representatives of twenty villages in the geographic area surrounding Bristol Bay as well as to the state senator and representative for the Bristol Bay area. The articles of incorporation also required that each representative be elected by democratic process, including secret ballot, within his or her village.[202] Membership and service, due to the funding source, were open to everyone regardless of race, color or creed.

Officers of the corporation included a president, vice-president and secretary-tresurer, all elected at an annual meeting. The chief executive officer was the executive director, appointed by a board of directors. The corporation's primary purpose at that time was to implement board policies and a work plan designed to eliminate or alleviate poverty problems in the Bristol Bay area. Accounting and disbursement of funds were handled in Anchorage at the RurAL CAP central office.

In January 1973, BBDC's articles of incorporation were amended to add an executive committee and the names of villages to be served. Late in the same month, an new corporation, the Bristol Bay Native Association (BBNA) was organized to serve Alaska Natives exclusively. Because BBNA and BBDC served the same geographic area and were formed for similar purposes, discussions concerning an eventual merger began; by January 1, 1975, the merger was complete.

Today, the Bristol Bay Native Association is the surviving nonprofit corporation serving Alaska Natives in the Bristol Bay area. Its purposes as stated in its articles of incorporation are as follows:

> To develop, adopt, undertake, finance, assist, foster, and otherwise promote nonprofit programs, projects, institutions, faculties, and endeavors of a social, welfare, charitable, educational, literary, or scientific nature for the native people of the Bristol Bay region of the State of Alaska.[203]

2. Organizational Structure

According to its articles of incorporation, members of BBNA "shall be stockholders of the Bristol Bay Native Corporation and the stockholders of the village corporations of the Bristol Bay Region," but membership can be further defined in the corporation's bylaws.[204] The bylaws, in turn provide that shareholder descendents of one-quarter or more Native blood shall also be eligible for membership.[205] The policies of the corporation are set by a thirty-member board of directors selected "by democratic process within each village";[206] four additional members are selected at-large by the board, and all members serve for three-year terms. The board meets at least once a year, but in the interim a ten-member executive board meets monthly to manage the association's affairs.[207]

As of 1984, the Bristol Bay Native Association served thirty villages in a widely dispersed area on the mainland and the Alaska Penninsula surrounding Bristol Bay. For administrative purposes these villages are divided into six subregions, and one board member from each subregion serves on the executive committee.[208] At its annual meeting the full board elects a president, vice-president, secretary and treasurer who then become the other four members of the executive committee. The association's chief executive officer is an executive director, hired by the board and responsible for the day to day operation of the association.

3. Recognition

Following ANCSA's passage, BBNA organized and incorporated the profit-making corporation known today as the Bristol Bay Native Corporation, Inc. BBNA remains as a separate, nonprofit corporation, incorporated under Alaska state statutes. BBNA also administers several Native programs funded by the BIA and the Administration for Native Americans and appears to qualify as a tribal or Indian "organization" under the Self-Determination Act and Indian Financing Act. However, as with both Tanana Chiefs Conference and Maniilaq, its recognition for federal Native programs appears derived from federal recognition of villages or ANCSA corporations as "tribes" under the Self-Determination Act and other such legislation.[209]

4. Present Activity

Although BBNA operates fewer programs relative to either Tanana Chiefs or Maniilaq, it has substantially expanded its program capability in the last five years. In 1978, BBNA had significant programs in three areas (regional economic planning, employment and training, and supplemental education); by 1983 it operated an array of thirteen programs delivered through six subregional structures at a cost of roughly $2.5 million. Furthermore, in 1978 the programs were solely federally funded, but by 1983 they were funded by ample funds from both state and federal agencies.[210]

These programs included one funded under the federal Indian Child Welfare Act to assist in adoptive placements and other Native child welfare services with offices in Naknek and Dillingham, as well as a more general social service program providing counseling and referral services to needy Native families. Other exclusively Native programs were available for employment assistance and higher education financial grants. Both Natives and non-Natives benefited from the elderly nutrition and infant learning programs BBNA provided in 1983. Similarly, both Natives and non-Natives benefit from BBNA's state-funded-programs.

Like both Tanana Chiefs and Maniilaq, BBNA provides village government services and sponsors village public safety officers in several communities. In 1983, using a combination of state and federal funding, BBNA also fielded three regional planning programs oriented toward economic development, land, and coastal zone management issues. Village government services also include assistance to both state-chartered municipalities and tribal governments with funding provided by the federal Administration for Native Americans.

5. Conclusion

The Bristol Bay Native Association provides many of the services to Native and other citizens in the Bristol Bay region that are traditionally provided by tribal or other local governments. As with the two non-profit associations examined before, BBNA has many characteristics of government and, like Maniilaq and the Tanana Chiefs Conference, might be considered governmental in function if not in law.

BBNA is recognized by the state as a nonprofit corporation, but its membership is clearly tied to ANCSA regional and village corporation shareholders and their descendents. In this last respect it differs from both the Tanana Chiefs and Maniilaq, each of which is organized as a consortium of Native traditional or IRA governing bodies rather than as a group of individuals. On the other hand, BBNA has specifically included the descendents of ANCSA shareholders in its membership and, like both Maniilaq and Tanana Chiefs, its board is clearly structured to afford equal representation of each village it serves. Moreover, as is the case also with Tanana Chiefs, BBNA has subdivided its numerous villages into subregions, to guarantee diverse, region-wide representation in its decision making.

E. General Conclusions

Unlike the Tlingit and Haida Central Council, discussed earlier, none of these nonprofit associations appear to be "tribes" or to be recognized as such by the federal government. Nonetheless, each of these associations is linked to Native villages or corporations which are recognized as "tribes" under federal legislation. That fact alone appears to afford them the status of recognized Native organizations under that legislation. Although Maniilaq is just as much a Native "organization" as either Tanana Chiefs or Bristol Bay, it differs from the latter two because its articles of incorporation appear to recognize a service obligation to both Natives and non-Natives. This is somewhat unique for a Native organization, but does not seem inconsistent with its federally recognized status. The organization is completely controlled by tribal governing bodies which, merely as a matter of choice, also provide services to non-Natives.

Similarly, the Bristol Bay Native Association also provides some programs to non-Natives. It too is an exclusively Native organization, although in terms of its organizational structure it is not tied as formally to Native governments as are both Maniilaq and Tanana Chiefs. Its membership is tied to ANCSA corporation shareholders and their descendents, but its board is made up of members elected "by democratic process within each village." It is thus not organized as a tribal consortium, but more generally as a service corporation responsive to primarily Native interests in the villages it serves.

No matter what their organizational structure, however, one thing is apparent about all the Native nonprofit associations we have discussed. Each grew substantially between 1978 and 1984 in terms of gross expenditures and the corresponding volume of programs provided. As others have demonstrated, these associations perform many of the service functions that one would expect of regional governments;[211] indeed, it appears these functions are still increasing. Yet these associations are not true governments, because they do not exercise any police power or political jurisdiction either as state or tribal governments. Even though they are not governments in the full sense of that term, these associations (as is demonstrated by their village government programs) do have the potential to assist communities in the development of governmental functions. The extent to which these functions can, either now or in the future, include traditional sovereign powers of tribal governments is considered more fully in chapter 10.

V. Multi-Regional Political Organizations

A. Introduction

The Alaska Federation of Natives (AFN) and the Alaska Native Brotherhood (ANB)[212] are unique among Alaska Native organizations. Both were formed in reaction to the important political issues of their day, and each has continuing relevance to the politics of the present. Neither organization has ever been federally recognized as a "tribe" nor do they administer programs under ANCSA or other federal Indian legislation. Nevertheless, each is a proven advocate for Alaskan Native political interests.

The ANB was responsible for obtaining the initial legislation which many years later resulted in the settlement of the Tlingit and Haida aboriginal claims; its support was also responsible for the extension of the IRA to Alaska. AFN, of course, was the unified political voice for Alaska Natives during the settlement of their land claims. Although the ANB and AFN have never been federally recognized as "tribes," their political representation of Alaska Native interests has long been recognized as legitimate. In that reality lies their necessity, their permanence and their strength.

B. Alaska Native Brotherhood and Sisterhood

1. History and Purpose

a. History

In 1912, at a meeting in Juneau, a group of Alaska Natives (one Tsimshian and twelve Tlingits from Sitka, Angoon, Wrangell, Juneau and Klawock) formed the Alaska Native Brotherhood (ANB). In 1915, the Alaska Native Sisterhood (ANS) was organized. Within the next ten years additional chapters called "camps" were formed throughout southeastern Alaska.[213] Both organizations are still active in southeastern and other parts of Alaska through some thirty-four local camps.

The Alaska Native Brotherhood and Sisterhood had three early goals: 1) recognition of Native citizenship rights, 2) education for Natives, and 3) abolition of "aboriginal customs." All three of these goals were compatible with the goals of the Dawes Act[214] and with Native assimilation into American society on an equal footing with non-Natives. According to one authority, the Alaska Native Brotherhood had no roots in aboriginal culture. Its goal was acculturation, and it was patterned after white men's clubs and societies which were then active in the struggle for a measure of Alaska self-government.[215] However, past Grand Camp President, Dr. Walter A. Soboleff, states that the Alaska Native Brotherhood and Sisterhood followed the traditional form of government for purposes of "tribal and clan operations."[216] The unique organizational structure of both the ANB and ANS may support Dr. Soboleff's statement; in any case, it appears to be an oversimplification to say that the ANB and ANS have "no" roots in aboriginal culture.

b. Purpose

As stated in its constitution, the purposes of the Brotherhood are:

> to assist and encourage the Native in his advancement among the cultivated races of the World, to oppose, discourage, and to overcome the narrow injustices of race prejudice, to commemorate the fine qualities of the Native races of North

America, to preserve their history, lore, art, and virtues, to cultivate the morality, education, commerce and Civil Government of Alaska, to improve individual and Municipal health and laboring conditions, and to create a true respect in Natives and in other persons with whom they deal for the letter and spirit of the Declaration of Independence and the Constitution and Laws of the United States.[217]

The purpose of the Alaska Native Sisterhood is "to complete the organization of the ALASKA NATIVE BROTHERHOOD."[218]

From the beginning, the Alaska Native Brotherhood involved itself with politics and political issues. These included such issues as labor relations on behalf of fishermen, territorial policies, economic development, the Indian Reorganization Act, the Alaska Native Claims Settlement Act and other Native concerns.[219] Felix Cohen confirms that the Brotherhood took a very active interest in legislation affecting Alaska Natives.[220] The Brotherhood was also active in Native voting rights; in 1924, one of its members, William L. Paul, Sr., an attorney, became the first Native elected to the territorial legislature.[221]

2. Structure and Organization

a. Membership

The Brotherhood's membership is open to all descendants (male and female) of aboriginal races of North America and to non-Natives who are married to such descendants. Non-Natives may vote and hold office in local ANB camps, but may not hold a Grand Camp office described below.[222] Membership in the Alaska Native Sisterhood is restricted to women who are accepted by unanimous vote of a local ANS Camp. Non-Native women may become members, but are not permitted to vote or hold even local office.[223] The rights of membership in the Sisterhood differ from the rights of Brotherhood membership in this respect.

b. Officers

The Brotherhood has six "Grand Officers": president, first vice-president, second vice-president, secretary, treasurer, and sergeant-at-arms. These officers are elected annually at a convention.[224] Additionally, all past ANB grand presidents are considered ANB "Grand Officers."[225]

The Sisterhood has four Grand Officers (president, vice-president, secretary and treasurer) who are, according to the *Brotherhood's* constitution, required to be elected "in the same manner and at the same time as the executive officers of the ALASKA NATIVE BROTHER-HOOD."[226] The executive committee consists of the Brotherhood's four Grand Officers, all past ANB Grand Presidents and the ANS Grand President. Five members constitute a quorum, and the executive committee is supposed to meet every three months between conventions.[227]

c. Organization

The Alaska Native Brotherhood and Sisterhood are organized into separate local camps subordinate to one elaborately interlocked "Grand Camp" or governing council. Between conventions, the Grand Camp is composed of the executive committee, the grand officers of the ANB and the ANS grand president. During the annual convention, the chairmen of the ANB subordinate camps and two specially elected delegates from each subordinate ANB and ANS camp are added to the Grand Camp.[228] The four grand officers of the Sisterhood constitute the ANS "Grand Camp Auxiliary," and the president of each local Sisterhood camp is also a member of the Sisterhood's "Grand Camp Council."[229]

Although the Sisterhood is organizationally separate from the Brotherhood, both its purpose and its representation on the Grand Camp place it in a supportive role. Although the ANB usually has a majority on the Grand Camp, the ANS Grand Officers, plus two specially elected ANS delegates also have Grand Camp seats during the annual convention.[230] Additionally, between conventions the ANS president is a member of the Grand Camp executive committee.

ANB and ANS policy matters are decided annually at a joint convention,[231] and are reflected in convention resolutions. Between conventions, the Grand Camp has the power to "formulate policies within the Constitution...and to appropriate money for the execution of such policies."[232] The ANS Grand Camp Council does not have similar constitutional authority; ANS policy formulation and implementation between conventions appears to be largely left to ANS local camps. Because of its central organization, the ANB Grand Camp therefore appears to be the unifying force for both ANB and ANS.

The executive committee acts for the Grand Camp when the convention is not in session, but it cannot act contrary to "the expressed will of the Convention" and is governed by such "instructions as they may receive from the Grand Camp." Although even public expressions by ANB officials are disfavored unless sanctioned by the Grand Camp, the executive committee does have the power, in spite of these restrictions, to act for the good of the Brotherhood in "any clear emergency."[233]

3. Recognition

As noted earlier, neither the Alaska Native Brotherhood nor Sisterhood are recognized by the federal government as eligible for Native programs nor are they considered "tribes."[234] In spite of that fact, the ANB has been accepted as representing the legitimate political interests of at least a portion of Alaska's Natives. The ANB was instrumental in first preventing and later permitting the Indian Reorganization Act to be applied to Alaska.[235] The Brotherhood was also instrumental in obtaining passage of the Tlingit-Haida Claims Act in 1935, which eventually resulted in recognition of Tlingit and Haida aboriginal claims to much of southeast Alaska.[236] Finally, the Alaska Native Brotherhood played an initial organizing role in the Alaska Native land claims settlement.[237]

4. Accomplishments and Activities

The Alaska Native Brotherhood, supported by the Alaska Native Sisterhood, can point to a long list of accomplishments furthering the political, social and economic status of Alaska Natives. In 1977, Dr. Walter A. Soboleff, ANB Grand President, noted that the ANB had among other things:

> lobbied for passage of [the] State Racial discrimination bill; gained recognition of Native rights as citizens, won the right of Natives to vote; integrated public schools; extended workmen's compensation laws to cover all; included Natives [in] aid-to-dependent children; secured relief for aged Natives; brought [the] IRA act to Alaska; brought hospitals for Natives to Alaska; in a time of great need encouraged establishment of boarding schools and further education of our youth; initiated [the] Tlingit and Haida land suit, and encouraged Native involvement in State and Federal Government.[238]

The Alaska Native Brotherhood continues to use its political position on behalf of Native interests; its members serve as directors and in other responsible positions of both Native and non-Native businesses, governments and other organizations. Its overall goal is to improve Native community life, and Dr. Soboleff has described it as a "training ground group for leadership."[239]

5. Conclusion

The Alaska Native Brotherhood does not provide direct governmental services nor does it serve in a governing capacity for specific communities; it is not recognized either by the state or federal governments for such purposes. Although it has no formal governmental authority, it is reportedly the oldest formally organized Indian group in the United States.[240] It has also had great political importance to many of Alaska's Native people. Long before any other organization was capable of doing so, it united Native people around common issues and obtained significant political and legal gains. It continues to be an effective political force on the Alaska Native scene.[241]

C. Alaska Federation of Natives (AFN)

1. History and Purpose

In the late 1960's many Alaska Native leaders felt a statewide organization was vital to solving land claims and other Alaska Native problems. In 1966, over four hundred Native people gathered in Anchorage, to discuss common problems and laid the groundwork for the Alaska Federation of Natives. According to the preamble to the original AFN constitution, Alaska Natives formed the statewide organization in order to:

> secure ourselves and our descendants the rights and benefits to which we are entitled under the laws of the United States, and the State of Alaska; to enlighten the public toward a better understanding of Native people; to preserve the Native cultural values; to seek an equitable adjustment of Native affairs and Native claims; to seek, to secure and to preserve our rights under existing laws of the Unites States; to promote the common welfare of the Natives of Alaska and to foster the continued loyalty and allegiance of the Natives of Alaska to the flag of the United States and the State of Alaska.

Objectives named in AFN's Articles of Incorporation pledge the federation:

> to promote pride on the part of the Natives of Alaska in their history and traditions; to preserve the customs, folklore, and art of the Native races; to promote the physical, economic, and social well-being of the Natives of Alaska; to discourage and overcome racial prejudice and inequities which such prejudice creates; and promote good government, by reminding those who govern and those who are governed of their joint and mutual responsibilities.

Funding for the organization during the early years came from membership dues, individual contributions, and loans. In the late 1960's, the Alaska Federation of Natives began to operate programs to deliver social services to Alaska Natives, but AFN's chief activity during that period was to seek a fair and just settlement of Alaska Native land claims.

On December 18, 1971, the Alaska Native Claims Settlement Act passed, initiating a new era for the federation. The settlement did not provide for a statewide Native organization, and many regional Native associations were dissatisfied with the then current AFN administration. Nineteen seventy-two was a year of crisis for the Alaska Federation of Natives; leadership in the federation changed, and the bylaws were amended to place the selection of the AFN president in the hands of a twelve-member board representing each of the then twelve regional corporations established under ANCSA. During this period, many Natives once again realized the need for a strong statewide organization. The Department of the Interior had promulgated regulations governing land selections, which regional corporations found to be completely contrary to the intent of the claims act. Utilizing AFN, they managed to secure more acceptable regulations.

In 1973, in response to Alaska Native human service needs, AFN reorganized and created two departments. One was a Land Claims Department—responsive to the profit-making corporations and to implementation of the Alaska Native Claims Settlement Act. The other was a Human Resources Department—responsive to the nonprofit Native associations and to Alaska Native health, education, and social service concerns.[242] Subsequently, the AFN board was restructured to include representatives from each of the thirteen regional profit corporations and eleven of the twelve regional nonprofit Native, associations discussed earlier. The full board was further divided into two executive committees called the "Land Claims" and "Human Resources" boards in order to better focus on the distinct interests of the profit corporations and nonprofit associations.[243]

2. Membership and Officers

There are five classes of membership in AFN. The only members entitled to vote are the regional corporations and nonprofit associations, through their representatives on the AFN Board of Directors and their delegates to the annual AFN convention. More than eighty thousand Alaska Natives are represented through AFN's voting member organizations.[244] Native individuals, non-Native individuals, organizations that are primarily Native to non-Native corporations and business compose the other (non-voting) classes. There are specific dues and membership requirements for each class.

AFN's annual goals and priorities are established by the delegates to its yearly convention (usually held in October) at which time the chairman of the full AFN board is also elected. Delegates to the convention are selected by each of AFN's voting members (i.e., the profit corporations and nonprofit associations) in proportion to the number of Natives enrolled under ANCSA to each regional profit corporation.[245] To achieve convention goals, the full board, Land Claims Board or Human Resources Board, depending on the issue, establish policies which are implemented by AFN staff under the direction of the president, who serves at the pleasure of the full board. The full board meets at least twice a year, but the full board chairman or the president may call special meetings.[246]

3. Recognition

Since the early days of the federation, AFN has been recognized by the state and federal governments for contracting and delivering services to Native people. Although AFN does not have formal recognition as a "tribe" or tribal governing body, it has long been acknowledged to be the legitimate political voice for most Alaskan Natives on statewide and national issues of mutual concern. Conceivably, AFN could be recognized as a Native "organization" under either 25 USCA 450b(c) of the Self-Determination Act or 25 USCA 1452(f) of the Indian Financing Act, but the practical obstacles in doing so seem almost insurmountable.[247]

4. Current Activity

AFN's role as the representative of the broad range of Alaska Native interests is dramatically emphasized by the events of the early 1980's. This period saw new concern with implementing the ANCSA settlement as well as with the possible negative effects if the restrictions on the alienation of Native stock are removed in 1991 as is required under ANCSA.[248] Subsistence, continued federal Native services and the emergence of the tribal government movement have also tested AFN's ability to be a unified voice for these diverse Alaska Naitve interests. AFN's response to these issues appears to be one calculted to build consensus where consensus is possible, coupled with pragmatic efforts to achieve goals upon which Alaska Natives can agree.

During 1982 and 1983, for example, AFN influenced the outcome of a number of federal and state policy deliberations and initiated a series of studies and conferences seemingly aimed at developing Native consensus on upcoming issues. On the federal level, AFN requested and obtained a committtment from the BIA to establish a "descendency roll" of the children of ANCSA shareholders to ensure that these descendents remain eligible for federal Native services. The federation also ensured that Alaska Natives were included in President Reagan's 1982 Indian policy statement and successfully opposed attempts to move the BIA's area office from Juneau to Portland.[249] At the state level, AFN spearheaded a successful drive to defeat a 1982 attempt to remove the subsistence priority from state fishing and hunting laws and successfully lobbied the governor to maintain a balance of urban-rural and commercial, sport and subsistence interests on the state Board of Fisheries. The federation also was instrumental in obtaining state legislation defining the scope of local government property taxing authority on ANCSA corporation lands.[250]

Regarding Native community consensus, AFN sponsored several studies, conferences and retreats seemingly aimed at defining and (ultimately) resolving issues of concern to Natives. During 1982 and 1983 the federation initiated studies on the effects of the 1991 ANCSA deadlines and sponsored a series of AFN board retreats which resulted in specific resolutions adopted at the 1983 AFN convention to address these issues.[251] During this same period AFN was actively involved in coordinating negotiations among the regional (and village) corporations over resolving the thorny 7(i) revenue sharing provisions of ANCSA.[252] Finally, AFN also sponsored a statewide conference in 1983 to examine and discuss the history and application of the Indian Reorganization Act in Alaska. This conference resulted in the formation of the United Tribes of Alaska, a new statewide Native organization of IRA and traditional village councils, to more specifically address the question of tribal government in Alaska.[253]

5. Conclusion

As the statewide political arm of the regional profit corporations and nonprofit associations, the Alaska Federation of Natives has represented statewide Native concerns since 1966. It was primarily responsible for the passage of the Alaska Native Claims Settlement Act. Since then it has been the primary advocacy organization for Alaska Native common concerns related both to land claims and human services. Although AFN is not a recognized Native "tribe," it fills a vital role as the statewide political arm of Alaska Natives and their regional profit and nonprofit corporations. During the early 1980's, it was using its position to lobby for favorable resolution of issues agreed upon by Natives and to build consensus among the Native community in response to upcomming issues.

D. United Tribes of Alaska

1. History and Purpose

As noted above, the United Tribes of Alaska grew out of an AFN sponsored conference on the Indian Reorganization Act. That was in March, 1983; the United Tribes held its first organizational meeting later that year in May at the University of Alaska campus in Anchorage. The meeting was attended by representatives from between thirty-seven and forty-two Alaska Native villages which comprised the charter members of UTA.[254] The organization held its first annual convention in October of the same year; by then its membership had grown to fifty-six villages.[255] Press reports from that time indicate that the possibility of using tribal governments as mechanisms to retain traditional village lands as well as institutions for local self-government were among the motivations of the new organization.[256]

2. Organization

The charter approved for ratification at the October, 1983 convention, disclaims any independent authority for United Tribes, but specifically provides that UTA's authority "derives from the governmental authority of its member Tribes."[257] This delegated authority is exercised through the "tribal council" which consists of "one representative from each member Tribe."[258] The tribal council may delegate authority to the UTA officers which consist of a chairman, vice-chairman, secretary and treasurer, who each serve a term of two years.[259] By the terms of its charter UTA, acting through the tribal council, has general powers to "formulate general policy on all issues relevant to members" and to "serve as a coordinating entity to further the interests and activities of members," but the charter explicitly provides that: "None of the rights and powers of the member Tribes shall be abridged" by the charter or any UTA action.[260]

3. Conclusion

The United Tribes of Alaska was specifically formed to advocate on behalf of tribal government interests in Alaska, and in that respect has a different focus from that of AFN, whose advocacy is principally directed toward land and human services isssues. Nonetheless, the initial organizers of the United Tribes disclaimed any intention to oppose AFN on these issuses, [261] and AFN openly supports UTA and is "committed to a positive working relationship with the new tribal organization." [262] The United Tribes appears to be an advocacy consortium for its member tribes and is similar in its organizational structure to both the Tanana Chiefs Conference and Maniilaq. Unlike those associations, however, UTA is strictly a political advocate for tribal governmental interests throughout Alaska and is not a service delivery organization.

VI. Tribal Operations Program

A. Introduction

The BIA Tribal Operations program is a loosely knit bureaucracy consisting of an area tribal operations officer in Juneau and one agency officer each in Anchorage, Fairbanks, Bethel, Nome and Juneau. [263] However, the area officer has no supervisory ("line") authority over the agency officers who are responsible to their respective agency superintendents; in the southeast agency (Juneau), the entire Tribal Operations program has been contracted out to the Tlingit and Haida Central Council.

Almost by definition, the Tribal Operations program requires the existence of Native "tribes" before there can be any "operations." Just as important, those tribes must have resources and "tribal" authority of some sort before they can become involved in the sort of activities which might require the assistance of the Tribal Operations program. The confusion about what was a "tribe" in Alaska, coupled with a chronic lack of tribal resources has historically meant that the scope of the Tribal Operations program was limited largely to servicing the needs of the Metlakatla Indian Community and those few IRA governments which had an active life. ANCSA and the Self-Determination and Indian Financing acts have changed this pattern.

Some 210 Alaska Native villages have been identified as eligible for benefits under Section 11(b) of ANCSA. Those villages and their associated village and regional corporations are specifically recognized as "tribes" in the Indian Self-Determination Act of 1975. The same entities qualify as "tribes" under the Indian Financing Act [264] as do certain Native groups which may not be eligible for benefits as ANCSA "villages." [265] However, the traditional functions of the Tribal Operations program appear to relate more to the concerns of tribal entities exercising governmental functions rather than tribal business enterprises. For that reason it is not yet clear that the Tribal Operations program would (or should) expand its area of operation to include the interests of the various corporations which are recognized as "tribes" or "organizations" under recent legislation. Conceivably those concerns might be better left to other BIA programs more directly involved with business and economic development matters or consolidated under a single program designed specifically to service Native business and economic development interests in general.

B. Tribal Operations Responsibilities

Generally, the Tribal Operations program acts as a liaison between a BIA area director and the various tribes within his jurisdiction. However, that role may be nonexistent if the area director prefers to retain personal control over area office tribal relations. Aside from this general liaison role, the present responsibilities of the Tribal Operations program are principally 1) approval of attorney contracts, 2) processing IRA constitutions and amendments to constitutions, 3)processing and monitoring Self-Determination Act tribal government improvement grants and 4) determining Native eligibility for BIA programs and services.

1. Attorney Contracts

Federal law requires that all attorney contracts with IRA[266] and traditional tribes[267] be approved by the Secretary of the Interior or his designee. The area directors have been delegated this authority,[268] and the Tribal Operations officer is the staff official who assists the area director in these matters. An IRA or traditional governing body or business council wishing to employ an attorney may first obtain a "tentative contract" from the BIA and at that time explain its reasons for hiring an attorney.[269] The tentative contract is a form contract which can be modified only with BIA approval; it is intended to protect the tribe from unscrupulous attorneys and ensure that the BIA exercises its trust responsiblity. Negotiation and execution of tribal attorney contracts for IRA organizations are governed by the provisions of the particular IRA constitution or charter,[270] but negotiation and execution for a tribe not organized under the IRA in controlled by BIA regulations.[271] However, these regulations do not apply to ANCSA corporations, because they are organized under state law and therefore have the power to select their own attorneys without BIA oversight.

2. IRA Constitutions

Under the terms of the Indian Reorganization Act, the Secretary of the Interior has the authority to approve (or disapprove) proposed constitutions and corporate charters of reorganized tribal governments.[272] As discussed earlier, this authority has been used in the past, until 1971, to approve the reorganization of some seventy-one communities throughout Alaska. Beginning in the late 1970's, and perhaps as a result of the influence of the Self-Determination Act, about thirty traditional village councils throughout Alaska submitted proposed new constitutions.[273] Although the constitutions must ultimately be approved in Washington, D. C., responsibility for the initial review of these new constitutions lies with the area Tribal Operations officer.

Although there are regulations describing the procedures to be followed in adopting new constitutions (elections, etc.), there are no definite guidelines about what provisions the constitutions should (or may) contain.[274] Typically though, IRA constitutions will describe the powers the particular government will exercise. Perhaps because the powers of tribal governments are less clearly defined in Alaska, the attempt to define them in these proposed IRA constitutions became the focus of an extented backroom political donnybrook involving the State of Alaska, the federal government and the applicant tribes. The state governor, in response to the Interior Department's approval of a proposed constitution in 1981, requested Secretary of the Interior Watt to delay further action on the constitution until the jurisdictional issues of the scope of the tribe's authority could be resolved.[275] As of mid-1984 there had been no action on this or any other IRA constitution.[276]

3. Tribal Government Improvement Grants

The Tribal Operations program also is charged with processing and monitoring grants to improve tribal government and the operations of tribal organizations under the Self-Determination Act.[277] In 1984 there were 155 grant applications under this program, ranging from six thousand to fifteen thousand dollars per application, depending on the population to be served by the tribal grantee. Tribal Operations is responsible for the initial review and evaluation of the grant applications and for monitoring their execution in the field.[278]

4. Determining Eligibility for Native Programs and Services

Although all ANCSA enrollment ended in 1977, and there is no continuing enrollment program for Alaska Natives,[279] the Tribal Operations program is nonetheless responsible for determining individual Native eligibility for BIA programs which are frequently based on a "blood quantum" requirement. Individual Natives applying for BIA benefits but who are not enrolled under ANCSA must be certified to meet the specific blood quantum requirements of each program or service for which they have applied.[280] The Tribal Operations program staff is responsible for researching the applicant's ancestry, usually using the ANCSA roll as a starting place, and issuing a "certificate of Indian blood" if the applicant qualifies. The BIA in Alaska issues between five and six *thousand* such certificates annually.[281]

C. Conclusion

The Tribal Operations program is the theoretical link between the tribes and the federal bureacracy which serves them, but unlike most other BIA programs, its duties and responsibilities are not even de scribed in the BIA Manual. This does not appear to be the fault of either the agency or area Tribal Operations officers but of the BIA central office in Washington, D.C. Tribal Operations is accorded a chapter in the BIA Manual (83 BIAM), but the provisions have become outdated and have never been revised. Although there are substantial guidelines for the approval of attorney contracts, one principle responsibility, there are no substantive guidelines for the review and approval of IRA constitutions. By 1984, this had become a particular embarassment in Alaska where the apparent aspirations of some thirty Native villages had seemingly become victim of backchannel bureaucratic politics. However, as noted earlier, the Self-Determination Act and similar legislation are breathing new life into Alaska Native "tribes" and "organizations." This legislation may have the same effect on the Tribal Operations program. That in turn may mean that its responsibilities will become more realistic—and complex.

ENDNOTES

[1]The term "nonsystem" is not intended to mean that there are no service delivery or political systems in rural Alaska, but rather to emphasize that there are a wide variety of systems which are not fully integrated into a unified network such as is found in urban Alaska. Nor is the term intended to imply that the absence of a unified system is necessarily inappropriate to the rural Alaska situation.

[2]T.A. Morehouse, et al., *Alaska's Urban and Rural Governments,* (New York: University Press of America, 1984), 169 ff., also discusses the multiplicity of governments and quasi-government organizations in rural Alaska. See also *Problems and Possibilities for Service Delivery and Government in the Alaska Unorganized Borough,* (Anchorage: Alaska Department of Community and Regional Affairs, 1981), 21-47.

[3]Service areas such as Rural Education Attendance Areas (REAAs), Coastal Resource Service Areas (CRSAs) and Aquaculture Service Areas are omitted from this discussion. See generally Morehouse, note 2, above, at 196-202.

[4]Morehouse, note 2, above, at 229. At present there appear to be no empirical studies of the effectiveness of diffuse service delivery and government in rural Alaska, but Morehouse concludes that the present arrangement "seems preferable to any other perceived alternative, as far as rural people are concerned." Id. See also *Problems and Possiblities,* note 2 above, at 65-80, Louis Weschler's discussion of the possiblities for "concurrent government" in rural Alaska.

[5]Indian Village Act of 1915, Session Laws of Alaska (SLA), Ch. 11. Amended, 1917 SLA Ch. 25; repealed 1929 SLA Ch. 23.

[6]See F. Cohen, *Handbook of Federal Indian Law,* (Washington, D.C.: G.P.O., 1942; reprinted New York: AMS, 1972) at 413, n. 200.

[7]See "Organized Boroughs and Cities," (Anchorage, Alaska Department of Community and Regional Affairs, 1980 map).

[8]Alaska Constitution, Art. X, Sec. 1.

[9]A.S. 29.48.010 (1983).

[10]A.S. 29.48.035 (1983).

[11]See D. S. Case, *Twenty-Four Ordinances to Enforce Local Law Through the Alaska "Village" Council (With Comments),* (Anchorage: Alaska Federation of Natives, 1977).

[12]See *Joint Task Force Report on Alaskan Native Issues,* (Washington, D.C.: American Indian Policy Review Commission, G.P.O., 1976) at 22.

[13]Id. at 21.

[14]Id. at 24.

[15]25 USCA 476. Section 16 of the IRA was originally applicable to Alaska, but certain other provisions were not. The IRA was made fully applicable to Alaska in 1936.

[16]Compare Federal Field Committee for Development Planning in Alaska, *Alaska Natives and the Land,* (Washington, D.C.: G.P.O., 1968) at 41 (fifty-nine IRA villages) and AIPRC Alaska Report, note 12, above, at 21 (seventy IRA villages).

[17]Phone conversation with Mary Schaeffer, Vice-President, Management and Planning, Maniilaq Assoc. (February 27, 1978).

[18]AIPRC Alaska Report, note 12, above, at 21.

[19]See e.g., *Powers of Indian Tribes,* 551 I.D. 14 (1934).

[20]F. Cohen, note 6, above at 122. See also F. Cohen, *Handbook of Federal Indian Law (1982 Edition),* (Charlottesville, Va.: Michie Bobs-Merrill, 1982) at 246-257.

[21]The extent to which Alaska Native tribes have been specifically deprived of these inherent powers is discussed in chapter 10. below.

[22]See 48 Fed. Reg. (No. 248) 56862, 56865-866 (Dec. 23, 1983), originally published in 47 Fed. Reg. (No. 227) 53130, 53133-135 (Nov. 24, 1982), for the BIA list. See Tribal Tax Status Act (Title II, P.L. 97-473, 96 Stat. 2650, as amended by P.L. 98-21, 97 Stat. 65) and Internal Revenue Service Bulletin No. 1983-50 (Dec. 12, 1983).

[23]The Juneau BIA area office recommended that all villages found eligible for ANCSA be included in the list as eligible for BIA services. Memorandum from Juneau Area Director to Deputy Assistant Secretary—Indian Affairs (Operations), "Publication of Alaska Villages Recognized as Tribes Receiving Services from the Bureau of Indian Affairs [25 CFR 545.6(b)]" (May 28, 1982). The following traditional councils which had previously received services were omitted from the published list:

Ninilchik	Andreafsky	Koliganek	English Bay
Unalaska	Chaloonawick	Nuiqsut	Salamatof
Yakutat	Kaltag	Ohagamuit	Seldovia

[24]Id. The four communities were: Pelican, Skagway, Tenakee and Tok. Twenty other communities listed below which reportedly had not received services prior to ANCSA were also excluded from the published list.

Afognak	Georgetown	Napaimute	Uganik
Ayakulik	Hamilton	Paimute	Umkumiute
Bells Flat	Kaguyak	Pauloff Harbor	Uyak
Bill Moore's	Litnik	Port William	Unga
Council	Mary's Igloo	Solomon	Woody Island

[25]Phone conversation with John Hope, then Tribal Operations Officer, BIA Area Office, Juneau (February 28, 1978). Mr. Hope subsequently served as BIA Juneau Area Director and at present is the president of the Tlingit and Haida Central Council.

[26]Id.

[27]Interview with Roy Peratrovich, then superintendent of the BIA Anchorage agency (February 9, 1978). See also 25 CFR 81.7.

[28]Constitution and Bylaws, Brevig Mission Community, on file with BIA, Anchorage agency.

[29]Roy Peratrovich interview, note 27, above.

[30]25 USCA 476.

[31]25 USCA 473a.

[32]55. I.D. 14 (1934). See notes 19 and 20, above, and accompanying text.

[33]All seventy-one of the Alaska IRAs are included in the published list of "Alaska Native Entities" which the BIA recognizes as eligible for service. See note 22, above. The initial publication of the list in 1982 noted that there was a "multiple, overlapping eligibility of native entities" in Alaska, presumably referring to the eligibility of ANCSA village and regional corporations under some statutes. The explanation accompanying the list advised that those entities included had "priority for purposes of funding and services." 47 Fed. Reg. at 53134. See also BIA memorandum of May 28, 1982, note 23, above.

[34]See chapter 6, above.

[35]See e.g., 25 USCA 450b(b) tribal definition, Self-Determination Act.

[36]See e.g., Art. II, Sec. 1, Constitution of the Kenaitze Indian Tribe (1971).

[37]See e.g., Art. II, Constitution of the Native Village of Deering (1945). Contained in *Charters, Constitutions and Bylaws of the Indian Tribes of North America,* "The Northwest and Alaska." George Fay, ed., (Greely, Colo.: University of Northern Colorado, 1972) Part XV.

[38]See 25 CFR Part 81.

[39]The enactment of the Administrative Procedure Act in 1955 (5 USCA) has probably eliminated the legal effect of the unpublished 1937 "Instructions" by requiring publication of all substantive administrative rules.

[40]AIPRC Alaska Report, note 12, above, at 21.

[41]25 USCA 450 et seq. (1975 Supp.) See also Morehouse, note 2, above, at 178-179, discussing the influence of the Self-Determination Act.

[42]See note 33, above, regarding the priority for IRAs and traditional councils. See also Morehouse, note 2, above, at 179.

[43]See John J. Kirlin, "Scenarios for the Political Development of Alaska," and Louis Weschler, "Three Approaches to Local/State Governance for Rural Alaska," in *Problems and Possibilities,* note 2, above, at 53-80. See also Michael Walleri, *Tribal-State Relations: A New Paradigm for Local Government in Alaska,* (Fairbanks: Tanana Chiefs Conference).

[44]See e.g., *The Maniilaq Association 1983 Annual Report and Directory of Services,* (Kotzebue, Alaska: Maniilaq Association), at 52-53; *Dena' Nena' Henash,* (Fairbanks: Tanana Chiefs Conference Inc., 1980) at 13; *Central Council of Tlingit and Haida Indian Tribes of Alaska Annual Report for the Year Ending September 30, 1983,* (Juneau: Tlingit and Haida Central Council) at 18.

[45]Interview with John Shively, Vice-President, NANA Development Corp. (February 27, 1978). See 43 USCA 1613(e) as amended by the Act of January 2, 1976. P.L. 94-204, 89 Stat. 1145, 1149.

[46]Morehouse, note 2, above at 177.

[47]Phone conversation of April 30, 1984, with Andrew J. Hope III, Executive Director Sitka Community Association.

[48]Board of Equalization v. Alaska Native Brotherhood, 666 P. 2d 1015, 1017 (Alaska 1983).

[49]Morehouse, note 2, above, at 178.

[50]Id.

[51]Under chapter 60 of the 1981 Session Laws of Alaska (60 SLA 1981), unincorporated communities, including those governed by IRA and traditional councils, were eligible for one-time grants of up to one thousand dollars per capita. AS 29.89.050, also provides annual grants of twenty five thousand dollars to unincorporated communities organized under the IRA. Other state grants are or have been available to unincorporated communities, including those governed by Native governments. See generally *Local Government Hi-Lites,* Cooperative Extension Service, University of Alaska (Vol. 10, No. 3, June 1982).

[52]Morehouse, note 2, above, at 179-180. See also R. Price, *Native Rights: A Report for the Alaska Statehood Commission,* (Fairbanks: Alaska Statehood Commission, 1982) at 113-116.

[53]Morehouse, note 2, above, at 180.

[54]Id. at 180-181. See also Johnson v. Chilkat Indian Village, 457 F. Supp. 384 (D. Alas. 1978), regarding Klukwan tribal jurisdiction.

[55]Native Village of Tyonek v. Puckett, No. A82-364 (D. Alas., filed September 26, 1982).

[56]"Akiachack seeks IRA status," *Tundra Times* (Nov. 9, 1983), and "State, tribal ways often differ," Id. (Nov. 16, 1983), describing the village of Akiachack's efforts to dissolve its state-chartered municipality and operate solely under an IRA form of government.

[57]IRA and traditional tribal governments have been suggested as possible vehicles to hold lands conveyed to ANCSA corporations in permanent tax exempt status. Unlike corporations, tribes have retained sovereign immunity from suit which may mean that their lands or other assets could not be reached by judicial process. Similarly, tribal governments can define their own membership terms to include children born after 1971, who may not necessarily become share holders in the ANCSA corporations. These and other issues related to tribal government in Alaska are discussed further in chapter 10.

[58]See ANB and ANS discussion, section V B, below. The ancestry of the Tlingit and Haida Central Council is also reflected in its organizational and executive committee structures which in several respects are similar to that of the ANB. Compare Art. III (The Grand Camp) and Art. V, sec. 6 (Executive Committee) of the 1963 ANB Constitution with Art. III (Composition of the Central Council) and Art. IX (Functions of the Executive Committee) of the Constitution of the Tlingit and Haida Indian Tribes of Alaska (April 17, 1973, as amended).

[59]See Constitution Alaska Native Brotherhood and Sisterhood (1963).

[60]Act of June 19, 1935, 49 Stat. 388.

[61]"A Development Planning Program for the Central Council of the Tlingit and Haida Indians of Alaska," (Tlingit and Haida Central Council, 1970) at 23.

[62]Art. I, T&HCC constitution, note 58, above.

[63]Tlingit and Haida Indians v. U.S., 389 F. 2d 778 (Ct. Cls. 1968).

[64]Cogo v. Central Council of Tlingit and Haida Indians, 465 F. Supp. 1286 (D. Alas. 1979), sovereign immunity with respect to enrollment and distribution of judgment funds. The Tlingit and Haida Indians are also listed as entities recognized for BIA service and contracting priority and are considered a tribal government by the Internal Revenue Service for purposes of the 1982 Tribal Tax Status Act, IRS Bulletin No. 1983-50 (Dec. 12, 1983) at 112. See note 22, above.

[65]Art. I, T&HCC constitution, note 58, above.

[66]Id., Art. VI, sec. 1.

[67]Id., Secs. 3 and 4, respectively.

[68]See discussion of IRA governments above. For example, IRA councils may hire attorneys only with the approval (albeit limited) of the Secretary of the Interior. IRA constitutions may only be amended with secretarial approval, see 25 USCA 476 and 25 CFR Part 81. Compare Art. X. T&HCC constitution, note 58, above, permitting amendment by the Tlingit and Haida delegates in assembly.

[69]Rule 20, Rules for the Election of Delegates to the Official Central Council Tlingit and Haida Indian Tribes of Alaska, as amended in 1983.

[70]Art. VI, sec. 1h of the T&HCC constitution, note 58, above, permits the Central Council to designate the communities which in turn elect delegates to the Central Council. Rule 1 of the T&HCC rules of election, note 69, above, lists the following communities as of 1983:

Anchorage	Hydaburg	Klawock	Saxman
Angoon	Juneau	Klukwan	Sitka
Craig	Kake	Metlakatla	Wrangell
Haines	Kasaan	Pelican	Yakutat
Hoonah	Ketchikan	Petersburg	San Francisco
			Seattle

[71]Rules 2 and 3, T&HCC rules of election, note 69, above.

[72]Art. IV, sec. 1 and Art. V, sec. 1, respectively, T&HCC constitution, note 58, above.

[73]See rules 5, 18 and 21(b), T&HCC rules of election, note 69, above.

[74]Art. VII, sec. 1 and Art IX, T&HCC constitution, note 58, above.

[75]Art. V, sec. 2, T&HCC constitution, note 58, above. The president or one-fourth of the delegates may also call special assemblies.

[76]Art. VIII, T&HCC constitution, note 58, above.

[77]49 Stat. 388, sec. 7.

[78]Tlingit and Haida Indians of Alaska et al. v. U.S., 177 F. Supp. 452 (Ct. Cls. 1959).

[79]Letter from Raymond E. Paddock, Jr., President, Tlingit and Haida Central Council to Senator James S. Abourezk, Chairman, American Indian Policy Review Commission (April 23, 1977) at 4.

[80]Act of August 19, 1965 (79 Stat. 543).

[81]Tlingit and Haida Indians of Alaska et al. v. U.S., 389 F. 2d 778 (Ct. Cls. 1968).

[82]Act of July 13. 1970, 84 Stat. 431 (25 USCA 1211).

[83]ANCSA Sec. 7(a)(10), 43 USCA 1606(a)(10).

[84]ANCSA Sec. 7(d), Id. 1606(d).

[85]Cogo v. Central Council of Tlingit and Haida Indians, 465 F. Supp. 1286 (D. Alas. 1979).

[86]See S. Rep. No. 91-848, 91st Cong., 2nd sess. at 1 (1970) and H.R. Rep. No. 91-881, 91st Cong., 2nd sess. at 1 (1970), cited in Paddock letter, note 79, above, at 9 and 10.

[87]Final Report of the American Indian Policy Review Commission, (Washington, D.C.: G.P.O., 1977) at 496.

[88]"Indian involvement" was the administrative predecessor to the Self-Determination Act. It relied in part on the 1910 Buy Indian Act (25 USCA 47) to permit contracting with Native organizations for Native services.

[89]25 USCA 450 et seq.

[90]AIPRC Final Report, note 87 above, at 496.

[91]25 USC 450b(b) and (c), respectively.

[92]24 USCA 450b(c).

[93]AIPRC Final Report, note 87 above at 496. See also 25 CFR 271.18-271.20, describing procedures for tribal resolutions approving new and renewal contracts.

[94]25 USCA 450b(b).

[95]The explanation accompanying the initial publication of the list of "Alaska Native Entities" recognized for BIA services notes that the entities listed have "priority for funding and services." No ANCSA corporations are included. See 48 Fed. Reg., note 22, above, at 53134.

[96]See "Meaning of 'Indian tribe' in section 4(b) of P.L. 93-638 for purposes of application to Alaska," Assistant Solicitor for Indian Affairs memorandum (May 21, 1976), concluding that any corporation or other tribe "benefiting" from the contract would have to approve it.

[97]T&HCC 1983 Annual Report, note 44, above, at 5.

[98]Id. at 19-20.

[99]Id. at 8-10.

[100]Id. at 12-15.

[101]Id. at 11.

[102]Id. at 17 and 23.

[103]See chapter 5, above, discussing the reindeer.

[104]25 USCA 477.

[105]John Hope conversation, note 25, above. See also Corporate Charter of the Native village of Deering, Alaska (1945) in *Charters and Constitutions,* note 37, above, at 1.

[106]Constitution and Bylaws of the Hydaburg Cooperative Association, (Washington, D.C.: G.P.O., 1957). See also Cohen (1942), note 6, above, at 414.

[107]Id.

[108]See note 31, above, and accompanying text.

[109]Deering Corporate Charter, *Charters and Constitutions,* note 105, above. The charter was "to be effective when duly agreed to, provided that the said Constitution and bylaws have been duly agreed to."

[110]See *Charters and Constitutions,* note 37, above, "Organized Villages of Nome District, Alaska," preceding page 1.

[111]Section 1, Deering Corporate Charter, *Charters and Constitutions,* note 37, above.

[112]See chapter 10, below, discussion of sovereign immunity. Interestingly, Metlakatla specifically amended its IRA corporate charter in 1949 to remove the "sue or be sued" clause from its list of corporate powers. See *Charters and Constitutions,* note 37, above, at 21.

[113]Tonuak Articles of Association, *Charters and Constitutions,* note 37, above, at 33.

[114]Preamble, Constitution and Bylaws of the Hydaburg Cooperative Association (1938), *Charters and Constitutions,* note 37, above, at 12.

[115]Id. Art. II, secs. 3(a) and 4(a).

[116]Id. Art. V, sec. 1.

[117]Id. Art. IV. See also Cohen, 1942, note 6, above, at 414.

[118]Deering Constitution, *Charters and Constitutions,* note 37, above, at 3.

[119]Through section 10 of the IRA (25 USCA 470), now merged with other loan funds under the Indian Financing Act (25 USCA 1461).

[120]43 USCA 1606(d), regional corporations and 1607(a), village corporations.

[121]A.S. 10.05.010 et seq. (Alaska Business Corporation Act).

[122]25 USCA 1451 et seq.

[123]43 USCA 1606(h). .

[124]The alienation provisions were modified in 1980 to permit corporations to perpetually restrict non-Native voting rights and impose a right of first refusal on all stock sales. In order to take advantage of these options, a corporation must amend its articles by majority vote of its shareholders by December 18, 1991. Title XIV, sec. 1410, Act of December 2, 1980, P.L. 96-487, 94 Stat. 2491 (Alaska National Interest Lands Conservation Act, amending section 7(h)(3) of ANCSA [43 USCA 1606(h)(3)]).

[125]See 25 USCA 450b(b) and (c) and 450f(a). 25 USCA 450b(b) defines "tribe." 25 USCA 450b(c) defines "tribal organization" in terms of the tribe's "governing body" and the "maximum participation" of Natives in its affairs. 25 USCA 450f(a) directs the Secretary of the Interior to contract only with tribes and tribal organizations.

[126]E.g., U.S. v. Sandoval, 231 U.S. 28, 46 (1913).

[127]43 USCA 1601(b).

[128]43 USC 1601(c). Curiously enough, the report was submitted to Congress sometime in 1974, but the secretary never made any recommendations. It is not clear at this writing (1984) to what extent the "1985 report", required under 43 USCA 1622, will address these questions.

[129]43 USCA 1606(d) requires that the corporations be organized for profit. Most village corporations are also incorporated as profit corporations.

[130]See A.S. 10.05.018 (Defense of Ultra Vires).

[131]See e.g., Art. III, Articles of Incorporation, Bristol Bay Native Incorporation, [sic] Inc., *Charters and Constitutions,* note 37, above, at 60. Compare: Art. III(c), Articles of Incorporation of AHTNA, Inc., id. at 44, permitting promotion of "economic, social, cultural and personal well-being of Natives enrolled to the Corporation."

[132]Substantially reenacted as the Community Services Act of 1974, P.L. 88-452, 88 Stat. 2292, but subsequently repealed by P.L. 97-35, Title VI, Sec. 683(a), Aug. 13, 1981, 95 Stat. 519, note following 42 USCA 2701.

[133]"Community Development," *2(c) Report: Federal Programs and Alaska Natives,* (Anchorage: Robert R. Nathan Associates, 1974). Task II, part B, sec. 6 at 1.

[134]Id. at 2.

[135]Conversation with Gordon Jackson, then Chairman of the Board, RurAL CAP (March 29, 1978).

[136]See Robert D. Arnold, *Alaska Native Land Claims,* (Anchorage: Alaska Native Foundation, 1976) at 108-117.

[137]*2(c) Report,* note 133, above, at 10.

[138]Phone Conversation with Phil Smith, then Executive Director, RurAL CAP (March 29, 1978).

[139]Id.

[140]"Juneau Area request for an exception to certain portions of 25 CFR Part 272," Memorandum from Assistant Solicitor for Indian Affairs, (September 1, 1976).

[141]See "Approval of Claims Attorney Contracts of Arctic Slope and AHTNA Tanah Ninnah Association (Copper River Indian Land Association)," Op. Sol. M-36744, (April 8, 1968), denying status as an Indian tribe for purposes of executing an attorney contract under 25 USCA 81.

[142]See AIPRC Final Report, note 87, above, at 139 suggesting that "lower forty-eight" tribal governments may gradually evolve from sovereign governments to "federal instrumentalities" if certain trends continue.

[143]See also Morehouse, note 2, above, at 198-196, discussing the Native non-profit corporations.

[144]Arnold, note 136, above, at 98.

[145]*Dena' Nena' Henash,* note 44, above, at 3.

[146]Dena' Nena' Henash, Articles of Incorporation (September 27, 1971).

[147]Dena Nena Henash Bylaws, Art. II, sec. 1(a) (March 1983).

[148]Id., sec. 1(b) and sec. 2, respectively.

[149]Id., sec. 3 and Art. IV, sec. 2.

[150]*Dena' Nena' Henash,* note 44 above, at 19.

[151]Dena' Nena' Henash Bylaws, note 147, above, at Art. IV, secs. 2 and 3.

[152]Id., Art. VII, secs. 1 and 2.

[153]Id. The six subregions are: Yukon-Tanana, Upper Tanana, Yukon Flats, Yukon-Koyukuk, Kuskokwim and Lower Yukon. See *Dena' Nena' Henash,* note 44, above, at 19 and at 21, describing the TCC region.

[154]Interview with Paul Sherry, TCC Director of Programs (Feb. 17 1984). The six subregional centers are: Fairbanks (Yukon-Tanana), Tok (Upper Tanana), Fort Yukon (Yukon Flats), Galena (Yukon-Koyukuk), McGrath (Kuskokwim) and Anvik (Lower Yukon).

[155]Dena' Nena' Henash Bylaws, note 147, above, at Art. VII, sec. 2.

[156]Id., Art. IV, sec. 2 and Art. V, sec. 2.

[157]Id., Art. V generally.

[158]Id., sec. 2.

[159]Id., Art. VI.

[160]25 USCA 450b(b) and 25 USCA 1452(c) respectively. See also 25 CFR 271.2(h), Self-Determination Act regulations and 25 CFR 101.1(e), Indian Financing Act regulations.

[161]25 USCA 450b(c) and 25 USCA 1452(f) respectively. See also 25 CFR 271.2(r), Self-Determination Act regulations and 25 CFR 101.1(j), Indian Financing Act regulations.

[162]Morehouse, note 2, above, at 192.

[163]*Dena' Nena' Henash,* note 44, above, at 18.

[164]Paul Sherry interview, note 154, above. TCC is also negotiating to take over Indian Health Service programs in its region during 1984. This will add approximately $7 million in health programs to TCC's current budget.

[165]Id.

[166]Tanana Chiefs organization chart (Sep. 1, 1983).

[167]Morehouse, note 2, above, at 195.

[168]Paul Sherry interview, note 154, above. See also *Dena' Nena' Henash,* note 44, above, at 7.

[169]Id. at 10 and 12.

[170]Interview with Al Ketzler, Sr., TCC Director of Community and Natural Resources (Feb. 17, 1984).

[171]*Dena' Nena' Henash,* note 44, above, at 13.

[172]Al Ketzler interview, note 170, above.

[173]25 USCA 1901 et seq. See also *Dena' Nena' Henash,* note 44, above, at 10.

[174]See AIPRC Final Report, note 87, above, at 495.

[175]Bylaws Kikiktugruk Area Community Development Corporation (February 14, 1969).

[176]Id.

[177]Conversation with Dennis Tiepelman, then President, Mauneluk Association (1978).

[178]Phone conversation with Matthew B. Conover, Vice-President/Development, Maniilaq Association (March 1984).

[179]Articles of Incorporation, Maniilaq Association, Art. III (June 26, 1973, as amended). Note: By its terms, this statement of purposes permits Maniilaq to serve all the people of northwest Alaska, not limiting its activity to Natives only.

[180]Bylaws, Maniilaq Association, Art. II, sec 3 (May 6, 1976, as amended).

[181]Id., Art. II, sec. 7 and Art. III.

[182]See notes 160 and 161, above.

[183]Phone conversation with Mary Schaeffer, then Vice-President, Management and Planning, Mauneluk Association (February 27, 1978). Maniilaq is eligible for tribal government improvement grants under 25 USCA 450h. See "Juneau Area request for an exception to certain portions of 25 CFR Part 272," unpublished solicitor's memorandum (September 1, 1976).

[184]*The Maniilaq Association 1983 Annual Report and Directory of Services,* (Kotzebue, Alaska: Maniilaq Assocation, 1984) at 8, 11 and 12. Also Matthew Conover, phone conversation, note 178, above. Maintnance is a fifth division; it is primarily responsible for maintenance of Maniilaq's physical facilities, but also provided emergency home repairs for elders and construction assistance on community projects. *Maniilaq Annual Report* at 56-57.

[185]Id. at 14-15.

[186]Id. at 17.

[187]Id. at 18.

[188]Id. at 17-33.

[189]Id. at 28.

[190]Id. at 24 and 28-29.

[191]Id. at 35-42.

[192]Id. at 42-43.

[193]Id. at 45-55.

[194]Id. at 48 (Coastal Management). See also *NANA Regional Strategy*, (Kotzebue, Alaska: Maniilaq Association, 1982) at vii (Regional Strategy Planning).

[195]*Maniilaq Annual Report*, note 184, above at 45-46.

[196]Id. at 47-48.

[197]AS 46.40.010 et seq. (Alaska Coastal Management Program). See also Morehouse, note 2, above, at 200-202, describing the coastal resource service areas.

[198]Matthew Conover, phone conversation, note 178, above.

[199]*Maniilaq Annual Report*, note 184, above, at 52-53.

[200]Matthew Conover, phone conversation, note 178, above.

[201]Articles of Incorporation, Bristol Bay Area Development Corporation (May 23, 1969)

[202]Id. Art. II.

[203]Articles of Incorporation, Bristol Bay Native Association, Art. III (Jan. 31, 1973). BBNA also provides services to non-Natives on a non-descriminatory basis through certain state-funded programs.

[204]Id. Art. VI.

[205]Bristol Bay Native Association Bylaws, Art. II (Circa 1973).

[206]Id., Art. III and Articles of Incorporation, note 203, above, Art. VII. Current board membership as described in personal communication from Kay E. Larson, BBNA Executive Director (January 19, 1984).

[207]Id.

[208]Id., describing the villages and regions as follows:

Nushagak Bay	Togiak Bay	Iliamna Lake
Aleknagik	Manokotak	Igiugig
Clark's Point	Togiak	Iliamna
Dillingham	Twin Hills	Kokhanok
Ekuk		Newhalen
		Nondalton
		Pedro Bay

Nushagak River	Kvichak Bay	Alaska Peninsula
Ekwok	Egegik	Chignik
Koliganek	King Salmon	Chignik Lake
Levelock	Naknek	Chignik Lagoon
New Stuyahok	Pilot Point	Ivanof Bay
Portage Creek	Port Heiden	Perryville
	South Naknek	Ugashik

[209]See notes 160 and 161, above.

[210]David S. Case, *The Special Relationship of Alaska Natives to the Federal Government*, (Anchorage: Alaska Native Foundation, 1978) at 141. Also personal communication from Kay E. Larson, note 206, above, and subsequent phone conversation (Apr. 2, 1984). See also Morehouse, note 2, above, at 192, comparing programs among nonprofit associations. It is difficult to draw careful comparisons among regions and the number of programs in each because programs may be catagorized differently and do not necessarily correspond to the same annual periods.

[211]Morehouse, note 2, above, at 193-194.

[212]The ANB is supported by the Alaska Native Sisterhood (ANS)—a separate, but organizationally related entity.

[213]Sources: Personal communication from Dr. Walter Soboleff, Past ANB Grand President, (May 3, 1978) and personal conversation with John Hope, Past ANB Grand President (March 24, 1978). See also Arnold, note 136, above, at 82-84.

[214]Id. at 83. The Dawes Act is the General Allotment Act of 1887. It permitted Natives to obtain citizenship by acquiring individual property and severing their tribal relations. See generally, chapter 4, above.

[215]Drucker, Philip, *Cultures of the North Pacific Coast*, (New York: Chandler Publishing, 1965) at 222-224.

[216]Dr. Walter Soboleff memorandum (September 16, 1977).

[217]Grand Camp Constitution, Alaska Native Brotherhood, Art. I (1983, as amended).

[218]Constitution for the Sisters of the Alaska Native Sisterhood, Art. 1 (1983, as amended).

[219]C.f. Drucker, note 215, above, at 223.

[220]Cohen, note 6, above, at 85.

[221]Arnold, note 136, above, at 85.

[222]Art. II, sec. 1, ANB Const., note 217, above, makes non-Natives married to Natives "eligible for full membership and all its rights and duties except that of holding a Grand Office."

[223]Art. III, ANS Const., note 218, above.

[224]Art. VI, sec. 7, ANB Const., note 217, above.

[225]Id., Art. V.

[226]Id., Art. VI, sec. 8.

[227]Id., sec. 6.

[228]Id., Art. IV and personal conversation with John Hope, note 213 above.

[229]Art. IV, ANS Const., note 218, above.

[230]Art. IV, ANB Const., note 217, above.

[231]See Arts. VI and IX, ANB Const., note 217, above, and Art. IV, ANS Const., note 218 above. Neither Constitution requires joint conventions, but that appears to be the intent.

[232]Art. IV, ANB Const., note 217, above.

[233]Art. VI, sec. 6, ANB Const., note 217, above.

[234]See 48 Fed. Reg., note 22, above.

[235]See Cohen, 1942, note 6, above, at 414.

[236]Arnold, note 136, above, at 91-92.

[237]Id. at 110.

[238]Dr. Walter Soboleff memorandum (September 14, 1977).

[239]Id.

[240]Phone conversation with John Hope, ANB Past Grand President (Feb. 2, 1984).

[241]See generally, Roy Peratrovich, interview, *Tundra Times* May 10, 1978, at 7. Roy Peratrovich was ANB Grand President from 1940-1945. See also, Drucker, note 215, above, at 224.

[242]Portions of this study were originally compiled and written in 1977 by Gordon Jackson, former AFN Executive Vice President for Human Resources.

[243]*Alaska Federation of Natives Bylaws*, Art. IV, sec. 2 (as amended October 22, 1980). See also 1983 Annual Report Alaska Federation of Natives (Anchorage: AFN, 1984) at 2.

[244]Id. at 1.

[245]AFN Bylaws, note 243, above, Art. III, sec. 8. Under this provision, the profit and nonprofit regional corporations are *each* entitled to one delegate and one alternate for "each two hundred persons (or major fraction thereof) which [sic] are Native shareholders in the Regional Corporation." Additionally, each class A member is entitled to five delegates and five alternates apart from the regional shareholder formula.

[246]See *AFN Report,* note 243, above.

[247]See Op. So. M-36772, Eligibility of Alaska Federation of Natives for Loan from Revolving Loan Fund (July 8, 1968), rejecting an AFN loan application because the federation was neither an "Indian-chartered corporation" under 25 USCA 470 nor a 'tribe, band or group' under 25 USCA 482. See also notes 160 and 161, above, discussing eligibility of Native "organizations" under the Self-Determination Act.

[248]AFN Report, note 243, above, at 5.

[249]Id. at 12-13.

[250]Id. at 14. See also chapter 97, 1983 Session Laws of Alaska (AS 29.53.020[k]), defining "developed" with respect to local property taxation of ANCSA lands.

[251]Id. at 19.

[252]Id. at 4. See also USCA 1606(i).

[253]Id. at 15 and 18.

[254]"Native leaders gather to form new federation," *Anchorage Daily News,* May 6, 1983, at b-1. See also "United Tribes of Alaska: New IRA Federation," *Tundra Times,* May 11, 1983, at 1. The author was also present at the meeting.

[255]United Tribes of Alaska membership list distributed at first annual UTA general meeting (Oct. 16, 1983).

[256]See *Anchorage Daily News* and *Tundra Times,* note 254, above.

[257]Art. II, United Tribes of Alaska Charter.

[258]Id., Art. IV.

[259]Id., Art. V.

[260]Id., Art. IX.

[261]*Anchorage Daily News,* note 254, above.

[262]*AFN Report,* note 243, above, at 15.

[263]Much of the information in this section is derived from a lengthy telephone interview with John Hope, then the BIA Juneau Area Office Tribal Operations Officer (February 28, 1978) and the author's subsequent experience as an attorney for the BIA in the Interior Department's Alaska solicitor's office from 1978 to 1982.

[264]25 USCA 450b(b), Self-Determination Act; 25 USCA 1452(c), Indian Financing Act, which also includes "groups" of less than 25 Alaska Natives established pursuant to 43 USCA 1613(h)(2).

[265]See e.g., 25 CFR 286.1(i), Indian Business Development Program; 101.1(g), Revolving Loan Fund and 103.1(g) Loan Guaranty, Insurance and Interest Subsidy, defining "Native group" for purposes at the Indian Financing Act.

[266]25 USCA 476.

[267]25 USCA 81.

[268]See generally 25 CFR 89.1 et seq.

[269]Id. 89.3.

[270]Id. 89.1.

[271]Id. 89.7 et seq.

[272]25 USCA 476 and 477.

[273]Robert E. Price, *Legal Status of the Alaska Natives: A Report to the Alaska Statehood Commission,* (Juneau: Alaska Department of Law, July 30, 1983) at 76-77.

[274]25 CFR Part 81. The conduct of secretarial elections necessary to adopt organic documents under the IRA is also the responsibility of the Tribal Operations Program in Alaska. Telephone interview with Michael J. Stancampiano, Assistant Tribal Operations Officer, Juneau BIA Area Office (May 17, 1984).

[275]Price, note 273, above.

[276]See e.g. "State, Feds Deadlocked on Sovereignty Issue," *Fairbanks Daily News-Miner,* May 17 1984 at 2.

[277]These grants are commonly known as "104 grants," because they are authorized under section 104 (25 USCA 450h) of the Self-Determination Act. Under the terms of the statute, they are specifically authorized for (1) the "improvement of tribal government" or (2) the planning, training, evaluation of [sic] other activities designed to improve the capacity of a tribal organization to enter into a contract...[under the Self-Determination Act]...."

[278]Stancampiano interview, note 274, above.

[279]Id.

[280]E.g., 25 CFR 20.1(n) defining "Indian" for purposes of eligibility for finincial assistance and social services programs as "a member or a one-fourth degree or more blood quantum descendant of a member of any Indian tribe;" 25 CFR256.2(e) defining "Indian" for purposes of the Housing Improvement Program, in part, as a "member" or person who "meets the membership requirements of a federally recognized tribe" or "a person of one-half or more degree Indian ancestry who is a descendant of a member of a tribe..."; 25 CFR 101.1(d), defining "Native" for purposes of the revolving loan program, in part, a "citizen...who is a person of one-fourth degree or more Alaskan Indian..., Eskimo or Aleut blood...."

[281]Stancampiano interview, note 274, above. The Tribal Operations Program has also been reponsible in the past for the administration of judgement funds awarded Alaska Native tribes by the U.S. Indian Claims Commission. E.g., Aleut Community at St. Paul Island v. U.S., 422 Indian Cls. Comm. 1 (1978); 25 CFR Part 77, regarding preparation of a membership roll to determine those eligible to participate in the judgement funds awarded the Pribilof Islands by the U.S. Court of Claims in dockets number 352 and 369-A. The final judgement came to $8.5 million, eighty percent of which was distributed per capita to eligible members of the Pribilof Island Aleut communities at St. Paul and St. George Islands.

CHAPTER TEN

"SOVEREIGNTY:" THE ALASKA NATIVE CLAIM TO SELF-GOVERNMENT

I. Introduction

A. The Meaning of "Sovereignty"

When discussing the concept of sovereignty as applied to Native American communities, one must keep in mind three important points. The first is that sovereignty is a western European legal concept originally used to define the political and legal existence of a nation-state.[1] The second is that, beginning with the earliest judicial decisions of the U. S. Supreme Court and continuing to the present, Native American communities have been consistently acknowledged to possess sovereignty.[2] Third, although sovereignty may once have implied complete political independence,[3] it no longer has such an absolute meaning. As applied to Native Americans by United States courts, "sovereignty" is a relative concept which connotes a more or less limited power of inherent self-government.[4] In other words, Native American communities are conceded to have *original* self-governing powers, *not granted* by the federal government, but subject to limitations established under federal law.

Alaska Native self-government also has cultural significance. Under the usual principles of federal "Indian" law, discussed below, Native American communities possess substantial political authority to govern their own affairs, shielded from the institutions and values of the surrounding non-Native society. In practical terms, this means that Native communities have substantial control over many institutions of political life upon which their own way of life depends. The cultural significance of such control is obvious when it relates to such matters as determining community membership, prescribing a form of government and regulating domestic relations among members. It is no less significant, however, when the question is one of raising revenue for community programs or regulating fish and game resources which are the very ground upon which Native cultures live.

The trouble is that the exercise of Native political authority in areas such as these latter two frequently conflicts with non-Native political institutions and values. Defining the boundary between the political authority of Native communities and that of surrounding non-Native communities is therefore often perceived as determining whether the Native way of life will survive. In the post-ANCSA era, the cultural significance of Native self-government appears to lend a sense of urgency to Alaska Native claims to "sovereignty."

B. Alaska Native Self-Government at a Crossroad

The Alaska courts have held in other contexts that federal laws defining the rights of Native Americans also apply to Alaska Natives, but vacillating federal policies and the false perception that Alaska Natives did not have traditional forms of political organization have often clouded the question of Alaska Native sovereignty.[5] By the early 1980's, the Alaska Natives found themselves at a crossroad in the development of their own forms of self-government.[6] The federal government had long treated Alaska Native villages like other "tribal" governments in the United States and seventy-one communities had been organized under the Indian Reorganizaton Act (IRA), but renewed attempts to establish IRA governments met with prolonged state resistance and confusion in the Interior Department.[7]

The question of Native self-government has been complicated by several factors. For example, both historically and recently, Alaska Native communities have been encouraged to incorporate as municipalities under territorial or state law.[8] Section 14(c)(3) of ANCSA also seems designed to promote this policy by requiring that village corportion land be conveyed to state incorported municipalities.[9] However, once incorporated as a state municipality, there is little guarantee that a Native community will retain political control over its destiny if significant numbers of non-Natives settle in it.[10] This possibility, among other factors, has prompted some villages to renounce municipal incorporation in favor of more traditional forms of Native government.[11]

The question of Alaska Native "tribal" status is another complicating factor. Alaska Natives are often characterized as not having the same "tribal" social organization as other Native American communities, but being organized instead as "village" societies. However, "tribe" is the term most often used in the legal literature to describe Native American communities which exercise powers of self-government. That the term is not historically applied to Alaska Natives often seems to imply (without analysis) that the typical Alaska aboriginal community (a village) did not have powers of self-government.

Unless law is simply a word game, whether a Native community exercises powers of self-government should not turn on whether it is described as a "tribe," a "village" or something else. Under the usual principles of Indian law, the correct question is whether the Native community has historically exercised or been recognized as having powers of political self-government. This can be a complex factual or legal issue, but one should not begin the inquiry confused about terminology. In this chapter, the terms "tribe," "village," "community" and their variants are all used to describe a political community with powers of self-government.

The status of Alaska Native lands is a final factor which complicates discussion of the scope of Native self-government. Powers of Native self-government are most often described in terms relating to tribal control of a federal reservation. Except for Metlakatla, Alaska Natives do not occupy reservations, so analysis of their governmental authority does not fit into this generally accepted framework. Before considering these and other issues further, however, it is probably necessary to review the basic principles of Native American self-government.

II. Native American Self-Government in General

A. The Interplay of History and Law

In the United States, the principles of Native American sovereignty originate in the historical fact that the "aboriginal" people were here first, literally "from the beginning." They governed the lands that came to be called the Americas, and themselves, according to a variety of political systems ranging from the imperial theocracies of South America to the village and nomadic societies of the North. The European immigrants, armed with a false perception of cultural superiority, an individualized concept of land ownership and the necessary population and technology to extend both ideas to the New World, in time displaced the aboriginal governments.[12] In what is now the United States, however, the immigrant invasion was tempered somewhat by federal statutes[13] and judicial principles derived from the history of the dealings (principally treaties) between the early immigrants and the aboriginals. The net effect of these statutes and judicial deliberations, given the American constitutional system of government, was to erect a federal bulwark against the complete destruction of the aboriginal governments and the cultures associated with them.

B. Inherent Sovereignty—The "Most Basic Principle"

Two of the first cases to examine the unique relationship that had developed between the aboriginals and the immigrants reached the U. S. Supreme Court within a year of each other. Together, they establish that while the aboriginal governments are no longer considered to be the independent foreign nations they once were, they are nonetheless "domestic dependent nations,"[14] acknowledged to be separate sovereigns and free from control by the states at least to the extent that they are protected by treaties or other federal law. As Chief Justice John Marshall summed up in *Worcester v. Georgia,* an 1832 case arising out of the conflicting political claims of the Cherokee Indian Nation and the State of Georgia:

> The Cherokee Nation, then, is a distinct community, occupying its own territory, with boundaries accurately described, in which the laws of Georgia can have no force, and which the citizens of Georgia have no right to enter but with the assent of the Cherokees themselves or in conformity with the

treaties and with the acts of Congress. The whole intercourse between the United States and this nation is, by our Constitution and laws, vested in the government of the United States.[15]

The common law rules defining the powers of Native American governments are constantly being refined in light of changing circumstances. Nevertheless, it is safe to say that the principles laid down in these and subsequent cases establish what Felix Cohen, the noted commentator on United States Indian law, has described as the "most basic principle" of all Indian law:

[T]hose powers which are lawfully vested in an Indian tribe are not, in general, delegated powers granted by express acts of Congress, but rather "inherent powers of a limited sovereignty which has never been extinguished."[16]

Under the United States Constitution, Congress has been held to have broad power to alter, and even extinguish, the federal-tribal relationship.[17] Thus, Congress can and has extinguished aboriginal land claims without compensation,[18] and has also seemingly terminated Indian political structures.[19] However, when Congress does act to extinguish Indian governmental powers, it must do so clearly and without equivocation, because the Supreme Court has held that all doubts or statutory ambiguities are to be construed in favor of the Native Americans. Extinguishment of aboriginal rights to land, other resources or self-government cannot be lightly implied.[20] In addition, executive or congressional "recognition" of tribal existence has uniformly been held to be a "political question" which prevents judicial examination of the sovereign status of any recognized "distinctly Indian community."[21]

C. Preemption and Infringement—Limits on the States

The frequent conflicts between state and tribal governments have produced many principles of United States Indian law. Most recently, the U.S. Supreme Court has described federal preemption and infringement on tribal sovereignty as "two independent but related barriers to the assertion of state regulatory authority over tribal reservations and members."[22] Under this analysis, if tribal self-government is guaranteed by a federal treaty, statute or executive order, state law over tribal members is superceded and the tribe's jurisdiction is exclusive, except as limited by other federal laws.[23] Moreover, the tradition of tribal sovereignty forms a " 'backdrop' against which vague or ambiguous federal enactments must always be measured."[24]

Federal "Indian" reservations, whether established by treaty, statute, executive order or other federal action, are perhaps the most familiar examples of those enactments which have been held to guarantee tribal self-government against state intrusion. However, the instruments creating the reservations were seldom explicit as to their effect on future assertions of state authority over the Indian tribe and its members occupying the reserved lands. It is under these circumstances that the tradition of tribal sovereignty has led the United State courts to interpret the often general language creating the reservations as precluding state authority where, "absent governing Acts of Congress," the assertion of such authority "infringed on the right of reservation Indians to make their own laws and be ruled by them."[25] Thus, for example, if the issue is whether the members of a tribe are subject to state fish and game laws, the absence of a reservation has been held sufficient to permit Alaska to apply its laws,[26] and the existence of a reservation has been held sufficient to prevent it from doing so.[27]

Under Public Law (P.L.) 280,[28] Congress has conferred the power on some states, including Alaska, to adjudicate civil disputes and to apply state criminal laws to most civil or criminal matters arising in the "Indian country" within the state. ("Indian country" is a term defined by a United States statute to mean: (1) reservations, (2) allotments and (3) dependent Indian communities.)[29] However, even P.L. 280 does not deprive a tribe of continuing (although concurrent) tribal jurisdiction over the same subjects as come under state jurisdiction.[30]

D. Powers of Native Governments

P.L. 280 has also been held not to extinguish tribal self-government,[31] and the lack of an Indian reservation land base does not extinguish either a tribe or its government.[32] In fact, the "most basic principle" of United States Indian law, that tribal sovereign powers are inherent, coupled with the requirement of clear congressional action to extinguish those powers, means just the opposite. Therefore, even tribes which have never occupied a federal reservation should theoretically retain those powers of self-government characteristic of aboriginal tribes generally.

Those powers include the power to: (1) adopt and operate a form of government of the tribe's choosing, (2) define conditions of tribal membership, (3) regulate domestic relations of members (4) prescribe rules of inheritance, (5) levy taxes, (6) regulate property within tribal jurisdiction and (7) control the conduct of tribal members.[33] Sovereign immunity from suit has long been held to be another aspect of tribal sovereignty, and it is also well established that tribes are not subject to the federal income tax.[34]

Under United States law, however, tribal governments are limited in at least three significant respects by virtue of their subordination to the superior sovereignty of the United States. Tribal governments cannot conduct foreign affairs;[35] they cannot alienate tribal lands without federal consent,[36] and they cannnot adjudicate crimes committed by non-Natives.[37] Moreover, absent a reservation or other "governing act of Congress," preemption of state authority is less likely.[38] That does not preclude *concurrent* state and tribal jurisdiction, however, and as to matters in which the tribe may have an overriding cultural, economic or social interest, it is possible that state authority may be precluded on the grounds of infringement alone.[39] For example, tribal sovereign immunity has been held to preclude state court enforcement of a monetary judgement even to collect state taxes legitimately levied against an Indian tribe.[40]

E. Vacillating Federal Policies

As more than one commentator has noted, federal policy has been far from consistent when it comes to Native sovereignty issues. These policies have vacillated between of assimilation on the one hand and of tribal autonomy on the other.[41] Early legislation, such as the Indian Trade and Intercourse Act, and court cases, such as *Worcester v. Georgia,* reflect a strong protectionist policy. On the opposite side, the 1887 General Allotment Act and the termination policies of the 1950's,[42] are the most significant manifestations of the assimilationist policy.

The allotment policy was reversed in 1934 with the passage of the Indian Reorganization Act,[43] and the termination philosophy was fully rejected by the Indian Self-Determination Act.[44] The effects of previous assimilationist legislation have not been erased, however, by this latest (and perhaps last) policy shift. Under these circumstances, generalizations about the scope or nature of Native sovereignty are somewhat perilous; they must take into account not only detailed statutory schemes but sometimes conflicting congressional policies and inconsistent court decisions. Generalization is particularly difficult in Alaska, because few court decisions have addressed self-government issues in the Alaska context.

III. Legal History of Alaska Native Sovereignty

A. Early History

The first reference to Alaska Native "tribes" in an American legal document is in Article III of the 1867 Russian-American Treaty of Cession. Article III permits the "inhabitants of the ceded territory," with the exception of the "uncivilized native tribes," to either return to Russia or become U.S. citizens. The "uncivilized tribes" were to be "subject to such laws and regulations as the United States may, from time to time, adopt in regard to aboriginal tribes of that country."[45] In spite of this language, there have been continuous attempts from 1867 to the present to distinguish the status of Alaska Natives from the status the United States accords to aboriginal Americans generally.

In the beginning, the federal government simply ignored the Alaska Natives, along with almost everyone else in the newly acquired territory.[46] It was not until the Organic Act of 1884[47] that a rudimentary government and the services of a federal court were extended to Alaska. Section 13 of this act also directed the Secretary of the Interior to provide for the education of school age children in Alaska "without reference to race" until a more permanent education system could be established.

The federal government's political relationship to Alaska Natives coalesced out of the Interior Department's Alaska Education program.[48] Sheldon Jackson was appointed as the department's first Alaska agent in 1885 to implement the education provisions of the Organic Act. Perhaps because the vast majority of the school age children in the territory were Natives, or perhaps because Sheldon Jackson was a former missionary to the Natives, he focused the resources of the Interior Department's Bureau of Education on the education of Alaska Natives.

During the next thirty years, the Bureau of Education developed a network of some seventy Native village schools from Barrow on the North Slope to Atka on the Aleutian chain and from Bethel in southwest Alaska to Hydaburg at the southern tip of the southeast panhandle.[48] More were added later, as congressional appropriations permitted. In addition to the schools, the Bureau of Education established the Native reindeer industry, extended medical care, and established village cooperative stores and other community commercial enterprises, including sawmills and salmon canneries.[49] In the process, some 150 reservations were also established for the benefit of the Natives, ranging in size from a few acres for schools to several thousand acres for reindeer herding or subsistence resource preservation.[50]

The most important point about all of these programs is that they were focused on Native villages, the essential units of self-government for most Alaska Native societies. As they had always done in the rest of the United States, the agents of the federal government dealt with the representatives of the aboriginal governments in the course of providing federal programs for their benefit. This history of government-to-government dealings seems sufficient to establish federal recognition of Alaska Native self-government.

In the early days of these programs, however, the relationship of the United States government to the Alaska Natives was considered to be distinguishable from its relationship with Native Americans generally. Because the Alaska Natives were not served by the Bureau of Indian Affairs and because their education was to be "without reference to race," the Interior Department Solicitor concluded in 1894 that certain laws applicable to "Indians" in "Indian country" were not applicable to Alaska Natives and implied, in general, that the status of Alaska Natives, politically and in other respects, was materially different from the other aboriginal American tribes.[51] Similarly, an early Alaska federal court case implied, in rejecting the practice of Tlingit slavery, that Alaska Natives were incapable of self-government, given the superior sovereignty of the federal government.[52]

B. Change in Status

Typical of a common law system, however, this point of view changed substantially over time and in light of new circumstances. The change was signaled by the Nelson Act of 1905,[53] which cast into statute what by that time had become an established fact—a separate system of education for Alaska Natives. The next year, Congress enacted the Alaska Native Allotment Act,[54] under which individual Alaska Natives became eligible for the same sort of individual restricted land entitlements as were applicable to other Native Americans at that time.[55] In 1918, the U.S. Supreme Court upheld the creation of the Metlakatla Indian Reservation in Alaska.[56] In 1923, relying in part on that decision, the Interior Department Solicitor approved commercial leasing on the Tyonek Reserve, concluding that:

> The relations existing between [the Natives] and the government are very similar and in many respects, identical with those which have long existed between the government and the aboriginal people residing within the territorial limits of the United States....[57]

In 1931, responsibility for the administration of Alaska Native affairs was transferred from the Bureau of Education to the Bureau of Indian Affairs, thereby conforming the Interior Department's administrative structure to the redefined status of the Alaska Natives. The administrative change also precipitated congressional interest. In early 1932, Edgar Howard, then Chairman of the House Committee on Indian Affairs, wrote the Secretary of the Interior to inquire about "the status of the Indian tribes in Alaska."[58] Within one month, the solicitor issued a comprehensive opinion reviewing the status of Alaska Natives. He concluded his discussion of the applicable cases, statutes and policies as follows:

> From the foregoing it is clear that no distinction has been or can be made between the Indians and other natives of Alaska so far as the laws and relations of the United States are concerned whether the Eskimos and other Natives are of Indian origin or not as they are all wards of the Nation, and their status is in material respects similar to that of the Indians of the United States. It follows that the natives of Alaska referred to in the treaty of March 30, 1867, between the

United States and Russia are entitled to the benefits of and are subject to the general laws and regulations governing the Indians of the United States....[59]

In another opinion issued the same year, the solicitor concluded that, like the tribes of the lower forty-eight states, the Natives of Alaska possessed attributes of sovereignty sufficient to regulate their own internal and social relations when it came to marriage and divorce.[60]

C. The Indian Reorganization Act

As originally enacted in 1934, the Indian Reorganization Act (IRA)[61] was not fully applicable to the Alaska Natives. First, the 1934 IRA was primarily oriented to the reorganization of Indian tribes "residing on the same reservation," and few Alaska Native communities were located on reservations.[62] Second, Alaska Natives were inadvertently excluded from the provisions of section 17, which provided for the incorporation of business corporations and from access to federal loan funds available under section 10.[63]

In the course of applying the 1934 act to Alaska, the Bureau of Indian Affairs surveyed some fifty Alaska Native villages to determine their forms of "tribal organization."[64] The survey was conducted through questionnaires completed by the bureau's principal teachers stationed in villages throughout Alaska. Although unscientific and fraught with ethnocentric judgements, the questionnaires present an interesting cross section of views on then extant Alaska Native village governing institutions. These included a system in Tatitlek of three "appointed chiefs...in existence as far back as any present can remember" and a seven-member council in Tanacross established in 1912 to "assist" the traditional chief. The Tanacross council was characterized as handling "purely local" matters such as "local government, and the settling of disputes between individuals."

There was also a seven-member council in Noatak established, according to the principal teacher, when the village was first founded in 1908. The council passed regulations, controlling such matters as house location, lot size, sanitation and dog control, but was not supported by the local U.S. commissioner in Kotzebue when it came to imposing fines for law and order violations. The commissioner reportedly viewed that as infringing on his prerogatives as commissioner. Nearby Selawik had an eight-member council originally established in 1915 under territorial law authorizing the incorporation of "Native villages."[65] When that law was repealed in 1929, it left the council's authority in legal limbo. Nevertheless, the teacher reported the council had passed "many ordinances" and was "doing the best it could under the circumstances." Further south, in Hooper Bay, the teacher (who had been there only five months) reported a "chief" assisted by a six-member council which had authority over such matters as "curfew enforcement, gambling, trails, etc. only."

When asked whether there were any weaknesses "of the present tribal organization," the most common response was that there was a lack of "legal authority" to enforce ordinances and decisions. This perception was often associated with the importance some teachers seemed to attach to written law, territorial legislation or the U. S. commissioner as a source of legal authority. The Angoon village council, for example, had been organized by a Native elder in 1916, and conducted its business "similar to any other local council government." It was characterized, however, as lacking "real power to enforce legislation." Hydaburg, on the other hand, was incorporated as a city in 1927 under general territorial statutes and was not perceived as having this difficulty. The communities were similarly characterized, however, as "trying to do away with all tribal ideas" (Angoon) or as having "no form of tribal organization" (Hydaburg).

Against this background the Interior Department proposed amendments in 1936 to meet the typical village focus of Alaska Native self-government. The Alaska IRA amendments provided first that Alaska Native "groups...not heretofore recognized as bands or tribes" could reorganize themselves for governmental and business purposes based on "a common bond of occupation, or association, or residence within a well-defined neighborhood, community or rural district...."[66] The House report explaining this provision noted that it was necessary:

> because of the peculiar nontribal organizations under which the Alaska natives operate. They have no tribal organizations as that term is understood generally. Many groups which would otherwise be termed "tribes" live in villages which are the bases of their organizations.[67]

By equating "villages" with "tribes" it seems likely that Congress was also confirming the self-governing status of the villages, thereby permitting them to enforce local ordinances even if they were not organized as territorial (or state) municipalities.[68]

A second provision, which was not repealed until 1976, permitted the Secretary of the Interior to create new Alaska Native reservations on lands "actually occupied" by Alaska Natives.[69] Although only six IRA reservations were established in Alaska,[70] sixty-nine villages were reorganized under federally approved constitutions.[71] Most villages which were organized under the new constitutions also adopted federally approved corporate charters to take advantage of the IRA loan provisions.[72]

Significantly, most villages in Alaska were required to reorganize their governmental structures under IRA constitutions as a condition to approval of a corporate (business) charter.[73] This approach emphasizes one of the main goals of the IRA nationally and in Alaska, which is to strengthen Native self-government.[74] It is important to understand that the IRA was specifically enacted to reverse previous federal Indian policy under the earlier allotment acts—policy which, in Theodore Roosevelt's words, was intended to "break up the tribal mass" by taking lands out of tribal control, thereby destroying the effectiveness of tribal government.[75] Accordingly, tribes were permitted to adopt federally approved constitutions which, in addition to their existing powers of self-government, also (1) prevented disposition of tribal assets without tribal consent; (2) entitled the tribe to hire attorneys with limited federal oversight, and (3) authorized tribes to negotiate with federal, state and local governments.[76] These and other major provisions of the IRA are still operative in Alaska and, as Felix Cohen noted when they were first enacted, have removed "almost the last significant differences" between the Alaska Natives and the Indians of the lower forty-eight states.[77]

D. Tribal Political Status

On the other hand, it is important to keep in mind that the IRA does not in any way weaken "the most basic principle" of Indian law. Tribal self-government is inherent in the historical existence of the tribe. Although the IRA does authorize the reorganization of governments of "Indians residing on one reservation" regardless of their historical tribal status,[78] an IRA constitution is not a requirement for a valid Native American government. Many tribes in the contiguous forty-eight states have never adopted IRA constitutions, but are nonetheless recognized as governments by the federal government.[79]

That is also the case in Alaska, where there is now a nearly one hundred-year history of federal recognition of Native self-government focused at the village level. Most of the more than two hundred villages in the state have a long history of self-government under traditional councils or other traditional political institutions.[80] In that respect, they are no different from many recognized "tribes" elsewhere in the United States which were originally organized as village communities or small bands of a few families or clans.[81] Even the subsequent adaptation of traditional forms of government to changing circumstances does not destroy tribal status.[82] The applicability of the IRA to these villages only confirms what has long been federal policy. Alaska Native villages are "tribes" in the political sense of that term and are similar in all significant respects to the tribes of the contiguous forty-eight states.[83]

The point is important, because it is at the core of the relationship between the descendants of the aboriginal and immigrant inhabitants of the United States. Although that relationship is colored by a good deal of racism,[84] it is legally not a relationship based on race but, rather, on the separate, self-governing, *political* status of the Native Americans. Thus, the U. S. Supreme Court has repeatedly upheld the constitutionality of programs and laws uniquely applicable to Native Americans, because they are focused on Natives as members of separate, political governments called "tribes." For example, the Court has upheld the validity of Indian preferential promotion within the BIA as required under the IRA because the preference was calculated to improve Native self-government by increasing the participation of tribal Indians in BIA operations.[85] Other federal programs available only to Native Americans because of their political status range widely from education, health care, housing and special welfare benefits to advantageous credit policies and business opportunities to special court procedures tailored to protect Native cultural values.[86]

Similarly, Native American tribes, because they are "unique aggregations possessing attributes of sovereignty over both their members and their territory," have been held to be valid recipients of congressionally delegated law enforcement authority to control the introduction of liquor into "Indian country."[87] The Department of the Interior Associate Solicitor for Indian Affairs has specifically concluded that Alaska Native villages may exercise this authority as "dependent Indian communities" occupying lands conveyed to a village corporation under the Alaska Native Claims Settlement Act of 1971.[88] Acting under this authority, the Interior Department has published two Alaska village ordinances exercising federally delegated authority to control the introduction of liquor into these communities.[89]

Since tribes are governments in their own right, it is also possible for states to delegate state governmental functions to them. At least seven states (Florida, Idaho, Maine, Montana, New York, South Dakota and Wisconsin) have done so in varying degrees.[90] In this same vein, the Alaska legislature has also recognized the inherent political status of village tribal governments by enacting legislation entitling a traditional or IRA "Native village government" in an unincorporated community to an annual $25,000 grant.[91]

Finally, the federal courts in Alaska have also upheld the self-governing status of Alaska Native villages. In 1958 the federal district court upheld the exclusive jurisdiction of the Tyonek tribe to try a tribal member accused of a crime not then covered under the federal Major Crimes Act.[92] Until this case, it was generally assumed that all territorial criminal laws applied to Alaska Natives regardless of their tribal status. This decision held that at least those self-governing Alaska Native communities which occupied lands set aside for them as dependent Indian communities were not subject to such laws.

The next year, Congress extended P.L. 280 to all "Indian country" in Alaska. As noted earlier, however, P.L. 280 does not extinguish tribal sovereignty;[93] it only extends state court jurisdiction to the adjudication of civil and criminal matters involving Native Americans in Indian country. The extension of state jurisdiction does not deprive Native governments of their previously existing authority. Therefore, Native and state governments which are subject to P.L. 280 exercise *concurrent* jurisdiction to adjudicate crimes and civil disputes.[94]

IV. ANCSA and Subsequent Events

A. General Observations

It was initially assumed by some that the Alaska Native Claims Settlement Act (ANCSA)[95] extinguished every aspect of special Native
American status in Alaska. While that assumption is perhaps true as to
aboriginal hunting, fishing and land rights,[96] it is not correct as to Native
rights of inherent self-government. ANCSA is explicit about the former,
but silent about the latter. Under the usual principles of federal Indian
law, termination of tribal self-government must be clear, and ambiguities
are construed in favor of the Natives.[97] Under these basic tests, it is most
unlikely that ANCSA terminated Alaska Native self-government, "the
most basic principle of all Indian law."

Nevertheless, ANCSA did cast substantial doubt on the practical
exercise of self-government. The unique feature of ANCSA is that, unlike previous[98] and subsequent[99] aboriginal settlements, it severed Native
land ownership from Native government. Under other settlements, an
ownership interest in the land and substantial governmental authority
over it were both confirmed to the tribal government. Under ANCSA,
the ownership interest in the lands was conveyed in fee simple to twelve
regional and more than two hundred village corporations chartered under
the laws of Alaska.[100] Although the villages were the focus of Alaska Native claims and traditional life, the aboriginal governments of the villages
were not designated as the owners of the land to be conveyed under the
act. The aboriginal political claims of the villages have not been settled,
but the remaining village land base is now owned by a state chartered
corporation.

This situation raises a number of practical and theoretical questions
about the jurisdiction of a Native government over private fee lands.
These lands may still be perceived as "belonging" to the whole village,
but they are now legally owned, at least indirectly, by those residents
of the village (and others) who are corporation shareholders. The village
political community, which may include others besides corporation
shareholders, may feel it is important to assert political control over corporate lands for a variety of purposes such as alcohol control, limiting
non-Native residency, regulating domestic relations among members,
zoning or even taxation. The extent to which a Native government can,
like other governments, exercise this sort of political authority over lands
it does not own is not fully decided, because most court decisions analyzing the scope of tribal sovereignty have arisen in a reservation or other
situations in which the Native political community also owned the lands
it governed.

B. The Jurisdiction Problem

Land ownership is not a prerequisite for Native governmental authority or "jurisdiction," any more than it is a requirement for non-Native

jurisdiction.[101] Thus it has been held that tribal determination of heirship of non-reservation, non-trust property is binding,[102] and that the governing authority of a tribe remains intact over the scattered allotments of its members long after the tribal reservation is extinguished.[103] Since, in addition, the Supreme Court has even concluded that lands "owned or occupied" by a "dependent Indian community" constitute "Indian country" for purposes of federal law,[104] the prevailing scholarly opinion is that "Indian country," whether within the confines of a reservation or not, is also the territorial boundary of tribal jurisdiction.[105]

One might assume that these principles are sufficient to establish inherent jurisdiction of Alaska Native village governments over ANCSA village corporation lands as lands "occupied" by dependent Indian communities. Such an assumption may be premature, however, because no court has yet been asked to decide the question.[106] Significantly, the Alaska Federal District Court has upheld the jurisdiction of an Alaska IRA government to adjudicate the title to artifacts located on IRA *owned* land.[107] On the other hand, as noted earlier, the U.S. Supreme Court decisions have focused only on the rights of *reservation* Indians to make their own laws and be governed by them. Thus, the jurisdiction of non-reservation Native American governments has not yet been fully examined.

One point seems certain; in a non-reservation, P.L. 280 state like Alaska, a significant measure of Native jurisdiction is likely to be exercised concurrently with the state, except as federal law may otherwise require. Thus it seems unlikely that a Native village could insulate its members against state criminal laws on ANSCA village corporation lands by passing an ordinance inconsistent with state law. On the other hand, P.L. 280 requires state courts to give "full force and effect" to any valid "tribal ordinance or custom...not inconsistent" with state civil law.[108] Thus, at least in the realm of civil (but not criminal) law, it seems that even under P.L. 280, many village ordinances and customs should be honored in the state courts. The scope of state and Native P.L. 280 jurisdiction is discussed further below.

C. Other Aspects of Sovereignty

Although the jurisdictional limits of Alaska Native governments are yet to be determined, other elements of their authority have become more clearly focused since ANCSA. Two Alaska Federal District Court decisions have confirmed their sovereign immunity.[109] The Alaska Supreme Court has also upheld the immunity of the Metlakatla Indian Community in a decision whose principles seem applicable to non-reservation governments as well.[110] The exemption of Native American governments from United States income tax laws has also been determined applicable to off-reservation Alaska Native IRA governments and corporations.[111] Another important development, is the growing ability of Alaska Native governments to provide meaningful services to their members and even to other citizens of the state. This is largely the result of post-ANCSA, federal Indian "self-determination" legislation and, recently, a pragmatic state approach to service delivery in the unincorporated rural Alaskan communities.[112]

ANCSA was but the first in a line of five major pieces of self-determination legislation. Together these statutes cement in place a federal policy which permits Native Americans to exercise real control over federal programs without the threat that the price of their independence will be termination of either the programs or the tribe's federal relationship. The keystone of the policy is the Indian Self-Determination and Education Assistance Act of 1975.[113] It was preceded by ANCSA in 1971[114] and followed by the Indian Financing Act of 1974,[115] the Indian Health Care Improvement Act of 1976,[116] and the Indian Child Welfare Act of 1978.[117]

Each of these acts define Alaska Native *villages* as described in ANCSA as "tribes" eligible for the various contract, grant and loan programs available to implement the new laws.[118] Significantly, the Indian Child Welfare Act also permits Alaska Native villages, regardless of their reservation status, to obtain retrocession of *exclusive* jurisdiction to adjudicate the child custody issues covered by the act.[119] Since only ANCSA "villages" are defined as tribes in this act, the clear implication is that they exercise enough governmental authority to decide child welfare cases. Finally, in 1983, the Internal Revenue Service published a list of some two hundred Alaska Native villages and other communities considered to be "Indian Tribal entities" exercising "governmental functions" for purposes of certain tax exemptions under the Indian Tribal Government Tax Status Act.[120] Cumulatively, these statutes and administrative actions tend to confirm that Alaska Native "villages" have the same political status as "tribes" in the lower forty-eight states.

The Self-Determination Act also *requires* the Bureau of Indian Affairs (BIA) and the Indian Health Service (IHS), upon request, to contract with Indian tribes or "tribal organizations" to provide BIA and IHS programs to tribal members.[121] Although relatively few IHS programs have been contracted, substantial portions of all BIA programs statewide are managed by Alaska Native villages as "tribes" or by their designated regional or subregional "tribal organizations."[122] In many parts of rural Alaska, these regional and subregional organizations are the only effective service delivery agencies, so the state relies on them to provide certain state services to rural Native and non-Native residents alike.[123] In 1984 the BIA also provided tribal government improvement grants of between six to fifteen thousand dollars each to some two hundred traditional and IRA villages statewide.[124] "Native village governments" located in unincorporated communities are also eligible for some annual grants under state statues.[125] Thus, drawing from a variety of sources, Alaska Native tribal governments and their sanctioned tribal organizations have been and may continue to be used by both federal and state governments as service delivery vehicles throughout rural Alaska.

D. The Cultural Aspect

Finally, it is important to understand that, as has been true of Native governments generally, Alaska Native villages and their "tribal" governments are and will likely remain the focus of Alaska Native cultural values. Unlike the village and regional corporations established under ANCSA, these governments are not enjoined either by statutory schemes or articles of incorporation to focus their attention on financial profit. Furthermore, Native governments are the logical way to ensure that those Natives born after December 18, 1971 have a focus of communal existence. Only Natives born on or before that date were eligible to enroll as shareholders to the ANCSA corporations.[126] Their descendants may eventually inherit corporation stock, but there is no guarantee of it, just as there is no assurance that present shareholders will not alienate their stock after 1991.[127] Tribal membership, however, is not subject to such limitations.

Without a doubt, ANCSA's corporate settlement of Native land claims has delivered substantial economic and political power into the hands of Alaska's Natives.[128] Nevertheless, whether the corporations, so efficient as engines of economic development and political influence, are appropriate for the maintenance of Native cultural and communal life is a persistent question. The prospect is especially problematic for the ANCSA corporations, since by 1991 roughly one third of Alaska's Native population (40,000 out of 120,000 people) will have been born after the date of the settlement and will likely have no direct stake in Native corporate life.[129] All Alaska Natives will, however, remain theoretically eligible for membership in their traditional village communities. One suspects that the growth of viable institutions of Native government is the key to the cultural viability of these communities. Nor is there anything inconsistent between the power of the ANCSA corporations and the traditional role of Native governments as the vessels of Native cultural and communal life. Indeed, there are several points at which Native governments and the ANCSA corporations could be mutually supportive and which enhance the importance of favorably resolving the claims of Alaska Native sovereignty.

V. State and Native Jurisdiction in Alaska

A. Jurisdiction in General

Before discussing the scope of state and Native jurisdiction, it is necessary to distinguish the components of any government's jurisdiction. "Jurisdiction" may be defined as the legitimate power of a government over people and property. The scope of a government's jurisdiction is described by the relationship of the political institutions exercising jurisdiction to the matters over which they exercise it. In the United

States, jurisdiction is typically divided among three institutions: (1) a legislature, (2) an executive branch and (3) a judiciary. These institutions exercise authority over either civil or criminal matters and more specifically as these matters may relate to: (a) a specific subject matter, (b) a specific territory and (c) defined people or their property.

Each institution has a particular jurisdictional function in any American governmental scheme, and to some degree Native American governments have incorporated these institutions as well. The legislature has jurisdiction to enact civil (regulatory) or criminal (prohibitory) laws; the executive branch has jurisdiction to implement these laws through civil regulations or criminal prosecutions, and the judicial branch has jurisdiction to adjudicate civil disputes or criminal offenses. These institutions along with their jurisdictional functions and their relationship to civil and criminal jurisdictional matters are diagramed on the following page.

The scope of state and Native jurisdiction in Alaska seems to revolve around four main questions. The first is the scope of state and tribal "subject matter" jurisdiction under P.L. 280. The second is the scope of state and tribal jurisdiction over territory, the "Indian country" question. The third is the scope of state and tribal jurisdiction over people and property, but this question is largely resolved by answering the first two. The fourth question, which is also related to the third, is that of the state's jurisdiction over Native governments, the issue of sovereign immunity.

The question of subject matter jurisdiction is particularly important in discussing the effect of P.L. 280 in Alaska, because the statute has been held to extend state jurisdiction only to the *adjudication* of civil disputes and to the legislative, executive and judicial control of *crime*. Notably, P.L. 280 does not extend state legislative or executive *regulatory* jurisdiction over Indian country. P.L. 280 also has ramifications for the other jurisdictional questions as well, so it is a good idea to review P.L. 280 generally before considering the other questions in more detail.

B.   P.L. 280 in General

P.L. 83-280,[130] an outgrowth of the termination policy of the 1950's, conferred automatic jurisdiction on five states over civil "causes of action" and criminal "offenses," involving people called "Indians" in "Indian country." Alaska was added as a sixth automatic state in 1958, but in 1970 Metlakatla was exempted from the criminal jurisdiction provisions of the act and specifically afforded concurrent jurisdiction with the state over misdemeanors.

The statute is "admittedly ambiguous,"[131] and the product of confusing congressional motives.[132] It began as a law and order measure intended to control criminality on Indian reservations at reduced federal expense; the addition of civil jurisdiction was a hastily considered afterthought.[133] For many years it was erroneously assumed that P.L. 280 was a broad grant of exclusive state criminal and civil jurisdiction over

JURISDICTION IN AMERICA

JURISDICTIONAL MATTERS	JURISDICTIONAL INSTITUTIONS AND FUNCTIONS		
	LEGISLATURE	EXECUTIVE BRANCH	JUDICIARY
CIVIL MATTERS -Subject Matter -Territory -People & Property	Enacts regulatory legislation	Regulates civil matters	Adjudicates civil disputes
CRIMINAL MATTERS -Subject Matter -Territory -People & Property	Enacts prohibitory legislation	Prosecutes crimes	Adjudicates crimes

Indians for all purposes, but it is now generally agreed that it does not deprive tribes of concurrent jurisdiction.[134] Moreover, the statute has consistently been narrowly interpreted to delegate to the states only that *court* jurisdiction which Congress clearly intended them to have and to preserve to the tribes exclusive jurisdiction over civil regulatory matters, such as taxing and zoning, not clearly transferred to the states.[135]

Specific provisions also prohibit states from exercising any jurisdiction which would "authorize the alienation, encumbrance, or taxation...or...regulation of the use of" any Indian property held in trust or restricted status.[136] This provision has been broadly construed to virtually prevent the application of any state laws to the adjudication or regulation of such property.[137] Every time it has been presented with the question, the Alaska Supreme Court has also denied state jurisdiction over restricted Alaska Native property, such as allotments,[138] except where federal law, such as ANCSA, specifically permits it.[139] Of course, there is *federal* jurisdiction to adjudicate entitlement to an allotment or restricted townsite lands,[140] as well as *tribal* jurisdiction to determine membership and individual interests in tribally owned trust property.[141]

C.   P.L. 280's Effect on Subject Matter Jurisdiction

Subject matter jurisdiction defines the disputes or cases over which a government may exercise power. In the case of civil matters, jurisdiction will be defined in statutes specifying the disputes which may be adjudicated and the courts having the power to adjudicate them. In the case of criminal matters, jurisdiction will be defined by statutes which specify the actions which are crimes and the penalties the government has the authority to impose. P.L. 280 authorizes the Alaska state courts to exercise jurisdiction over the adjudication of both civil "causes of action" and criminal "offenses" involving "Indians" in "Indian country." However, the limits P.L. 280 imposes on the state's authority are perhaps as significant as the authority granted.

1. P.L. 280's Limits on State Civil Jurisdiction

P.L. 280 places three important limitations on state civil jurisdiction. First, consistent with the language of the statute, the U. S. Supreme Court has limited such jurisdiction to the judicial adjudication of "civil causes of action,"[142] thus prohibiting the application to Indian reservations of state civil regulatory laws, such as relate to taxation. Similarly, the Ninth Circuit Court of Appeals has refused to apply local municipal zoning ordinances to an Indian reservation because they were not state laws of "general application to private persons or private property."[143] Finally, state civil authority is limited by a specific provision of P.L. 280 which requires that in state judicial proceedings:

> Any tribal ordinance or custom heretofore or hereafter adopted by an Indian tribe, band, or community in the exercise

of any authority which it may possess shall, if not inconsistent with any applicable civil law of the State, be given *full force and effect* in the determination of civil causes of action pursuant to [P.L. 280] (emphasis added).[144]

Interpretation of this latter provision is likely to depend on the meanings given "inconsistent" and "applicable." One commentator suggests that "applicable," when referring to state civil laws means only laws of general, statewide application, which would not include the purely local laws of a state chartered municipality.[145] Under this analysis, IRA or traditional council ordinances or customs would not be "inconsistent" unless state law specifically precluded the enforcement of the council ordinances or customs. This approach is similar to the scope of authority accorded Alaska home rule municipalities under the state constitution[146] and statutes relating to local governments.[147]

a. The Alaska "Home Rule" Analogy

Alaska home rule municipalities are distinguished from general law municipalities[148] by the authority of the former to adopt and be governed by a home rule charter. Although the powers of general law municipalities are to be broadly construed,[149] home rule municipalities may exercise "all legislative powers not prohibited by law or by charter."[150] Thus, in determining the validity of home rule municipal ordinances versus state statutes, the Alaska Supreme Court has held that:

A municipal ordinance is not necessarily invalid in Alaska because it is *inconsistent* or in conflict with a state statute. The question rests on whether the exercise of authority has been *prohibited* to municipalities. The prohibition must be either by express terms or by implication such as where the statute and ordinance are so *substantially irreconcilable* that one cannot be given its substantive effect if the other is to be accorded the weight of law (emphasis added).[151]

The test accorded Alaska home rule municipal ordinances suggests that a similar test might apply to the substantive ordinances and customs of traditional and federally chartered IRA Native governing councils. Although neither form of government derives its authority from state laws, the substantive provisions of their laws may specifically be enforced in state courts under P.L. 280 if they are "not inconsistent" with state statutes. The concept of inherent sovereignty implies home rule authority for traditional governing councils. The analogy is even clearer with IRA governments established under community approved constitutions, because the IRA as applied to Alaska was intended to "grant certain rights of home rule to Indians."[152]

b. The Attitude of the Courts

The Alaska Supreme Court appears to recognize that "Indian tribes are sovereign, self-governing entities subject only to the plenary power of Congress" and that their "affairs are subject to state law only to the extent that Congress explicitly so provides."[153] This narrow interpretation of state jurisdiction, coupled with liberal interpretation of P.L. 280 to benefit Natives,[154] suggests that affording Native ordinances and customs "full force and effect" in Alaska state courts may permit the exercise of substantial Alaska Native civil authority.

For example, the U.S. Supreme Court has judicially acknowledged that "[t]raditional tribal justice tends to be informal and consensual rather than adjudicative."[155] Commentators have made similar observations about the nature of contemporary justice measures in Alaska Native villages.[156] It has even been suggested that incorporated Alaskan municipalities could regulate minor forms of misconduct by incorporating traditional values in ordinances and procedures of an essentially civil nature.[157] Thus, at least as to their members, Alaska Native governments might also be able to resolve disputes and correct misconduct by traditional, informal or consensual means so long as such authority is not specifically forbidden by state laws of general application.[158]

Significantly, the Alaska Federal District Court has confirmed the authority of an Alaska Native IRA government to adjudicate rights to cultural artifacts located on IRA owned land.[159] Similar authority might well extend to regulation of other Native interests even arising on lands not owned by the Native government, but over which it nonetheless has authority.[160] Regulation of these interests could, of course, be enforced in Native village forums. They should also be upheld in state courts, unless doing so would be "inconsistent" with state law. Of course, if village authority were questioned in state courts, the ultimate test would be the extent to which those courts would truly give "full force and effect" to village ordinances and customs. Several decisions of the Alaska Supreme Court indicate that it is cautious to assume jurisdiction over Native affairs.[161] A reverse implication is that it may be equally careful to preserve Native governing authority where it seems to be required by the third specific limitation on state P.L. 280 jurisdiction.

2. P.L. 280's Limits on State Criminal Jurisdiction.

Prior to 1885, all enforcement of Indian criminal law was within the exclusive jurisdiction of reservation tribal governments.[162] The Major Crimes Act of 1885 and the subsequent U.S. Supreme Court decision in *U.S. v. Kagama*[163] permitted Congress, by specific legislation, to intrude federal enforcement of United States criminal law on what had previously been an area of exclusive tribal authority.[164] P.L 280 extended this principle to the states by permitting certain states (including Alaska) to exercise criminal jurisdiction over "Indian country...to the same extent that such State...has jurisdiction over offenses committed elsewhere within the State...."[165]

As with the civil provisions of P.L. 280, it was originally assumed that the criminal provisions also granted exclusive jurisdiction to the states over Indian "offenses" and prohibited all tribal enforcement of tribal criminal statutes. For example, several years after P.L. 280 was extended to Alaska in 1958, the Metlakatla tribal government was informed that it no longer had jurisdiction to prosecute even minor offenses occurring on the reservation, because the state had exclusive jurisdiction. The Metlakatlans then ceased enforcing their local laws and relied on the state to control criminal conduct on the reservation.

It soon became obvious that Metlakatla's isolation and the state's then limited resources meant that the state could not adequately enforce its criminal laws on the reservation. Both Metlakatla and the state petitioned Congress for relief. Congress responded in 1970 by amending P.L. 280 to permit Metlakatla and the state to exercise concurrent criminal jurisdiction. The congressional reports and debates accompanying the amendment demonstrate that the 1970 Congress interpreted P.L. 280 to confer state exclusive criminal jurisdiction unless Congress provided otherwise.[166] However, more recent scholarly opinion, legal analysis and administrative practice has consistently interpreted P.L. 280 as a grant of concurrent jurisdiction to the states rather than a totally gratuitous ouster of continued tribal authority.[167]

Nonetheless, state jurisdiction does extend to all "offenses" against state law committed by Indians in Indian country. Unlike the corresponding provisions governing state civil jurisdiction, there is no requirement that state adjudication of such offenses give any force to tribal ordinances and customs. On the other hand, as with civil court proceedings, state criminal prosecutions are limited in so far as they cannot result in the "encumbrance" of trust or restricted property.[168]

State criminal prosecutions are also limited to "offenses," which has been interpreted to mean only activities which are "prohibited" under state law. Thus, the Ninth Circuit Court of Appeals has refused to approve state P.L. 280 jurisdiction to enforce state gambling regulations on Indian reservations where gambling is regulated but not prohibited as a matter of state public policy. Conversely, where gambling is prohibited, the same court seems willing to permit state enforcement as an element of its P.L. 280 criminal jurisdiction.[169]

D. Jurisdiction Over Territory—The "Indian Country" Question

1. Territorial Jurisdiction in General

Territorial jurisdiction describes the geographic extent of a government's power which, for Native communities, is largely a question of defining the meaning of "Indian country."[170] The phrase has a long legislative and judicial history dating back to the early trade and intercourse acts and is now defined by a comprehensive federal statute as the land within: 1) "Indian reservations," 2) "dependent Indian communities" or 3) "Indian allotments."[171] All three definitions have some application to Alaska, but the "dependent Indian community" concept is the one that has the most significance.

The concept originated in *U.S. v. Sandoval* wherein the U.S. Supreme Court held that the lands owned by a New Mexico Pueblo were "Indian country" for purposes of enforcing the federal Indian liquor laws, thus prohibiting the distribution of liquor on the Pueblo's lands.[172] The argument in *Sandoval* was that the Pueblo lands were not Indian country because they were owned in fee simple. In rejecting that argument, the Supreme Court concluded that the Pueblo constituted Indian country under the liquor laws because it was treated by the United States as a "dependent Indian community" entitled to federal protection.[173]

Twenty years later, the U. S. Supreme Court again considered the meaning of "Indian country" as applied to a New Mexico Pueblo. This case, *U.S. v. Chavez,* was a federal prosecution of a non-Indian for larceny against Pueblo Indians.[174] The prosecution was under the so-called General Crimes Act[175] which makes the general criminal laws of the United States applicable (with certain exceptions) to Indian country. The Supreme Court expanded on its definition in *Sandoval* to include within the concept "any unceded land owned or occupied by an Indian nation or tribe of Indians."[176] This was the same definition which the Alaska Federal District Court later applied to the Tyonek reservation in the case of *In re McCord,* previously noted.[177]

That case was a federal prosecution for statutory rape under territorial law. The defendant argued he was subject only to tribal jurisdiction, because his crime was committed in Indian country, and because statutory rape was not then included among the crimes which could be prosecuted under the Indian Major Crimes Act.[178] The prosecution argued, in part, that the Tyonek lands were not Indian country because they were not really "reservation" lands. The court concluded that the Tyonek lands were within the statutory definition of Indian country because, as interpreted by *Chavez,* the term included "any unceded lands owned or occupied by an Indian nation or tribe of Indians...."[179]

2. "Indian Country" After ANCSA

McCord carefully restricted its holding to only those lands "set aside for the use of and...governed by an operational tribal unit."[180] Nevertheless, lands conveyed under the Alaska Native Claims Settlement Act might fall within the broader *Chavez* Indian country definition. Indeed the Interior Department has gone so far as to conclude that ANCSA selected lands are Indian country at least for purposes of villages exercising federally *delegated* powers under the Indian liquor laws.[181] Additionally, Natives occupying those lands do so as "dependent communities" in so far as they are dependent on the United States for many of the public services they receive.[182] Several federal courts have held that this sort of dependency is an influential factor in determining whether nonreservation, tribally owned lands are "Indian country."[183] Prevailing scholarly opinion does not tie the existence of Indian country to the existence of either federally or tribally owned land,[184] but one court has concluded that whether the United States retains title to the lands occupied by the Natives is also a relevant factor.[185]

The extent to which ANCSA lands, owned by a Native village corporation, may be "governed by an operational tribal unit" as "Indian country" is theoretically an open question.[186] However, the U.S. Supreme Court has characterized the "Indian country" concept as a flexible one which "may be considered in connection with the changes which have taken place in our situation, with a view of determining from time to time what must be regarded as Indian country where it is spoken of in the statutes"[187] Furthermore, subsequent to ANCSA, lands in Alaska actually owned by a Native government have been judicially treated as Indian country over which a Native government may exert jurisdiction.[188] It is also likely that allotments and restricted townsite lands, given the language of the federal Indian country statute, are Indian country for some purposes of tribal jurisdiction.[189] Finally, it is clear, even in Alaska, that lands, such as the Metlakatla reservation, which are held in federal trust are also Indian country.[190]

Indeed, the U.S. Supreme Court has upheld the existence of Indian country in a variety of land ownership situations.[191] In all of these situations it seems clear that federal jurisdiction could displace state jurisdiction when it comes to the exercise of authority over Indian country. What is not clear is the extent to which Native jurisdiction could exclude state jurisdiction on *nonreservation* lands. Generally, tribal jurisdiction is exclusive of state authority within the confines of a federal reservation,[192] but even within reservations, the U.S. Supreme Court has permitted some exercise of authority infringe on important tribal interests.[193] On the other hand, exclusive tribal authority on allotments no longer within a reservation has also been sustained.[194] It therefore seems that the mere existence of "Indian country" will not be the only factor in deciding whether tribal authority can be exercised free of concurrent state jurisdiction.

3. Off-Reservation Civil Regulation

In addition to permitting state adjudication of civil "causes of action," P.L. 280 also provides that:

> [T]hose civil laws of [a] State...that are of general application
> to private persons or private property shall have the same
> force and effect within...Indian country as they have else-
> where within the State....[195]

It was long contended that this provision permitted states to regulate and tax nontrust property even on Indian reservations.[196] The U.S. Supreme Court rejected that argument in *Bryan v. Itasca County*[197] and drew a broad distinction between a state's jurisdiction to "adjudicate" and jurisdiction to "regulate" under P.L. 280.

Itasca County argued in *Bryan* that it could levy a personal property tax against a trailer occupying reservation land. It contended that P.L. 280 extended all state civil laws of "general application" to Mr. Bryan's reservation, and that the county was therefore authorized to tax his trailer under state law.[198] The Court held that the legislative history of P.L. 280 revealed a restrictive purpose to apply to reservations only those laws of the state related to "adjudication" of disputes between private individuals. Under this interpretation, the Court ruled that regulatory laws, such as those relating to taxation, could not be applied to Indian reservations in P.L. 280 states. In spite of P.L. 280, state tax laws were "preempted" from application to individual private property on federally guaranteed reservations.[199] The decision has effectively insulated federal reservations from a wide variety of state regulatory laws, notably, for example, laws relating to gambling.[200]

However, the *Bryan* Court specifically noted that the preemptive analysis "usually yields different results" when applied to "tribal Indians who have left or never inhabited Federally established reservations."[201] The statement illustrates the presumption, clarified in later cases, that tribal interests are considered stronger, and therefore state preemption is more easily found, within the boundaries of federal reservations.[202] Because there are no reservations (except Metlakatla) in Alaska, that presumption may not be available as a means of excluding state jurisdiction in most of Alaska's "Indian country." The U.S. Supreme Court has implied as much in at least three cases, one of which arose in Alaska.

In *Mescalero Apache Tribe v. Jones* (1972),[203] the Court permitted state taxation of gross receipts from a tribal ski resort located *off* the Mescalero reservation. *McClanahan v. Arizona State Tax Commission*[204] was a companion case to *Mescalero Apache,* and in both cases the Supreme Court noted that *Kake v. Egan* was authority for the power of a state to tax and otherwise regulate *off*-reservation Indian enterprises. The general implication seems to be that in these particular off-reservation situations, the interests of the tribe did not outweigh the interests of the state in regulating the particular activity. Unless some more significant tribal interests were at stake, it is likely that the state would have regulatory authority over other off-reservation Native interests in Alaska, even if the affected territory were considered "Indian country." State authority in these circumstances is not derived from any provison of P.L. 280 but rather from a "balancing" of tribal, state and federal interests which the Supreme Court has employed to determine the relative scope of each government's jurisdiction under the related but distinct doctrines of "preemption" and "infringement." These concepts are discussed in more detail in section VI of this chapter.

However, even if the State of Alaska were to have regulatory jurisdiction over off-reservation Indian country, there is nothing in P.L. 280 or the general jurisdictional principles of federal Indian law to preclude a Native village government from exercising concurrent regulatory authority over the same lands. This could, at least theoretically, include the usual powers of tribal governments such as zoning, taxation and other forms of civil regulation.[205] The actual authority of the Native government could be substantial. On the other hand, the existence of a state chartered municipality with jurisdiction over some of the same lands[206] would likely preclude, as a practical matter, the exercise of duplicate authority by a Native government. In the absence of state chartered governments, however, Alaska Native traditional or IRA councils could provide effective local government.

4. Delegation and Other Expansions of Tribal Jurisdiction

As communities with inherent rights of political self-government, Alaska Native village traditional and IRA councils can also exercise federally delegated criminal and civil authority in Indian country.[207] The Indian liquor laws are perhaps the most prominent example of this sort of delegated authority,[208] and by the specific terms of P.L. 280 they are specifically excepted from state criminal jurisdiction.[209] Under these statutes, Indian tribes have been held to have concurrent authority with states to regulate the introduction of liquor into Indian country even though the tribes supposedly did not exercise such authority traditionally.[210] As previously noted, this authority has been delegated to villages in Alaska and provides these villages with an alternate and locally enforceable means of preventing the introduction of liquor into their communities.[211] Although it is not exactly analogous, under the Indian Child Welfare Act, Alaska Native villages may also obtain retrocession of exclusive jurisdiction over child custody cases involving children domiciled within Indian country governed by the tribe.[212] Similarly, 1981 amendments to the Lacey Act, discussed in chapter 7, permit Native fish and game ordinances as applied to Indian country to be enforced as federal law.[213]

E. Jurisdiction Over Persons and Property

As a general principle, Native governments have large measures of criminal and civil jurisdiction over the persons and property of persons (especially tribal members) living within Indian country.[214] Within the limits discussed above, P.L. 280 affords the State of Alaska concurrent jurisdiction over criminal "offenses" and civil "causes of action" involving "Indians" arising within "Indian country." The state may even be able to exercise concurrent civil regulatory jurisdiction over Indian persons and unrestricted property within off reservation Indian country. One significant unresolved question is whether, under some circumstances, the interests of the tribe in the exercise of exclusive jurisdiction over particular matters might outweigh the interests of the state over such matters out-side a reservation. Assuming the existence of such circumstances, it seems likely that Alaska Native village traditional or IRA councils could also have exclusive jurisdiction over persons and property within off-re-servation Indian country.

F. Sovereign Immunity

1. In General

Because they are governmental entities, Indian tribes have long been acknowledged to possess governmental immunity from suit, also known as "sovereign immunity."[215] Under this doctrine, a government cannot be sued without its consent, which means, significantly, that sovereign immunity is also a barrier to court jurisdiction to enforce mone-tary or other sanctions which would deplete governmental assets or hamper governmental functions. In general, tribal sovereign immunity exempts Native governments and their officers from state court jurisdic-tion,[216] but it may not be a bar to actions against a tribe by the United States or those acting under its authority.[217] Congress can also waive tribal sovereign immunity as an exercise of plenary power,[218] and it has been held that a Native government can waive its own immunity as an exercise of its inherent sovereignty.[219] Additionally, suits against tribal officials acting outside the scope of their authority may also be permitted under a narrow but established exception to the sovereign immunity doc-trine.[220]

Since sovereign immunity is an attribute unique to governments, an issue which frequently arises in litigation is whether a particular Native community claiming sovereign immunity is truly a government or "tribe." Although sovereign immunity does not depend on federal recognition of tribal political status,[221] it seems well established that federal recognition is sufficient to establish sovereign immunity,[222] and, thereby, to insulate a tribe from judicial examination of its political status. In the absence of such recognition, Native communities claiming sovereign status can be subjected to detailed requirements of proof, often with mixed results.[223]

The Alaska Supreme Court has specifically held that the Metlakatla Indian Community, as a "recognized" Indian tribe, possesses gov-ernmental immunity from suit.[224] However, on two subsequent occas-sions when it was presented with the issue of whether a traditional tribal council[225] or an IRA organized community[226] also had sovereign immunity, it assumed that they did without deciding the question. The Alaska Dis-trict Federal Court has not been so reluctant, holding in one case that the Chilkat Indian Village IRA could not be joined in a lawsuit because the parties agreed it was immune[227] and in another that the Tlingit and Haida Central Council was immune as a recognized Indian tribe.[228] It seems particularly clear that Alaska Native communities organized under Indian Reorganization Act constitutions have sovereign immunity, be-cause section 16 of the IRA specifically confirms it.[229] In any event, the

BIA's inclusion of nearly two hundred Alaska Native entities in its 1982 and 1983 annual publications of recognized "Indian Tribal Entities" all but settles the question of whether Alaska Native communities have sovereign immunity. [230]

2. Waivers of Immunity

a. In General

Whether and under what circumstances a tribe or Congress might waive tribal immunity, has become an increasingly litigated issue. As noted above, it seems well established that Congress can waive the immunity of a tribe, but the rule is that any such waivers must be explicit and cannot be implied. [231] Nevertheless, for many years it was argued that P.L. 280 and the Indian Civil Rights Act constituted fairly broad congressional waivers of tribal governmental immunity. Two decisions of the U.S. Supreme Court laid these arguments to rest. [232] A more current issue, especially in Alaska, is the circumstances under which a tribe might be construed to have waived its own immunity in the course of its dealings with business interests or state government.

b. Congressional Waivers

During the 1960's and early 1970's it was sometimes argued that P.L. 280's grant of jurisdiction to a state constituted a congressional waiver of tribal sovereign immunity. The Alaska Supreme Court has firmly rejected that argument in *Atkinson v. Haldane,* a case arising on the Metlakatla Indian reservation. Using reasoning analagous to that of the U.S. Supreme Court in *Bryan v. Itasca County,* [233] the Alaska court concluded that P.L. 280 should be read narrowly to extend state jurisdiction only to those matters explicitly covered in the statute. It may be recalled that P.L. 280 only explicitly authorized state jurisdiction over "causes of action" and application of state laws governing "private" persons or property. Because Metlakatla was a governmental entity, not a private person, the *Atkinson* court concluded that P.L. 280 did not constitute a congressional waiver of Metlakatla's sovereign immunity. The decision is also consistent with the U.S. Supreme Court's conclusion in *Bryan* that P.L. 280 did not confer state jurisdiction "over the tribes themselves." [234]

For about ten years after its passage, the 1968 federal Indian Civil Rights Act [235] was frequently held to be a congressional waiver of tribal immunity for purposes of federal court enforcement of its provisions against tribal governments. With some significant exceptions, the Indian Civil Rights Act incorporates the U. S. constitutional guarantees of civil liberty and makes them applicable to the actions of Indian tribes. [236] At least in the Ninth Circuit Court of Appeals, the civil rights guaranteed under the act were never applied literally the same as they would have been under the U. S. Constitution, but were to be interpreted "with due regard to, historical, governmental and cultural values of an Indian tribe."[237] Nonetheless, other decisions from the same court had permitted lawsuits against tribes to recover damages or enjoin tribal actions which allegedly violated civil rights.[238]

The U. S. Supreme Court's 1978 decision in *Santa Clara Pueblo v. Martinez,* eliminates, with one narrow exception, the possibility of future such lawsuits against tribes or their officers.[239] The *Martinez* case arose out of disparate treatment of women under the membership laws of the Santa Clara Pueblo located in northern New Mexico. Consistent with its patrilinial culture, the Pueblo barred children from membership if their fathers were not members even if their mothers were members. The Supreme Court construed the Indian Civil Rights Act narrowly, concluding that it did not explicitly waive sovereign immunity and that no waiver could be implied.[240] The Court went on to conclude that the Indian Civil Rights Act had a dual purpose of not only requiring tribes to afford civil rights to those subject to their jurisdiction but also to encourage tribes to do so through their own governments and not federal judicial intervention.[241] The only exception to this rule is if a tribal violation of civil rights results in illegal imprisonment. In those circumstances, the Indian Civil Rights Act specifically permits a federal *habeas corpus* remedy.[242]

It should also be noted that state jurisdiction to enforce state civil rights laws[243] against Alaska Native governments has not been granted unless it is under P.L. 280—the only federal grant of state civil jurisdiction. The Alaska Supreme Court's decision in *Atkinson v. Haldane,* previously discussed, construed P.L. 280 narrowly to permit state jurisdiction only in cases involving *private* parties. Since Native governments are not "private" parties, they and officers acting on their behalf should be immune from suit under Alaska's civil rights laws.

c. Tribal Waivers

The tribal waiver issue arises in Alaska in the context of the dealings Native governments have had with private businesses and various state programs. Unless waived, governmental immunity is a bar to the enforcement of any contract against a Native government, so any time such a government enters into a contract there is a potential waiver issue in the event of a contract dispute. Also a number of state statutes authorize state contracts, services and grants for unincorporated traditional or IRA village councils.[244] Administration of these statutes has raised the question of how the state might enforce state grant and contract provisions, therefore raising the question of tribal waivers of immunity.[245] Although the U.S. Supreme Court has not decided the issue, it appears likely that Native governments can waive governmental immunity as an exercise of inherent political authority.[246] Litigation of the issue suggests that Native governments might be held to have waived immunity under several circumstances. These include: (i) contractual waivers, (ii) the purchase of insurance, (iii) provisions in tribal constitutions or corporate charters, (iv) the mingling of tribal government and business activities and (v) the actions of tribal officers acting beyond their authority.

i. Contractual Waivers

At least one federal court has found a waiver of sovereign immunity where a Native community entered into a contract with the federal government to provide police services and agreed in the contract to assume liability for damages arising out of the wrongful conduct of tribal police officers.[247] More recently, the Alaska Supreme Court has construed the arbitration clause of a construction contract to be a waiver of tribal sovereign immunity.[248] Although the latter decision is inconsistent with the normal requirement that such waivers must be clear and explicit, cases such as these are clear warnings to Native governments that they must be cautious not to inadvertently waive sovereign immunity in signing business or other agreements.

ii. Purchase of Insurance

It has been held in a line of cases involving non-Native municipal governments that the purchase of liability insurance satisfies one of the functions of immunity and therefore should be construed as a waiver.[249] One reason for supporting sovereign immunity is to provide protection of public funds and public property from diversion into the payment of private damage claims. However, in *Atkinson v. Haldane,* discussed earlier, the Alaska Supreme Court found that Native governments, because of their limited resources, could not adequately protect their public assets merely by purchasing insurance. The *Atkinson* court therefore held that tribal purchase of liability insurance was not a waiver of sovereign immunity.[250] The same principles ought to apply to other Alaska Native governments, so the purchase of insurance by itself does not appear to threaten tribal sovereign immunity. On the other hand, liability insurance required for contracts under the Indian Self-Determination Act does constitute a limited waiver of the contracting tribes sovereign immunity, but only up to the amount secured by the insurance policy.[251]

iii. Tribal Constitutions and Charters

Sovereign immunity can also be waived through specific provisions of a tribal constitution or corporate charter. Approval of such documents by the Secretary of the Interior under the Indian Reorganization Act constitute a waiver.[252] Corporate business charters adopted under section 17 of the IRA typically include a "sue and be sued" clause.[253] However, IRA constitutions now in effect in Alaska do not appear to waive sovereign immunity in either general or specific terms.[254] Similarly, the constitutions adopted by traditional governing councils do not appear to effect a waiver of immunity.[255] In any event, even corporate waivers of immunity should be narrowly drawn to prevent exposure of the tribal government's assets except to the extent those assets are specifically assigned to a corporate enterprise.[256]

iv. Mingling of Government and Business

When a Native government establishes a tribal business corporation, whether under the IRA or otherwise, it is important that it maintains its separate identities as a government and as a business by careful drafting of corporate articles and other organizing documents. In a Colorado case, a tribe, organized under both sections 16 and 17 of the IRA, was held to have consented to suit through business incorporation under section 17 and to have thereby waived its *governmental* immunity.[257] In analyzing the Colorado opinion, the Alaska Supreme Court found that the tribe had not clearly distinguished its governmental and business functions in the business corporation charter; that error was sufficient to find a waiver of governmental immunity.[258]

It is also important to keep the day to day operation of a tribe's government and business interests separate. The Alaska Federal District Court has noted that confusion often surrounds the distinction between the two spheres of activity. The result of not clearly separating the two can be a finding that the tribe itself was acting in a corporate capacity and therefore that its immunity was waived under the "sue and be sued" clause of a corporate charter.[259] The purpose of providing for the two forms of organization under the Indian Reorganization Act is to permit the Native government to protect tribal assets from rapid dissipation (as government assets) while at the same time taking limited risks on business enterprises, which typically require accountability.[260] Any mingling of government and business which jeopardizes a tribe's immunity defeats the pupose of *maintaining* two separate entities.

It should be noted that the necessity of careful separation of operations may be a particularly difficult notion to accept in many Alaskan communities. As was pointed out in chapter 8, typical Alaska Native "tribal" units have been relatively small, cooperative units. Villages have generally taken a wholistic approach to their affairs. In a small community, where positions in both "government" and "business" may be held by the same individuals, maintaining the distinction between the two may well appear to be a senseless exercise.

v. Tribal Officials

Federal officials who are acting "beyond their authority" can typically be sued to prevent such actions or to recover damages on the theory that since they are acting beyond their authority they are not acting on behalf of the sovereign.[261] Although this is not technically a "waiver" of sovereign immunity it accomplishes the same result—judicial intervention in governmental affairs. The principle appears applicable to tribal officials as well,[262] but this is a complex area of law which is still evolving, so it is not clear precisely when tribal officials might be considered to be acting "beyond their authority."

Although, circumstances involving denials of civil rights are one of the notable instances where federal officials can be sued individually as acting beyond their authority,[263] except for *habeas corpus* actions, suits in similar circumstances do not appear to be permitted against tribal officials. In *Santa Clara Pueblo v. Martinez,* disucssed earlier, the U.S. Supreme Court concluded that tribal officials were exempt from all but *habeas corpus* actions even though their actions may have been a denial of rights under the Indian Civil Rights Act.

One Ninth Circuit Court of Appeals decision suggests that the limitations of *Martinez* are generally applicable to "intratribal" disputes between tribal members and tribal officials.[264] Another federal circuit court has suggested, in a suit brought by a non-Indian oil company to enjoin tribal officials from terminating an oil lease, that whether the officials could be sued or not depended on whether the tribal government could legally authorize them to terminate the lease. That in turn was said to turn on whether the tribe's power to terminate the lease trespassed on the "overriding interests of the National Government," or was "necessary to protect tribal self-government or to control internal relations."[265] There is a disquieting hint in both these cases that federal courts may be more willing to find ways to assert jurisdiction over cases involving conflicts between non-Indians and tribal officials than in cases involving Indians and tribal officials, but it is simply too early to predict circumstances under which tribal officials may be held to be acting beyond their authority for purposes of asserting federal jurisdiction to review their actions.

G. Conclusions

Tribal jurisdiction in a nonreservation, P.L 280 state like Alaska is perhaps subject to a greater degree of state interference than is the case on reservations in other P.L. 280 states. Nonetheless, it is important to realize that P.L. 280 is not a grant of either exclusive or general state jurisdiction over "Indians" in "Indian country." The statute has been specifically limited to civil "causes of action" and criminal "offenses," and in neither case can state jurisdiction interfere with Native property held in restricted or trust status. Significantly, in civil cases, P.L. 280 also requires state courts to give "full force and effect" to certain tribal ordinances or customs. In Alaska this may mean that enactments and customary practices of Native governments must be accorded a deference similar to that afforded the ordinances of home rule municipalities chartered under Alaska state law. Finally, P.L. 280 does not grant any state jurisdiction over tribal governments themselves, but only authority over private causes of action and individual criminal offenses.

In many respects, therefore, P.L. 280 in Alaska is not so important as a grant of state jurisdiction over Native affairs as it is for the restrictions it imposes on the exercise of state authority. Furthermore, whether the state can exercise more general regulatory authority over Alaska Natives in off-reservation Indian country than is possible in a reservation situation is something of an open question, which has little to do with P.L. 280. Instead, the degree to which the state may have concurrent regulatory jurisdiction with off-reservation tribes seems likely to depend on the relative interests of the state and tribal governments in the subject matter being regulated.

VI. The Nature of the Alaska Native Claim to Self-Government

A. Politics or Property

Aboriginal powers of self-government or "sovereignty" are not founded on a claim to property ownership or "title," but rather on inherent political independence which incidentally enables a government to assert authority over people and property subject to its jurisdiction. The discovery of what came to be known as the Americas generated a vigorous European debate over the rights of the original inhabitants of the "new world."[266] The debate, initially among the Spanish clergy of the mid-sixteenth century,[267] influenced the theory, if not usually the practice, of Spanish aboriginal policy.[268] The debate was taken up in the seventeenth century by the Dutch jurist and statesman, Hugo Grotius and was carried on through the eighteenth century by the Swiss jurist, Emmerich Vattel,[269] both of whose thoughts influenced the early Indian cases decided by John Marshall.[270]

The focus of these early debates was on the relative rights of the aboriginal inhabitants of the newly discovered lands to both property and sovereignty.[271] At least under the English common law, with its feudal heritage, the concepts of property ownership and political authority were joined together in the person of the sovereign.[272] However, the British negotiation of treaties with the North American aboriginal tribes implied, Marshall later held, that the aboriginal people were also sovereign.[273] The purpose of the treaties was the acquisition of aboriginal property rights to the land held by the Indians,[274] to which the British asserted an *exclusive* right of acquisition by virtue of their "discovery."[275] However the title of the British (and later the Americans) could not be realistically equated to complete political control, because the Indians were able to oppose early assertions of such sovereignty militarily.[276] The result was that the concepts of sovereignty and land title were judicially distinguished so that even though the land titles of the aboriginal inhabitants were theoretically impaired by the doctrine of discovery (i.e.' they could only sell to the "discovering" nation), their inherent right to political self-government was not.[277]

Thus, under the domestic law of the United States, the concepts of aboriginal property rights and aboriginal sovereignty are legally distinct; political authority is not linked to land ownership.[278] It follows, therefore, that the extinguishment of aboriginal title to land does not by implication extinguish aboriginal political authority.[279] Furthermore, it has been held that even in terminating the federal-tribal relationship, the United States does not extinguish the tribe or its inherent political authority.[280]

It is therefore arguable that since aboriginal self-government cannot be "taken" by the United States it can never be "lost" by a tribe[281] and so is not a compensable right under the Fifth Amendment to the United States Constitution.[282] Moreover, it is difficult to see how the "value" of self-government could be qualified in monetary terms.

Finally, as suggested above, aboriginal claims of self-government go beyond claims of mere property ownership to include claims of political control over people and territory within the tribe's jurisdiction even though these are not associated with tribally owned property.[283] Furthermore, it is only because Indian "tribes" possess "attributes of sovereignty over both their members and their territory" that the federal government can delegate its own political authority to them.[284] Thus, to confine Native American claims of inherent political authority to mere property claims in some sense lessens their significance.

B. The Meaning of "Tribe"

Whether a particular Native American community possesses sovereignty, however, has generally turned on the question of whether or not it is a "tribe." The answer depends on two sometimes related but independent inquiries. In the first place, a community may be considered a tribe ethnologically. Whether a community is an ethnological tribe can require a complex factual and historical analysis, but the U.S. Supreme Court has defined a tribe as:

> a body of Indians of the same or a similar race, united in a community under one leadership or government, and inhabiting a particular though sometimes ill-defined territory....[285]

Even if a community does not qualify as a tribe ethnologically, it is clear that there is also a separate legal sense of the term which arises out of federal recognition of a tribe politically. Along with foreign affairs and certain other matters identified in the U.S. Constitution, questions of:

> whether, to what extent, and for what time [distinctly Indian communities] shall be recognized and dealt with as dependent tribes requiring the guardianship and protection of the United States are to be determined by Congress, and not by the courts.[286]

As noted before, whether a Native American community constitutes a "tribe" with powers of self-government is a "political question" so that if the legislative or executive departments (the "political" branches of government) recognize its independent existence, the question is no longer subject to independent judicial inquiry. [287]

Courts can, as mentioned earlier, determine that a Native American community is a tribe whether or not it is federally recognized. [288] Although procedures are now in place to ensure that all ethnological tribes are federally recognized, [289] federal recognition is not a prerequisite to either tribal existence or the exercise of tribal self-government. Nevertheless, a clearly established pattern of recognition does confirm that a given Native American community possesses certain powers of self-government and is entitled to federal "Native" programs even though it may not be, strictly speaking, an ethnological tribe. [290] The recognition issue has become especially relevant in Alaska because of past characterizations that Alaska Natives are not organized as ethnological "tribes" and because the burden of proving the factual and historical existence of more than two hundred Native village governments would be excessive.

C. Whether Alaska Native Communities Have Sovereignty

Quite logically, the beginning point for the Alaska Native sovereignty debate is the question of whether Alaska Natives ever exercised political control over themselves. Although it is difficult to believe that any community of human beings could long exist without some means of internal political authority, what constitutes "political" authority is likely to depend as much on the cultural perspective of the mind defining it as on the reality of life in the society living it. Most Native American societies were probably not "political societies" in the sense that concept was understood to apply to the European nation-state. The political character of such states was often perceived as derived from the obedience "'of the bulk of its members...to a certain and common superior.' "[291]

The problem, of course, is that few Native American societies really had a "certain and common superior" equivalent to a sixteenth century European absolute monarch. Instead, the members of aboriginal societies were more often obedient to the force of shared customs and established traditions. "Political" leadership in this context was more often based on earned respect than on enforced obedience, and to those who came from a European tradition might not appear to be "political" at all. A less ethnocentric and more realistic view is that a "political society" is one composed of:

> a considerable number of persons who are permanently united by habitual obedience to a certain and common superior, or whose conduct in regard to their mutual relations habitually conforms to recognized standards. [292]

Using this concept of "political society," it seems obvious that Alaska Native societies were no less (or more) political than were the so-called tribal societies of the contiguous United States. Nevertheless, the perception has crept into the legal treatment of Alaska Natives that they were not "grouped as bands or tribes" as in the lower forty-eight states.[293] Recently, this alleged distinction has become the focus for the suggestion that the absence of "tribal" organization implies an absence of political organization as well.[294] On the other hand, it is generally accepted that the village was the usual form of Alaska Native community organization and government prior to western contact.[295]

Owing to the pernicious influence of contact, it is questionable whether many present-day Native American communities are organized as true "tribes" in the ethnological sense.[296] Many ethnic tribes were split apart on separate reservations, and frequently federal representatives would designate diverse bands of Indians as a "tribe" for purposes of negotiating a federal treaty.[297] In addition, other Indian communities organized as villages, specifically the Pueblos of southwest America, have long been treated as Native sovereignties and are often compared with the Alaska Native villages in this regard.[298] Furthermore, the exhaustive study of the status of Alaska Natives which was undertaken to provide a background for ANCSA confirms that the village was the principal Alaska Native political organization.[299] Some anthropological investigations go even further to suggest that Alaska Natives were politically organized as small nations prior to western contact.[300]

Nonetheless, the difficulty of proving the historical existence and political independence of every village in Alaska tends to focus the Alaska Native sovereignty debate on the question of whether these villages have been federally "recognized" as separate political communities or "tribes." There is ample evidence, beginning with the 1867 Russian Treaty of Cession, that the United States government has long treated Alaska Natives according to the principles applied to other Native American communities. As noted earlier, Article III of the treaty implies a distinction between the "uncivilized tribes" and the other "inhabitants of the ceded territory." The latter, if they remained in the territory, were to be "admitted to all the rights, advantages and immunities of citizens of the United States." The "uncivilized tribes," however, were to be "subject to such laws and regulations as the United States may, from time to time, adopt in regard to aboriginal tribes of that country."[301]

Although, early opinion tended to treat Alaska Natives differently from the Indians of the rest of the United States,[302] that view was substantially reversed by the beginning of the twentieth century. One early case involved the right of an Alaska Native to citizenship under the terms of the 1867 treaty. The Alaska Federal District court concluded that the Native had abandoned his tribal relations and so was entitled to the rights of a citizen as one of the other "inhabitants" of the territory, but in reaching this conclusion the court said that:

> [The 1867 treaty] *gave the Indian tribes of Alaska the same status before the law as those of the United States,* and , unless a different intention appears on the face of the law, extends *all acts of Congress, applicable and of a general nature, relating to the Indians of the United States, to Alaska* (emphasis added).[303]

Subsequent opinions of the Interior Department Solicitor reached the same conclusion, including, as noted earlier, the decision that Alaska Native self-government was sufficient to validate marriage among tribal members outside of territorial law.[304]

In 1931, the administration of Alaska Native affairs was transferred from the Interior Department's Office of Education to the Bureau of Indian Affairs,[305] and, as discussed earlier, the comprehensive Indian Reorganization Act (IRA) was specifically amended in 1936 to suit the Alaska Native "non-tribal," village form of organization. It has been suggested that the Alaska application of the IRA to "groups" with a "common bond" implies that the basis of reorganization in Alaska is something other than that of a community's historical political existence, the implication being that Alaska Native communities may not have inherent powers of self-government characteristic of tribes generally.[306] On the other hand, the current regulations implementing the IRA include Alaska Native communities within the meaning of the term "tribe" without distinction as to their historic political existence so long as they are "recognized and receiving services from the Bureau of Indian Affairs."[307]

The BIA and its predecessor, the Bureau of Education, have provided services to Alaska Native villages since about 1885.[308] The BIA has provided these services to Alaska Native villages at least since 1931 under the comprehensive authority of the Snyder Act.[309] Furthermore, every major piece of national Indian legislation enacted since ANCSA has consistently included Alaska Native "villages" within the scope of eligibility for the services and benefits these enactments provide.[310] Significantly, Indian education regulations adopted in 1979 specifically note that "Tribes and Alaska Native villages" are "distinct cultural and governmental entities" with "a government to government relationship...with the Federal Government."[311] In 1982 and 1983, the BIA included 197 "Alaska Native Entities" in its annual publications of "Indian Tribal Entities Recognized and Eligible to Receive Services from the United States Bureau of Indian Affairs."[312] Most recently, the BIA has published ordinances adopted by two traditionally organized Alaska Native villages under provisions of the federal Indian liquor laws delegating federal authority over liquor control to tribal sovereigns.[313]

In many respects, Alaska Native claims of self-government are in the same position as their claims of aboriginal title immediately before the passage of ANCSA. Then there was no definitive judicial or congressional determination that all Alaska Natives had valid claims of aboriginal land title. The Tlingit and Haida Indians had successfully adjudicated their land claims to all of southeast Alaska, but it had taken thirty-three years.[314] All manner of technical and historical questions had been raised about the validity of aboriginal land claims in Alaska,[315] and it appeared unlikely that the issue would ever be resolved in any then living person's lifetime. The objections to Alaska Native sovereignty claims have a similar ring, but the historic evidence of Alaska Native aboriginal political organization and the history of federal recognition both support the validity of the Alaska Native claims to inherent self-government.

D. The "Scope of Sovereignty" Questions

As a practical matter, the scope of Native sovereignty in the United States often depends on the degree to which its exercise is free of federal control or state interference. Federal control is generally expressed in the form of specific statutes,[316] although there are a few limitations which are derived as a "necessary result of [tribal] dependent status"[317] or because the tribal exercise of some powers would be "inconsistent with the overriding interests of the National Government."[318] In any event, the federal limitations are relatively specific and few in number. Rather, it is in regard to the states that Native American sovereignty issues have had their greatest visibility.

To a substantial degree the extent to which Native government is free from conflicting state laws is largely determinative of the effective scope of Native political authority. The issue is often presented as one of the relative jurisdiction of tribal and *state* governments,[319] and in the case of a P.L. 280 state like Alaska may be governed in part by *federal* statutory law.[320] However, as noted elsewhere, the U.S. Supreme Court has also developed two related but independent tests to adjust the boundaries between tribal and state political power. One of these tests is based on federal preemption of state authority as seen against the historical "backdrop" of tribal sovereignty.[321] The other test is whether, in the absence of governing acts of Congress, the asserted state authority "infringes" on the right of "reservation Indians to make their own laws and be ruled by them."[322] The two tests are related through the tribal sovereignty doctrine. In the case of preemption, the federal and tribal interests at stake are interpreted in light of a common goal: the enhancement of Native American self-government. These interests are weighed against competing state interests, which by themselves are seldom sufficient to overcome any combination of Native and federal interests reflected in federal law.[323]

1. Preemption

The federal preemption doctrine is founded on the supremacy clause of the United States Constitution.[324] Federal treaties and laws are the "supreme law of the land," and to the extent necessary to accomplish their purposes, they "preempt" state laws. It is a flexible doctrine, but it has special force in the field of Indian affairs, because this subject is one in which the federal interest is so dominant as to be presumed to displace any countervailing state interest.[325] Federal preemption in the field of United States Indian law also has special force because federal statutes and treaties are viewed against the "backdrop" of the tradition of Native American sovereignty.[326] Thus, treaties or statutes which are ambiguous or even silent on their relationship to the exercise of Native American tribal sovereignty are consistently read to protect the exercise of Native self-government from state infringement.[327]

Nonetheless, the preemption doctrine seems to have its greatest vigor when applied either to activities on an Indian reservation or in the context of specific federal laws related to off-reservation activities.[328] Thus, where the tribe regulates fish and game on its reservation with substantial federal assistance, the states have been held preempted from applying inconsistent controls to reservation activity.[329] In the absence of a reservation, however, the U.S. Supreme Court has held (in an Alaska case) that state law also applies.[330] On the other hand, there are federal laws, such as the Indian Child Welfare Act, which preempt state authority even outside the reservation.[331] This law preempts inconsistent Alaska laws in a variety of contexts even though the custody dispute may not arise on an Indian reservation. Moreover, at least one state court has upheld the recognized tribal status of an off-reservation Alaska Native community in the context of this act.[332] The Alaska Supreme Court has also sustained the general application of these laws to Alaska.[333]

2. Infringement

The "infringement" test has always arisen in the context of state infringement on the right of *"reservation* Indians to make their own laws and be ruled by them,"[334] but the U.S. Supreme Court has suggested that it is applicable when the issue is either state control of non-Indians on the reservation or state control of Indian activities off the reservation. "In these situations," the Court noted:

> both the tribe and the State could fairly claim an interest in asserting their respective jurisdictions. The [infringement] test was designed to resolve this conflict by providing that the State could protect its interest up to the point where tribal self-government would be affected.[335]

This language suggests that where there is a Native government, it can also have interests, even outside a federal reservation, which are subject to exclusive tribal governmental control and correspondingly free from state interference. It suggests, at the very least, that there is an irreducible core of off-reservation tribal sovereignty to which state interests must give way.

In reviewing the status of Alaska Native "tribes" in 1977, the American Indian Policy Review Commission concluded that, even in the absence of reservations, Native governments retained the "attributes and powers" of tribal sovereigns except those "specifically denied or taken from them by Congress."

> Vital among these are power to act in a corporate capacity; immunity from State and Federal income taxation; immunity from suit without consent; power to determine membership; and power to regulate conduct of members as such.[336]

Both the Alaska Federal District Court and State Supreme Court have upheld Alaska Native governmental immunity and authority on several of these points.[337] The Alaska attorney general's office has even concluded that recognized Alaska Native governments have inherent authority to charter their own corporations outside the provisions of the state's corporation laws.[338] Although a satisfactory doctrine describing the borders between tribal and state authority remains to be fully developed, the U.S. Supreme Court, in a 1981 decision, has suggested several areas in which tribal interests are most likely to outweigh state interests. Tribal interests are likely to be strongest in matters internal to the tribe, most notably those which involve tribal members. These include: tribal membership decisions as well as punishment for offenses, regulation of domestic relations and regulation of inheritance among tribal members. Tribes are also acknowledged to have civil jurisdiction over non-members, particularly in matters of taxation or regulation which arise in the course of consensual relations between non-members and the tribe. Tribal civil authority also extends to non-members where their conduct threatens tribal political integrity, economic security, or health and welfare.[339]

3. Manifesting Native Self-Government

Theories of Native government are important, but they mean little unless they are accompanied by the actual exercise of political authority. In the final analysis, whether a Native government has an "interest" protected from state infringement may depend on the Native government's ability to demonstrate the relationship of that interest to Native internal affairs, political integrity, economic security or health and welfare of the Native community. If the Native government exercises no authority over these matters, then it will have difficulty demonstrating the existence of a protected interest.

Several U.S. Supreme Court, as well as lower court, decisions demonstrate the point. For example, in a 1942 Oklahoma case, the Supreme Court held that the estates of certain Oklahoma Indians were subject to state probate taxes because "these Indians have no effective tribal autonomy."[340] More recently, in *Bryan v. Itasca County,* the Court specifically noted that the preemption of state law was less likely with respect to nonreservation Indians and those who " 'do not possess the usual accoutrements of Tribal self-government.' "[341] It is also significant that when the Alaska Federal District Court upheld the exclusive jurisdiction of the Tyonek Indians in the *McCord* case, it did so on the express determination that their lands were "governed by an operational tribal unit."[342]

Decisions such as these imply that a threshold consideration in any future determination of the scope of Alaska Native sovereignty is likely to be whether Alaska Natives do in fact have active systems of self-government. Organization under the Indian Reorganization Act is one way to establish evidence of active self-governance. IRA organization requires a community to adopt a constitution which, when accepted by the Secretary of the Interior, constitutes both an official link to the federal government and evidence of the community's self-governing structure. Even communities which do not wish to organize under the IRA may find it wise to adopt a written constitution. For better or worse, formal organization of Alaska Native governments, whether under the IRA or otherwise, seems likely to enhance their political status.

Finally, the continued exercise of Native government over a period of time might lead to the gradual acceptance and reasonable expansion of this form of political authority. Failure to exercise powers of self-government is likely to mean further atrophy and the eventual replacement of Native governing bodies with state incorporated municipalities. Although that might not necessarily be a bad result, some time and thought should be given to what would be lost and what would be gained in the exchange.

4. Concurrent Jurisdiction

Finally, the possibilities for Native and state concurrent jurisdiction should not be overlooked. Although state concurrent jurisdiction infringes on Native self-government when it is inconsistent with Native laws,[343] it is not necessary that the two should conflict. Moreover, as noted earlier, P.L. 280 specifically requires state courts to give "full force and effect" to any valid "tribal ordinance or custom" so long as it is "not inconsistent" with state law.[344] The delegation of authority to tribes to regulate liquor in Indian country is also to be exercised "in conformity" with both state and tribal laws.[345] The problem in Alaska is often not that state and Native laws conflict so much as it is an *absence* of locally directed and culturally appropriate regulatory and law enforcement authority in unincorporated communities.[346] Alaska Native governments, acting under either delegated or inherent authority, offer one possibility for filling the void.

In the absence of reservation lands or other manifestations of federal protection, the likelihood is reduced that Native jurisdiction can be exercised in a manner inconsistent with legitimate state interests. Nonetheless, it is just as likely that there are legitimate Native governmental interests which the state cannot adversely affect even in the absence of a reservation or some "governing act of Congress." Moreover, Native concurrent self-government may also be a significant source of political authority, especially in Alaska's unincorporated communities.

E. Resolving the Issues

There are at least three ways, not necessarily mutually exclusive, in which to resolve Alaska Native sovereignty claims. They could be resolved judicially on a case by case basis in much the same manner as these claims have been resolved in the rest of the United States over the last two hundred years. They could be resolved by federal legislation in a manner similar to that used recently to describe the jurisdiction of the Passamaquoddy, Penobscot and Maliseet Indians in the State of Maine.[347] They could also be at least partially resolved through state legislation (including constitutional amendments) specifically acknowledging the jurisdiction of Native governments over mutually agreeable matters. As noted earlier, other states have already taken this step, and several Alaska statutes also acknowledge the existence of "Native village governments" for particular purposes.[348] Finally, they could be resolved administratively in the context of federal recognition of Alaska Native governments and the promulgation of individual tribal constitutions, either under the terms of the Indian Reorganization Act or on independent Native initiative.

Each approach is characterized by its own set of advantages and disadvantages. Litigation is time consuming, expensive and haphazard, but avoids the necessity of coming to grips with the very difficult political issues of state and tribal jurisdiction. Federal or state legislation would require negotiation of some of the most difficult and elusive issues in United States law and political theory, but it holds the promise of a more comprehensive and politically stable solution. Administrative resolution inevitably pits small, sometimes unsophisticated, communities against a distant federal bureaucracy, subject to often subtle political pressures, but it seems to avoid some of the risks inherent in either litigation or a more comprehensive legislative solution. In all likelihood, resolution of these claims will involve elements of all three approaches.

Little controversy surrounds some of the sovereignty issues. For example, a Native government's control over membership and even its members, especially with respect to many matters related to Native cultural life, would seem to be of little consequence to most state interests. Similarly, Native criminal prosecution of members for minor offenses is probably of little concern to the state, and Native governments would likely welcome state prosecution of felonies. It might even be possible to resolve such seemingly thorny problems as tribal taxing authority if ANCSA Native corporations could be given federal and state tax deductions or credits for payments made to Native governments to fund services otherwise provided by the state or federal government.[349] Doing so would support stated federal policies favoring tribal self-government and at the same time permit Alaska Native corporation resources, which would otherwise be lost to taxes, to remain in the Alaska Native community. Practical questions such as these seem susceptible to legislative solution.

It also seems feasible to work out in general terms the powers Alaska Native tribes could exercise under IRA or traditional constitutions without necessarily specifying each such power. In any event adopting IRA or traditional constitutions would more clearly establish the parameters of a community's asserted authority. IRA constitutions might more clearly have this effect, not because they would grant powers not already vested in Native governments (a common misconception), but because they establish a formal link to federal support for self-government. Other issues which could not be clarified in either federal or state legislation or Native constitutions would, perhaps, have to be left for judicial resolution. The task, however, would be more sensibly narrowed, less expensive and not so politically disruptive if the issues were first better defined legislatively and administratively.

VII. Conclusion

Native American claims in the United States have historically revolved around three issues: land, subsistence (hunting and fishing rights) and self-government. Alaska Native Land Claims were substantially resolved in 1971 under ANCSA; following another protracted political initiative, their subsistence claims were addressed nine years later in the Alaska National Interest Lands Conservation Act.[350] It seems likely that their claims to self-government will also have to be addressed before the Alaska Native settlement can be considered complete. By 1983, Alaska Natives had begun to organize to assert these claims.[351] The then Governor of Alaska characterized the issue as "one of the bigger issues" that will face his administration; it has also had the attention of the Alaska congressional delegation.[352] There appeared to be some hope that self-government, perhaps the final Alaska Native claim, would receive at least the same level of consideration as did the earlier ones to land and subsistence.

One thing seems certain, if the sometimes tragic history of aboriginal Americans elsewhere is any guide; long after most of the aboriginal lands and even many of the people have been lost, the tribal governments remain. They remain as the rekindling sparks of proud cultures. Perhaps in Alaska, in the waning days of the twentieth century, we will at last find one place where the relationships between immigrant and aboriginal Americans can be structured so that each may enrich the other, and thereby ensure the diversity that is the hallmark of a free society.

ENDNOTES

[1]See American Indian Policy Review Commission, *Task Force Four: Federal, State and Tribal Jurisdiction,* (Washington: U.S. Govt. Printing Off., 1976) at 1. See generally J.S. Clinebell and J. Thomson, *Sovereignty and Self-Determination: The Rights of Native Americans Under International Laws,* 27 Buffalo L. Rev. 669 at 679-683 (Fall 1978). See also K. Kickingbird, "Indian Sovereignty: The American Experience," in *Pathways to Self-Determination Canadian Indians and the Canadian State,* L. Little Bear et al, eds. (Toronto: University of Toronto Press, 1984).

[2]Cherokee Nation v. Georgia, 30 U.S. (5 Pet.) 1 (1831), coining the phrase "domestic dependent nations." Merrion v. Jicarilla Apache Tribe, 455 U.S. 130 (1982), upholding tribal inherent sovereignty to impose oil severence tax.

[3]See Buffalo L. Rev., note 1, above.

[4]See e.g., White Mountain Apache Tribe v. Bracker, 448 U.S. 136 at 141- 145 (1980). See also *Final Report of the American Indian Policy Review Commission,* (Washington: U.S. Govt. Printing Off. 1977) at 154-156; but see 27 Buffalo L. Rev., note 1, above, at 683-700, arguing that these limitations are illegal under principles of international law. It is important to understand that the legal principles defining the politically dependent status of Native Americans are the doctrines of United States domestic law and not established principles of international law.

[5]See e.g., In re Minook, 2 Ak. Rpts. 200 (D.C. Ak. 1904) citizenship under federal law, U.S. v. Berrigan, 2 Ak. Rpts. 442 (D.C. Ak. 1904), protection of land rights. See also chapter 8, regarding traditional forms of Alaska Native political organization.

[6]Contemporary forms of Alaska Native government are discussed in chapter 9. There are three forms of Native government in Alaska: (1) traditional governing councils, (2) Indian Reorganization Act (IRA) governing councils and (3) the Tlingit and Haida Central Council. State organized municipalities are not Native although they are governments. ANCSA corporations are not governments, although they will likely remain Native so as long as there are restrictions on the alienation of ANCSA stock.

[7]R. Price, *Native Rights A Report for the Alaska Statehood Commission,* (Juneau: Alaska Department of Law 1982) at 76-77, describing resistance to the Circle Village constitution in 1981 and federal indecision. See also "Native Sovereignty Issue Puts Heat on Sheffield," *Fairbanks Daily News-Miner,* April 20, 1984, describing opposition to the Eagle village constitution in 1984, and "Clark Says U.S. Won't Deal With Natives as Sovereign People," *Anchorage Daily News,* May 1, 1984, describing the conflicting responses of the Interior Department.

[8]See American Indian Policy Review Commission, *Special Joint Task Force Report on Alaska Native Issues,* (Washington, D.C.: U.S. Govt. Printing Off. 1976) at 21-24. Hereafter *"AIPRC Alaska Report."* See also 1915 Sess. Laws of Alaska (SLA) ch. 11, providing for "local self-government in certain Native vil-

lages in the Territory of Alaska;" amended by 1917 SLA ch. 25 to prohibit local jurisdiction "over the property of white residents," repealed by 1929 SLA ch. 23. See also F. Cohen, *Handbook of Federal Indian Law*, (Washington, D.C. U.S. Govt. Printing Off. 1942; reprinted New York: AMS Press, 1972) at 413, n. 200 and 201. Accord F. Cohen, *Handbook of Federal Indian Law*, (Charlottesville, Va.: Michie Bobbs-Merrill, 1982) at 751.

[9]Section 14(c)(3) originally required reconveyance of "no less than 1,280 acres" either to an existing municipality or in trust to the state for a future municipality. The provision was amended in 1980 by section 1405 of the Alaska National Interest Lands Conservation Act (ANILCA) to permit village corporations, municipalities or the state to agree to a lesser amount. Act of December 21, 1980, P.L. 96-487, 94 Stat. 2494, 43 USC 1613.

[10]*AIPRC Alaska Report*, note 8, above, at 22.

[11]See "State disputes legality of Akiachak move," *Tundra Times* (Anchorage) November 9, 1983.

[12]The earliest decisions of the U.S. Supreme Court acknowledge and describe the factors leading to European dominance in stark and often unflattering terms. E.g., Johnson v. M'Intosh, 21 U.S. (8 Wheat.) 543 at 573:

> The potentates of the old world found no difficulty in convincing themselves that they made ample compensation to the inhabitants of the new, by bestowing on them civilization and Christianity, in exchange for unlimited independence.

and at 590:

> The Europeans were under the necessity either of abandoning the country, and relinquishing their pompous claims to it, or of enforcing those claims by the sword, and by the adoption of principles adapted to the condition of a people with whom it was impossible to mix, and who could not be governed as a distinct society....

[13]E.g., The Northwest Ordinance, Act of August 7, 1789, art. 3, 1 Stat. 50:

> The utmost good faith shall always be observed toward the Indians; their lands and property shall never be taken from them without their consent; and in their property, rights, and liberty they shall never be invaded or disturbed, unless in just and lawful wars authorized by Congress; but laws founded in justice and humanity shall, from time to time, be made, for preventing wrongs being done to them, and for preserving peace and friendship with them.

See also Indian trade and intercourse acts, e.g., Act of June 30, 1834, ch. 161, sec. 12, 4 Stat. 730, 25 USC 177, prohibiting alienation of tribal lands unless by "treaty or convention entered into pursuant to the Constitution."

[14]Cherokee Nation v. Georgia, 30 U.S. (5 Pet.) 1 (1831). The issue in this case was whether the Cherokee Nation was a "foreign State" for purposes of federal court jurisdiction under Art. III, Sec. 2, Cl. 1 of the U.S. Constitution. Chief Justice John Marshall noted that "the condition of the Indians in relation to the United States is perhaps unlike that of any other two people in existence," *Id.* at 15. He concluded that the Cherokee were not a foreign state because they were within the boundries of the United States ("domestic") and relied on the United States for protection ("dependent"), but were nonetheless a "distinct political society" (a "nation").

[15]Worcester v. Georgia, 31 U.S. (6 Pet.) 515 at 561 (1832). Chief Justice Marshall, speaking for a majority of the court, concluded that various provisions of the U.S. Constitution (relating to wars, treaties and commerce) were sufficient to vest the intercourse between the Cherokee Nation and the United States in the government of the United States. *Id* at 559. Under Art. VI, Cl. 2 of the Constitution, the Constitution and all treaties or laws "made in Pursuance" of the Constitution are the "Supreme Law of the land" and override conflicting state laws.

[16]Cohen (1982), note 8, above, at 231, citing U.S. v. Wheeler, 435 U.S. 313, 322-323 (1978). See also Cohen (1942), note 8, above, at 122.

[17]E.g., Lone Wolf v. Hitchcock, 187 U.S. 553 (1903), upholding congressional authority to unilaterally abrogate Indian treaties. Congressional power over Indian affairs has been characterized as "plenary," but the term does not imply congress' power is unlimited. See U.S. v. Sioux Nation of Indians, 448 U.S. 371 (1980), requiring compensation for the taking of the Sioux reservation and Delaware Tribal Busines Committee v. Weeks, 430 U.S. 73, 84-85, reh. den. 431 U.S. 960 (1977), concluding that the exercise of congressional power must "be tied rationally to the fulfillment of Congress' unique obligation toward the Indians."

[18]Tee-Hit-Ton Band of Indians v. U.S., 348 U.S. 272 (1955).

[19]See e.g., Cohen (1982), note 8, above, at 782, discussing the abolition of the tribal courts of the Five Civilized Tribes in Oklahoma under the 1898 Curtis Act and at 170-175, discussing the termination legislation of the 1950's and its effect on some 115 tribes.

[20]E.g., Menominee Tribe v. U.S., 391 U.S. 404 (1968); Alaska Pacific Fisheries v. U.S., 248 U.S. 78 at 89 (1918). See also U.S. *ex. rel.* Hualpai Indians v. Santa Fe Pac. R.R., 314 U.S. 339, 354 (1941) regarding extinguishment of aboriginal rights, and Washington v. Yakima Indian Nation, 439 U.S. 463 at 502, n.1 (1978), Marshall J., dissenting, collecting cases.

[21]U.S. v. Sandoval, 231 U.S. 28 at 46 (1913), describes the scope of the "political question" doctrine in Indian affairs. So long as the recognized community is "distinctly Indian," whether and for what purposes and for how long it will be treated as such is a matter for the "political" branches of government, not the courts, to decide. See also U.S. v. Holliday, 70 U.S. (3 Wall.) 407 (1866).

[22]*White Mountain Apache Tribe v. Bracker,* note 4, above, at 142-143 (1980).

[23]E.g., Warren Trading Post v. Arizona Tax Commission, 380 U.S. 685 (1965), Indian trade statutes held to preempt state taxation of gross receipts of non-Indian trader; McClanahan v. Arizona State Tax Commission, 411 U.S. 164 (1973), general provisions of the Navajo treaty held to prohibit state income tax on reservation earnings of a Navajo tribal member; Ramah Navajo School Board v. Bureau of Revenue, ____U.S.____, 73 L. Ed. 2d 1174 (1982), state gross receipts tax on tribal construction contractor preempted by several federal statutes.

[24]*White Mountain Apache Tribe v. Bracker,* note 4, above, at 143, citing *McClanahan,* note 23, above.

[25]E.g., Williams v. Lee, 358 U.S. 217 at 220 (1959), prohibiting state adjudication of a civil dispute between a non-Native trader and a Navajo tribal member arising out of a credit sale made on the Navajo reservation.

[26]Kake v. Egan, 369 U.S. 60 (1962).

[27]Metlakatla v. Egan, 369 U.S. 45 (1962).

[28]Act of Aug. 15, 1953, 67 Stat. 588 (now codified as amended in scattered parts of 18, 25 and 28 USC). Some provisions of P.L. 280 were repealed and reenacted in revised form under the Indian Civl Rights Act of 1968, P.L. 90-284, Apr. 1, 1968, 82 Stat. 77 (25 USC 1301 *et seq.*)

[29]18 USC 1151. See note 170, below, for full statutory definition.

[30]*Criminal Jurisdiction on the Seminole Reservations in Florida,* 85 I.D. 433 (Op. Sol. M-36907, Nov. 14, 1978).

[31]Bryan v. Itasca County, 426 U.S. 373, at 388-389 (1976).

[32]DeCoteau v. District County Court, 420 U.S. 425 at 446 (1975), holding that allotments which were no longer part of an Indian reservation remained subject to the exclusive jurisdiction of the tribal and federal governments. See also Jones v. Meehan, 175 U.S. 1 at 29 (1899), holding that tribal laws of inheritance applied to the allotment of a tribal member which had never been part of an Indian reservation. Accord *U. S. v. Sandoval,* note 21, above, applying the federal Indian liquor laws to Pueblo Indian communities occupying lands owned in unreserved, communal fee title. See also Kimball v. Callahan, 590 F. 2d 768,776 (9th Cir.), cert. den. 444 U.S. 826 (1979) and Settler v. Lameer, 507 F. 2d 231 (9th Cir. 1974), upholding off-reservation tribal authority for certain purposes under treaties.

[33]Cohen (1942) at 122; accord Cohen (1982), at 246-257; both at note 8, above. See also U.S. v. Quiver, 241 U.S. 602 at 603-604 (1916), regarding tribal control over personal and domestic relations.

[34]E.g., Santa Clara Pueblo v. Martinez, 436 U.S. 49 at 58 (1978), sovereign immunity; Cohen (1982), note 8, above, at 390, regarding income tax immunity.

[35]*Cherokee Nation v. Georgia,* note 14, above, at 17-18.

[36]*Johnson v. M'Intosh,* note 12, above. See also, 25 USC 177, note 13, above, prohibiting alienation of tribal lands except by treaty or other convention authorized by Congress. However, the Interior Department Solicitor has concluded that these restrictions do not apply to lands transferred under ANCSA even though they may now be owned by an Indian tribal government. Letter from the then Interior Solicitor, Clyde Martz, to John E. Rougeot and Paul S. Williams (Jan. 16, 1981).

[37]Oliphant v. Suquamish Tribe, 435 U.S. 191 (1978).

[38]E.g., *Kake v. Egan,* note 26, above.

[39]See *McClanahan,* note 23, above, at 179, discussing the relationship of the *Williams v. Lee* "infringement" test to matters affecting non-Indians and off-reservation disputes, citing *Kake v. Egan* with respect to the latter.

> In these situations, both the tribe and the State could fairly claim an interest in asserting their respective jurisdictions. The *Williams* test was designed to resolve this conflict by providing that the State could protect its interest up to the point where tribal self-government would be affected.

Accord *White Mountain Apache Tribe v. Bracker,* note 4, above, at 145, discussing the necessity of a "particularized inquiry into the nature of the state, federal and tribal interest at stake." See also Montana v. U.S., 450 U.S. 544 at 563-567 (1981), regarding the relative importance of the tribe's internal authority and its political, economic and social interests in balancing state and tribal interests.

[40]Chemehuevi Indian Tribe v. California Board of Equalization, 492 F. Supp. 55 (N.D. Cal. 1979).

[41]E.g., C. E. Goldberg, *Public Law 280: The Limits of State Jurisdiction Over Reservation Indians,* 22 UCLA L. Rev. 535, 536 (1975).

[42]See generally chapter 4 regarding the effects of allotment policies. See Cohen (1982), note 8, above, at 152-177, describing the termination policies of the 1950's.

[43]Act of June 18, 1934, ch. 576, 48 Stat. 984, 25 USC 461 *et seq.,* applied to Alaska by the Act of May 1, 1936, ch. 254, sec. 1, 49 Stat. 1250, 25 USC 473a. See generally e.g., G. D. Taylor, *The New Deal and American Indian Tribalism,* (Lincoln, NE.: University of Nebraska Press, 1980) for a scholarly description and analysis of the history and consequences of the IRA.

[44]Act of Jan. 4, 1975, P.L. 93-638, 88 Stat. 2203, 25 USC 450 *et seq.* Among other things, the Self-Determination Act states that:

> [T]he prolonged Federal domination of Indian service programs...has denied to the Indian people an effective voice in the planning and implementation of programs for the benefit of Indians.

and further acknowledges that:

> [T]he Indian people will never surrender their desire to control their relationships both among themselves and with the non-Indian governments, organizations, and persons. 25 USC 450(a).

and reaffirms a congressional commitment to:

> the maintenance of the Federal Government's unique and continuing relationship with a responsibility to the Indian people....25 USC 450a(b).

The U.S. Supreme Court recently noted that the Self-Determination Act and several similar statutes embody a joint federal-tribal goal of promoting tribal self-government, New Mexico v. Mescalero Apache Tribe, ____U.S.____, 76 L. Ed. 2d 611, 5l U.S. Law Week (U.S.L.W.) 4741 at 4744, n. 17 (June 13, 1983). Other self-determination era legislation is discussed in section IV C of this chapter, "Other Aspects of Sovereignty."

[45]Art.III, Treaty of March 30, 1867, 15 Stat. 539, discussed further in chapter 2, V B, "Treaty of 1867."

[46]C.M. Naske and H. E. Slotnick, *Alaska A history of the 49th State,* (Grand Rapids, Mich.: Eerdmans Publishing, 1979) at 58 and 133. See also E. Gruening, *The State of Alaska,* (New York: Random House, 1968) at 47-52.

[47]Act of May 17, 1884, 23 Stat. 24. Prior to this time, the Oregon Federal District Court had jurisdiction over Alaska cases. See e.g., U.S. v. Seveloff, 1 Ak. Fed. Rpts. 64 (D.C. OR. 1872).

[48]See chapter 5, II A4, "Missionary Schools," for a more detailed description of these events.

[49]*Work of the Bureau of Education for the Natives of Alaska, 1916-1917,* Bulletin No. 5, (Washington, D.C.: U.S. Dept. of the Interior, Bureau of Education, 1918) at 10-11.

[50]See chapter 3, II, "Development and Decline of the Alaska Reservation Policy."

[51]*Alaska—Legal Status of Natives,* 19 Land Decisions (L.D.) of the Interior Department 323 (1894).

[52]In re Sah Quah, 1 Ak. Fed. Rpts. 136 at 140 (D. Ak. 1886).

[53]Act of January 27, 1905, 33 Stat. 617.

[54]Act of May 17, 1906, 34 Stat. 197, as amended 43 USC 270-1 *et seq.* (1970), repealed with a savings clause by the Alaska Native Claims Settlement Act, P.L. 92-203, sec. 18(a), 85 Stat. 688 at 710, 43 USC 1617(a).

[55]See *Authority of the Secretary of the Interior to Dispose of Reindeer Belonging to Estates of Deceased Natives of Alaska,* 54 I.D. 15 at 18-19 (1932), holding that the usual, Indian probate proceedings were applicable to reindeer and Alaska allotments.

[56]*Alaska Pacific Fisheries v. U.S.,* note 20, above.

[57]*Leasing Lands Within Reservations Created for the Benefit of the Natives of Alaska,* 49 L.D. 592, at 594-595 (1923). Accord *Status of Natives of Alaska With Respect to the Title to Tidelands Near Ketchikan,* 50 L.D. 315 (1924).

[58]Letter from Edgar Howard to Ray Lyman Wilbur, Secretary of the Interior (Jan. 28, 1932) and Secretary Wilbur's reply (Mar. 14, 1932), Alaska Division, General Correspondence, Status of Alaska Natives, NARS, RG 75.

[59]*Status of Alaska Natives,* 53 L.D. 593, at 605-606 (1932). See also H. D. Anderson and C. Eells, *Alaska Natives: A Survey of their Sociological and Educational Status,* (London: Stanford University Press, 1932) at 146, noting that for the Eskimos: "Tribal distinctions based upon linguistic differences, however, were sufficiently marked to denote distinct tribes." Among the 24 villages Anderson and Eells studied: "[E]ighteen had adopted a form of government similiar to that in use among whites, while six still clung to their traditional form." But see Wilbur reply, note 58, above, which states that "the aborigines of Alaska" have not "been recognized as independent tribes with a government of their own." Inconsistently, however, Wilbur concludes that under the Treaty of Cession "no native *tribes* or parts of *tribes* occupied the status of civilized people (emphasis added)."

[60]*Validity of Marriage by Custom Among the Natives or Indians of Alaska,* 54 Interior Decisions (I.D.) 39, at 42-45 (1932). The opinion was prompted by a letter from an missionary stationed in St. Timothy, Alaska, describing the refusal of the local U. S. commissioner to grant a marriage license to a Native couple who wanted a church marriage although previously married by a village chief. The commissioner refused the license because the couple had been "living together unlawfully." Letter from E. A. McIntosh to Hon. Scott Leavitt, House of Representatives, Washington, D.C. (April 11, 1932) and associated correspondence, Alaska Division, General Correspondence, Status of Alaska Natives, NARS, RG 75.

[61]Note 43, above.

[62]25 USCA 476. See generally House Report No. 2244, accompanying H.R. 9866, 74th Cong., 2nd sess. (May 26, 1936). Accord Senate Report No. 1748, 74th Cong., 2nd sess. (Apr. 7, 1936).

[63]Id., regarding exclusion from section 17. See 25 USCA 477 and 470, describing respectively the corporate and loan provisons.

[64]Questionnaires Concerning Tribal Organization in Alaska 1934-35, Indian Organization Division, NARS, Washington, D.C., RG 75. See also "Questionnaire on Local Self Government," memorandum from Chas. W. Hawksworth to Prin-

cipal Teachers (Aug. 16, 1934), General Correspondence, Wheeler-Howard Act, Alaska Division, NARS, RG 75. See also Anderson and Eells, note 59, above, at 46-50 and 144-150 describing "social organization and government" among the Alaska Eskimos.

[65]See note 8, above, and accompanying text, regarding incorporation of Native villages under the territory's "Indian Village Act."

[66]Act of May 1, 1936, sec. 1, 49 Stat. 1250, 25 USCA 473a. The precise language was based on the language of section 9 of the Federal Credit Union Act of June 26 1934, 48 Stat. 1216 and was proposed in a joint memorandum to the Commissioner of Indian Affairs signed by William L. Paul, Felix S. Cohen and Paul W. Gordon (Jan. 22, 1936), copy on file with the author.

[67]H. Rept. No. 2244, note 62, above, at 1-2. Accord S. Rept No. 1748, id. But see Anderson and Eells, note 59, above, at 28-30, describing "twenty tribal groups" among the Eskimos stretching around the coast of Alaska from the Copper River to Point Barrow in "adjacent and sometime overlapping territory."

[68]But see Price, note 7, above, at 74-75, suggesting a contrary interpretation. Ironically, however, congressional recognition of village self-government seems even more pronounced following enactment of ANCSA. See section IV C of this chapter, "Other Aspects of Sovereignty."

[69]Act of May 1, 1936, sec. 2, 49 Stat. 1250, repealed by the Federal Land Policy and Management Act of 1976, P.L. 94-579, Oct. 21, 1976, sec. 704(a), 90 Stat. 2743 at 2792.

[70]See chapter 3, II, D-F, relating to IRA reservations in Alaska.

[71]Two regional IRAs were organized in 1971, the Inupiat Community of the Arctic Slope and the Kenaitzie Indian Tribe. Prior to that only villages had been reorganized. See "Publication of Alaska Villages Recognized as Tribes Receiving Services from the Bureau of Indian Affairs (25 CFR 54.6[b])," memorandum from BIA Juneau Area Director to Deputy Assistant Secretary—Indian Affairs (Operations), May 28, 1982, listing villages.

[72]See note 63, above, and accompanying text. Several communities, particularly in southeast Alaska, were organized as cooperative associations under federally approved constitutions and charters. See Cohen (1942), note 8, above, at 414, describing the Hydaburg Cooperative Association.

[73]"Instructions for Organization in Alaska Under the Reorganization Act of June 18, 1934 (48 Stat. 984), and the Alaska Act of May 1, 1936 (49 Stat. 1250), and Amendments Thereto," approved by the Secretary of the Interior Dec. 22, 1937, at 5 (Para. III[i]).

[74]Fisher v. District Court, 424 U.S. 382, 387 (1976); accord *New Mexico v. Mescalero Apache Tribe,* note 2, above, at 4744, n. 17.

[75]See S. L. Tyler, *A History of Indian Policy*, (Washington, D.C.: U.S. Department of the Interior, 1973) at 104, citing Theodore Roosevelt's Dec. 8, 1901 message to Congress. Sections 1 and 2 of the IRA (25 USCA 461 and 462) prohibited future allotment of reservations and extended trust periods indefinitely.

[76]25 USCA 476.

[77]Cohen (1942), note 8, above, at 406. See also "Taxing Powers of Village of Saxman," *Opinions of the Solicitor on Indian Affairs*, (Washington, D.C.: U.S. Govt. Printing Off., circa. 1975), Vol. II, 1337, letter opinion from Felix S. Cohen, Acting Solicitor, to George W. Folta, Esq., Counsel at Large, (July 7, 1945), concluding that "[I]f the village has continued its aboriginal character as a tribe or band, [it]...has the right to impose [property] taxes on its members...."

[78]See 25 USCA 476, authorizing reorganization of "tribes" and 25 USC 479, defining "tribe."

[79]See 47 Federal Register (Fed. Reg.) 53130 (No. 227, Wednesday, Nov. 24, 1982), for the annual publication of "Indian Tribal Entities" recognized by the Bureau of Indian Affairs. Compare 48 Fed. Reg. 56862, 56865 (No. 248, Friday, Dec. 23, 1983), publishing the same list without the qualifying remarks of the 1982 publication. There is some indication, however, that the BIA distinguishes between "historical" and "non-historical" tribes as far as their powers of self-government are concerned. See *Powers of an Indian Group Organized Under IRA but Not as Historical Tribe*, 1 Opinions of the Solicitor on Indian Affars (Op. Sol. Ind. Aff.) 813 (Apr. 15, 1938), concluding without analysis that a "non-historical" community of Indians residing on the same reservation could exercise the powers of a property owner but not those of a sovereign unless delegated by the federal government.

[80]Significantly, the exhaustive sociological, historical and anthropological study which formed the factual basis for the Alaska Native Claims Settlement Act also characterizes the villages as the essential historical unit of political organization for most Alaska Native societies. See, Federal Field Committee for Development Planning in Alaska, *Alaska Natives and the Land*, (Washington, D.C.: U.S. Govt. Printing Off., 1968) at, e.g., 144 (villages generally), 130 (Arctic Slope Eskimos), 179 (Southwest Coastal Eskimos), 197 (Koyukuk-Lower Yukon Eskimos and Indians), 206-207 (Upper Yukon-Porcupine Indians), 222-223 (Bristol Bay Eskimos), 239 and 245 (Aleuts), 264-266 (Chugach and Eyak Indians). Tlingit and Haida Indians were also organized in villages, but governed by clans, Tlingit and Haida Indians v. U.S., 177 F. Supp. 452, 455-456 (Ct. Cls. 1959). See also Anderson and Eells, note 59, above, at 48-50, describing traditional Eskimo village government. See generally chapter 8, above.

[81]Washington v. Commercial Passenger Fishing Vessel Assn., 443 U.S. 658, 664, n. 5 (1979). See generally Taylor, note 43, above, at 2, discussing the nature of traditional Native American political organization.

[82]U.S. v. Washington, 641 F.2d 1368, 1373-1374 (9th Cir. 1981), but denying tribal status to certain northwest coast Indian groups who had not continued to function as tribal governments settled in "distinctively Indian residential areas."

[83]Federal recognition is clearly not required to establish the political existence of a tribe, Joint Tribal Council of Passamaquoddy Tribe v. Morton, 528 F.2d 370 (1st Cir. 1975), but federal recognition alone has been held sufficient to establish tribal sovereign immunity in Alaska, Atkinson v. Haldane, 569 P.2d 151 at 163 (Ak. 1977). But see Board of Equalization of Ketchikan Borough, Alaska Native Brotherhood and Sisterhood, 666 P.2d 1015, 1023, Rabinowitz J., concurring, concluding that the Ketchikan Indian Corporation (IRA) was not "clearly" recognized even though it was organized under the IRA and listed in the Federal Register as "recognized and eligible to receive services" from the BIA.

[84]See e.g., R. Drinnon, *Facing West: Metaphysics of Indian-Hating and Empire-Building*, (Minneapolis: University of Minnesota Press, 1980), for an historical account and analysis of the role of racism in United States aboriginal (and foreign) policy.

[85]Morton v. Mancari, 417 U.S. 535 at 543 (1974), Indian preference in employment. See generally R. Johnson, *Indians and Equal Protection*, 54 Wash. L. Rev. 587 (1979), discussing other examples of Indian preference legislation.

[86]See Alaska Chapter, Associated General Contractors of America, Inc. v. Pierce, 694 F.2d 1162 at 1168-1169, n. 10 (9th Cir. 1982), discussing the various services and benefits available to Native Americans, given their "special relationship" with the federal government and upholding the application of these principles to Alaska Natives even though they have allegedly "not historically been organized into reservations or into tribal units."

[87]U.S. v. Mazurie, 419 U.S. 544 at 557 (1975), upholding the described delegation under 18 USCA 1161.

[88]*Liquor Ordinance, Village of Allakaket, Alaska,* Op. Assoc. Sol. Ind. Aff. (Oct. 1, 1980).

[89]Village of Chalkyitsik, 48 Fed. Reg. 21378 (No. 93, Thursday, May 12, 1983) and Village of Northway, 48 Fed. Reg. 30195 (June 30, 1983).

[90]Florida, F.S. 285.16 et seq., enforcement of state laws on Indian reservations; Idaho, I.S. 67-2327 et seq., joint exercise of powers between state agencies and Indian tribes; Maine, 30 M.S. 6205 et seq., implementing the jurisdictional provisions of the federal legislation resolving the Maine land claims; Montana, M.S. 18-11-101 et seq., permitting cooperative agreements between state agencies and Indian tribes; New York, 81 N.Y.S. 4101 et seq., relating to Indian schools; South Dakota, S.D.S. 13-15-1 et seq., intergovernmental cooperation in education and S.D.S. 1-24-1 et seq., joint exercise of governmental powers; Wisconsin, W.S. 20.002(13), permitting state grants to Indian tribes for the same purposes as to state chartered local governments.

[91]A.S. 29.89.050. However, the Alaska State Attorney General has concluded on several occassions that Article X of the Alaska Constitution permits only state chartered boroughs and cities to function as local governments within Alaska; therefore, general powers of local government cannot be delegated to Alaska tribal governments. E.g., *Co-operation agreement between city and IRA Council of Saxman,* (File No. J66-406-82, Mar. 2, 1982).

[92]In re McCord, 151 F. Supp. 132 (D. Ak. 1957), refusing to apply the federal Indian Major Crimes Act (18 USCA 1153), which permits federal prosecution of Indians for certain crimes. *McCord* has significant implications for the territorial jurisdiction of Alaska Native tribal villages and is disucssed further below.

[93]See *Bryan v. Itasca County,* note 31, above, and accompanying text.

[94]See 85 I.D. 433, note 30, above, concluding that P.L. 280 mandates concurrent state and tribal criminal jurisdiction.

[95]P.L. 92-203, Dec. 18, 1971, 85 Stat. 688, as amended, 43 USCA 1601 et seq.

[96]43 USCA 1603. Special "subsistence" hunting and fishing preferences for predominately Native "rural Alaska residents" were subsequently established under Title VIII of the Alaska National Interest Lands Conservation Act (ANILCA), P.L. 96-487, Dec. 2, 1980, 94 Stat. 2422, 16 USCA 3111 et seq. See also, U.S. v. Atlantic Richfield Co., 435 F. Supp. 1009 (D. Ak. 1977), aff'd 612 F.2d 1132 (9th Cir. 1980); cert. den. 449 U.S. 888 (1980), holding that claims for trespass to aboriginal title in Alaska were also extinguished under ANCSA. Accord, Inupiat Community of the Arctic Slope v. U.S., 680 F.2d 122 (Ct. Cls. 1982); cert. den. 103 S. Ct. 299. See also Inupiat Community of the Arctic Slope v. U.S., 548 F. Supp. 185 (D. Ak. 1982), rejecting aboriginal claims beyond the territorial sea, now on appeal.

[97]E.g., Ex Parte Crow Dog, 109 U.S. 556 at 572 (1883), limitation on tribal government's authority to impose sanctions for murder not implied. Accord, Menominee Tribe v. U.S., 391 U.S. 404 at 411-412 (1968), statute terminating reservation held not to extinguish associated hunting and fishing rights by implication.

[98]E.g., Treaty With the Wyandot, Etc., 7 Stat. 16 (Jan. 21, 1785). See Art. III and IV, establishing reservation boundaries and hunting rights; Art. V, permitting tribes to punish U.S. citizens trespassing on reservation.

[99]E.g., see P.L. 96-420, Oct. 10, 1980, 94 Stat. 1785, 25 USCA 1721 et seq., resolving Pasamaquoddy, Penobscot and Maliseet claims in Maine. 25 USCA 1725 details the jurisdiction of the State of Maine *vis a vis* the three tribes. 25 USCA 1726 provides for the organization of each tribal government. 25 USCA 1727 permits the Passamaquoddys and Penobscots to assume exclusive jurisdiction under the Indian Child Welfare Act, P.L. 95-608, Nov. 8, 1978, 92 Stat. 3069, 25 USCA 1901 et seq.

[100]See generally, R. Arnold, *Alaska Native Land Claims,* (Anchorage: Alaska Native Foundation, 1978 ed.) at 234-272.

[101]E.g., Merrion v. Jacarilla Apache Tribe, 455 U.S. 130 (1982). See also Cohen (1942), note 8, above, at 143-145.

[102]Jones v. Meehan, 175 U.S. 1 at 29 (1899).

[103]*DeCoteau v. District County Court,* note 23, above, at 446. See also Kimball v. Calahan, 590 F. 2d 768 (9th Cir. 1979), cert. den. 444 U.S. 826, tribal hunting and fishing rights on disestablished reservation.

[104]U.S. v. Chavez, 290 U.S. 357, 364 (1933).

[105]Cohen (1982), note 8, above, at 27-26. "Indian country" is now defined by federal statute, 18 USCA 1151, quoted at note 170 below.

[106]The question is one of the issues, however, in a case now pending in the Alaska Federal District Court, Native Village of Tyonek v. Puckett, Civ. No. A82-369 Civil. Among other things, the Tyonek Tribe seeks a declaration that it has authority to exclude non-members of the tribe from ANCSA village corporation lands.

[107]Johnson v. Chilkat Indian Village, 457 F. Supp. 384 (D. Ak. 1978).

[108]28 USCA 1360(c). Significantly, as discussed further below, the statute does not require the tribal ordinance to be *consistent* with state law, only that it not affirmatively contradict state law, Alaska employs a similar test to determine the scope of the powers of its home rule municipalities. See Jefferson v. State, 527 P.2d 37 at 43 (Ak. 1974).

[109]*Johnson v. Chilkat Indian Village,* note 107, above, sovereign immunity stipulated for IRA tribe exercising jurisdiction over tribally owned land; Cogo v. Central Council of Tlingit and Haida Indians, 465 F. Supp. 1286 (D. Ak. 1979), sovereign immunity of landless non-IRA tribe in tribal membership dispute.

[110]*Atkinson v. Haldane,* note 83, above. Two subsequent Alaska Supreme Court decisions have avoided the issue. See Native Village of Eyak v. G. C. Contractors, 658 P.2d 756 (Ak. 1983), sovereign immunity of traditional village government assumed, but deemed waived under terms of a contract; *Board of Equalization of Ketchikan Borough v. Alaska Native Brotherhood and Sisterhood,* note 83, above, assuming sovereignty, but finding in favor of a local property tax levied on the IRA organized Ketchikan Indian Corporation's leasehold based on a balancing of city and tribal interests. The majority opinion does not discuss the potential sovereign immunity defense to attempts to collect the tax; but see, Rabinowitz, J., concurring, note 83, above, concluding that the Ketchikan Indian Corporation was not a sovereign because it was neither an "historic" tribe nor "clearly" recognized by the federal government.

[111]Letter from J.E. Griffith, Chief IRS Rulings Section, Exempt Organizations, Technical Branch, to BIA, Nome Superintendent (May 10, 1982), applying Rev. Rul. 67-284 as modified by Rev. Rul 74-13 and 81-295. See generally, Cohen, 1982, note 8, above, at 390.

[112]See chapter 9, IV, "Nonprofit Development and Service Corporations," discussing the service delivery role of Native nonprofit corporations.

[113]P.L. 93-638, Jan. 4, 1975, 88 Stat. 2203, 25 USCA 450 et seq.

[114]Note 95, above. It is not clear that ANCSA is truly self-determination legislation except in the sense that it established independent Native corporations to pursue Native economic purposes. If the corporations fail, however, it can be argued that ANCSA cynically intended to strip the Alaska Natives of the very assets confirmed to them under the settlement.

[115]P.L. 92-262, Apr. 12, 1974, 88 Stat. 77, 25 USCA 1451 et seq.

[116]P.L. 94-437, Sep. 30, 1976, 90 Stat. 1400, 25 USCA 1601 et seq.

[117]P.L. 95-608, Nov. 8, 1978, 92 Stat. 3069, 25 USCA 1901 et seq.

[118]ANCSA, 43 USCA 1602(c); Self-Determination Act, 25 USCA 450b(b); Indian Financing Act, 25 USCA 1452(c); Indian Health Care Improvement Act, 25 USCA 1603(d) and Indian Child Welfare Act, 25 USCA 1903(f). The definitions also include, variously, ANCSA village, regional and urban corporations and "groups," implying that since "villages" are named separately, the term refers to an entity separate from the various ANCSA corporations.

[119]25 USCA 1918(2), permitting "tribes" to obtain jurisdiction regardless of their reservation status. See 1978 U.S. Code Cong. and Admin. News (USC-CAAN) 7530 at 7547, regarding intent that this provision apply specifically to the Alaska situation. Retrocession does not seem to be required for tribal courts to exercise concurrent jurisdiction over child custody matters, because such jurisdiction was not surrendered to the state under P.L. 280.

[120]Revenue Bulletin No. 1983-50 at 6 and 11-12 (Dec. 12, 1983), applying Title II of P.L. 97-473, 96 Stat. 2605, as amended by P.L. 98- 21, 97 Stat. 65.

[121]25 USCA 450b(c) defines "tribal organization" as the "governing body of any Indian tribe" or "any legally established organization of Indians which is controlled, sanctioned or chartered by such governing body."

[122]See chapter 9, II D, "Tlingit and Haida Central Council," IV B, "Tanana Chiefs Conference," IV C, "Maniilaq" and IV D, "Bristol Bay Native Association."

[123]See *Problems and Possibilities for Service Delivery and Government in the Alaska Unorganized Borough*, (Anchorage: Alaska Department of Community and Regional Affairs, 1981) at 22. See also T. A. Morehouse and G. A. McBeath, *Alaska's Urban and Rural Governments*, (Lanham, MD.: University Press of America, 1984) at 185-195, discussing the role of the nonprofits.

[124]Telephone interview with with Michael J. Stancampiano, BIA Juneau Area Office Assistant Tribal Operations Officer (May 17, 1984). The grants are provided under section 104 of the Self-Determination Act, 25 USCA 450h. Recent restrictions in federal funding have reportedly substantially reduced the level of these grants from earlier levels.

[125]E.g., A.S. 29.89.050.

[126]16 USCA 1604(2).

[127]ANCSA stock cannot be alienated except by inheritance until Jan. 1, 1992. On that date "all stock previously issued shall be deemed to be cancelled." Corporations are then required to issue new shares of unrestricted stock, 43 USCA 1606(3)(A). Under amendments to ANCSA enacted in 1980, corporations may,

by majority vote of their shareholders on or before December 18, 1991, amend their articles of incorporation to restrict voting rights to Natives and to give corporations the right of first refusal for any stock sales, 43 USCA 1606 (3)(B).

[128]E.g., "Alaska's natives are bringing off the biggest corporate takeover," Smithsonian, August, 1981 at 30.

[129]"Descendancy Role of Alaskan Natives," *1991 Issues Report,* (Anchorage: Alaska Native Foundation, Oct. 7, 1982).

[130]Codified in part at 18 USCA 1162 (criminal jurisdiction):

> (a) Each of the States...listed in the following table shall have jurisdiction over offenses committed by or against Indians in the areas of Indian country listed opposite the name of the State...to the same extent that such State...has jurisdiction over offenses committed elsewhere with the State..., and the criminal laws of such State...shall have the same force and effect within such Indian country as they have elsewhere within the State...:

State	Indian Country Affected
Alaska	All Indian country within the State, except that on Annette Islands, the Metlakatla Indian community may exercise jurisdiction over offenses committed by Indians in the same manner in which such jurisdiction may be exercised by Indian tribes in Indian country over which State jurisdiction has not been extended....

> (b) Nothing in this section shall authorize the alienation, encumbrance, or taxation of any real or personal property, including water rights, belonging to any Indian or Indian tribe, band, or community that is held in trust by the United States or is subject to a restriction against alienation imposed by the United States; or shall authorize regulation of the use of such property in a manner inconsistent with any Federal treaty, agreement, or statute or with any regulation made pursuant thereto; or shall deprive any Indian or any Indian tribe, band, or community of any right, privilege, or immunity afforded under Federal treaty, agreement, or statute with respect to hunting, trapping, or fishing or the control, licensing, or regulation thereof.

> (c) The provisions of sections 1152 and 1153 of this chapter shall not be applicable within the areas of Indian country listed in subsection (a) of this section as areas over which the several States have exclusive jurisdiction.

28 USCA 1360 (civil jurisdiction):

> (a) Each of the States...listed in the following table shall have juris-diction over civil causes of action between Indians or to which In-dians are parties which arise in the areas of Indian country listed op-posite the name of the State...to the same extent that such State...has jurisdiction over other civil causes of action, and those civil laws of such State...that are of general application to private persons or private property shall have the same force and effect within such Indian country as they have elsewhere within the State...:

State	Indian Country Affected
Alaska -----------------------	All Indian country within the State....

> (b) Nothing in this section shall authorize the alienation, encumbr-ance, or taxation of any real or personal property, including water rights, belonging to any Indian or any Indian tribe, band, or commu-nity that is held in trust by the United States or is subject to a restric-tion against alienation imposed by the United States; or shall au-thorize regulation of the use of such property in a manner inconsis-tent with any Federal treaty, agreement, or statute or with any reg-ulation made pursuant thereto; or shall confer jurisdiction upon the State to adjudicate, in probate proceedings or otherwise, the owner-ship or right to possession of such property or any interest therein.

> (c) Any tribal ordinance or custom heretofore or hereafter adopted by an Indian tribe, band, or community in the exercise of any author-ity which it may possess shall, if not inconsistent with any applicable civil law of the State, be given full force and effect in the determina-tion of civil causes of action pursuant to this section.

Provisions permitting other states to assume civil and criminal jurisdiction over Indian country with the consent of the affected tribes were enacted as part of the Indian Civil Rights Act of April 11, 1968, P.L. 90-284, Title IV, 82 Stat. 78, codified at 25 USCA 1321-1326.

[131]*Bryan v. Itasca County,* note 31, above, notes that the statute is "admittedly ambiguous."

[132]See Goldberg, note 41, above, at 537-538.

[133]Santa Rosa Band of Indians v. Kings County, 532 F.2d 655, 661 (9th Cir. 1975), citing Goldberg, note 41, above, at 540-544.

[134]Cohen, (1982), note 8, above, at 344-345. See also 85 I.D. 433, note 30, above, concluding that P.L. 280 is a grant of concurrent state jurisdiction.

[135]*Bryan v. Itasca County,* note 31, above, state chartered local government held without jurisdiction to tax personal property on a reservation; *Santa Rosa Band of Indians v. Kings County,* note 133, above, state local government held to be without jurisdiction to zone reservation land.

[136]18 USCA 1162(b), relating to criminal "offenses" and 28 USCA 1360(b), relating to civil "causes of action." See note 130, above.

[137]In re Humboldt Fir, Inc. 426 F. Supp. 292, 296 (N.D. Cal. 1977), aff'd. 625 F.2d 330 (9th Cir. 1980). See also State of Alaska v. Agli, 472 F. Supp. 70, 72-74 (D. Ak. 1979) and People of South Naknek v. Bristol Bay Borough, 466 F. Supp. 870 (D. Ak. 1979).

[138]Fondahn v. Native Village of Tyonek, 450 F. 2d 520 (9th Cir. 1971), denying federal jurisdiction over tribal membership dispute; accord, Ollestead v. Native Village of Tyonek, 560 P.2d 31 (Ak. 1977), cert. den. 434 U.S. 938 (1977), denying state jurisdiction over tribal trust assets. Heffle v. Alaska, 633 P. 2d 264 (Ak. 1981), cert. den. 455 U.S. 1000 (1982), denying state jurisdiction over restricted allotment. But see Sheppard v. Sheppard, 655 P.2d 895 (Idaho 1982) and Fisher v. Fisher, 656 P.2d 129 (Idaho 1982), upholding state court jurisdiction to take value of reservation trust property into account in calculating property division incident to divorce in spite of P.L. 280.

[139]Calista Corporation v. DeYoung, 562 P.2d 338 (Ak. 1977) and Calista Corporation v. Mann, 564 P.2d 53 (Ak. 1977), probate jurisdiction over restricted ANCSA stock.

[140]Aguilar v. U.S. (Aguilar II), 474 F. Supp. 840 (D.C. Ak. 1979), allotments, and Carlo v. Gustafson, 512 F. Supp. 833 (D.C. Ak. 1981), townsites. See generally Scholder v. U.S. 428 F.2d 1123, 1129 (9th Cir. 1970) and chapter 4, IV B, "Federal Court Jurisdiction."

[141]*Fondahn v. Native Village of Tyonek* and *Ollestead v. Tyonek,* note 138, above, denying state jurisdiction to determine individual right to tribal trust proceeds derived from oil leases when tribe had denied membership to plaintiffs.

[142]Bryan v. Itasca County, note 31, above. See note 130, above, quoting statute.

[143]See note 130, above, quoting statute and *Santa Rosa Band of Indians v. Kings County,* note 133, above. See also Cohen (1982), note 8, above, at 363-365.

[144]28 USCA 1369(c), quoted in note 130, above.

[145]Goldberg, note 41, above, at 582. This intepretation is based on language in 28 USCA 1360(a) which permits only state civil laws of "general application" to be extended over Indian country.

[146]Art. X, secs. 9, 10 and 11 of the Alaska Constitution.

[147]AS 29.08.010 defines the nature of a "home rule municipality" and the general scope of its powers. In 1984, a bill (HB 172) was pending in the Alaska legislature to substantially revise Title 29 of the Alaska Statutes, relating to state municipal government, but it is not anticipated that the revision (if adopted) will alter the fundamental nature and general scope of home rule municipal authority.

See generally, Duvall, *Delineation of the Powers of the Alaska Home Rule City: The Need for a Beginning,* 8 Alaska L. J. 232 (Oct. 1970) and Sharp, *Home Rule in Alaska: A Clash Between the Constitution and the Court,* 3 UCLA-Alaska L. Rev. 1 (1973).

[148]AS 29.08.030. The pending revision to Title 29 of the Alaska Statutes is not expected to alter this fundamental distinction.

[149]Art. X, sec. 1, Alaska Constitution.

[150]Art. X, sec. 11, Alaska Constitution. See also AS 29.08.010, note 147, above.

[151]*Jefferson v. State,* note 108, above. See also e.g., Kenai Peninsula Borough v. Kenai Peninsula Board of Realtors, Inc., 652 P. 2d 471 (Ak. 1982) and Anderson v. Municipality of Anchorage, 645 P. 2d 205 (Ak. Ct. App. 1982), applying the test in civil and criminal cases, respectively to invalidate a "inconsistent" municipal ordinances.

[152]Act of May 1, 1936, ch. 254, 49 Stat. 1250.

[153]*Ollestead v. Tyonek,* note 138, above, at 33, n. 2.

[154]*Bryan v. Itasca County,* note 31, above, at 379. See also *Alaska Pacific Fisheries v. U.S.,* note 20, above, at 89.

[155]U.S. v. Wheeler, 435 U.S. 313 at n. 34 (1978), citing cases.

[156]E.g., A. Hippler and S. Conn, *The Village Council and Its Offspring: A Reform for Bush Justice,* 5 UCLA-Alaska L. Rev. 22 (1975).

[157]D. S. Case, *Twenty Four Ordinances to Enforce Local Law in Alaska Native "Villages" (With Comments),* (Anchorage: Alaska Federation of Natives, 1977) at Part I, 16-17. See also Baker v. City of Fairbanks, 471 P. 2d 385 (Ak. 1970), Alexander v. City of Anchorage, 490 P. 2d 910 (Ak. 1971), defining the nature of criminal prosecution for due process purposes.

[158]Of course, due process and other requirements of the Indian Civil Rights Act, 25 USCA 1301, et seq., note 130, above, would also apply.

[159]*Johnson v. Chilkat Indian Village,* note 107, above.

[160]E. g., Jones v. Meehan, 175 U.S. 1 (1899), tribe held to have authority over inheritance of a member's unrestricted lands within Indian country even though never owned by the tribe. See generally, Cohen (1982), note 8, above, at 632-633. See also *DeCoteau v. District County Court,* note 32, above, at 445, holding that allotments remaining from an abolished reservation were deemed an "adequate fulcrum" for tribal government and were subject to exclusive tribal and federal jurisdiction.

[161]It seems significant that several of the Alaska Supreme Court's decisions have favored continued exercise of Native governing authority. Atkinson v. Haldane, 569 P. 2d 1151 (Ak. 1977), confirmed tribal sovereign immunity for the

Metlakatla Indian Community and implied similar immunity for other "recognized" Alaska Native governments. Two subsequent cases have assumed, without deciding, that off-reservation Alaska Native villages retained elements of political sovereignty. *Board of Equalization for the Borough of Ketchikan v. Alaska Native Brotherhood and Sisterhood,* note 83, above, and *Native Village of Eyak v. G. C. Contractors,* note 110, above.

The state supreme court has also accorded traditional governments a measure of legitimacy under state law. Alaska v. Aleut Corp., 541 P.2d 730 (Ak. 1975), recognized that organized civil governments, even if they were the product of "cultural tradition" were entitled to notice of state land sales when such notice was required under AS 28.05.305 for state incorporated communities and "other organized communities."

The court's solicitude for Native culture is also apparent in *Calista Corp. v. Mann,* note 139, above, upholding the validity of "cultural adoptions" in determining the rights of Eskimo children to Native corporation stock. See also Alvarado v. State, 486 P.2d 891 (Ak. 1971), requiring selection of a jury panel for a Native defendant from a fair cross-section of the community in which the crime allegedly occurred; Carle v. Carle, 503 P. 2d 1050 (Ak. 1972), court may not award custody of a Native child to an urban parent instead of a village parent on theory that doing so would facilitate child's adjustment to urban culture; Aguchak v. Montgomery Ward Co., 520 P.2d 1352 (Ak. 1974), rural defendants entitled to notice of right to change of venue in small claims action; Gregory v. State, 550 P.2d 374, 379, n. 5 (Ak. 1976), acknowledging that certain Native cultural values might contribute to an involuntary guilty plea; Frank v. State, 604 P. 2d 1068 (Ak. 1979), permitting taking of moose out of season for a funeral potlatch as a protected right of religion under the state and federal constitutions; E.A. v. State, 623 P. 2d 1210 (Ak. 1981), upholding application of the Indian Child Welfare Act to future adoptive proceedings; Jimmie v. Alaska Village Electric Co-op., Inc., 624 P. 2d 1258 (Ak. 1981), acknowledging unique circumstances related to winter life in an Alaska Native village.

[162]See Ex Parte Crow Dog, 109 U.S. 556, 571 (1883), holding that the United States could not by "argument and inference" alone extend its laws over reservation Natives.

[163]118 U.S. 375 (1886).

[164]The full scope of the Major Crimes Act has never been determined. Prevailing scholarly opinion is that it does not exclude tribal prosecution of major crimes. Cohen (1982), note 8, above, at 339-341. The Indian Civil Rights Act, cited in note 130, above, limits tribal punishment for any offense to a maximum of six months imprisonment and a $500 fine.

[165]18 USCA 1162(a), note 130, above.

[166]Act of November 25, 1970, P.L. 91-523, 84 Stat. 1358, 18 USCA 1162, as amended. See 1970 USCAAN 4783 and 116 Cong. Rec. 32585-86 and 37353-56 for Senate and House consideration and discussion of the background to the amendment. See especially, remarks of Sen. Ervin at 116 Cong. Rec. 32585, quoting excerpts from S. Rep. No. 91-1108, Senate Judiciary Committee, Sep. 16, 1970, accompanying S. 902.

[167]Cohen (1982), note 8, above, at 344-345. See also 85 I.D., note 30, above. The 1970 debates should also have little weight in determining the meaning of a 1953 statute.

[168]18 USCA 1162(b), note 130, above.

[169]Compare Barona Group of the Capitan Grande Indians v. Duffy, 694 F. 2d 1185 (9th Cir. 1982) with c.f. U.S. v. Farris, 624 F. 2d 890 (9th Cir. 1980). See also note 200, below, and accompanying text.

[170]Cohen, (1982), note 8, above, at 27-28.

[171]18 USCA 1151 defines "Indian country" as follows:

> Except as otherwise provided in sections 1154 and 1156 [Indian liquor laws] of this title, the term "Indian country," as used in this chapter, means (a) all land within the limits of any Indian reservation under the jurisdiction of the United States government, notwithstanding the issuance of any patent, and including rights-of-way running through the reservation, (b) all dependent Indian communities within the borders of the United States, whether within the original or subsequently acquired territory thereof, and whether within or without the limits of a state, and (c) all Indian allotments, the Indian titles to which have not been extinguished, including rights-of-way running through the same.

Although it is defined in a criminal statute, the U.S. Supreme Court has repeatedly applied the concept of Indian country to civil matters as well. *Decoteau v. District County Court,* note 32, above, at 427, n. 2 and Moe v. Confederated Salish and Kootenai Tribes, 425 U.S. 463, 478-479 (1976).

[172]*U.S. v. Sandoval,* note 21, above, applying 18 USCA 1154.

[173]*U.S. v. Sandoval,* note 21, above, at 47.

[174]290 U.S. 357 (1933).

[175]18 USCA 1152.

[176]*U.S. v. Chavez,* note 174, above, at 364.

[177]Note 92, above and accompanying text.

[178]18 USCA 1153.

[179]Note 92, above, at 135. See also U.S. v. McGowan, 302 U.S. 535 (1938), construing land set aside as an Indian "colony" to be Indian country and U.S. v. Pelican, 232 U.S. 442 (1913), construing allotments to be Indian country.

[180]Id. at 136.

[181]*Liquor Ordinance, Village of Allakaket, Alaska,* note 88, above.

[182]The Alaska District Court case of U.S. v. Booth, 161 F. Supp. 269 (D.C. Ak. 1958) does not alter this conclusion. *Booth* holds that the Metlakatla reservation was not Indian country on the dubious finding that it was neither a dependent Indian community nor an Indian reservation. Specific congressional application of P.L. 280 to Metlakatla is inconsistent with this conclusion. Under 18 USCA 1162(a), note 130, above, Metlakatla exercises concurrent criminal jurisdiction with the state "over offenses committed by Indians in the same manner in which such jurisdiction may be exercised by Indian tribes in Indian country over which State jurisdiction has not been extended." See also *Metlakatla v. Egan,* note 27, above, denying state jurisdiction to control fishing on the reservation.

[183]U.S. v. Martine, 442 F.2d 1022, 1023 (10th Cir. 1971), holding that Navajo tribal property purchased from a corporate owner was Indian country under 18 USCA 1151 in part because of the "established practice of government agencies toward the area." Accord *Johnson v. Chilkat Indian Village,* note 107, above, permitting tribal court to adjudicate ownership of personal property located on tribally owned land in Alaska subsequent to ANCSA. See generally Cohen (1982), note 8, above, at 27-46.

[184]Id. at 764-767, relating particularly to Alaska.

[185]U.S. v. South Dakota, 665 F.2d 837, 839 (8th Cir. 1981), citing Weddell v. Meierhenry, 636 F.2d 211, 212 (8th Cir. 1980), cert. den. 451 U.S. 941 (1981).

[186]Price, note 7, above, at 110-111.

[187]*Ex Parte Crow Dog,* note 162, above, at 561, rejecting the argument that repeal of the 1834 definition of "Indian country" opened Indian lands to federal criminal law.

[188]C.f. *Johnson v. Chilkat Indian Village,* note 107, above, the court did not specifically hold that the lands were Indian country, however.

[189]Cohen, 1982, note 8, above, at 347, discussing whether off-reservation allotments might be Indian country, and at 766, relating specifically to Alaska allotments. See also People of South Naknek v. Bristol Bay Borough, 466 F. Supp. 870, 877 (D. Ak. 1979), holding that restricted Native townsite lots were not "reservations" but not deciding whether they were "Indian country" either.

[190]*Metlakatla v. Egan,* note 27, above.

[191]*U.S. v. Sandoval,* note 21, above, tribally owned fee land held to be Indian country for purposes of federal jurisdiction. *DeCoteau v. District County Court,* note 32, above, at 446, allotments in disestablished reservation held to be Indian country for purposes of exclusive tribal and federal jurisdiction; accord *U.S. v. Pelican,* note 179, above.

[192]*McClanahan v. Arizona State Tax Commission,* note 23, above, no state income tax jurisdiction on a reservation. Accord *White Mountain Apache Tribe v.*

Bracker, note 4, above. See also Colville Tribe v. Walton, 647 F. 2d 42 (9th Cir.), cert. den. 454 U.S. 1092 (1981), state regulation of water preempted by creation of reservation.

[193]*Moe v. Confederated Salish and Kootenai Tribes,* note 170, above, Indian retailer required to collect state cigarette tax from non-Indian purchasers on the reservation because the tax was imposed on the purchasers rather than the Indian vendors; see also Washington v. Confederated Tribes of the Colville Indian Reservation, 447 U.S. 134 Montana v. U.S., 450 U.S. 544 (1981), upholding exclusive state authority over non-Native fishing on non-Native fee land where the Indian tribe had not traditionally relied on fishing as an important source of food and fish were not shown to have cultural importance.

[194]*DeCoteau v. District County Court,* note 32, above.

[195]28 USCA 1360(a), note 130, above.

[196]C. f. Goldberg, note 41, above, at 576-580.

[197]Note 31, above.

[198]Id. at 378.

[199]The relationship of federal preemption to tribal jurisdiction is discussed further below in section VI of this chapter.

[200]E.g., Seminole Tribe v. Butterworth, 658 F.2d 310 (1981), cert. den. 455 U.S. 1020, prohibiting application of Florida's gambling laws to the operation of a tribal bingo parlor, because state law regulated but did not *prohibit* gambling. See also note 169, above, and accompanying text.

[201]*Bryan v. Itasca County,* note 31, above, at 376, n. 2, citing *McClanahan v. Arizona State Tax Commission,* note 23, above, at 167-168.

[202]See e.g., *White Mountain Apache Tribe v. Bracker,* note 4, above, and the discussion, in section VI of this chapter, of the role "balancing" of tribal, state and federal "interests" apparently plays in the preemption of state jurisdiction.

[203]411 U.S. 145 (1972).

[204]Note 23, above. See also Puyallup Tribe v. Department of Game (Puyallup I), 391 U.S. 392 (1968) and *Kimball v. Callahan,* note 32, above, permitting state regulation of off-reservation fishing in some circumstances for "conservation" purposes. See generally R. Johnson, *The States Versus Indian Off-Reservation Fishing: A United States Supreme Court Error,* 47 Wash. L. Rev. 207 for a more complete discussion of the Indian off-reservation fishing jurisdiction question.

[205]Indeed none other than Felix Cohen has specifically concluded that Alaska Native villages have such powers even if they are not situated on a reservation.

"Taxing Powers of Village of Saxman," *Opinions of the Solicitor on Indian Affairs,* (Washington, D.C.: U.S. Govt. Printing Off., circa 1975), Vol. II, 1337, letter opinion from Felix S. Cohen, Acting Solicitor, to George W. Folta, Esq., Counsel at Large (July 7, 1945). The Interior Solicitor's office apparently still adheres to this conclusion some ten years after the passage of ANCSA, *Taxing Authority of the Alaska Native Community of Circle,* memorandum from Robert Thompson, Attorney-Advisor, to Assistant Solicitor, Tribal Government and Alaska (Sep. 9, 1981).

[206]Such jurisdiction seems implied by the conveyance provisions of section 14(c)(3) of ANCSA, 43 USCA 1613(c)(3).

[207]E.g., *U.S. v. Mazurie,* note 87, above.

[208]18 USCA secs. 1154, 1156, 1161, 3055, 3113, 3488, 3618-3619. See generally Cohen (1982), note 8, above, at 305-308, discussing similar federal statutes prohibiting various activities on tribal lands without tribal consent. Although these statutes do not necessarily delegate federal jurisdiction to tribes, they nonetheless enhance tribal authority by transforming actions on Indian lands without tribal consent into federal crimes.

[209]18 USCA 1162(c), note 130, above, but all states have been held to have concurrent jurisdiction with tribes to license liquor sales under 18 USCA 1161. See note 210, below.

[210]Rice v. Rehner,____U.S.____, 77 L. Ed. 2d 961 (1983), analyzing scope of delegated tribal jurisdiction under 18 USCA 1161.

[211]See notes 88 and 89, above.

[212]25 USCA 1903(10), defines a "reservation" as "Indian country" as defined under 18 USC 1151; section 1911(a) permits exclusive tribal jurisdiction on the tribe's "reservation," and section 1918 permits retrocession of exclusive tribal jurisdiction over child custody proceedings in P.L. 280 states as permitted in section 1911(a).

[213]See chapter 7, V E, "Lacey Act Amendments."

[214]Cohen (1982), note 8, above, at 335-344 and 763-767, relating to Alaska. Tribes, of course, may not adjudicate crimes committed by non-Natives, *Oliphant v. Suqumish Tribe,* note 37, above, see also section IID, above, "Powers of Native Governments."

[215]See generally Cohen, 1982, note 8, above, at 324-328.

[216]E.g. *Atkinson v. Haldane,* note 83, above. Sovereign immunity also precludes jurisdiction over counterclaims, U.S. v. U.S. Fidelity & Guaranty Co., 309 U.S. 506 (1940) and has been held to preclude jurisdiction to judicially enforce collection of legitimately imposed state taxes, *Chemehuevi Indian Tribe v. California Board of Equalization,* note 40, above, distinguishing *Mescalero Apache Tribe v. Jones,* note 203, above. However, states may be able to encourage payment of taxes by other means. E.g., *Washington v. Confederated Tribes*

of Colville Indian Reservation, note 193, above, confiscation of cigarettes bound for reservation stores; U.S. v. Alabama, 313 U.S. 274 (1940), lien on federal property permitted as an encumbrance on the property even though the tax was not judicially enforceable against the federal government.

[217]See Federal Power Commission v. Tuscarora Indian Nation, 362 U.S. 99, 119-120; reh. den. 362 U.S. 956 (1960), permitting condemnation of tribally owned fee lands even though federal legislation did not specifically permit it and holding that 25 USC 177, which implies tribal consent for the taking of tribal lands, was "not applicable to the sovereign United States." But see Black J., dissenting at 142, concluding that "Great nations, like great men, should keep their word."

[218]Santa Clara Pueblo v. Martinez, 436 U.S. 49 (1978).

[219]U.S. v. Oregon, 657 F.2d 1009, 1012-1016 (9th Cir. 1981).

[220]*Santa Clara Pueblo v. Martinez,* note 218, above, at 71 and Puyallup Tribe, Inc. v. Department of Game (Puyallup III), 433 U.S. 165, 168, n. 3 and 173 (1977). See also e.g., Kennerly v. U.S., 721 F.2d 1252 (9th Cir. 1983), preventing tribal member's suit against tribal officials.

[221]Bottomly v. Passamaquoddy Tribe, 599 F.2d 1061 (1st Cir. 1979), noting also that neither a prolonged course of dealing with the federal government nor continued full exercise of a tribe's sovereign powers is necessary to establish sovereign immunity.

[222]E.g., Haile v. Saunooke, 246 F.2d 293, 297 (4th Cir. 1957). Accord Green v. Wilson, 221 F.2d 769 (9th Cir. 1964); *Atkinson v. Haldane,* note 83, above, at 162, and e.g., Maryland Casualty v. Citizens National Bank, 261 F.2d 520 (5th Cir.), cert. den. 385 U.S. 918 (1966).

[223]Compare Joint Tribal Council of Passamaquoddy Tribe v. Morton, 528 F.2d 370 (1st Cir. 1975), tribal status upheld on stipulated facts, with Mashpee Tribe v. New Seabury Corp, 592 F.2d 575 (1st Cir. 1979), cert. den. 444 U.S. 866 (1979), upholding jury verdict that community had voluntarily abandoned tribal status. See generally Montoya v. U.S., 180 U.S. 261 (1901), defining "tribe," and discussed further below in section VI A, "Politics or Property." See generally section VI B, below, "Whether Alaska Natives Have Sovereignty."

[224]*Atkinson v. Haldane,* note 83, above.

[225]*Native Village of Eyak v. GC Contractors,* note 110, above.

[226]*Board of Equalization of Ketchikan Borough v. Alaska Native Brotherhood and Sisterhood,* note 83, above.

[227]*Johnson v. Chilkat Indian Village,* note 109, above.

[228]Cogo v. Central Council of Tlingit & Haida Indians, 465 F. Supp. 1286 (D. Ak. 1979).

[229]Section 16, 48 Stat. 987, 25 USCA 476, provides in pertinent part that:

> In addition to all powers vested in any Indian tribe...by existing law, the constitution adopted by said tribe shall also vest in such tribe or its tribal council the following rights and powers:...to prevent the sale, disposition, lease, or encumbrance of tribal lands, interests in lands, or other tribal assets without the consent of the tribe....

See also Cohen (1982), note 8, above, at 326, n. 381.

[230]See note 79, above, citing annual publication of "recognized tribal entities." But see *Board of Equalization of Ketchikan Borough v. Alaska Native Brotherhood and Sisterhood,* note 83, above, Rabinowitz J., concurring.

[231]*Martinez v. Santa Clara Pueblo,* note 218, above, at 58-59.

[232]Bryson v. Itasca County, note 31, above, notes that P.L. 280 was not a waiver. *Martinez v. Santa Clara Pueblo,* note 218, above, held that the Indian Civil Rights Act did not waive sovereign immunity.

[233]*Atkinson v. Haldane,* note 83, above, at 163-167. See also *Bryan v. Itasca County,* note 31, above.

[234]*Atkinson v. Haldane,* note 83, above, at 166-167, and *Bryan v. Itasca County,* note 31, above, at 389.

[235]25 USCA 1301 et seq., note 130, above.

[236]The Indian Civil Rights Act does not prevent Indian tribes from establishing a religion, 25 USCA 1302(1); does not require free counsel in criminal cases, 25 USCA 1302(6) and requires a jury of only six persons in a criminal prosecution, 25 USCA 1302(10).

[237]Tom v. Sutton, 533 F.2d 1101, 1104, n. 5 (9th Cir. 1976), citing cases and holding that the Indian Civil Rights Act did not require a tribe to appoint counsel at public expense and that the act itself was a limitation on the broad language of a tribal constitution purporting to grant rights under the United States Constitution. See generally Johnson, *Indians and Equal Protection,* note 85, above.

[238]See e.g., Johnson v. Lower Elwha Tribal Community, 484 F.2d 200 (9th Cir. 1973), finding federal civil rights jurisdiction in right to vote action brought by tribal member under 28 USCA 1343(4).

[239]*Santa Clara Pueblo v. Martinez,* note 218, above.

[240]Id. at 58.

[241]Id. at 62.

[242]25 USCA 1303. But see Dry Creek Lodge v. Arapahoe and Shoshone Tribes, 623 F. 2d 682 (10th Cir. 1980), cert. den. 449 U.S. 1118, reh. den. 101 S. Ct.

1421 (1981), permitting federal judicial relief against a tribe when non-Natives allegedly had no tribal forum in which to litigate entitlement to a right-of-way on Indian lands. But see White v. Pueblo of San Juan, 728 F. 2d 1307 (10th Cir. 1984), refusing to apply *Dry Creek Lodge* when there was a tribal forum.

[243]AS 18.80.010 et seq. are the Alaska State human rights provisions prohibiting discrimination.

[244]See "Tribal Status of Alaska Natives Research Request 81-132," memorandum from Peter B. Froehlich, Alaska State Legislature House of Representatives Research Agency, to Representative Hoyt "Pappy" Moss (June 24, 1981) at 12-13, citing the following statutes with dates of enactment or latest amendment indicated in parentheses:

AS 04.21.040 (1980) - Defining "local governing body" to include traditional village councils for alcoholic beverage control statutes.

AS 18.75.040 (1966) - Grants village councils dog control authority within a twenty-mile radius of a village.

AS 29.89.090 [sic] (Probably .050) - Grants $25,000 per year in state aid to "Native village governments" to include IRA or traditional councils, "the paramount chief" or other governing body of a Native village which meets the requirements of the Alaska Native Claims Settlement Act.

AS 35.30.010(a)(2) (1977) - Requires plan review and comment on public projects by village councils.

AS 41.20.480(b) (1978) [renumbered as 41.21.163 in 1983] - Allows certain village councils to submit nominations to governor for appointments to the Wood-Tikchik State Park Management Council.

AS 44.47.150 (1975) - Requires approval by "appropriate village entity," including traditional councils, of any transfer of lands held in state trust under section 14(c)(3) of ANCSA.

AS 44.74.070 (1962) - Allows transfer of state automotive and construction equipment to a political subdivision of the state including IRA village councils.

AS 44.83.170(b)(2) (1980) - Allows the Alaska Power Authority to make loans for power projects for which village council is responsible.

AS 46.40.130(a)(2) (1977) - Allows organization of coastal resource service areas to be initiated by resolution of traditional village councils.

AS 46.40.180(a) - Requires review and approval of a district coastal management program by traditional village councils.

AS 46.07 - Refers to "village governing body" in several subsections without defining it for purposes of the Village Safe Water Act.

[245]Peter B. Froehlich memrandum, note 244, above, at 14-15, discussing sovereign immunity issues and a then recent, informal assistant attorney general's opinion regarding immunity of IRA councils.

[246]*U.S. v. Oregon*, note 219, above. See also Merrion v. Jicarilla Apache Tribe, 617 F.2d 537, 540 (10th Cir. 1980), aff'd. on other grounds, 455 U.S. 130 (1982).

[247]Loncassion v. Leekity, 334 F. Supp. 370 (D.N.M. 1971).

[248]*Native Village of Eyak v. GC Contractors*, note 110, above. The court's conclusion that an arbitration clause in a contract is an explicit waiver of sovereign immunity is somewhat suspect.

[249]*Atkinson v. Haldane*, note 83, above, at 168, n. 60, citing cases.

[250]Id. at 169-170.

[251]25 USCA 450 f(c) and 450 (g)(c), requiring liability insurance and prohibiting insurance carriers from asserting the tribe's immunity as a defense. See also 25 CFR 271.45 and 274.39, requiring public liability and motor vehicle liability insurance in the context of Self-Determination Act contracts.

[252]*Merrion v. Jicarilla Apache Tribe*, note 246, above.

[253]Section 17, 25 USCA 477, authorizes tribal charters to include such "powers as may be incidental to the conduct of corporate business...." The "sue and be sued" clauses of IRA tribal corporate charters have been construed to be waivers of sovereign immunity, e.g., Parker Drilling Co. v. Metlakatla Indian Community, 451 F. Supp. 1127, 1136-1137 (D. Ak. 1978). See generally charters reprinted in G. E. Fay, ed., "The Northwest and Alaska," in *Charters, Constitutions and Bylaws of the Indian Tribes of North America*, Occassional Papers in Anthropology Ethnology Series (Greeley, CO.: University of Northern Colorado, 1972).

[254]Id.

[255]See e.g., "Constitution and Bylaws of the Brevig Mission Community Alaska," Village Files, BIA, Anchorage agency.

[256]See e.g., *Maryland Casualty Co. v. Citizens National Bank of West Hollywood*, note 222, above, at 521, discussing scope of waivers.

[257]Martinez v. Southern Ute Tribe, 374 P.2d 691 (Co. 1962).

[258]*Atkinson v. Haldane*, note 83, above, at 173-174.

[259]*Parker Drilling Co. v. Metlakatla Indian Community*, note 253, above, at 1132-1133.

[260]"Separability of Tribal Organizations Organized Under Secs. 16 and 17 of the I.R.A.," *Opinions of the Solicitor on Indian Affairs,* Vol. II at 1846, 65 I.D. 483 (M-36515 Nov. 20, 1958). See also *Atkinson v. Haldane,* note 83, above, at 171-175 and at 174-175, noting that:

> Recognition of two legal entities, one with sovereign immunity, the other with the possibility for waiver of that immunity would enable the tribes to make maximum use of their property. The property of the corporation would be at risk, presumably in an amount necessary to satisfy those with whom the tribe deals in economic spheres. Yet some of the tribal property could be kept in reserve, safe from judgement execution which could destroy the tribe's livelihood, in recognition of the special status of the Indian tribe.

[261]Larson v. Domestic & Foreign Commerce Corp., 337 U.S. 682, 689-690 (1949). See generally Cohen (1982), note 8, above, at 318-323.

[262]*Santa Clara Pueblo v. Martinez,* note 218, above, at 59 and *Puyallup Tribe III,* note 220, above, at 168, n. 3 and 173.

[263]E.g., Bivens v. Six Unknown Named Agents, 403 U.S. 388 (1971).

[264]*Kennerly v. U.S.,* note 220, above, prohibiting suit against tribal officials to recover money allegedly illegally paid from member's BIA trust account to repay debts owed the tribe.

[265]Tenneco Oil Co. v. Sac and Fox Tribe, 725 F.2d 577, 580 (10th Cir. 1984), citations omitted. See also *Puyallup III,* note 220, above, at 168, n. 3 and 173, permitting suit against tribal officers to enforce legitimate state fish and game conservation regulations which the officers allegedly violated.

[266]M.F. Lindley, *The Acquisition and Government of Backward Territory in International Law.* (London: Longmans, Green and Co., Ltd., 1926; reprinted New York: Negro Universities Press Print, 1969) at 10-20, discussing the views of Victoria, Las Casas, Grotius, Pufendorf and Vattel.

[267]See L. Hanke, *All Mankind is One,* (DeKalb, Ill.: Northern Illinois University Press, 1974), a study of the opposing views of Bartolome de Las Casas and Juan Gines de Sepulveda on the rights of the American aboriginals.

[268]F. Cohen, *The Legal Conscience,* "The Spanish Origin of Indian Rights in the Law of the United States," (New Haven: Yale University Press, 1960; reprinted Archon Books, 1970) at 239-40.

[269]Id. at 248 and Lindley, note 266, above, at 13 (Grotius) and 17 (Vattel).

[270]*The Legal Conscience,* note 268, above, at 248.

[271]Id. at 242-243.

[272]H. R. Berman, *The Concept of Aboriginal Rights in the Early Legal History of the United States,* 27 Buffalo L. Rev. 637, 650 (1978).

[273]*Cherokee Nation v. Georgia,* note 14, above, at 16 and *Worcester v. Georgia,* note 15, above, at 555-556.

[274]D. V. Jones, *License for Empire,* (Chicago: University of Chicago Press, 1982). This is an enlightening study of the American Indian treaty systems under both the British and United States governments. See particularly chapter 5, "Transformation of the Treaty System 1768-75," regarding the transformation of the treaties from instruments of mutual "accomodation" to instruments of land acquisition. Accord Cohen, 1982, note 8, above, at 66.

[275]*Johnson v. M'Intosh,* note 12, above, at 588-589. See generally chapter 2, I B, "The Rule of Discovery."

[276]Jones, note 274, above, at 147-156 and 164-169. Accord Cohen, 1982, note 8, above, at 59-60 and 70-73, discussing the abandonment of George Washington's early "conquered provinces" theory as applied to Indian tribes.

[277]Berman, note 272, above, at 650.

[278]The 1840 Treaty of Waitangi in New Zealand illustrates the obverse of this proposition. Although the Maori now dispute the question, the English language version of the treaty surrenders Maori sovereignty to the British crown, but Maori rights to property are separately protected. See Lindley, note 266, above, at 41-42. Compare A. H. Snow, *The Question of Aborigines in the Law and Practice of Nations,* (Washington, D. C.: U.S. Govt. Printing Off., 1919; Northbrook, Ill.: Metro Books reprint, 1972) at 120-122, quoting from the Treaty of Waitangi, but criticizing it for the "dangers and difficulties" it allegedly illustrates in "the attempt to deal with aboriginal tribes by treaty."

[279]At least one Alaska Native representative tribal organization has taken the position tthe political authority of its member villages persists over lands Native title to which was extinguished under ANCSA. See letter from William C. "Spud" Williams, President, Tanana Chiefs Conference, Inc., to The Honorable Bill Sheffield, Governor, State of Alaska (October 6, 1983) at 8 concluding that:

> [I]f the Alaska Natives are truly unique, the State must accept the full and true implications of such uniqueness. In the context of Native jurisdictional claims, the State must recognize the historical fact that Native territorial jurisdiction has never been diminished and that congressional, executive and judicial actions recognize the failure to settle these claims.

[280]E.g., *Menominee Tribe v. U.S.,* 388 F.2d 998 at 1000 (Ct. Cl. 1967), *aff'd.,* 391 U.S. 404 (1968). See generally, Cohen, 1982, note 8, above, at 19 and 815-816.

[281]Although tribal existence cannot be "taken" by the United States so that it requires compensation, it can be abandoned by the aboriginal people. It has been held repeatedly that once a tribal community abandons its tribal relationships, it ceases to exist as political community or "tribe." The Kansas Indians, 72 U.S. (5 Wall.) 737, 757 (1867). See also e.g., *U.S. v. Washington,* note 82, above,

and Mashpee Tribe v. New Seabury Corp., 592 F.2d 575 (1st Cir.), cert. den. 444 U.S. 866 (1979). However, federal recognition, coupled with the political question doctrine, probably preclude any judicial analysis of the continued existence of a federally recognized tribe. See Cohen, 1982, note 8, above, at 9.

[282]The Fifth Amendment provides in part that:

> No person shall be...deprived of life, liberty or property, without due process of law; nor shall private property be taken for public use, without just compensation.

The Fifth Amendment has been held applicable to the taking of tribally owned reservation lands, e.g., *U.S. v. Sioux Nation of Indians,* 448 U.S. 371 (1980), but "unrecognized" aboriginal land (and other) rights have been held not to be "property" in the Fifth Amendment sense, e.g., *Tee-Hit-Ton Band of Indians v. U.S.,* note 18, above.

[283]*Jones v. Meehan,* note 102, above, upholding tribal jurisdiction over inheritance of tribal member's land which was never owned by the tribe. See also, e.g., *Merrion v. Jicarilla Apache Tribe,* note 101, above, at 137-144 (1982), tribe's authority to impose severence tax on oil extracted from reservation lands based on its inherent sovereignty, not only proprietary powers.

[284]E.g., *U.S. v. Mazurie,* note 87, above, at 557.

[285]Montoya v. U.S., 108 U.S. 261 at 266 (1901).

[286]*U.S. v. Sandoval,* note 21, above, at 46.

[287]U.S. v. Holliday, 70 U.S. (3 Wall.) 407 (1866). See generally, Cohen, 1982, note 8, above, at 3-5, discussing current limitations on the political question doctrine in Indian "taking" cases. See also L.R. Weatherhead, *What is an "Indian" Tribe"?—The Question of Tribal Existence,* 8 Amer. Ind. L. Rev. 1 (Norman, Ok.: University of Oklahoma College of Law, 1981).

[288]*Joint Tribal Council of Passamaquoddy Indians v. Morton,* note 83, above, and accompanying text.

[289]"Procedures for Establishing that an American Indian Group Exists as a Tribe," 25 CFR Part 83.

[290]E.g., *Atkinson v. Haldane,* note 83, above, at 162, confirming the sovereignty of the Metlakatla Indian Community on the independent ground of federal recognition.

[291]Lindley, note 266, above at 21, quoting Austin's test for "political character."

[292]Id. at 23. As Lindley discusses it "considerable number" means only something more than a few "isolated individuals" and does not imply an urban or similar large community.

[293]Cohen (1942), note 8, above, at 414, n. 208.

[294]Price, note 7, above, at 61.

[295]Id. and Cohen (1942), note 8, above, at 414. See generally, chapter 8. See also Anderson and Eells, note 59, above, at 48-50.

[296]Taylor, note 43, above, at 2, cited also in *U.S. v. Washington*, note 82, above, at 1373.

[297]E.g., Id., describing the negotiations surrounding the fishing treaties in western Washington State. For an exhaustive discussion of the Washington treaties and their implications see U.S. v. Washington, 384 F. Supp. 312 (W.D. Wash. 1974), aff'd. 520 F. 2d 676 (9th Cir. 1975), cert. den. 423 U.S. 1086 (1976), decision subsequently aff'd. *Washington v. Washington Commercial Passenger Fishing Assn.*, note 81, above.

[298]Hearings on S. 2037 and S.J. Res. 102 before the subcommittee of the Committee on Interior and Insular Affairs, 80th Cong., 2nd Sess. at 149 (1948), testimony of W.H. Haas, then Chief Counsel to the Bureau of Indian Affairs.

[299]See *Alaska Natives and the Land*, note 80, above. See also *Handbook of North American Indians*, vol. 6, *Subarctic*, (Washington, D.C.: Smithsonian Institution, 1981), at 664-665 and 705-707.

[300]See generally chapter 8, II, "Southeast Alaska Indians." See also E. S. Burch, Jr., "Studies of Native History as a Contribution to Alaska's Future," Special Lecture to the 32d Alaska Science Conference, Fairbanks, Ak. (Aug. 25, 1981). Accord Anderson and Eells, note 59, above, at 48, noting that among the Eskimos "a tribe occup[ied] several adjacent villages in a given territory."

[301]15 Stat. 539.

[302]E.g., In re Sah Quah, 1 Ak. Fed. Rpts. 136 at 140, implying that the Tlingits had no powers of self-government.

[303]In re Minook, 2 Ak. Rpts 200 (D. Ak. 1904) at 220-221.

[304]54 I.D., note 60, above, at 46.

[305]Chapter 1, II B1, "Change in the Relationship—1904-1936."

[306]Price, note 7, above, at 75-76. See also 1 Op. Sol. Ind. Aff. 813, note 79, above, regarding the powers of "non-historic" tribes.

[307]25 CFR 81.1(w). By 1971, seventy one Alaska Native communities had been organized under the IRA. See chapter 9, I C1, relating to traditional and IRA governments. As of 1981, approximately 30 new communities had requested constitutions and corporate charters. Price, note 7, above, at 76.

[308]See chapter 1, II B1, "Change in the Relationship—1904-1936," discussing Native services provided by the early Office of Education under Sheldon Jackson's administration. See generally chapter 5.

[309]Act of Nov. 2, 1924, 42 Stat. 208, 25 USCA 13. The Snyder Act is the general appropriations authorization for all Indian services in the United States. See, chapter 1, II B3, "Human Services Under the Snyder Act—1931-1971" and chapter 5, generally.

[310]See text accompanying notes 113-117, above. See also, Morton v. Ruiz, 415 U.S. 199 at 212 (1973), describing the service eligibility of "off-reservation" Alaska Natives.

[311]25 CFR 32.3, "Indian Education Policies."

[312]47 Fed. Reg. 53130 at 53133 and 48 Fed. Reg. 56862 at 56865, note 79 above. But see, *Board of Equalization of Ketchikan Borough v. Alaska Native Brotherhood,* note 110, above, Rabinowitz J., concurring, concluding that the list does not "clearly" recognize an IRA entity as a sovereign.

[313]See note 89, above. The Inupiat Community of the Arctic Slope (ICAS) had also been judicially characterized as a "reconized tribe," Inupiat Community of the Arctic Slope v. U.S. (ICAS I), 680 F. 2d 122 (Ct. Cls. 1982; cert. den. 51 USLW 3339 (1982).

[314]Tlingit and Haida Indians of Alaska v. U.S., 177 F. Supp. 452 (Ct. Cls. 1959).

[315]E.g., chapter 2, V E, "Events After Statehood."

[316]E.g., the Indian Civil Rights Act, note 130, above, imposing certain constitutional requirements on Indian tribal governments, but permitting only limited remedies. See generally, *Santa Clara Pueblo v. Martinez,* note 218, above.

[317]*U.S. v. Wheeler,* 435 U.S. 313 at 326 (1978), describes only three such limits on Indian tribes: (1) the ability to freely alienate the lands they occupy to non-Indians, (2) the ability to enter into direct commercial or governmental relations with foreign nations and (3) the ability to criminally prosecute nonmembers in tribal courts (citing cases).

[318]*Washington v. Confederated Tribes of the Colville Reservation,* note 193, above, at 153-154, construing the limits imposed by the "overriding interests of the National Government" to be the same three as described in *U.S. v Wheeler,* note 317, above.

[319]E.g., compare *Montana v. U.S.,* note 193, above, upholding exclusive *state* fish and game jurisdiction over non-Indian, fee land within reservation boundaries with New Mexico v. Mescalero Apache Tribe, ____U.S.____, 76 L. Ed. 2d 611 (1983), upholding exclusive *tribal* fish and game jurisdiction on tribally owned, reservation lands. See also section V of this chapter, "State and Native Jurisdiction in Alaska."

[320]See section V B of this chapter, "P.L. 280 in General."

[321]*McClanahan v. Arizona State Tax Commission,* note 23, above, at 172. See also section II of this chapter, "Native American Self-Government in General."

[322]*Williams v. Lee,* note 25, above, at 220; both tests are summarized in *White Mountain Apache Tribe v. Bracker,* note 4, above, at 142-143.

[323]*New Mexico v. Mescalero Apache Tribe,* note 319, above, 72 L. Ed. 2d at 620, summarizes the modern preemption rule for a unanimous court as follows:

> State jurisdiction is preempted by the operation of federal law if it interferes or is incompatible with federal and tribal interests reflected in federal law, unless the State interests at stake are sufficient to justify the assertion of State authority.

[324]Article VI, cl. 2 of the U.S. Constitution provides that:

> This Constitution, and the laws of the United States which shall be made in pursuance thereof; and all treaties made, or which shall be made, under the authority of the United States, shall be the supreme law of the land; and the judges in every state shall be bound thereby, anything in the Constitution or law of any state to the contrary notwithstanding.

[325]E.g., Cohen (1982), note 8, above, at 273.

[326]*McClanahan v. Arizona State Tax Commission,* note 23, above, at 172-173.

[327]E.g., Cohen (1982), note 8, above, at 273, citing cases.

[328]*New Mexico v. Mescalero Apache Tribe,* note 319, above, 72 L. Ed. 2d at 621, n. 18.

[329]Id. generally.

[330]*Kake v. Egan,* note 26, above.

[331]Indian Child Welfare Act, P.L. 95-608, Nov. 8 1978, 92 Stat. 3069, 25 USCA 1901.

[332]Application of Angus, 655 P. 2d 208 at 212, n. 9 (Or. App. 1982), review denied ___ U.S. ___, 78 L. Ed. 2d 109, (1983), concluding that the Sitka Community Association is a "federally recognized tribe." See also *ICAS I,* note 313, above.

[333]*E. A. v. State,* 623 P. 2d 1210 (Ak. 1981); A.B.M. v. M. H 651 P. 2d 1170 (Ak. 1982), discussed and criticized in *The Indian Child Welfare Act: Does It Cover Custody Disputes Among Extended Family Members.* Alaska L. Rev. 157 (Durham, N.C.: Duke University School of Law, 1984).

Section 4 of the Alaska Statehood Act of July 7, 1958, P.L. 85-508, sec. 4, 72 Stat. 339, as amended, exempts "lands or other property" belonging to Alaska Natives from state taxation "except when held by individual natives in fee without restrictions on alienation." Section 21(d) of ANCSA permits state taxation of "developed" ANCSA corporate property and all ANCSA lands 20 years after they are received, but it is possible that section 4 of the Statehood Act would still exempt property owned by tribal governments from state taxation. It has been held to protect restricted allotments and townsite lots. People of South Naknek v. Bristol Bay Borough, 466 F. Supp. 870, 874 (D. Ak. 1979). See also Cohen (1982), note 8, above, at 767-768.

[334]*Williams v. Lee*, note 25, above, at 220.

[335]*McClanahan v. Arizona State Tax Commission*, note 23, above, at 179, citing *Kake v. Egan*, note 26, above, at 75-76.

[336]*American Indian Policy Review Commission, Final Report* (Washington, D.C.: U.S. Govt. Printing Off., 1977) at 490-491. Accord *Montana v. U.S.*, note 339, below, and accompanying text.

[337]*Atkinson v. Haldane*, note 83, above, Metlakatla's sovereign immunity; Cogo v. Central Council of Tlingit and Haida Indians, 465 F. Supp. 1286 (D. Ak. 1979), off-reservation, Alaska Native tribe has sovereign immunity from suit to determine membership; c.f. *Ollestead v. Native Village of Tyonek*, note 138, above, state court adjudication of tribal membership prohibited under P.L. 280 because it would involve adjudication of trust property; *Johnson v. Chilkat Indian Village*, note 109, above, tribe could not be joined as an indespensable party because of sovereign immunity, but held to have sufficient jurisdiction over tribally owned (non-reservation) land to adjudicate title to tribal artifacts.

[338]"Alaska Native Villages," letter opinion by Robert Price, Assistant Attorney General, to Palmer McCarter, Director, Division of Local Government Assistance, Alaska Department of Community and Regional Affairs (File No. J66-355-82, Mar. 5, 1982).

[339]*Montana v. U.S.*, note 39, above, at 563-567. See generally R.G. McCoy, *The Doctrine of Tribal Sovereignty: Accomodating Tribal, State and Federal Interests*, 13 Harvard Civil Rights-Civil Liberties L. Rev. 357 1978).

[340]Oklahoma Tax Commission v. U.S., 319 U.S. 598, 603 (1942).

[341]*Bryan v. Itasca*, note 31, above, at 376, n.2, citing *McClanahan v. Arizona State Tax Comm.*, note 23, above.

[342]*In re McCord*, note 92, above, at 136. See also *U.S. v. Washington*, note 82, above, at 1373, denying the appellant tribes the status of treaty fishing tribes in part because the formally established tribal governemnts "have not controlled the lives of the members." But see *U.S. v. Washington*, note 297, above, at 403, permitting tribal regulation of off-reservation treaty fishing where the tribe had a competant legal system. See also Settler v. Lameer, 507 F. 2d 231 (9th Cir. 1974), upholding tribal jurisdiction over off-reservation treaty rights of members.

[343]E.g., *New Mexico v. Mescalero Apache Tribe*, note 44, above.

[344]28 USCA 1360(c), discussed in section V, C I of this chapter, "P.L. 280's Limits on State Civil Jurisdiction."

[345]18 USCA 1161. See also *Rice v. Rehner,* note 210, above, holding that the delegation to the tribe does not preempt state licensing laws.

[346]C.f. *Problems and Possibilities for Service Delivery and Government in the Alaska Unorganized Borough,* note 123, above, at 26-27. See also Hippler and Conn, note 156, above.

[347]25 USCA 1725-1727.

[348]See note 90, above, and accompanying text describing other state statutes. The Alaska statutes are listed at notes 91 and 244.

[349]Deductions and credits for certain contributions and taxes paid to Indian tribes determined by the Secretary of the Interior "to exercise governmental functions" are already possible under the Tribal Tax Status Act, P.L. 97-473, Jan. 14, 1983, 96 Stat 2608, 26 USCA 7871.

[350]P.L. 96-487, Title VIII, 94 Stat. 2422, 16 USCA 3117 et seq. See generally chapter 7, III, "Subsistence and ANCSA."

[351]See e.g., "United Tribes of Alaska new IRA federation," *Tundra Times* (Anchorage) May 11, 1983 at 1.

[352]See e.g., "Sovereignty Meeting Proposed" and "Sovereignty Has 'Ingredients of Strife,' Stevens Says," *Fairbanks Daily News-Miner,* Saturday, July 9, 1983.

SELECTED BIBLIOGRAPHY
BY PARTS AND CHAPTERS

PART I: INTRODUCTION

CHAPTER ONE
THE FEDERAL RELATIONSHIP TO ALASKA NATIVES

A. Selected Books and Articles

Alfedson, G. "Greenland and the Law of Political Decolonization." *German Yearbook of International Law* 25. Berlin: Dunckner & Humblot (1982): 290-308.

"American Indian Policy Review Commission." *Final Report.* Washington, D.C.: Government Printing Office, 1977.

―――. *Special Report on Alaska.* Washington, D.C.: Government Printing Office, 1976.

Anderson, H. D. and W. C. Eells. *Alaska Natives A Survey of Their Sociological and Educational Status.* Stanford: Stanford University Press, 1935.

Arnold, R. D. *Alaska Native Land Claims.* 2d ed. Anchorage: Alaska Native Foundation, 1976.

Barsh, R. L., and J. Y. Henderson, *The Road.* Berkley: Univ. of Cal. Press, 1980.

Barcott, P. A. "The Alaska Native Claims Settlement Act: Survival of a Special Relationship," *Univ. of San Francisco L. Rev.* (Fall 1981).

Berry, M. C. *The Alaska Pipeline: The Politics of Oil and Native Land Claims.* Bloomington: Indiana University Press, 1975.

Cohen, F. *Handbook of Federal Indian Law.* 1982 ed. Charlottesville, Va.: Michie Bobbs-Merrill, 1982.

―――. *Handbook of Federal Indian Law.* Washington, D. C.: Government Printing Office. 1942. Reprint. New York: AMS Press, Inc., 1972.

Coulter, R. T. "The Denial of Legal Remedies to Indian Nations Under U.S. Law." *Rethinking Indian Law.* New York: National Lawyers Guild, 1982.

Davis, K. C. *Administrative Law Treatise.* St. Paul, Minn.: West Publishing Co., 1958.

Federal Field Committee for Development Planning in Alaska. *Alaska Natives and the Land.* Anchorage: Federal Field Committee, 1968.

"Federal Plenary Power in Indian Affairs After *Weeks* and *Sioux Nation.* U. of Penna. L. Rev." 131 (1982).

Getches, D. H.; D. M. Rosenfelt, and C. F. Wilkinson. *Federal Indian Law Cases and Materials.* St. Paul: West Publishing Company, 1979.

Gruening, E. *The State of Alaska.* New York: Random House, 1968.

Hulley, C. C. *Alaska Past and Present.* Portland, Ore.: Binfords & Mort, 1970.

"Indian Law Symposium." *N. Dak. L. Rev.* 48 (1972), 49 (1973).

Jones, R. S. *Alaska Native Claims Settlement Act of 1971 (Public Law 92-203) History and Analysis.* Washington, D.C.: Congressional Research Service, 1972.

Keon-Cohen, B. A. "Native Justice in Australia, Canada, and the U.S.A.: A Comparative Analysis." *Monash Univ. L. Rev.* 7 Clayton, Victoria, Australia: Monash University (1981).

"Law and Indigenous Populations." *Buffalo L. Rev.* (1978).

Merriam, L., tech. dir. *The Problem of Indian Administration.* Baltimore: Johns Hopkins Press, 1928.

Miller, D. H. *The Alaska Treaty.* Kingston, Ont., Canada: Limestone Press, 1981.

Morehouse, T. A., G. McBeath and L. Leask. *Alaska's Urban and Rural Governments,* New York: University Press of America, 1984.

Naske, C-M., and Herman E. Slotnick. *Alaska: A History of the 49th State.* Grand Rapids, Mich.: William B. Eerdmans Publishing Company, 1979.

Nathan, Robert P. and Associates, Inc. *2(c) Report: Federal Programs and Alaska Natives,* Anchorage: Robert P. Nathan and Associates, Inc. [1975].

Price, M.E. "Region-Village Relations Under the Alaska Native Claims Settlement Act," *UCLA L. Rev.* 5 (1975).

Price, M.E. and Robert N. Clinton. *Law and the American Indian Readings Notes and Cases.* 2d ed. Charlotesville, Va.: The Michie Company Law Publishers, 1983.

Price, R. *Native Rights A Report to the Alaska Statehood Commission.* Juneau: Alaska Department of Law, 1982.

Sand, C. D. [Sutherland]. *Statutes and Statutory Construction.* Chicago: Callagahan & Company, 1972.

Scott, A. W. *The Law of Trusts.* 2d ed. Boston: Little Brown and Company, 1967.

Stoebner, K. "Alaska Native Water Rights as Affected by the Alaska Native Claims Settlement Act." *American Indian Journal.* Washington D.C.: Institute for the Development of Indian Law 4 (March 1978): 1-26.

Tyler, L. S. *A History of Indian Policy.* Washington, D.C.: Government Printing Office, 1973.

Ulibarri, G. S. *Documenting Alaskan History Guide to Federal Archives Relating to Alaska.* Fairbanks: University of Alaska Press, 1982.

U.S. Congress, House. Presidential Message to Congress. *Recommendations for Indian Policy.* 91st Cong., 2d sess., 1970. H. Doc. 91-363.

U.S. Congress, Senate. *Russian Administration of Alaska and the Status of the Alaskan Natives.* 81st Cong., 2d sess., 1950. S. Doc. 152.

Walleri, M. *Tribal-State Relations: A New Paradigm for Local Government in Alaska.* Fairbanks: Tanana Chiefs Conference, n.d.

B. Archival Material

Bureau of Indian Affairs. Files of the Juneau Area Office. Village File Series 307.3. Including files on the following villages: Elim, Karluk, Tyonek, Eklutna, Tetlin, and Gambell.

Federal Records Center, Seattle, Wash. Files of the Territorial Governor of Alaska. Record Group 348. Microfilm: M-393, Roll Nos. 274, 268 and 269.

National Archives, Files of the Bureau of Indian Affairs. Record Group 75. "Letter Press (1898-1901)," Metlakatla. Series 801.

———. "Alaska Trust Fund." Series 801.

———. Executive Orders. Series 822.

———. General Correspondence Files, Alaska Division, Bureau of Education. Series 806. Boxes:

No.   1,   "Natives (Reserves) 1910-1911."
No.   4,   "Copper Center-6."
No.   21,   Several Files.
No.   37,   "Reindeer (Reserves) 1911-1912."
No.   41,   "Hydaburg (1911-1912)."
           Hydaburg (1912-1913)."
           "Klawock (1912-1913)."
           "Klawock (1913-1914)."

National Archives. Files of the Territorial Governor of Alaska. Record Group 348. Box 462, Folders:
40-4d #1 "Aboriginal Rights"
40-4f "BIA Misc."

C. Cases and Legal Opinions

13 L.D. 120 (1891). "Alaska Lands-Indian Occupancy."

19 L.D. 323 (1894). "Alaska-Legal Status of Natives."

49 L.D. 592 (1923). "Leasing of Lands Within Reservations Created for the Benefit of the Natives of Alaska."

53 I.D. 593 (1932). "Status of Alaska Natives."

54 I.D. 39 (1932). "Validity of Marriage by Custom Among the Natives or Indians of Alaska."

55 I.D. 14 (1934). "Powers of Indian Tribes."

70 I.D. 166 (1962). "Oil and Gas Leasing on Lands Withdrawn by Executive Order for Indian Purposes in Alaska."

81 I.D. 316 (1974). "Authority to Determine Eligibility of Native Villages after June 18, 1934."

Alaska v. Udall, 420 F. 2d 938 (9th Cir. 1969).

Alaska Chapter, Associated General Contractors of America, Inc. v. Pierce, 694 F.2d 1162 (9th Cir. 1982).

Alaska Pacific Fisheries v. U.S., 248 U.S. 78 (1918).

Alaska Pacific Fisheries v. U.S., 250 F. 274 (9th Cir. 1917).

Alaska Public Easement Defense Fund v. Andrus, 435 F. Supp. 664 (D.C. Ak. 1977).

Aleut Corp. v. Arctic Slope Regional Corp., 410 F. Supp. 1196 (D.C. Ak. 1976).

Aleut Corp. v. Arctic Slope Regional Corp., 417 F. Supp. 900 (D.C. AK. 1976); rev'd sub nom Doyon Ltd. v. Bristol Bay Native Corp., 569 F. 2d 491 (9th Cir.); cert. den. 439 U.S. 954 (1978).

Aleut Corp. v. Arctic Slope Regional Corp., 421 F. Supp. 862 (D.C. Ak. 1976).

Aleut Corp. v. Arctic Slope Regional Corp., 484 F. Supp. 482 (D.C. Ak. 1980).

Aleut Corp. v. Tyonek Native Corp., 725 F.2d 527 (9th Cir. 1983).

Application of Angus, 655 P. 2d 208 (Or. Ct. App. 1982); cert. den. sub nom Woodruff v. Angus, 52 USLW 3263 (1983).

Atkinson v. Haldane, 569 P. 2d 151 (Ak 1977).

Board of Equalization for the Borough of Ketchikan v. Alaska Native Brotherhood and Sisterhood, Camp No. 14, 666 P.2d 1015 (Ak. 1983).

Board of Regents v. Roth, 408 U.S. 564 (1972).

Bryan v. Itasca County, 426 U.S. 373 (1976).

Cape Fox Corp. v. U.S., 456 F.Supp. 784 (D.C. Ak. 1978); rev'd. on jurisdictional grounds, 648 F.2d 399 (9th Cir. 1981).

Carlo v. Gustafson, 512 F. Supp. 833 (D.C. Ak. 1981).

Central Council Tlingit and Haida Indians of Alaska v. Chugach Native Ass'n., 502 F. 2d 1323 (9th Cir. 1974) cert. den. 421 U.S. 948.

Cherokee Nation v. Georgia, 30 U.S. (5 Pet.) 1 (1831).

Choctaw Nation v. United States, 119 U.S. 1 (1886).

Cogo v. Central Council of Tlingit and Haid Indians, 465 F. Supp. 1286 (D. Ak. 1979).

Cook Inlet Region v. Kleppe, Slip Op. A-40-73 Civ, 2 ILR No. 4 at 29 (D.C. Ak. February 20, 1975).

Dandridge v. Williams, 397 U.S. 471 (1970).

Davis v. Sitka School Board, 3 Ak. Rpts. 481 (1908).

Delaware Tribal Business Committee v. Weeks, 430 U.S. 73 (1977).

Edwardsen v. Morton, 369 F. Supp. 1359 (D.C.D.C. 1973).

Eric v. Secretary of U.S. Department of Housing and Urban Development, 464 F. Supp. 44 (D.C. Ak. 1978).

Fisher v. District Court, 424 U.S. 382 (1976).

Fondahn v. Native Village of Tyonek, 450 F.2d 520 (9th Cir. 1971).

Fox v. Morton, 404 F. 2d 254 (9th Cir. 1974).

Gila River Pima-Maricopa Band of Indians v. U.S., 427 F. 2d 1194 (Ct. Cls. 1970).

Goldbcrg v. Kelly, 397 U.S. 471 (1970).

Hamilton v. Butz, 520 F. 2d 709 (9th Cir. 1975).

Heffle v. Alaska, 633 P.2d 264 (Ak. 1981); cert. den. 455 U.S. 1000 (1982).

Johnson v. Chilkat Indian Village, 457 F. Supp. 384 (D.C. Ak. 1978).

Johnson v. M'Intosh, 21 U.S. (8 Wheat) 543 (1823).

Kake v. Egan, 369 U.S. 60 (1962).

Koniag, Inc. v. Kleppe, 405 F. Supp. 1360 (D.C.D.C. 1975); aff'd in part sub nom Koniag v. Andrus, 580 F. 2d 601, (D.C. Cir. 1978).

"Liquor Ordinance, Village of Allakaket, Alaska." Unpublished Memorandum. Op. Assoc. Sol. Ind. Aff., October 1, 1980.

Lone Wolf v. Hitchcock, 187 U.S. 553 (1903).

McClanahan v. Arizona State Tax Commission, 411 U.S. 164 (1973).

In re McCord, 151 F. Supp. 132 (D.C. Ak. 1957).

Menominee Tribe of Indians v. U.S., 391 U.S. 404 (1968).

Metlakatla v. Egan 369 U.S. 45 (1962).

Miller v. U.S., 159 F. 2d 997 (9th Cir. 1947).

In re Minook, 2 Ak. Rpts. 200 (1904).

Morton v. Mancari, 417 U.S. 535 (1975).

Morton v. Ruiz, 415 U.S. 199 (1973).

Native Village of Eyak v. G.C. Contractors, 658 P.2d 256 (Ak. 1983).

"Native Village of Karluk and the [R]eservation at Karluk." Unpublished Memorandum. Alaska Regional Solicitor, January 22, 1968.

Ollestead v. Native Village of Tyonek, 560 P. 2d 21 (Ak. 1977); cert. den. 434 U.S. 938.

Pence v. Kleppe, 529 F. 2d 135 (9th Cir. 1976).

Quick Bear v. Leupp, 210 U.S. 50 (1908).

Rockbridge v. Lincoln, 449 F.2d 567 (9th Cir. 1971).

In re Sah Quah, 1 Ak. Fed. Rpts. 136 (D.C. Ak. 1886).

Santa Rosa Band of Indians v. Kings County, 532 F. 2d 655 (9th Cir. 1976).

Seminole Nation v. U.S., 216 U.S. 286 (1942).

Sutter v. Heckman, 1 Ak. Rpts, 188 (D.C. Ak. 1901).

Tee-Hit-Ton Band of Indians v. U.S. 348 U.S. 272 (1955).

13th Regional Corp. v. Department of the Interior, 654 F. 2d 758 (D.C. Cir. 1980).

Tlingit and Haida Indians of Alaska v. U.S., 177 F. Supp. 452 (Ct. Cls. 1959).

Ukpeagvik Inupiat Corp. v. Arctic Slope Regional Corp., 517 F. Supp. 1255 (D.C. Ak. 1981).

U.S. v. Alaska Pacific Fisheries, 5 Ak. Rpts. 484 (D.C. Ak. 1916); aff'd. 250 F. 275 (9th Cir. 1917); aff'd. 248 U.S. 78 (1918).

U.S. v. Antelope, 430 U.S. 641 (1976).

U.S. v. Berrigan, 2 Ak. Rpts. 442 (D.C. Ak. 1904).

U.S. v. Booth, 161 F. Supp. 269 (D.C. Ak. 1958).

U.S. v. Cadzow, 5 Ak. Rpts. 125 (D.C. Ak. 1914).

U.S. v. Candelaria, 271 U.S. 432 (1925).

U.S. v. Libby, McNeill and Libby, 107 F. Supp. 697 (D.C. Ak. 1952).

U.S. v. Sioux Nation, 448 U.S. 371 (1980).

U.S. v. Wheeler, 435 U.S. 313 (1978).

Waters v. Campbell, 1 Ak. Rpts. 91 (D.C. Or. 1876).

White v. Califano, 437 F. Supp. 543 (D.C.S.D. 1977); aff'd. 581 F.2d 697.

Williams v. Lee, 358 U.S. 217 (1959).

Wilson v. Watt, 703 F. 2d 395 (9th Cir. 1983).

Worcester v. Georgia, 31 U.S. (6 Pet.) 515 (1832).

PART II: ALASKA NATIVE LANDS AND RESOURCES

A. Books, Articles and Memoranda

Bennett, G. I. "Aboriginal Title in the Common Law: A Stony Path Through Feudal Doctrine." *Buffalo L. Rev.* 27 (Fall 1978): 617-636.

Berman, H. R. "The Concept of Aboriginal Rights in the Early Legal History of the United States." *Buffalo L. Rev.* 27 (Fall 1978): 637-668.

Cohen, F. *Handbook of Federal Indian Law.* 1982 ed. Charlottesville, VA.: Michie Bobbs-Merrill, 1982.

———. *Handbook of Federal Indian Law.* Washington, D.C.: Government Printing Office, 1942. Reprint. New York: AMS Press, Inc., 1972.

———. Memorandum to Commissioner of Indian Affairs regarding Cohen's visit to Alaska. July 10, 1944. RG 348, Box 462, Folder 40-4d #1, Terr. Gov. Files. Federal Records Center, Seattle.

"Entitlement of the Akutan Village Council to Rental Proceeds from Ls. No. E00C14200079." Op. Alaska Reg. Sol., November 2, 1978.

"Executive Order Reservations: A Compensable Indian Right." *Yale L.J.* 69 (1960).

"Extent of the 'Fair and Honorable Dealings' Section of the Indian Claims Commission Act." *N. Mex. L. Rev.* 48 (1972): 729.

Federal Field Committee for Development Planning in Alaska. *Alaska Natives and the Land.* Anchorage: Federal Field Committee, 1968.

Gruening, E. *The State of Alaska.* New York: Random House, 1968.

Henderson, J. Y. "Unraveling the Riddle of Aboriginal Title." *Amer. Ind. L. Rev.* 5 (1977).

Jackson, S. *Annual Report on Introduction of Domestic Reindeer in Alaska.* 16 vols. Washington, D.C.: Government Printing Office, 1890-1906.

Janson, L., ed. *Alaska Native Management Report.* Anchorage: Alaska Native Foundation, 1971-78.

Jones, Richard S. *Alaska Native Claims Settlement Act of 1971 (Public Law 92-203) History and Analysis.* Washington, D.C.: Congressional Research Service, 1972.

National Resources Committee *Alaska, Its Resources and Development.* Washington, D.C.: Government Printing Office, 1938.

Otis, D. S. *The Dawes Act and the Allotment of Indian Lands.* Norman, OK.: University of Oklahoma Press, 1973.

Price, Monroe E. "Region Village Relations Under the Alaska Native Claims Settlement Act." Parts 1 and 2. *UCLA-Alaska L. Rev.* 5 (1975 and 1976): 58 and 237.

Prucha, F. *Americanizing the American Indian: Writings by the "Friends of the Indian" 1880-1900.* Cambridge: Harvard University Press, 1973.

———. *American Indian Policy in the Formative Years.* Lincoln, NB.: University of Nebraska Press, 1962.

Taylor, G. D. *The New Deal and American Indian Tribalism The Administration of the Indian Reorganization Act, 1934-45.* Lincoln, NB.: University of Nebraska Press, 1980.

Windahl, E. and W. H. Timme. "Application of Sec. 19 of the Alaska Native Claims Settlement Act to the St. Lawrence Island Reserve." Brief to U.S. Dept. of Interior, 1973. On file with Regional Solicitor, Anchorage.

B. CHAPTER TWO
ABORIGINAL TITLE—Cases and Opinions

13 L.D. 120 (1891). "Alaska Lands—Indian Occupancy."

24 L.D. 312 (1897). "Alaska Lands—Survey—Indian Occupancy."

26 L.D. 512 (1898). "Alaskan Lands—Rights of Natives—Application for Survey."

26 L.D. 517 (1896). "Alaskan Lands—Rights of Natives—Water Supply."

37 L.D. 334 (1908). "Alaskan Townsites—Status and Rights of Indian Occupants."

Aleut Community of St. Paul v. U.S., 480 F. 2d 831 (Ct. Cls. 1973).

Alaska v. Udall, 420 F. 2d 938 (9th Cir. 1969).

Cherokee Nation v. Hitchcock, 187 U.S. 294 (1902).

Davis v. Sitka School Board, 3 Ak. Rpts. 481 (1908).

Edwardsen v. Morton, 159 F. Supp. 1359 (D.C.D.C. 1973).

Heckman v. Sutter, 119 F. 83 (9th Cir. 1902).

Inupiat Community of the Arctic Slope v. U.S. (ICAS I), 680 F. 2d 122 (Ct. Cls.); cert. den. 51 USLW 3339 (1982).

Inupiat Community of the Arctic Slope v. U.S. (ICAS II), 548 F. Supp 185 (D.C. Ak. 1982).

Johnson v. Pacific Coast S.S. Co., 2 Ak. Rpts. 224 (D.C. Ak. 1904).

Johnson v. M'Intosh, 21 U.S. (8 Wheat) 543 (1823).

Miller v. U.S., 159 F. 2d 997 (9th Cir. 1947).

In re Minook, 2 Ak. Rpts. 200 (1904).

Oneida Indian Nation v. County of Oneida, 414 U.S. 661 (1974).

Passamaquoddy Tribe v. Morton, 388 F. Supp. 649, (1975) aff'd. 528 F. 2d 370 (1st Cir. 1975).

Sutter v. Heckman, 1 Ak. Rpts. 188 (D.C. Ak. 1901).

Tee-Hit-Ton Band of Indians v. U.S., 348 U.S. 272 (1955).

Tlingit and Haida Indians of Alaska v. U.S., 177 F. Supp., 452, (Ct. Cls. 1959).

Tlingit and Haida Indians of Alaska v. U.S., 389 G. 2d 778 (Ct. Cls. 1968).

U.S. v. 10.95 Acres of Land, 75 F. Supp. 841 (D.C. Ak. 1948).

U.S. v. Alaska, 201 F. Supp. 796 (D.C. Ak. 1962).

U.S. v. Alaska, 422 U.S. 184 (1975).

U.S. v. ARCO, 435 F. Supp. 1009 (D.C. Ak. 1977); aff'd. 612 F.2d 1132 (9th Cir.); cert. den. 499 U.S. 888 (1980).

U.S. v. Berrigan, 2 Ak. Rpts. 442 (D.C. Ak. 1904).

U.S. v. Cadzow, 5 Ak. Rpts. 125 (D.C. Ak. 1914).

U.S. v. Gemmill, 535 F. 2d 1145 (9th Cir. 1976).

U.S. v. Libby McNeil and Libby, 107 F. Supp. 697 (D.C. Ak. 1952).

U.S. v. Lynch, 7 Ak. Rpts. 568 (1927).

U.S. v. Mitchell (Mitchell I), 445 U.S. 535 (1980).

U.S. v. Mitchell (Mitchell II),_____U.S.____, 51 USLW 4999 (1983).

U.S. v. Santa Fe R. Co., 314 U.S. 339 (1941).

U.S. v. Seveloff, 1 Ak. Fed. Rpts. 64 (1872).

Waters v. Campbell, 1 Ak. Fed. Rpts. 91 (1876).

Worcester v. Georgia, 8 U.S. (6 Pet.) 515 (1832).

Worthen Lumber Mills v. Alaska-Juneau Gold Mining Company, 229 F. 966 (9th Cir. 1916).

C. CHAPTER THREE
RESERVATIONS—Cases and Legal Opinions

49 L.D. 592 (1923), Leasing Lands Within Reservations Created for the Benefit of the Natives of Alaska.

51 L.D. 155 (1925), Power of the Territorial Legislature to Impose a Tax Upon Reindeer Held or Controlled by the Natives of Alaska.

53 I.D. 111 (1930), Creation of Reservation for Alaska Natives (Pertaining to Vocational Education Reserves).

56 I.D. 110 (1937), Authority of the Secretary of Interior to Reserve Waters in Connection with, and Independently of Land Reservations for Alaska Natives under the Act of May 1, 1936.

70 I.D. 166 (1963), Oil and Gas Leasing on Lands Withdrawn by Executive Order for Indian Purposes in Alaska.

M-36761, Op. Sol., Leasability of Lands in Vicinity of Eklutna (May 1, 1967).

34 Op. Attys. Gen. 171 (1924) (Pertaining to Mineral Leasing on Executive Order Reserves).

Alaska Pacific Fisheries v. U.S., 240 F. 274 (9th Cir. 1917); aff'd. Alaska Pacific Fisheries v. U.S., 248 U.S. 78 (1918).

Atkinson v. Haldane, 569 P. 2d 151 (Ak. 1977).

Cape Fox Corp. v. U.S., 456 F. Supp. 784 (D. Ak. 1978); rev'd. on jurisdictional grounds 646 F. 2d 399 (9th Cir. 1981).

Federal Records Center, Seattle. Files of the Territorial Governor. Record Group 348, Box 462, Folder 40-4d #1.

"Hearings on claims of Natives of the Towns of Hydaburg Klawock, and Kake, Alaska, pursuant to the provisions of Section 201.216 of the Regulations for Protection of the Commercial Fisheries of Alaska." Report of Presiding Chairman.

Hynes v. Grimes Packing Co., 337 U.S. 86 (1949).

Kake v. Egan, 369 U.S. 60 (1962).

Menominee Tribe of Indians v. U.S., 391 U.S. 404 (1968).

Metlakatla Indian Community, Annette Island Reserve v. Egan, 369 U.S. 45 (1962).

"Native Village of Karluk and the [R]eservation at Karluk." Unpublished Memorandum. Alaska Regional Solicitor, January 2, 1968.

Sioux Tribe v. U.S., 316 U.S. 317 (1942).

Nagle v. U.S., 191 F. 141 (1911).

U.S. v. Alaska Pacific Fisheries, 5 Ak. Rpts. 484 (D.C. Ak. 1916); aff'd. Alaska Pacific Fisheries v. U.S., 240 F. 2d 274 (9th Cir. 1917); aff'd. Alaska Pacific Fisheries v. U.S., 248 U.S. 78 (1918).

U.S. v. Midwest Oil Co., 236 U.S. 459 (1915).

D. CHAPTER FOUR
NATIVE ALLOTMENTS AND TOWNSITES—Cases and Legal Opinions

13 L.D. 120 (1891). "A. S. Wadleigh."

26 L.D. 104 (1898). "George Kostrometinoff."

26 L.D. 512 (1898). "Louis Greenbaum."

26 L.D. 558 (1898). "Pacific Steam Whaling Co."

28 L.D. 427 (1899). "Kittie Cleogeuh."

28 L.D. 535 (1899). "John G. Brady."

37 L.D. 334 (1908). "Alaskan Townsites—Status and Rights of Indian Occupants."

39 L.D. 597 (1911). "Alaska Commercial Co.;" rev'd. on reconsideration, 41 L.D. 75 (1912).

44 L.D. 113 (1915). "Charlie George."

48 L.D. 362 (1921). "Yakutat & Southern Railway v. Setuck Harry, Heir of Setuck Jim."

52 L.D. 597 (1929). "Frank St. Clair."

53 L.D. 194 (1930). "Frank St. Clair."

54 I.D. 15 (1932). Authority of the Secretary of the Interior to Dispose of Reindeer Belonging to Estates of Deceased Natives of Alaska; reprinted as, "Regulation of Reindeer Owned by Alaska Natives," 1 Op. Sol. on Ind. Aff. 320.

66 I.D. 212 (1959). Disposal of Lots in Saxman Alaska.

67 I.D. 410 (1960). Herbert H. Hilscher.

71 I.D. 340 (1964). Allotment of Lands to Alaska Natives.

83 I.D. 47 (1976). City of Klawock v. Andrew.

88 I.D. 373 (1981). U.S. v. Flynn.

"Administrative Appeal of Nels W. Nelson, Jr., Assoc. Sol., Indian Affairs Memo (March 2, 1981).

Aguilar v. Kleppe (Aguilar I), 424 F. Supp. 433 (D.C. Ak. 1976).

Aguilar v. Kleppe (Aguilar II), 474 F. Supp. 840 (D.C. Ak. 1979).

Alaska v. Agli, 472 F. Supp. 70 (D. C. Ak. 1979).

Alaska v. Udall, 420 F. 2d 938 (9th Cir. 1969).

Aleknagik Natives, Ltd. v. Andrus, 648 F. 2d 496 (9th Cir. 1980).

Archie Wheeler, 1 IBLA 139 (1970).

Assiniboine & Sioux Tribe v. Nordwick, 378 F. 2d 426 (9th Cir. 1967).

Carlo v. Gustafson, 512 F. Supp. 833 (D.C. Ak. 1981).

Choate v. Trapp, 224 U.S. 665 (1912).

City of Klawock v. Andrew, 24 IBLA 85 (1976).

Cramer v. U.S., 261 U.S. 219 (1923).

Critzer v. U.S., 597 F.2d 708 (Ct. Cls. 179); cert. den. 444 U.S. 920.

Eluska v. Andrus, 587 F.2d 996 (9th Cir. 1978).

Fisher v. Fisher 656 P.2d 129 (Ida. 1982).

Frederick Howard, 67 IBLA 157 (1982).

Germina Iron Co. v. U.S., 165 U.S. 379 (1897).

Heffle v. Alaska, 633 P.2d 264 (Ak. 1981).

Herman Joseph, 21 IBLA 199 (1975).

Heckman v. Sutter, 119 F. 83 (9th Cir. 1902).

Henrietta Roberts Vaden, 70 IBLA 171 (1983).

In re Incorporation of Haines Mission, 3 Ak. Rpts. 588 (D.C. Ak. 1908).

John Nusunginya 28 IBLA 83 (1976).

Johnson v. Pacific Coast SS. Co., 2 Ak. Rpts. 224 (1904).

Klawock v. Gustafson, 585 F.2d 428 (9th Cir. 1978).

Lucy Ahvakana 3 IBLA 341 (1971).

McKay v. Kalyton, 204 U.S. 458 (1907).

Mary Olympic, 47 IBLA 58 (1980).

Mary Olympic (On Reconsideration), 65 IBLA 26 (1982).

Nagle v. U.S., 191 F. 141m (9th Cir. 1911).

Northern Cheyenne Tribe v. Hollowbreast, 425 U.S. 649 (1976).

Oklahoma Tax Commission v. U.S., 319 U.S. 598 (1943).

Pence v. Kleppe (Pence I), 529 F. 2d 135 (9th Cir. 1976).

Pence v. Andrus (Pence II), 586 F. 2d 733b (9th Cir. 1978).

People of South Naknek v. Bristol Bay Borough, 466 F. Supp. 870 (D. Ak. 1979).

Royal Harris, 45 IBLA 87 (1980).

Russian American Co. v. U.S., 199 U.S. 570 (1905).

Scholder v. U.S., 428 F.2d 1123 (9th Cir. 1970); cert. den. 400 U.S. 942.

Seminole Nation v. U.S. 613 (1913).

Sheppard v. Sheppard, 655 P.2d 895 (Ida. 1982).

Shields v. U.S., 504 F. Supp. 1216 (D.C. Ak. 1981); aff'd. Shields v. U.S., 698 F.2d 987 (9th Cir. 1983).

Squire v. Capoeman, 351 U.S. 1 (1956).

Starr v. Long Jim, 227 U.S. 613 (1913).

State of Alaska, 45 IBLA 318 (1980).

Stephen Kenyon (On Reconsideration), 65 IBLA 44 (1982).

Tooahnippah v. Hickel, 397 U.S. 598 (1970).

U.S. v. 10.95 Acres of Land, 75 F. Supp. 841 (D.C. Ak. 1948).

U.S. v. Alaska, 201 F. Supp. 796 (D. C. Ak. 1962).

U.S. v. Anderson, 625 F.2d 910 (9th Cir. 1980); cert. den. 450 U.S. 920.

U.S. v. Bowling, 256 U.S. 484 (1921).

U.S. v. Clarke, 445 U.S. 253 (1980).

U.S. v. Flynn, 53 IBLA 208 (1981).

U.S. v. Jackson, 280 U.S. 183 (1930).

U.S. v. Lynch, 7 Ak. Rpts. 568 (D.C. Ak. 1927).

U.S. v. Mitchell (Mitchell I), 445 U.S. 535 (1980).

U.S. v. Mitchell (Mithcell II), 5l USLW 4999 (1983).

U.S. v. Rickert, 188 U.S. 432 (1902).

West v. Oklahoma Tax Commission, 334 U.S. 717 (1948).

Yellowfish v. City of Stillwater, 691 F.2d 926 (10th Cir. 1982); cert. den. 51 USLW 3825.

PART III: FEDERAL HUMAN SERVICE OBLIGATIONS

CHAPTER FIVE
HISTORY OF NATIVE SERVICES IN ALASKA

CHAPTER SIX
NATIVE ENTITLEMENT TO SERVICES

A. Selected Books, Articles and Memoranda

Anderson, H. D., and W. C. Eells. *Alaska Natives A Survey of Their Sociological and Educational Status.* Stanford: Stanford University Press, 1935.

Andrews, C.L., ed. *The Eskimo,* Vol. 7, No. 4, 1-6. Seattle, Wash, Oct. 1940. Microfilm M939, #273, Terr. Gov. Files 40-40c, "Natives." Federal Records Center, Seattle.

Cohen, F. *Handbook of Federal Indian Law.* 1982 ed. Charlottesville, Va.: Michie-Bobbs Merrill, 1982.

———. *Handbook of Federal Indian Law.* Washington, D.C.: Government Printing Office, 1942. Reprint New York: AMS, 1972.

Davis, K. C. *Administrative Law Treatise.* St. Paul, Minn.: West Publishing Co., 1958.

Federal Field Committee for Development Planning in Alaska. *Alaska Natives and the Land.* Anchorage: Federal Field Committee, 1968.

Getches, D. H. *Law and Alaska Native Education.* Fairbanks: University of Alaska, Center for Northern Educational Research, 1977.

Hawkins, J. E. *A Preliminary Profile of Federal Programs Provided to Alaska Natives.* Washington, D.C.: Assistant Secretary of Indian Affairs, 1982.

Jackson, S. *Annual Report on Introduction of Domestic Reindeer into Alaska.* 16 vols. Washington, D. C.: Government Printing Office, 1890-1906.

Jones, Richard S., *Federal Programs of Assistance to American Indians.* Report to the Senate Select Committee on Indian Affairs, 96th Cong., 2d sess., Dec. 1982.

Juneau Area Activities 1975-1976. Juneau: Bureau of Indian Affairs, 1976.

Lindley, M. F. *The Acquistion and Government of Backward Territory in International Law.* 1926. Reprint. New York: Negro Universities Press, 1969.

Marsh, W. R. *North to the Future, Alaska Department of Education and Education in Alaska, 1785-1967.* Juneau: State of Alaska, Department of Education, 1967.

"Memorandum of General Agreement." Alaska State Department of Education—Bureau of Indian Affairs, March 1, 1962.

Nathan, Robert R. and Associates, Inc. *2(c) Report: Federal Programs and Alaska Natives.* Anchorage: Robert R. Nathan and Associates, Inc. [1975].

Rainey, F. G. "Memorandum Concerning Control and Ownership of Native Reindeer in Arctic Alaska." Files of Terr. Gov., M-939, #237, File 40-04, "Native Misc," 1939. Federal Records Center, Seattle.

Scott, A. W. *Law of Trusts.* vol. 1. Boston: Little Brown and Co., 1967.

Snow, A. H. *The Question of Aboriginies in the Law and Practice of Nations.* 1919. Reprint. Northbrook, Ill.: Metro Books, Inc., 1972.

B. Cases and Opinions

89 I.D. 196 (1982) Aleutian-Pribilof Island Assoc. v. Acting Deputy Assistant Secretary Indian Affairs (Operations).

Alaska Chapter, Associated General Contractors of America v. Pierce, 694 F. 2d 1162 (9th Cir. 1980).

Alaska Pacific Fisheries v. U.S., 248 U.S. 78 (1918).

Aleut Community of St. Paul Island v. United States, 480 F. 2d 831 (Ct. Cls. 1973).

Aleutian-Pribilof Islands Assoc. v. Acting Deputy Assistant Secretary Indian Affairs (Operations), 9 IBIA 254 (1982).

Board of Regents v. Roth, 408 U.S. 564 (1972).

In re Carr, 1 Ak. Rpts., 75 (D.C. Or. 1875).

Cherokee Nation v. Georgia, 30 U.S. (5 Pet) 1 (1831).

Dandridge v. Williams, 397 U.S. 471 (1970).

Eric v. Secretary of U.S. Dept. of Housing and Urban Dev., 464 F. Supp. 44 (D.C. Ak. 1978).

Fox v. Morton, 505 F. 2d 254 (9th Cir. 1974).

Gila River Pima-Maricopa Band of Indians v. U.S., 427 F.2d 1194 (Ct. Cls. 1970).

Goldberg v. Kelly, 397 U.S. 254 (1970).

Gritts v. Fisher, 224 U.S. 640 (1912).

Hamilton v. Butz, 520 F. 2d 709 (9th Cir. 1975).

Hootch v. Alaska State-Operated School System, 536 P. 2d 793 (Ak. 1975).

Hydaburg Cooperative Association v. U.S., 667 F.2d 64 (Ct. Cls. 1981).

Koniag v. Kleppe, 495 F. Supp. 1360 (D.C.D.C. 1975).

Lewis v. Weinberger, 415 F. Supp. 652 (D.C. N. Mex. 1976).

McClenahan v. Arizona, 411 U.S. 164 (1973).

Menominee Tribe v. U.S., 391 U.S. 404 (1968).

Morton v. Ruiz, 415 U.S. 199 (1972).

Pence v. Kleppe, 529 F. 2d 135 (9th Cir. 1976).

Perrin v. U.S., 232 U.S. 478 (1914).

Rockbridge v. Lincoln, 449 F. 2d 567 (9th Cir. 1971).

"Scope of the Snyder Act of November 2, 1921." Op. Sol., M-36857, February 22, 1973.

Seminole Nation v. U.S., 316 U.S. 286 (1942).

Squire v. Capoeman, 351 U.S. 1 (1956).

Territory of Alaska v. Annette Island Packing Co., 289 F. 671 (9th Cir. 1923).

13th Regional Corporation v. Department of the Interior, 654 F. 2d 758 (D. C. Cir. 1980).

Tiger v. Western Investment Co., 221 U.S. 286 (1911).

"Tlingit and Haida Community Councils and Second Class City Councils—Status Under P.L. 93-638." Op. Alaska Reg. Sol., January 5, 1977.

"Transfer of BIA School Sites in Alaska." Op. Alaska Reg. Sol., May 14, 1982.

U.S. v. Berrigan, 2 Ak. Rpts. 442 (D.C. Ak. 1905).

U.S. v. Candelaria, 271 U.S. 432 (1925).

U.S. v. Chavez, 290 U.S. 357 (1933).

U.S. v. Holliday, 70 U.S. (3 Wall.) 407 (1852).

U.S. v. Kagama, 118 U.S. 375 (1886).

U.S. v. McGowen, 302 U.S. 535 (1938).

U.S. v. Lomen & Co., 8 AK. Rpts. 1 (D.C. Ak. 1921).

U.S. v. Mitchell (Mitchell I), 445 U.S. 535 (1980).

U.S. v. Mitchell (Mitchell II), 51 USLW 4999 (1983).

U.S. v. Sandoval, 231 U.S. 28 (1913).

U.S. v. Seveloff, 1 Ak. Rpts. 64 (D.C. Or. 1872).

U.S. v. Thomas, 151 U.S. 577 (1894).

White v. Califano, 437 F. Supp. 543 (D.C.S.D. 1977); aff'd. per curiam, 581 F. 2d 697 (8th Cir. 1978).

White v. Matthews, 420 F. Supp. 882 (D.C.S.D. 1976).

Wilson v. Watt, 703 F. 2d 395 (9th Cir. 1983).

PART IV: THE FEDERAL OBLIGATION TO
PROTECT SUBSISTENCE

CHAPTER SEVEN
SUBSISTENCE IN ALASKA

A. Selected Books, Articles and Memoranda

"Alaska Native Claims Settlement Act Implementation and Policy Review." Asst. Secretary, Land and Water Resources, Dept. of the Interior. Memorandum, March 3, 1978.

Arnold, R. D. *Alaska Native Land Claims.* 2nd ed. Anchorage: Alaska Native Foundation, 1978.

Camerino, v. "Subsistence in Alaska and the Effect of H.R. 39." *American Indian Law Journal.* 3 (December 1976): 16-22.

———. "Case of the Bowhead Whale." *American Indian Law Journal.* 3 (December 1976): 23-25.

Davidson, A. *Does One Way of Life Have to Die So Another Can Live? A Report of Subsistence and the Conservation of the Yupik Life-Style.* Bethel, Ak.: Yupiktak Bista, 1974.

Dunnigan, J. H. *Alaskan Natives and Marine Mammals Law and Policy Affecting Life Style.* Unpublished Paper. Seattle, WA.: Indian Legal Problems Seminar, University of Washington School of Law, 1974.

History and Implementation of Ch. 151 SLA 1978, The State's Subsistence Law. Draft Report. Juneau: Alaska House of Representatives Special Committee on Subsistence, May 15, 1981.

Johnson, R. W. "The States Versus Indian Off-Reservation Fishing: A United States Supreme Court Error." *Wash. L. Rev.* 47 (1971): 207.

Jones, D. V. *License for Empire: Colonialism by Treaty in Early America.* Chicago: University of Chicago Press, 1982.

Kelso, D. D. "Legal Issues in Federal Protection of Subsistence on the Proposed National Interest Lands." Reprinted in *Hearings on Inclusion of Alaska Lands in National Park, Forest, Wildlife Refuge and Wild and Scenic Rivers Systems.* House Committee on Interior and Insular Affairs. Subcommittee on General Oversight and Alaska Lands. 95th Cong., 1st sess., April 21 and 22, 1977. Serial 95-16, pt. 1.

McBeath, G. *North Slope Borough Government and Policymaking.* Fairbanks: Institute for Social and Economic Research, University of Alaska, 1981.

Mitchell, D. "Alaska Native Subsistence and H.R. 39." Unpublished Memorandum. Anchorage: Rural Alaska Community Action Program, July 10, 1978.

"Policy Statement on Subsistence Utilization of Fish and Game." Alaska Department of Fish and Game and Board of Fish and Game. Joint Memorandum, May 4, 1973.

Spicer, E. *A Short History of the Indian of the United States.* New York: Van Nostrand Co., 1969.

"Subsistence law: real and perceived problems." Op. Ak. Atty. Gen. File No. 166-448-83, February 25, 1983.

Udall, S. L. "The Alaska Natives and Their Subsistence Rights: A Discussion of the Constitutional Questions." Unpublished Memorandum. Anchorage: Alaska Federation of Natives, July 1977.

B. Cases and Opinions

54 I.D. 517 (1934) Migratory Bird Treaty Act and Swinomish Indian Reservation.

Adams v. Vance, 570 F. 2d 950 (D.C. Cir. 1978).

Alaska Pacific Fisheries v. U.S., 248 U.S. 78 (1919).

Alaska Public Easement Defense Fund 435 F. Supp. 664 (D.C. Ak. 1977).

Antoine v. Washington, 420 U.S. 194 (1975).

Cheyenne-Arapaho Tribes v. Oklahoma, 618 F. 2d 665 (10th Cir. 1980).

Cheyenne-Arapaho Tribes v. Oklahoma, 681 F. 2d 705 (10th Cir. 1982).

Committee for Humane Legislation, Inc. v. Richardson, 414 F. Supp. 297 (D.C.D.C. 1976) aff'd. 540 F. 2d 1141 (D.C. Cir. 1976).

Fouke Company v. Mandel, 386 F. Supp. 1341 (D.C. Md. 1974).

Frank v. State, 604 P. 2d 1068 (Ak. 1979).

Hopson v. Kreps, 462 F. Supp. 1374 (D. Ak. 1979); rev'd., 622 F. 2d 1375 (9th Cir. 1980).

Kake v. Egan, 369 U.S. 60 (1962).

Kenai Penninsula Fishermen's Cooperative Assoc. v. State, 628 P. 2d 897 (Ak. 1981).

Kimball v. Callahan, 493 F. 2d 564 (9th Cir.); cert. den., 419 U.S. 1019 (1974).

Kimball v. Callahan, 590 F. 2d 768 (9th Cir.); cert. den., 444 U.S. 826 (1979).

Lone Wolf v. Hitchcock, 187 U.S. 553 (1903).

Menominee Tribe v. U.S. 391 U.S. 404 (1968).

Metlakatla v. Egan, 369 U.S. 552 (1962).

Missouri v. Holland, 252 U.S. 416 (1920).

Montana v. U.S., 450 U.S. 544 (1981).

Morton v. Mancari, 417 U.S. 535 (1974).

Nevada v. U.S., ____ U.S. ____, 51 USLW 4974 (1983).

New Mexico v. Mescalero Apache Tribe, ____ U.S. ____, 76 L. Ed. 2d 611, 51 USLW 47412 (1983).

North Slope Borough v. Andrus, 486 F. Supp. 332 (D.C.D.C. 1980); rev'd. in part, 642 F. 2d 589 (D.C. Cir. 1980).

People of Togiak v. U.S., 470 F. Supp. 423 (D.C.D.C. 1979).

Puyallup Tribe v. Department of Game (Puyallup I), 391 U.S. 392 (1968).

Puyallup Tribe v. Department of Game (Puyallup III), 433 U.S. 165 (1977).

Pyramid Lake Paiute Tribe of Indians v. Morton, 354 F. Supp. 252 (D.C.D.C. 1973).

Recommended Decision Concerning Resumption of State Management Over Nine Species of Marine Mammals, MMPA Docket No. WASH 76-1, June 30, 1977.

State v. Tanana Valley Sportsman Association, 582 P. 2d 854 (Ak. 1978).

State of California v. Watt, 668 F. 2d 1290 (D.C. Cir. 1981).

Tulee v. Washington, 315 U.S. 863 (1942).

U.S. v. Michigan, 471 F. Supp. 192 (W.D. Mich. 1979); aff'd. in pertinent part and remanded, 653 F. 2d 277 (6th Cir. 1981).

U.S. v. Washington, 384 F. Supp. 312 (W.D. Wash. 1974); aff'd. 520 F. 2d 676 (9th Cir. 1975); cert. den., 423 U.S. 1086.

U.S. v. Winans, 198 U.S. 371 (1905).

Village of Kaktovik v. Watt, 689 F. 2d 222 (D. C. Cir. 1982).

Washington v. Washington State Passenger Fishing Vessel Association, 443 U.S. 658 (1979).

Washington Game Department v. Puyallup Tribe (Puyallup II), 414 U.S. 44 (1973).

White Mountain Apache Tribe v. Arizona, 649 F. 2d 1274 (9th Cir. 1981).

PART V: ALASKA NATIVE SELF-GOVERNMENT

CHAPTER EIGHT
TRADITIONAL ALASKA NATIVE SOCIETIES

Birket-Smith, K. *The Chugach Eskimo.* Copenhagen: Natinal Musseets Skrifter, Ethnografisk, Raekke, 1953.

————., and F. de Laguna. *Eyak Indians of the Copper River Delta, Alaska.* Copenhagen: Lavin and Monksgaard, 1938.

Burch, E. S., Jr. "Traditional Eskimo Societies in Northwest Alaska." Senri Ethnological Studies 4. Osaka, Japan: National Museum of Ethnology, 1980.

————. *The Traditional Eskimo Hunters of Point Hope, Alaska: 1800-1975.* Barrow, Ak.: North Slope Borough, 1981.

————. "The Caribou/Wild Reindeer as a Human Resource." *American Antiquity* 37 (1972): 356.

————. *Eskimo Kinsmen: Changing Family Relationships in Northwest Alaska.* San Francisco: West Publishing Co., 1975.

————. "Indians and Eskimos in North Alaska, 1816-1977: A Study in Changing Ethnic Relations." *Arctic Anthropology* 16 (1969): 123-151.

Burch, E.S., Jr. and T. C. Correll. "Alliance and Conflict: Inter-Regional Relations in North Alaska." *Alliance in Eskimo Society.* Edited by D. L. Guemple. Proceedings of the American Ethnological Scoiety, 1971, Supplement. Seattle: University of Washington Press, 1972.

Chance, N. *The Eskimo of North Alaska.* New York: Holt Rinehart and Winston, 1966.

Collins, H. B., et al. *The Aleutian Islands: Their People and Natural History.* Smithsonian Institution War Background Studies, No. 21. Washington, D.C.: Government Printing Office, 1945.

Davydov, G. L. *Two Voyages to Russian America, 1802-1807.* Edited by R. A. Pierce. Kingston, Ontario: The Limestone Press, 1977.

de Laguna, F. "Under Mount St. Elias: The History and Culture of the Yakutat Tlingit." Vol. 7, pt. 1. *Smithsonian Contributions to Anthropology.* Washington, D.C.: Smithsonian Institution, 1972.

———. "Matrilineal Kin Groups in Northwestern North America." Proceedings of the Northern Athapaskan Conference, 1971. Paper No. 27. *Canadian Ethnology Service* 1 (1975).

———. "Aboriginal Tlingit Sociopolitical Organization." In *The Development of Political Organization.* Edited by E. Tooker. Proceedings of the American Ethnological Society, 1979. Washington, D.C.: The American Ethnological Society, 1983.

———. *The Story of A Tlingit Community: A Problem in Relationship Between Archaeological, Ethnological, and Historical Methods.* Bulletin 172, Smithsonian Institution, Bureau of American Ethnology. Washington, D.C.: Government Printing Office, 1960.

———., McClellan, C. "Ahtna." In *Handbook of North American Indians.* Vol 6, *Subarctic.* Washington, D.C.: Smithsonian Institution, 1981.

Drucker, P. *Indians of the Northwest Coast.* Garden City, N. Y.: Natural History Press, 1955.

Cultures of the North Pacific Coast. New York: Chandler, 1965.

Ellanna, L. J. *Bering Strait Insular Eskimo: A Diachronic Study of Economy and Population Structure.* Technical Paper 77. Juneau: Alaska Department of Fish and Game, Division of Subsistence, 1983.

Fall, J. A. "Patterns of Upper Inlet Tanaina Leadership, 1741-1918." Ph.D. diss., University of Wisconsin, 1981.

Fienup-Riordan, A. *The Nelson Island Eskimo: Social Structure and Ritual Distribution.* Anchorage: Alaska Pacific University Press, 1983.

Garfield, V. E. *Tsimshian Clan and Society.* Seattle: University of Washington Publications, 1939.

Garfield, V.E. and P. S. Wingert. *The Tsimshian Indians and Their Arts.* Seattle: University of Washington Press, 1966.

Gedeon, F. "Memoirs." In *One Hundredth Anniversary of Orthodoxy in America.* St. Petersburg, Russia: Valaam Monastery, 1804.

Goldschmidt, W. R. and T. Haas. *Possessory Rights of the Natives of Southeastern Alaska.* Mimeographed Report to the Commissioner of Indian Affairs. Washington, D. C.: U.S. Department of the Interior, [1942].

Gubser, N. J. *The Nunamiut Eskimos: Hunters of Caribou.* Forge Village, Mass.: Murray Printing Co., 1965.

Guedon, M-F. *People of Tetlin, Why Are You Singing?* Mercury Series, Paper 9. Ottawa: National Museum of Man, Ethnology Division, 1964.

Gunther, E. *Indian Life of the Northwest Coast of North America.* Chicago: University of Chicago Press, 1972.

Helm, J. et al. *The Contact History of the Subarctic Athapaskans: An Overview.* Proceedings of the Northern Athapaskan Conference, 1971. Paper No. 27, vol. 1. Canadian Ethnology Service, 1975.

Hosley, E. H. "Environment and Culture in the Alaska Plateau." In *Handbook of North American Indians.* Vol. 6 *Subarctic.* Washington, D.C.: Smithsonian Institution, 1981.

Hughes, C. C. *An Eskimo Village in the Modern World.* Ithaca, N.Y.: Cornell University, 1960.

Jones, D. *A Century of Servitude: Pribilof Aleuts Under U.S. Rule.* Lanham, Md.: University Press of America, 1980.

Kari, P. *Land Use and Economy of Lime Village.* Technical Paper 80. Juneau: Alaska Department of Fish and Game, Division of Subsistence, 1983.

Krauss, M. E. *Alaska Native Languages: Past Present and Future.* Alaska Native Language Center Research Paper No. 4. Fairbanks: University of Alaska, 1980.

Krause, A. *The Tlingit Indians.* (1885) Trans. by E. Gunther. Seattle: University of Washington Press, 1956.

Lantis, M. "The Social Culture of Nunivak Eskimo." N.S. Vol. 35, Pt. 3 *Transactions of the American Philosophical Society* (1946).

————. *The Aleut Social System, 1750-1810, from Early Historical Sources.* Ethnohistory in Southwestern Alaska and the Southern Yukon, Studies in Anthropology, No. 7, pt. 2. Lexington, Ky.: The University Press of Kentucky, 1970.

————, ed. *Ethnohistory in Southwestern Alaska and the Southern Yukon.* Studies in Anthropology No. 7. Lexington, Ky.: University Press of Kentucky, 1970.

Laughlin, W. S. *Aleuts: Survivors of the Bering Land Bridge.* New York: Hall, Rinehart and Winston, 1980.

Lisiansky, U. *A voyage around the World in the Years 1803, 1804, 1805, and 1806.* 1814.

McClellan, C. "Culture Contacts in the Early Historic Period Northwestern North America." *Arctic Anthropology* 2 (1964):3-15.

McFadyen, C. "Koyukon." In *Handbook of North American Indians.* Vol. 6, *Subarctic.* Washington, D.C.: Smithsonian Institution, 1981.

McKennan, R. *The Chandalar Kutchin.* Technical Paper No. 17. Arctic Institute of North America, 1965.

Merculieff, L. "Traditional Living in a Modern Society." *Alaska Geographic: Islands of the Seals, the Pribilofs* 9 (1982).

Morgan, L., ed. *Alaska Geographic: The Aleutians* 7 (1980).

Murdock, J. "Ethnological Results of the Point Barrow Expedition." *Ninth Annual Report of the Bureau of American Ethnology, 1887-1888.* Washington, D. C.: Government Printing Office, 1892.

Nelson, E. W. *The Eskimo About Bering Strait.* Part 1, 18th Annual Report. Bureau of American Ethnology, 1896-97. Washington, D.C.: Government Printing Office, 1889.

Nelson, H., H. Graburn, and B. S. Strong. *Circumpolar Peoples: And Anthropological Perspective.* Pacific Palisades, Calif.: Goodyear, 1973.

Nelson, R. K. *Athapaskan Subsistence Adaptations in Alaska.* Senri Ethnological Study 4. Osaka, Japan: National Museum of Ethnology, 1980.

———. *The Athabaskans: People of the Boreal Forest.* Alaska Historical Commission Studies in History No. 27. Fairbanks: University of Alaska Museum, 1983.

Oberg, K. *The Social Economy of the Tlingit Indians.* Seattle: University of Washington Press, 1973.

Osgood, C. *Contributions to the Ethnography of the Kutchin.* Yale University Publication in Anthropology No. 14, 1936.

———. *Ethnography of the Tanaina.* Yale University Publications in Anthropology No. 16 1937.

———. *Ingalik Social Culture.* Yale University Publications in Anthropology No. 53, 1958.

Oswalt, W. *Napaskiak, An Alaskan Eskimo Community.* Tucson, Ariz.: University of Arizona Press, 1963.

———. *The Ethnoarchaeology of Crow Village.* Smithsonian Institute, Bureau of American Ethnology, Bulletin No. 199. Washington, D.C: U.S. Government Printing Office, 1967.

———. "The Tlingit." In *This Land Was Theirs.* New York: John Wiley and Sons, 1966.

———. *Alaskan Eskimos.* San Francisco: Chandler, 1967.

———. *Mission of Change in Alaska.* San Marino, Calif.: The Huntington Library, 1963.

Patty, S. H. "A Conference with the Tanana Chiefs: A Memorable Gathering at Fairbanks in the Summer of 1915." *Alaska Journal.* 1 (1971): 2-18.

Paul, W., Sr. "My Family Came to Claim This Land." *Alaska Geographic* 3 (1979): 235.

Pribilof Island Logs, Reel No. 20, October 21, 1902. University of Alaska Archives, Fairbanks.

Ray, D. J. *The Tribes of Bering Strait, 1650-1898.* Seattle: University of Washington Press, 1975.

Rogers, G. W. *Alaska in Transition: The Southeast Region.* Baltimore: Johns Hopkins, 1960.

Shinkwin, A. and M. Case. *Modern Foragers: Wild Resource Use in Nenana Village, Alaska.* Technical Paper 91A. Juneau: Alaska Department of Fish and Game, Division of Subsistence, 1984.

Slobodin, R. "Kutchin." In *Handbook of North American Indians.* Vol. 6, *Subarctic.* Washington, D.C.: Smithsonian Institution, 1981.

Snow, J. H. "Ingalik." In *Handbook of North American Indians.* Vol. 6, *Subarctic.* Washingnton, D.C.: Smithsonian Institution, 1981.

Townsend, J. B. "Tanaina." In *Handbook of North American Indians.* Vol 6, *Subarctic.* Washington, D.C.: Smithsonian Institution, 1981.

———. *Ranked Societies of the Alaskan Pacific Rim.* Senri Ethnological Study 4. Osaka, Japan: National Museum of Ethnology, 1980.

Van Stone, J. W. *Point Hope, An Eskimo Village in Transition.* Seattle: University of Washington Press, 1966.

———. *Eskimos of the Nushagak River.* Seattle: University of Washington Press, 1967.

———. *Athapaskan Adaptations.* Chicago: Adeline Publishing Co., 1974.

Wolfe, R. J. "Food Production in a Western Eskimo Population." Ph.D. diss., University of California, Los Angeles, 1979.

———. *Sound/Yukon Delta Sociocultural Systems Baseline Analysis.* Technical Paper 59. Juneau: Alaska Department of Fish and Game, Division of Subsistence, 1981.

———. "Alaska's Great Sickness, 1900: An Epidemic of Measles and Influeza in a Virgin Soil Population." *Proceedings of the American Philosophical Society* 126 (1982).

Zagoskin, L. A. *Lieutenant Zagoskin's Travels in Russian America, 1842-1844.* Toronto: University of Toronto Press, 1967.

CHAPTER NINE
MODERN ALASKA NATIVE GOVERNMENTS
AND ORGANIZATIONS

A. Books, Articles and Memoranda

1975-76 Juneau Area Activities Report. Juneau: Bureau of Indian Affairs, 1976.

1983 Annual Report Alaska Federation of Natives. Anchorage: Alaska Federation of Natives, n. d.

American Indian Policy Review Commission. *Joint Task Force Report on Alaskan Native Issues.* Washington, D.C.: Government Printing Office, 1976.

————. *Final Report of the American Indian Policy Review Commission.* Washington, D.C.: Government Printing Office, 1977.

"Approval of Claims Attorney Contracts of Arctic Slope and AHTNA Tanaah Ninnah Association (Copper River Indian Land Association)." Op. Sol. M-36744, April 8, 1968.

Arnold, R. D. *Alaska Native Land Claims.* Anchorage: Alaska Native Foundation, 1976.

Case, D. S. *Twenty-Four Ordinances to Enforce Local Law Through the Alaska "Village" Council (With Comments).* Anchorage: Alaska Federation of Natives, 1977.

Dena' Nena' Henash. Fairbanks: Tanana Chiefs Conference, Inc., [1980].

A Development Planning Program for the Central Council of the Tlingit and Haida Indians of Alaska. Juneau: Tlingit and Haida Central Council, 1970.

"Eligibility of Alaska Federation of Natives for Loan from Revolving Loan Fund." Op. Sol. M-36772, July 8, 1968.

McKenzie, E. *Report of the Third Bush Justice Conference.* Anchorage: Alaska Federation of Natives, 1977.

The Maniilaq Association 1983 Annual Report and Directory of Services. Kotzebue, Ak.: Maniilaq Association, n. d.

Mauneluk Report 1 (August 1977).

Morehouse, T. A., G. McBeath and L. Leask. *Alaska's Urban and Rural Governments.* New York: University Press of America, 1984.

NANA Regional Strategy. Kotzebue, Ak.: Maniilaq Association, 1982.

Problems and Possibilities for Service Delivery and Government in the Alaska Unorganized Borough. Anchorage: Alaska Department of Community and Regional Affairs, 1981.

"Publication of Alaska Villages Recognized as Tribes Receiving Services from the Bureau of Indian Affairs [25 CFR 54.6(b)]." Memorandum. from Juneau Area Director to Deputy Assistant Secretary— Indian Affairs (Operations), May 28, 1982.

Tlingit and Haida Indian Tribes of Alaska Annual Report for the Year Ending September 30, 1983. Juneau: Tlingit and Haida Central Council, n. d.

Walleri, M. *Tribal-State Relations: A New Paradigm for Local Government in Alaska.* Fairbanks: Tanana Chiefs Conference, n. d.

B. Constitutions and Other Organic Documents

AHTNA Regional Corporation. *Articles of Incorporation* (1972). Juneau: Alaska Department of Commerce.

Alaska Federation of Natives, Inc. *Articles of Incorporation* (1967). Juneau: Alaska Department of Commerce.

———. *ByLaws* (October 22 1980). Anchorage: Alaska Federation of Natives, Inc.

Alaska Native Brotherhood and Sisterhood. *Constitution and By-Laws* [1984].

———. *Constitution* (1963).

Brevig Mission. *Community Constitution and By-Laws* (n. d.) On file with BIA, Anchorage Agency.

Bristol Bay Area Development Corporation. *Articles of Incorporation* (May 23, 1969).

Bristol Bay Native Association. *Articles of Incorporation* (January 21, 1973). Juneau: Alaska Department of Commerce.

Bristol Bay Native Association. *By-Laws* (n. d.) Dillingham, Ak.: Bristol Bay Native Association.

Fay, G., ed. *Charters, Constitutions and By-Laws of the Indian Tribes of North America.* Part 15. *Northwest and Alaska.* Greeley, Colo.: University of Northern Colorado, 1972.

————. *Charters, Constitutions and By-Laws of the Indian Tribes of North America.* Part 16. *Eskimo and Indian Villages of Alaska.* Greeley, Colo.: University of Northern Colorado, 1980.

Hydaburg Cooperative Association. *Constitution and By-Laws of the Hydaburg Cooperative Association Alaska* (April 14, 1938). Washington, D.C.: U.S. Department of the Interior.

————. *Corporate Charter of the Hydaburg Cooperative Association Alaska* (April 14, 1938). Washington, D.C.: U.S. Department of the Interior.

Kenaitze Indian Tribe. *Constitution of the Kenaitze Indian Tribe* (1971). Washington, D.C.: U.S. Department of the Interior.

Maniilaq Association. *Articles of Incorporation* (1973), as amended. Juneau: Alaska Department of Commerce.

————. *By-Laws* (May 6, 1976), as amended. Kotzebue, Ak.: Maniilaq Association.

Metlakatla Indian Community. *Constitution and By-Laws of the Metlakatla Indian Community Annette Islands Reserve Alaska* (August 23, 1944). Washington, D.C.: U.S. Department of the Interior.

————. *Corporate Charter of the Metlakatla Indian Community* (December 19, 1944). Washington, D.C.: U.S. Department of the Interior.

Tanana Chiefs Conference, Inc. *Articles of Incorporation of Dena' Nena' Henash* (September 27, 1971). Juneau: Alaska Department of Commerce.

———. *Bylaws of Dena' Nena' Henash (Tanana Chiefs Conference, Incorporated)* (March 1983). Fairbanks: Tanana Chiefs Conference.

Tlingit and Haida Central Council. *Constitution of the Central Council of the Tlingit and Haida Indian Tribes of Alaska* (April 17, 1973, as amended through 1984). Juneau: Tlingit and Haida Central Council.

———. *Rules for the Election of Delegates to the Official Central Council of Tlingit and Haida Indian Tribes of Alaska* (November 1977, as amended through 1984). Juneau: Tlingit and Haida Central Council.

Tonuak Indian Credit Association. *Articles of Association and By-laws for the Tonuak Indian Credit Association, Dillingham, Alaska* (1951). Juneau: Bureau of Indian Affairs.

CHAPTER TEN
"SOVEREIGNTY": THE ALASKA NATIVE CLAIM TO SELF-GOVERNMENT

A. Books, Articles and Memoranda

American Indian Policy Review Commission. *Final Report of the American Indian Policy Review Commission.* Washington, D.C.: U.S. Government Printing Office, 1977.

———. *Task Force Four: Federal, State, and Tribal Jurisdiction. Washington, D.C.: U.S. Government Printing Office, 1976.*

———. *Special Joint Task Force Report on Alaskan Native Issues.* Washington, D.C.: U.S. Government Printing Office, 1976.

Anderson, H.D. and W.C. Eells. *Alaska Natives: A Survey of Their Sociological and Educational Status.* Stanford, Calif.: Stanford University Press, 1935.

Arnott, S. "Legislation: The Alaska Native Claims Settlement Act: Legislation Appropriate to the Past and the Future." *Amer. Ind. L. Rev.* 8 (1981): 135.

Berman, H. R. "The Concept of Aboriginal Rights in the Early Legal History of the United States." *Buffalo L. Rev.* 27 (Fall 1978): 637.

Chambers, R. P. "Judicial Enforcement of the Federal Trust Responsibility to Indians." *Stanford L. Rev.* 27 (1975): 1213.

Clinebell, J. S. and J. Thomson. "Sovereignty and Self-Determination: The Rights of Native Americans Under International Laws." *Buffalo L. Rev.* 27 (Fall 1978): 669.

Cohen, F. *Handbook of Federal Indian Law.* 1982 ed. Charlottesville, Va.: Michie Bobbs-Merrill Law Publishers, 1982.

———. *Handbook of Federal Indian Law.* 1942. Reprint. New York: AMS Press, Inc., 1972.

———. "The Spanish Origin of Indian Rights in the Law of the United States." In *The Legal Conscience.* New Haven, Conn.: Yale University Press, 1960. Reprinted Archon Books, 1970.

Drinnon, R. *Facing West: Metaphysics of Indian-Hating and Empire-Building.* Minneapolis: University of Minnesota Press, 1980.

Duvall. "Delineation of the Powers of the Alaska Home Rule City: The Need for a Beginning." *Alaska Law J.* 8 (October 1970): 232.

Federal Field Committee for Development Planning in Alaska. *Alaska Natives and the Land.* Anchorage: Federal Field Committee, 1968.

Getches, D. H., D. M. Rosenfelt, and C. F. Wilkinson. *Federal Indian Law Cases and Materials.* St. Paul, Minn.: West Publishing Co., 1979.

———. *Federal Indian Law Cases and Materials.* 1983 Supp. St. Paul, Minn.: West Publishing Co., 1983.

Goldberg, C. E. "Public Law 280: The Limits of State Jurisdiction Over Reservation Indians." *UCLA L. Rev.* 22 (1975): 535.

Gruening, E. *The State of Alaska.* New York: Random House, 1968.

Hanke, L. *All Mankind is One—A Study of the Disputation Between Bartolome de Las Casas and Juan Gines de Sepulveda on the Religious and Intellectual Capacity of the American Indians.* DeKalb, Ill.: Northern Illinois University Press, 1974.

Hippler, A. and S. Conn. "The Village Council and Its Offspring: A Reform for Bush Justice." *UCLA L. Rev.* 5 (1975): 22.

"The Indian Child Welfare Act: Does It Cover Custody Disputes Among Extended Family Members?" *Alaska L. Rev.* 1 (Summer 1984): 157.

Johnson, R. W. "Indians and Equal Protection." *Wash. L. Rev.* 54 (June 1979): 587.

Jones, D. V. *License for Empire.* Chicago: University of Chicago Press, 1982.

Kickingbird, K. "Indian Sovereignty: The American Experience." In *Pathways to Self-Determination: Canadian Indians and the Canadian State.* L. Little Bear et al., eds. Toronto: University of Toronto Press, 1984.

Lindley, M. F. *The Acquisition and Government of Backward Territory in International Law Being a Treatise on the Law and Practice Relating to Colonial Expansion.* 1926. Reprint. New York: Negro Universities Press, 1969.

McCoy, R. G. "The Doctrine of Tribal Sovereighty: Accomodating Tribal, State and Federal Interests." *Harvard Civil Rights-Civil Liberties L. Rev.* 13 (1978): 357.

Martone, F. J. "American Indian Tribal Self-Government in the Federal System: Inherent Right or Congressional License." *Notre Dame Lawyer* 57 (April 1976): 600.

Miller, D. H. *The Alaska Treaty.* Kingston, Ontario: The Limestone Press, 1981.

Naske, C-M. and H. E. Slotnick. *Alaska: A History of the 49th State.* Grand Rapids, Mich.: William B. Eerdmans Publishing Co., 1979.

Price, M. and R. N. Clinton. *Law and the American Indian: Readings, Notes and Cases.* 2nd Edition. Charlottesville, Va.: The Michie Company Law Publishers, 1983.

Price, R. *Native Rights A Report for the Alaska Statehood Commission.* Juneau: Alaska Department of Law, 1982.

"Publication of Alaska Villages Recognized as Tribes Receiving Services from the Bureau of Indian Affairs [25 CFR 54.6(b)]." Memorandum from Juneau Area Director to Deputy Assistant Secretary—Indian Affairs (Operations), May 28, 1982.

Sharp. "Home Rule in Alaska: A Clash Between the Constitution and the Court." *UCLA-Alaska L. Rev.* 3 (1973): 1.

Snow, A. H. *The Question of Aborigines in the Law and Practice of Nations.* 1919. Reprint. Northbrook, Ill.: Metro Books, Inc., 1972.

Taylor, G. D. *The New Deal and American Indian Tribalism: The Administration of the Indian Reorganization Act, 1934-45.* Lincoln, Neb.: University of Alaska Press, 1980.

"Tribal Self-Government and the IRA of 1934." *Mich. L. Rev.* 76 (1972): 955.

"Tribal Status of Alaska Natives Research Request 81-132." Memorandum from Peter B. Froehlich to Representative Hoyt "Pappy" Moss. Juneau: Alaska State Legislature House of Representatives Research Agency, June 24, 1981.

Tyler, S. L. *A History of Indian Policy.* Washington, D.C.: U.S. Department of the Interior, 1973.

Weatherhead, L. R. "What is an 'Indian Tribe'?—The Question of Tribal Existence." *Amer. Ind. L. Rev.* 8 (1981): 1.

Work of the Bureau of Education for the Natives of Alaska, 1916-1917. Bulletin No. 5. Washington, D.C.: U.S. Department of the Interior, Bureau of Education, 1918.

B. Archival Material

National Archives. Files of the Bureau of Indian Affairs, Indian Reorganization Division. Record Group 75. Questionnaires Concerning Tribal Organization in Alaska 1934-1935.

———. Files of the Bureau of Indian Affairs, Alaska Division, General Correspondence, Wheeler-Howard Act. Record Group 75. "Questionnaire on Local Self-Government." Memorandum from Chas. W. Hawksworth to Principal Teachers, August 16, 1934.

———. Files of the Bureau of Indian Affairs, Alaska Division, General Correspondence, Status of Alaska Natives. Record Group 75. Letter from Representative Edgar Howard to Ray Lyman Wilbur, Secretary of the Interior, January 28 1932.

———. ———. Letter from Ray Lyman Wilbur, Secretary of the Interior, in Reply to Representative Edgar Howard, March 14, 1932.

———. ———. Letter of April 11, 1932, from E. A. McIntosh to Hon. Scott Leavitt, House of Representatives and associated correspondence regarding marriage among Alaska Natives by tribal custom.

C. Cases and Legal Opinions

19 L.D. 323 (1894). "Alaska—Legal Status of Natives."

49 L.D. 592 (1923). "Leasing of Lands Within Reservations Created for the Benefit of the Natives of Alaska."

50 L.D. 315 (1924). "Status of Natives of Alaska With Respect to the Title to Tidelands Near Ketchikan."

53 L.D. 593 (1932). "Status of Alaska Natives."

54 L.D. 39 (1932). "Validity of Marriage by Custom Among the Natives or Indians of Alaska."

55 I.D. 14 (1934). "Powers of Indian Tribes."

56 I.D. 137 (1957). "The Protection of Indians and other Natives of Alaska from the Liquor Traffic."

65 I.D. 483 (1958). "Separability of Tribal Organizations Organized Under Secs. 16 and 17 of the I.R.A."

85 I.D. 433 (1978). "Criminal Jurisdiction on the Seminole Reservations in Florida."

Alaska v. Aleut Corp. 541 P. 2d 730 (AK 1975).

Alaska Chapter, Associated General Contractors of America, Inc. v. Pierce, 694 F. 2d 1162 (9th Cir. 1982).

Alaska Pacific Fisheries v. U.S., 248 U.S. 78 (1918).

Application of Angus, 655 P. 2d 208 (Or. App. 1982); rev. den. _____ U.S. _____, 78 L. Ed. 2d 109 (1983).

Atkinson v. Haldane, 569 P. 2d 151 (Ak. 1977).

Barona Group of the Capitan Grande Indians v. Duffy, 694 F. 2d 1185 (9th Cir. 1982).

Board of Equalization for the City and Borough of Ketchikan v. Alaska Native Brotherhood, Camp No. 16, 666 P. 2d 1015 (Ak. 1983).

Bottomly v. Passamaquoddy Tribe, 599 F. 2d 1061 (1st Cir. 1979).

Bryan v. Itasca County, 426 U.S. 373 (1976).

In re Carr, 1 Ak. Fed. Rpts. 75 (1875).

Chemehuevi Indian Tribe v. California Board of Equalization, 492 F. Supp. 55 (N.D. Cal. 1979).

Cherokee Nation v. Georgia, 30 U.S. (5 Pet.) 1 (1831).

Cogo v. Central Council of Tlingit and Haida Indians, 465 F. Supp. 1286 (D.C. Ak. 1979).

"Co-operation agreement between city and IRA Council of Saxman." Unpublished Memorandum. Op. Asst. Alaska Atty. Gen. File No. J66-406-82, March 2, 1982.

DeCoteau v. District County Court, 420 U.S. 425 (1975).

Delaware Tribal Business Committee v. Weeks, 430 U.S. 73, reh. den. 431 U.S. 960 (1977).

Department of Game v. Puyallup Tribe (Puyallup II), 414 U.S. 44 (1973).

Dry Creek Lodge v. Arapahoe and Shoshone Tribes, 623 F. 2d 682 (10th Cir. 1980); cert. den. 449 U.S. 1118; reh. den. 101 S. Ct. 1421 (1981).

Ex Parte Crow Dog, 109 U.S. 556 (1883).

Federal Power Commission v. Tuscarora Indian Nation, 362 U.S. 99; reh. den. 362 U.S. 956 (1960).

Fisher v. District Court, 424 U.S. 382 (1976).

Fondahn v. Native Village of Tyonek, 450 F.2d 520 (9th Cir. 1971).

Green v. Wilson 221 F. 2d 769 (9th Cir. 1964).

Haile v. Saunooke 246 F. 2d 293 (4th Cir. 1957).

In re Humboldt Fir, Inc., 426 F. Supp. 292 (N.D. Cal. 1977); aff'd. 625 F.2d 330 (9th Cir. 1980).

Inupiat Community of the Arctic Slope (ICAS) v. U.S. (ICAS I), 680 F.2d 122 (Ct. Cls.); cert. den. 51 USLW 3339 (1982).

Jefferson v. State, 527 P.2d 37 (Ak. 1974).

Johnson v. Chilkat Indian Village, 457 F. Supp. 384 (D.C. Ak. 1978).

Johnson v. Lower Elwha Tribal Community 484 F. 2d 200 (9th Cir. 1973).

Joint Tribal Council of the Passamaquoddy Tribe v. Morton, 528 F. 2d 370 (1st Cir. 1975).

Jones v. Meehan, 175 U.S. 1 (1899).

Kake v. Egan, 369 U.S. 60 (1962).

The Kansas Indians, 72 U.S. (5 Wall.) 737 (1867).

Kennerly v. U.S., 721 F.2d 1252 (9th Cir. 1983).

Kimball v. Callahan, 493 F.2d 564 (9th Cir.); cert. den. 419 U.S. 1019 (1974).

Kimball v. Callahan, 590 F.2d 768 (9th Cir.); cert. den. 444 U.S. 826 (1979).

"Liquor Ordinance, Village of Allakaket, Alaska." Unpublished Memorandum. Op. Assoc. Sol Ind. Aff., October 1, 1980.

Loncassion v. Leekity 334 F. Supp. 370 (D.N.M. 1971).

Lone Wolf v. Hitchcock, 187 U.S. 553 (1903).

McClanahan v. Arizona State Tax Comm'n., 411 U.S. 164 (1973).

In re McCord, 151 F. Supp. 132 (D.C. Ak. 1957).

Maryland Casualty v. Citizens National Bank, 261 F. 2d 520 (5th Cir. 1966).

Mashpee v. New Seabury Corp., 592 F.2d 575 (1st Cir.); cert. den. 444 U.S. 866 (1979).

"Meaning of 'Indian tribe' in Section 4(b) of P.L. 93-638 for purposes of application to Alaska." Unpublished Solicitor's Memorandum, May 21, 1976.

Menominee Tribe v. U.S., 391 U.S. 404 (1968).

Merrion v. Jicarilla Apache Tribe, 455 U.S. 130 (1982).

Mescalero Apache Tribe v. Jones, 411 U.S. 145 (1973).

Metlakatla v. Egan, 369 U.S. 45 (1962).

In re Minook, 2 Ak. Rpts. 200 (D.C. Ak. 1904).

Moe v. Confederated Salish and Kootenai Tribes, 425 U.S. 463 (1976).

Montana v. U.S., 450 U.S 544 (1981).

Montoya v. U.S., 180 U.S. 261 (1901).

Morton v. Mancari, 417 U.S. 535 (1974).

Namekagon Dev. Co. v. Bois Forte Res. Housing Auth. 395 F. Supp. 23 (D. Minn. 1974) aff'd 517 F. 2d 508 (8th Cir. 1975).

Native Village of Eyak v. G. C. Contractors, 658 P.2d 756 (Ak. 1983).

New Mexico v. Mescelaro Apache Tribe, ＿＿U.S. ＿＿, 76 L. Ed. 2d 611 (1983).

Oklahoma Tax Commission v. U.S., 319 U.S. 598 (1942).

Oliphant v. Suquarmish Tribe, 435 U.S. 191 (1978).

Ollestead v. Tyonek, 560 P. 2d 31 (1977).

Parker Drilling Co. v. Metlakatla Indian Community, 451 F. Supp. 1127 (D.C. Ak. 1978).

People of South Naknek v. Bristol Bay Borough, 466 F. Supp. 870 (D.C. Ak. 1979).

"Powers of an Indian Group Organized Under IRA but Not as Historical Tribe" (April 15, 1938). Reprinted in 1 Op. Sol. on Ind. Aff. 813 (1975).

Puyallup Tribe v. Department of Game (Puyallup I), 391 U.S. 392 (1968).

Puyallup Tribe v. Department of Game (Puyallup III), 433 U.S. 165 (1977).

Rice v. Rehner, _____ U.S. _____, 77 L. Ed. 2d 961 (1983).

In re Sah Quah, 1 Ak. Fed. Rpts. 136 (D.C. Ak. 1886).

Santa Clara Pueblo v. Martinez, 436 U.S. 49 (1978).

Santa Rosa Band of Indians v. Kings County, 532 F. 2d 655 (9th Cir. 1975).

Seminole Tribe v. Butterworth, 658 F.2d 310 (1981); cert. den. 455 U.S. 1020.

Settler v. Lameer, 507 F.2d 231 (9th Cir. 1974).

Settler v. Yakima Tribal Court, 419 F.2d 486 (9th Cir. 1969); cert. den. 398 U.S. 903 (1970).

"Taxing Authority of the Alaska Native Community of Circle." Unpublished Memorandum. Robert Thompson, Attorney-Advisor, to Asst. Sol., Tribal Govt. and Alaska, September 9, 1981.

"Taxing Powers of Village of Saxman." Letter Opinion from Felix Cohen, Acting Solicitor, to George W. Folta, Esq., Counsel at Large (July 7, 1945). Reprinted in 2 Op. Sol. on Ind. Aff. 1337 (1975).

Tenneco Oil Co. v. Sac and Fox Tribe, 725 F.2d 577 (10th Cir. 1984).

"Tlingit and Haida Community Councils and Second-Class City Councils-Status under P.L. 93-638 ('the Act')." Unpublished Memorandum. Field Solicitor, Juneau, January 5, 1977.

Tlingit and Haida Indians of Alaska et al. v. U.S., 177 F. Supp. 452 (Ct. Cls. 1959).

Tom v. Sutton, 533 F. 2d 1101 (9th Cir. 1976).

U.S. v. Berrigan, 2 Ak. Rpts. 442 (D.C. Ak. 1904).

U.S. v. Booth, 161 F. Supp. 269 (D.C. Ak. 1958).

U.S. v. Chavez, 290 U.S. 357 (1933).

U.S. v. Farris, 624 F.2d 890 (9th Cir. 1980).

U.S. v. Holliday, 70 U.S. (3 Wall.) 407 (1866).

U.S. ex rel Hualpai Indians v. Santa Fe Pac. R.R., 314 U.S. 339 (1941).

U.S. v. Kagama, 118 U.S. 375 (1886).

U.S. v. McBratney, 104 U.S. 621 (1881).

U.S. v. McGowan, 302 U.S. 535 (1938).

U.S. v. Martine, 442 F. 2d 1022 (10th Cir. 1971).

U.S. v. Mazurie, 419 U.S. 544 (1975).

U.S. v. Oregon, 657 F.2d 1009 (9th Cir. 1981).

U.S. v. Pelican, 232 U.S. 442 (1913).

U.S. v. Quiver, 241 U.S. 602 (1916).

U.S. v. Sandoval, 231 U.S. 28 (1913).

U.S. v. Sioux Nation of Indians, 448 U.S. 371 (1980).

U.S. v. South Dakota, 665 F. 2d 837 (8th Cir. 1981).

U.S. v. United States Fidelity & Guaranty Co., 308 U.S. 506 (1940).

U.S. v. Washington, 641 F. 2d 1368 (9th Cir. 1981).

U.S. v. Wheeler, 435 U.S. 313 (1978).

Warren Trading Post Co. v. Arizona Tax Commission, 380 U.S. 685 (1965).

Worcester v. Georgia, 21 U.S. (6 Pet) 515 (1832).

White v. Pueblo of San Juan, 728 F. 2d 1307 (10th Cir. 1984).

White Mountain Apache Tribe v. Bracker, 448 U.S. 136 (1980).

Williams v. Lee, 358 U.S. 217 (1959).

INDEX

INDIAN SELF-DETERMINATION ACT. *See* SELF-DETERMINATION; TRUST RESPONSIBILITY; RELATIONSHIP, FEDERAL OR SPECIAL

INDIAN TITLE. *See* ABORIGINAL TITLE

INTERNATIONAL WHALING CONVENTION. *See* TRUST RESPONSIBILITY; SUBSISTENCE

INUPIAT ILITQUSIAT. *See* MANIILAQ ASSOCIATION

JACKSON, SHELDON. *See* EDUCATION

JOHNSON-O'MALLEY ACT. *See* EDUCATION

JURISDICTION. *See also* P.L. 280 and INDIAN COUNTRY
Alaska issues described, 451
allotments and townsites generally, 168
ANCSA's effect on, 447
before P.L. 280, 14
competing state and tribal interests, 472-476
described generally, 450-452
federal
   allotments and townsites, 169, 171
   criminal, 455
government, tribal and state, 440
Indian liquor laws and, 460
infringement and, 438-439, 459, 473-474
Indian Child Welfare Act and, 449
land ownership and, 447-448, 458-460
off-reservation tribal jurisdiction, 458-460, 473-474
over persons and property, 460-461
P.L. 280. See headings under P.L. 280
preemption and, 438-439, 459, 472-473
subject matter jurisdiction defined, 453
subsistence and, 310-313
territorial. See heading under INDIAN COUNTRY